1997

Advance Directives
and the Pursuit of Death
with Dignity

MEDICAL ETHICS SERIES

David H. Smith and Robert M. Veatch, *Editors*

Advance Directives and the Pursuit of Death with Dignity

Norman L. Cantor

Indiana University Press

Bloomington and Indianapolis

The paper used in this publication meets the minimum requirements of American National Standard for Information Sciences—Permanence of Paper for Printed Library Materials, ANSI Z39.48-1984.

♾™

Manufactured in the United States of America

Library of Congress Cataloging-in-Publication Data

Cantor, Norman L.
    Advance directives and the pursuit of death with dignity / Norman L. Cantor.
      p. cm. — (Medical ethics series)
    Includes bibliographical references and index.
    ISBN 0-253-31304-X
    1. Right to die. 2. Euthanasia. 3. Medical ethics. I. Title.
II. Series.
R726.C34   1993
179'.7—dc20   92-46072

1 2 3 4 5 97 96 95 94 93

Contents

On Restraining Life-Preserving Medical Technology

AT ONE TIME, most people wanted to live as long as possible, and the medical profession sought to prevent death at all costs. That approach could prevail so long as medical capabilities to forestall death were limited. In the middle of the twentieth century, however, medical science developed an array of mechanisms able to extend life well beyond previous bounds.

Mechanical ventilators could sustain breathing processes for protracted periods. Techniques for artificial nutrition and hydration could sustain patients whose ingestion-digestion systems had failed. Immunosuppressive drugs made organ transplantation an option. Sophisticated resuscitation techniques could often revive patients whose breathing had ceased. These and many other developments made it possible to sustain life long after the human body had lost its natural ability to perform critical tasks.

For the most part, these developments were salutary. This was particularly so when the new technology assisted in restoring an ailing person to something close to a prior level of functioning. Yet there was and is a downside. Medical technology can sustain—for protracted periods—gravely debilitated, dying individuals who have no hope of recovering their former capacities. This technological capability has cast doubt on the prior strategy of activating all possible life-preserving medical means.

In the modern era, death increasingly results from chronic maladies and gradual body failure. Cancer, cardiovascular ailments, and cerebrovascular diseases often cause progressive degeneration and protracted dying processes.[1] Alzheimer's disease offers an example. Its gradual impairment of mental functions continues inexorably for an average period of 8.1 years. In its final stages, severe dementia necessitates constant care until death ensues from pneumonia, heart disease, or kidney failure.[2] Such possibilities of grave deterioration of mental faculties and total loss of function have implications both for the aging American population and the medical profession.

Many people have come to view a degenerative dying process as a fate worse than death itself. They dread a difficult and protracted dying process, featuring total helplessness and dependence, increasing dementia, and astronomical expenses. The ultimate specter is one of prolonged suspension in a helpless state, sustained by an array of tubes and machines.[3] Medical intervention then preserves the shell of life but is unable to restore the previously vital patient to anything resembling the patient's previous status.

That specter may or may not include physical and emotional suffering. But it almost certainly entails a status deemed degrading by the typical adult considering his or her own demise. People wonder how they can avoid such a fate. They wonder how medical intervention in the dying process might be restrained sufficiently to permit death with dignity or, at least, death without prolonged suspension in a gravely deteriorated state.

The physician's role has inevitably shifted in the face of modern medicine's awesome capabilities. When medical science had very limited means to arrest fatal conditions, it made sense to activate all medical tools to keep the patient alive for the maximum period possible. With the advent of modern capacity to prolong a difficult dying process beyond "natural" bounds and to preserve the patient in a debilitated state, common sense dictated that the lifesaving imperative sometimes be relaxed. Accordingly, the physician's role has changed. The physician has become a *manager* of medical intervention. Not every life-preserving device need be activated, and a device once activated need not be maintained indefinitely. A stage may be reached when further medical intervention is unwarranted and the patient may be allowed to expire.

This altered approach to life-preserving medical intervention has been acknowledged by numerous physicians and medical bodies.[4] The question is how this altered approach will be administered. What are the circumstances in which medical intervention may properly be withheld or withdrawn? What criteria govern conduct which will lead to the death of a patient? How can a person control a post-competence dying process in a fashion which preserves a personal vision of dignity?

One vehicle for controlling medical intervention is an advance directive. By advance directive, I mean a writing issued by a competent person intending to govern post-competence medical care. That directive might contain substantive instructions which stand by themselves, taking the form of what is commonly known as a living will. Such a document is aimed at guiding any and all decision makers responsible at the moment for critical post-competence decisions. (Usually, the decision makers are a close family member in conjunction with an attending physician.) Alternatively, an advance directive might simply designate a health-care agent (sometimes called a proxy or surrogate or attorney-in-fact) who will be charged with making post-competence medical decisions for the patient. Appointment of an agent can be accompanied by substantive instructions to that agent—a course which I vigorously endorse.[5]

This book considers the legal, moral, and practical bounds of advance directives. Because the concept of an advance directive is rooted in respect for self-determination and autonomy, chapter 1 examines the scope which current law accords to medical decisions by competent patients shaping their contemporaneous medical handling. Chapter 2 works from that foundation to consider the scope of any "right" to direct in advance the degree of medical intervention which will be rendered during a post-competence dying process. That chapter considers the inherent difficulties of *prospective* autonomy as confronted in directives governing future medical contingencies.

Chapter 3 looks at the state statutes—whether living-will type laws or durable power of attorney for health-care measures (DPOA-HC)—which are potentially applicable to advance directives. The nature and impact of such measures is analyzed. Chapter 3 then discusses the various formats which might be used for an advance directive in light of the statutory framework.

Chapter 4 turns to the practical task of drafting advance directives. That chapter first surveys the formulations which have commonly been used to instruct health-care agents or other decision makers. It then examines deficiencies in current versions of advance directives and suggests ways in which such instructions might be improved.

Chapters 5 and 6 address problems of administering advance directives. Chapter 5 presents the principles which guide those persons charged with interpreting and implementing an advance directive. It also considers circumstances which might warrant deviation from the apparent terms of a directive. Chapter 6 examines perhaps the hardest issue faced in administration of an advance directive: a conflict between the instructions previously issued and the now incompetent patient's contemporaneous well-being. That chapter treats the moral and legal bounds applicable when such a conflict is encountered. Included are discussions of both professional conscience and institutional conscience as they bear on implementation of advance directives.

Chapter 7 examines the mechanisms which might be available to enforce advance directives. It discusses what might ensue when either a health-care provider or a relative of the patient refuses to comply with the terms of an advance directive.

The final chapter examines New Jersey's recent (effective January 1992) Advance Directives for Health Care Act. That enactment represents perhaps the most comprehensive and forward-looking piece of legislation regulating advance directives. For reasons that are outlined in chapter 8, the New Jersey legislation might well serve as a model for states seeking to update their statutory frameworks for advance directives.

The stakes are high in the modern effort to shape a humane approach to medical technology's capacity to prolong moribund medical patients far beyond previous bounds. Pressures are increasing to employ new responses (such as assisted suicide and active euthanasia) to people's widespread apprehensions of dying in a prolonged, debilitated status. The key question is whether medicine and law can adapt existing techniques for shaping limits to medical intervention in the dying process in order to assure people that they can avoid a distasteful and prolonged demise.

The advance directive is supposed to be an important tool in achieving that goal. Failure of that tool will almost certainly precipitate more widespread resort to assisted suicide and active euthanasia. This book seeks to promote the understanding, use, and effectiveness of advance directives. The hope is that by allowing persons to shape the contours of medical intervention they can secure a modicum of dignity in the dying process.

**Advance Directives
and the Pursuit of Death
with Dignity**

1

The Bounds of Autonomy for Competent Medical Patients

FOR PURPOSES of analyzing advance directives, it is useful to understand the bounds imposed on patient autonomy to reject life-preserving medical intervention. Both an advance directive (exercising prospective autonomy) and a contemporaneous decision (exercising immediate autonomy) allow a person to shape his or her own dying process in accord with personal values and preferences. While prospective autonomy is not identical to contemporaneous autonomy,[1] they share a common foundation in self-determination. The judicial determinations concerning contemporaneous patient decisions illuminate both the precise nature of the patient's interests in making such decisions and the conflicting interests which might warrant limitations upon fatal choices. The same kind of interests and the same kind of conflicts sometimes surface in the context of advance directives. Analysis of these tensions in the context of contemporaneous decisions can therefore cast light on similar tensions when an advance directive is applied to an incompetent patient.

The prerogative of a competent individual to determine if and when to receive life-preserving medical intervention is now firmly entrenched in American jurisprudence. Every decision by a highest state court has upheld a competent patient's right to control medical intervention even when the consequence will be the patient's death.[2] And medical sources have largely acquiesced in this precept of patient autonomy.[3]

This legal and medical consensus about patient autonomy was by no means a foregone conclusion. Medical tradition had long favored a view of doctor-patient relations in which the patient's handling was determined primarily by the physician's professional judgment (which usually called for maximum life preservation).[4] And many sources believed—for religious or philosophical reasons—that stricken persons ought not be accorded dominion over their own dying process. Only recently have notions of individual autonomy and bodily integrity come to prevail over medical paternalism. In any event, despite the shaky foundation in medical practice,

1

respect for a competent patient's control over medical intervention has now become both the legal and medical norm. This development reflects a widespread sentiment that individual self-determination is an integral element of human dignity and of humane medical treatment.

Yet there are still uncertainties about the source and bounds of a patient's prerogative to reject life-preserving medical intervention. The roots of patient autonomy are found in common-law sources. The doctrine of battery protected all persons against unconsented invasions of their bodies.[5] The doctrine of informed consent adapted this concept of bodily integrity to the physician-patient context. Informed consent became a key element in the tort law governing the physician-patient relationship. But these common-law protections of medical patient autonomy are not the exclusive legal protections available.

Within the last twenty years, many courts have reinforced the common-law prerogative to reject life-preserving care by incorporating it into the constitutional sphere. Numerous decisions declare that a patient's control of medical intervention is anchored in the federal Constitution's protection of liberty (and often in a comparable state constitutional provision as well).[6] At the same time, these cases note that the constitutional "right" involved is not absolute. The individual's constitutional interest will occasionally yield to some asserted government interest in limiting a patient's decision to reject life-preserving medical care.

It is important to decide the precise degree of constitutional protection accorded to patient autonomy. For if a patient's right to reject life-preserving medical intervention is indeed anchored in a constitutional source, both state legislatures and state judiciaries must respect that constitutional constraint. Constitutional doctrine can thus affect the rules—whether legislatively or judicially created—which govern the substance and effect of advance directives.

Constitutional protections have the potential to overcome governmental policies which purport to confine terminal decisions to patients who are facing unpreventable death within a short time or which limit the types of medical intervention which a patient can reject. (These kinds of constraints will be discussed later in this chapter and in chapter 3.) Further, even in the absence of explicit substantive instructions from a competent patient, constitutional law might impact on terminal medical decisions. It is possible that a person's designation of an agent to make post-competence health-care decisions is entitled to constitutional protection as an exercise of liberty.[7] A state might be constitutionally obligated to respect a person's designation of a surrogate decision maker, and that health-care agent might even be constitutionally entitled to make the same range of decisions that the patient could have made if competent.[8] This last possibility makes it even more important to define the constitutional scope of a competent patient's right to reject life-preserving medical treatment. That right might become the measure of an appointed health-care agent's authority.

IS A DECISION TO REJECT LIFE-PRESERVING MEDICAL INTERVENTION A FUNDAMENTAL ASPECT OF PERSONAL LIBERTY UNDER THE FEDERAL CONSTITUTION?

The starting point for analysis is the June 1990 U.S. Supreme Court decision in *Cruzan v. Director, Missouri Department of Health.*[9] That case addressed the medical fate of a permanently unconscious patient who, according to the trial court's findings, had not issued clear-cut prior instructions. *Cruzan* thus contains no definitive determination about the scope of autonomy of a competent person who issues advance medical instructions. Nonetheless, *Cruzan* was the Supreme Court's first pronouncement concerning the constitutional interests of medical patients. It is, therefore, a source of guidance about constitutional doctrine in the area.

Cruzan dealt with the fate of Nancy Cruzan, a woman mired in a permanently unconscious state in the wake of severe brain injuries sustained in an automobile accident. Ms. Cruzan's parents had sought judicial authorization to act on their daughter's behalf and to end the artificial nutrition maintaining her existence. Ms. Cruzan had previously made informal oral declarations indicating she would not wish to be maintained in a permanently vegetative state. However, the Missouri courts had ruled that there was insufficient evidence to establish the now incompetent patient's preferences in a clear-cut fashion. Without clear and convincing evidence of the patient's wishes, the Missouri Supreme Court refused to permit a guardian's decision to withdraw life-preserving medical treatment from an incompetent patient. The parents appealed to the U.S. Supreme Court contending that Ms. Cruzan's constitutional right to reject unwanted medical treatment had been violated.

The holding, or thrust, of *Cruzan* goes to Missouri's approach to *in*competent medical patients. By a five to four margin, the U.S. Supreme Court rejected the constitutional challenge to Missouri's approach. Chief Justice Rehnquist's majority opinion ruled both that a state may (but need not) confine terminal decisions on behalf of incompetent patients to instances when the patient has previously expressed such a preference and that the state may demand clear-cut evidence of the patient's previous expressions. These precautions were reasonable, the majority declared, in order to safeguard incompetent patients from terminal decisions inconsistent with the patient's preferences and in order to safeguard against abuse of the helpless patients involved.

The U.S. Supreme Court accepted the Missouri Supreme Court's finding that Nancy Cruzan had not made clear-cut expressions about her post-competence medical fate. By definition, then, there was no autonomous patient choice involved in the case. Nonetheless, Nancy's parents had grounded their petition on the premise that their daughter had possessed, as a competent adult, a constitutionally protected right to reject life-preserving medical intervention. Their threshold contention was that the word "liberty" in the due process clause of the Fourteenth Amendment affords a competent adult a right to reject unwanted medical care.[10]

The majority opinion in *Cruzan* assumed, for purposes of discussion alone, that a competent person does enjoy "a constitutionally protected right to refuse life-saving hydration and nutrition."[11] Nonetheless, a number of commentators have suggested that *Cruzan* forebodes a contrary conclusion: that a decision to reject medical treatment is *not* a fundamental aspect of liberty protected by the Fourteenth Amendment.[12] Those commentators base their conclusion on the majority opinion's references to a liberty "interest" in rejecting treatment (as opposed to a liberty "right"). Their premise is that a Supreme Court opinion would not use the term *interest* if it were thought that a fundamental aspect of liberty was involved.

My own analysis is different. To my mind, the *Cruzan* decision lends impetus to the notion that a competent patient's rejection of medical intervention *is* a fundamental aspect of liberty. Use of the term "liberty interest" is explainable by judicial caution in crafting constitutional jurisprudence. The majority was reserving decision about the ultimate scope of a competent patient's constitutional prerogative. It had already assumed that a constitutional right existed. There was no need to specify whether that right was part of fundamental liberty or not. The government interests surrounding care of an *in*competent patient were strong enough to prevail in either event.

While the majority opinion in *Cruzan* is inconclusive, there are some indications even in that opinion that a majority of the Supreme Court will ultimately declare that a competent patient's decision to reject life-preserving medical intervention is a fundamental aspect of liberty. The majority opinion surveys (without any hint of disapproval) some of the many state court decisions establishing patients' control of medical intervention in a natural dying process as a right grounded in common law, state constitutional law, or federal constitutional law.[13] The majority acknowledges as well that the "logic" of prior Supreme Court cases regarding fundamental liberty interests could easily be extended to the competent medical patient. However, Chief Justice Rehnquist's opinion refuses to go the last step and declare a medical patient's constitutional right. Instead, it "assumes," for purposes of the *Cruzan* case alone, that such a constitutional right does exist.[14]

Justice O'Connor's concurring opinion expresses strong sympathy for the claim that a competent patient has a fundamental liberty interest in rejecting medical care. Justice O'Connor comments: "[T]he due process clause must protect, if it protects anything, an individual's deeply personal decision to reject medical treatment."[15] Her opinion, in combination with the four dissenting voices in *Cruzan*, means that there were five Justices in June 1990 who supported that notion. Only Justice Scalia disparaged the idea of a competent person's constitutional right to reject unwanted medical treatment. That leaves current Justices Kennedy, Souter,

Thomas, and Chief Justice Rehnquist (as well as Justice White's successor) free to join Justices O'Connor, Stevens, and Blackmun and acknowledge the fundamental liberty status of the patient's autonomy interest.

Judicial acceptance of a competent patient's autonomy interest as fundamental depends on whether the patient's interest is deemed "so rooted in the traditions and conscience of our people as to be ranked as fundamental."[16] That is the standard used by the modern Supreme Court for defining fundamental aspects of liberty.[17] Employing that standard, there is a considerable basis for deeming the competent medical patient's liberty interest to be fundamental.

As noted, even Chief Justice Rehnquist's majority opinion recounted the string of modern cases upholding a competent medical patient's prerogative to reject life-preserving medical intervention. That line of authority helps demonstrate how self-determination and bodily integrity have become integral aspects of a medical patient's interests. The doctrine of informed consent—a doctrine premised on a patient's prerogative to reject medical intervention—has found universal acceptance in American jurisprudence. Moreover, the doctrine has universally been transposed to life-and-death decisions in the face of medical afflictions. Thus, there is a solid foundation for the conclusion that control of life-sustaining medical intervention has become a fundamental aspect of personal liberty in the context of modern American society.

The *Cruzan* opinions of Justices Stevens (dissenting) and O'Connor (concurring) eloquently explain why autonomy to reject unwanted treatment during a natural dying process can be deemed a fundamental aspect of liberty. Justice Stevens is particularly sensitive to the dilemma posed to modern society by medical technology's capacity to prolong a dying process. He therefore urges application of autonomy principles to the context of human dying. He comments:

> Choices about death touch the core of liberty. Our duty, and the concomitant freedom, to come to terms with the conditions of our own mortality are undoubtedly "so rooted in the traditions and conscience of our people" as to be ranked as fundamental. . . . [18]

Both Justices Stevens and O'Connor elucidate the important human dignity elements which underlie patient self-determination. One element identified is the blow to human dignity which accompanies a patient's inability to secure his or her wish regarding the important and intimate matter of death. Justice Stevens in particular notes patients' interests both in a closure of life consistent with individual values and beliefs and in preservation of a particular self-image during the dying process.[19] Thus, both fulfillment of chosen values and avoidance of subjective degradation or embarrassment (during debilitation in the dying process) are seen as important components of human dignity and personhood. Another element recognized is the indignity or humiliation entailed in the forced subjection of a patient to unwanted medical intervention. Justice O'Connor in particular uses graphic images of physical "restraint" and the patient as "captive" of the care givers.[20]

The Stevens and O'Connor opinions, along with the dissenting opinion of Justice Brennan, highlight how a right to select medical treatment honors the intrinsic worth of human choice in this context. Autonomy is afforded not just to promote a patient's material best interests but to enable a patient to fulfill self-selected values. This focus on self-determination (as opposed to bodily integrity) as the key ingredient within the patient's interests will help define the ultimate scope of the right or interests involved. This focus helps refute the notion that a patient's right is confined to declining particularly invasive or burdensome forms of medical care—a notion that has sometimes been voiced.[21] If autonomy or self-determination is the key interest, even relatively unobtrusive medical interventions (such as blood transfusions or simple medications) may be resisted by the competent patient. A diminished concern with the physical invasiveness of medical intervention is consistent with the trend of state court decisions. Those decisions have attached less and less importance to the invasiveness of the medical intervention being rejected.[22]

Identification of the integral tie between choice and human dignity in the context of death-and-dying decisions follows the path of prior state court decisions in the field. Some of those decisions had stressed the blow to dignity when a patient's autonomous preferences regarding medical interventions are not respected.[23] Other decisions had acknowledged the relation between human dignity and the avoidance of both suffering and a dying process deemed undignified or degrading according to the affected individual.[24] All these voices emphasized the importance of an individual's choice to reject medical interventions deemed distasteful or to decide when a prospective existence is so painful or dismal that life-preserving intervention is unwanted. These judicial expressions form part of the "collective conscience" which will ultimately determine the constitutional status of a patient's autonomy interest.

It isn't just the failure of the majority opinion in *Cruzan* to disparage the jurisprudence linking medical self-determination and fundamental human dignity which encourages me to think that rejection of life-preserving medical intervention will eventually be recognized as a fundamental aspect of liberty. Note that the majority opinion acknowledges the value and importance of self-determination in the death-and-dying context. Indeed, one of the governmental interests which is recognized and upheld in *Cruzan* is an interest in safeguarding a patient's choice.[25] (The majority regarded Missouri's demand for clear and convincing evidence of prior patient expressions as necessary to ensure that any guardian's decision would be consistent with the patient's own wishes.) Chief Justice Rehnquist adds that he doesn't think that due process of law requires government "to repose judgment on these [life-and-death] matters *with anyone but the patient herself* [emphasis added]."[26]

(The irony, of course, is that Missouri's scheme actually frustrated personal choice as applied to Nancy Cruzan and to many medical situations. For example, polls demonstrate that the vast majority of Americans prefer not to be maintained in a permanently vegetative state.[27] Yet Missouri insists on maintaining a permanently vegetative patient in the absence of clear and convincing prior instructions to the contrary. The state's policy accomplishes a result opposite to what the vast majority of patients would want and opposite to the best judgment of what Nancy Cruzan would have wanted.)

It is true that the current Supreme Court is not inclined to expansively define fundamental liberty interests. The marked trend is to confine the notion of fundamental interests to those explicitly mentioned in the Constitution (such as free speech) or to those relating to marriage, procreation, and family living.[28] Even *Roe v. Wade*[29] and its inclusion of a woman's abortion interest within the realm of fundamental liberties was recently assaulted, though not vitiated.[30] Some perspective on this trend is appropriate.

The vulnerability of *Roe v. Wade* lay not in the general concept of fundamental aspects of liberty but in its specific application to an abortion decision. Fundamental liberty is supposed to be rooted in "the traditions and collective conscience of the people." Yet at the moment *Roe v. Wade* was decided in 1973 almost half the states punished the performance of abortions, and a very significant portion of the population regarded abortion as a form of homicide. There was arguably a dissonance between the Supreme Court's 1973 declaration of fundamentality and widespread societal perceptions. A similar dissonance affects the effort to have homosexual relations declared a fundamental aspect of personal liberty. Sexual relations are generally viewed as intimate and part of personal liberty. Yet certain forms of sexual behavior have traditionally been deemed abominable by a very significant segment of American society.

By contrast, there is no widespread aversion to a competent patient's prerogative to reject life-preserving medical intervention. As noted, notions of bodily integrity and control of medical intervention have strong grounding in twentieth century American jurisprudence and in societal attitudes of the last few decades. Self-determination in shaping medical response to a fatal affliction appeals not just to archliberals, like Justice Brennan, but to judicial conservatives as well. A prime example is former Chief Justice Warren Burger. While still a lower court judge in 1964, Warren Burger authored a ringing judicial endorsement of the notion of individual autonomy to reject life-preserving medical intervention.[31]

To be sure, respect for self-determination of a medical patient is not universal. There are right-to-life groups which are opposed to allowing preservable patients to expire. Some religious groups view life-and-death decisions as exclusively within the domain of a divine being (rather than in the dominion of the patient). But in a pluralistic society, there are almost no universal moral precepts. These ripples of dissent do not undermine the basic point that a competent patient's prerogative to reject life-preserving medical intervention has wide-ranging support in modern American society. That support—as well as the roots in well-established concepts of bodily integrity and informed consent—bode well for eventual Supreme Court recognition of a patient's prerogative as a fundamental aspect of liberty. Another positive sign is that post-*Cruzan* state court decisions continue to view a competent patient's rejection of life-preserving medical treatment as a fundamental aspect of liberty under both the federal and state constitutions.[32]

Calling something a fundamental aspect of liberty does not determine the ultimate contours of the right involved. Even fundamental liberties can be impinged in response to "compelling" governmental interests. There is still need, then, to define the scope of a competent patient's right to reject life-preserving medical intervention.

IS A PATIENT'S INTEREST IN REJECTING LIFE-SUSTAINING TREATMENT OUTWEIGHED BY A STATE INTEREST IN PRESERVING LIFE OR IN PRESERVING RESPECT FOR THE SANCTITY OF LIFE?

Many state supreme court decisions have considered a competent patient's decision to reject life-sustaining medical intervention where the patient was preservable for a considerable period of time. Those decisions commonly confront a putative governmental interest in the "sanctity of life." That sanctity-of-life interest can be divided into two components. One element is the protection of individuals against the harm normally entailed in the deprivation of life. A second element is promotion of societal respect for the concept that human life is sacrosanct. This element arguably includes maintaining social respect for all human existence by preventing human intermeddling which prematurely shortens a preservable life. Government could argue that any patient's judgment that a life is no longer worth living is morally offensive and that the state refuses to condone such a judgment. Or government might argue, as some people have done, that allowing debilitated persons to choose death broadcasts a message that life is not worth living for some handicapped persons. The concern is that this message will devalue the lives of handicapped persons and will weaken the social fabric.[33]

The legitimacy of a governmental interest in the preservation of life is indisputable. Such an interest suffuses much of American criminal law and significant parts of tort law. The question, though, is how this interest plays out when arrayed against what has been identified as an individual's fundamental liberty interest in shaping life-sustaining medical intervention. While a government interest in preserving life is potentially a compelling one, is it predominant in the context of competent medical patients rejecting life-preserving care?

Several state supreme court decisions declare that a competent patient's autonomy interests simply outweigh government interests encompassed within the sanctity-of-life rubric. The New Jersey Supreme Court's pronouncement is fairly typical: "[T]he state's indirect and abstract interest in preserving the life of the competent patient generally gives way to the patient's much stronger personal interest in directing the course of his own life."[34] The U.S. Supreme Court's *Cruzan* decision does nothing to undermine this determination. Indeed, eight of the Justices there seemed ready to rule that if Nancy Cruzan's wish to resist life-preserving medical intervention had been clearly expressed, it would have prevailed against any asserted state interests.

Some commentators have wondered why autonomy interests so easily prevail against sanctity-of-life concerns in the medical context.[35] To my mind, the judicial balance in favor of patient control of medical intervention is correct. But the balance deserves further explanation, beyond merely stressing the importance of a patient's autonomy and bodily integrity interests.

As noted, one legitimate governmental concern is protection of each individual against the harm entailed in deprivation of life. Yet that individual interest is really a protection against *unconsented* conduct which threatens a premature demise. Government can and should protect individuals against life-threatening abuse and mistreatment. But where a patient makes a deliberate determination that medical intervention will precipitate a status worse than death (from the perspective of that patient), government frustration of that choice does not promote the individual patient's self-defined interest. From the patient's perspective, the death which ensues is not a harm but, rather, a chosen and timely relief. (Government does have an interest in ensuring an informed and deliberate choice—but not in frustrating a considered choice.)[36]

Alternatively, government might assert—under the sanctity-of-life rubric—a collective interest in frustrating what government terms a morally offensive determination that some life is no longer worth living. The major defect in this argument is the premise that a person's choice not to struggle against a potentially fatal affliction is morally offensive. Modern medicine's capacity to preserve life long beyond previous bounds has undermined that premise. There is now societal understanding that prolonged suffering or prolonged indignity in the face of a fatal affliction can be a fate worse than death. People understand that a cancer patient may prefer death to the subjectively intolerable consequences of chemotherapy. People understand that an ALS patient (a victim of amyotrophic lateral sclerosis, a degenerative disease of the muscles known also as Lou Gehrig's disease) may reach a stage of helplessness and debilitation where continued respirator maintenance is intolerable.

In short, no moral condemnation currently accompanies the proposition that not every life-extending medical means must be maintained in the face of a naturally occurring dying process. There is widespread acknowledgment that, for some persons facing fatal afflictions, nonexistence may be preferable to medical maintenance. Once the morality of that posture is accepted, it makes eminently good sense to respect an individual's judgment that the dying process has become sufficiently torturous or degrading to warrant the cessation of medical intervention.

No one can assess the individual's suffering or sense of indignity better than the individual. Thus, it is not surprising that a competent patient's self-determination interests have been deemed dominant over the state interest in promoting respect for the sanctity of life.

The final government interest in this context is in avoiding endorsement of judgments that certain lives are not worth preserving. It is understandable that government wishes to avoid conveying a public message that *it* sees certain lives as so lacking in quality that further protection is unwarranted. But that is not the necessary consequence of government acquiescence in a competent patient's determination that medically maintained existence is so painful or dismal as to warrant foregoing life-sustaining treatment.

Judicial upholding of a patient's control over medical intervention does not constitute government endorsement of a determination that a particular life is not "worth living" or preserving. Indeed, judges upholding a patient's decision to reject life-preserving medical treatment frequently disclaim any judgment that the patient's decision is wise, desirable, or commendable.[37] Judicial respect for the patient's decision can therefore be viewed as an affirmation of human dignity as embodied in the patient's exercise of self-determination.[38] As one judge explained, with respect to a decision to terminate life support made by a woman suffering from a fatal degenerative muscle disease (ALS):

> This poor woman is not anti-life and her decision is not anti-life. . . . She has suffered much. It simply is not wrong in any sense for this good woman to want relief from her suffering. Hospitals and health care providers do not deal with life in the abstract. They deal with living people. Eventually, all those living people become dying people, and those people must be dealt with in a way which fully respects their dignity, including as part of that dignity the right to choose one's treatment.[39]

The New Jersey Supreme Court has added that "the value of life [is] desecrated not by the decision to refuse medical treatment but by the failure to allow a competent human being the right of choice."[40] In sum, when a competent, dying patient makes a determination that prospective physical or mental pain warrant rejection of continued medical intervention, this is not seen as an antilife posture undermining the state interest in promoting sanctity of human life. A person's coming to terms with a natural dying process is not seen as an affront to respect for the value of life.

IS THE RIGHT TO REJECT LIFE-PRESERVING MEDICAL INTERVENTION CONFINED TO TERMINAL PATIENTS NEARING THE END OF LIFE?

The answer to this question has implications for advance directives. Many people's directives seek to avoid prolonged medical maintenance in a stable, but severely debilitated, status. At the same time, termination of medical treatment to a stabilized patient, preservable for an extended period, has been attacked as a form of medical homicide which ought not be tolerated. Insight into this tension can be gleaned from consideration of competent patients who have rejected medical intervention capable of preserving their existence for long periods.

Is the patient's prerogative to reject life-sustaining medical intervention confined to the last stages of an inevitably terminal illness or condition? Early cases dealing with a patient's rejection of life-preserving medical treatment cautiously suggested that the governmental interest in preserving life could be overridden only because the patient's existence was nearing its end anyway.[41] According to that early perspective, the state's interest in preservation of life diminished as the duration of preservable existence diminished. Under such an approach, the patient's constitutional right to resist life-sustaining treatment might be limited to situations where an unpreventable death is near. Otherwise, the governmental interest in sanctity of life would prevail and a state could (if it wished) dictate continued life-preserving medical intervention.[42]

There are at least two reasons why the long potential duration of a patient's existence cannot determine the scope of a patient's right to resist life-preserving medical intervention. First, the government interest in sanctity of life does not increase just because the potential life span is longer. The government concern is both with promoting general respect for life and with the implicit judgment that a patient's quality of life is no longer worth preserving. That state interest is present and constant whether the patient's death is imminent or whether the dying process could be extended for years. (Even if the treatment rejected could only extend life for an hour, there is an implicit judgment that the hour of life was not worth preserving.) Second, the patient's autonomy interest in controlling medical intervention in a naturally occurring dying process[43] actually increases as the preservable existence lengthens. The patient's principal interest is in determining when a prospective existence (following contemplated treatment) would be so painful, distasteful, or degrading that further medical intervention is unwanted. The long prospective duration of a dying process only enhances the importance of the patient's choice. That is, the longer a prospective dying process, the more important choice is to a patient who views the prospective existence as torturous or degrading.

A number of state court decisions confirm this judgment: that a competent patient's autonomy interest prevails regardless of the duration of the preservable existence in issue.[44] That judicial posture is easiest to understand where the motive for the patient's rejection of treatment is avoidance of suffering. (The relevant cases generally involve patients afflicted with degenerative diseases or severe chronic debilitations.) Judges express understanding of a patient's powerful self-determination interest where medical intervention, while extending the patient's existence, will leave the patient in a gravely debilitated status. They understand that such a patient may wish to avoid the suffering and/or indignity which the patient associates with prolonged incapacitation. They also recognize that a patient's suffering is subjective—largely beyond judicial capacity to measure and weigh—and that such suffering can continue for a protracted period.[45] Accordingly, the cases uniformly refuse to supplant a competent patient's judgment that, for that patient, the prospective existence following continued medical intervention will be intolerable.[46] In that fashion, the courts avoid endorsing any particular judgment that a quality of life is so deteriorated as not to be worth preserving, and they avoid having to determine what length of preservable existence would override a patient's normal autonomy interest.

All the discussion so far goes to the right of a competent patient who is faced with an unpreventably fatal condition. A harder question is whether the competent patient's constitutional prerogative extends beyond terminal patients. (By terminal patients, I mean those afflicted with a pathological condition triggering an inexorable dying process—whatever its duration. I am including within terminal conditions both diseases such as ALS, which themselves cause a patient's death, and diseases such as AIDS, which affect the body's systems and lead to death from intervening causes.)[47] The hardest application of the issue comes when a medical patient is salvageable to a "healthful" existence and nonetheless seeks to reject lifesaving medical intervention.

Some state court decisions do mention the incurable status of the patient when discussing why a state interest in the preservation of life may be overridden.[48] Such a position is at least understandable. The offense to the state interest in sanctity of life seems intuitively greater if the patient is curable. A patient who resists treatment which could restore him or her to a healthful existence is behaving in a manner reminiscent of a suicide. (The interest in preventing suicide will be addressed separately in the next subsection.) The patient is not simply acquiescing in an unpreventable dying process. Many people see a salvageable patient's decision to resist medical intervention as morally less defensible than an inexorably dying person's decision.[49] It would, then, be theoretically possible to distinguish between the prerogative of an inexorably dying patient and a patient restorable to a "healthful" status.[50]

The likelihood is that a competent patient's medical autonomy will be upheld regardless of whether the patient is facing unavoidable death. One context in which competent, salvageable patients have been accorded a right to resist lifesaving medical intervention involves religiously motivated patients. (The typical case involves a Jehovah's Witness opposing a lifesaving blood transfusion.) Numerous decisions uphold the religiously motivated patient's decision, usually invoking constitutional grounds.[51]

The religious patient's autonomy interest is reinforced by the federal Constitution's explicit protection of religious freedom. However, it is unlikely that a competent patient's prerogative will be confined to religiously motivated patients.

The general patient interests reflected in medical decisions—self-determination, bodily integrity, and maintenance of dignity—are likely to reach the same constitutional plane as freedom of religion. Not surprisingly, then, the most recent state supreme court decision upholding a religiously motivated patient's rejection of treatment is grounded on constitutional interests in liberty and privacy (without reliance on the free exercise clause).[52]

This suggested constitutional approach to the religiously motivated patient is consistent with recent decisions upholding, as a matter of common law, a salvageable patient's right to resist life-preserving medical intervention.[53] The premise of such cases is that a competent patient's self-determination and bodily integrity interests simply outweigh the state's interest in preservation of life—even when the patient is preservable to a healthful existence. Such determinations regarding the common-law scope of the patient's right will in turn help shape the ultimate bounds of the constitutional right in issue.[54] (This is so because the constitutional right is shaped in part from the "traditions and collective conscience" of the people. State common law is one important index of the collective conscience.)

Just as a patient is entitled to resist life-preserving medical intervention even if that patient is salvageable to a healthful existence, a patient is entitled to resist intervention which would leave him in a chronically debilitated condition (though preservable for an extended period). A variety of patients fit this category. There is the gangrene patient facing an amputation operation. There is the patient with acute kidney disease who is sustainable for many years but will be perpetually dependent on burdensome medical intervention (kidney dialysis). There is the quadriplegic patient who is dependent on a mechanical respirator or on artificial nutrition because of chronic pathological conditions. In all these instances, courts have upheld competent patients' decisions to refuse further life-sustaining medical intervention.[55]

This result is sound. It would not be sensible to confine a patient's autonomy right to those patients who are beyond recovery (i.e., unpreventably dying). An inevitable issue under such a standard would be the definition of patient "recovery." Can the patient with gangrene "recover" (and therefore be deemed nonterminal and not entitled to resist life-preserving intervention) if the contemplated operation will leave him or her an amputee? Is the cancer patient with a fifteen percent chance of recovery a dying patient? And what about the patient with acute kidney disease who is salvageable for many years but can't stand the burden of the dialysis process? If the competent patient's constitutional prerogative depended on the length and quality of the preservable existence, courts would be implicated in the assessment of when the nature of the salvageable life is so dismal or uncertain as to preclude state interference with the patient's decision. This is a troubling specter for the judiciary.[56]

All this makes sense. Yet, when a patient's condition has stabilized and the patient is preservable for an extended period, a decision to forego further treatment (knowing that the result will be death) has overtones of suicide. The similarity to suicide warrants examination.

IS RELINQUISHMENT OF AN EXISTENCE PRESERVABLE FOR AN EXTENDED PERIOD INCOMPATIBLE WITH SOCIETY'S TRADITIONAL ANTIPATHY TOWARD SUICIDE?

When the issue of rejection of life-sustaining medical treatment arose in the 1950s and 1960s, hospitals argued that society's long-standing antipathy toward suicide warrants medical refusal to cooperate with a patient's rejection of treatment. The argument had appeal, particularly where the patient was salvageable to a healthful existence or where the patient's condition had stabilized and the patient was preservable for an indefinite period. In such instances, a decision to reject or discontinue medical support precipitates a prompt and foreseeable death. Isn't that suicide? This contention found some early judicial support.[57] And the contention was recently echoed by Justice Scalia in his opinion concurring in the result in *Cruzan*.[58]

Despite Justice Scalia's plaintive cry, the basic assertion has been thoroughly repudiated. Every decision of the last fifteen years has refused to equate suicide with a competent patient's rejection of life-sustaining medical intervention.[59] The only issue is the precise rationale for this result.

One common explanation is that suicide entails a specific intent to die and that a person declining medical intervention lacks such an intent. That rationale is convincing with regard to some patients. For example, a patient motivated by religious tenets (such as a Jehovah's Witness refusing a blood transfusion) has no specific intent to die. That patient hopes and expects a healing process to ensue and is merely adhering to a religious injunction in rejecting the particular treatment at hand. Likewise, a patient rejecting a highly expensive lifesaving procedure might well lack any specific intent to die.

However, the specific intent rationale is more problematic as applied to a terminally ill patient seeking to avoid a distasteful dying process. If the patient's main objective is avoidance of suffering or indignity, and that objective can be achieved only by death, then the intent behind the rejection of life-preserving treatment is close to the specific intent of any suicide who finds existence painful or meaningless.[60] Thus, the element of specific intent does not provide a comprehensive basis for distinguishing suicide.

Another basis to distinguish suicide from rejection of medical treatment is to see the former as involving a self-initiated destructive action.[61] This conforms with the commonsense understanding of suicide. When we think of suicide, we commonly think of taking pills, slitting wrists, or firing a shot. By contrast, rejection of medical treatment entails acquiescence in a natural disease process or trauma not initiated by the patient. Letting nature take its course is seen as different from inflicting an injury upon oneself.[62]

There is a simpler explanation for the distinction between rejection of life-preserving treatment and suicide. Over the past twenty-five years, both popular and judicial perceptions have come to regard a patient's decision about medical intervention in the face of a critical condition as part of a competent person's fundamental self-determination prerogatives.[63] A decision to resist life-preserving medical intervention involves important elements of both bodily integrity (resisting bodily invasions) and self-determination (shaping one's dying process). Recognition of these elements as engendering "rights" in the context of a critically stricken medical patient has simply removed the matter from the realm of suicide.[64]

It was inherent in the recognition of informed consent in the context of critical medical care that the patient would sometimes choose to die. Often, the patient's motive in rejecting medical intervention was distaste for the prospect of a gravely debilitated existence. (Among others, we're talking about the cancer patient, the gangrene patient, or the quadriplegic dependent on artificial aids.) Such refusal of medical intervention might well entail a suicide-like thought or state of mind. But no court could accept the notion that a patient might be foreclosed from exercising a right to refuse treatment because the patient might be deliberately preferring death over the anticipated, subjective hell of continued existence. A recent Massachusetts opinion commented: "There is a clear distinction between respecting the right of individuals to decide for themselves whether to refuse treatment and endorsing the idea that it is acceptable for individuals to take their own lives."[65]

Once the patient is deemed to be exercising a right to self determination, the motives behind the action are irrelevant. This is not such a surprising notion. For example, if a death-row prisoner waives a promising appeal or refuses to assert a possible defense, this is seen as a legitimate exercise of self-determination and part of the person's human dignity.[66] So long as the prisoner is competent, it shouldn't matter if he has an underlying wish to die because of a belief that the prospective punishment is warranted. While the prisoner's decision might be loosely analogized to a suicidal step, common sense tells us that it is not suicide.

The competent patient's decision to resist life-preserving medical treatment falls in the same realm. There is no occasion to differentiate among decisions motivated by religious convictions, by economic concerns, by distaste for a particular form of treatment, or by distaste for the dismal, debilitated condition facing the patient if treatment is accepted. The decision, whatever the precise motive, lies within the patient's self-determination prerogative.

The above perspective on a patient's acquiescence in death from natural causes applies even when the patient's condition has stabilized and life could be extended indefinitely. Some poignant examples have involved quadriplegics dependent on medical machinery (either respirators or artificial nutrition) who have been permitted to terminate life support.[67] Despite both the patient's specific intent to die and the fact that the withdrawal of medical intervention would be a "but for" cause of death, the withdrawal has been regarded as a permissible rejection of medical care and treated as distinct from suicide.[68] The underlying disease or trauma which is permitted to run its course by removal of the artificial intervention is considered the determinative legal cause of death.

A further wrinkle on the suicide theme occurs where the patient's condition has not only stabilized, but the medical support has been in place for an extended period. This situation triggers an assertion that life support has become such an integral part of the patient's being that any removal of life support constitutes a self-destructive, suicide-like act.

That contention recently surfaced in a dissenting opinion in *McKay v. Bergstedt*,[69] a Nevada case. In that instance, a thirty-nine-year-old quadriplegic sought to cease life-sustaining mechanical ventilation after twenty-three years of such treatment. The majority upheld the patient's decision. Judge Springer's dissent argued that the ventilator should be viewed as an integral part of the dependent patient so that its withdrawal would constitute a self-destructive act.[70] He saw the act as equivalent to removal of a pacemaker, prosthetic device, or artificial organ from a stabilized patient.

My perspective is that medical intervention doesn't cease to be medical intervention even if maintained for a long period and even if installed within the body. With degenerative ailments and with experimental treatments, it is understood that a patient's condition might deteriorate and reach a point when maintenance of the technology becomes intolerable. This is the case, for instance, with kidney dialysis. Many patients accept that treatment for years before ultimately deciding to terminate the burdensome intervention. A respirator, a pacemaker, or an artificial organ ought to fall into the same category. If, after months or even years, the patient's condition deteriorates or the patient's emotional tolerance is exhausted, a halt to medical intervention ought to be possible. Judge Springer's effort to anthropomorphize the medical machinery in order to make the process seem more like suicide is neither helpful nor persuasive.

There are situations where a person's self-harmful behavior exceeds mere rejection of medical intervention and is closely akin to suicide. A healthy person's attempt to donate a liver or other vital organ to a needy recipient might be an example. No health-care provider would cooperate with such an enterprise, even if it were motivated by admirable altruistic motives. At the same time, a person stricken with a potentially fatal pathology could reject medical intervention with the intention of dying and donating an organ to a needy recipient. This is only to say what was already asserted: that the prerogative to reject medical intervention may be exercised by a competent patient no matter what the patient's motive.

Another patient behavior which exceeds mere rejection of medical intervention is a refusal to accept oral feeding. The usual context is an elderly, grievously debilitated person who refuses to eat even though swallowing and digestive capabilities are still intact. I'll address this matter below, in the context of rejection of nutrition.

DOES A COMPETENT PATIENT'S RIGHT TO CONTROL MEDICAL INTERVENTION INCLUDE REJECTION OF ARTIFICIAL NUTRITION AND/OR MANUAL FEEDING?

Trauma or degenerative disease sometimes causes loss of a patient's swallowing reflex or disruption to the normal ingestion-digestion system. A range of interventions (including insertion of a nasogastric tube or surgical installation of a gastrostomy tube) may be available to sustain the patient's life. Does the competent patient's self-determination prerogative encompass refusal or withdrawal of such artificial nutrition? (I use artificial nutrition here as a shorthand applicable to artificial hydration as well.) The issue has provoked strong emotions and controversy over the last ten years.[71]

If there were strong grounds to distinguish artificial nutrition from regular medical intervention, it might be possible to exclude artificial nutrition from the scope of the patient's constitutional prerogative to control medical intervention. Even a fundamental liberty interest can be circumscribed when certain applications exceed the accepted or traditional bounds of the liberty principle involved.[72] In the case of artificial nutrition versus conventional medical treatment, the kind of distinction which would warrant separate constitutional handling probably does not exist. This conclusion flows from consideration of the claims raised by those commentators who seek to differentiate artificial nutrition from conventional medical intervention.[73]

One common assertion is that because cessation of nutrition inevitably leads to the patient's death, such cessation is tantamount to killing the patient. The patient is allegedly being dehydrated (or starved) to death instead of merely being permitted to die from a natural disease process.[74]

There is another perspective on causation. From this latter perspective, the trauma or disease process which incapacitated the patient's alimentary system ought to be viewed as the legal cause of death. This pathology, which permanently ended the patient's ingestion-digestion capacity, created the need for artificial intervention to maintain the patient's existence. Absent artificial nutrition, the patient would have died naturally from the underlying illness or trauma. Removal of that artificial nutrition merely allows the natural dying process to follow its terminal course. Death through dehydration stems from the original incapacitating trauma and not from introduction of a new external element into the scenario. While dehydration may be a "but for" cause of death (along with the underlying pathology), the death may still be viewed as "acquiescence in the natural shutting down of a critical bodily function."[75] The underlying pathology can be deemed the legally determinative cause of death so long as the withdrawal of artificial nutrition accords with the applicable standards of physician responsibility to a competent patient.[76]

From the perspective of causation, the situation is not significantly different from a patient who rejects life-preserving mechanical ventilation or kidney dialysis. Legal responsibility for withdrawal of life-preserving intervention is assessed according to the scope of medical duty to the particular patient. This approach prevails whether the intervention is a respirator for lung or heart malfunction, a dialysis machine for kidney malfunction, or artificial nutrition for alimentary malfunction. In all these instances, the normal medical duty to preserve life is modified by the competent patient's instructions.

A separate claim is that the provision of nutrition has a special symbolic significance which differentiates it from medical treatment. Some commentators contend that feeding is inherently a symbol of human interdependence and caring, a symbol which should always be preserved.[77]

Yet any symbolic distinction between artificial nutrition and conventional medical care seems forced. The caring embodied in artificial feeding seems little different from the caring involved in furnishing antibiotics, blood transfusions, medicines, or chest massage. While feeding normally carries a salutary symbolic message, that is not always the case. In the context of a competent, fatally afflicted patient, feeding may carry no benefit for the patient; the act may lose its usual symbolic cast.[78] This is especially so when the patient is undergoing a torturous dying process being prolonged by artificial nutrition. When that stage is reached, it is palliative care (nursing care aimed at easing the pain, anxiety, or discomfort of the patient) which may connote the caring and humane consideration that people expect and deserve.

Some health-care providers may have special qualms about withdrawing artificial nutrition. One survey indicated that as late as 1983, seventy-three percent of physicians surveyed would continue artificial nutrition even for a hopelessly comatose, terminally ill patient.[79] Intravenous fluids were apparently considered by some to be an entrenched therapy at that time. Yet the survey is deceptive. As of that time, there was still uncertainty about the legal consequences of withdrawing artificial nutrition. Recall that some of the first legal expressions concerning refusal of medical intervention spoke in terms of a prerogative to reject "extraordinary" means. Most of the early cases dealt with respirators or other forms of regular medical intervention. Only between 1983 and 1985 did the courts begin to indicate that artificial nutrition could be regarded like conventional medical intervention.[80] Moreover, physicians in 1983 may have had concerns about the pain and aesthetics involved in a death by dehydration, concerns which have since been largely resolved.

When the issue of withdrawing artificial nutrition first arose, an effort was made to portray the consequences for the "starving" patient as painful and repulsive. A Massachusetts lower court in 1986 devoted twenty pages to the gruesome consequences allegedly attached to death by dehydration.[81] However, contemporary medical opinion repudiates that portrayal.[82] By use of basic palliative techniques (including sedatives, analgesics, and moistening of passages) health-care providers can mitigate the harsh effects of death from dehydration. One expert analogizes the end stage (following cessation of artificial nutrition) to the process by which patients often died thirty years ago, before artificial nutrition techniques were available.[83]

Having repudiated the specter of agonized, grotesque creatures being starved to death, the medical community has tended to regard artificial nutrition like other forms of medical intervention. A wide range of physicians' groups and ethicists have adopted the position that no logical distinction exists between removal of artificial nutrition and removal of other life-preserving technology. For example, the American Medical Association Council on Ethical and Judicial Affairs includes artificial nutrition among those life-prolonging medical interventions which may ethically be foregone at some phase in the decline of a terminally ill patient.[84] Similar stands were taken both by the President's Commission for the study of Ethical Problems in Medicine and by the Hastings Center Task force on Death and Dying.[85]

Not surprisingly, the judiciary has adopted the same perspective. State cases virtually unanimously view artificial nutrition as a form of medical intervention that is governed by standards applicable to conventional medical procedures.[86] Respirators, dialysis machines, and artificial nutrition are all seen as medical technology performing bodily functions when the body's normal processes have shut down. All are therefore subject to the patient's prerogative to control medical intervention. The Supreme Court's tacit acceptance of this proposition in *Cruzan* speaks thunderously for this conclusion. Although the justices were well aware of the arguments seeking to distinguish nutrition from medical treatment, no opinion embraces that idea.

The only dissonance in this emerging attitude toward artificial nutrition comes from state legislative voices. In some states, living-will type laws or durable power-of-attorney measures differentiate between nutrition and other forms of medical intervention. That dissonance and its limited practical effect will be discussed in chapter 3, which deals with the legal status of advance medical directives.

If a competent patient has a prerogative to reject artificial nutrition, does that prerogative include a right to reject manual feeding? The issue seems to arise when a patient is afflicted with debilitating chronic conditions, none of which yet necessitates life-sustaining medical intervention. The patient may seek to accelerate death by declining oral feeding while simultaneously refusing permission for artificial nutrition. (The assumption here is that the patient is capable of ingesting food without distress but simply chooses not to.) Some persons would avoid this juncture by a pill overdose or other means of suicide. Other persons, though, will be so physically incapacitated, weakened, or isolated that suicide is not a viable alternative. Because a food-rejecting course of conduct is sometimes prompted by extreme depression, the competency of the patient deserves careful scrutiny.[87] However, such scrutiny may well disclose that the patient is competent and the legal issue must then be faced.

All discussion to this point recognizes a legal prerogative to reject *medical intervention*. A threshold question, then, is whether hand-feeding is medical in nature. The answer is probably negative. While such feeding is commonly provided in institutional settings by health-care providers, the same assistance could presumably be provided by lay persons. There may be borderline cases, as when oral nutrition is being provided through a syringe or where professional guidance is crucial to shaping the patient's diet. Nonetheless, simple hand-feeding in most instances may be deemed to fall outside the bounds of medical intervention. The Illinois Supreme Court recently commented that spoon-feeding and bottle-feeding are "analytically distinguishable" from the artificial nutrition considered part of medical intervention.[88]

There is also a causative relation problem when hand-feeding is equated with the medical intervention previously discussed. In one sense, the patient may be tired of coping with chronic afflictions and may be seen as acquiescing in a natural dying process. Yet if a chronically ill patient is capable of ingesting and digesting, a death by starvation (or dehydration) is arguably not a proximate result of natural processes. (This is unlike the situation where ALS or some other degenerative disease disables the patient's swallowing capacity.) The decision to stop eating is a self-initiated deviation from customary human conduct in a fashion which jeopardizes survival. It is also undertaken with the intention of dying. The conduct closely resembles suicide—even though it involves passive behavior and is, therefore, technically distinguishable from typical means of suicide.

All these factors suggest that rejection of manual feeding is not part of a person's fundamental constitutional prerogative to reject life-sustaining medical intervention. The patient's accepted prerogative is to decline medical intervention in the face of a naturally occurring pathological condition. This does not encompass a patient's decision to prompt a life-threatening condition by refusing to ingest food.[89] Consistent with this view, the majority opinion in *Cruzan* remarked: "We do not think that a State is required to remain neutral in the face of an informed and voluntary decision by a physically able adult to starve to death."[90]

This conclusion—that a competent patient does not have a constitutional right to reject manual feeding—is also supported by the bulk of cases which have dealt with hunger strikers. Especially where the hunger striker was a prisoner seeking to extract concessions in return for resumption of eating, the judiciary has rejected the striker's reliance on a right to decline medical intervention.[91] It might be tempting to distinguish these cases on the ground that they involve unfair coercion being utilized by prisoners to blackmail administrative officials; that is, a prison administrator ought to be free to make policy judgments without the emotional blackmail of a prisoner's life hanging in the balance. Yet judicial hostility has also surfaced where the prisoner refusing nutrition has sought no concessions.[92]

The likely explanation is that courts see a moral distinction between self-initiated distress situations, such as hunger strikes, and situations where natural afflictions have prompted the necessity of artificial nutrition. Where a healthy person simply refuses to eat, this is seen as an act of passive suicide differentiable from a decision whether to accept medical intervention in the face of natural disease.

At the same time, there are a few cases where lower courts have indicated unwillingness to interfere with a debilitated elderly person's determination to refuse all nutrition (even though the person was physically capable of receiving such nutrition).[93] These courts have refused petitions by health-care providers to authorize forced feeding of the persons in question.

I suggest that the explanation for such results is revulsion at the prospect of physically restraining (for extended periods) persons who are both competent and determined to resist nutrition. This demeaning restraint constitutes such a significant harm to human dignity and self-respect that courts may be unwilling to interfere, at least where the person is already involved in an inexorable dying process.[94] Many sources have noted the distasteful specter projected by forcible restraint of a patient.[95]

This concern for the indignity of restraints has not always prevailed. The forced treatment of hunger strikers provides one example. In addition, courts have sometimes authorized forcible medical intervention toward resisting medical patients.[96] But this intervention usually occurs where an *in*competent patient is engaged in self-destructive behavior. That is, restraints are frequently used for patients who uncomprehendingly tend to harm themselves or others.[97]

The judicial attitude may well be different where competent patients facing serious afflictions determine to resist all forms of nutrition. In that context, the likelihood is that solicitude for the competent patient's dignity will impel courts to refrain from interference when nutrition is knowingly declined by wearied chronic patients. This approach might well prevail in the future even where hunger-striking prisoners are involved (so long as they are not seeking to exert coercion on administrators or others). That is, the revulsion toward forced administration of nutrition against the considered will of competent individuals may well overcome the moral qualms about acquiescing in a form of passive suicide.

IS A PERSON FACING A FATAL AFFLICTION ENTITLED TO ACCOMPLISH DEATH BY MEANS OTHER THAN REJECTION OF MEDICAL INTERVENTION?

Some commentators have sought to expand the notion of a right to refuse life-preserving medical treatment to include a "right to die."[98] These commentators see the self-determination implicated in rejecting treatment as encompassing a prerogative to dictate the circumstances in which life may be ended. This would include not only self-administered suicide but assistance from others in committing suicide.

Some persons would even include active euthanasia (the introduction by others of external agents, such as poisons, to end a patient's life).

As a matter of constitutional law, the argument that recognition of a patient's right to decline medical intervention compels recognition of a right to die is not very persuasive. The tradition which impelled acknowledgment of a right to refuse life-preserving medical intervention was grounded in bodily integrity and self-determination as reflected in the doctrine of informed consent. Bodily integrity has included a prerogative to resist many bodily invasions. But bodily integrity has never meant a prerogative to introduce whatever elements into the body that a person wishes. Laws against narcotics, prostitution, and consensual sodomy tend to refute such a notion. And laws against assisting suicide tend to undermine the notion that there is a traditional prerogative to control the timing of one's demise or to use active means to terminate one's existence.

Consider the healthy person who decides to contribute a vital organ to a critically ill person. However commendable the motivations involved may be, any physician who performs such an organ-harvesting operation is probably committing homicide. The same analysis is applicable to the technician who freezes a patient to death pursuant to the patient's wish to utilize cryonics. The motives of all parties involved may be life-preserving or life-exalting in nature, but the deed is still a homicide unlikely to find constitutional protection.[99] The motive for accomplishing another person's death has not generally provided a legal defense. (Self-defense and defense of others constitute exceptions.) There is certainly room for legislative change if and when resurrection of frozen corpses becomes a realistic possibility. In the meantime, freezing persons to death will likely remain a crime.

All this is not to say that persons suffering natural afflictions will never be accorded a "right" to secure a quick and painless death. Assisted suicide and even active euthanasia deserve careful analysis as society devises responses to the modern life-extending capability of medical technology. The conflicting policy considerations surrounding those issues are beyond the scope of this book. My only point here is that if such steps are to take place, they will follow from legislative authorization or from common-law development and not from constitutional law.

2

Advance Directives and Problems of Prospective Autonomy

MODERN MEDICINE'S ability to preserve persons indefinitely in gravely debilitated states has prompted a search for ways to cope with technology. One such way is patient control over medical intervention. Chapter 1 described the evolution of legal doctrine aimed at permitting competent individuals to govern their contemporaneous medical fates. This chapter addresses the adaptation of this autonomy principle to future-oriented decisions.

Advance directives have emerged as a vehicle for people to control post-competence medical intervention in a dying process. The object is to permit individuals to prescribe personal preferences in advance and so to maintain a measure of autonomy even after incompetency. I refer to this technique as *prospective autonomy*.

By formulating advance instructions, a declarant (directive maker) can seek to shape future medical handling according to his or her personal values. An advance directive may also designate an agent who will ultimately be responsible for implementing the declarant's instructions or, in the absence of discernible instructions, for making medical decisions on behalf of the incompetent patient. Such a person is variously known as a health-care agent, representative, surrogate, attorney-in-fact, or proxy; but I'll use the term health-care agent. (Note also that in this book the term *advance directive* includes an instruction directive, a directive appointing an agent, or a document combining both elements.)

The potential benefits of an advance directive are plain. Not only can persons prospectively promote personal values and concepts of dignity, but the ultimate decision makers on behalf of the incompetent patient can receive crucial guidance. An advance directive can guide health-care providers as to the agent to be responsible for decision making, as to substantive wishes of the declarant regarding care, or both. A health-care agent or, in the absence of a designated agent, any person acting as formal or informal guardian of the incompetent patient also can receive guidance as to the wishes of the patient. This guidance might mitigate the anxiety, uncertainty, or conflicts sometimes surrounding terminal decisions on behalf of incompetent patients.

As noted, an advance directive exercises prospective autonomy. Prospective autonomy is clearly different in some respects from the contemporaneous personal choice described in chapter 1. Those differences raise certain practical problems. One problem flows from the complexity of decision making in the death and dying area. Future-oriented decisions may involve hypothetical facts and a multitude of prospective circumstances which complicate decision making.[1] To formulate a comprehensive advance directive, a person might have to consider a spectrum of potential mental states (within the range of incompetency), infinite combinations of mental and physical dysfunction, and a variety of possible factors bearing on a decision whether to receive life-sustaining medical intervention.

Additional problems in formulating advance directives flow from the limited perspective of a person looking toward future, post-competence events. A directive may not always be drafted proximate to the moment of its implementation, so it may involve prediction about remote and abstract developments. A person's feelings about death and incapacity might even change with maturity or greater proximity to critical events. Moreover, a person shaping future medical handling is speculating about feelings and sentiments (in a future state of incompetency) which are inherently unknowable in advance.

These difficulties concerning the complexity, remoteness, and perspective of future-oriented death-and-dying decisions prompted initial uncertainty about the legal status of advance directives.[2] In the early 1970s, it was thought that an advance directive constituted a hortatory instrument—an instruction that the declarant *hoped* would be followed but which had no legally binding effect. It was assumed that extending life was an integral part of a guardian's and health-care provider's responsibilities toward an incompetent, dying person. There was no confidence that removal of life support would be consistent with traditional responsibility to act in the "best interests" of a helpless ward. In that era, even if a now incompetent patient would apparently have preferred to relinquish life-preserving medical intervention, the doctrine of parens patriae (a state's authority to protect incompetent persons) loomed as a possible basis to override the patient's prior choice. That implication might have been drawn from cases of the period ordering lifesaving treatment for Jehovah's Witnesses despite their previously stated religious objections.[3] A possible reading of those decisions was that an incompetent patient's guardian should be guided by the patient's current health interests rather than by the patient's prior values and expressed preferences.

Subsequent legal doctrine has repudiated those initial hesitations. Courts have come to recognize that prospective autonomy in shaping medical intervention is not only a legitimate concept but an integral part of the self-determination which society respects. This judicial posture was reached only by overcoming both the practical concerns mentioned above and skepticism about the role of autonomy in the context of incompetent beings. The arguments which countered the initial concerns are worth attention. Their persuasiveness will determine the ultimate scope accorded to advance directives.

DO THE PRACTICAL DIFFICULTIES AFFECTING PROSPECTIVE AUTONOMY OBVIATE THE UTILITY OF THE ADVANCE DIRECTIVE INSTRUMENT?

As noted, practical difficulties confront a person formulating instructions concerning future medical handling in a state of incompetency. First, incompetency can encompass a wide spectrum of mental states—from total unconsciousness to acute awareness (but lacking the mental ability to process the impressions being absorbed).[4] A person's attitudes toward future handling may vary widely across this spectrum of possible states. Further, a person might ultimately face a wide range of physical afflictions and disabilities. This range of afflictions in turn engenders a host of medical contingencies. Each affliction carries its own prognosis uncertainty as well as a multitude of possible combinations of physical and mental dysfunction.

A patient contemplating this range of mental and physical states must also consider a multiplicity of factors in planning future medical intervention. Personal attitudes toward physical pain, physical appearance, physical incapacity, diminished mental function, helplessness, dependence, religious precepts, economic burdens, and well-being of surrounding family and friends represent some of the elements which might influence a person's future-oriented medical decisions. The sheer complexity of the issue therefore raises concern about a person's ability to make an informed and considered choice about dying in a future state of incompetency.[5]

Despite the difficulties involved, the multiplicity of prospective medical situations should not prevent effective advance directives. While a comprehensive directive anticipating all possible situations might not be possible (given the limits of human imagination), every competent person is capable of addressing a few precepts or guidelines regarding future medical care.[6] A person can articulate certain principles—whether grounded on religious scruples, personal philosophy, or personal notions of dignity—which will be relevant across a wide spectrum of medical conditions.

Religiously based principles are likely to be simple (such as an aversion to blood transfusions or a belief that life should be preserved to the maximum extent possible). Dignity-based principles may be more complex, but they may also be reducible to understandable terms. First, a person may have well-developed dignity concepts about a particular status, such as permanent unconsciousness. Such a preference can be expressed in a simple and clear-cut fashion. Second, even if a person is seeking to avoid a conscious, but severely debilitated, existence, it may be possible to describe a few key factors (such as level of dementia) which would make life-sustaining intervention unwanted regardless of the particular medical condition at hand. In short, an outcome-oriented directive—one that describes a debilitated status which is personally intolerable—cuts across a wide range of potential medical interventions.

Additional problems regarding future-oriented decisions flow from the distance of the competent person looking toward future events.[7] A person might well formulate medical instructions far in advance of the anticipated events. (Indeed, this is sound policy because one can't know when an unexpected accident might precipitate a permanent state of incompetency.) This distance sometimes necessitates predictions about remote and abstract circumstances.

This problem of immediacy generates several concerns. One is that the abstract nature of the initial decision making reduces the scrutiny and consideration which would otherwise be given to deviant or morally problematic decisions.[8] A patient making a contemporaneous decision to reject life-preserving medical intervention (e.g., because of religious scruples or views about post-treatment indignity) will likely be subjected to counterarguments and supplications by surrounding staff and concerned observers. The person drafting a directive to shape prospective treatment may not receive similar input or confrontation. This can make the advance decision less informed or considered than might be ideal.

Another concern relates to the fact that the directive may be based on projections about feelings which might not in fact materialize. Professors Rebecca S. Dresser and John A. Robertson argue that the difficulty of foreseeing personal interests in a remote and abstract state make an advance directive an unreliable device.[9] They observe that a person's condition, feelings, and sensations (as they materialize in a future state of incompetency) might be radically different from those contemplated at the time of making an advance directive. For example, a debilitated status which in advance seems demeaning may turn out to have some redeeming value to the incompetent patient. If that is the case, a lack of proximity to actual events may have distorted the substance of the directive. A healthy declarant may have undervalued the potential satisfactions of a debilitated status.[10]

A further concern is the hypothetical nature of projected feelings in a future state of incompetency. A person shaping future medical handling is speculating about feelings and sentiments which are inherently unknowable in such a state. A person cannot precisely anticipate the feelings and experiences of an incapacitated existence—whether positive feelings of satisfaction or negative feelings of frustration and humiliation.[11] If a person can only *guess* about the nature of personal reactions to a future debilitated state, should society respect life-and-death judgments made from such a divorced perspective? In some other contexts, significance is attached to the abstract perspective of the decision maker toward actual consequences. For example, there is great reluctance to bind a woman to prebirth decisions regarding the adoption or future custody of a prospective child.[12] An inability to accurately envision the feelings of childbirth and bonding supposedly undermines the reliability of the advance decision.

The difficulties of remoteness and perspective in making future-oriented death-

and-dying decisions ought not preclude giving binding effect to advance medical directives. While a person cannot be certain what conditions will develop post-competency, it may well be that a declarant correctly anticipates the suffering and/or debilitation associated with his or her dying process. And there is no reason to assume (absent contrary evidence) that a declarant's views or priorities have in fact changed since the advance directive was signed. An adult may have well-developed and firm attitudes about some important issues (e.g., a vision of personal dignity or concern for the surrounding family's emotional and/or fiscal interests) which apply across a spectrum of medical conditions and which are likely to remain firm.

Those sources who oppose prospective autonomy on grounds of remoteness and lack of proximity have yet to explain what chronological lines could be drawn. That is, it is evident that some prospective autonomy must be honored. If a competent person gives instructions about the scope of prospective surgery, that instruction will be honored while the patient is under general anesthesia the next day. This is an exercise of prospective autonomy. The same is true if the surgery is to take place in a week or a month. Unless there were some material reason to think that the patient had altered his or her decision, the initial, competently made instruction would govern. If the initial instruction speaks to the situation later encountered, at what point is the instruction too remote to be upheld?

Of course, a person's philosophy and attitude toward death *might* change over time. It is, therefore, appropriate for the eventual administrator of an advance directive to examine whether the patient's values did vary or change after the directive was issued. Yet the *potential* changeability of people's feelings should not be a basis to bar future-oriented directives.

Certainly, law does not withhold enforcement of future-oriented disposition of property by will, irrevocable trust, or contract, even though the disposer's inclinations might change over time. In those contexts, documents are enforced as written even if it is later shown that the disposer's inclinations changed in fact (but no alteration was made in the relevant document while the actor was still competent). In the context of advance medical directives, it should at least be assumed that a directive maker's wishes persist over time unless there is some showing to the contrary.

The unknowability of a person's prospective feelings in a state of incompetency should also not constitute a bar to advance directives. This unknowability factor ought to impel some serious deliberation (by the declarant) about the content of an advance directive. A person ought to ponder the possible range of feelings in various debilitated states before dictating the rejection of life-preserving intervention in those states. But a person is generally capable of contemplating states of incompetency and fixing his or her basic parameters of personal dignity in those states. Sometimes, prospective feelings or sensations will not be particularly important, as when the condition being contemplated is an unconscious or semiconscious state. Even if future feelings are relevant, a person is capable of making an informed prediction about those feelings and of considering the importance of such feelings in relation to other elements relevant to post-competence medical intervention.

Consider some illustrations. For some persons, an altruistic concern for the interests and well-being of surrounding loved ones will be an overriding factor even if prospective existence does not entail great suffering. For some persons, a personal vision of dignity—grounded on the image which the person wants to leave for posterity—will be a determinative factor even if a feared sense of embarrassment or humiliation does not in fact materialize. In short, the problems of remoteness and perspective associated with advance directives dictate care in formulating such instruments but do not vitiate their utility.

Nor does remoteness (and the possible abstract nature) of a determination mean that inadequate deliberation has gone into the advance instructions. We are considering a written document drafted with the expectation that it will govern life-and-death decisions. A person would indeed be well advised to consult with someone knowledgeable and caring concerning the practical and moral implications of the person's advance instructions. But the reduction to writing and the signing themselves have a cautionary impact on the declarant, thus impelling reflection.

A prerequisite that an advance directive be signed only after certain consultations would entail costs likely to make such instruments accessible only to upper income people. Again, the nature of the deliberation surrounding an advance directive might be a proper inquiry for any health-care agent (or other person) eventually implementing the instructions. That agent might inquire whether the declarant was aware of the considerations making a particular instruction problematic. (Chapter 5 explores this and other aspects of administration of an advance directive.) But the signing of an advance directive ought to be presumed—subject to rebuttal—to carry with it sufficient deliberation to make it binding. Every person knows that he or she might be disabled tomorrow, and so the specter of incapacity has to prompt a certain amount of contemplation even if the maker of an advance directive is currently hale and hearty.

There is no better way to respect future-oriented self-determination than an advance directive. A person's own projections about preferred choices are more likely to accurately reflect that person's will than the approximations and reconstructions of that will performed by other parties at a later date when the subject is incompetent. Thus, if society wants to uphold self-determination in the context of medical decisions for incompetent patients, advance directives must be respected.[13]

A public policy which upholds advance directives is likely to benefit the peace of mind of competent persons in general and persons afflicted with degenerative disease in particular. Many persons experience anxiety in contemplating the prospect of prolonged existence in a status regarded by them as degrading. That anxiety can be acute for persons who see a protracted, severely debilitated dying process as a significant detriment to a lifetime image. Some persons may even be so wary of the aggressiveness of health care providers as to forego treatment for life-threatening disorders. For all such persons, the knowledge that advance instructions will be honored may be a source of relief and reassurance.[14] Limited studies tend to confirm both that loss of control over events prompts patients to suffer negative physical and emotional effects[15] and that discussion of advance directives causes patients to worry less.[16] Future-oriented control of medical intervention may also promote competent persons' self-respect.

Such factors as reduced anxiety and increased self respect add a general, morale-promoting value to a public policy upholding advance directives. Another utilitarian benefit is the saving of public resources. That is, widespread use and implementation of advance directives might well result in reduced resort to expensive life-preserving medical machinery. This would be an incidental public benefit flowing from the upholding of future-oriented autonomy. I am not contending that these general public benefits provide a morally sufficient basis for enforcing advance directives. They do, however, reinforce the self-determination arguments for upholding a competent person's advance directive.

IS A RIGHT TO SELF-DETERMINATION MEANINGFUL IN THE CONTEXT OF AN INCOMPETENT PATIENT?

Self-determination normally entails a conscious weighing of the options at hand. For a medical patient, this means considering and weighing the consequences of nontreatment or various forms of treatment. By definition, an incompetent patient is incapable of performing these functions. Many sources therefore argue that notions of autonomy and personal decision making have no place in regard to an irreversibly incompetent patient.[17] For those sources, a right to refuse medical treatment is dependent upon capacity for choice.[18]

The obvious response is that an advance directive reflects a competently made declaration of a person's wishes and, therefore, is an exercise of self-determination. Not everyone is satisfied with this response. Some commentators insist that the problems of uncertainty, proximity, and perspective mentioned in the previous section subvert the notion of autonomy with regard to advance medical directives. For them, a person contemplating a prospective dying process can never be sufficiently informed in advance to make an effective and binding determination.[19]

The counterarguments were presented above. I argued that prospective autonomy is entitled to respect despite the practical difficulties of anticipating future medical scenarios. The advance directive mechanism for self-determination may not be perfect. There will always be some residual doubt about whether the declarant fully grasped the implications of his or her determination or whether the declarant might have changed his or her mind in the interim. But these flaws don't destroy the importance of advance directives in a society which highly values self-determination.[20]

A declarant ought to be presumed to have deliberately formulated and constantly adhered to the sentiments of an advance directive unless the record rebuts that presumption. A dying process—particularly a protracted dying process—is too integral a part of a person's life to be removed from the realm of self-determination. People care mightily about the image and memories to be left during a period of decline and death. People strive to cultivate an image during a lifetime, and they don't want to see that image despoiled by a protracted demise in a gravely debilitated condition.[21] These personal aspirations seem worthy of respect. Disregard of prior choices relegates the now incompetent patient to the status of an object whose fate is determined for it rather than of a human who has etched his or her own fate.

The question now is which view will prevail. Do obstacles of proximity and perspective bar recognition of prospective autonomy in the context of death and dying? Or are people entitled to shape in advance the degree of medical intervention provided in their post-competence existences?

In law, the concept of prospective autonomy has been almost universally accepted—as a matter of state common law, state constitutional law, or federal constitutional interpretation. A number of state court decisions ascribe to an incompetent person the "same right to autonomy in medical decisions as a competent patient."[22] This broad declaration ignores the cognitive incapacity of an incompetent patient and cannot be taken literally. But at the least, the statement means that a person who has competently expressed his or her wishes (as in an advance directive) is entitled to have post-competence medical care shaped according to those wishes.

Judicial willingness to preserve self-determination in the context of an incompetent patient spawned what is known as the "substituted judgment" approach. The idea was to decide the incompetent patient's fate in the same manner the patient would decide if the patient were miraculously competent for a few moments.[23] Replicating a patient's choice might be a difficult goal to attain, at least in the absence of the patient's considered judgment about life-sustaining medical intervention. But an advance directive can constitute an explicit judgment about that issue. Most authorities therefore recognize that a person's advance directive is the best evidence of the now incompetent patient's wishes.[24] And all authorities endorsing the substituted judgment approach regard the patient's competently expressed wishes as binding.

Recognition of the binding effect of prior expressions could have come through common-law development (judicial structuring of the physician-patient and guardian-patient relationships). As courts began to recognize a constitutionally based right to reject life-sustaining medical intervention, however, they quickly acknowledged prior expressions as a source of constitutional rights for an incompetent patient. That is, the courts readily viewed implementation of the prior wishes of an incompetent patient as fulfilling a constitutional "right" of self-determination.[25]

The ready acceptance of prospective autonomy reflects judicial appreciation of the importance of self-determination and personal visions of dignity in shaping a dying process. Many of the relevant cases arose in the context of permanently unconscious patients who, while competent, had indicated that they would not want life-preserving medical treatment if reduced to a permanently vegetative status. Those cases regard a prior declaration as a statement about what the declarant would regard as a degrading existence. They regard such a declaration as a way for a person to preserve humanity and dignity in the face of an incapacitating condition. And they regard this determination as an integral part of the self-determination which properly belongs to an individual either under the common law or the Constitution.

The U.S. Supreme Court's disposition of *Cruzan* does not alter this judicial pattern. I've already argued that *Cruzan* does not repudiate the notion that a competent person's rejection of medical intervention is a fundamental aspect of liberty. *Cruzan* holds only that it is constitutional for a state to prevent withdrawal of life-sustaining care *in the absence of clear-cut instructions* from the previously competent patient.

The *Cruzan* decision may even reinforce the respect which has been accorded to advance directives as a vehicle of prospective autonomy. Eight of the nine justices seemed to indicate that if there had been clear proof of the incompetent patient's previously expressed wishes, the state would have been required to respect that determination. This would be consistent with prior Supreme Court acknowledgement that rights involving choices for incompetent persons can only be given meaningful expression via agents acting on behalf of the incompetent individuals.[26] *Cruzan* may well mean that the clear exercise of future-oriented autonomy will be deemed to prevail (as a matter of constitutional law) against a state's asserted interest in promoting sanctity of life principles. An advance directive is, potentially, a clear expression of the patient's autonomy.

This possible constitutional status for advance directives has significant implications for efforts of some states to circumscribe the scope of living wills or other advance directives. The next chapter examines those implications while setting out the legal framework governing interpretation and administration of advance directives.

Before turning to that topic, some last words about *Cruzan*. The Supreme Court ruled there that in the absence of clear-cut prior expressions, a comatose patient's constitutional liberty interest was not violated by a state requirement of continued medical intervention. That ruling was probably sound in terms of a liberty interest in self-determination. That is, in the absence of a patient's prior expressions on the topic of life-sustaining medical intervention, no genuine choice can be attributed to the now incompetent patient.[27]

Self-determination, though, is not the only constitutional interest which could have surfaced in *Cruzan*. The practical effect of Missouri's legal framework was to relegate to an indefinite limbo every incompetent patient who had not left prior instructions. Absent prior expressions, Missouri mandated continued life support no matter how painful or degraded the status of the incompetent patient. This course denied the guardians of Nancy Cruzan any option to act in her best interests or in order to preserve her dignity. This preclusion of medical approaches consistent with the best interests of the incompetent patient deprived Nancy Cruzan of a highly humane course and relegated her to a permanently insensate status. The Missouri statute was thus arguably unconstitutional in denying liberty—liberty not in the sense of choice but in the sense of a range of humane treatment options.[28] Denial of that range of options relegates some patients to an indefinite, undignified status arguably inconsistent with constitutional respect for human dignity.

In sum, it would have been possible to rule in *Cruzan* that liberty and due process under the Fourteenth Amendment demand that states respect the basic dignity of incompetent patients. That would mean, at least, that the standard fixed for guardianship must permit a medical decision consistent with the incompetent patient's best interests, including personal dignity.

This idea—that the due process clause compels states to use guardianship decision-making standards which permit choices consistent with the well-being and dignity of an incompetent being—has implications beyond the death-and-dying area. Liberty as dignity would mean, for example, that a state must furnish protection and at least a minimum level of dignified care to any incompetent whom the state decides to shelter.[29] Similarly, a state could not preclude a sterilization (or other medical procedure) for a gravely mentally disabled person if such a procedure were necessary to that person's happiness and well-being.

The topic of rights of incompetents (in the absence of competently expressed, advance instructions) is beyond the scope of this book. My only point here is that *Cruzan* could have been resolved on a basis broader than Nancy's self-determination interest or her parents' familial decision-making authority. As it is, *Cruzan* does not constitute an impediment to advance directives. But that case could have been better argued (and decided).

3

Choosing the Best Format in Light of the Statutory Framework for Advance Directives

IN ORDER to decide on the proper format and content for an advance medical directive, it is important to understand the governing legal structure. There are variations from state to state, so before counseling anyone, an adviser must check the statutes in effect in the particular locale.[1] However, there are common features, and this chapter examines the most prominent patterns.

Parallel to the post-1976 development of judicial doctrine establishing the importance of prior expressions (as described in the previous chapter), state legislatures have widely endorsed the concept of advance directives designed to govern medical handling of incompetent patients. This legislative recognition of prospective autonomy has taken two forms. The most prevalent vehicle is living-will legislation—laws recognizing the binding effect of prior instructions reduced to writing in accord with certain formalities. Another vehicle is legislation authorizing a competent person (a principal) to appoint a health-care agent charged with making the principal's post-competence health-care decisions. The principal may also accompany appointment of a health-care agent with written guidelines or instructions to the agent.

In the next sections, I'll look at the strengths and weaknesses of these respective techniques for shaping post-competence care. Thereafter, I'll suggest a preferred format for an advance directive.

LIVING-WILL TYPE LEGISLATION

Starting with California's fledgling effort in 1976, forty-seven states have endorsed the use of written substantive instructions aimed at governing future medical intervention.[2] These living-will type measures typically provide that a now incompetent patient's prior instructions should be given binding force. The typical statutory preamble declares legislative recognition of the autonomy and dignity of incompetent patients and dictates respect for living wills as a means to promote those values. The typical statute then prescribes certain formalities for creation of a living will, usually the witnessing of a declarant's signature by two persons. In a few states, the statute provides a form document which must be followed; more often, the statute provides a sample form which can be adopted or varied at the option of a declarant.[3] Usually, the statute mandates that health-care providers either honor the terms of a living will or act to transfer the patient to a provider who will cooperate with the patient's will. (The sanction for noncompliance is usually stated as "professional discipline".)

The potential utility of living-will type legislation was considerable.[4] In the many states where the judiciary had not addressed the issue, living-will statutes removed any legal cloud over the concept of future-oriented autonomy. The legislation clarified that a now incompetent patient's prior instructions could and should be given binding force. It also clarified that medical compliance with a living will would not be deemed assistance to suicide or any other impropriety. Indeed, health-care providers were assured by the legislation that good-faith compliance with a living will would immunize providers from legal liability.

Living-will type legislation also offered considerable practical promise. By encouraging written documentation of a person's wishes regarding life support, such legislation seemed to promise important help to future decision makers acting on behalf of incompetent patients. A written format provides the opportunity for elaboration of a person's preferences and for deliberation on the complex issues involved. As an evidentiary tool, a writing is clearly preferable to testimony about prior oral declarations. As a practical aid, an instruction directive might reduce the uncertainty and anguish of those decision makers responsible for the medical fate of an incompetent patient. Accordingly, a directive might reduce disagreement and conflict among decision makers.

Despite the considerable potential of living-will type laws, major disappointments must be noted regarding the bulk of such legislation to date. (New Jersey provides an exception, for reasons to be explained in chapter 8.) First, the legislation in most jurisdictions is seriously flawed. The state political processes have clearly been impacted by a variety of interest groups: health-care providers, religious groups, and right-to-life organizations, as well as patients' rights advocates.[5] The result has been serious limitations on the circumstances in which state legislatures have given their endorsement to the implementation of living wills. (The nature and effects of these limitations are considered below.) Second, the living will has not yet emerged as a popular tool for the exercise of control over a future dying process. The best estimates are that only fifteen to twenty-five percent of adults have signed a living will, though the percentage is higher for persons over age sixty-four.[6]

There are significant obstacles to the widespread use of living-will type instruments. One obstacle is people's common unwillingness to confront their own mortality. That unwillingness has always been reflected in the low percentage of people who draft regular wills, and it is probably a factor contributing to the low percentage who draft instructions regarding terminal medical treatment.[7]

Another obstacle may be a public perception that living-will instruments will not effectively control critical medical decisions.[8] There is some empirical evidence which would explain such a perception. One recent study and some anecdotal reports show that physicians in charge of medical intervention in a dying process may be influenced more by the wishes of surrounding family members than by the incompetent patient's living will.[9] This order of influence flows in part from physicians' sensitivity to the possibility of lawsuits.[10] In the typical terminal care scenario, it is the surrounding family which looms as a litigation threat if their wishes are contravened and not the helpless, moribund patient. A similar phenomenon has occurred in the context of prior instructions regarding organ donation, where the surrounding family's wishes tend to prevail in practice.[11]

Two developments in 1990 might provide impetus to the use of living-will type documents. The July 1990 *Cruzan* decision received extensive publicity and highlighted the importance of clear-cut prior instructions in the context of incompetent patients. In the months following *Cruzan*, right-to-die oriented organizations received over a million requests for living-will forms. And in October 1990, Congress passed the federal Patient Self-Determination Act[12] requiring health-care institutions receiving federal funds to provide to their patients information about advance medical directives.[13]

These two 1990 developments have certainly promoted public consciousness about advance directives, including living-will type instruments. The ultimate success of a living will depends, however, on its utility in achieving the basic goal— extensive control over medical intervention in a subsequent dying process.

As noted, the living-will legislation in most jurisdictions is flawed. And the principal flaw stems from provisions in many living-will laws significantly qualifying the circumstances in which legislative endorsement is accorded to implementation of advance instructions.[14] Because such legislation appears to limit the scope of a declarant's autonomy (in contrast to the broad common-law acceptance of prospective autonomy), it threatens to have a negative effect on the responsiveness of health-care providers to living-will type instruments. Statutory restrictions may well cause health-care providers to have hesitations about the legal effect of certain living-will instructions. The providers' risk-aversive tendencies would then prompt irresolution and thus hamper the implementation of advance instructions. The statutory limitations therefore warrant examination.

STATUTORY CONSTRAINTS CONTAINED IN LIVING-WILL TYPE LAWS

Living-will type statutes almost universally confine authorized removal of life support to a patient in a "terminal condition."[15] The precise definition of a terminal condition varies from state to state, but the thrust of many such provisions is to limit legislative endorsement of cessation of life support to unpreventably dying patients in the last stages of decline (as opposed to gravely debilitated individuals whose lives are indefinitely preserveable despite serious medical pathology). A legislative limitation of this sort is unresponsive to the needs of people who dread protracted maintenance in a chronic, debilitated status or of people stricken with degenerative disease and on the brink of what will be inexorable decline toward total helplessness. "Persons suffering from Alzheimer's disease and strokes, from chronic kidney failure, or from certain malignancies may not be terminal but nevertheless consider aggressive, life-sustaining medical interventions to produce a disproportionate burden."[16]

A number of living-will statutes define a terminal condition as an "incurable and irreversible" condition which, "regardless of" medical intervention, makes death imminent.[17] The irreversibility notion raises the possibility that the technical maintenance of lost bodily functions can preclude finding a terminal condition and thus undermine an advance directive aimed at preventing indefinite lingering in a gravely debilitated condition. For example, dialysis machines can substitute for the waste-disposal function of damaged kidneys. And artificial nutrition can substitute for normal ingestion of food after brain trauma incapacitates the swallowing reflex. Yet, end-stage kidney disease may so ravage the patient that dialysis merely prolongs the dying process without relieving suffering or restoring a meaningful level of function.[18] And artificial nutrition may sustain a patient in a permanent vegetative state, forestalling death but leaving the patient utterly insentient. In short, if a condition is deemed "reversible" when medical intervention can preserve bodily function (but the patient is left with insidious consequences from the pathological condition), then the purpose of many advance directives would be frustrated.[19]

As noted, a number of living-will statutes define a terminal condition as one which, *regardless of* medical intervention, will cause death imminently. If the words "regardless of medical intervention" are read literally to mean death will result imminently even with medical intervention, then such a provision is pointless. Where death is imminent anyway with or without medical intervention, the prerogative to relinquish further medical intervention has no practical consequence.[20]

A few state courts have recognized the pointlessness of such language and have ruled that proximity of death must be assessed without regard to the particular medical intervention in dispute. The Illinois Supreme Court recently commented: "If the very delay caused by the [life-preserving] procedures [in dispute] were allowed to govern the assessment of imminence, the Act's definition of a terminal disease would be rendered circular and meaningless."[21] That court ruled that imminence must be judged "as if the death-delaying procedures were absent."[22] This means, for example, that if a respirator is sought to be detached from a patient with chronic respiratory incapacity, the condition would be deemed terminal if death would be imminent without the disputed respirator. However, there is no assurance that all state courts facing similar statutory language will similarly interpret their living-will legislation.

Even where the "terminal condition" limitation is understood to mean terminal

in the absence of the disputed medical intervention, a problem occurs with living-will statutes which include a proximity of death limitation. For example, some
statutes in defining a terminal condition require that death be "imminent" (in the
absence of medical intervention). A narrow interpretation of such a provision
would exclude conditions involving artificial nutrition and would necessitate extended treatment for many cancers. Moreover, where a gradual illness, like pneumonia, afflicts a severely demented and incapacitated person whose underlying
physical condition is stable, such a provision apparently means that antibiotics
must be provided. In all these instances, death might not be considered imminent
even in the absence of medical intervention. (Also, there is a hazard that the intervening pneumonia might be deemed a curable or reversible condition, so that
the stabilized, deteriorated patient might still not be in a terminal condition.)

In some jurisdictions, the imminence requirement has been altered to say that
death must occur "within a relatively short time" in the absence of medical intervention.[23] Even this relaxation of the requisite time proximity between cessation
of treatment and death does not fully meet the exigencies of advance directives.
For one thing, the phrase "a relatively short time" is imprecise and subject to
grudging interpretation by health-care providers so inclined. In addition, people
ought to be able to provide in advance for medical response to protracted dying
processes such as cancer or other degenerative diseases. "The two leading killers
in the U.S.—heart disease and cancer—as well as degenerative diseases—M. S.
and Alzheimer's—and any of the immune disorders—such as AIDS—are all
chronic illnesses that frequently lead to a [protracted] terminal period of incompetence."[24] In the absence of living-will legislation, the judicial proclivity would
probably be to respect clear prior directives without respect to death proximity or
life-expectancy limitations.[25]

The impetus for the original legislative tendency to endorse advance directives
only for the last stages of unpreventable dying processes is understandable. Legislators were influenced in part by the early judicial formulations of a competent
patient's prerogative to resist life-preserving treatment. These early formulations
had hinted that the patient's prerogative might be limited to situations where unpreventable death is near.[26] It was thought that, otherwise, government interests in
promoting sanctity of life might override even a competent patient's self-determination prerogative.[27] In addition, legislators were concerned about helpless beings
and their possible exploitation in a medical setting. When most living-will laws
were adopted, there had been little experience with standards and practices of removal of life support. The specter of government-endorsed quality-of-life judgments
about indefinitely preservable beings alarmed some people.[28] Finally, legislative
hesitancy to endorse full-blown autonomy in the context of future-oriented terminal
medical decisions also stemmed from political pressure. State legislative processes
have commonly been impacted by a variety of interest groups (including religious
groups and right-to-life organizations).[29] Right-to-life organizations, in particular,

have sought to circumscribe the circumstances in which living wills might lead to a patient's demise via removal of life support.

The problem is that confining advance directives to the last stages of an unavoidable dying process intolerably restricts the scope of future-oriented autonomy. Many persons drafting advance directives are concerned with the effects of progressive deterioration of organ systems and the combined effects of chronic disorders. Previously vital persons often wish to oppose medical intervention capable of prolonging existence for extended periods if the status preserved entails extreme suffering or a gravely incapacitated and (subjectively) degrading status. When medical intervention cannot restore an individual to even a semblance of a former status, that individual may seek the prerogative to reject further medical intervention via an advance directive. The "terminal illness" limitation—as contained in some living-will type legislation—inhibits the exercise of that prerogative. (Later in this chapter I'll suggest means to circumvent this limitation for persons preparing an advance directive in jurisdictions with restrictive legislation.)

Other common restraints within living-will statutes relate to the scope of "life-sustaining procedures" deemed rejectable pursuant to a living will. One common subject of special attention is artificial nutrition and hydration. (For simplicity's sake, I'll use the term nutrition as a shorthand for both nutrition and hydration.)

As noted in chapter 1, some commentators sought to draw a distinction between artificial nutrition and other forms of life-sustaining medical treatment. There were two contentions. One was that provision of nutrition carries a symbolic import—commitment to the well-being of fellow humans—absent in other types of medical intervention. A second contention related to causation; withdrawal of nutrition was claimed to cause a patient to starve to death, while withdrawal of mechanical life support would merely allow a natural disease process to run its course.

Almost all courts addressing the issue have rejected the notion that artificial nutrition is differentiable from other medical intervention. A wide range of physicians' groups and ethicists have also rejected the asserted distinctiveness of artificial nutrition. I already explained the reasons for this triumph of logic and common sense. Nonetheless, the living-will statutes in a number of states still single out artificial nutrition. This statutory distinction poses a serious concern for a declarant (maker of an advance directive) who is fearful of being mired either in a permanent vegetative condition or in a barely conscious state caused by severe strokes or other brain trauma. In those situations, a person may well wish to forego artificial nutrition as well as other forms of medical intervention.

The statutory constraints on rejection of artificial nutrition take a variety of forms. As of 1986, seventeen states had excluded artificial nutrition from the scope of treatment rejectable pursuant to a living-will. Since that time, a number of those seventeen state legislatures have mitigated that exclusionary policy. Several of those states now include nutrition within rejectable life support.[30] Several others among them now allow for the withdrawal of artificial nutrition if the declarant has explicitly authorized that course.[31]

There are still approximately six states which seek to bar withdrawal of artificial nutrition pursuant to a living will.[32] And a few other states closely confine the circumstances in which nutrition can be withdrawn. For example, Illinois bars withdrawal of nutrition if it "would result in death solely from dehydration or starvation rather than from the existing terminal condition."[33] North Dakota allows nutrition cessation only if continued nutrition would be "harmful or painful" to the patient.[34]

The overall picture with regard to artificial nutrition is more permissive. In the majority of states, artificial nutrition is either not mentioned (thus leaving room for judicial determinations equating nutrition with other forms of life support) or can be foregone if the declarant has explicitly authorized such a course. Nonetheless, as noted, a number of states' living-will laws still seriously circumscribe a declarant's options regarding artificial nutrition.

A more minor legislative constraint is found in living-will statutes excluding "comfort care" from life-sustaining measures which can be withheld pursuant to a living will.[35] The legislative intent is to require provision of palliative care—meaning drug relief of pain or anxiety, skin care, hygiene, and grooming. In large measure, such a requirement coincides with people's preferences. The vast majority of people presumably prefer to receive intervention promoting their own comfort. However, there may be some patients who have religious or philosophical reasons for opposing drugs which will diminish suffering and/or alertness. And there may be instances when "palliative" relief would incidentally either shorten or prolong a dying process and therefore be unwanted by a declarant. In some instances, then, a legislative mandate of comfort care would impinge on the preferences of persons formulating an advance directive.

There is another objectionable feature of some living-will laws as to the scope of rejectable "life-sustaining procedures." A number of state statutes include a sample form which must either be substantially followed or is at least suggested (and even if not "suggested" would often be adopted as a matter of convenience by unsophisticated declarants). Many declarants will find the prescribed form inadequate for the declarant's needs.

Often, the prescribed or suggested form describes the treatment to be withheld as that which "only prolongs the process of dying."[36] This formulation for unwanted treatment is extremely opaque and uninformative.[37] A prime object of a living will is to indicate a level of deterioration and incapacity and/or suffering at which the formerly vital individual no longer desires life-sustaining intervention. Yet the form declaration does not describe factors which would determine when a patient's condition is so dismal or painful that treatment "only" prolongs the dying process. Is it the intendment of the formulation that any possible benefit from further existence, any iota of interactional capacity, means that treatment should be extended because it does not only prolong dying? Even if the incompetent patient's condition is burdened by unrelievable suffering? Even if the patient is physically helpless and severely demented—a status which would be deemed intolerably demeaning by many people directing their own future medical fates? And how does the notion of treatment only prolonging a dying process relate to chances for a temporary and partial remission? Does a one percent chance of a brief remission mean that treatment is not "only" prolonging the dying process? In short, the typical "forms" suggested by living-will laws are deficient in their vague formulation of the circumstances in which life-preserving medical intervention is to be withheld. (Chapter 4, on drafting advance directives, suggests solutions.)

There exist other minor defects in typical living will legislation. One example is a provision in approximately thirty living-will laws which suspends the effect of such a document while a female declarant is pregnant.[38] The defect is minor only in the sense that it will impact on few people. But at least in the approximately twenty jurisdictions which nullify a declarant's directive during an entire pregnancy, the defect is major in that the provision is unconstitutional. A sweeping nullification during an entire pregnancy disregards the viability line drawn by *Roe v. Wade* and would be struck down.[39]

Another common defect is a revocation clause providing that the maker of a living will revokes the document by any statement or expression to that effect, regardless of the maker's mental state at the time of the expression.[40] Such a provision has been roundly criticized as inconsistent with the living will's underlying object of promoting autonomy. To quote one source:

> The revocation of a declaration by an incompetent patient or one unable to understand what he or she is doing should not be effective, since it negates the very essence of what the act seeks to promote: self-determination.[41]

A broad revocation policy has been defended as erring on the side of life and as reflecting commitment to respect for human life.[42] Yet a revocation provision ignoring the mental status of the declarant creates considerable potential for the manipulation of an incompetent patient who possesses a living will. Under it, a severely demented patient could repeatedly be asked whether he or she wants to rescind the prior directive, and eventually a positive response would be forthcoming. Or an observer might simply misrepresent that verbal repudiation of the directive had occurred.[43] It makes more sense to say, as some state laws do,[44] that the competently expressed desires of a declarant at all times supersede any inconsistent expression contained in a prior directive.

Alternatively, any expression by an incompetent patient apparently inconsistent with a prior directive ought to provoke reassessment of the patient's mental capacities and desires. It is conceivable that an incompetent patient might have enough cognitive understanding so that a desire to continue to receive life-sustaining treatment ought to be respected. This requires some comprehension of death (and of the significance of the decision) on the part of the incompetent patient. However, a patient's expression ought not be followed without regard to the level of dementia involved.[45]

The preceding discussion about the meaning of terms like "terminal condition" and "life-sustaining procedures" showed how some living-will statutes appear to constrict the autonomy of makers of living wills. The prime objectives of living-will statutes were salutary: to offer an approved vehicle for prospective autonomy and to reassure health-care providers about legal liability. The results, as shown, were sometimes confusing and problematical. A leading commentator, Professor Alexander Capron, has suggested that living-will statutes "have sown much confusion and have probably detracted as much from patients' real rights as they have added."[46]

The key question—at least in jurisdictions whose statutes bear some of the defects previously addressed—is whether to utilize the living-will vehicle provided by the state legislature. Before resolving that issue, it is useful to examine another possible vehicle for exercising prospective autonomy: appointment of a health-care agent.

ADVANCE DESIGNATION OF A HEALTH-CARE AGENT

It is usually important to make advance selection of a person—whom I call a health-care agent, although alternate names include proxy, surrogate, attorney-in-fact, or health-care representative—who will be responsible for post-competency medical decisions. The assumption is that a reliable person will be chosen as future agent and that such agent will be conversant with, and sympathetic to, the declarant's wishes regarding medical intervention in the dying process.

If such a trustworthy person is available, selection of a personal agent offers an extremely useful means to promote self-determination in the dying process. In the first place, selection of a personal agent should provide an occasion for the principal (the person designating an agent) to contemplate and discuss the substance of future-oriented instructions regarding medical intervention. The principal naturally needs to discuss the contents of instructions with the contemplated agent in order to be sure that the agent both understands and sympathizes with the principal's goals. Indeed, no self-respecting person would agree to serve as agent without understanding at least the essence of the principal's wishes. Second, an agent serves as an authoritative source to whom health-care providers can turn regarding critical decisions. The presence of a designated agent can thus mitigate confusion about decision-making authority and reduce conflict among relatives or others surrounding a moribund patient.[47] Finally, an agent can serve both as an advocate and potential enforcer of a patient's wishes in the event that health-care providers seem to be ignoring or deviating from those wishes.[48]

A health-care agent's advocacy role is important during the current era in which advance directives are still an unfamiliar device. As noted, there are indications that physicians in charge of terminal care may be influenced more by the wishes of surrounding family members than by the incompetent patient's prior instructions.[49] Yet, if advance directives are to become a widespread and effective vehicle, people will have to be reassured that their wishes will in fact be implemented. Presence of a trusted agent (with authority to act as an advocate) ought to increase the probability that an advance directive will be faithfully observed. No one can be certain that a trusted agent won't turn renegade and deviate from prior instructions. But the chances of faithful adherence to prior wishes would seem to be better through a specially selected and instructed representative than through reliance on the happenstance of which family members are on hand at critical moments.

Assuming that a suitable person can be found to act as agent, a question may arise about what legal mechanism to utilize for appointment of that agent? The object, of course, is to secure binding effect for the agent's determinations and to afford the agent full authority to implement the principal's wishes.

In a growing number of states (now approximately twenty), the living-will legislation permits a declarant to designate a person to be in charge of implementing the declarant's living will. The problem with this mechanism is that the designated agent is presumably confined by the limitations contained within the relevant living-will statute. This means that in some states constraints described in the preceding section—concerning a "terminal condition" and "life-sustaining treatments" —would apply.[50]

A more promising mechanism is use of a durable power of attorney (DPOA). This is a simple document giving the named agent (sometimes known as a proxy, surrogate, or attorney-in-fact) authority to make post-competence decisions on behalf of the principal. The DPOA document is effective without any judicial proceedings, and the principal can generally define the scope of the agent's authority. Statutes providing for durable powers of attorney exist in every state.

A first task, though, is to make sure that the jurisdiction in question will recognize the authority of the DPOA holder (the agent) to make decisions as to life-sustaining medical intervention. The general DPOA statutes were primarily intended to cover property-related decisions for incompetents, and the statutes usually did not mention health-care decisions (let alone terminal medical decisions). There was doubt in many jurisdictions whether authority over intimate and personal life-and-death decisions could be delegated in a regular DPOA. However, the uncertainty has been resolved in many states in a manner allowing a DPOA to be used for medical decisions.

Legislatures in approximately thirty states have adopted special statutes authorizing a durable power of attorney for health care (DPOA-HC).[51] (The mechanism might be called appointment of a health-care proxy, as in New York, or of a health-care representative, as in New Jersey; but the concept is the same.) A competent person (principal) appoints an agent who will have binding authority over post-competency medical decisions, including authority to reject life-preserving medical intervention.

Even in the absence of a DPOA-HC law, a person may well have authority to designate an agent who will have power to make critical medical decisions. In several states, the general DPOA statute mentions health-care decisions and will likely be interpreted to include critical medical decisions. Moreover, several courts have indicated that written designation of a prospective health-care agent should be respected either under a general DPOA law (even without statutory mention of health care decisions) or as a matter of common law.[52]

Even if a mechanism exists for appointment of a health-care agent, a question remains whether that agent will possess full authority to implement the principal's wishes. (Again, the answer may vary from jurisdiction to jurisdiction, but certain generalities can be described here.) Most DPOA-HC laws do afford the agent full authority. Many such measures instruct a health-care agent to carry out the principal's wishes as gleaned from the appointing document or elsewhere. And the agent is given authority to make the same range of decisions regarding life-preserving medical intervention that the principal could make if competent.[53] For example, New York's enactment empowers an agent to make "any and all health care decisions on the principal's behalf that the principal could make."[54]

By potentially enabling a health-care agent to make the same range of decisions that the principal could have made if competent, these broad DPOA-HC type laws permit the maximum scope possible for prospective autonomy aimed at shaping post-competence medical handling. The only clear limitations are those (like bans on assisted suicide or active euthanasia) which would be imposed even on the decisions of competent patients. (A further possible limitation—conflict between a principal's instructions and the contemporaneous best interests of the now incompetent patient—will be discussed in chapter 6.)

Not all DPOA-HC type statutes confer plenary authority on a health-care agent to carry out the wishes of the principal with regard to life-preserving medical intervention. In a few instances, a DPOA-HC measure replicates the same kind of restrictions contained in the state's living-will law.[55] As noted, this usually means a "terminal condition" restriction on the circumstances in which life support may be withdrawn and some restraint on removal of artificial nutrition. Other constraints may also exist. For example, Kentucky does not require an agent to carry out the wishes of a principal; rather, the agent must consider physicians' recommendations as well as the patient's best interests in shaping medical handling.[56] Nonetheless, the majority of DPOA-HC type laws offer a broad, effective device for exercising prospective autonomy.

CHOOSING A FORMAT FOR AN ADVANCE DIRECTIVE

The principal modes for advance directives have now been described: a living-will type document (instruction directive) and appointment of a health-care agent. Which format, or combination of formats, is best suited to effectuating a declarant's object of controlling post-competence medical intervention?

Circumstances may dictate the appropriate response. If there is no trustworthy, sympathetic, and willing person to serve as a health-care agent, then a declarant's only option is an instruction directive aimed at directing anyone who is eventually in charge of the incompetent patient's medical care. Also, the particular statutes within a state—their degree of deference to a declarant's autonomy—will help determine what format to employ.

If we assume both that a suitable person is available and that the particular state's DPOA-HC law (or comparable statute) affords an agent broad authority to carry out a principal's wishes, it makes good sense to utilize that statutory mechanism to designate an agent. In the absence of a designated agent, attending medical personnel would customarily turn to an incompetent patient's spouse, or next of kin, or other close acquaintance willing to assume responsibility for medical decision making. This might seem like a satisfactory arrangement, depending on the declarant's circumstances. That is, a person might be confident that his or her spouse (or other trusted person) will be on hand at the critical moments and that the spouse will faithfully implement the incompetent patient's wishes.

Yet, there are almost always good reasons to formally appoint an agent. First, if there are children or siblings in the picture (among those likely to be on hand during a dying process), there is always potential for disagreement and confusion. One child or sibling (or other relative, for that matter) may become so grief-stricken or guilt-ridden as to oppose implementation of the patient's wishes. Or that child or sibling may have a different interpretation of what the patient's wishes actually are. Designation of a single authoritative agent (as well as alternate agents in the event the main agent is unavailable) will diminish the disruption and confusion which might otherwise prevail.

A second reason to formally designate an agent is to enhance that agent's authority in the event of opposition from health-care providers. This is particularly a concern if the now incompetent patient's wishes are idiosyncratic or otherwise not to the tastes of the surrounding medical personnel. In many states, in the absence of designation as a health-care agent, the spouse or next of kin (or whoever is on hand) has no formal legal authority to make decisions on behalf of the incompetent patient. Health-care providers commonly rely on the decisions of surrounding family only as a matter of convenience. At the moment that an attending physician is troubled by the course which the family is seeking in reliance on the patient's wishes, the physician can contend that the family has no formal legal status. To regain control, the family might have to institute costly and time-consuming guardianship proceedings. By contrast, an agent appointed pursuant to a DPOA-HC law (or comparable statute) is armed with explicit authority to implement the wishes of the now incompetent patient.

The problem of who's in control of decision making is mitigated somewhat in the approximately nineteen states which have adopted statutory provisions regarding surrogate decision making for incompetent persons. These provisions list, in order of priority, the persons authorized to make medical decisions on behalf of an incompetent patient who has not designated his or her own agent. The list of authorized surrogates usually begins with a spouse and then reaches blood relatives in a descending order of proximity.[57]

These family-surrogate decision-making provisions will often be unsuited to declarants seeking to shape their post-competence medical fates. First, the close relative delegated decision-making power by statute may not be the person whom the declarant believes would be most suited to the task. Second, there may be disagreements or frictions among relatives of equal status (disputes among children or siblings or relatives of another degree). Third, many of these provisions appear within the state's living-will type statute and are therefore subject to the constraints (such as a terminal condition limitation) found in the relevant living-will type statute.[58] In other words, these legislative efforts may not satisfactorily fill the void when a declarant has failed to designate a health-care agent.

My only hesitance to use a statutory mechanism for appointment of a health-care agent would arise where the relevant DPOA-HC contains limitations on an agent's authority which are distasteful to the principal. (This might be the case, for example, where the DPOA-HC law itself imposes a narrowly defined "terminal condition" limitation.) In that instance, I would recommend a "nonstatutory" designation of a health-care agent. That is, the principal's appointment document would be signed with the same formality (number of witnesses, etc.) dictated by the DPOA-HC law, but the principal would make clear that he or she was relying on common-law and constitutional prerogatives rather than the DPOA-HC statute. In that fashion, the appointed agent could assert that he or she is not bound by the distasteful (to the principal) restraints contained in the DPOA-HC law. This effort to escape the unwanted limitations of a particular DPOA-HC law might not succeed, but it's probably worth a try.

If an agent is designated—whether through a DPOA-HC type law or otherwise —a question arises as to whether the document should contain substantive instructions (beside just naming an agent and alternates). My response is affirmative.

There are important reasons to accompany designation of a health-care agent with substantive instructions representing the principal's basic perspectives on post-competence medical handling. In the first place, any decision maker, including a designated agent, ought to be instructed on several critical considerations. These include the principal's personal attitudes toward pain, incapacitation, and indignity, as well as financial costs and the emotional interests of surrounding family and friends.

Reliance on familiarity with the principal's general values, as culled from the agent's casual interactions with the principal, is probably inadequate. A recent study shows a significant divergence between competent chronic patients' actual wishes (regarding CPR) and the perceptions of family members and physicians close to the patient.[59] This divergence tends to emphasize the need for precise articulation of the principal's wishes regarding terminal care. Moreover, even pointed discussions about a principal's medical preferences may be inadequate. Oral conversations may considerably predate the critical events, and an agent ought not rely on memory alone.

Written instructions to the health-care agent can be useful for reasons beyond assuring the agent's full understanding of the principal's wishes. Written instructions will help repel any challenges or objections posed by family or medical staff opposed to the incompetent patient's wishes.[60] A written substantive directive can thus serve as an important evidentiary tool for the agent, especially where the directive's content reflects idiosyncratic wishes of the patient which otherwise might be opposed by family or staff.

Even in a jurisdiction which ostensibly accords an appointed agent potential power to make the same range of decisions the patient could make if competent, the presence of written instructions may well assist the agent in securing adherence to the principal's wishes. The agent is supposed to be acting according to the wishes of the principal. The agent may contend that the principal's wishes were communicated orally; but if those purported wishes are unusual or controversial (e.g., a rejection of all life-sustaining care should the principal be placed in a nursing home), health-care providers may be reluctant to accept that contention. Then, in the absence of written confirmation of the incompetent patient's wishes, the agent may be hard put to implement the principal's wishes. For if the agent can't show that the patient's wishes were in fact consistent with the controversial course which the agent is seeking, then the health-care providers might well refuse to follow the course sought. Moreover, even recourse to the courts may be unavailing in such a case. When the wishes of the principal are unknown (or, as in the present hypothetical, unprovable), an agent is supposed to act in accord with the patient's best interests. And those contemporaneous best interests might diverge from what the principal really wanted, but didn't express in writing, and now can't be proven.

Of course, an agent may be able to convince the surrounding health-care providers even in the absence of written instructions. That is, an agent in some instances might credibly and persuasively argue that he or she is following the principal's wishes as orally conveyed. But there is a risk that the agent's representations will be disbelieved. And even the presence of a broad statutory authorization to make any decision the patient could have made, if competent, may not be enough to overcome physicians' or other observers' doubts (in the absence of written instructions).

Written instructions also serve as a check against an agent's abuse of authority. Because the principal has provided a written standard or guideline, medical staff or other observers can be reassured that the agent's decisions conform with the incompetent patient's previously expressed wishes.[61] Again, a health-care agent is a fiduciary entrusted with carrying out a patient's wishes. If an agent unjustifiably deviates[62] from the principal's instructions, health-care providers are supposed to resist (and secure judicial appointment of a guardian to supplant the designated agent).

Nothing prevents use of written substantive instructions in a jurisdiction which provides for appointment of a health-care agent. Indeed, such laws generally require the agent to implement the principal's wishes and thus contemplate existence of instructions. Nothing prevents the reduction of such instructions to writing, whether the instructions are incorporated into the document appointing an agent or contained in a separate writing. (The substantive instructions might be lengthy; and while appointment of a health-care agent can usually be accomplished by a short form, the instructions might be contained in an attachment or appendix incorporated by reference into the appointment document.)

In some jurisdictions, it may be important to label the instructions as adjuncts to appointment of a health-care agent rather than as a separate living-will document. This would be true, for example, where the state living-will law contains unwanted (by the principal) limitations on implementing a declarant's wishes regarding terminal care. It would also be true in the odd jurisdiction, such as Illinois, whose DPOA-HC law states that appointment of an agent makes a living will inoperative.[63]

So far, I've suggested that the ideal format for an advance directive is a document appointing a health-care agent together with written substantive instructions. While these instructions are intended primarily to direct a health-care agent, they should also bind any future decision maker on behalf of the incompetent patient. This is so because almost all states give effect to clear-cut prior expressions by the now incompetent patient in shaping the bounds of medical intervention.[64] As a precaution, even if written instructions accompany appointment of an agent and are labeled accordingly they ought to include a sentence clarifying that the same instructions are intended to bind any eventual decision maker (if the agent is unavailable for any reason).

What about the person who cannot recruit a suitable health-care agent? What advance directive format should that person follow? In a state like New Jersey whose living-will type legislation accords broad autonomy to a declarant, that statutory mechanism should be utilized. (By "statutory mechanism" I mean personalized instructions complying with the formalities of a living-will statute, not necessarily any sample form recommended within the statute itself.) A living will fully conforming to the applicable statute should likewise be the format if the particular state's limitations on declarant autonomy don't conflict with the declarant's preferences.

A statutory living will binds all decision makers ultimately in charge of an incompetent patient's medical handling (including health-care providers and surrounding family).[65] Using the living-will statute also reassures physicians that they will be immune from liability for good-faith compliance with the document. At the same time, any statutory penalty for noncompliance with a declarant's instructions will be applicable.

In a state whose living-will type statute contains unwanted constraints, a nonstatutory advance directive—which I will call a *nonstatutory instruction directive*[66]—appears to be the best course. This is a writing, signed and witnessed in accord with the formalities demanded by the jurisdiction's living-will law, expressing the declarant's personal wishes with regard to post-competence medical intervention. (Compliance with the statutory formalities is designed to demonstrate the requisite seriousness and deliberation which the relevant legislature deemed appropriate to an instruction directive.) The distinctive feature of this nonstatutory document is that it invokes the declarant's common-law and constitutional prerogatives rather than the statutory authority provided in the relevant living-will law.[67]

The object of a nonstatutory instruction directive is to prescribe post-competence medical handling while avoiding the substantive statutory constraints of most living-will laws. Can these statutory "restrictions" be so easily circumvented?

The answer is probably yes. Most living-will statutes explicitly preserve the legal prerogatives of persons who have not invoked the statutory living-will mechanism. A typical "preservation-of-rights" provision specifies that the living-will law "shall have no effect or be in any manner construed to apply to persons not executing a directive pursuant to this [living-will law] nor shall it in any manner affect the rights of any such persons. . . . "[68] This language preserves common-law rights, including any rights applicable under the doctrines of substituted judgment or best interests of the patient. Under those judicially developed doctrines, persons charged with responsibility for incompetent patients are expected to follow the patients' expressed wishes.[69] Accordingly, courts have used an instruction directive as convincing proof of the patient's wishes even in a jurisdiction which did not have a living-will law.[70] And several courts have dictated compliance with oral instructions which exceeded the "terminal condition" or artificial nutrition limitations of living-will statutes.[71]

How can this be, you ask? What was the point of living-will legislation if its "restrictions" can so easily be circumvented?

The answer requires historical perspective. State legislatures adopting living-will laws wanted to endorse the concept of prospective autonomy, but in a restrained fashion. The legislators were generally wary about shaping the fate of helpless patients (only since 1976 have the courts and legislatures seriously dealt with this issue), and they were sensitive to political pressure from right-to-life oriented groups. At the same time, the legislators did not seek to disrupt the judicial doctrines which had developed or to foreclose continued judicial developments. The typical legislature adopting a living-will law was saying in effect: "We approve advance directives, and we'll even provide explicit immunity for health-care providers who comply with advance directives. But our official stamp of approval applies only so long as the patients affected are in a terminal condition (or aren't deprived of nutrition, or are 'only' having their dying process prolonged by medical intervention). We are wary about encouraging living wills beyond these bounds. But we are willing to leave it to the courts, if they are intrepid enough, to shape people's autonomy rights regarding medical intervention in the dying process."

If this interpretation of legislative intent is correct, then nonstatutory instruction directives exceeding the ostensible legislative bounds ought to be enforceable. The legislative object was to withhold *its* endorsement from instruction directives going beyond "terminal illness" or "life-sustaining procedures" (as defined by the living-will statute) but not to make such provisions unlawful or unenforceable by the courts.[72] Such an interpretation would be reinforced in a jurisdiction which has adopted a DPOA-HC type law conferring authority on health-care agents to implement their principals' instructions in circumstances beyond those mentioned in that jurisdiction's living-will law. Such a DPOA-HC underscores the legislature's willingness to permit terminal decisions beyond the bounds endorsed in the living-will statute.

There are two major problems with reliance on a nonstatutory instruction directive—at least until there has been authoritative judicial confirmation of the approach. First, health-care providers may be influenced in practice by the apparent facial limitations of a living-will statute's language. Physicians and health-care administrators are notoriously sensitive to possible traversing of legal bounds. Even when the health-care provider is confident of winning a legal test, there may be reluctance to incur the time, expense, and publicity accompanying litigation. The provider may therefore choose to follow the superficial meaning of the statutory language (constraints like terminal condition) rather than the underlying statutory intent described above. (Indeed, there is a danger that health-care providers will ignore the preservation-of-rights clause and regard the living-will mechanism as the exclusive one for withholding life-preserving care. In other words, there is a hazard that health-care providers would infer that the statutory immunity conferred under a living-will law implies that liability is possible for any provider who removes life-preserving care in circumstances beyond those enumerated in the living-will law.)

The primary solution to this misapprehension of the legal framework is vigorous education of health-care providers as to the legal status of a nonstatutory directive. It will be incumbent upon agencies concerned about advance directives—including state health departments and voluntary professional or consumer organizations—to inform health-care providers about the common-law and constitutional rights embodied in nonstatutory instruction directives.

That informational task will be supplemented, over time, by health-care agents acting pursuant to DPOA-HC and comparable laws. Those agents will act as advocates of incompetent patients' interests, and they will no doubt press for adherence to principals' instructions despite the ostensible constraints of some living-will type statutes. However, the topic at this point is use of nonstatutory instruction directives where a person could not find a suitable agent and where the relevant living-will law is narrow and confining. In the absence of an agent, compliance with the incompetent patient's nonstatutory instruction directive may be dependent on the degree of awareness of legal rights and responsibilities among the surrounding medical staff. Again, a conglomeration of health-care consumer groups, medical professional organizations, and state and federal agencies will have to endeavor to apprise health-care providers about the legal effect of a nonstatutory instruction directive. (It would be nice if they circulated large quantities of this book as part of that endeavor.)

Some commentators suggest that a nonstatutory instruction directive be used as a *supplement* to a conventional living will conforming to all statutory limitations.[73] That is, they recommend signing a statutorily correct document *and* a nonstatutory instruction directive. The latter is supposed to "amplify" the declarant's wishes and, by invoking common-law and constitutional rights, avoid the limitations of the relevant legislation. This nonstatutory instruction directive would state that the declarant's signing of the prescribed living-will form should not be construed as limiting the nonstatutory document's instructions—the latter representing the declarant's genuine wishes.

I can understand the rationale for this approach. By signing a conforming living will, the declarant hopes to secure whatever benefits (such as sanctions for noncompliance with instructions and assurance of nonliability for good-faith compliance) that the relevant statute provides. Medical personnel are presumably bound by this document meeting all statutory conditions. At the same time, the medical personnel are presented with an expanded document (a nonstatutory directive) expressing the patient's real wishes without reference to statutory restrictions like a "terminal condition" constraint. The commentators' hope is that the medical personnel can be persuaded to follow the more expansive wishes expressed in this nonstatutory instruction directive.

While I understand and sympathize with this strategy, I can't endorse it. The effect is to present two documents which on their face seem inconsistent or contradictory. That situation seems rife with potential uncertainty and confusion, and it may even be an invitation to obstructionism. It is true that the reasons for two documents are readily understandable, as explained above. The declarant is hoping to effectuate the minimum provided by statute and to expand upon that minimum by invoking other legal sources. Yet, purposeful preparation of inconsistent instructions seems quite problematic. The problem would be even greater if it happened that the conforming living will were prepared *after* the nonstatutory directive—the obvious hazard being that the latter document would be viewed as controlling despite the declarant's contrary intention.

My own preference, as stated, is to prepare a single, nonstatutory instruction directive. This unequivocal expression of the declarant's wishes, explicitly relying upon common-law and constitutional prerogatives, ought to be effective. As noted, the nonstatutory directive would be prepared with all the formality (witnesses, etc.) prescribed in the living-will statute, so its seriousness of purpose could not be questioned. And the document should fall within the preservation-of-rights provision contained in most living-will laws.

The down side of my strategy seems modest. True, the enforcement machinery provided by a living-will statute would not technically be applicable to a nonstatutory document. But the enforcement machinery provided under a living-will statute is minimal anyway (a point to be discussed in chapter 7, which deals with enforcement of advance directives). Similar enforcement devices can be utilized for a nonstatutory directive.

It is also true that voluntary medical cooperation might be more easily obtained pursuant to a conforming living will than pursuant to a nonstatutory instruction directive. This is because the immunity from liability provision of a living-will statute is, technically, not applicable to a nonstatutory directive. Nonetheless, use of a conforming living will (along with a nonstatutory advance directive) would risk either thwarting the desired scope of the declarant's substantive instructions or creating confusion because of inconsistent instructions. On balance, my advice is to spell out a declarant's actual preferences in the format of a single, nonstatutory instruction directive.

A second problem with a nonstatutory instruction directive may be that not all courts will adopt the generous view of legislative intent which I have outlined. An alternative view of legislative intent is that statutory limitations on living wills— such as those relating to terminal conditions or artificial nutrition—express a public policy antagonistic to any activity exceeding those limitations. Under this view, the public policy expressed in a living-will measure might be extended to decision makers deciding the fate of all incompetent patients, even without a statutory living will in the picture. The restrictive legislative policy might then be applied to a nonstatutory instruction directive, to prior oral expressions, and to incompetent patients who left no prior instructions at all.

This was the approach suggested by the Missouri Supreme Court in the *Cruzan* case.[74] The Missouri living-will law excluded nutrition from rejectable life-sustaining medical procedures. Ms. Cruzan, a permanently unconscious patient, had made certain verbal statements indicating that she would not want life-preserving intervention in such a status, but she had not issued a living will. The court chose to respect the policy reflected in that living-will law (supposedly opposing any withdrawal of artificial nutrition) even though no living will was actually involved in the case.[75]

A similar approach was followed by an Ohio appellate court in a case called *Couture v. Couture*.[76] Ohio's DPOA-HC law[77] had restricted a health-care agent's authority with regard to nutrition and with regard to a patient in a nonterminal condition. Even though no power of attorney was involved in the case, the *Couture* court relied on the public policy expressed in the DPOA-HC law to circumscribe the authority of a guardian seeking to implement an incompetent patient's prior oral instructions.[78]

In a jurisdiction where the inclination of lower court judges is to give broad public policy effect to the limitations contained in living-will or DPOA-HC laws, the ultimate resort for patients' advocates is constitutional attack on those limitations. Chapter 2 described prospective autonomy (as exercised via an advance medical directive) as an extension of a competent individual's fundamental liberty interest in shaping medical intervention in a dying process.[79] That perspective has prevailed in decisions both under the federal constitution and under some state constitutions.

This possible judicial responsiveness to constitutional claims has important implications for state statutes restricting the circumstances under which life-preserving medical intervention can be withdrawn. For example, a statutory bar to withdrawal of artificial nutrition would appear to be unconstitutional in the face of a patient's prior authorization of nutrition cessation.[80] Several state courts have already reached that conclusion, relying primarily on state constitutional provisions.[81] And that conclusion is probably reinforced by the U.S. Supreme Court's 1990 decision in *Cruzan*. None of the justices there endorsed a distinction between nutrition and other forms of medical intervention. Indeed, the majority opinion even recounted, with no hint of disapproval, prior state judicial determinations upholding the withdrawal of artificial nutrition.

There is also significant doubt about the constitutionality of statutory provisions confining implementation of advance directives to patients in a "terminal condition." A number of courts have suggested that the "rights" of incompetent patients with regard to prior autonomous expressions rejecting treatment are identical to those of competent patients.[82] At the same time, numerous decisions have indicated that competent patients are entitled to reject life-preserving medical intervention even in circumstances when the patient is not in a terminal condition (meaning that death might still be forestallable for years). At least where a patient has left clear-cut contrary instructions, then, a statutory terminal-condition limitation would appear to be unconstitutional. A few courts have already subscribed to this conclusion.[83]

Ultimate resort to a constitutional attack is likely to provide small consolation to the lingering, gravely debilitated patient in a jurisdiction with broad public-policy constraints on the permissible scope of advance instructions. If the particular state judiciary is inclined to expansively interpret the import of statutory limitations on a declarant's autonomy, those same judges may prove unsympathetic to constitutional attacks on the statutory restrictions. Even if the constitutional attack is ultimately successful—for example, at the state supreme court level—the litigation will entail substantial delay and expenditures.

Hopefully, the constitutional attack strategy will only be necessary in a few states. Many jurisdictions have legislation giving expansive scope to declarants' autonomy by means of appointment of a health-care agent. And most jurisdictions should be willing to respect nonstatutory instruction directives invoking common-law and constitutional prerogatives. That result should be reachable without extensive litigation.

I've now indicated the preferred format for an advance medical directive. In a jurisdiction providing for a DPOA-HC or other means to appoint a health-care agent with broad authority to implement a declarant's wishes, that mechanism should be utilized. That appointment document should be accompanied by substantive instructions to the agent. For the person who cannot find an appropriate agent, a living will should be utilized, unless the state's statutory limitations on declarant autonomy are distasteful to the particular declarant. In the latter event, a nonstatutory instruction directive provides an appropriate vehicle. In all these instances, the declarant issues substantive instructions to guide those ultimately in charge of decision making on his or her behalf. I turn now to the problem of formulating those instructions.

4

Drafting Advance Instructions

THE OBJECTIVE of an advance medical directive is to design a good death, a death with dignity as personally defined by the declarant. That definitional task might be easy for some people. For example, there are some persons who want all available means to be used to forestall death. This approach might appeal to someone who believes that all life, whatever its quality, is preferable to death. Or to someone who believes that dominion over death is solely a divine prerogative. Or to someone who doubts the ability of others to make appropriate "terminal" decisions, even with the benefit of advance instructions. For all such persons, it should be easy to dictate maximum medical intervention. One formula reads: "I want my life to be prolonged to the greatest extent possible without regard to my condition, the chances I have for recovery, or the cost of the procedures."[1]

Variations on this maximum-intervention theme are easily imaginable. A person could prescribe that all life-preserving measures are to be undertaken and continued *until* irreversible coma ensues. Or one could dictate medical intervention until death is, according to medical judgment, unpreventably imminent (specifying the brief time span intended by the word imminent). The thrust of this approach is that life support is to be vigorously maintained until the patient is really in extremis.

The task of defining a death with dignity is much harder for most people. Most people believe that circumstances do exist in which life-preserving medical intervention would be unwanted—circumstances in which existence for the individual would constitute a fate worse than death. Defining these circumstances entails fixing a stage in a future dying process at which life has become intolerably painful or undignified. For most people, this means defining a level of mental and physical dysfunction which is personally unacceptable. That, in turn, can be a daunting task. As noted in the discussion of prospective autonomy in chapter 2, a multitude of problems hamper this definitional task.

There are an infinite number of potential medical situations which may occur in a dying process. There are infinite gradations of mental deterioration and physical disability. There are infinite combinations of mental and physical dysfunction. There are always uncertainties attached to medical diagnosis and prognosis, including chances of error and statistical possibilities of remission or recovery. Moreover, a plethora of factors might shape a person's conception of dignity in the dying process.[2] Physical pain, emotional suffering (feelings of embarrassment, frustration, and dependency), immobility and physical helplessness, mental incapacity, use of physical restraints, and physical appearance are common elements in defining an undignified or degrading state. Beyond personal well-being and dignity, a person might wish to consider the interests of surrounding persons—for example, loved ones and health-care providers. The interests of surrounding persons might include the emotional strain of protracted care, the economic costs of care, and the allocation of medical resources.

The multitude of variables involved makes it impossible to anticipate and specifically provide for all post-competence health-care decisions. One consequence is that considerable disagreement exists about the best strategy for designing advance instructions. Advice ranges from leaving nothing in writing to articulating detailed instructions about forms of unwanted medical treatment, or about a level of debilitation deemed personally intolerable, or about both. In the following pages, I'll comment on some of the major approaches before describing my own preferred solution.

THE "NO WRITTEN DIRECTIVE" OPTION

A couple of years ago, a noted physician in the bioethics field published an article explaining why she would not prepare an advance directive.[3] She was confident that her next of kin would be present during any critical moments in her future dying process and that those persons could be counted on to understand and implement her preferences regarding medical intervention. Likewise, she was confident that the health-care providers likely to be on hand would be compassionate, understanding, and cooperative. Finally, she was dubious whether a typical instruction directive would be very informative to the ultimate decision makers.[4] She regarded the typical instructions as too vague to be useful.

My first quarrel is with the good doctor's failure to designate in writing a health-care agent. In the previous chapter, I described the inevitable potential for confusion or dispute if more than one close family member or loved one is on hand for critical decisions. Naming an authoritative agent (and alternates) seems to me a vital step in avoiding that hazard.

My second quarrel goes to the absence of written instructions. Is it enough to appoint an agent and orally instruct that agent?

This is a tempting option for the multitudes of people who are repulsed or intimidated by the prospect of spelling out their vision of an intolerable, incapacitated existence. An attorney active in the field of death and dying described to me her clients' common impulse to rely on appointment of a health-care agent. She explained:

Most people are not caught up in the details of medical conditions in which they would or would not want to be maintained. Rather, they feel that if there is no chance they would be restored to a quality of life they define as worthwhile, they would not want treatment continued. They believe that the people who know them and love them understand their values enough to draw the cutoff lines, and they are willing to abide by the decision those people would make. They usually feel more strongly about the decisionmaker than the decision itself—they trust the decision their loved ones would make and do not trust a decision that would be made by others involved, including hospital personnel and (in the worst possible situation) courts. Thus, the most crucial aspect of the advance directive is the appointment of the health care representative. (It seems to create a feeling of security comparable to appointment of a guardian in a testamentary will to take care of one's children.) Indeed, for many people who do not want to contemplate all of the possible medical conditions which could arise, completing a proxy directive, without more, fulfills their concerns.[5]

There is another argument (besides aversion to the seemingly complex and morbid drafting job) against issuing written instructions. When the time arrives for implementing instructions, a hazard exists that some observer (relative or friend of the patient, or health-care provider) will use the imprecision of the advance directive to contest and obstruct implementation of the now incompetent patient's wishes. Many such documents use language leaving considerable room for interpretation, including room for a grudging interpretation by anyone so inclined. A person disagreeing with a health-care agent's interpretation of an advance directive can seek intervention from hospital administrators, from an institutional ethics committee, or even from the courts. Such intervention might disrupt or delay the smooth effectuation of the principal's wishes.[6]

I am totally unconvinced of the wisdom of refraining from written instructions. In the first place, I feel that helpful and informative instructions *can* be prepared, even for people who are reluctant to confront their mortality and contemplate the circumstances of their eventual demise. (This chapter is largely devoted to that drafting enterprise.) Second, reliance on prior oral instructions (or, worse, impressions from prior general interactions between the agent and principal) seems quite unsound. Memories fade, and the time span between instructions and implementation can be considerable. Third, the eventual health-care providers may not be as cooperative as anticipated so that some reinforcement of the agent's chosen course of treatment might be necessary. Written instructions can serve that function. This tool is especially useful if the instructions are unusual or idiosyncratic.[7] Fourth, written instructions may serve as a check on the designated agent or other decision maker. That is, an observer may in good faith note that an agent is being swayed by personal predilections rather than the declarant's instructions. Returning the agent to the declarant's prescribed track may then be entirely consistent with the declarant's wishes.

Having articulated my strong preference for written advance instructions, I'll now examine several approaches to that drafting problem.

THE SHORT-FORM OPTION

The multiplicity of potential medical situations during a dying process and/or common aversion to spelling out an intolerable debilitated status have often prompted resort to short, sweeping formulations of the criteria for withdrawing life-preserving medical intervention.[8] Many short-form living wills (or instruction directives) condense the operative language to one sentence. One of the first living-will forms was drafted in 1969 and distributed to over 500,000 persons over the years by the Euthanasia Education Council, an organization later known as Concern for Dying.[9] The operative portion of that directive read:

> If a situation should arise in which there is no reasonable expectation of my recovery from physical or mental disability, I request that I be allowed to die and not be kept alive by artificial means or heroic measures. I do not fear death itself as much as the indignities of deterioration, dependence, and helpless pain.[10]

The deficiencies of that form are patent. Ambiguous language such as "heroic measures" is one weakness. Terms such as "heroic" or "extraordinary" are too often used in instruction directives to describe types of unwanted medical intervention. The terms have no commonly understood content and serve only to confuse.[11]

The even more serious fault is the opaque phrase used to define the point at which life-sustaining intervention is to be omitted. The form refers to "physical or mental disability" from which no recovery is reasonably likely. No definition is provided for the level of disability expected to trigger withholding of life-sustaining intervention. Does the form really intend to reject intervention from the point at which mental incapacity (according to its legal definition) is reached? Aren't there some degrees of mental incapacity which would be tolerable, at least if the declarant is restorable to physical health? And aren't there some physical incapacitations which would be tolerable (to the typical declarant) so long as the incompetent patient were still mentally capable of pleasure and interaction with the environment?

More recent short-form efforts fare only slightly better. One living-will version, distributed as of late 1990 by the Society for the Right to Die,[12] reads:

> If I should be in an incurable or irreversible mental or physical condition with no reasonable expectation of recovery, I direct my attending physician to withhold or withdraw treatment that merely prolongs my dying. I further direct that treatment be limited to measures to keep me comfortable and to relieve pain.[13]

Another 1990 model reads, in operative portion:

> If I am permanently unconscious or there is no reasonable expectation of my recovery from a seriously incapacitating or lethal illness or condition, I do not wish to be kept alive by artificial means.

These forms provide precious little guidance as to the nature and degree of deterioration which the declarant considers a fate worse than death.[14] One possible interpretation of the latter form is that once the declarant becomes incompetent (i.e., loses decision-making capacity for serious medical decisions), life-sustaining care should be omitted starting from the onset of any incurable, "seriously incapacitating" chronic condition. Does the typical declarant really want to reject all life-preserving care at that point, even if the incompetent patient is capable of enjoying continued existence? How "serious" must the incapacitating condition be?

As mentioned in the preceding chapter, the sample living wills sometimes provided within living-will statutes are even more problematic. In the first place, they commonly state that the patient must be in a "terminal condition" as defined in the particular statute.[15] As noted, such a limitation may well be inconsistent with a typical declarant's wish to avoid a prolonged, highly debilitated existence or a protracted period of decline associated with degenerative diseases. Second, statutory short forms frequently employ the opaque language dictating removal of care which serves "only to prolong the dying process."[16] It is dubious that such statutory forms satisfactorily reflect the wishes of the majority of persons seeking to shape a dignified dying process.

Numerous other efforts have been made to condense a declarant's substantive instructions into a single sentence or paragraph. Professor Robert Veatch prescribed cessation of life-sustaining care "which is either . . . gravely burdensome to me or will sustain life in a way that is gravely burdensome to me or others."[17] Another example is contained in a "power of attorney for health care" prepared by Charles P. Sabatino for the A. B. A. Commission on Legal Problems of the Elderly. Beside providing for appointment of a health-care agent, that document offers an interesting option regarding substantive instructions to the agent. It mentions "best interests" of the patient as a general standard, but it contains the following language as well:

> I do not want my life to be prolonged nor do I want life-sustaining treatment to be provided or continued if my Agent believes the burdens of the treatment outweigh the expected benefits. I want my Agent to consider the relief of suffering, the expenses involved and the quality as well as the possible extension of my life in making decisions concerning life-sustaining treatment.[18]

Short-form documents of this nature are not entirely useless. They provide a statement that the declarant does not want life-sustaining medical intervention in all circumstances. This is important information dispelling any notion that the patient seeks maximum medical maintenance. These documents also express the declarant's concern about indignity in the dying process and about the burdens upon surrounding parties. Given an agent who has consulted with the declarant and understands the precise intendment of the language, and given sympathetic and cooperative health-care providers, such a document *might* work very well.

A short-form effort like the Sabatino document thus seems appealing. It appears to maximize a health-care agent's flexibility in interpreting the declarant's wishes regarding a dignified dying process. It obviates the daunting task of spelling out the kinds of deteriorated conditions which would be intolerable for the declarant.

To my mind, however, the Sabatino formulation is still too spare. There is not much practical guidance for the ultimate implementers of the instructions, particularly as to the deteriorated quality of life which the declarant deems intolerable. The deficiency is especially acute if there is no health-care agent in the picture, and the de facto decision makers are not familiar with the details of the declarant's wishes. Even if a health-care agent has been designated, the criteria or guidelines are so spare that they create a risk of nonimplementation in the event that any surrounding party (family, friend, or health-care provider) challenges the agent's interpretation of intolerable indignity.

An illustration is provided in a 1987 New York case.[19] A stricken AIDS patient had named a health-care agent and specified that treatment should be withdrawn when "extreme mental deterioration" made a "meaningful quality of life" no longer possible. The patient deteriorated, became incompetent, and reached a stage at which the trusted agent sought the removal of life support. A court refused to order the hospital to cooperate, finding the term "meaningful quality of life" to be too amorphous to be enforceable.

My own feeling is that it is usually important to provide detailed guidance to the ultimate decision makers. If the indignity of a debilitated condition is a declarant's central concern, I would at least seek to define the main attributes of indignity which would make existence intolerable for that declarant. The issue is how to accomplish this objective without making the task so complex and distasteful as to deter masses of people from going beyond the short forms described above.

THE OPTION OF SKETCHING OUT INTOLERABLE DEBILITATION

A number of sources agree with me that it is desirable to provide detailed substantive instructions in an advance directive.[20] We agree that detailed instructions can amplify otherwise vague directives, can reinforce a health-care agent's determinations, and can help establish the thoughtfulness and seriousness of the declarant.[21] Questions exist, though, about how to inject the desired detail without intimidating or frustrating the declarant and without investment of long professional hours in counseling the declarant.

One undesirable technique is to address a whole spectrum of medical interventions, from routine and simple diagnostic tests to complicated procedures (i.e., from blood tests, to various machines, to receipt of organ transplants). There are authorities who recommend specifying the kinds of medical intervention which the declarant would or would not want.[22] I am not one of them. From my perspective, the crucial guidance in an instruction directive goes to the criteria for an intolerable quality of life—particularly the level of debilitation which renders existence degrading to the declarant. In other words, the substantive instructions should be result oriented, focusing on the consequences of medical intervention for the patient's status rather than the nature of the medical procedures.[23]

Of course, there are exceptions to this principle. A declarant's attitude about artificial nutrition ought to be registered, because nutrition constitutes a controversial subject warranting explicit guidance. Or a person might have a particular aversion to some form of treatment (such as a permanent respirator) which would warrant special mention. Beyond such instances, detailed consideration of a spectrum of medical treatments seems superfluous to me. I would concentrate on defining the kind of existence which the declarant deems intolerable.

In defining an intolerable status, most people view some level of dementia as a critical element. For example, the vast majority of people regard maintenance in a permanently unconscious state as a pointless burden on the emotional and financial resources of those surrounding the patient's dying process. They see no benefit to be derived from lingering in a permanently insentient state.

Many people also consider lesser forms of dementia intolerable, though viewpoints obviously differ. A number of commentators focus on the point at which an incompetent patient can no longer recognize the persons around them. From their perspective, interaction with loved ones is a sine qua non for a meaningful existence. Other persons stress the mental capacity to understand and communicate with surrounding persons. Some people insist on full mental capacity, expressing unwillingness to receive life-sustaining medical intervention once mental competence is irretrievably lost.[24]

For many people, physical debilitation accompanying mental incapacity may be an important factor in determining an intolerable quality of life. Immobility, helplessness, dependence, or being an emotional and/or financial burden on others may be extremely distasteful prospects.[25] For some people, an intolerable level of physical incapacity might be readily definable. It is not unusual, for example, to see a living will which renounces life-sustaining medical intervention if the patient becomes permanently dependent on nursing care. That degree of helplessness and dependence, together with mental incompetence, represents an intolerably degrading specter for these declarants.

For most people, though, it seems extremely hard to identify the levels and combinations of mental and physical dysfunction which would make continued existence intolerable, warranting the cessation of life-sustaining medical intervention. A sample form circulated by the New Jersey Bioethics Commission illustrates one approach to the problem. That form first provides an operative paragraph in which the declarant accepts the principle that a debilitated existence may be so personally degrading and distasteful as to be intolerable. That paragraph states:

> I realize that there may come a time when I am diagnosed as having an incurable and irreversible illness, disease, or condition which may not be terminal. My condition may cause me to experience severe and progressive physical or mental deterioration and/or a permanent loss of capacities and faculties I value highly. If, in the course of my medical care, the burdens of continued life with treatment become greater than the benefits I experience, I direct that life-sustaining measures be withheld or discontinued. I also direct that I be given all medically appropriate care necessary to make me comfortable and to relieve pain.[26]

The document's drafters apparently recognized that "severe . . . deterioration [to the point that] burdens of continued life . . . become greater than the benefits I experience" is an imprecise formula. They therefore added a paragraph suggesting that the declarant spell out the kinds of debilitation which would make existence personally intolerable. That explanatory paragraph reads:

> [The above paragraph] covers a wide range of possible situations in which you may have experienced partial or complete loss of certain mental and physical capacities you value highly. If you wish, in the space provided below you may specify in more detail the conditions in which you would choose to forego life-sustaining measures. You might include a description of the faculties or capacities, which, if irretrievably lost, would lead you to accept death rather than continue living. You may want to express any special concerns you have about particular medical conditions or treatments, or any other considerations which would provide further guidance to those who may become responsible for your care.

The idea is sound. Ideally, declarants should specify the levels of debilitation which would make continued life support unwanted. Yet the reality is that most people are either unwilling (because of refusal to face their mortality) or unable (because of unfamiliarity with the relevant terms and concepts) to articulate the desired guidelines.

There are a couple of possible solutions, besides reversion to the short forms previously described. One is to adopt or adapt my own existing effort to express in detail a vision of an unacceptably degrading medical status. Another solution is to utilize a "values profile" in which the declarant is asked to fill out—by checking the relevant boxes—a form covering attitudes about critical elements of degradation in a dying process. I'll address those "solutions" in succession.

THE CANTOR OPTION

In 1990, I first drafted my advance directive.[27] (It was then labeled a living will, though it was really a comprehensive advance directive including both appointment of a health-care agent and substantive instructions.) An updated and shortened version of that directive appears herein as Appendix A. At this juncture, I will articulate the major features of my directive, describing the objectives and concerns which governed my preparation of the document. In particular, I want to show how I handled the dignity-related criteria designed to govern post-compe-tence medical intervention.

The first part of my directive names a health-care agent to be responsible for administering the directive. I strove to select someone reliable, sympathetic with my concerns (as expressed in the document), and who would not be overly affected by the emotional difficulty of "letting go." An alternate agent is designated in the event of unavailability of the primary agent.[28] (As previously noted, in the absence of a designated agent, attending medical personnel would customarily turn to an incompetent patient's spouse or next of kin or other close acquaintance willing to assume responsibility for medical decision making. But for reasons already ar-ticulated, I preferred to designate an authoritative agent familiar with my wishes and presumptively able to implement my instructions in a clear-headed fashion.)

It might be advisable explicitly to detail certain authority intended for the health-care agent, such as power to access medical records, to hire and fire health-care personnel, to move the incompetent patient to a different setting, and to initiate litigation.[29] The health-care agent might ultimately have to act as an advocate, and even enforcer, of the directive—if health-care providers refuse to cooperate with its instructions. An enumeration of powers is intended to facilitate the agent's performance of these administrative and enforcement functions. Enumeration would be unnecessary, however, in a jurisdiction whose DPOA statute already confers the desired authority.

Having appointed a health-care agent, I devote most of the advance directive to providing substantive guidance for the agent or any other ultimate decision mak-ers. An introductory paragraph relates to types of medical intervention. There is no effort to enumerate attitudes about a full range of treatments. Rather, a few summary principles are set out.

My concern was threefold in mentioning these "principles" relating to types of care. First, I wanted to clarify that all forms of medical care are, for me, po-tentially rejectable—not just "extraordinary" or "heroic" or complex means. Sec-ond, I wished to clarify that artificial nutrition holds no magic significance for me and should be considered part of potentially rejectable medical intervention. Third, I specified my general preference for palliative care—meaning maintenance in a clean and comfortable environment and relief of extreme pain. This provision regarding palliative care was probably unnecessary, ranking as intuitively self-evi-dent. I included it in an excess of caution only because the use of advance directives is still at a primitive stage of development.

In the section relating to substantive instructions, I present a short statement of criteria or guiding principles for my agent or any other decision maker on my behalf. There, I invoke "best interests" in the sense of burdens of prospective existence exceeding benefits. My intendment is that burdens in this context include any discernible suffering (physical or emotional) and that benefits include any possible gratification from interaction with the environment. This is consistent with the customary meanings given the terms *burden* and *benefit*.

My advance directive also makes it clear, however, that considerations of dignity, as defined in the body of the advance directive, are to be deemed an integral part of my best interests. This latter point is important because often, when a patient has reached a severely deteriorated and debilitated status, commonly understood burdens such as physical and emotional suffering are difficult to assess.[30] It is useful to specify that notions of indignity and degradation are to come into play as part of the best-interests formula. This is consistent with an emerging realization that existence can be burdensome not just because of pain but because of indignity or other subjectively intolerable considerations (like emotional drain on others).[31]

A substantial part of my advance directive then seeks to define my concept of a status sufficiently undignified to warrant withholding or withdrawing life-preserving medical intervention. The instructions are not confined to a "terminal condition" in the sense of an unpreventably fatal illness. Rather, I have sought to control intervention in the face of any potentially life-threatening pathology once a certain level of deterioration and dysfunction has been reached or when the result of medical intervention would be to relegate me to such a deteriorated status.

Such a level of deterioration might be reached suddenly, as through trauma to the brain, or gradually, as the result of a degenerative process. In the latter case, there will not be any single magic moment when a degrading status is reached; the deterioration will be gradual, both in physical and mental terms. Nonetheless, a stage may ultimately be reached when my status has become degrading according to my agent's good-faith application of my criteria.[32] At that stage, I would want no further life-preserving intervention to combat potentially life-threatening pathology. This is consistent with one of my basic objects: the avoidance of prolonged lingering in a self-defined, degrading status.

The first substantive instruction regarding dignity relates to permanent unconsciousness or a permanent vegetative state (PVS). An existence devoid of all awareness is to my mind a demeaning state for a human being, and I don't wish to be maintained in such a condition. I make it clear that all life-preserving medical intervention, including artificial nutrition, should be withheld if such a condition occurs. Medical criteria have been developed for definitive diagnosis of permanent unconsciousness,[33] and I ask only that sound medical practice be followed in verifying the diagnosis.

PVS represents an easy case. The harder task is defining the degree of mental and physical debilitation which—while an individual is still conscious or semiconscious—constitutes an intolerably undignified state for a previously acute and active individual. For me, as I imagine for most people, not all mental incapacity can be deemed degrading. Obviously, a person lacking competence (unable to understand and process data at a level sufficient to make his or her own decisions) can still derive enjoyment and benefits from existence. A person can be "pleasantly senile" despite significant loss of mental faculties. Even though I don't relish being remembered in such a deteriorated state, I don't instruct that life support be withheld solely because of this level of mental dysfunction.

At the same time, my mental dysfunction could become so extreme that my condition would be demeaning or degrading for me. One clear index of such a status would be permanent inability to recognize and/or interact with my relatives or loved ones. I have therefore made this a per se determinative criterion of an undignified status warranting withholding of life support.

This does not mean that such profound dementia is to be the exclusive determinant of an intolerably demeaning status. I further explain that lesser but still extreme mental deterioration (such as the inability to read and understand simple material) would constitute a significant element of indignity to be considered in conjunction with other indices of indignity and suffering in assessing my overall best interests.

Extreme physical disability is articulated as another factor to be considered under the rubric of indignity in assessing my best interests in an incompetent state. As with the case of mental dysfunction, I make it clear that not all levels of physical incapacity are to be deemed intolerable (even in combination with the mental incompetence which is a prerequisite to any application of an advance directive). My assumption is that I am life-affirming enough in character to adjust to a significant degree of physical incapacity. Of course, if my mental deterioration deprives me of the ability to cope with whatever physical disabilities are involved, that fact will have to be included in calculating my best interests. That is, a level of physical incapacity together with extreme mental deterioration may result in discernible suffering or dignity loss to the point that my best interests dictate the cessation of medical intervention in the face of a life-threatening condition. This thought concerning the interrelation of mental and physical incapacity is expressed in my advance directive.

My advance directive also specifies some aspects of physical dysfunction which are particularly relevant to an assessment of indignity. In my mind, certain types of incapacity are associated with extreme helplessness and dependence and may well evoke feelings of frustration and embarrassment. My advance directive mentions three such factors: inability to feed myself, inability to dress (or bathe) myself, and incontinence necessitating either diapering or being otherwise attended. Each of these elements is labeled a significant blow to dignity to be considered in the best-interests calculus. While none of these elements is deemed sufficient, by itself, to prompt a finding of intolerable indignity, each is a relevant consideration.

It may well be that in a debilitated mental state I will not actually sense the frustration, humiliation, or degradation which I associate with an undignified status.

Nonetheless, it is important to me (and, I imagine, to most people) to be remembered in a certain fashion. I have therefore directed that my prospective medical intervention be shaped with my conception of indignity in mind regardless of the extent of perceptible suffering. I also assume that my lingering in a severely degraded status would extract a significant toll from surrounding relatives and friends. This furnishes an additional impetus for bringing indignity into play whether or not I will sense that indignity in a state of incompetency.

All this is not to say that contemporaneous, perceptible feelings will not be factors in the best-interests calculus. My directive specifies that irremediable physical pain (or pain that is remediable only through drug intervention producing a prolonged stuporous state) should be considered a significant factor adverse to best interests. The same instruction applies to perceptible emotional pain (embarrassment, frustration, anxiety, or whatever). The problem, again, is that these various elements of suffering are not susceptible to accurate measurement when a person has reached an extremely debilitated mental state. For that reason I have taken pains to define indignity as a potentially determinative factor.

Any person seeking to formulate a comprehensive advance directive ought to ponder some interests extrinsic to the incompetent patient's own personal status. Principal candidates for attention would be the emotional and financial interests of surrounding loved ones. Most persons, myself included, care about the emotional toll extracted from loved ones by a prolonged deathwatch or chronic care of an extremely deteriorated person. Beyond the anguishing mental and physical burdens imposed upon surrounding persons, the economic costs of terminal care may be relevant. Economic concerns can range from a diminished estate for descendants to actual dependence on the resources of others.

My personal strategy was to try and regulate medical intervention in my dying process in a fashion which would minimize the burdens imposed on others. My advance directive aims to avoid a prolonged dying process at a level of suffering or indignity likely to extract a severe toll from others. In that fashion, I express my solicitude for the anguish or burden suffered by those around me during my dying process. At the same time, I have not explicitly instructed my agent to weigh these extrinsic interests.

An alternative strategy would be to articulate economic costs and/or emotional burden on others as relevant factors in assessing best interests. For example, one could say that if a decision regarding best interests is otherwise borderline, the extreme expense of prospective care and the anguish of loved ones should be considered as factors weighing against initiation or continuation of life-preserving medical intervention.

My advance directive defines one level of mental incapacity (inability to recognize and/or interact with loved ones) as per se so undignified as to warrant cessation of life-preserving medical intervention. In addition, I specify that lesser degrees of dementia, together with other incapacities, would make my existence intolerably demeaning. In order to assist my agent in applying the concept of a demeaning existence, I identify several factors as "significant blows" to dignity. But the ultimate judgment about a demeaning condition is left to my health-care agent.

A difficult issue is presented when a person reaches an extremely debilitated mental status but is still physically healthy. (By "healthy," I mean that there are no current life-threatening conditions, even if there are chronic disabilities.) How should preventive or curative medical care be handled at this juncture? I am referring to future pathological conditions which by themselves are not life-threatening but which, if not treated, will develop into fatal conditions. These include both minor infections which are treatable with antibiotics and minor organ dysfunctions which are curable but which will lead to fatal dysfunctions if not treated. Once what has been defined as a demeaning state has been reached, should preventive and curative measures be withheld in order to facilitate the onset of a liberating dying process?

My personal disposition was to dictate the qualified omission of such medical measures once I have reached a demeaning status. Thus, if I become either permanently unable to recognize relatives and friends or otherwise trapped in a self-defined degrading existence, I anticipate that even medical intervention for curable infections and organ dysfunctions will be withheld. My one major caveat is that the sequelae of nontreatment be considered in applying the governing best interests standard. That is, any pain, discomfort, or indignity which would accompany the ensuing dying process (following nontreatment) must be considered. The decision makers must weigh whether the prospective negative consequences of nontreatment (any additional suffering or additional indignity during the ensuing dying process) outweigh the relief which death would, by definition, provide from a currently demeaning status.[34]

My determination to renounce even preventive and curative intervention—once my condition has reached a self-defined demeaning status—may be controversial. The consequence is to relinquish life for a being (my future, incompetent persona) who is still aware of the environment and perhaps capable of extracting some net pleasure from interactions with that environment. (I'm thinking here about a state of extreme, but "pleasant" senility, for example.)

Some moral issues arise in this context. First, some persons might question my moral right to dictate the demise of a helpless future persona not actually suffering from the deteriorated (though undignified) status. My response to this objection is presented at length in chapter 6. There, I argue that individual self-determination includes a moral prerogative of shaping a post-competence dying process according to a personal concept of dignity—even if that vision of dignity does not coincide with the contemporaneous well being of the incompetent persona. A person who has developed a character during a lifetime deserves an opportunity to shape post-competence recollections of that character. Just as I think I have a right to dispose of my property—even in a way which might disadvantage my future, incompetent persona—I think I have a right to dictate my post-competence medical fate.

Second, there may be tension between my preferences regarding preventive and curative care and the conscientious positions of some medical personnel. I have no desire to force medical personnel to violate their scruples. In the event that attending medical personnel cannot in good conscience implement my preferences, my health-care agent will be expected to seek alternative personnel who can willingly cooperate. In the event that an institutional host (such as a private hospital or nursing home) has conscientious objections to my prescribed course of treatment (or nontreatment), my agent might seek my transfer to another facility in which cooperation is available. Only if these recourses are not viable would I want my agent to seek to legally coerce the objecting personnel or institution. (Chapter 5, which deals with administration of advance directives, devotes further attention to the issue of conscientious scruples of health care providers.)

THE VALUES-PROFILE OPTION

When my advance directive was published in 1990, one criticism voiced was that the document was so elaborate that only persons who could afford a fancy lawyer (and/or medical consultant) would be able to utilize such an instrument. Frankly, I was surprised by this criticism. My conceit had been that my prescription about intolerable debilitation and indignity represented an "every (wo)man" position that would capture the fancy of masses of people. Judging from the dearth of reprint requests, my conceit was sadly misplaced. Apparently, people's preferences about life-sustaining medical treatment are too diverse to be captured in any single document, or standard form. (I hasten to point out, however, that at least a few friends and relatives have replicated my advance directive reprinted herein as Appendix A).

If people's advance directives must be individually constructed, with careful consultation about each element, the prospects for widespread usage of advance directives will diminish. (Recall that best estimates indicate that only between five and twenty-five percent of people currently have an advance directive, even in the prevalent short-form formats). People are notoriously reluctant to deal with the "grisly" task of designing their own dying process. They will be even more reluctant if they have to pay significant sums to accomplish the already distasteful task. Yet if an advance directive is to be a detailed, hand-tailored document, then some expense may well be entailed for medical and/or legal consultations.

Nor are physicians and other health-care providers anxious to perform the consultative function. Physicians have heavy demands on their time and are reluctant to deal with the "hypothetical" death-and-dying process of a healthy person. "[T]he [consultative] process is unfamiliar, time consuming and inherently distasteful to many physicians who have been trained to preserve life whenever possible."[35] There is generally little economic incentive to perform the consultative function, as third-party reimbursements (government and private insurance) usually don't cover the fees involved.

A possible solution is to allocate the consultative task to nonphysicians. Authorities assert that consultation and guidance must initially be available to declarants and that an interactive process is essential (either contemporaneous with or after preparation of a directive) in order that declarants can explain their choices.[36] It is not at all clear that physicians or lawyers are essential ingredients in the initial consultative process.[37] A social worker, patient's advocate, physician's assistant, or other medical-staff person might be trained to fulfill the function of introducing people to advance directives and even assisting in preparation of the documents.

For anyone responsible for initially assisting a declarant in preparation of an advance directive, as well as for the ultimate administrators or decision makers, a "values profile" might serve as an important adjunct or supplement to an advance directive. A values profile is basically a questionnaire aimed at eliciting a declarant's attitudes toward issues commonly arising in the context of medical intervention in a dying process.[38] This device offers the potential both for succinctly laying out the critical issues for a declarant and for providing a handy format for a range of responses. At the very least, an appropriate questionnaire can furnish a useful guide to issues to be raised by a person seeking to assist a declarant in preparation of an advance directive. Even better, the profile could get attached to the directive itself and become an interpretive guide in the ultimate implementation of that directive.

To my mind, efforts to formulate an effective values profile have not been very successful. One effort in the direction of a values profile is called a "values history" and was prepared at the Institute of Public Law of the University of New Mexico Law School.[39] That document provides a series of open-ended questions concerning general attitude toward typical forms of life-preserving medical intervention (e.g., respirators and dialysis machines), permanent unconsciousness, diminished mental and physical function, and chronic illness. This values history seems deficient for a couple of reasons. First, it does not pointedly focus either on particular elements of indignity or on identifying a person's minimally tolerable level of function. Second, its open-ended solicitation of subjective responses may not sufficiently focus respondents' attention upon those critical issues. Moreover, it is difficult for the average declarant to formulate responses to open-ended inquiries.[40]

Another relevant document, called a "medical directive," was prepared by E. Emanuel and L. Emanuel.[41] Its distinctive feature is a questionnaire asking the respondent to signal choices about various forms of medical intervention in four paradigmatic illness circumstances. As with the values history, the object is to explore the declarant's wishes about "the process of dying."[42] However, the four scenarios covered relate only to two extreme stages of mental incapacity: severe dementia, to the point where the patient is unable to recognize people or to speak understandably, and PVS. No inquiry is made about lesser forms of mental incapacity, or about physical deterioration, or about an overall definition of intolerable indignity. This medical directive anticipates that a designated health-care agent will deal with circumstances not covered in the document itself.

The medical directive was published in 1989. In 1990, the Emanuels published an expanded version.[43] Their questionnaire scenarios continue to focus on a rather narrow range of dementia. However, they have added inquiries touching on physical immobility, dependence on others, ability to communicate, and place of habitation. These additions represent an improvement. Yet the added inquiries are still not phrased to identify what the declarant would consider an intolerable status—a fate worse than death.

These previously published documents point in the right direction. The object is to provide a questionnaire format focusing on issues critical to most persons thinking about post-competence medical intervention. Moreover, the questionnaire should supply a list of possible responses allowing the declarant to identify an intolerable existence without having to formulate new language.

My own effort to draft a values profiles is set out herein as Appendix D. It focuses on dementia, physical immobility, helplessness, expense, pain, and burden on others. The hope is that this sample document will advance the pursuit of a values profile which can serve as a handy tool for masses of people to amplify what they really mean by the language of a short-form advance directive.

MISCELLANEOUS OPTIONAL PROVISIONS

To my mind, the central issue in an advance directive is preparation of substantive instructions which convey a declarant's wishes concerning post-competence medical intervention. That instructional task is particularly important if the declarant does not have a health-care agent to administer the advance directive. For that reason, the prior two subsections in this chapter focused on methodology for conveying detailed substantive instructions about post-competence care.

Robert Veatch offers an additional way to provide interpretive guidance as to the meaning of general instructions.[44] His living will is innovative in listing individuals who can be consulted in the course of administering the document. It mentions both persons whose views on post-competence care coincide with the declarant's and medical professionals whose judgment the declarant respects.

There are a variety of other provisions which, at a declarant's option, might be included in an advance directive. A person who cares particularly about the locus of post-competence care (e.g., someone with an aversion to a nursing home) can use an advance directive to articulate that preference. An advance directive could also contain provisions relating to donation of organs or bodily tissue, performance of an autopsy, or even burial instructions.

It might be useful to include an immunity clause expressing the declarant's wish that the ultimate administrators of a directive (including any health-care agent and attending medical personnel) be immune from liability. One option would be to absolve these actors for "good-faith" adherence to the directive.[45] An alternative approach would be to relieve health-care providers from liability only for conduct that meets "reasonable medical standards." This is the standard imposed on decision makers under most living-will type statutes.[46]

The effect of a good-faith standard of immunity might well be to relieve an agent or health professional from liability for negligent conduct. For example, a careless (but good-faith) judgment about the hopelessness of an incompetent patient's condition would be immune from liability. Only reckless conduct would incur liability under a good-faith standard.

The advantage of a good-faith standard is its reassurance to the eventual administrators; they receive a message that the declarant intended to encourage implementation of the directive by conferring immunity for good-faith adherence to instructions. The good-faith standard does not seem like an excessive risk. Many commentators argue that overly aggressive medical intervention poses a greater hazard than undertreatment, at least in hospital settings.

A propos of overly aggressive intervention, one source has suggested a clause threatening dire consequences for physicians' failure to implement an advance directive's request for termination of life-sustaining treatment. The clause provides:

> I will consider such treatment [i.e., medical continuation of life-preserving care] an act of criminal assault, and want my proxy to file a criminal assault and battery complaint against those involved in this violation of my basic right to refuse treatment. Additionally, I want my family members to file a multi-million dollar civil damage suit against those involved in treating me against my will.[47]

My own thoughts on enforcement methods are set out in chapter 7. At this point, I'll just comment on the above paragraph. In essence, the paragraph is bluster aimed at intimidating recalcitrant health-care professionals. The chances of launching a criminal-assault proceeding in the context of a moribund, incompetent patient are somewhere between zero and nil. The chances of launching a successful "multimillion-dollar" damage suit are slim—for reasons to be articulated in chapter 7.

The above effort at bluster and intimidation is a matter of strategy. Personally, I don't see the above paragraph's threats as doing much to promote good will and sympathy from the attending medical personnel. I prefer an approach which reassures the personnel that good-faith implementation of instructions will incur no liability. Of course, a health-care agent or surrounding family member might some day have to threaten suit against recalcitrant personnel or a recalcitrant institution. But I would hold such threats in abeyance in the hope and expectation that they would never become necessary. On the other hand, I can understand an argument that the above paragraph graphically conveys the declarant's seriousness and determination about renouncing life support in accord with the advance directive.

5

Interpretation and Administration of Advance Directives

THE CHALLENGE of interpreting an advance directive is almost inevitable. Millions of short-form directives have been distributed containing only the most rudimentary instructions.[1] This effectively means that hundreds of thousands of people have now dictated a halt to medical intervention which "only prolongs the dying process" once the declarant has become incapacitated with "no reasonable hope of recovery."

The language "*only* prolongs the dying process" cannot be taken literally. Even for a person diagnosed as permanently vegetative, there is some infinitesimal hope either of a misdiagnosis or of a miraculous recovery which would restore some measure of function. Arguably, continued life support then wouldn't *only* prolong the dying process. Yet the declarant's intention was presumably to avoid continued medical intervention in circumstances of grave incapacity and indignity. The challenge is to interpret the imprecise language in a manner fulfilling the declarant's actual wishes.

Even if an advance directive seeks to provide detailed instructions—as in my own document, Appendix A—considerable interpretive discretion may well be lodged in the health-care agent or other person charged with administration. Because "the number of plausible combinations and permutations of [medical] interventions and clinical contexts is virtually limitless . . . ,"[2] even a lengthy document cannot provide for all situations. A common response will be for an advance directive to articulate a general standard or guideline, such as "best interests" of the declarant, in addition to particularized instructions.

A general standard usually confers broad discretion on decision makers acting on behalf of the incompetent patient. For example, a best-interests standard incorporates notions like pain, suffering, indignity, and countervailing benefits—leaving a delicate balancing task in the hands of the agent or other administrator. Application of such a best-interests standard entails a weighing of largely unquantifiable benefits and detriments. The eventual decision makers must make a judgment not only about the extent of suffering being incurred by an incompetent (and perhaps noncommunicative) patient[3] but also about the patient's potential for satisfaction despite a debilitated condition. Elements of indignity must be brought into the balancing process if consistent with the declarant's wishes.

The use of a generalized standard, as well as the frequent imprecision of advance directive terminology, underlines the importance of consultation between a declarant and those persons (including health-care agents and medical professionals) likely to be involved in administration of an advance directive. Virtually every commentator on advance directives stresses the utility of such communication. These conversations have a dual purpose. They illuminate the real wishes of the declarant via amplification of unclear language. And they give the agent or health-care provider a chance to express any discomfort or hesitancy about implementation of the declarant's wishes. In the event of tension between the declarant's wishes and the decision makers' willingness to cooperate, a declarant can either modify those wishes or seek alternative agents or health-care providers.

It would theoretically be possible to demand, as a prerequisite to a binding advance directive, a showing that the document is the product of consultation. Certainly, awareness of all the document's implications and reflective deliberation are a desirable foundation for such a fateful document. Nonetheless, such a heightened standard for validity of an advance directive would impede the utility of such directives and would be unwise.

Any requirement of consultation with a medical or legal source would impose economic costs and diminish people's accessibility to the advance directive mechanism. It might also be difficult to establish in retrospect (sometimes years after the event) that the advance directive was prepared with sufficient consultation (or deliberation). A consultation prerequisite would be subject to manipulation by any physician (or other eventual decision maker) uncomfortable with the substance of an advance directive.

The normal standard for documentary capacity—the ability to understand and appreciate the nature and consequences of the decision—should govern the validity of advance directives.[4] Some commentators suggest that "informed consent" be a prerequisite for a directive (drawing an analogy to the consent expected for a contemporaneous decision to forego medical intervention). This would require receipt of information about the nature of the pathology, the benefits and risks of contemplated medical intervention (or nonintervention), and the available alternatives.

Such an informed-consent or consultation prerequisite for an advance directive would impose an impossible burden where a declarant is healthy and simply anticipating the eventual prospect of incapacity and a dying process. (And that is the usual situation surrounding the making of an advance directive.) The myriad of variables makes customary informed consent impractical. Even if a declarant is aware of particular pathology at the time of making an advance directive, the normal standard for documentary capacity should prevail.

If emotional trauma apparently surrounded making of the directive, that would be a basis for investigation of competency by the health-care agent or other decision maker. That is, a health-care agent aware of traumatic circumstances surrounding preparation of a directive should seek assurance that the declarant at least understood the nature and consequences of the document being signed. It is conceivable that temporary depression or other severe upset unduly influenced the content of an advance directive. However, the starting presumption should be that a declarant who signed an advance directive in the presence of two witnesses was competent to understand the nature and consequences of the decision.

THE BASIC GUIDELINE: THE DECLARANT'S WISHES

The central guideline for any health-care agent or other administrator of an advance directive must be implementation of the desires and preferences of the now incompetent declarant. This conclusion applies whether the advance directive takes the form of a statutorily approved living will, a nonstatutory living-will type document, or a durable power of attorney for health care (or similar mechanism for appointment of a health-care agent).

As the preambles to most living-will type statutes attest, the thrust of such legislation is to recognize a person's autonomy in shaping medical intervention in a future dying process. Not surprisingly, then, the statutes—subject to limitations earlier discussed—anticipate fulfillment of a declarant's wishes.[5] Physicians are commonly accorded legal immunity for compliance with a living will. Under some statutes, a legal proceeding is explicity authorized against a party (whether health-care agent or medical professional) acting inconsistently with the declarant's instructions.[6]

The legal injunction to interpret and apply a declarant's wishes applies to a nonstatutory advance directive as well. That result would follow in most jurisdictions under the judicially developed doctrine of "substituted judgment."[7] A precept of that doctrine is respect for a person's autonomy to shape medical intervention. If a now incompetent patient's previous wishes can be determined, those wishes govern provision of post-competence medical care. The U.S. Supreme Court's decision in *Cruzan* only lends impetus to this judicial trend by suggesting constitutional status for the clearly expressed wishes of a previously competent patient. A written instruction directive will constitute an important index of those wishes.[8]

A similar framework—giving preeminent force to a declarant's wishes—applies to a durable power of attorney or other mechanism for designation of a health-care agent. The typical DPOA-HC statute requires the agent to act in accord with the principal's wishes or, if those wishes are unknown, in accord with the patient's best interests.[9] This approach is consistent with law's traditional approach to fiduciaries acting on behalf of legal incompetents. A guardian, trustee, or other fiduciary is supposed to implement the discernible or inferrable wishes of a ward (expressed while the ward was competent).[10] A health-care agent is a form of fiduciary and is expected to adhere to the patient's wishes.[11]

This does not mean that a declarant's wishes must be comprehensively or precisely expressed in order for a designated agent to seek withdrawal of life-sustaining medical intervention. An important object of a designated-agent mechanism is to secure a person to implement the principal's vision of a dignified dying process without forcing the principal to spell out detailed instructions. When a DPOA-HC statute prescribes that an agent shall act according to "best interests" when the patient's wishes are "unknown," the agent is being enjoined to act consistently with the principal's articulated values and preferences even if an explicit instruction covering the situation at hand is not available. The designated agent is being authorized to interpret and apply the principal's will; the agent's interpretation should prevail so long as that interpretation does not conflict with the principal's known wishes.[12]

Alternatively phrased, the statutory reference to best interests encompasses the values and preferences of the principal.[13] If a designated agent is making a good-faith assessment of the principal's wishes, as gleaned from the express or apparent concerns of the principal, that agent's decision about life-sustaining medical intervention ought to be upheld. This conclusion is inapplicable only in a few jurisdictions (like Missouri) where clear-cut prior expressions have been made an absolute prerequisite to withdrawal of life-sustaining care of an incompetent patient.[14] In the vast majority of locales, though, a designated health-care agent need only act consistently with the known wishes, values, and preferences of the principal. Clear and convincing evidence of the principal's precise instructions is not then essential.

All the preceding material suggests that application of an advance directive will not always be easy. The imprecision endemic to advance instructions will hamper fulfillment of the declarant's wishes. Nonetheless, the key object is implementation of those wishes. The starting point, and perhaps best index of an incompetent patient's wishes, is the document itself. But because the document will sometimes be vague or uninformative, further interpretive guides will be necessary.

Where language of an advance directive is fuzzy or ambiguous, consideration of the background and circumstances of the directive's adoption is appropriate in order to discern a declarant's actual desires. This is what occurred in a recent Florida case. In *Browning v. Herbert*,[15] an elderly woman had executed a written directive indicating that she wanted life-prolonging procedures suspended if she should reach a terminal condition and death was "imminent." A year later, she suffered a massive stroke and was reduced to a barely conscious (but not vegetative) state. She could survive for up to a year in that debilitated status. The question was whether death was imminent within the meaning of her directive. Looking to the nature and purposes of the entire directive, the court determined that death was imminent within the intendment of the patient.

A similar task has to be undertaken with regard to all imprecise language within an advance directive. Suppose an advance directive employs a term like

"heroic means" or "extraordinary treatment" in defining unwanted medical intervention. Was the underlying concern with *expensive* machinery which might deplete
the estate? Was the concern *intrusive* machinery which might disturb the comfort
of the patient? Or did the declarant intend to dispense with any life-preserving
medical intervention once the patient has reached an extremely incapacitated state?
If the latter, what incapacitated status did the declarant consider as warranting the
withholding of such intervention? In all cases of imprecision, the advance directive's
history and background can be examined to try and determine the directive maker's
actual intent.

Obviously, a variety of tools might be employed in the effort to fathom a
directive's actual intent. One index would be the declarant's statements preceding
or contemporaneous with the preparation of the directive. These statements could
have come in any of an infinite variety of contexts, from casual chats with friends
to pointed discussions with any persons consulted in the preparation of the directive.
Each statement must be considered "for what it is worth."[16] That is, a casual,
passing remark may carry less force than a considered consultation with a prospective health-care agent or medical care provider.

A declarant's expressions subsequent to the advance directive must also be
considered. An advance directive may predate its ultimate implementation by a
considerable period. During that period, the maker may have occasion to elaborate
on the meaning of the original document, or even to supplement it. Those elabo-
rations or clarifications can prove helpful in discerning the advance directive's
intended meaning.

Consideration of a declarant's post-directive statements may even, in rare instances, curtail reliance on the advance directive document. A person's values or
perspectives may change over time, and the declarant may have altered or con-
tradicted the original directive, even without formally revoking it. Statutes relating
both to living wills and durable powers of attorney commonly recognize this possibility by providing for revocation of the relevant directive by any expression "evi-
dencing an intent to revoke the document."[17]

In other words, revocation of an advance directive can occur without the formality usually demanded for the original creation of the document. This liberal
approach to revocation is grounded on the common policy favoring preservation
of life. Legislators apparently anticipated a situation where a declarant would repudiate his or her original life-relinquishing inclinations upon being confronted
with real life-threatening prospects. Though allowance of informal revocation might
tempt some of the declarant's family to invent conversations, the strong public
policy favoring preservation of life warrants the risk involved. My objection is to
those jurisdictions which allow revocation regardless of the patient's mental condition when "revoking," a topic to which I will soon turn.[18]

As part of the background and circumstances to be examined in gleaning the
meaning of an advance directive, should the health-care agent or other decision

maker look to the declarant's prior behavior and lifestyle? The answer is that there is some limited utility in resort to such evidence. A person's general lifestyle does not usually provide a pointed or reliable index regarding medical preferences during a dying process.[19] A vigorous and independent person who previously disdained medical intervention may still wish to cling to life at its fringe.

On the other hand, the behavioral patterns of the individual may provide some guidance in interpretation of an advance directive. If the declarant has indicated that dignity and quality of life are important considerations in shaping his or her medical fate, then certain strong dispositions expressed in lifestyle and behavior may help form an understanding of what was undignified in the eyes of the declarant. A person's prior attitude toward family and loved ones might also be examined in deciding whether the suffering of such third parties is a relevant consideration in shaping the declarant's terminal care.[20] Finally, the personal values of the declarant may inform interpretation of terms used in the directive. For example, a devout Catholic who uses the term "extraordinary means" may well intend to adopt the definition of that term found in church doctrine.

JUSTIFIED AND UNJUSTIFIED DEVIATIONS FROM THE TERMS OF AN ADVANCE DIRECTIVE

Even an elaborately drafted advance directive—to say nothing of the sparse, short forms frequently used—cannot anticipate the multitude of conditions and variables that may accompany an eventual dying process. One consequence is that a health-care agent (or other administrator of a directive) will sometimes be justified in deviating from the literal terms of a directive. The question is when such deviations are warranted.

A. Unforeseen Developments

One justification for overriding the terms of an advance directive is changed circumstances from those anticipated by the declarant. This excuse would not be acceptable in the context of a regular will disposing of property, where finality and certainty are deemed preeminent values. Despite occasional injustices, an unrevoked will is enforced according to its terms even in the face of a showing that the expectations or desires of a testator had changed. (A testator's legacy to her trusted son Bob is not vitiated by a demonstration that Bob turned out to be a bum who stole money from his mother, or even by a showing that the testator wanted to disinherit Bob though she neglected to revise her will.) The fact that human life is in issue in administering an advance directive compels a more flexible approach, including some consideration of changed circumstances.

An illustration of a warranted deviation from a directive comes when technological developments give a new cast to the medical situation being confronted.

Suppose, for example, that a directive specifies that treatment for an incurable, degenerative disease be withdrawn when a certain point of deterioration has been reached. Later, that point is reached, but in the interim a drug has been discovered which promises a significant remission. If the declarant's object was to forego treatment only in the face of an irremediable dying process, the development of this drug would furnish a possible basis to override the letter of the advance directive.

Or suppose an advance directive calls for cessation of life-preserving care if the patient should be "continuously unconscious for a period of one week."[21] If the declarant's intent was to permit accurate diagnosis of a permanently unconscious state, and it will now take more than one week to make an accurate medical assessment, the relevant decision makers are clearly warranted in overriding the precise instruction. In these instances, the letter of the advance directive is overridden, in light of unforeseen developments, in order to fulfill the advance directive's spirit.

A changed circumstance might take the form of a negative development impelling deviation from a prior instruction to maintain life-sustaining care. For example, a directive may have dictated administration of a particular medication which had previously produced, or was expected to produce, a therapeutic benefit. If post-competence developments in the patient's condition demonstrate that the medication is no longer achieving the expected benefits, withdrawal of the medication would be consistent with the spirit of the advance directive.[22]

It's not always easy to reconcile tensions between the letter and the supposed "spirit" of an advance directive. Suppose that the patient has been definitively diagnosed as being in a permanently vegitative state (PVS), a state in which the directive unequivocally calls for cessation of medical intervention (consisting at this point of a respirator and artificial nutrition). But Cousin Joe from Des Moines has phoned and said that he wants a chance to take a last farewell from the patient. This will take a couple of days. The patient knew Cousin Joe, and liked him, but had no particular attachment to him. Should the health-care agent delay the instructed demise of the patient in order to accommodate Cousin Joe?

On the one hand, the patient liked Cousin Joe and *might* have favored accommodating him if the patient had anticipated such a circumstance. And the patient will never sense or suffer from the extended survival period. On the other hand, the directive explicitly deems permanent unconsciousness to be a demeaning state and the document does not articulate the interests of relatives as a concern. If I were the health-care agent, I think I would express regrets to Cousin Joe and I would instruct the attending medical staff to pull the respirator plug. But I couldn't fault an agent who chose to accommodate Cousin Joe.

In the last hypothetical, the decision makers must fill a gap in the instructions resulting from an unanticipated circumstance (Cousin Joe's desire to make a parting).[23] It is entirely appropriate to turn to the underlying objects or spirit of the directive and to seek to further those objects. In this particular instance, it's simply not clear whether the contemplated action (delay to accommodate Cousin Joe), while inconsistent with the letter of the directive, is consistent with its spirit. Since one clear object of the directive is to salvage the patient's self-defined dignity, and that dignity is inconsistent with PVS, my inclination is to adhere to that discernible object and uphold the letter of the directive.

Other sources have recognized that the literal terms of an advance directive should not always govern. For example, the 1983 President's Commission for the Study of Ethical Problems in Medicine suggested that deviation from the terms of a directive might be grounded on a "finding that the patient did not adequately envision and consider the particular situation within which the actual medical decision must be made."[24] This position is sound in its implicit recognition that unforeseen developments can make a provision within an advance directive inconsistent with the declarant's objectives (i.e., inconsistent with the spirit of the document). The New Jersey Bioethics Commission's 1990 report also expresses understanding that changed circumstances (such as therapeutic advances) might warrant noncompliance with the terms of an advance directive.[25] That report recognizes that ostensibly clear language can become ambiguous when applied to unforeseen developments.

B. Conflicts with the Patient's Current Best Interests

A strong temptation to deviate from an advance directive will arise where the declarant's instructions conflict with the current interests of the now incompetent patient. This situation should not occur very frequently. Most people desire to cling to life so long as there is a modicum of benefit to continued existence. Only in case of extreme neurological and physical impairment do they really seek removal of life-sustaining medical support.[26] Nonetheless, there will be instances when advance directives prescribe courses which are in tension with an incompetent patient's ostensible well being or immediate best interests.[27]

An advance directive might seek to preserve the declarant's personal vision of dignity (as a vital, fully functional human being) by directing that life support be withheld whenever the person becomes permanently mentally incompetent and is relegated to a nursing home.[28] Such an instruction might be based either on the specter of dependence on others or on the declarant's wish to avoid emotional and financial burdens to attending family during a protracted dying process.[29] Such an instruction—if implemented—could prompt withholding of antibiotics and cause the ensuing demise of an incompetent patient ostensibly enjoying existence but stricken with pneumonia. The patient admitted to the nursing home may be mentally impaired and incompetent yet still be alert, retaining awareness of the environment and apparently enjoying the impaired existence.

Further examples of possible dissonance between an advance directive and a now incompetent patient's immediate interests (meaning immediate well-being) will be presented in chapter 6. In that chapter, I address the moral implications of an agent's acting counter to the current well-being of a now helpless being. (I conclude there that implementation of prior instructions counter to current well-being is not intrinsically immoral.) At this juncture, the question is whether a health-care agent is entitled to use the patient's current well-being as a justification for not implementing the terms of an advance directive.

As noted, there will be considerable temptation to override an advance directive calling for the demise of a helpless patient (the new nursing-home resident) contrary to the patient's immediate well-being (the patient is still aware and getting some satisfaction from existence). The agent (or other decision maker) who succumbs to that temptation may seek to invoke the notion that the declarant did not sufficiently envision or consider the consequences. Recall the suggestion of the President's Commission that deviation from an advance directive might be grounded on "a finding that the patient did not adequately envision and consider the particular situation within which the actual medical decision must be made." That standard deserves some explanation and refinement.

In some instances, an agent's decision to override a directive's ostensible instruction may represent a good-faith interpretation of the declarant's intent—a judgment that the declarant simply did not intend to encompass the situation at hand. The declarant who prescribed that medical treatment should be withheld upon subsequent admission to a nursing home may have contemplated a status of either total immobility or acute embarrassment. That declarant may not have intended to cover a period of "pleasant" ambulatory senility or a situation where anticipated embarrassment did not materialize in fact. Then, if the now incompetent patient does not seem to be suffering in the nursing home, the agent would be warranted in ignoring the literal scope of the instruction regarding nontreatment after admission to a nursing home.

There is, however, a variation of the above scenario which must be considered. The decision not to implement the instruction regarding nontreatment in a nursing-home setting might be grounded on the agent's (or medical personnel's) distaste for the instruction. That is, the declarant may have fully intended the literal meaning of the directive, but refusal to implement flows from the conviction that the instruction was imprudent or ill-considered.

The obstacle to following this course does not come from any serious threat of legal liability. Medical staff, surrounding family, and courts are likely to acquiesce in decisions to maintain an apparently happy patient—despite the tension with the terms of an advance directive. The chances are therefore slim that a health-care agent or other decision maker would face the threat of a lawsuit, let alone actual liability, for providing treatment to a pleasantly senile patient or, generally, for acting according to the contemporaneous well-being of a now incompetent patient. In the unlikely event of a legal proceeding, the sympathies of any trier of fact would be with the decision to respect the material, current interests of the patient. Even if the decision maker were found "liable," any "damages" would be assessed with awareness of the benefits to the patient derived from the actual decision.

Nonetheless, I submit that it is not appropriate for decision makers to override advance directives merely because the declarant's expressed preferences do not coincide with current, material best interests.[30] If the declarant did in fact contemplate the situation actually encountered and still provided for a course contrary to material best interests, that course ought to be respected. Self-determination includes a prerogative to make decisions that most people would regard as foolish or unsound. If a person has considered the prospect of "harm" to his or her own future incompetent persona and nonetheless makes certain personal values predominant, that decision should ordinarily be respected.

I agree, however, with commentators who say that steps should be taken to examine the circumstances surrounding the formulation of an advance directive that appears to subordinate the perceptible current interests of a now incompetent patient. As noted, future-oriented autonomy entails projections, and a problematic decision can no longer be reconsidered by the now incompetent person. It is therefore sensible to ground implementation of a "problematic" life-and-death decision on a determination of whether the declarant really intended the problematic result ostensibly prescribed by the directive. But where good-faith examination discloses that the maker of an advance directive deliberately dictated the result in issue, that directive ought to be upheld.

Indeed, I only reluctantly endorse a limited prerogative to avoid the ostensible terms of an advance directive (in favor of a now incompetent patient's current well-being) conditioned upon a good-faith judgment that the declarant did not really intend to encompass the situation actually confronted. The high stakes involved— the life of an incompetent human being—warrant this limited prerogative. And the reality probably is that some people sign an advance directive without really contemplating some of the graver consequences and dilemmas. When those grave dilemmas occur (such as a clear conflict between a directive and current best interests), I favor allowing the decision makers to make a good-faith inquiry about the directive maker's contemplation of the dilemma confronted. Yet this authorization to avoid an apparent instruction might be misused.

The standard suggested by the President's Commission—involving the "adequacy" of a declarant's consideration of a directive's application—is fraught with danger of manipulation.[31] An agent (or other decision maker) may always contend that the declarant did not "adequately" envision the consequences. The standard supplies an opening for overriding idiosyncratic preferences of the declarant that prove distasteful to the eventual decision makers.

An adequacy of contemplation standard thus threatens to undermine any confidence that idiosyncratic preferences will be followed. One of the benefits of an advance directive is the comfort it can supply to the individual while that person is still competent. That comfort flows from confidence that the advance directive has regulated the future care of the individual in a fashion consistent with personal preferences and values. If eventual decision makers abuse their authority and readily circumvent advance directives, much of the value of such instruments will be lost.

There is only a fine line between saying that a declarant did not contemplate or intend to include the situation at hand (in rejecting care) and saying that the declarant's instruction was ill considered. The former involves interpretation of the directive's meaning, with the conclusion that the declarant simply did not intend the literal scope of the directive's language. The latter involves overriding the declarant's preferences because they are not congruent with the immediate well-being of the now incompetent patient and are, therefore, distasteful to decision makers. I suggest that deviation from the apparent terms of a directive is warranted only upon a good-faith judgment that the declarant did not intend to reject treatment in the situation at hand—whether his or her ostensible well-being would be sacrificed or not.[32]

C. Expressions of Incompetent Patients

By definition, an advance directive represents an autonomous expression of will which becomes effective only after the declarant has lost legal capacity to make the medical decisions at hand. It may seem strange, then, to utilize an incompetent patient's utterances in administering an advance directive. Nonetheless, there is an appropriate role for such expressions. The challenge is to define the bounds of that role.

The starting point of analysis is recognition that incompetency may cover a wide range of mental incapacity. While some patients may be barely aware of their environment and totally unable to comprehend information, others may have some understanding of data relating to their medical condition and proposed treatment (even if they are incapable of making a considered judgment about the data). Utterances from the former class may be incoherent ravings while the latter class may be making meaningful communication. The appropriate response to incompetent patients' utterances depends, in part, on where the patient fits within the range of incompetency.

Some living-will statutes fail to make an appropriate differentiation among incompetent patients. The offending statutes provide that the declarant may revoke a directive "at any time and in any manner, without regard to the declarant's mental or physical condition."[33] This apparently means that any statement countering a living will or contradicting a previous instruction will effectively revoke such instructions, no matter how deteriorated the declarant's mental condition at the time of this "revocation." (Following such a revocation, the declarant would presumably revert to the status of an incompetent patient who had left no prior instructions as to the matter in issue, and the general rules governing the handling of such patients would then prevail.[34] There would be no possibility of the patient issuing further, binding instructions since the patient would lack the requisite mental capacity.)

This extreme statutory receptivity toward revocation of a prior directive is problematic at best. As several commentators have noted,[35] the extreme deference to incompetents' expressions tends to subvert notions of self-determination. A carefully considered advance directive can, in theory, be undermined by the babble of a gravely demented patient. And potential for the manipulation of a demented patient is patent. The decision makers surrounding the patient (perhaps uncomfortable with the substance of a living will) can simply keep asking the patient whether he or she renounces the document until an affirmative response is attained.[36]

A variation on this theme appeared in a recent New York case. There, the now incompetent patient had appointed her daughter as health-care agent. The disgruntled son, apparently upset at the daughter's inclinations regarding care, sought to obtain the mother's "revocation" of the proxy appointment. He recorded a phone conversation with the incompetent patient, using leading questions to elicit one or two word responses. The son then petitioned for removal of his sister as health-care agent. The ploy failed. The judge recognized that the incompetent mother had not comprehended the conversation, and he rejected the petition.[37] Still, the incident underscores the vulnerability of incompetent patients to manipulation of their utterances.

The motivation behind the liberal revocation provisions in living-will statutes is easy to understand. There is a natural revulsion toward removing life-preserving care from a person who is articulating a wish to live.[38] This is so even when the patient is confused and uncomprehending of the real significance of the utterances. At the same time, giving determinative force to incompetent declarations, no matter how demented the patient, seems excessive.

The impropriety of giving force to the expressions of severely demented patients becomes more evident when we consider such a patient calling for death via the removal of life support. Not infrequently, such a patient will ask to be allowed to die or will consistently struggle to remove life-preserving intervention (such as artificial feeding tubes). Many sources have recognized that interpreting such behavior as meaningful choice is inappropriate.[39] Sometimes, this conclusion is grounded on the ambiguity of nonverbal conduct. Indeed, physical resistance to medical intervention can sometimes be ambiguous—possibly reflecting annoyance, anger, or desire for attention, rather than a deliberate choice to die.[40] But the more convincing explanation for reservations regarding such conduct is that the "choices" of grievously demented patients cannot be regarded as meaningful acts of self-determination. If a nondying patient were at a similar stage of mental incapacity, that person's choices would not be accorded binding force. This would be true with regard to medical choices, such as sterilization, or nonmedical decisions, such as disposition of property. There is no reason to accord greater weight to such expressions for purposes of a life-and-death treatment decision.

All this does not mean that the expressions of demented patients should be ignored. If an incompetent patient has any degree of comprehension and ability to communicate, the patient should be consulted about the proposed course of medical handling and the patient's reactions should be considered.[41] Again, this does not mean that the incompetent patient's responses should necessarily be determinative of the course to be followed but only that those responses should be sought and considered by the relevant care providers and decision makers.[42] There are several rationales for this consultation requirement.

First, it is a mark of human respect and dignity to consult with the incompetent patient, even if that patient is not very comprehending. The incompetent patient is a human being, albeit with reduced capacities. It would be inhumane to simply ignore the will and feelings of the incompetent patient while implementing the medical course fixed by the decision makers (even if this course conforms to the patient's advance directive). Nonconsultation and straight performance of fateful medical procedures constitute manipulation of the patient as though he or she were an inanimate object. Consultation thus has a symbolic significance, reminding staff, observers, and perhaps the patient that a human life is at stake.

In addition, the patient may have enough mental capacity to respond with assent to the proposed course.[43] Simple assent, without the capacity for full understanding and mental deliberation, is not informed consent or a genuine exercise of autonomy. But the consultative effort involved in attaining assent recognizes the patient's humanity, and the assent may assuage the patient and ease the ensuing course of treatment in some degree.[44]

The expressions of an incompetent patient can also furnish important insights into the emotional and physical feelings of the patient—insights which are relevant to the implementation of advance directives. The thrust of an advance directive may be to dictate omission of life-sustaining intervention where the burdens of continued existence in a debilitated, incompetent state exceed the benefits. The expressions of the incompetent patient are, in turn, one index of either the burdens (pain, suffering, and indignity) or benefits (emotional satisfaction) being experienced.[45] Even when a patient is totally incapable of making deliberate decisions, the patient may be capable of expressing feelings. If those feelings can be discerned and understood, they can be useful in the administration of an advance directive.

An additional reason for consulting with the incompetent patient and for paying heed to the incompetent's expressions is to assess prospective physical resistance to proposed medical procedures. The patient's resistance may necessitate physical restraints or heavy sedation. Depending on the nature of the medical procedure, the restraints may even be prolonged or repeated in nature. (Resistance to artificial nutrition tubes, frequent blood transfusions, or dialysis attachment provide examples.) Particularly in the case of an incapacitated patient who cannot comprehend the reasons for the treatment, restraints may provoke frustration and anger. The consequence of continued medical intervention in such circumstances would then be prolonged maintenance in an inhumane status—perhaps in a fashion inconsistent with the terms of an advance directive.

The expressions of the incompetent patient may therefore be important both to assessing in advance the patient's reactions to proposed medical intervention and to assessing the patient's feelings and status while undergoing actual restraints. The specter of prolonged or repeated restraint or sedation also helps explain the purpose of seeking assent from a mentally incompetent patient. That assent may diminish the chances that a resisting patient will be relegated to an undignified status during the dying process.

A final possible rationale for consultation with an incompetent patient would be to secure clues as to what the patient would choose if the patient were competent. Resort to such a rationale might occur, for example, where an advance directive is vague and the decision makers are seeking to determine what the declarant would have wanted in the current medical circumstances. This object (to discern what the patient would have wanted, if competent) has been cited in decisions of the Washington State Supreme Court relating to the handling of incompetent patients.[46] That court suggested that current expressions of an incompetent patient might furnish "a strong indicator of the treatment she would choose if competent to do so."[47] However, the same court cautioned that the weight attributed to the incompetent's expressions must depend on the extent to which the patient understands the issue at hand.

This last admonition is consistent with the diminished role of choice in the context of incompetent patients. If the incompetent patient has a substantial understanding of the circumstances, and the patient's "choice" corresponds to the patient's values as consistently held while competent, perhaps there is a meaningful autonomy element in the response obtained.[48] However, if the patient is so demented as not to understand or appreciate the nature and consequences of the choices involved, it is an illusion to talk in terms of autonomy and self-determination. Giving dominion to the deranged expressions of such persons would make a mockery of self-determination when the expressions override a carefully considered advance directive.

In sum, the expressions of an incompetent patient can sometimes be useful guides in shaping administration of a dying process in accord with an advance directive. Their utility, however, varies markedly according to the mental capacity of the patient and the ability of decision makers to accurately interpret the expressions. Statutory provisions which give substantive force to all incompetent expressions inconsistent with prior directives (as by treating them as effective revocations of a living will), are clearly overbroad. The ravings of a deeply demented patient ought not be permitted to override an advance directive. At most, an understanding (even if not deliberately considered) expression by an incompetent patient ought to suspend implementation of an advance directive which conflicts with the expression.[49] That is, in order to suspend the force of an advance directive calling for withdrawal of life support, a life-affirming expression must come from an incompetent patient who at least understands the concept of death. Even then, the force of such an expression probably ought to continue only so long as the position is being communicated by the patient. Thereafter, a considered and clear advance directive ought to govern.

THIRD PARTY OPPOSITION: FAMILY, PHYSICIANS', OR HOSPITALS' OBJECTIONS

To this point in the discussion, the difficulty of interpreting terse or vague language has posed the main obstacle to effective administration of an advance directive. Another obstacle materializes when one of the parties surrounding an incompetent patient—whether family member, physician, or institutional administrator—objects to implementation of a directive's instructions.

Appointment of a health-care agent is one technique for dealing with this hazard. The hope is that the agent will serve as an advocate to secure fulfillment of the declarant's wishes. But in many instances there will be no designated agent. Or the designated agent himself or herself may wonder how to deal with opposition from one of the above sources. Various mechanisms or techniques for enforcement of an advance directive will be discussed in chapter 7. Here, I address the legal status of the parties' objections to implementation of the declarant's apparent instructions.

A. Family Members' Opposition

There are indications that physicians sometimes fail to adhere to advance directives because of opposition by family members surrounding the moribund, incompetent patient.[50] This tendency is not surprising in light of the strong practical disincentives for an attending physician to contest a surrounding family's instructions. The family represent a potentially vocal and disruptive element. They pose a threat of legal recourse if a physician terminates life support contrary to the family's wishes. A specter of controversy, time investment, expense, and adverse publicity therefore looms before any physician who contemplates contravening the family. The much easier course is to go along with the family's wishes. (Similar incentives for deference to family wishes exist if it is a health-care agent who is confronted with a family's opposition to implementation of the now incompetent patient's directive.)

Family opposition might be grounded on either of two bases. One basis would be a family's contention that they understand the patient's real wishes—even if the family interpretation conflicts with the ostensible meaning of the advance directive. In such instances, acquiescence in the family position might be appropriate. As the previous material indicated, compliance with the incompetent patient's actual preferences may sometimes entail deviation from the apparent meaning of an advance directive. The family may be making a good-faith and plausible interpretation of the patient's actual intentions.

Another possible scenario exists. The family's opposition to fulfilling a directive's terms may stem from reasons other than good-faith interpretation of the patient's wishes. For example, the family may simply be emotionally unable to cope with the prospective death and may therefore seek to prevent it. Or the family may be seeking to substitute their view of the patient's best interests for what they deem the patient's aberrational or ill-considered instructions.

Under the second scenario—in which the family want to counter the patient's wishes because of their own preferences—the appropriate course for medical staff (and for a health-care agent, if present) is clear. The patient's wishes are supposed to prevail. If a health-care agent is present and determines that the advance directive dictates cessation of life support, and that determination appears accurate, medical personnel ought to follow that course. Life support should be withdrawn in accord with the directive. If there is no designated health-care agent, physicians should not simply acquiesce in the distorted position pushed by the family. The medical staff (or hospital administration) ought to petition for judicial appointment of a guardian who will be willing to adhere to the advance directive.

In the real world, the disincentives mentioned above will often come into play. As a practical matter, medical staff, and possibly even health-care agents, will defer to the wishes of the surrounding family. This will particularly be the case if the family seek life extension while the advance directive calls for cessation of life support.

B. Physicians' Opposition

Physicians might raise principled objections to implementing an advance directive. One objection would be that sound medical practice impels nonadherence to the now incompetent patient's wishes. A second objection would be that the physician's conscientious scruples don't permit compliance with the course prescribed in the directive. Sometimes these objections overlap.

A physician's objections might pull in either of two directions. Sometimes, a physician might object because an advance directive calls for cessation of life support at a stage considered premature according to the physician's assessment of good medical practice. Sometimes, a directive will call for continuation of life-preserving intervention to a point deemed inappropriate or futile by the physician or by professional standards. The principles to be presented here apply to both these happenstances.

The first inquiry regards an advance directive which prescribes cessation of medical intervention at a stage deemed premature and inappropriate by an attending physician relying on sound medical practice (i.e., professional standards). For example, a declarant, sensitive to personal notions of dignity, may have mandated cessation of life-preserving medical intervention at any point after admission to a nursing home. Later, although the patient is physically "healthy," mental deterioration prompts the patient's admission to a nursing home. Suppose the declarant (now a nursing-home resident) is stricken with pneumonia. Many physicians would object to withholding medical care from such a salvageable patient,[51] even though the patient is incapable of independent living because of chronic ailments and/or mental incapacity—a status deemed intolerable in the patient's advance directive.

Where the physician's objection to "premature" cessation of life-sustaining care is grounded on the rationale of sound medical practice, the patient's wishes ought ordinarily to prevail. This is so because social norms, as judicially interpreted, establish the primacy of patient self-determination over most conflicting professional preferences.

The primacy of social norms over medical preference has been established in many contexts. The whole doctrine of informed consent imposed duties which many physicians viewed as being in tension with their professional role.[52] Yet the contours of that doctrine were fixed by courts and legislatures despite professional qualms and objections. Similarly, as to the standard of skill required of physicians, the courts and legislatures may choose to accept professional custom and practice as the governing legal norm, but they need not do so.[53]

In short, while professional notions of sound medical practice form an important consideration in shaping the legal bounds of physicians' duties, those professional preferences are not paramount. For example, professional judgment received a rude setback when the federal government fixed regulations limiting abortion counseling in medical facilities receiving federal funding. Despite the bitter complaint that the federal rules violated professional standards, those rules were sustained.[54]

A similar lesson has been applied in the context of rejection of life-sustaining medical care. When patients or their representatives sought to reject such treatment, physicians commonly objected that medical standards outweighed patient self-determination.[55] Patients turned to the courts. The judicial response was that a patient's choice "must be accorded respect even when it conflicts with the advice of the doctor or the values of the medical profession as a whole."[56] Though such ringing declarations often appear in the context of competent patients, a similar order of priorities is likely to prevail with regard to incompetent patients and advance directives. A number of courts have accorded binding force to now incompetent patients' prior expressions despite medical practitioners' opposition.[57] The noncontemporaneous nature of advance medical instructions is unlikely to affect the upholding of patient self-determination over professional qualms.[58]

It is true that many legislative measures relating to advance directives mention "reasonable medical standards" or "accepted medical practice."[59] Most of this statutory language resembles that of the Uniform Rights of the Terminally Ill Act, which provides: "A physician or other health-care provider, whose action under this [Act] is in accord with reasonable medical standards, is not subject to criminal or civil liability, or discipline for unprofessional conduct, with respect to that action."[60] The relevant statutory language generally appears in the provision according physicians immunity for compliance with a statutorily approved advance directive.

At first blush, such expressions might be understood as endorsing physician adherence to good medical practice rather than the contrary terms of an advance directive. But it is unlikely that these statutory provisions will upset the understood priority of patient wishes over professional preferences.

The relevant statutory language about "reasonable medical standards" may simply be aimed at preserving claims of medical malpractice when compliance with patient instructions is undertaken in a technically shoddy fashion. For example, a physician who withdraws life support from a supposedly permanently unconscious patient might be liable for having negligently failed to perform the requisite tests of permanent unconsciousness. The language of some states' immunity provisions tends to support this focus on technical proficiency. Connecticut law states:

> [There shall be] no liability in removal or withholding [life support], provided that . . . the decision to withhold or remove such life support system is based on the best medical judgment of the attending physician in accordance with the usual and customary standards of medical practice. . . . "[61]

Delaware explicitly uses the word "negligence" in its immunity provision. The language reads:

> Physicians or nurses who act in reliance on a document exercised in accordance with this [statute] . . . by withholding medical procedures for an individual who executed such document shall be presumed to be acting in good faith, and unless negligent shall be immune from civil or criminal liability.[62]

In sum, the references to "reasonable medical practice" in immunity provisions were not intended to authorize physicians to impose their professional preferences to the detriment of patient choice expressed in advance directives. Moreover, the constitutional status accorded patient choice might mandate that patient choice prevail over professional hesitations concerning the soundness of the patient's chosen course.

There may be some practical limits to the primacy of patient wishes over professional judgment. A medical practitioner is probably not obligated to practice "bad medicine" or violate his or her professional judgment in order to comply with patient preferences.[63] At the same time, the physician may not simply impose his or her will on the patient. The physician's normal recourse is to withdraw from the case and arrange transfer of the patient's care to medical professionals willing to cooperate with the patient's chosen course.

Modern medicine recognizes a broad role for patient autonomy. While some physicians may object, on grounds of good medical practice, to implementation of certain instructions, other practitioners will see fit to comply. Thus, withdrawal from the case will often be a satisfactory outcome. There will be a fellow physician whose professional judgment differs from that of the original attending physician and who can step in and implement the patient's desired medical handling. Such divergence of opinion about professional and ethical issues is not uncommon. It occurs with regard to abortion. It occurs with regard to artificial nutrition. And it may occur with regard to the "premature" stage at which an incompetent patient may be permitted to die. While some physicians may be unwilling to withhold antibiotics from a "healthy" but gravely demented nursing-home resident, other physicians may have no qualms about respecting the patient's advance directive which dictates such a course. In short, the fact that some segments of the medical profession might regard a practice as ethically problematic should not preclude implementation of a patient's desire to follow the problematic practice. (The principal legal boundary on respecting patient choice would be the criminal law, with its constraints against assisted suicide and active euthanasia.)

There may be instances, however, when the advance directive's prescribed course is so problematic—from the perspective of medical judgment or ethics—that few if any practitioners will be willing to cooperate. Transfer of the patient to a cooperating physician may then not be a viable option. The proper resolution of this situation is still unclear.

One option might be to take the patient home, at least if the patient can be made comfortable in that setting. Another option might be litigation to try and force the resisting physician to follow the advance directive. That step would entail considerable expense and effort, and the legal resolution is far from certain. (Courts may be reluctant to compel conduct by physicians which is uniformly regarded as medically unsound. At the same time, modern medicine acknowledges the importance of patient choice, and the patient's self-determination interest might be ruled predominant.) As a practical matter, I suspect that many practitioners will simply impose their preferences by continuing life support in the face of an advance directive which dictates what the practitioner deems "premature" withdrawal of medical intervention.

Suppose the physician's objection to premature withdrawal is based on a strongly felt, personal moral judgment. In other words, on occasion a physician who objects to implementation of an advance directive may rely on personal conscience rather than just professional judgment or sound medical practice. Will such physicians be required to act in violation of their scruples?

Ordinarily, the tension between professional conscience and patient wishes is resolved—as in the case of tension with professional judgment—by respect for both physician and patient interests. That is, a patient (or person acting on behalf of the patient) cannot normally force a health-care professional to violate personal scruples. However, the objecting physician is expected to act to transfer the patient's care to fellow professionals who can, in good conscience, implement the advance directive.

Solicitude for physicians' conscientious objections first surfaced in the context of abortion and sterilization services. In the 1970s, numerous states adopted statutes providing that medical personnel cannot be coerced into providing abortion or sterilization services in violation of their moral scruples.[64]

Similar solicitude for professional conscience has been shown in the context of termination of life-sustaining medical intervention. Cases express unwillingness to compel a physician to violate moral precepts (in order to fulfill a patient's wishes), at least where transfer of care to another health-care provider can be accomplished.[65] Living-will statutes in many states take a similar approach. A physician is not required to follow a medical course violative of his or her conscience, but the physician is expected to seek transfer of the patient to another health-care provider. The main divergence among these statutes relates to the degree of effort the physician must make in arranging a transfer.[66]

Superficially, this legal framework seems to work a commonsense accommodation of patient and professional interests. The patient is entitled to shape the degree of medical intervention into a dying process, even when the decision was made far in advance of implementation and even if the choice is idiosyncratic. Health-care providers are not required to sacrifice their personal or professional scruples. Their alternative is to withdraw from the case while assisting the patient's representatives in finding a provider who can cooperate in implementing the advance directive. So long as a cooperating provider can be found, providers' individual scruples won't prevent implementation of patient choices.

Transfer of the incompetent patient's care to a cooperating physician may be feasible. Sometimes it merely entails referral to another physician within the same institution. Sometimes, though, complications disturb the nice theoretical structure just outlined.

The moribund patient may have developed an attachment to the particular health-care provider, so that transfer to an alternative provider entails a significant emotional price. Or the incident may occur in a relatively isolated geographical area so that transfer to a distant alternative provider imposes a significant burden upon surrounding family and loved ones continuing a deathwatch. Or a particular case may have generated so much publicity that alternative providers are reluctant to get involved. What happens when one of these complications prevents smooth transfer of the patient to alternative medical hands? Does the patient's interest yield, or does the health-care provider's?

If a health-care provider's personal scruples conflict with a declarant's chosen course, and transfer of the patient is not feasible, the provider can probably be compelled to violate his or her conscience. While states have often chosen to respect professional conscience, no constitutional or moral imperative requires that result when there is a conflict with patient choice. This conclusion is drawn by analogy from other contexts in which important public policies have been found to override the conscientious scruples of service providers. An example is enforcement of bans on race or gender discrimination despite the discriminator's conscientious belief in the discriminatory practice.[67] A patient's interest in obtaining medical treatment consistent with an advance directive probably occupies a comparable value status relative to professional conscience.

The little judicial precedent available suggests that a health-care provider can be compelled to violate his or her conscience when an alternative arrangement to accommodate the patient cannot feasibly be made.[68] This has been the case, for example, where the patient has developed a strong emotional bond to personnel within a particular institution,[69] where transfer of the patient would entail hardship for the surrounding family,[70] or where no alternative setting could be found.[71] In effect, the physician is being required, as a condition of medical licensure, to extend a full range of services to anyone accepted as a patient (where withdrawal and transfer is not feasible).[72] This does not seem like an unreasonable burden, at least within the range of medical conduct upheld as legal under the criminal law and not uniformly deemed ethically intolerable by the medical profession as a whole.

The same framework applies when a physician's objection to honoring an advance directive is grounded on a conviction that the requested treatment is medically inappropriate or "futile." (Start thinking about an advance directive which dictates continued life support even as to a permanently unconscious status and about an attending physician who feels that life support in such an instance is pointless.) Often, a claim of medical futility or pointlessness is really one of professional judgment about sound medical practice. Therefore, the same theoretical structure applies as applied to a physician's objection to premature withdrawal of life support. This means that while a physician can not ordinarily be forced to provide care which that physician deems medically unsound or futile, there is an obligation to assist in transfer of the patient to a physician who will implement the patient's chosen course. The patient's autonomy interest is acknowledged and accommodated.[73]

This topic of futile or pointless medical intervention is complex, and it warrants more detailed explanation. Some commentators do assert a physician's prerogative to refuse to provide treatment which is futile, meaning that it carries not even a modicum of benefit to the patient.[74] To the extent the assertion implies a medical prerogative to simply ignore or override a patient's preference for continuance of life-sustaining care, the assertion seems much too simplistic. As several other sources have noted, the concept of futility must differentiate between medical means which will have no physiological effect and means which are believed by the physician to carry no benefit for the patient (even though the means are life-extending).[75] When life-preserving techniques are in issue—as in the case of life support for a permanently unconscious patient—the issue is not technical capacity but values (i.e., is continued life support warranted?).[76]

The answer to that question involves patients' perceptions of the value of gravely debilitated existence and social judgments about allocation of resources, not just medical judgment. Medical professionals are not peculiarly qualified to weigh the interests involved. "[D]eciding whether the life of a severely ill person is worth saving—whether a patient's state of existence is sufficiently good to justify further medical treatment—is not a question that doctors are uniquely, or even specially, qualified to answer."[77]

In short, complex value judgments underlie any contention that life-extending medical intervention is futile. The underlying question is the dispensability of a human life, and the relevant standard for that judgment is a societal issue to be resolved by courts and legislatures after consideration of many perspectives, including those of the medical profession. A medical judgment that an intervention is pointless is relevant but not determinative. Even some *medical* sources agree that medical judgment cannot be paramount in fixing the parameters of the duty of life-preservation. The Society of Critical Care Medicine, for example, recognizes that it is appropriate for a physician to provide service which is meaningful to the patient even though it has "no reasonable medical benefit."[78]

An illustration of the possible tension between physicians' preferences and patients' advance instructions occurred in a 1991 case.[79] A Minnesota hospital sought court appointment of a guardian for an eighty-seven-year-old woman immersed in a permanent vegetative state. The hospital's ultimate object was to secure authorization to end life support (a respirator) because it supposedly constituted "inappropriate medical treatment that is not in the patient's medical interests."[80] The family insisted that treatment should continue because the patient would have wanted continued life support. Their appraisal was based on the patient's prior religious convictions and on alleged prior statements.

Assuming there was a firm basis for the family's contention that the now incompetent patient would have wanted continued life support,[81] the petition for appointment of a new guardian should have been (and was) dismissed. The relevant principles have been presented. The physicians' assertion that continued respirator maintenance would be futile is a claim based on professional judgment about sound medical practice. Physicians ordinarily cannot be forced to practice bad medicine, but their judgment cannot be imposed upon patients' preferences.[82] This means that the attending physician and hospital could not simply override the patient's wishes. They could turn over care to more cooperative physicians but, in the absence of such cooperative physicians, the original attending physicians would be obligated to continue medical maintenance.[83]

There might be rare instances when professional judgment (such as that asserted by the doctors in the Minnesota hospital) is reinforced because the patient's prescribed course is so inhumane as to be beyond the bounds of acceptable professional behavior. (In chapter 6, I speculate about a situation where the now incompetent patient has dictated maximum life support but is later suffering agonizingly and irremediably while begging that life support be withdrawn.) If the patient's prescribed course is inhumane according to widely accepted standards, physician resistance will probably be upheld and allowed to overcome the patient's advance directive.[84]

This possible exception for inhumane treatment does not apply to an advance directive which prescribes medical maintenance in a permanently vegetative state (PVS). It is true that most people regard permanent unconsciousness as a distasteful and undesirable prospect. This is readily understandable, given the horrible void of a permanently vegetative state. Nancy Cruzan's attending physician testified about her "alternating constipation and diarrhea, stomach troubles, eye problems, rashes, bleeding gums, contorted limbs, seizures and vomiting."[85] But PVS is not yet considered so utterly degrading that continued life support is widely regarded as inhumane. The thousands of PVS patients being maintained[86] undermines any notion that medical maintenance in a PVS is currently considered so inhumane as to be beyond the bounds of acceptable medical practice. (However, it is conceivable that societal norms will eventually evolve to the point that preservation in a PVS is widely considered inhumane.)

The result in the Minnesota case might be different under somewhat different facts. If the patient had never indicated a wish to be preserved in a PVS, and if there were no religious beliefs or other indices that she would have wanted such a course, the family's effort to continue life support might conceivably be supplanted. This displacement of the family's preference would be grounded not on medical futility but on a judgment that the permanently unconscious patient's best interests dictate withdrawal of life support. The standard of best interests is generally used where a now incompetent patient has never expressed personal preferences with regard to life-sustaining medical intervention.[87] Under this standard, a decision maker on behalf of the patient is supposed to decide whether the burdens of potential existence with treatment outweigh the potential benefits.

It may legitimately be asked why a permanently unconscious patient's best interests lie in termination of life support, given that the patient is insensate and is not suffering. The answer is that best interests can include dignity. And the vast majority of people, considering what they want for their own prospective medical handling, regard permanent unconsciousness as an undignified and unwanted status. (People may also be influenced by the perception that care of PVS patients poses an emotional and economic burden on others.) If the vast majority of people would regard termination of life support as being in their own best interests as PVS patients, and the particular patient has never given reason to think that he or she deviates from that perspective, then removal of life support seems most consistent with the best interests of that patient.

In short, the day may soon come when—in the absence of prior instructions to the contrary—decision makers on behalf of permanently unconscious patients will be expected to permit such patients to expire. Such a result will be based on a societal perception that the vast majority of persons would want that result for themselves and that it would coincide with humane and dignified medical handling. That was the instinctive judgment of the New Jersey Supreme Court in 1976 in *Quinlan*. Increasing empirical data confirms that the *Quinlan* court's intuition was correct. Accordingly, courts continue to uphold guardians' decisions to remove PVS patients from life support.[88]

The United States is currently at a juncture where withdrawal of life support from a PVS patient is regarded as a permissible course, consistent with the patient's best interests. Such withdrawal will eventually be the expected course (in the absence of prior patient expressions to the contrary or other indicia of patient will).[89] Again, this position is anchored in the perception that most people define their own best interests in such a fashion and that a permanently unconscious patient has no significant interest in medical maintenance.

In the recent Minnesota case, the family was contending that the patient either expressed or would have expressed a preference for continued life support. They properly sought to ground their assessment of best interests in the values and preferences of the patient herself. Therefore, their decision on behalf of the incompetent patient should prevail over the physicians' judgment about the pointlessness of continued care.[90]

In the Minnesota case, no issue arose about the financing of the disputed care. As in *Cruzan*, public sources were willing to foot the bill. In other instances, however, implementation of an advance directive may raise serious concerns about the allocation of expensive and/or scarce medical resources.[91] Those concerns are legitimate and must ultimately be confronted. Society is and will continue to be unwilling to fund all critical care for all patients. But those resource-allocation issues should be resolved by social judgment—as reflected in considered regulatory and legislative determinations—and not by individual practitioners' judgments that public funds might better be expended elsewhere rather than in the "futile" care sought by a particular advance directive.[92]

C. Institutional Conscience

A hospital may resist implementation of an advance directive on the ground that *its* moral precepts (as opposed to the precepts of staff members) would be offended. In recent years, that claim has most commonly been raised in cases where removal of artificial nutrition was sought by or on behalf of a patient.[93] Is there such a thing as institutional conscience? If there is, does it override a patient's desires regarding medical treatment?

The notion of institutional conscience has aroused some controversy. A few commentators contend that an inanimate object like a hospital can have no conscience. From their perspective, only persons, not bricks and mortar, can have conscientious scruples.[94] By contrast, other observers assert that the development of separate missions or philosophies by health-care-provider institutions "may serve an important purpose in our morally pluralistic society."[95]

My sentiments lie with those who believe that institutions not only can but should have cognizable moral positions. It is true that institutions can't experience the shame or anguish that accompanies an individual's compelled betrayal of conscience.[96] But the institution's founders, owners, board of directors, administrators, and staff could presumably have these feelings. Moral integrity can have a role in determining what goes on within an institution.

On many issues of medical practice, a range of ethical postures is possible. Within that spectrum, it seems desirable that institutions take ethical stands and seek high moral ground. Suppose, for example, the issue were experimentation on human or animal subjects, and the institution took a stricter moral position than required by government regulations. Most people, whether they agree with the particular institutional policy or not, would acknowledge that institutional moral integrity is a meaningful concept in these instances.

Recognition of the concept of institutional conscience does not mean that the institution's interest must always prevail. An institution which believes that AIDS patients are sinners and don't deserve treatment may not necessarily be entitled to turn away AIDS patients. There are many instances when an institutional policy— including positions taken on religious or philosophical grounds—can be overridden by strong public policies. To cite an example, employers or schools which conscientiously believe in their discriminatory policies can be compelled to cease gender or race discrimination. Antidiscrimination laws have been upheld despite the discriminators' deeply held beliefs. But while government may choose to override institutional conscience, it may also decide to recognize and accommodate that conscience.

In the context of health-care providers, both courts and legislatures have generally expressed sympathy with the concept of institutional conscience, especially in the private sector. The first expression of that sympathy came in the 1970s when health care providers were exempted from performing abortions or sterilizations in violation of their conscientious scruples. That relief came both from legislatures[97] and courts.[98]

In the late 1980s and the 1990s, the issue became institutional objections to patients' and guardians' requests for withdrawal of life-preserving treatment. On that issue, there has been limited responsiveness to claims of institutional conscience. The judicial inclination has been to seek an accommodation of both patients' and institutional interests. If it is feasible to transfer a patient to an alternative setting, that step must be taken rather than forcing an institution to provide objectionable care.[99] Transfer to a health-care provider which can conscientiously follow the patient's preferred course both allows the patient ultimately to control the degree of medical intervention and permits the original host institution to maintain its moral integrity. (The original host institution is expected to assist in securing transfer to another health-care provider.)

As in the case of an attending physician with conscientious objections, transfer of a patient from an objecting institution is not always practicable. Publicity attached to a case may deter other institutions from getting involved. Or nearby institutions may share the same scruples as the host institution. Or the patient may have an emotional attachment to particular personnel. Or inconvenience to surrounding family may impede transfer of the patient to another locale.

In the event that transfer cannot practicably be accomplished, an institution will probably be required to cooperate in implementation of the controversial advance directive. This has been the result, for example, where institutions did not give the patient (or family) advance notice about the institution's conscience-based policy.[100]

The implications are plain for health-care agents or others seeking implementation of a "problematic" advance directive. As long as the host institution had served notice about its conscientious policy (such as refusal to remove artificial nutrition), and as long as the moral policy is genuine (as opposed to a contrivance to get rid of an unwanted patient), that policy is entitled to respect. Some effort will have to be made to move the patient to a more responsive setting (or to demonstrate hardship to the patient) before the institution can be compelled to provide the controversial service in violation of its conscience. The health-care agent can expect the institution to take "reasonable steps" to assist in the search for an alternative setting.

6

The Moral Boundaries of Shaping
Post-Competence Medical Care

AN ADVANCE DIRECTIVE seeks to impose a person's own values on a future dying process. A declarant's personal conception of self-respect in dying might be grounded on religious precepts, personal philosophy, or a personal vision of dignity in the dying process. This personal conception of dignity might or might not coincide with the immediate well-being of the incompetent patient at the later moment for implementation of the advance directive.

It is easy to envision instances of extreme dissonance between an advance directive and the perceptible interests of a later incompetent patient. For example, in chapter 4 I mentioned the advance directive of a declarant so sensitive to helplessness that she dictated cessation of life-sustaining intervention beginning at the moment of admission to a nursing home. That declarant might later become mentally impaired and incompetent but remain alert, retaining significant awareness of the environment and ostensibly enjoying existence in a nursing home. If such a person later contracts pneumonia, contemporaneous patient interests would dictate medical intervention, while the advance directive prescribes that the patient should be permitted to die.

In a converse fashion, contemporaneous interests might favor allowing a patient to die while the advance directive prescribes maintaining life-preserving intervention. A person who is a "vitalist," who believes that life is so sacred as to demand preservation to the last possible moment, may issue an advance directive requesting continuation of all life-preserving treatment no matter how dismal the patient's ultimate condition. Subsequently, as a mentally incapacitated patient stricken with terminal cancer, that person might experience unbearable, unremitting pain.[1] Continuing all possible medical intervention would then conflict with the incompetent patient's contemporaneous interests, which impel withdrawal of life-preserving machinery.[2]

These examples test the limits of future-oriented autonomy. In each, a person has issued an advance directive which defines a personal concept of dignity and self-respect, including the upholding of certain personal values. That directive now appears to conflict with the contemporaneous interests of the incompetent persona.[3]

A conflict between personal choice and immediate well-being would not impede effectuation of choice if the person were competent. For a competent person exercising contemporaneous autonomy, personal choice regarding medical treatment need not coincide with material best interests. The respect accorded contemporaneous autonomy extends to personal decisions which deviate from mainstream conceptions of wisdom or best interests. A competent patient may refuse a medical procedure that would leave her in a debilitated state (e.g., an amputation) even though most reasonable people would choose otherwise. Autonomy in contemporaneous medical decision making thus embodies a prerogative to impose personal values and preferences whether they are "sound" or not. Does a similar prerogative attach to prospective autonomy—decisions aimed at post-competence medical handling?[4]

As explained in chapter 2, prospective autonomy is different in some respects from contemporaneous personal choice. That chapter canvassed the problems—including a multiplicity of variables, multiple combinations of variables, medical uncertainty, and declarants' limited perspective—which handicap prospective autonomy. While those problems certainly complicate the task of a declarant seeking to control a future, incompetent dying process, they don't nullify the concept of advance directives. Chapter 2 outlined the rationale for advance directives, a rationale widely accepted in contemporary America. Both courts and legislatures have recognized and even expressed strong sympathy with the principle of advance directives. Yet these sources have not settled the potential conflict between an advance directive and contemporaneous patient well-being.

The cases decided to date do not really resolve the conflict between advance instructions and contemporaneous best interests. There are decisions which speak in fairly absolute terms of a person's "right to avoid circumstances in which the individual himself would feel that efforts to sustain his life demean or degrade his humanity."[5] But these cases do not involve situations in which the previously competent patient's vision of dignity clashes with that patient's subsequent perceptible interests. A few decisions suggest that a previously competent patient's clear directive prevails against a subsequent guardian's appraisal of the incompetent patient's best interests.[6] Yet these judicial expressions occur in cases in which the incompetent patient had reached a permanently unconscious or stuporous state. As such, the cases do not address any real conflict between a prior directive and the perceptible interests of the incompetent patient.[7]

In addition to the above judicial expressions, DPOA-HC laws in many states purport to give a health-care agent the authority to make the same range of decisions that the principal could make if competent.[8] It is a truism that a competent patient would be entitled to reject life-sustaining medical intervention or to consent to nontherapeutic medical procedures even if such a decision did not conform to the apparent well-being of the patient. Thus, in theory, these statutes confer authority on an agent to implement an advance directive which conflicts with the immediate well-being of the incompetent persona. However, the theoretical scope of these statutory measures has not been tested.

The above-cited legal authorities suggest that a person's clear-cut advance directive can prevail over that person's subsequent well-being. Even if that is a legally tolerable course, is it moral to override the immediate well-being of a helpless, incompetent being? At least two concerns have surfaced in the discussions to date.

The first issue involves the moral stature of future-oriented autonomy. It pertains to definition of an incompetent patient's interests and the status of previously declared values whose importance can no longer be appreciated by the now incompetent patient. Via an advance directive, a declarant is seeking to effectuate personal perceptions of self-respect and dignity. Yet at the moment for implementation of those personal values, the incompetent patient may not sense or appreciate the fulfillment of those values. Do that patient's interests encompass elements which can no longer be sensed by the patient (such as nonadherence to the patient's previously articulated conception of a dignified existence)? If the patient can no longer sense invasions of the patient's values, aren't the patient's interests confined to the contemporaneous benefits and burdens being experienced?

Assuming that a person can have interests in having previously important values and choices respected, what about the contemporaneous interests of the incompetent persona who has succeeded the formerly competent patient? Doesn't withdrawal of life-preserving medical support grievously harm a pleasantly senile patient? The possibility of "harming" a helpless, incompetent patient by withdrawing a life-preserving treatment leads to an additional moral contention. The idea is that a person may lose moral authority to dictate the fate of a later, incompetent persona if the later persona is so changed as to have a different "personal identity."

A continuous personal identity supposedly requires some measure of psychological continuity, either through continued memories or beliefs. In the context of death, dying, and advance directives, a competent declarant might become so demented and lacking in psychological continuity as to be considered a new person for moral purposes. If so, it is arguable that one person, the maker of the directive, cannot morally harm or dictate the death of another person—namely, the demented, new persona.[9] In other words, "self-determination" no longer prevails because the original "self" no longer exists. From this perspective, an advance directive might lose its moral stature if, at the moment for implementation, it conflicts with the contemporaneous interests of the incompetent persona.

The remainder of this chapter offers my resolution of the tension between prospective autonomy (as found in an advance medical directive) and an incompetent patient's immediate well-being. First, I present five "scenarios" intended to exemplify the kinds of dilemmas which might arise. Then, I describe and critique the major positions favoring solicitude for immediate patient interests as opposed to previously expressed preferences. Finally, I offer my own resolution of the five scenarios—a resolution giving considerable scope to the declarant's autonomy interest, even to the detriment of immediate patient well-being.

SCENARIOS RAISING CONFLICT AMONG AN INCOMPETENT PATIENT'S INTERESTS

Several examples may help crystallize the potential tension between an advance directive and the contemporaneous interests of an incompetent patient. In the following scenarios, assume that all patients were fifty years old at the time of making an advance directive and that the critical medical decisions are confronted five years later. Assume also that no evidence exists that the patient changed his or her mind or wavered in resolve between preparation of the advance directive and losing competence.

Scenario 1: Person A, a Jehovah's Witness, prescribes in an advance directive that blood transfusions should not be administered regardless of the life-saving potential of such medical intervention. She is aware of the life and death implications of this religiously motivated instruction. Later, A becomes prematurely senile and incompetent. Still later, the senile patient develops bleeding ulcers which demand blood transfusions. With a blood transfusion, she will survive and continue to live as a "pleasantly senile" person for a number of years. The senile A no longer has recollection of, or interest in, religion; however, she remained an avid Jehovah's Witness up until the time of incompetency. Should the attending physician administer a life-saving blood transfusion?

Scenario 2: Person B believes both that life should be preserved to the maximum extent possible and that suffering is preordained and carries redemptive value in an afterlife. B prepares an advance directive in which all possible life-extending medical intervention is requested and all pain relief is rejected. At the time of the preparation of the directive, B has a conversation with a physician in which the physician explicitly warns him that many terminal illnesses entail excruciating pain. Despite that admonition, B directs that all means to preserve life be utilized and that analgesics be omitted. Subsequently, B suffers from cancer, which both affects his brain, rendering him incompetent, and causes him to suffer excruciating pain. Further medical treatment such as radiation or chemotherapy will extend B's life but will not itself relieve the pain or cause any remission in which competence would return. Should the attending physician sedate the patient, or cease the life-prolonging medical intervention, or both?

Scenario 3: Person C is an individual with chronic heart problems. Physicians have informed C that at some stage he will need a heart transplant in order to survive. C prepares an advance directive stating that if he becomes incompetent and survival becomes dependent on a heart transplant, then such a transplant should be rejected because of its expense. C prefers to leave a substantial monetary legacy to his children. Later, C becomes prematurely senile and incompetent. Still later,

C's heart deteriorates and a heart transplant becomes necessary to preserve C's life. With the transplant, C will very likely continue to live for three to five years. Without it, C will die within a few months. The transplant will cost $100,000 and is not covered by any insurance or government benefit program. C's estate totals $100,000. Should a life-extending heart transplant be performed?

Scenario 4: Person D is a health-care professional sensitive to society's needs for organ and tissue donations. In her advance directive, D provides that if she should become incompetent but remain physically healthy, then she wishes to donate a kidney and bone marrow to needy recipients. Later, D is afflicted with Alzheimer's disease and reaches a point of profound dementia. Needy recipients for kidney and bone-marrow transplants have been located. The prospective transplant operations will pose only a slight risk to D and entail only mild pain. At the same time, the now incompetent D has no recollection of her prior instruction and no appreciation of the altruism involved in donating an organ or tissue. She will derive no con-temporaneous gain from the contemplated operations. Should the transplants be performed in accord with D's advance directive?

Scenario 5: Person E is a sociology professor known for her intellectual sharp-ness. E takes enormous pride in that intellectual acuity. E drafts an advance directive prescribing that if she should become mentally impaired and incompetent to the point where she can no longer read and comprehend a sociology text, then all life-preserving medical intervention should be withheld. When reminded by her spouse about the potential for happiness in an incompetent state, E replies that she deems significant mental dysfunction to be degrading and personally distasteful. For her, such a debilitated existence is a fate worse than death. Later, E suffers a serious stroke which renders her permanently incompetent and incapable of reading or performing intellectual tasks. E is also unable to swallow and is therefore de-pendent on artificial nutrition. At the same time, E does not appear to be in any pain and seems to derive some pleasure from listening to music. Should the life preserving nasogastric tube be continued?

In each of the above situations, people have issued advance directives which effectuate their personal values and concepts of dignity. Yet implementation of those prior instructions conflict in some measure with the contemporaneous in-terests or well-being of the incompetent persona. Can the advance directive prevail? Does prospective autonomy encompass the prerogative to impact negatively on the incompetent persona?

DEFINING THE INTERESTS OF INCOMPETENT PATIENTS

Law Professors Rebecca Dresser and John Robertson have been prime spokes-persons for a position which denigrates reliance on advance instructions. They assert that it is wrong to use advance instructions as a guide to managing the medical treatment of a helpless, incompetent patient.[10] Their basic premise is that the autonomy interests reflected in a person's prior choices become "meaningless" once the incompetent patient can no longer understand and appreciate the violation of those choices. That is, the patient's previously cherished ideas about dignity, religion, or altruism lose importance when their nonimplementation cannot be sensed. For Dresser and Robertson, an incompetent patient "lacks interests in privacy, dignity, and other values that presuppose some conscious appreciation of those concerns."[11]

Professors Dresser and Robertson go even further. They do not just discount the significance of autonomy interests once violation of such interests can no longer be appreciated. They also speculate that if incompetent patients could miraculously be given momentary competence to decide their fate, those patients would focus on their current material interests and not any prior abstract, philosophical, or dignity-related concerns.[12]

A concomitant precept for Dresser and Robertson is that a helpless, incompetent patient's contemporaneous interests (in a debilitated status) ought to be the predominant guide to care so long as the patient retains any significant interest in continued life (which to them includes any patient with the capacity to interact with his or her environment). Dresser and Robertson focus on the current welfare of the incompetent patient. For them, that focus demonstrates moral concern for the debilitated human being. By contrast, it would be morally wrong to allow "meaningless" prior values to prevail over the patient's current interests in continued life.[13]

The Dresser-Robertson position would certainly obviate some hard problems associated with advance directives. Unclear, ill-considered, or deviant instructions could simply be ignored. Health-care providers would be following a humane course by acting according to the contemporaneous, perceptible interests of an incompetent patient. However, the Dresser-Robertson approach seems critically flawed.

The most fundamental flaw is the thesis that incompetent patients are not harmed by rejections of their prior directives. This thesis certainly does not conform to common perspectives and ways of thinking. For instance, if a dying, incompetent Jehovah's Witness receives a blood transfusion in contravention of a prior instruction (in a vain attempt to prompt a remission), we tend to say that the person's religious values have been affected and that this constitutes harm to the patient. If a person dictates in an irrevocable trust that funds be expended in a particular way and the trustee absconds with those funds after the person's incompetency, we tend to say that the now incompetent and unaware grantor has been injured by this breach of faith (as have the intended beneficiaries). If a person expresses a desire to receive all possible life-preserving intervention, yet a life-sustaining ventilator is subsequently withdrawn in order to save another patient, then we tend to see an impingement of the patient's self-determination even if the patient was comatose at the moment of the deed.[14]

There are other examples of societal respect for the unsensed interests of incompetent persons. Assume that a permanently unconscious patient has left no instructions about medical intervention, and assume that he has no surrounding family or friends. What prevents the medical staff from carving up the patient in order to harvest nonvital organs or tissue for the benefit of others? What prevents the conduct of nontherapeutic medical experiments on the insensate being? The obstacle is social respect for the intrinsic dignity interests of persons, even when violations of those interests cannot be felt by the affected individual.[15] Society can and does attribute dignity interests to incompetent persons despite their incapacity to sense or appreciate breaches of those interests.

Attribution of some significance to abstract, unappreciated values of incompetent patients does not resolve the issue at hand. The question remains whether these abstract interests (as articulated in an advance directive) can prevail in the critical context of life-preserving medical intervention, especially when the immediate well-being of the helpless patient would seem to dictate life preservation. If the answer is positive, and I think it is, the key lies in understanding the integral link between prospective autonomy and the success of a person's life.

The late Professor Nancy K. Rhoden was an articulate advocate of the moral force of prospective autonomy in the death-and-dying context.[16] Professor Rhoden argued that the advance instructions of a competent person have considerable moral force, even if that person reaches an incompetent state in which failure to honor prior wishes cannot be felt or appreciated. For Rhoden, it is highly "humane" and respectful of human dignity to give force to future-oriented decisions, even at the expense of some contemporaneous interests of a now incompetent persona. She comments:

> The competent person's primacy derives from his status as moral agent [autonomous individual]. Moral agency is inherently future directed, and the future may . . . encompass one's incompetency. Prior directives are the tools for projecting one's moral and spiritual values into the future. These values seem to me worthy of respect even when they conflict with the subsequent, purely physical, interests of an incompetent.[17]

Rhoden further states:

> Viewing the patient only in the present divides her from her history, her values and her relationships—from all those things that made her a moral agent. . . . If a person has stated, "treat me, when incompetent, as if my competent values still hold," respect for persons demands that we do so.[18]

Professor James F. Childress adds: "The principle of respect for persons, which supports respect for the autonomous patient's choices, also supports reliance on the nonautonomous person's prior autonomous directives."[19]

Is all this convincing? Or is the Dresser-Robertson position more appropriate in emphasizing the contemporaneous, material interests of the incompetent patient? Does that position reflect a morally correct focus on the helpless patient's immediate interests? Just because people want others to treat them in post-competency as if they had their prior sense of dignity intact does not necessarily mean that society should promote such a "delusion." In other words, the moral foundation for allowing persons to impose choices about dignity and personal values upon a future incompetent persona needs elaboration.

A starting point in examining the moral foundation is to note the importance people commonly attach to prospective control over the dying process. It is apparent that many people care mightily about their post-competence medical handling, and they hope (if not expect) to shape their own fates in the face of potentially fatal afflictions. The hundreds of thousands of requests for advance directive forms provide one index of public interest. The 1991 Danforth Act, federal legislation requiring health-care institutions to inform patients about advance directives, provides another index of the perceived importance of advance directives.

Why do people care so much about controlling a post-competence dying process? Beyond noting the fact of widespread interest, it is useful to understand the rationale which moves people in this direction. Of course, a variety of motives may impel people to try and direct their post-competence medical fate. In part, the concern may be avoidance of the suffering sometimes incurred during a fatal affliction. But I suggest that the central concern is maintenance of a personal conception of dignity and self-respect, which includes shaping of a dying process consistent with one's character and values.

Post-competence maintenance of dignity and character may be important to avoid feelings of embarrassment or humiliation.[20] But avoidance of unpleasant emotions is not the sole or even dominant object. In significant part, a person's control over a post-competence dying process is an effort to mold other people's posthumous recollections of the person's character and values. This desire to shape recollections is grounded on common recognition of a tie between human dignity and a personal image projected to others. And because of a perceived tie between dignity and lifetime image, individual self-fulfillment and self-respect are seen as dependent not just on dominion over important decisions while the person is still competent and acutely aware but on dominion over a lifetime image.

The self-realization value of autonomy is commonly seen, then, as encompassing control of medical intervention in the intimate matter of dying, even at post-competence stages. A person views control over the post-competence dying process as part of an effort to shape the subsequent images and recollections of his or her life. Those images include both the self-image which the person may hold while still mentally aware and the post-competence images which surrounding people and survivors may hold.

People understand that a lifetime image can be critically affected by the portion of existence involving their incompetent persona. Professor Ronald Dworkin has observed that "it seems essential to someone's control of his whole life that he be able to dictate what will happen to him when he becomes incompetent."[21] This is so because the nature of how one is remembered is considered important to the success of one's life and survivors' recollections are affected by the lingering impressions of the moribund persona.[22] The ultimate specter is a protracted period of demeaning debilitation or of burden (emotional and/or economic) being imposed on surrounding loved ones. Justice Stevens, dissenting in *Cruzan*, recognized the important interest in not having memories sullied by a protracted and undignified dying process. He remarked: "Nancy's interest in life . . . includes an interest in how she will be thought of after her death by those whose opinions matter to her. . . . How she dies will affect how that life is remembered."[23]

The advance instructions actually issued by people tend to confirm a preoccupation with shaping lifetime recollections and framing a lifetime image consistent with a declarant's character. A common goal is to avoid a debilitated status which the declarant regards as undignified or demeaning. Living wills and other advance instructions frequently focus on avoiding existence in a degraded state. For example, the cases dealing with the prior expressions of patients in a permanently vegetative state (PVS) reflect that focus. Courts hearing such cases understand and empathize with people's distaste for the utter helplessness, the wasted bodily status, and the devitalized personality associated with PVS.[24]

Another common object of a person's advance instructions is to avoid emotional and financial burdens to attending family during the dying process.[25] In *Cruzan*, Justice Brennan noted the understandable wish of people to prevent "a prolonged and anguished vigil" for surrounding family.[26] Public surveys disclose that many persons wish to avoid future medical maintenance in the event of total and permanent dependence on others.[27] Such predilections might be grounded either on a wish to avoid what is perceived as a helpless, undignified state or on a concern for the surrounding persons burdened by the future patient's care.

This common solicitude for family interests reflects understanding that the recollections a person leaves behind are shaped by more than the visual images of the deteriorated, incompetent persona. A person's altruistic nature and concern for the interests of family and others are also part of the character and recollections which the individual cultivates. That character influences the human relationships one has with others, human relationships which form part of a person's individual image and legacy. A person who has nurtured certain relationships during competency may seek to advance those relationships even during post-competency, perhaps by an advance directive which dictates that the emotional and financial interests of surrounding family be considered in shaping the person's post-competence medical handling.[28] Implementation of such an instruction helps an individual perpetuate a relationship which he or she has sought to cultivate as part of a lifetime character. It honors an autonomous person's effort to build a life image and legacy.

A similar phenomenon occurs with regard to a person's dedication to religious or philosophical beliefs or to other personal ideals. Adherence to those ideals is part of an individual's personal integrity and character.[29] Implementation of those ideals at a post-competence stage of life carries forward the person's character and affects other people's recollections of that character.

From all the above, it is clear that respect for prospective autonomy (as reflected in an advance medical directive) honors the same kind of values applicable to autonomy generally. Self-determination in shaping medical intervention during any naturally occurring dying process upholds personal priorities and thus honors human capacity for choice. When that self-determination is upheld at a post-competence stage of existence, society honors the *fulfillment* of human capacity for choice as represented in each person's shaping of his or her lifetime priorities and character.[30] In prescribing post-competence care, every declarant seeks to preserve a personal vision of dignity, to imprint his or her own character on this critical juncture, and to continue personal ideals.

Even given the important autonomy interests at stake, can those interests prevail when arrayed against the immediate well being of a helpless, incompetent persona? We know that autonomy in the death-and-dying context is so valued by society that it is upheld against many competing interests. As noted in chapter 1, competent persons may reject life-sustaining intervention even when they are salvageable to healthful existences. This means that society waives any interest in the patient's productive capacity in order to uphold self-determination. Moreover, a choice to reject life support will be upheld even if the decision impacts negatively on other persons. A patient may reject life support in contravention of strong physician preferences to continue treatment. A patient may choose to reject life support and expire even if terrible grief will be caused to surrounding loved ones. A parent may even reject life support when the ensuing death will adversely affect a dependent minor.[31]

A similar priority of interests is likely to prevail in extension of the self-determination prerogative to the setting of post-competence medical decisions. Competing interests (such as medical preferences about sound medical practice) will not likely be permitted to override prior patient choice. Courts already view implementation of the prior instructions of a now incompetent patient as fulfillment of a "right" to self-determination. To ignore such instructions would relegate the patient to the status of an object whose fate is determined by others rather than of a human who has shaped his or her own fate.

The moral foundation for upholding prospective medical autonomy seems sound. In effect, society is saying that people have "earned" the right to shape their post-competence care and thus to shape recollections of each individual's lifetime. Each person, while competent, cultivates and nurtures a particular vision of body and soul, thereby fulfilling the potential of human autonomy. By preserving the body and developing the character associated with it, a person earns the moral prerogative of shaping the post-competence images and recollections other persons will have of the previously competent individual.[32] (By the way, there are burdens, not just privileges, associated with being the lifetime master of a particular body. When an incompetent patient is languishing in a hospital, the assets accumulated during the competent phase of existence are being dispensed to cover costs of care.) The bottom line, though, is that a competent person justifiably views control over a post-competence dying process as part of the earned prerogative to shape the subsequent images and recollections of his or her life.

A competent person's prerogative of shaping post-competence developments is recognized in numerous situations. I've already referred to the judicial acceptance of advance medical instructions. A similar solicitude for prospective autonomy underlies the disposition of property by will, contracts for post-competence care (e.g., nursing-home residency), and requests regarding disposal of a cadaver. Society conceivably could choose to intervene and direct the allocation of wealth upon a person's death, but it chooses, rather, to afford people wide discretion in the distribution of their property. In part, this choice reflects a utilitarian concern for the encouragement of wealth accumulation; but in part, it also reflects a moral judgment that people have earned a right to dispose of their property. That prerogative is important to people partly because they seek to shape the images and memories which will survive their competency and their lives.

People's expectations that future-oriented decisions will be respected upon incompetency are not grounded simply on personal preferences or aspirations. Social structures and conventions have also supplied a foundation for such expectations. Even before the development of legislative mechanisms for promoting control of post-competence medical intervention, society demonstrated considerable respect for individuals' future-oriented autonomy. Irrevocable trusts and durable powers of attorney furnished legal mechanisms for persons to prospectively control the post-competence disposition of property. Conventional wills served as a vehicle for disposition of property after death. Contract law allowed for post-competence implementation of a person's preferences in such matters as care setting and disability insurance. Additionally, families commonly honored a person's prior requests regarding burial or other disposition of his or her cadaver, including a subsequent gift of anatomical parts.[33]

In these respects, as well as others, society commonly upheld a person's future-oriented decisions even when the person no longer had capacity to appreciate violations of those personal values or preferences. Professors Dresser and Robertson would distinguish death-and-dying decisions from other exercises of future-oriented autonomy on the basis of the serious, negative consequences involved, such as the death of an incompetent patient when an advance decision dictates the withdrawal of life-preserving medical intervention. A maker of an advance directive can thus be materially harmed by being allowed to die while still possessing significant interests in life. According to Dresser and Robertson, this is unlike the maker of a will who is dead and therefore cannot be affected by implementation of an ill-considered or unwise disposition of property.[34]

I doubt that the potential for inflicting serious "harm" to one's future interests provides a sufficient basis to distinguish advance medical directives. First, if one recognizes the continuing, prospective autonomy interests of the moribund patient, implementation of an advance directive is not inflicting net harm to that patient. Second, accepted forms of future-oriented autonomy also have the capacity to harm a future, incompetent persona. A person can bind oneself to disadvantageous contracts and dispose of wealth in a fashion which negatively impacts on a future, incompetent persona. The latter could be accomplished by outright gifts, by irrevocable trusts, or perhaps by durable powers of attorney. In all these instances—as in the instance of shaping medical intervention in a dying process—respect for a person's competent prospective decisions is morally justified by respect for the person and the lifetime image being cultivated.

The above depiction of the common importance attached to abstract interests, such as dignity and altruism, in a post-competence state underlines another flaw in the Dresser-Robertson thesis. Specifically, they claim that if persons could miraculously regain momentary cognition in order to make an informed decision in their present state of incompetency, they would act according to their contemporaneous interests (apparent benefits and burdens) rather than their prior values. However, it is impossible to test the premise and no reason can be seen to accept it a priori.

There is no reason to assume that a person's values and priorities would change while the person is in a permanently incapacitated status. If a person previously cared about the indignity of a severely deteriorated status, or if a person cared about the emotional and financial well-being of surrounding family, those deeply rooted values would presumably persist.[35] Those values were felt deeply enough that the individual, when competent, knowingly used them to dictate her or his death-and-dying process. Experience shows that competent persons commonly issue instructions that they not be maintained in a permanently unconscious state even though they are aware that they will not sense or experience the degradation of such a state. This can best be explained by people's acute concern about how they will be remembered and the distasteful image which may be left behind. In short, the Dresser-Robertson premise regarding noncontinuity of a person's priorities seems dubious at best.

PERSONAL IDENTITY AND THE STATUS OF AN INCOMPETENT PERSONA

Some commentators suggest that a person can lose "personal identity" via loss of the memory and character which distinguish an individual.[36] From this perspective, an incompetent persona may be, in effect, a different person from the being who previously formulated an advance directive. The declarant, then, would arguably have no moral right to "harm" the incompetent persona by directing the withholding of life-sustaining medical treatment. Harm would be inflicted at least so long as the incompetent persona's pain and suffering did not make life so torturous as to be considered a fate worse than death.

The notion of personal identity seems to be of limited utility. No source employing this concept defines the degree of memory loss or character change that would make an incompetent persona a "new" person. Even if an administrable standard were defined, it would probably have limited practical application. In many instances, an incompetent persona retains a significant measure of long-term memory of a prior, competent status, thereby retaining his or her original personal identity. If an incompetent persona is so severely demented as to have lost all or almost all memories, the resulting being (a new personal identity) would have very limited contemporaneous interests. This is true, for example, for the incompetent persona who is in a permanently vegetative or barely conscious state and lacks relational or interactional capacity.[37]

Professors Allen E. Buchanan and Dan W. Brock use the limited interests of a severely demented patient to partially finesse the personal identity dilemma. They argue that a persona so severely demented as to lose basic cognitive or interactive capacity is no longer a "person" with cognizable moral interests. Thus, a competent person can dictate the fate of a future persona in a persistent vegetative state because that latter persona is not, for Buchanan and Brock, a person with equal moral status.[38] For them, such a nonperson has radically truncated interests. However, if a profoundly demented persona is still aware, that persona does have cognizable interests. For example, if a demented persona is still subject to pain, Buchanan and Brock would question the moral status of a prior directive which would produce a painful death. Similarly, Buchanan and Brock would probably deem it morally necessary to protect a profoundly demented person with clear capacity for pleasurable sensations from a prior directive dictating termination of care.[39]

This last situation does suggest an instance when the personal identity argument seems most troubling. A person has total or almost total loss of memory (perhaps an individual with advanced Alzheimer's disease) yet is aware and capable of experiencing pleasure. From the perspective of memory, at least, it is as if the original declarant had miraculously undergone a brain transplant. Is the declarant entitled to dictate the medical fate of this new persona?

I would argue that the answer is yes—that a declarant ought to be permitted to control medical intervention via an advance directive regardless of the degree of memory retained by the incompetent persona. From a legal perspective, "although each individual goes through many stages and transformations of varying significance in the passages of a lifetime, the individual nevertheless remains ultimately and essentially the same person from cradle to grave."[40] In other words, the life span of each person's embodiment is a unitary event even if the persona associated with the embodiment becomes so severely demented that he or she retains no recollection of the prior competent persona. Along these lines, Professor

Dworkin asserts that "the competent and demented stages of life are steps in a single life, . . . [and] the competent and demented selves are parts of the same person."[41] Under this vision of a person's singular lifetime, the fates of various personas that may emerge over time are inextricably entwined.

This judgment about a single, unified life conforms to the way people see their own lives, as shown by the effort to employ advance directives. Someone who makes a prior directive sees herself or himself as the unified subject of a human life. Such people see their concern for their bodies, their goals, or their families as transcending their (future) incapacity.[42] For most persons, then, it is self-evident that they ought to be given prospective dominion over post-competence matters such as medical intervention, property dispositions, residency locus, organ donations, autopsy, and funeral arrangements.

The notion of a single integrated existence encompassing both competence and post-competence stages also conforms to the way others view a person's life. A person is remembered as one being, even if that being undergoes radical changes during a lifetime. The incompetent persona is viewed by surrounding persons as a reflection or extension of the former self, still embodying the values and beliefs previously associated with the now incompetent person. Thus, we still think of the incompetent individual as a Catholic, Jew, or whatever faith he or she previously professed. Similarly, that person is perceived as maintaining a character (self-centered, altruistic, or whatever) even if that character is no longer discernible. In short, the concept of a unitary existence—with a competent and post-competent being viewed as having a single personal identity—conforms both with how people see themselves and how others see them.

The moral foundation for permitting a competent person to control the fate of a later, incompetent persona has already been presented. The competent person nurtured and developed the body, character, and relationships later associated with the incompetent persona. The competent person thus *earned* a certain prerogative to direct the fate of the succeeding, incompetent persona as that fate impacts on the recollections of a person's integrated lifetime. As noted, the competent person has lifetime burdens as well as privileges. That person's accumulated assets will fund all care provided to the later, incompetent persona.

The incompetent patient, no matter how demented, is still a human being and possesses certain immediate interests. The demented persona may not only have physical sensations but might even be in an ostensibly pleasant emotional state. While I have argued that an advance directive has considerable moral status and ought usually to prevail, there is a question about limits. To what extent should prospective autonomy interests yield to the contemporaneous interests of the incompetent patient or to the interests of others?

My response to this question comes via resolution of the scenarios previously outlined. For me, the key element in circumscribing autonomy is the concept of humane conduct toward an incompetent being. There are boundaries to what basic humanity permits people to do to themselves. Just as society limits what a competent person can do to his or her competent self, there is a limit on what a person can dictate for his or her future, incompetent persona. In the next section I will explain how this notion of humane treatment impacts on actual medical situations.

RESOLUTION OF THE SCENARIOS

As already suggested in chapter 5 in dealing with administration of advance directives, an ostensible clash between advance instructions and contemporaneous patient interests will seldom require judicial resolution. As a practical matter, the health-care agent or other decision makers will tend to "interpret" an advance directive to accord with the clear-cut contemporaneous interests of the patient. It is legitimate for administrators of an advance directive to examine whether the declarant really contemplated and intended to encompass the situation now confronted. And when obvious harm to the now incompetent patient is threatened by implementation of a directive, the decision makers may well find that the declarant did not envision the situation that has now unfolded.

Even if the advance directive's administrators are knowingly misinterpreting or distorting the declarant's (perhaps idiosyncratic) wishes, a decision to favor the perceptible, contemporaneous interests of a now incompetent patient will seldom be challenged or overturned. Medical staff, surrounding family, and courts are likely to acquiesce in decisions to maintain an ostensibly happy patient or to allow a severely anguished patient to die, regardless of the apparent intention of the directive.[43]

Even if administrators of an advance directive are, as a practical matter, often guided by clear-cut contemporaneous interests of an incompetent patient, a question remains regarding what *should* be the result. Should the declarant's considered wishes be derogated to the immediate interests of the patient?

Commentators have expressed diverse views on the subject. A few simply assert that prior choices, if specific, must prevail over contemporaneous patient interests.[44] By contrast, Professor Dresser argues that an advance directive should not be followed if the incompetent patient has any significant interest in continued life—meaning a capacity to interact with the environment.[45] As we know, she accords little status to prior expressions. Even commentators who generally respect advance directives tend to draw a line in situations when the directive calls for withholding life-preserving medical intervention from an apparently content, though demented, patient. Professors Rhoden, Buchanan, Brock, Nancy M.P. King, and Sanford H. Kadish seem to agree that an advance directive should not be implemented if to do so would terminate a life that "clearly contains more pleasure and enjoyment than suffering and pain."[46]

The commentators' restraint regarding advance directive implementation appears to flow from two considerations. First, future-oriented autonomy may have somewhat less force than contemporaneous autonomy. With contemporaneous self-determination, one can be sure that an effort is made to dissuade the competent patient from a foolish choice, allowing the competent patient to continue to reassess the competing personal interests right up to the moment of implementation of a terminal decision. By contrast, an advance directive is based on projections and speculation about prospective interests, and it may not be clear how much the declarant actually considered the situational conflict now confronted by the decision makers. In particular, it may be difficult to determine how much the declarant was confronted and challenged concerning any morally problematic instructions issued. Second, there seems to be a moral compunction or instinctive revulsion about allowing a helpless, ostensibly content individual to die—even when the decision is grounded on that individual's own prior direction.

My own position would be to implement, in most instances, a considered, future-oriented determination even at the expense of an incompetent patient's contemporaneous interests. As noted, advance directives have moral stature because a person's self-determination and self-realization goals naturally include a strong interest in shaping future images and recollections. Because those recollections become embodied in, and associated with, an incompetent persona, thus affecting other people's lifetime memories of the unitary person, the person's prior autonomous decisions deserve respect.

Moreover, there is no intrinsic bar to competent decisions which may entail future harm. A person can give away one's wealth, subject to rules involving fraud against creditors, even though that act might cause substantial hardship to a future incompetent persona. Self-determination includes a prerogative to make decisions which most people would regard as foolish or unsound. Once a person has made a considered judgment, even an imprudent future-oriented decision should ordinarily be respected.

It is acceptable that special steps be taken to examine the circumstances surrounding the formulation of an advance directive that appears to subordinate the perceptible contemporaneous interests of an incompetent patient. As noted, future-oriented autonomy entails projections, and a problematic decision can no longer be reconsidered by the now incompetent person. Therefore, it is sensible to require that implementation of a "problematic" life and death decision be predicated on an examination of whether the maker of the advance directive really considered and intended the problematic result ostensibly dictated.

This means that the ultimate decision makers should at least inquire whether the directive maker was aware of the problematic consequences now being faced. For example, did the vitalist declarant realize that excruciating pain might be encountered during an extended dying process? Did the future-oriented person seeking to avoid indignity realize that the incompetent persona might derive some pleasure from a debilitated existence? Such inquiries are legitimate. But when good-faith examination discloses that the maker of an advance directive knowingly dictated the result in issue, then that directive ought ordinarily to be upheld.

With regard to the scenarios presented above, I take the position that the advance directives should be implemented in each instance. I'll address each case to indicate where I think constraints might properly come into play.

Scenario 1 (the Jehovah's Witness who has prospectively rejected all blood transfusions): A person's autonomy should include the prerogative to choose religious precepts that govern the competence and post-competence portions of a lifetime. This is so whether or not violations of those religious precepts will be sensed or felt by the person. The premise is, as already explained, that persons may be harmed by disrespect for their values and self-defined dignity even if that disrespect is not sensed or appreciated. If prospective autonomy is a meaningful concept, as I think it is, then the injury to autonomy interests from disregarding the advance directive outweighs the harm to the incompetent persona. The result is similar to that of the competent Jehovah's Witness who rejects a life-saving blood transfusion.

The fact that the critical moment comes years after the original directive should not matter so long as the directive reflects a deliberate judgment and so long as there is no indication that the person's values changed while still competent. The situation here is different from that of parents who are legally precluded from imposing religious precepts on immature minors in a fashion that will seriously harm the incompetent minor. Here, a mature adult has adopted a religious tenet with the understanding that the decision may subsequently disadvantage her own material interests as an incompetent persona.

Scenario 2 (the vitalist patient in excruciating pain): If a person has made a considered decision that, for purposes of future medical intervention, sanctity-of-life principles should prevail over distaste for suffering, then that choice ought to be respected. It is certainly a heartrending spectacle to contemplate the helpless, anguished patient being sustained in reliance on prior instructions. There will be a great temptation to find that the patient did not sufficiently anticipate or appreciate the prospective pain and, therefore, ought to be spared the consequences of an "imprudent" directive.

Yet, when the advance directive seems considered and unambiguous, it is not immoral to hold the patient to the bargain. Respect for autonomy justifies such a result. People may have strong philosophical or religious beliefs in both the sanctity of life and the meaning of suffering. Those beliefs can form a legitimate part of the personal character and self-image which an individual may seek to project during a lifetime, including the post-competence dying process.

A possible rationale for nonimplementation of an advance directive might arise where an incompetent patient has reached such a degraded and undignified status that it is simply inhumane to allow a patient's prior directive to dictate prolongation of that status. For example, B (who left an advance directive dictating all possible intervention) may not only be groaning in agony but also thrashing to the point at which continuous physical restraint is necessary to keep his life-preserving medical intervention in place. Is not the specter of this helpless, agonized, and tethered human being enough to conclude that basic humanity demands some relief despite the patient's carefully considered advance directive? Have we not reached the moral boundary of autonomy? Just as a self-determination prerogative cannot morally encompass self-mutilation or consent to slavery, can we not say that the prospective imposition of an utterly degrading status on an incompetent patient is simply beyond tolerable bounds?

My answer is yes. There are limits to what even I can stomach under the rubric of autonomy. However, a few caveats should be imposed on a boundary to future-oriented autonomy governed by intrinsic human dignity.

First, the criterion ought to be intrinsic human dignity as understood by a clear majority of the population. The fact that a guardian's subjective version of human dignity will be offended by adherence to advance instructions ought not be determinative. This caveat has application to B's case in scenario 2. Many people would not be offended by continued administration of life-preserving treatment, in accord with the patient's prior instructions, despite the incompetent patient's significant suffering. Many people would acquiesce in a person's prerogative to design a dying process consistent with personal views about the nature and value of suffering. Only when actual suffering reaches the level most people would label intrinsically inhumane should the patient's directive be overridden.

Second, the directive should be breached only to the minimum extent necessary to avoid inhumane handling. In scenario 2, for example, B ought to be given analgesics (in contravention of the directive), but the life-sustaining intervention should be continued in accord with the directive. In this way, the patient's intrinsic human dignity is preserved as consistently as possible with the patient's advance instructions.

Another wrinkle might be added to the scenario if B, the now incompetent patient, were not only in obvious distress but also verbally begging to have the life-preserving medical intervention withdrawn (contrary to his advance instructions). I touched on the matter of contemporaneous expressions in chapter 5. There, I explained that declarations by a currently incompetent patient can be given only limited force. That force depends on the degree of dementia involved. (While some patients may be barely conscious and totally unable to comprehend, others may have some degree of understanding of their conditions.)

If B understands his situation and comprehends the prospect of death, the pleading for cessation of medical care warrants consideration. At the very least, the expressions are an index of the patient's degree of suffering. At some point, extreme suffering may convince the relevant decision makers that continued intervention is inhumane.

Contemporaneous expressions will also influence those decision makers whose natural inclination is to follow the incompetent patient's clear-cut current interests. The previously vitalist patient's current requests to be allowed to die may then reinforce the decision makers' determination to override the advance directive prescribing prolongation of the tortured existence. The decision makers may see the patient's utterances as confirmation of their choice to act according to that patient's contemporaneous interests.

As the patient is incompetent, the expressions cannot be regarded as acts of genuine self-determination. Nonetheless, an aware (though legally incompetent) patient may be able to give assent to a proposed course of medical handling, and that assent is entitled to some recognition.[47] By contrast, the utterances of a gravely demented patient can reflect neither self-determination nor assent. Such deranged utterances certainly cannot be permitted to override a clear advance directive. If the patient is severely demented, reliance on the verbal "revocation" of a vitalist advance directive is inappropriate.[48]

Even when the incompetent persona is aware and has some comprehension, ascribing binding force to contemporaneous utterances is problematic. Suppose the patient had been a devout Catholic who always believed in the reception of last rites. He or she, however, is now an incompetent persona with some, but limited, understanding of the issue and is declining last rites. Should we follow the incompetent's current wishes, or should we adhere to the advance directive? Unambiguous, competently made instructions should prevail so long as the treatment dictated for the incompetent persona is not fundamentally inhumane. Receipt of the last rites would not be widely perceived as inhumane.

Another obstacle to implementation of B's directive might be posed by attending physicians or other health-care providers. They might be contending either that continued medical intervention is "futile," because the patient's condition is so dismal as not to benefit the patient, or that continued treatment conflicts with the providers' personal scruples.

This issue was touched on in chapter 5, which deals with administration of advance directives. The proper resolution is to uphold the patient's advance instructions (here calling for continued life support) despite the tension with the physicians' views of sound medical practice or medical ethics. This is not to say that health-care providers will be compelled to furnish care they deem medically or ethically inappropriate. Accommodation of all interests is sought by transfer of the patient's care to another professional who is willing to cooperate with the patient's chosen course.[49] This disposition is particularly appropriate when preservation of life is the patient's chosen course.

In some instances, professional scruples might be reinforced by a determination that the patient's previously prescribed course is so inhumane (in application) as to be beyond the bounds of acceptable medical behavior. That is, a universally accepted professional standard of conduct might prohibit implementation of the patient's wishes. A court would be reluctant to order compliance with such a problematic instruction. Even though courts, as agents of society as a whole, are not compelled to accept medical norms, the impetus is strong to adopt a universally respected professional norm. And without judicial intervention it would be difficult to find medical professionals to implement the disputed directive.

Another practical constraint is the availability of resources to finance B's protracted medical struggle. There is no constitutional obligation or societal inclination to finance all beneficial medical services. The impetus to fund a medical service is even less for care which is torturous to the incompetent patient and inappropriate from the perspective of some medical staff. Health-care providers may prove unwilling to provide this latter type of care to the impecunious "vitalist" patient.

Scenario 3 (the expensive heart transplant): If C were still competent, there would be little question that the patient would be entitled to reject a heart transplant for the sake of preserving a fiscal stake for his or her descendants. The patient would then be permitted to die despite the possibility of preserving a clearly meaningful existence for a number of years. Should C's altruistic nature and impulses be denied merely because the critical personal decision was made years before the moment for its implementation? Should the contemporaneous interests of the now incompetent persona impel life-preservation?

For the same reasons future-oriented autonomy permits a person to impose his or her religious precepts on a subsequent incompetent persona, a person's articulated, altruistic principles should prevail.[50] A person should be able to shape the collective memory of that person's lifetime, including recollections of the person's character and principles. Continued respect for those principles are part of the contemporaneous interests of the now incompetent patient.[51]

Professor Yale Kamisar posed to me a hypothetical variation on this scenario. Suppose, he suggested, C's descendants (the people whose economic stake C sought to protect) renounce their economic interest. In other words, suppose C's family prefers to preserve his incompetent existence even if it costs them a $100,000 legacy. They are therefore telling the attending physician to ignore C's advance directive and to perform the life-extending surgery.

This is a tough dilemma. The very beneficiaries of C's altruism are seeking to waive their interest in favor of extending his life. As a practical matter, many physicians would probably follow their instructions.

Yet, the whole point of prospective autonomy is to allow a declarant to fix priorities in a post-competence dying process. C made the considered judgment that he would prefer death rather than expensive preservation of his debilitated existence. The concept of advance directives would be endangered by acquiescence in the family's reordering of C's priorities. After all, many declarants prescribe a post-competence course in order to spare their loved ones burdens and suffering. If those loved ones can simply renounce their interest and thereby alter the declarant's wishes, that altruistic type of advance directive would have little force.

Of course, my response might be different if circumstances had markedly changed subsequent to the preparation of the advance directive. Suppose, for example, the family show that the economic status of the children (the economic beneficiaries of C's demise) had substantially changed over time. They no longer need the $100,000 nearly to the degree they did when C's advance directive was issued. If the economic circumstances changed *after* C's incompetence, the family's argument seems strong. C himself might well have preferred life-saving surgery in light of the family's diminished economic need. If the changed circumstances occurred before C became incompetent, but he did not alter his advance directive, the picture is more murky. Arguably, C's failure to alter his directive means that his assessment of the importance of the $100,000 legacy did not change.

Scenario 4 (harvesting an organ and tissue): Like the advance directive in scenario 3, D's advance directive to donate a kidney and bone marrow upon death is grounded in altruism. In this case, her solicitude is directed toward some future unknown organ recipients rather than known family members. Also, the altruistic gesture takes the form of authorizing removal of an organ or tissue rather than mere rejection of life-sustaining medical intervention.

Use of a prospective organ donation to fulfill an altruistic impulse is consistent with the previously expressed notion that a person's body is associated with a single, unitary existence. That is, the competent declarant tends to see the kidney (or bone marrow) as his or her own. The credit for altruism is registered in recollections about the unitary person even though the incompetent persona may not sense satisfaction from the altruism involved or from the approbation engendered. D will be remembered as the generous donor of the life-saving organ and tissue. Thus, the advance directive ought to be implemented even though the operation involved will have no therapeutic value for the now incompetent patient.

In the hypothetical case as presented, the harvesting operations would pose slight risk and create only mild pain for the incompetent persona. Suppose, though, that the incompetent patient is debilitated to a point at which the operation would pose a significant mortal risk for that patient.

One reaction is that the prescribed course now resembles suicide more than the rejection of life-sustaining medical intervention in the face of a naturally occurring dying process. This person is initiating a course of conduct involving a bodily invasion which will place his or her life in jeopardy. It may well be that health-care professionals would refuse to cooperate with such a venture even if the patient were competent. If that is the case (i.e., the patient's prescribed course would not be followed even if the patient were competent) then a fortiori that course need not be followed for the now incompetent patient.

Assume again that D's risk is slight and the pain modest. Suppose now the incompetent persona does not assent to the operations so she will have to be restrained and forced to undergo the procedures. In other words, implementation of the course prescribed in the advance directive will subject the incompetent persona to a measure of indignity. How does this element get factored in?

If good-faith investigation discloses that the declarant never considered the possible degradation of the incompetent persona, that fact might provide a rationale for deviation from the prescribed course. At least if the declarant was extremely sensitive to bodily restraint, a good-faith judgment might be that D would have altered her resolve in the face of the indignity of restraint. But if good-faith investigation discloses that the declarant probably would want the transplant performed (regardless of the implications for the incompetent persona), then the advance directive should be implemented.

Just as an advance directive can prescribe the withdrawal of life support and arguably "harm" an incompetent persona, a directive should be able to dictate a course which subjects the incompetent persona to a measure of indignity. The limit to this principle has been discussed above in the context of scenario 2. At some point the course prescribed by the advance directive becomes so intrinsically inhumane that decision makers may justly refuse to fulfill the directive. But that point would not be reached in the present scenario so long as the restraint of the incompetent persona would only be temporary.[52]

Scenario 5 (the demented professor): For E, maintaining a dignified image was crucial. Similar to her, some people wish to preserve for posterity their images as vital, active, and acute individuals. Part of the self-respect and dignity that they value is grounded on avoiding a deteriorated status which they regard as degrading.

A declarant's concern about deterioration may reflect apprehensions of frustration, embarrassment, or humiliation of being viewed in a state of incompetency. If that is the rationale for the original instructions, and if the feared emotions don't materialize (as best the decision makers can tell), then there might be a legitimate basis to override E's advance directive. But such apprehensions might not be the core of the declarant's concern. Previously active and vital people may seek to avoid an undignified status (such as permanent unconsciousness or extreme dementia) even if they understand that there will be no emotional suffering in the debilitated state. In part, their concern may be to avoid mental anguish or burdens for surviving relatives who must cope with the debilitated individual. Or, the person may simply view a life image (and the personal investment in cultivating that image) as being debased by a gravely deteriorated period of existence.

In principle, this aspiration to maintain dignity deserves as much respect as the religious or altruistic motivations discussed in previous scenarios. Indeed, religious precepts, concern for survivors' interests, and concern about a dignified image are all part of the self-respect, values, and character which an individual seeks to cultivate in a lifetime.

As a result of strokes, brain trauma, or degenerative neural diseases, many persons reach a point of grave physical and mental debilitation. The names Conroy,

Clark, Dinnerstein, Foody, and O'Connor all represent a court case in which the saga of such a person is recounted. The formerly vigorous person has become a helpless patient, confined to bed, unable to feed himself or herself, and usually incontinent. The patient is conscious, but barely so. It is difficult to determine if the patient is in physical or emotional pain. The patient may occasionally groan, sigh, or smile. The patient may be aware of surrounding people but cannot recognize or communicate with friends or loved ones. The patient has no hope of recovery. The patient is indefinitely sustained by artificial nutrition, by kidney dialysis, or by mechanical ventilation.

In such a situation—when the contemporaneous benefits and burdens of the incompetent patient can no longer be measured with any confidence—the patient's previously articulated, dignity-based instructions ought unquestionably to prevail. The incompetent patient has reached a level of incapacitation which many previously vital persons would view as demeaning. If a person has indicated in an advance directive that such a status is personally distasteful, then that judgment ought to be respected. This is so even if the uncomprehending, deteriorated patient is not perceptibly suffering and has some remaining capacity for pleasure.

Some commentators would draw the line at an incompetent patient whose potential for pleasure and satisfaction seems to clearly outweigh any material detriments (such as perceptible pain and suffering). An illustrative case is the "pleasantly senile" person. This incompetent individual may have lost all short-term memory and may be incapable of functioning intellectually at anything resembling the person's previous level. Nonetheless, the person seems "happy" and capable of deriving certain simple pleasures from life (such as E's listening to music). The commentators' thesis seems to be that it is inhumane or immoral to withhold or withdraw life-preserving medical intervention from such a person, even in reliance on an explicit advance directive. I'm not so sure.

One premise accepted above (in scenario 2) is that certain handling of an incompetent patient might be so intrinsically degrading or undignified as to be inhumane (according to widely shared societal standards). That principle has some relevance to the present context. For example, if the withholding of medical intervention would prompt an agonizing dying process for the ostensibly content, yet incompetent patient, that result might be labeled inhumane and impermissible. In many situations, though, the withholding of life-preserving medical intervention could be accompanied by palliatives to provide a painless dying process.

The further question is whether it is intrinsically immoral to implement an advance directive which calls for withholding life-preserving medical intervention from a gravely deteriorated, previously vital individual when the incompetent persona still has clear capacity for net pleasure or satisfaction from continued existence. From a perspective that values prospective autonomy, it is not immoral for E to seek to preserve an image of vitality—a certain version of self-respect—by dictating the withholding of further medical intervention from his or her incompetent deteriorated persona. This is so even if E's incompetent persona is still capably of deriving some pleasure from existence (such as by listening to music). As long as withholding medical intervention will not impose cruel suffering on the incompetent patient, an unambiguous and considered directive should be upheld.

I'm not sure how often this issue will arise. I would think that most people would not want to prompt the demise of their ostensibly happy future persona. Yet it is not intrinsically immoral for a person to shape future medical intervention in a way which will minimize any period of substantially deteriorated existence. Avoidance of a personally demeaning dying process is, ordinarily, part of the self-realization and self-respect furthered by future-oriented autonomy.

Of course, my moral perspective on E's case may be perverted by an obsessive-compulsive preoccupation with notions of autonomy. If my perspective is indeed aberrational as tested by prevalent social standards, it perhaps ought to be ignored. I concede that if allowing E to die is widely deemed immoral, then that judgment ought to instruct the legal norm governing those responsible for the medical fates of incompetent patients. However, the intrinsic moral nature of withholding life-preserving medical treatment from a contented but severely demented patient is still an open issue. It is a subject for continued public debate informed by medical, legal, and philosophical inputs. For me, giving expansive scope to advance directives, even to the detriment of the ostensible immediate interests of an incompetent persona, is both morally and legally sustainable.

7

Enforcing Advance Directives

THE LEGAL VALIDITY of an advance directive means little if the document is ignored or resisted in practice. To date, a fair amount of informal and anecdotal evidence indicates that living wills are frequently ignored.[1]

The reasons for this phenomenon could be several. Surrounding family members may be moved by their own concerns—often emotional inability to "let go"—or their own perceptions of the incompetent patient's best interests. (And medical staff may be acquiescing in the family's preferred course because the family represent the most vocal and immediate force seeking to influence care.) Or medical staff may be unfamiliar with the binding legal status of an advance directive and therefore may be pushing for their version of good medical practice. Or medical personnel may have ethical qualms about the course laid out in the advance directive. Or the medical staff may be puzzled about the meaning and content of a particular advance directive. (Chapter 4 recounted how some instruction directives can be singularly uninformative.)

Appointment of a health-care agent is a device intended in part to deal with these impediments to fulfillment of advance instructions. An agent is supposed to be familiar with a principal's wishes and dedicated to seeing that they are implemented. However, appointment of an agent is not a panacea. Some declarants will be unable to enlist a suitable agent. In those instances, an instruction directive—without designation of a health-care agent—will be the only document at hand. Moreover, presence of a designated health-care agent provides no guarantee that surrounding family and/or medical personnel will adhere to an advance directive. And an agent encountering such resistance to the principal's instructions may well be unfamiliar with institutional dynamics and may well be unsure how to cope with resistance from medical staff or from the patient's family.

All these scenarios involving deviation from an advance directive suggest that mechanisms for enforcement of such documents will have to be found. To date, no widespread ethic of respect for advance directives has emerged in the medical profession and in health-care institutions. There is no culture which accepts advance directives as a natural and integral part of medical practice.

Educating the lay and medical publics about the advance directive technique may spur some change in attitude. The federal Patient Self-Determination Act of 1991 (PSDA) is aimed at accomplishing that educative task.[2] But education alone is unlikely to impel uniform compliance with advance directives. Inevitably, there will be some need to coerce medical respect for advance instructions. The availability of coercive measures will reinforce the message supplied by the PSDA: that an advance medical directive is a legitimate and important means for a person to try and impose a measure of dignity on his or her dying process.

Experience with advance directives is still too sparse to determine whether effective enforcement machinery is possible. In this chapter, I will consider the primary existing routes for securing implementation of an advance directive in the face of hesitancy or resistance from those parties surrounding the incompetent patient.

All enforcement machinery is dependent on an advocate on behalf of the now incompetent patient. Ordinarily, a designated health-care agent will serve as that advocate. The succeeding descriptions of possible enforcement mechanisms are in large part intended to guide health-care agents in performing their advocacy role. As a preliminary matter, though, I'll address the problem of a declarant who couldn't or didn't name an agent.

In the absence of a health-care agent, deviations from an instruction directive (at least deviations in the direction of extending life) will be difficult to curb. In some such instances, any surrounding family and attending medical staff will reach a mutual understanding to follow a medical course counter to the patient's advance directive. When that occurs, no advocate of the patient's wishes is present to contest that mutual understanding. Only if a dissident family member or a dissident staff person surfaces will there be a voice for adherence to the patient's advance directive. And, as chapter 5 pointed out, dissent will not likely surface so long as the treatment course seems consistent with the incompetent patient's immediate well being.

This advocacy void will surely plague the patient without a health-care agent. Eventually, the void may be filled by patients' advocates employed by health-care institutions or by government-paid guardians on behalf of the institutionalized disabled.[3] Such paid advocates could conceivably monitor care of incompetent patients and could be charged with promoting adherence to an advance directive. But the United States is still a long way from that solution. Not every institution has a patient's advocate. Not every such advocate is schooled about advance directives and their legal framework. And it may well be that no patient's advocate would intervene without being summoned by some party connected to the incompetent patient. Similar problems exist with regard to those few jurisdictions which have special guardians on behalf of the institutionalized disabled.

All this points me to one conclusion with regard to the unrepresented incompetent patient: compliance with an advance directive will be largely dependent on the good will and good faith of surrounding family and medical staff.[4] Coercive mechanisms will seldom impact on those parties because there will be no advocate to initiate action. An important question becomes: how can a declarant, in advance, promote the desired voluntary, good faith compliance with an advance directive?

The most obvious tool is frank discussion with the family and physicians likely to be attending a declarant's dying process. We already established that such discussion is critical for the purpose of explaining the declarant's wishes—as so many advance directives contain only cursory, cryptic instructions. It is now evident that a further purpose can be served by discussions between the declarant, on the one hand, and family and physicians on the other. That purpose is enlisting sympathy for, and willingness to adhere to, the declarant's instructions.

It is very important, then, for a declarant who will not be naming a health-care agent to conduct a serious discussion with the likely attending physician about the contents of the declarant's advance instructions. Beside elucidating the meaning of the directive, the conversation should aim at conveying the declarant's seriousness and deliberateness. The conversation can thus dispel any question about the declarant's determination to have his or her wishes carried out. Beyond that, the declarant should seek assurance from the physician that the latter understands and intends to comply with the directive. While this verbal promise won't be readily enforceable by the subsequently incompetent patient, it at least creates a moral incentive for the physician to comply. The physician will have made an explicit promise to the declarant. A cynic might observe that this promise, plus $1.25, will get the declarant on the subway (in New York City). I have more faith than that in physicians' moral rectitude.

In the best of all possible worlds, a declarant would enter into a written contract with the prospective attending physician. The patient would agree to seek post-competence medical care from the physician and to pay for that care. The physician would agree to adhere to a good-faith interpretation of the declarant's advance instructions. In addition, the physician might agree to a schedule of liquidated damages (preagreed sums) payable to the declarant's estate for any period during which the declarant's wishes are flaunted. Finally, an immunity provision in the contract would reaffirm that the physician will incur no liability for good-faith adherence to the directive.

Why is such a contract confined to "the best of all possible worlds?" The problem is lack of incentive for a physician to enter into such a contract. If the physician has had an enduring relationship with the declarant, that physician will both expect to be the eventual attending physician and to be paid—all without any advance contract. Why should such a physician agree in writing to honor the advance directive and to pay damages for disrespecting the directive? At the moment, there aren't incentives for a physician to enter the advance contract described.

On the other hand, perhaps market forces will someday make the above hypothetical contract a reality. Perhaps physicians will compete for the business of servicing the needs of an increasingly aged population. Physicians might then seek to reassure patients and prospective patients about the caring, sensitive treatment being offered. And the above-described contract might be one element in the effort to communicate the desired solicitude.

Of course, what good is this "contract" if the patient will be incompetent at the critical moments? Who's going to enforce the contract against the nonadhering physician? If there had been a suitable "advocate" at hand, the declarant would have designated that person as a health-care agent and wouldn't particularly have needed the contract.

Again, my only hope is an economic incentive. If the declarant has any descendants or beneficiaries, the declarant's "estate" has a financial interest in the liquidated damages for any violation of the hypothetical contract. So, at the time of making the advance contract, the declarant would provide a copy to all persons connected to the estate and inform the contracting physician about that step. There would then be a financial disincentive to the physician's dishonoring of the advance contract.

This advance contract idea obviously needs fine tuning. Can liquidated damages be fixed so that they at least roughly correspond to projected actual damages? (That is a prerequisite to a valid liquidated-damages clause.) Should we be wary about creating a financial interest (in the beneficiaries of the estate) in having life-sustaining care extended in violation of an advance directive? Is there a hazard that such beneficiaries would intervene in terminal decisions and encourage violations of the declarant's instructions? And, of course, will there be sufficient incentives to induce any physician to enter into such an advance contract? But my starting point was the discouraging conclusion that, in the absence of a health-care agent, declarants will be hard put to assure implementation of their advance directives. The advance contract is simply one suggestion for filling the void. An alternative might be sought in institutions whose protocols require an ethics committee to monitor administration of all advance directives.

So far in this chapter, the assumption has been that a health-care agent (an advocate of the incompetent patient) offers the best hope for securing adherence to an advance directive. How good is that hope? The underlying question is whether a health-care agent has effective means for enforcing an advance directive.

Suppose that an advance directive both designates Pat, the declarant's daughter, as health-care agent and instructs that life-sustaining treatment cease if her father becomes demented to the point of being unable to read and understand a newspaper. Later, the declarant suffers a series of strokes which leave him permanently incompetent, bedridden, and incapable of reading a newspaper.

This incompetent patient is living in a long-term care facility. He is aware of his environment and smiles when given a back rub or when visited by loving family. There is no indication that the patient is in pain. The patient could live for many months in this state.

Now suppose this incompetent patient contracts pneumonia. Without antibiotics, the patient will die of pneumonia within ten days. The patient's son (i.e., the health-care agent's brother) and the attending physician both favor giving the patient antibiotics in order to cure the pneumonia. Both are aware of the patient's advance directive, but both have reasons for continuing care. The son cannot bear the thought of letting the father die while the father still derives some pleasure from existence. The attending physician considers it unsound medical practice to allow a patient in this condition to go untreated.

Pat (the patient's daughter and health-care agent) is determined to follow her father's considered instructions. She is convinced that he is presently in precisely the kind of debilitated state that he wanted to avoid. What mechanisms can Pat, as health-care agent, use to enforce her father's directive?

INTERNAL INSTITUTIONAL ROUTES

Pat should not want to make a federal case out of this controversy. The object is to secure prompt, caring, and careful implementation of her incompetent father's advance instructions. Litigation is an expensive, time-consuming, and exhausting process. (Only a few barracuda populating major law firms *want* to litigate.) Because Pat wants expeditious resolution of her dispute, her first recourse ought to be to gentle (but increasingly not so gentle) persuasion.

The obvious starting point is the attending physician. Armed with the document designating her as health-care agent and any other evidence of her father's wishes, Pat ought to try and persuade that physician to conform care to the advance instructions. If the physician continues to voice concern about sound medical practice, Pat might express interest in consulting with an institutional ethics committee. Or she might mention the possibility of bringing in another practitioner who would be comfortable with the advance directive. The physician will undoubtedly express concern about Pat's brother, who is insisting on full medical treatment. Pat should remind the physician that she is her father's designated agent and charged with responsibility for his post-competence care.

Chances are that this first interchange between Pat and the attending physician will not move the latter. If the physician remains resistant, I can imagine two principal strategies: a confrontation mode and a mediation mode. They could be undertaken together or in succession, starting with confrontation.

The confrontation mode could start with a second conversation with the attending physician and proceed up the supervisory ladder, first to the relevant department head and then to the hospital administrator. The main feature of the confrontation mode is threats. Pat is convinced of the legal and moral soundness of her effort to implement her father's directive; she is determined to accomplish that object. She can seek to convey the seriousness of her effort by warning about the recourse she intends to pursue if her object is thwarted. What exactly are the steps she is threatening?

The first threat is aimed at the pocketbook. In all her conversations with the relevant health-care providers, Pat will insist that no payment will be forthcoming for services which she did not authorize or which would have been obviated if her orders had been followed. Pat is asserting that no payment is due for treatment provided counter to a patient's wishes as expressed in an advance directive and as interpreted by an authorized health-care agent. Her contention has a solid legal foundation. Commentators agree that no payment is due for such unwanted services,[5] and there is legal precedent supporting that contention.[6]

The nonpayment threat is most realistic if the patient's assets are funding the current services and if Pat, as health-care agent, has some control over those payments. If some other source has control of the now incompetent patient's assets, (like, God forbid, Pat's brother), Pat's threat looms hollow. Similarly, if medical services are being financed by a private insurer or government benefit program, Pat's threat carries less clout. She would have a hard time prompting a third-party payor to cease payments for life-sustaining treatment. This would be so either because of the insurer's bureaucratic maze, which likely has to be negotiated, or because of sluggish response from third-party payors. A 1992 anecdote recounts how the Medicare Inspector General's office, reponding to an allegation of $150,000 in unauthorized hospital service, said it did not have resources to even investigate such a piddling abuse.[7] Nonetheless, Pat can, in good conscience, state her intention to contact the relevant third-party payor in order to prompt a refusal to pay for unauthorized services to her father.

Pat's second threat is to turn to outside agencies having some sort of regulatory power over the health-care providers. In some states, for example, the state health department will have regulations obligating providers to recognize and honor advance directives.[8] Pat can threaten to file a complaint about violation of the applicable regulation.

An alternative (or additional) regulatory channel is the federal Department of Health and Human Services (HHS). That agency administers compliance with federal regulations governing recipients of Medicaid and Medicare funds. (Virtually every hospital receives such funds.) The Patient Self-Determination Act (PSDA) of 1991 requires every funds recipient to "ensure compliance" with state law applicable to advance directives.[9] Pat can justifiably contend that nonadherence to her father's instructions breaches that obligation of compliance with state law. (As discussed in chapter 2, state law generally recognizes and enforces a declarant's prospective-autonomy interests.)

It is unclear whether Pat's threat to resort to HHS will be effective. The ultimate sanction available to that agency is disqualification of the health-care provider from participation in the federal program. The chances of that sanction being used to remedy a complaint about continuation of life-sustaining care are somewhere between zero and nil. Nonetheless, no hospital administrator or medical practitioner relishes having a federal investigator nosing about in response to a complaint. And if Pat's complaint uncovers an offending institutional pattern or practice, there might be some hope of engendering a serious HHS response, short of a termination of funds. So there is at least some chance that the institution will take seriously Pat's warning about resort to HHS.

A threat of invoking an administrative-type remedy might also be leveled at the attending physician. He or she might well be a health-care provider subject to the same PSDA obligation (and same HHS jurisdiction) described above. Moreover, the physician's professional obligation—as is becoming increasingly clear—is either to implement an advance directive or to transfer care to a fellow professional willing to cooperate with the patient's instructions. This means that Pat can threaten to invoke professional discipline against the attending physician who is violating that professional duty. This conclusion is reinforced by statutory provisions in approximately ten states whose living-will statutes explicitly label as "unprofessional conduct" a physician's failure to fulfill obligations such as the duty to honor a directive or transfer care of the patient.[10]

Pat's threat to file a complaint about unprofessional conduct may not move the attending physician very much. First, the channels of professional discipline (proceedings before a state board of medical examiners or other professional body) are notoriously slow and cumbersome. Second, the relevant professional board may not apply very stringent standards for compliance with advance directives. The physician may be given room to maneuver on issues such as the clarity of the patient's instructions, norms of sound medical practice, medical judgment about the patient's prognosis, or solicitude about the incompetent patient's immediate well-being. Third, even if the professional board were to find some violation of professional norms, the sanction imposed would be light. A private letter of reprimand might turn out to be the only penalty imposed.

For all these reasons, the specter of professional discipline might not seem very imposing. Still, no physician wants to have to account for his or her conduct before a group of peers authorized to impose sanctions such as suspension from medical practice. If Pat genuinely believes that the attending physician is not conforming to professional norms or legal obligations, the threat to initiate a disciplinary proceeding seems highly appropriate.

The final step in the confrontation mode is to threaten litigation. In theory, suit might be brought seeking to compel the attending physician to implement the father's advance directive[11] and/or to obtain monetary damages for the physician's failure to implement the directive. The chances of success in this hypothetical suit will be analyzed below. For the moment, I want to comment on the impact of a threat to litigate.

The attending physician knows that litigation is costly, time-consuming, and wearing. He is anxious to avoid litigation. At the same time, he knows that Pat is not likely to sue. Litigation is costly and exhausting for the plaintiff as well as the defendant. If Pat has no control over her father's assets, there is no assurance that she will be reimbursed. Pat is unlikely to invest the time, money, and effort unless she is confident that significant relief will be forthcoming. Therefore, the impact of a litigation threat depends in part on Pat's chances of success in that suit and the likely relief (to be analyzed below).

Even if the chances that Pat really would sue are slim, and even if her chances of substantial monetary relief are not great (issues still open), a threat to sue in this context strikes me as a legitimate tactic. First, Pat's legal claim seems sound. She is indeed entitled to seek enforcement of her father's advance directive. Second, physicians continue to operate under the misapprehension that their main hazard of liability stems from a wrongful-death action for implementing prior instructions.[12] They need to be apprised that money damages can flow from *failure* to implement such instructions.[13] (Interestingly, though, in the instant scenario, Pat's brother might be making noises about a wrongful-death suit at the same time that she is threatening to sue because of continued life support. The attending physician, now certainly in a tizzy, needs sound legal advice.)

Pat might try a mediation strategy rather than launching the confrontation mode. The most likely vehicle for the mediation strategy is the internal Institutional Ethics Committee (IEC), which exists in most hospitals today.[14] The IEC is usually an interdisciplinary body composed of some combination of physicians, administrators, nurses, clergy, a psychiatrist, and a lawyer. Often there will be a lay community representative as well. The articulated function of the IEC will vary from institution to institution. Sometimes, its task is simply to design institutional policy regarding sensitive ethics issues. While that task may include fixing policy about advance directives, it might not include intervention in particular patients' cases. Often, though, the IEC is available to serve a consultative function regarding a dispute surrounding a patient's dying process.

Let's assume that the particular IEC has jurisdiction to provide consultation on particular cases. Whether Pat should indeed turn to that IEC depends on the circumstances in the particular institution.[15] She must first examine the composition of the particular IEC and determine, to the extent possible, whether it has adopted an approach sympathetic to patients' rights. In some instances, the IEC will be captive to institutional interests and will not offer any realistic hope of a favorable response to Pat's position.

In other instances, though, there is hope for constructive IEC input. The IEC might remind the attending physician about the legal prerogatives of patients and their health-care agents. The IEC might reassure the attending physician that compliance with the advance directive is within professional bounds. The IEC might examine the advance directive and confirm Pat's conclusion that its terms apply to the patient's current condition. All these might be constructive inputs encouraging the attending physician and/or hospital administration to facilitate Pat's effort to implement her father's wishes.

In outlining Pat's main options in enforcing her father's advance directive, I've focused on using internal institutional channels to cajole or cudgel the relevant health-care providers. I don't pretend that this will be an easy or assuredly successful route.

A poignant reminder of the difficulties involved appears in an April 1992 op-ed piece in the New York Times.[16] The piece recounts the saga of a veteran physician and his lawyer brother seeking to effectuate their father's prior instructions during the father's bout with terminal cancer. The father, himself a physician, had determined to reject nonpalliative medical intervention. Despite conferences with medical personnel and hospital administrators, and despite pointed reminders about possible legal recourse, the sons' efforts proved unavailing. Vigorous, unwanted diagnostic and therapeutic procedures continued for two weeks until the father was moved to a hospice for his final hours.

The op-ed piece graphically illustrates how daunting and frustrating it can be to cope with busy physicians and an institutional bureaucracy. The author, the physician son, wonders how lay persons will fare where two experienced professionals failed.

I still recommend pursuing internal institutional channels, at least as a starting point. Perhaps the brothers in the op-ed piece would have had more success if they had been armed with a written instruction directive. Perhaps the lawyer in the story could have been clearer or firmer about the external options that the brothers intended to pursue. In any event, internal channels seem to offer the best hope of expeditiously securing the desired object: compliance with the declarant's instructions. Litigation should be regarded only as an ultimate resort.

SUING THE HELL OUT OF THEM

In our litigious society, the notion of suing for enforcement of an advance directive automatically strikes a responsive chord. If the attending medical personnel and/or host institution are resisting implementation of her father's advance directive, why shouldn't Pat "sue the hell out of them"?

The theoretical framework for liability of the health-care providers certainly exists.[17] One possible source of liability is contract law. When a physician undertakes care of a patient, an implied contract is created. One of the implied terms of that contract is that the patient is entitled to shape medical intervention. That prerogative can be exercised in a prospective fashion by use of an advance directive. A physician thus arguably breaches an implied contract by contravening the terms of an advance directive. Under contract-remedies doctrine, a breaching party is liable for the foreseeable damages flowing from the breach. In a typical case, those damages may include the patient's medical expenses for unwanted treatment and the patient's pain and suffering associated with that unwanted treatment.[18]

Tort law also provides a potential legal handle. Under the doctrine of informed consent, a physician ordinarily commits a battery by administering unauthorized medical treatment. While an exception might apply for emergency treatment, that exception would not apply where, as here, the patient's advance directive rejects the care in question. A tortfeasor physician would be potentially liable for all proximate damages caused by unauthorized treatment (including associated medical expenses and, perhaps, pain and suffering). A possibility even exists that surrounding family could recover for *their* pain and suffering during the physician's prolongation of existence counter to an advance directive.

The common-law claims grounded in contract and tort law would be reinforced in the few states whose living-will statutes provide for "civil liability" as a statutory remedy for violation of a physician's duties.[19] (Usually, the physician's duty is to comply with an advance directive or secure transfer of the patient's care to a cooperative professional.) While the extent of the "civil liability" is not specified in those statutes, recoverable damages probably mirror those available pursuant to the common law.[20]

In the vast majority of states, however, living-will statutes will not be helpful in imposing liability on health-care providers for noncooperation with an advance directive. This is not surprising given the background for adoption of these legislative measures. A key object of living-will statutes was to insulate physicians against liability for voluntary implementation of living wills.[21] Much less exertion went into designing sanctions for noncompliance with such documents. In approximately twenty-two states, no penalty at all is prescribed for such noncompliance.[22] In most of the remaining states, the sole sanction suggested is "professional discipline"—a recourse whose flaws have already been mentioned.

If the noncooperating institution is government owned, the federal Constitution might provide a legal handle for liability. I argued in chapters 1 and 2 that a patient's autonomy to shape medical intervention in a dying process is a fundamental aspect of liberty. If that is so, a public institution which knowingly violates a clear-cut advance directive should be liable in damages for committing a constitutional tort.[23]

At this point, Pat's supporters are probably salivating with enthusiasm to file suit. She ostensibly has at least two, and possibly four, causes of action: in contract, in tort, in constitutional tort, and (in a few locales) under a living-will type statute.

I hate to be a spoilsport, but I have to dampen that enthusiasm somewhat. First, a reminder about the practical disincentives to suit. Litigation is expensive, both because of attorneys' fees and court costs. In the kind of suit under discussion, experts will have to be recruited and their fees paid. Litigation is time-consuming, even when a case involving a dying patient is given accelerated consideration. Both sides need a modicum of time to prepare their cases, and postponements are common to accommodate one side or another or the court. (There will be multiple sides because the institution and health-care professionals may have separate representation and a guardian ad litem may be appointed on behalf of the incompetent patient.) Litigation concerning a helpless, dying patient also draws media attention.

Pat can expect to see her name prominently displayed in the local papers, if not broadcast over the local airwaves. All these practical elements might dissuade Pat from filing suit.

Even if Pat has the temerity to face the above practical obstacles, she can anticipate a variety of defenses on behalf of the defendant health-care providers. The defendants may be contending that the advance instructions are unclear and that the patient's wishes are therefore too murky to justify removal of life support. They may be contending that "reasonable medical standards" dictate continued treatment and that they are entitled to adhere to such professional standards.[24] The defendants may be contending that the advance directive in issue exceeds the permissible bounds of the state's living-will law.[25] The hospital may be contending that it made reasonable efforts to transfer care to a cooperating professional but that such efforts proved futile.[26] These defendants' claims raise debatable issues. Pat and her attorney may ultimately succeed in refuting or overcoming the claims, but their existence means that an eventual favorable outcome is far from assured.

Let's assume for the moment that Pat overcomes all the hurdles listed, both practical and doctrinal. She wins the lawsuit. What has she accomplished? Did she secure for her father a death conforming to his conception of dignity as expressed in his advance directive? Did she succeed in socking it to the recalcitrant physician and hospital in terms of money damages?

As to the first question (Did Pat's father achieve a death consistent with his vision of dignity?), the answer is maybe. The suit to compel respect for his advance directive would have continued for weeks, if not months. If Pat won at the trial court level, the defendants might have appealed. Appeals would postpone the final disposition for more months. It's quite possible that her father would die in the interim, having received the unwanted medical intervention. On the other hand, it's conceivable that Pat would win a quick victory at the trial court level and that the defendants would choose not to appeal. At least after a few weeks of litigation, Pat would have secured either defendants' adherence to her father's instructions or transfer of care to a cooperating health-care provider. (Of course, the physicians may have administered antibiotics pending the outcome of the litigation, with the result that Pat's father would have survived at least one bout with pneumonia.)

As to the second question (Did Pat sock it to the defendants for money damages?), the answer is probably no. The one clearly compensable item of damages is medical expenses associated with the unwanted medical treatment. Depending on the period Pat's father survived with treatment, and depending on the nature of the treatment, those expenses might be considerable. However, in many instances third-party payors will have financed the relevant care. Those payors are subrogated to Pat's potential award for medical expenses. Thus, the sums actually recovered by Pat (or her father's estate) would turn out to be only those amounts not covered by third-party payors.

Pat's attorneys' fees might be a compensable item if incurred in an effort, while her father was still alive, to compel compliance with her father's advance directive.[27] Similarly, fees paid to expert witnesses and other costs associated with such an injunctive proceeding might be compensable. However, in a litigation aimed at securing monetary damages, counsel fees connected with *that* litigation are not ordinarily recoverable.

The really juicy potential item of damages is pain and suffering. Juries are capable of awarding very large sums as compensation for mental anguish, and that item is theoretically recoverable here.[28] Unfortunately, in the context of a patient like Pat's father, there are significant obstacles to recovery of pain and suffering damages.

The first obstacle is a practical one: establishing that pain and suffering in fact occurred. In many instances, an incompetent patient will not be perceptibly suffering during a period when life-sustaining treatment is continued counter to advance instructions. This is certainly so for a patient who is comatose or only semiconscious during the period in question. It may also be so for patients who are still conscious and aware. Pat's father, for example, may not have experienced significant embarrassment and humiliation from his debilitated existence—even if apprehension of those feelings had partially motivated his advance directive.

The second obstacle is a theoretical one involving judicial reluctance to impose damages for "wrongful life." A damage suit on behalf of Pat's father contends, in effect, that he should have been allowed to die and that defendants owe damages for keeping him alive and causing him pain and suffering. The strong judicial presumption, however, is that life is worthwhile and valuable. There is understandable judicial reluctance to endorse the assessment by Pat's father that he would have been better off dead.[29] Such judicial endorsement might be inferred from a damage award for pain and suffering, for the defendants will contend both that they conferred a benefit upon Pat's father by extending his life and that the value of any enjoyment or satisfaction derived from his extended life ought to be set off against the pain and suffering experienced. Because courts are sensitive to the notion that they should not be evaluating the emotional benefits and detriments of a life, they will continue to drag their feet in assessing damages for pain and suffering in this context.[30]

It is true that Pat's father—not any judge—initially made the decision (expressed in his advance directive) that death would be preferable to a debilitated life without further capacity to read. His autonomy interest entitled him to make that judgment and to resist medical efforts to coerce continued treatment. But recognition of that autonomy right does not necessarily demand award of monetary damages for continued existence when any such award impliedly assigns a low monetary value to that continued life. That Pat's father considered life without reading so distasteful as to warrant dying does not mean that a court must ignore the value or benefit derived from his continued existence.

The final obstacle is a likely tendency by triers of fact (judges and juries) to sympathize with the health-care providers' perspective in cases like those of Pat's father. Defendants will point out that they strove to preserve the life of an aware, functioning human being (albeit in contravention of that human being's advance directive). There will be enough empathy with this position to prevent assessment of mammoth damage awards.

To sum up, and to paraphrase James Joyce, the way of the health-care agent is hard. The first recourse is to institutional channels, and those channels are likely to prove difficult and frustrating. Pat, as health-care agent, will need extraordinary determination to convince the resisting health-care providers to implement her father's advance directive. This is especially so here because Pat's brother is on hand contending that his father should not be permitted to die. The second recourse, to an IEC, might prove successful. But that will depend on the nature and composition of the particular IEC. Moreover, even if the IEC responds sympathetically, its advice will not bind the relevant health-care providers. They might continue to resist.

The ultimate recourse, litigation, might prove successful. But it is more likely to prove expensive, exhausting, and frustrating to Pat.

8

New Jersey's Model Legislation

MOST READERS should stop at this point. The central mission of this book has been completed. I have presented advance directives from all the salient angles: historical foundation, legal framework, format, content, interpretation, and enforcement. My insights have all been communicated.

This last chapter is intended for people interested in reforming current state legislation governing advance directives. (This group might include not just legislators but many physicians, health-care providers of all sorts, lawyers who deal with issues of death and dying, and lay people who care deeply about society's response to medical technology's capacity to sustain a prolonged, debilitated moribund existence.) The need for some reform has already been explained. Chapter 3 noted a variety of common statutory defects which may handicap people's ability to exercise full control over post-competence medical intervention.

This chapter's focus is New Jersey because that state's new legislation—the Advance Directives for Health Care Act adopted in July 1991[1]—comes as close as any existing legislation to meeting the criticisms articulated in chapter 3. In some respects, the New Jersey legislation (hereinafter the A.D. Act) can serve as a useful model for new legislation or for reform of existing legislation in other states.

The succeeding part of this chapter highlights the ways in which the A.D. Act surpasses the bulk of prior legislation treating advance directives. As will be shown, the A.D. Act provides expansive scope for the autonomy of competent persons to shape post-competence medical intervention. In addition, the New Jersey Bioethics Commission has provided informative material aimed at assisting the public in understanding and using advance directives. These sources (the A.D. Act and the Commission's booklet) offer sensitive guidance not only for persons preparing advance directives but also for health-care agents, medical personnel, and other decision makers ultimately charged with implementing an advance directive. At the same time, the A.D. Act is not perfect. The last section of this chapter comments on a few question marks which, to my mind, might mar what is, on the whole, a very sound piece of legislation. But first, the kudos.

ADVANTAGES OF NEW JERSEY'S ADVANCE DIRECTIVE ACT

A. An Integrated Statute

Many states have more than one statute relating to advance directives. Often this means a living-will type statute along with a durable-power-of-attorney-for-health-care (DPOA-HC) type statute. These separate measures can easily be a source of confusion and uncertainty. They sometimes give conflicting signals as to the scope of a health-care agent's authority, or they cause confusion about the relationship between a living will and a document appointing an agent.[2]

By contrast, the A.D. Act takes a comprehensive, integrated approach. It provides both for an instruction directive (a living-will type document) and a proxy directive (designation of a health-care agent). The Act encourages an "integrated" document, combining both elements. But it recognizes that some persons will rely solely on an instruction directive and others solely on a proxy directive.

The Act's melding of the two major approaches to advance directives should minimize the tension and confusion that sometimes flows from separate statutes. In addition, explanatory material circulated by the New Jersey Bioethics Commission helpfully offers a variety of options to a declarant.[3] Forms are provided for a proxy directive, for an instruction directive, and for a combined instrument. The same booklet succinctly explains the advantages and disadvantages of each format.

In a few states, most notably New York, the primary legislative input comes in the form of a broad DPOA-HC type measure (without a living-will type law).[4] A person is permitted to designate an agent who may be empowered to make "any and all health care decisions on the principal's behalf that the principal could make."[5] By enabling a health-care agent to make the same decisions that the principal could have made if competent, such measures may avoid the limitations concerning "terminal condition" and artificial nutrition often found in living-will statutes. A broad DPOA-HC statute thus offers wide scope to a person's prospective autonomy interest in shaping post-competence medical handling.

The question arises: should legislative intervention in this area be confined to authorization of proxy directives, as was done in New York? The New York State Task Force on Life and the Law, which developed New York's legislation, specifically considered, and ultimately rejected, the idea of combining, in one law, provisions relating to substantive instructions and those relating to a health-care agent.[6] Statutory attention to instruction directives was deemed superfluous since the New York courts had already recognized prior instructions as evidence of an incompetent patient's wishes which govern the decisions of a designated health-care agent.[7] The Task Force believed that further professional education of health-care providers concerning the force of a living will (or other evidence of a patient's prior expressions) was all that would be necessary for the successful utilization of advance instructions.[8] A proxy directive was seen as "a better, more effective vehicle" than an instruction directive (living will), because the latter supposedly would require that the declarant anticipate a wide range of medical contingencies.[9]

My perspective is that exclusive statutory focus on proxy directives (as in New York) undervalues the utility and importance of instruction directives in achieving results truly consistent with a declarant's wishes. It is true that nothing prevents use of instruction directives in a jurisdiction which provides statutorily only for a proxy directive. Indeed, such laws require the agent to implement the principal's wishes and thus contemplate the existence of some substantive instructions. Nonetheless, the A.D. Act's comprehensive approach—combining in one law provisions regarding substantive instructions and proxy designation—seems preferable.

Equal statutory focus on substantive instructions should promote public and professional awareness of the importance and status of a written instruction directive. This awareness is particularly important for people who cannot recruit a suitable person to serve as a health-care agent (as is the case, for example, for some isolated elderly people).

The A.D. Act clarifies the effect of an instruction directive as a means to effectuate personal preferences in the absence of a designated health-care agent. One section makes an instruction directive "legally operative" upon an attending physician and any other decision maker responsible for an incompetent patient. All such decision makers are directed to uphold the specific terms of an instruction directive and to "exercise reasonable judgment" to implement the intent and spirit of the directive when its terms do not provide clear-cut guidance regarding the incompetent patient's current condition.[10] This provision eliminates any doubt about the validity and binding force of a written instruction directive (a living-will type instrument).

B. Expansive Scope of Prospective Autonomy

In chapter 3, I criticized provisions found in many living-will laws (and some DPOA-HC statutes) confining the substantive content of an advance directive. I mentioned, among other things, limitations relating to terminal condition, artificial nutrition, and pregnancy. To my mind, New Jersey does it better. Although the language of the A.D. Act is still subject to judicial interpretation, my reading is that the Act overcomes all the common pitfalls and gives extremely expansive scope to a declarant's self-determination prerogative.

The most important New Jersey improvement relates to the "terminal condition" limitation—the notion in some living-will laws that life-sustaining care can only be withdrawn when an incompetent patient is facing unpreventable death within a short period of time. Such a limitation is plainly inconsistent with many declarants' desires to avoid indefinite medical maintenance in a gravely debilitated condition. Many people view a gravely debilitated, protracted dying process as intolerable—perhaps because of the indignity or frustration of utter helplessness and dependence, or because of distress over the image and recollections to be left with survivors, or because of the emotional toll on loved ones, or because of depletion of a potential legacy. Such apprehensions are not confined to permanent unconsciousness; they apply as well to medical prolongation of a severely debilitated state such as a barely conscious condition provoked by a severe stroke or other brain trauma.

The new A.D. Act appears to respond sympathetically to the dignity-related concerns of persons intent on avoiding a protracted, debilitated dying process. Section 67(a) addresses the circumstances in which life-sustaining medical intervention may be withdrawn pursuant to an advance directive. Three subsections of Section 67(a) mitigate the harsh effects of the terminal condition precondition found in some living-will statutes.[11]

Subsection (2) speaks to permanent unconsciousness and authorizes cessation of life-sustaining medical intervention (in accord with an advance directive) for a patient in that status. Subsection (3) speaks to a declarant whose instructions refer to a "terminal condition." That term is broadly defined as "the terminal stage of an irreversibly fatal illness, disease, or condition."[12] The Act explains that there is no specific life expectancy limitation intended. A prognosis of six months or less (absent the contemplated life-sustaining medical intervention) is deemed a terminal condition, but that period is given as a guideline only.[13] In other words, the A.D. Act does not confine a "terminal condition" to the very last stage of a fatal illness, when death is fairly imminent.

Subsection (4) of Section 67(a) goes even further. It authorizes cessation of life-sustaining treatment (consistent with an advance directive) when the patient has reached a "serious irreversible condition" and "the likely burdens associated with the medical intervention . . . may reasonably be judged to outweigh the likely benefits . . . or imposition of the medical intervention on an unwilling patient would be inhumane."

Subsection (4) is the key provision for purposes of advance directives which seek to cover nonprolongation of a gravely debilitated (but conscious) state unwanted by the declarant. For that purpose, it is important to establish that the "burdens" mentioned in Section 67(a)(4) can include dignity concerns (such as dysfunction, helplessness, and dependence) as well as other values and preferences of the patient—in addition to pain and suffering, which would customarily be considered burdens.[14] Examination of the language and background of the A.D. Act indicates that the term *burdens* was indeed intended to have such an expansive meaning.

The A.D. Act and the report of the New Jersey Bioethics Commission that preceded the Act's passage are replete with indications that an advance directive can encompass a person's full range of values and preferences. Section 61(f) of the Act enjoins any designated health-care agent to make the same decision the patient would have made under the circumstances now confronted.[15] The report stresses both that a critical goal of the advance directive is to assure respect for a declarant's wishes and that those wishes should embody the patient's own concept of important considerations in shaping medical handling.[16] "The patient possesses knowledge of his or her own personal values and goals without which the risks, benefits, and burdens of proposed treatment options, and therefore the patient's true wishes and best interests, cannot be meaningfully evaluated."[17]

Even where no instruction directive exists, or where the principal's instructions are not clear, the health-care agent is admonished to act in a manner consistent with the intent and spirit of the patient's wishes as best they can be discerned. The governing standard becomes "best interests" of the now incompetent patient; best interests, in turn, are to be assessed in accord with the patient's wishes.[18] "The authority . . . to act in the patient's best interests rests on the understanding that such a judgment will in fact be grounded in and consistent with the available evidence of the patient's own values and objectives."[19] The report explains that the Act seeks to further the patient's well-being, which is "grounded in the patient's own values and objectives."[20] In short, the statutory language and background offer ample support for the proposition that the "burdens" in Section 67(a)(4) include a declarant's predilections regarding indignity and other personal values.

An expansive interpretation of the burdens to be considered in administering advance directives pursuant to Section 67(a)(4) would also be consistent with the A.D. Act's express object of preserving relevant constitutional rights. Section 67(c) explicitly disclaims legislative intent to abridge any right to refuse treatment under either the New Jersey or federal constitutions. In New Jersey, In re *Peter*[21] indicates that a person is entitled to shape post-competence medical handling according to personal values without limitation to customary notions of burden such as physical pain. That prerogative likely enjoys constitutional status pursuant to either the New Jersey or federal constitutions.[22]

The New Jersey Supreme Court has declared that an incompetent patient enjoys the "same right to autonomy in medical decisions as a competent patient."[23] This apparently means that a person may use an advance directive to direct future medical intervention to the same extent that a competent person can direct contemporaneous medical care. A competent person, in turn, is entitled to bring considerations of dignity and other personal concerns into play in shaping medical intervention in a dying process.[24]

A broad reading of Section 67(a)(4)—one which permits an advance directive to reject life-sustaining care even when a patient is preservable indefinitely and not perceptibly suffering—is essential. I previously noted that many declarants seek to avoid maintenance in a gravely debilitated condition which they regard as demeaning or undignified. If burdens, for purposes of Section 67(a)(4), were confined to pain and suffering, then rarely would a debilitated patient attain the relief from indignity often being sought via an advance directive. As many commentators have noted, it is extremely difficult to assess the degree of emotional or physical suffering of a severely demented patient.[25] A health-care agent can more easily and accurately implement an advance directive grounded on the principal's delineation of a severely debilitated status which the principal deems subjectively intolerable.

The sample advance directives prepared by the New Jersey Bioethics Commission are sensitive to the possible desire to avoid the "burden" of prolonged medical maintenance in a gravely debilitated condition. One of the options offered to a declarant is to decline treatment for an irreversible illness or condition which is not necessarily fatal. The option is aimed at a future condition in which the patient is experiencing "severe and progressive physical or mental deterioration and/or permanent loss of capacities and faculties" valued highly by the patient.[26] The form document suggests to the principal that he or she use the blank space provided to describe "the faculties or capacities which, if irretrievably lost, would lead you [the declarant] to accept death rather than continue living."[27] The clear implication is that the subjectively distasteful nature of a gravely debilitated existence (as outlined in an advance directive) is to be considered as part of the burdens to be assessed by the agent administering the advance directive.[28] In short, there is cause for optimism that the A.D. Act, in application, will fully uphold a declarant's prospective autonomy.

Another area in which the A.D. Act affords flexibility is with regard to artificial nutrition. The living-will laws of some states differentiate between artificial nutrition and conventional medical treatment. I previously considered and rejected the arguments supporting this differentiation—notions that removal of artificial nutrition "causes" a patient's death in some unique way or conveys a negative symbolic message about human caring. The New Jersey legislature confronted these arguments, ultimately rejecting them in the A.D. Act's final version.

In the New Jersey Bioethics Commission's draft bill proposing an advance directive law, as originally adopted by the New Jersey Senate,[29] a distinction was maintained between artificial nutrition and other medical treatment. Section 16 of the bill significantly circumscribed the conditions in which artificial nutrition might be withdrawn pursuant to an advance directive. The incompetent patient would have to be in a terminal condition (the end stage of an irreversible dying process).[30] In addition, the patient would have had to explicitly authorize removal of nutrition, and the implementation decision by an agent would have to be reviewed by an institutional ethics committee (or other review body) prior to implementation. The Commission's report justified the special treatment of artificial nutrition, as opposed to conventional medical intervention, on grounds of "social policy."[31] The report mentioned "respect for and protection of human life, and the preservation of public confidence in the caring role of health care professionals."[32]

The final A.D. Act rejects the original bill's policy which differentiates artificial nutrition from conventional medical technology. The original Section 16, restricting cessation of artificial nutrition, is stricken. Section 55, as amended, explicitly includes "artificially provided fluids and nutrition" within the broad definition of life-sustaining treatment which can be withheld pursuant to an advance directive, even without explicit authorization.

Despite the New Jersey Bioethics Commission's original suggestion that "respect for . . . human life" and "preservation of public confidence in the caring role of health care professionals" might warrant special status for artificial nutrition, the A.D. Act's final approach seems sound. Numerous medical and legal sources have considered and rejected the asserted distinctiveness of artificial nutrition. For example, the President's Commission for the Study of Ethical Problems in Medicine, the New York State Task Force on Life and the Law, the New York Academy of Medicine, and the Hastings Center Task Force on Death and Dying all found no logical distinction between cessation of artificial nutrition and cessation of other life-sustaining technology.[33] New Jersey's final approach thus coincides with popular perspectives, with uniform judicial reaction and with the expressions of numerous medical organizations.

Another concession to declarants' autonomy comes in the A.D. Act's handling of pregnancy. Sections 56 and 58(a)(5) provide that a female declarant may, but need not, include special instructions with regard to the impact of pregnancy on instructions for life support. New Jersey thus avoids the unconstitutional approach present in states which purport to suspend the effect of a female's advance directive during the entire period of pregnancy. The A.D. Act leaves the issue of life support during pregnancy entirely in the female declarant's hands. No mention is made of fetal interests, even those of a third trimester fetus.

The thorniest autonomy issue is advance instructions which conflict with an incompetent patient's contemporaneous well-being, and this issue is not definitively resolved by the A.D. Act. I argued in chapter 6 that a considered advance directive ought to be upheld even to the detriment of some current interests of an incompetent patient. It is at least arguable that the A.D. Act adopts that approach—anticipating implementation of advance directives despite tension with a patient's current material interests.

The A.D. Act's whole focus is on respect for a declarant's wishes. It contemplates that an advance directive will be implemented according to its terms if it provides "clear direction" or "clear and unambiguous guidance under the circumstances."[34] "Best interests" of the incompetent patient are mentioned as a default standard to be used only when the actual wishes of the declarant cannot be determined by the persons applying an advance directive.[35] The clear implication is that the declarant's expressed preferences govern even if in tension with immediate well-being.

There is additional support for the proposition that a declarant's competently expressed preferences govern. Best interests, for purposes of the A.D. Act, probably encompass a patient's personal preferences (including dignity-related concerns and altruistic values) as well as physical well-being. The Bioethics Commission report accompanying the relevant bill stated: "[T]he authority . . . to act in the patient's best interests rests on the understanding that such a judgment will in fact be grounded in and consistent with the available evidence of the patient's own values and objectives."[36]

Finally, the Act confers authority to withdraw life-sustaining treatment (consistent with a directive) for a chronically debilitated patient suffering from a "serious irreversible illness or condition [where] the likely risks and burdens associated with the medical intervention . . . may reasonably be judged to outweigh the likely benefits."[37] So long as the burdens mentioned include offense to the patient's personal values and preferences, the A.D. Act apparently allows the declarant's self-determination interest to prevail. I already argued that burdens under the Act do include such personal-value considerations. Recall also that New Jersey courts declare both that an incompetent patient retains the *same* autonomy right as a competent patient and that a competent patient clearly may reject treatment which most people would consider prudent.

The only doubt about the dominance of self-determination over immediate patient well-being stems from some cryptic phrases in the background report to the A.D. Act prepared by the New Jersey Bioethics Commission. In discussing the circumstances in which the administrator of an advance directive might deviate from the terms of the directive, that report notes, in passing, that the administrator should be "most attentive" to whether the directive is "contrary to the patient's best interests."[38] The comment is not clarified. At another juncture, the report suggests that a directive could be interpreted in a fashion inconsistent with its terms "to protect patient well being."[39] Both comments probably refer to instances when unanticipated changes in medical technology (or other unforeseen circumstances) make the literal terms of the declarant's directive inconsistent with the patient's current best interests. In that event, the terms of the advance directive can be ignored in order to achieve a result consistent with the spirit of the document as a whole.[40] This is not the same as saying that a declarant's clearly expressed preferences can be overridden whenever they are not congruent with material "best interests" of the patient in the narrow sense of that term.

C. Guidance to Administrators of Advance Directives

Provisions within the A.D. Act anticipate many of the difficulties associated with application of an advance directive, and they offer sufficient flexibility for sensible administration. Take, for example, the vagueness that plagues many short-form advance directives. The A.D. Act acknowledges that an advance directive's language will not always be clear and may not even be the declarant's final and definitive expression. A health-care agent is enjoined to "give priority" to an in-struction directive.[41] But the agent is also authorized to consider other evidence of the now incompetent patient's wishes, including statements of the declarant outside the advance directive itself.[42] Administrators of an advance directive are generally enjoined to follow the "intent and spirit" of directives that do not furnish clear-cut instructions.[43] In light of the frequent imprecision of advance directives, referral of decision makers to additional indices of the declarant's intentions is probably constructive.

The A.D. Act also seems sufficiently flexible to permit a health-care agent or other administrator to deviate from the terms of an advance directive when appropriate. For example, although the Act normally contemplates that a directive's "clear direction" will be followed, it also urges a health-care agent to "make the health care decision the patient would have made."[44]

This ought to furnish sufficient authorization to deviate from a directive's language where changed circumstances make the literal text inconsistent with the declarant's discernible objectives. The background report accompanying the New Jersey Bioethics Commission's draft bill expresses an understanding that changed circumstances (such as therapeutic advances) might warrant noncompliance with the terms of an advance directive.[45] The report recognizes that ostensibly clear language can become ambiguous when applied to unforeseen circumstances.[46]

The A.D. Act also appears to address sensibly the difficult issue of post-com-petence expressions by a declarant. Section 63(b) requires a health-care agent to discuss treatment options with the incompetent patient "to a reasonable extent" and to "take the patient's expressed wishes into account in the decision making process." This statutory enjoinder to consult with an incompetent patient makes sense for reasons already explained in chapter 5. Consultation has a symbolic func-tion in recognizing the patient's human status. It also has an instrumental value in furnishing insights into the emotional and physical feelings of such patients, feelings which are important in the administration of an advance directive.

All this does not mean that an incompetent patient's expressions should be determinative of the medical course to be followed. I argued in chapter 5 that an incompetent patient's input ought to be sought and considered but not necessarily followed in administration. The first portion of Section 63(b), dictating that de-cision makers "take the patient's expressed wishes into account," is consistent with that approach. An additional paragraph in Section 63(b) goes further and compels adherence to certain expressions by the incompetent patient. The relevant language provides:

> [I]f a patient who lacks decision making capacity clearly expresses or manifests the contemporaneous wish that medically appropriate measures utilized to sustain life be provided, that wish shall take precedence over any contrary decision of the health care representative and any contrary statement in the patient's in-struction directive.

The motivation behind this provision is understandable and admirable. There is a natural revulsion toward removing life-preserving care from a person who is articulating a wish to continue living.[47] At the same time, according determinative and continuing force to incompetent declarations, no matter how demented the patient, is excessive. (Certainly, it would be inappropriate to give such status to the deranged utterances of a patient expressing a wish to die.) Giving deference to the expression of a gravely demented patient (in preference to a carefully considered advance directive) could subvert self-determination. The potential for the manipulation of a demented patient is patent. Decision makers on behalf of the patient, if uncomfortable with the substance of the advance directive, could simply keep asking the patient whether he or she renounces the original instruction until an affirmative response is attained.

It is possible to interpret Section 63(b) in a fashion that makes it consistent with common sense and with respect for a declarant's self-determination. An utterance from a gravely demented patient should not be regarded as a "clear" expression for purposes of Section 63(b). Only if a patient comprehends the concept of death and the significance of his or her life-affirming utterance should such an utterance override a clear and considered advance directive.

Even in the latter situation, the effectiveness or "precedence" of contemporaneous expressions (over a conflicting advance directive) should continue only as long as the life-affirming position is being communicated by the patient. Afterward, a clear and apparently considered advance directive should regain its effective status. In effect, an advance directive renouncing life support should only be "suspended" by an incompetent patient's life-affirming expression.

As to problems of administration faced when health-care providers pose conscientious objections to implementing an advance directive, the A.D. Act breaks little new ground. New Jersey has adopted the same basic structure prevailing under most living-will legislation. That is, professional conscience is recognized, but professionals with conscientious objections are expected to assist in arranging transfer of responsibility to more accommodating health-care professionals.

A.D. Act Sections 62(b) and 62(c) authorize individual health-care professionals to invoke "sincerely held personal or professional convictions" in order to decline to participate in withdrawal of life-sustaining measures pursuant to an advance directive. An objecting physician is required to act to transfer the patient's care to fellow professionals who can cooperate in good conscience with the course prescribed in the advance directive. Although the Act doesn't articulate a "reasonable efforts" standard, that is probably the scope of the transfer duty imposed on the objecting physician.

The A.D. Act does not resolve the question of what happens when transfer of the patient cannot be accomplished even after reasonable efforts. The physician cannot simply withdraw from the case, leaving the patient to fend for himself or herself.[48] At the same time, the Act itself does not require a physician to implement a personally repugnant course in the event that transfer cannot be arranged. The background report accompanying the original bill underlying the A.D. Act indicates that "judicial intervention" may then become necessary.[49] It does not suggest what the result of such intervention should be. I argued in chapter 5 that the tension might well be judicially resolved in favor of the patient's autonomy interest. That is, a patient's interest in controlling medical care by means of an advance directive might well override an individual health-care provider's scruples where transfer cannot practicably be arranged.

As to institutional health-care providers, the A.D. Act deviates somewhat from the prevailing pattern. In most states, institutional conscience is recognized, and the objecting institution is expected to assist in securing transfer of the problematic patient to a more accommodating institution. While A.D. Act Section 54(d) acknowledges the importance of the "ethical integrity" of health-care institutions, only a "private, religiously-affiliated health care institution" is accorded a right to refuse participation in withdrawal of life-sustaining measures.[50] Private nonsectarian institutions are not entitled to invoke institutional conscience in order to refuse implementation of "offensive" advance directives.

The explanation is plain for excluding nonsectarian institutions from a right to conscientious objection in this context. Drafters of the legislation were apprehensive that recognition of such a right would "risk unduly diminishing the number of institutional settings in which patients and families can properly expect their rights and wishes to prevail."[51] The concern was that institutions would manufacture "moral" policies either in order to shun difficult cases that had engendered or might engender unwelcome publicity or in order to avoid economic costs associated with certain types of moribund patients.[52] The conscience-based concerns of sectarian institutions would, by contrast, presumably be bona fide. Moreover, a claim based on religious conscience would be reinforced by the Constitution's Free Exercise Clause.

The statutory differentiation between religiously affiliated and nonsectarian health-care institutions parallels a distinction intimated by the New Jersey Supreme Court in the abortion context. In *Doe v. Bridgeton Hospital*,[53] the New Jersey Supreme Court required three private, nonsectarian hospitals to permit elective abortions despite the moral objections of the hospitals' boards of directors. The court ruled that hospitals are "quasi-public" institutions and therefore subject to certain public-service obligations despite their conscientious scruples.[54] As in the case of Section 65(b) of the A.D. Act, the court was apprehensive that adequate health-care facilities would not be available to meet the needs and preferences of the consumer population.

The apprehension concerning availability of health-care providers willing to implement controversial or idiosyncratic advance directives is understandable.

Families seeking to transfer patients from objecting institutions have often encountered widespread institutional refusal to accept a transfer patient for the purpose of implementing an advance directive. Nonetheless, it is by no means clear that a total exclusion of conscience claims by private, nonsectarian institutions is a necessary measure.

New York's recent legislation concerning health-care agents takes a different approach. There, a private hospital is entitled to formulate and implement a policy against cooperating with terminal decisions if the policy is based on "religious beliefs or sincerely held moral convictions central to the facility's operating principles."[55] In addition, patients and family must be informed in advance about the policy, and the hospital must seek to transfer the patient in the event of conflict. If transfer to a more accommodating facility is not arranged, the objecting hospital must either honor the health-care agent's decision or "seek judicial relief."[56]

Experience under the New York model should help determine whether the A.D. Act's nonrecognition of institutional conscience in the private, nonsectarian sector is excessively accommodating to patients' interests. That is, if private New York institutions do not use the available exemption in a fashion which overly impedes the honoring of advance instructions, it will indicate that New Jersey's approach was unnecessarily broad.

I would issue another caveat with regard to the A.D. Act provisions relating to professional conscience. Section 65(c) mentions that nothing in the A.D. Act requires a health-care institution to act contrary to "accepted medical standards." This provision recalls the discussion in chapter 5 of professional refusals to provide "medically futile" care which might be requested in an advance directive. In that discussion, I warned that medical judgments that life-extending care is futile and expendable ought rarely to prevail in the face of an advance directive prescribing continued medical intervention. I would hope that Section 65(c) of the A.D. Act would not be interpreted as generally elevating professional judgment over patient self-determination.

The success or failure of the A.D. Act will offer an important clue to the fate of advance directives. The New Jersey legislation provides a comprehensive and forward-looking approach to advance directives. It ought to promote the effective use and administration of such instruments and thus help persons shape the contours of medical intervention in order to secure a modicum of dignity in the dying process.

I'll end with the same warning given in the Introduction. The stakes are high in the effort to shape a humane approach to medical technology's capacity to prolong patients far beyond previous bounds. Pressures are mounting to employ new responses (such as assisted suicide and active euthanasia) to people's apprehensions about dying in a prolonged, debilitated status. The advance directive is supposed to be an important tool in achieving a death with a modicum of dignity without resort to those radical responses. Failure of this tool, and a failure of medicine and law to shape medical intervention in the dying process in a fashion consistent with what most people would want, would assure that assisted suicide and/or active euthanasia will proliferate. In short, a lot depends on the sensitive promotion, interpretation, and administration of advance medical directives. This book was aimed at advancing those objects.

Advance Directive for Health Care

There may come a time when I am unable, due to mental incapacity, to make my own health-care decisions. In order to provide the guidance and authority needed to make decisions on my behalf:

I, Norman L. Cantor, hereby declare my instructions and wishes for my future health care. This advance directive for health care shall take effect in the event I become unable to make my own health-care decisions, as determined by the physician who has primary responsibility for my care and my designated health-care representative. I direct that this document become part of my permanent medical records. My two current physicians, ———— and ————, have been provided with copies of this document.

Part One: Designation of a Health-Care Representative

I hereby designate:

Name
Address
Telephone

as my health-care representative to make any and all health-care decisions for me, including decisions to accept or to refuse any treatment, service, or procedure used to diagnose or treat my physical or mental condition, and decisions to provide, withhold or withdraw life-sustaining measures. I authorize my representative to secure all medical records and take all steps, including litigation or transfer from one locale to another, which she may deem appropriate in implementing this directive.

I have discussed the terms of this designation with my health-care representative, and she has willingly agreed to accept the responsibility for acting on my behalf.

If the person I have designated above is unable, unwilling, or unavailable to act as my health-care representative, I hereby designate the following person to act as my health-care representative, in the order of priority stated:

1. Name
   Address
   Telephone

2. Name
   Address
   Telephone

Part Two: Instructions for Care

I direct my representative to make decisions on my behalf in accordance with my wishes as stated in this document or as otherwise known to her. In the event my wishes are not clear, or if a situation arises I did not anticipate, my health-care representative is authorized to make decisions in my best interests, as defined in this document.

I direct that the central guideline shaping my medical handling be my best interests, including consideration of pain and suffering and all the dignity-related factors mentioned in this document. This means that if, in the course of my medical care, the burdens of continued life with treatment become greater than the benefits I experience, or if my condition is demeaning (as I've defined it below), life-sustaining measures are to be withheld or discontinued.

Before I turn to instructions relating to particular types of circumstances, I mention certain guidelines which apply to all post-competence decisions on my behalf. First, while my instructions call for withholding of life-preserving medical care in various situations, palliative care is always to be provided. That is, pain relievers or sedatives should be provided to relieve intractable pain or extreme emotional upset insofar as the need for such palliative agents can be discerned. Also, I would always expect to be maintained in a clean, sheltered, and comfortable environment. Nursing care aimed at providing a clean and dignified environment should therefore always be furnished.

Second, medical treatment to be rejected may include all forms of medical intervention whether complex, like respirators, or simplistic, like blood transfusions or antibiotics. Artificial nutrition and hydration are also included. Different treatments may entail different consequences and side effects (e.g., the long-term dependence on a dialysis machine) so that differentiations among types of treatment may have to be made in the course of actual decision making. Yet there is no intention here to categorize certain treatments as ordinary and others as extraordinary for purposes of shaping my medical future. Best interests will have to be assessed on a case-by-case basis with regard to my specific condition and various proposed treatments.

I now turn to the circumstances in which life-sustaining medical intervention should be foregone. If there should come a time when I become permanently unconscious, and it is determined by my attending physician and at least one additional physician with appropriate expertise who has personally examined me, that I have irreversibly lost consciousness, I direct that life-sustaining measures be withheld or discontinued.

I realize that there may come a time when I am diagnosed as having an incurable and irreversible illness, disease, or condition which may or may not be terminal. My condition may cause me to experience a permanent loss of capacities and faculties I value highly. My best interests and my dignity are to be the general guidelines in shaping medical intervention in such instances. I direct that those guidelines be administered in accord with the following considerations.

1. *Physical Pain.* To the extent that analgesics still leave significant physical pain or produce prolonged stupor, this should be deemed a significant factor adverse to my best interests.

2. *Indignity.* There are certain conditions which for me, an independent person who has been extremely active in both intellectual and physical pursuits, would be demeaning and degrading. I understand that in my state of incompetency I may not feel or sense the humiliation or degradation with which I am concerned. Nonetheless, it is important to me, as a currently autonomous being, to shape my medical future in accord with my conception of dignity. It is important to me to be remembered as a person possessing certain characteristics, whose absence I consider undignified or demeaning. I direct that medical intervention be guided by my conception of personal dignity described herein. In other words, my best interests as an incompetent person should be judged with the following elements of indignity in mind.

A major element of indignity for me is helplessness. If, for example, I permanently lose the capacity to feed myself, this is a significant blow to my dignity. Inability to dress or bathe myself should also be considered a significant blow to my dignity. Similarly, if I lose control of my bodily evacuations so that I must be diapered or otherwise attended, this constitutes a significant blow to my dignity.

Another aspect of helplessness is physical restraint. It may be that in my incompetence I will physically resist administration of medical treatment or otherwise act out so as to necessitate physical restraint in order to protect myself or others. Such conduct may be purely instinctive without any awareness or reason behind the actions. Nonetheless, it is demeaning to be trussed up or physically restrained for significant periods. If prolonged or repeated restraint (or, alternatively, prolonged or repeated sedation reducing me to a stupor) is necessary, this involuntary restraint is to be considered a significant blow to my dignity.

3. *Mental Deterioration.* By definition, this advance directive is relevant only when I have lost competence to make my own medical decisions. While it is difficult for me to conceive of life without such mental capacity, I understand that persons lacking such capacity can still derive enjoyment and benefit from their existences. Therefore, while the prospect of mental incompetence is troubling to

me, that fact, by itself, should not be deemed a basis for withholding or withdrawing medical treatment.

At the same time, there is a level of severe mental dysfunction which for me is demeaning and repugnant. For example, permanent inability to recognize and/or interact with my relatives or friends would, by itself, constitute an intolerable, demeaning status. Along these lines, incapacity to read and understand a newspaper or magazine would reflect a level of mental dysfunction very troubling to me. If I am permanently reduced to such a level of dysfunction, this would at least constitute a significant blow to my dignity, to be considered along with the other elements of indignity and burden mentioned in this document. Thus, for example, if my mental deterioration reaches this level, and I am also physically immobilized or afflicted by other significant elements of indignity, I would want cessation of life-sustaining medical intervention.

4. *Physical Disability*. I have always been a vigorous person. Thus, it is hard to imagine existence without capacity to engage in physical pursuits. Nonetheless, I consider myself resilient enough and life-affirming enough to adjust to a significant degree of physical disability, including even blindness or inability to walk. Consequently, physical incapacity by itself should not be regarded in my case as a demeaning or degrading state.

While severe physical disabilities would not by themselves be a basis for ending life-preserving care, such disabilities in combination with extreme mental deterioration or other significant blow or blows to my dignity might well prompt a determination that my best interests dictate the cessation of medical intervention in the face of a potentially life-threatening disease or condition. This last statement refers to the conditions which I have described above as depriving me of dignity (such as incontinence or inability to feed myself). I reiterate that such extreme incapacities should be considered significant blows to my dignity.

My degree of actual or prospective physical disability should be considered in conjunction with my level of mental dysfunction. That is, if my mental deterioration deprives me of the ability to cope with whatever physical disabilities are involved, that fact should be included in calculating my best interests.

5. *Chronic and Degenerative Disease*. I am aware that there are a number of incurable diseases and conditions which gradually and insidiously cause physical and/or mental deterioration over a prolonged period, before eventually leading to death. Alzheimer's disease and ALS (Lou Gehrig's disease) provide two examples known to me. If my incompetence coincides with such an affliction, I direct that medical intervention be shaped in accord with the formula outlined above. This instruction means that when irreversible deterioration has reached a point which can be defined as demeaning by my standards, life-preserving medical care should not be continued. I understand that as a consequence death may be permitted much earlier than it would ensue if medical intervention were maintained until the most advanced stages of the disease process. My wish is to avoid those stages of the

dying process in which my existence has become demeaning according to the standards described in this document.

At any point when my condition is demeaning, my wish is that life-preserving medical treatment be withheld or withdrawn. Again, this instruction applies to all forms of treatment, whether simplistic or complex, and includes artificial nutrition where normal alimentary processes have been incapacitated (whether by the underlying degenerative disease or by any other pathology which has developed). This instruction also applies to preventive measures (such as antibiotics) and measures capable of curing intervening diseases (such as pneumonia). However, in making a determination whether to employ preventive and curative measures once my condition is demeaning, my agent should consider any pain or discomfort or indignity associated with a nonintervention course; that is, consideration should be given to whether these negative consequences of withholding preventive or curative measures would make the dying process inhumane.

Part Three: Signature and Witnesses

By writing this advance directive, I inform those who may become entrusted with my health care of my wishes and intend to ease the burdens of decision making which this responsibility may impose. I understand the purpose and effect of this document and sign it knowingly, voluntarily, and after careful deliberation.

Signed this _____ day of _____, 19_____.
Signature _____

I declare that the person who signed this document did so in my presence, that he is personally known to me, and that he appears to be of sound mind and free of duress or undue influence. I am eighteen years of age or older, and I am not designated by this or any other document as the person's health-care representative nor as an alternate health-care representative.

1. witness _____
   address _____
   city _____ state _____
   signature _____

2. witness _____
   address _____
   city _____ state _____
   signature _____

Form Health-Care Power of Attorney

The following form is based on a form first prepared by Charles Sabatino for the American Bar Association and the American Association of Retired Persons. It has been adapted by Elizabeth Patterson, and her version is printed at 42 So. Car. L. Rev. 582–87. I have revised her version.

HEALTH-CARE POWER OF ATTORNEY

1. *DESIGNATION OF HEALTH-CARE AGENT*

I, _____, hereby appoint:
   (Principal)

_____
   (Agent's name)

_____
   (Address)
Home Telephone: _____ Work Telephone: _____
as my Agent to make health- and personal-care decisions for me, as authorized in this document, during any period of mental incompetence which I may undergo.

2. *AGENT'S POWERS AND DUTIES*

I grant to my Agent full authority to make decisions for me regarding my health care. In exercising this authority, my Agent shall follow my desires as stated in this document or as otherwise expressed by me or known to my Agent.

In making any decision, my Agent shall attempt to discuss the proposed decision with me to determine my desires if I am able to communicate in any way. In the event my wishes as previously expressed are unclear, my Agent shall make a choice for me based upon what my Agent believes to be in my best interests as expressed by me in this document or elsewhere. My Agent's authority to interpret my desires is intended to be as broad as possible, except for any limitations I may state below.

Accordingly, unless specifically limited by Section H below, my Agent is authorized as follows:

A. To consent, refuse, or withdraw consent to any and all types of medical care, treatment, surgical procedures, diagnostic procedures, medication, and the use of mechanical or other procedures that affect any bodily function, including, but not limited to, artificial respiration, nutritional support and hydration, and cardiopulmonary resuscitation;

B. To authorize, or refuse to authorize, any medication or procedure intended to relieve pain, even though such use may lead to physical damage, addiction, or hasten the moment of, but not intentionally cause, my death;

C. To authorize my admission to or discharge from, even against medical advice, any hospital, nursing-care facility, or similar facility or service;

D. To take any other action necessary to making, documenting, and assuring implementation of decisions concerning my health care, including, but not limited to: the granting of any waiver or release from liability required by any hospital, physician, or other health-care provider; the signing of any documents relating to refusals of treatment or the leaving of a facility against medical advice; and the pursuing of any legal action, in my name and at the expense of my estate, either to force compliance with my wishes, as determined by my Agent, or to seek actual or punitive damages for the failure to comply;

E. To have access to medical records and information to the same extent that I am entitled to, including the right to disclose the contents to others;

F. To contract on my behalf for placement in a health-care or nursing-care facility, or for health-care related services, without incurring personal financial liability for the contract;

G. To hire and fire medical, social-service, and other support personnel responsible for my care;

H. The powers granted above do not include the following powers or are subject to the following rules or limitations:

_____

_____

_____

3. *ORGAN DONATION* (INITIAL ONLY ONE)

My Agent may _____ or may not _____ consent to the donation of all or any of my tissue or organs for purposes of transplantation.

4. *STATEMENT OF DESIRES AND SPECIAL PROVISIONS*

With respect to any life-sustaining treatment, I direct the following: (INITIAL WHICHEVER OF THE FOLLOWING THREE PARAGRAPHS REFLECTS

YOUR WISHES. IN PARAGRAPH D YOU MAY ADD TO WHICHEVER
PARAGRAPH YOU CHECKED OR YOU MAY PROVIDE INSTRUCTIONS
IN YOUR OWN WORDS IF YOU WISH.)

(A). _____ GRANT OF DISCRETION TO AGENT. I do not want my
life to be prolonged nor do I want life-sustaining treatment to be provided or
continued if my Agent believes the burdens of the treatment outweigh the expected benefits. I want my Agent to consider the relief of suffering, my personal
beliefs, the expense involved, and the quality as well as the possible extension
of my life in making decisions concerning life-sustaining treatment.

OR

(B). _____ DIRECTIVE TO WITHHOLD OR WITHDRAW TREAT-
MENT. I do not want my life to be prolonged, and I do not want life-sustaining
treatment if either:

1. I have a condition that is incurable or irreversible and, without the administration of life-sustaining procedures, is expected to result in death within
   a relatively short period of time; or
2. if I am in a state of permanent unconsciousness.

OR

(C). _____ DIRECTIVE FOR MAXIMUM TREATMENT. I want my
life to be prolonged to the greatest extent possible, within the standards of accepted medical practice and without regard to my condition, the chances I have
for recovery, or the cost of the procedures.

AND/OR

(D). _____ DIRECTIVE IN MY OWN WORDS:

_____

_____

_____

_____

5. *STATEMENT OF DESIRES REGARDING TUBE-FEEDING*

With respect to artificial nutrition and hydration, including by means of a nasogastric tube or tube into the stomach, intestines, or veins, I wish to make clear
that (INITIAL ONLY ONE)

(A). _____ I *do not* want to receive these forms of artificial nutrition and
hydration, and they may be withheld or withdrawn under the conditions given
above.

OR

(B). _____ I *do* want to receive these forms of artificial nutrition and hydration.

6. *SUCCESSORS*

If an Agent named by me refuses to serve or becomes otherwise unavailable (or if an Agent is my spouse and is divorced from me or separated from me), I name the following as successors to my Agent, each to act alone and successively, in the order named. The word *Agent* in this document includes a Successor Agent who has assumed authority to act pursuant to this section.

A. First Alternate Agent:

      _____

      Address: _____

    Telephone: _____

B. Second Alternate Agent:

      _____

      Address: _____

    Telephone: _____

7. *PROTECTION OF MY AGENT AND THIRD PARTIES WHO RELY ON MY AGENT*

No health-care provider or other person or entity that either reasonably relies upon a person's representation that he or she is the person named as my Agent or relies in good faith on a health-care decision made by my Agent shall be liable to me, my estate, my heirs or assigns, for recognizing the Agent's authority or relying on the decision.

No Agent who in good faith makes a health-care decision pursuant to the authority granted herein shall be liable to me, my estate, or my heirs or assigns, on account of the substance of the decision.

8. *ADMINISTRATIVE PROVISIONS*

A. This power of attorney is intended to be valid in any jurisdiction in which it is presented.

B. My Agent shall not be entitled to compensation for services performed under this Health-Care Power of Attorney, but he or she shall be entitled to reimbursement for all reasonable expenses incurred as a result of carrying out the Health-Care Power of Attorney.

C. The powers delegated under this power of attorney are separable so that the invalidity of one or more powers shall not affect any others.

9. *UNAVAILABILITY OF AGENT*

If at any relevant time the Agent and Successor Agents named herein are unable or unwilling to make decisions concerning my health care, and those decisions are to be made by another surrogate, I direct that the surrogate make all decisions in accord with my directions as stated in this document.

BY SIGNING HERE I INDICATE THAT I UNDERSTAND THE CONTENTS OF THIS DOCUMENT AND THE EFFECT OF THIS GRANT OF POWERS TO MY AGENT.

I sign my name to this Health-Care Power of Attorney on this _____ day of _____, 19____. My current home address is:

_____

_____

Signature: _____

Name: _____

WITNESS STATEMENT

I declare, on the basis of information and belief, that the person who signed or acknowledged this document (the principal) is personally known to me, that he/she acknowledged this Health-Care Power of Attorney in my presence, and that he/she appears to be of sound mind and under no duress, fraud, or undue influence.

Witness No. 1

Signature: _____ Date: _____

Print Name: _____ Telephone: _____

Residence Address: _____

_____

Witness No. 2

Signature: _____ Date: _____

Print Name: _____ Telephone: _____

Residence Address: _____

_____

The New Jersey Bioethics Commission's Combined Advance Directive for Health Care (Combined Proxy and Instruction Directive)

I understand that as a competent adult I have the right to make decisions about my health care. There may come a time when I am unable, due to physical or mental incapacity, to make my own health care decisions. In these circumstances, those caring for me will need direction concerning my care and will turn to someone who knows my values and health care wishes. I understand that those responsible for my care will seek to make health care decisions in my best interests, based upon what they know of my wishes. In order to provide the guidance and authority needed to make decisions on my behalf:

I, _____ hereby declare and make known my instructions and wishes for my future health care. This advance directive for health care shall take effect in the event I become unable to make my own health-care decisions, as determined by the physician who has primary responsibility for my care, and any necessary confirming determinations. I direct that this document become part of my permanent medical records.

In completing Part One of this directive, you will designate an individual you trust to act as your legally recognized health care representative to make health care decisions for you in the event you are unable to make decisions for yourself.

In completing Part Two of this directive, you will provide instructions concerning your health care preferences and wishes to your health care representative and others who will be entrusted with responsibility for your care, such as your physician, family members and friends.

Part One: Designation of a Health Care Representative

A) CHOOSING A HEALTH CARE REPRESENTATIVE:
I hereby designate:

name _____
address _____
city _____ *state*_____
telephone _____

as my health care representative to make any and all health care decisions for me, including decisions to accept or to refuse any treatment, service or procedure used to diagnose or treat my physical or mental condition, and decisions to provide, withhold or withdraw life-sustaining measures. I direct my representative to make decisions on my behalf in accordance with my wishes as stated in this document, or as otherwise known to him or her. In the event my wishes are not clear, or a situation arises I did not anticipate, my health care representative is authorized to make decisions in my best interests, based upon what is known of my wishes.

I have discussed the terms of this designation with my health care representative and he or she has willingly agreed to accept the responsibility for acting on my behalf.

B) ALTERNATE REPRESENTATIVES: If the person I have designated above is unable, unwilling or unavailable to act as my health care representative, I hereby designate the following person(s) to act as my health care representative, in the order of priority stated:

1. *name* _____   2. *name* _____
   address _____   *address* _____
   city _____ *state* _____   *city* _____ *state* _____
   telephone _____   *telephone* _____

Part Two: Instruction Directive

In Part Two, you are asked to provide instructions concerning your future health care. This will require making important and perhaps difficult choices. Before completing your directive, you should discuss these matters with your health care representative, doctor, family members or others who may become responsible for your care.

*In **Sections C and D,** you may state the circumstances in which various forms of medical treatment, including life-sustaining measures, should be provided, withheld or discontinued. If the options and choices below do not fully express your* *wishes, you should use* **Section E,** *and/or attach a statement to this document which would provide those responsible for your care with additional information you think would help them in making decisions about your medical treatment.* **Please familiarize yourself with all sections of Part Two before completing your directive.**

C) GENERAL INSTRUCTIONS. To inform those responsible for my care of my specific wishes, I make the following statement of personal views regarding my health care:

Initial ONE of the following two statements with which you agree:

1. _____ I direct that all medically appropriate measures be provided to sustain my life, regardless of my physical or mental condition.

2. _____ There are circumstances in which I would not want my life to be prolonged by further medical treatment. In these circumstances, life-sustaining measures should not be initiated and if they have been, they should be discontinued. I recognize that this is likely to hasten my death. In the following, I specify the circumstances in which I would choose to forego life-sustaining measures.

If you have initialed statement 2, on the following page please initial each of the statements **(a, b, c)** *with which you agree:*

a. _____ I realize that there may come a time when I am diagnosed as having an incurable and irreversible illness, disease, or condition. If this occurs, and my attending physician and at least one additional physician who has personally examined me determine that my condition is **terminal,** I direct that life-sustaining measures which would serve only to artificially prolong my dying be withheld or discontinued. I also direct that I be given all medically appropriate care necessary to make me comfortable and to relieve pain.

In the space provided, write in the bracketed phrase with which you agree:

To me, terminal condition means that my physicians have determined that:

_____ **[I will die within a few days]** _____ **[I will die within a few weeks]**
_____ **[I have a life expectancy of approximately** _____ **or less** *(enter 6 months, or 1 year)*]

b. _____ If there should come a time when I become **permanently unconscious,** and it is determined by my attending physician and at least one additional physician with appropriate expertise who has personally examined me, that I have totally and irreversibly lost consciousness and my capacity for interaction with other people and my surroundings, I direct that life-sustaining measures be withheld or discontinued. I understand that I will not experience pain or discomfort in this condition, and I direct that I be given all medically appropriate care necessary to provide for my personal hygiene and dignity.

c. _____ I realize that there may come a time when I am diagnosed as having an **incurable and irreversible** illness, disease, or condition which may not be terminal. My condition may cause me to experience severe and progressive physical or mental deterioration and/or a permanent loss of capacities and faculties I value highly. If, in the course of my medical care, the burdens of continued life with treatment become greater than the benefits I experience, I direct that life-sustaining measures be withheld or discontinued. I also direct that I be given all medically appropriate care necessary to make me comfortable and to relieve pain.

(Paragraph c. covers a wide range of possible situations in which you may have experienced partial or complete loss of certain mental and physical capacities you value highly. If you wish, in the space provided below you may specify in more detail the conditions in which you would choose to forego life-sustaining measures. You might include a description of the faculties or capacities, which, if irretrievably lost, would lead you to accept death rather than continue living. You may want to express any special concerns you have about particular medical conditions or treatments, or any other considerations which would provide further guidance to those who may become responsible for your care. If necessary, you may attach a separate statement to this document or use Section E to provide additional instructions.)

Examples of conditions which I find unacceptable are:

_____

_____

_____

_____

D) SPECIFIC INSTRUCTIONS: Artificially Provided Fluids and Nutrition; Cardiopulmonary Resuscitation (CPR). _Above you provided general instructions regarding life-sustaining measures. Here you are asked to give specific instructions regarding two types of life-sustaining measures—artificially provided fluids and nutrition and cardiopulmonary resuscitation._

In the space provided, write in the bracketed phrase with which you agree:

1. In the circumstances I initialled on page 3, I also direct that artificially provided fluids and nutrition, such as by feeding tube or intravenous infusion,

[be withheld or withdrawn and that I be allowed to die]
[be provided to the extent medically appropriate]

2. In the circumstances I initialled on page 3, if I should suffer a cardiac arrest, I also direct that cardiopulmonary resuscitation (CPR)

[not be provided and that I be allowed to die]
[be provided to preserve my life, unless medically inappropriate or futile]

3. If neither of the above statements adequately expresses your wishes concerning artificially provided fluids and nutrition or CPR, please explain your wishes below.

_____

_____

_____

E) ADDITIONAL INSTRUCTIONS: *(You should provide any additional infor-mation about your health care preferences which is important to you and which may help those concerned with your care to implement your wishes. You may wish to direct your health care representative, family members, or your health care pro-viders to consult with others, or you may wish to direct that your care be provided by a particular physician, hospital, nursing home, or at home. If you are or believe you may become pregnant, you may wish to state specific instructions. If you need more space than is provided here you may attach an additional statement to this directive.)*

_____

_____

_____

F) BRAIN DEATH: *(The State of New Jersey recognizes the irreversible cessation of all functions of the entire brain, including the brain stem (also known as whole brain death), as a legal standard for the declaration of death. However, individuals who cannot accept this standard because of their personal religious beliefs may request that it not be applied in determining their death.)*

Initial the following statement only if it applies to you:

_____ To declare my death on the basis of the whole brain death standard would violate my personal religious beliefs. I therefore wish my death to be declared solely on the basis of the traditional criteria of irreversible cessation of cardio-pulmonary (heartbeat and breathing) function.

G) AFTER DEATH—ANATOMICAL GIFTS: *(It is now possible to transplant human organs and tissue in order to save and improve the lives of others. Organs, tissues and other body parts are also used for therapy, medical research and education. This section allows you to indicate your desire to make an anatomical gift and if so, to provide instructions for any limitations or special uses.)*

Initial the statements which express your wishes:

1. _____ **I wish** to make the following anatomical gift to take effect upon my death:
    A. _____ any needed organs or body parts
    B. _____ only the following organs or parts

for the purposes of transplantation, therapy, medical research or education, or
    C. _____ my body for anatomical study, if needed.
    D. _____ special limitations, if any;

If you wish to provide additional instructions, such as indicating your preference that your organs be given to a specific person or institution, or be used for a specific purpose, please do so in the space provided below.

_____

_____

_____

2. _____ **I do not wish** to make an anatomical gift upon my death.

Part Three: Signature and Witnesses

H) COPIES: The original or a copy of this document has been given to the following people *(NOTE: If you have chosen to designate a health care representative, it is important that you provide him or her with a copy of your directive.):*

1. *name* _____   2. *name* _____
    address _____   *address* _____
    city _____ *state* _____   *city* _____ *state* _____
    telephone _____   *telephone* _____

I) SIGNATURE: By writing this advance directive, I inform those who may become entrusted with my health care of my wishes and intend to ease the burdens of decisionmaking which this responsibility may impose. I have discussed the terms of this designation with my health care representative and he or she has willingly agreed to accept the responsibility for acting on my behalf in accordance with this directive. I understand the purpose and effect of this document and sign it knowingly, voluntarily and after careful deliberation.

Signed this _____ **day of** _____, **19**____.
signature _____
address _____
city _____ *state* _____

J) WITNESSES: I declare that the person who signed this document, or asked another to sign this document on his or her behalf, did so in my presence, that he or she is personally known to me, and that he or she appears to be of sound mind and free of duress or undue influence. I am 18 years of age or older, and am not designated by this or any other document as the person's health care representative, nor as an alternate health care representative.

1. *witness* _____
   address _____
   city _____ *state* _____
   signature _____
   date _____

2. *witness* _____
   address _____
   city _____ *state* _____
   signature _____
   date _____

Prepared by the New Jersey Commission on Legal and Ethical Problems in the Delivery of Health Care (New Jersey Bioethics Commission) March 1991.

A Values Profile

I. Introduction

The following questionnaire is designed to guide your medical treatment after you have become incompetent (that is, you are unable to understand the nature and consequences of important medical decisions). The object is to instruct about what level of deterioration would warrant cessation of life-sustaining medical intervention on your behalf. Unless you indicate otherwise, you can assume that comfort care (care intended to keep you clean and comfortable) will always be provided.

Listed below are factors which some people consider important in shaping post-competence medical care. You are asked to give your own reactions to the various factors.

Some people's main concern is that their existence not be prolonged during the last stages of an unavoidable dying process (i.e., when they have been stricken with an incurable fatal condition). If that is your main concern, Section II below gives you a chance to indicate the time span which you consider the "last stage" of an unavoidable dying process.

Some people are more concerned about medical prolongation of their lives—whatever the possible survival period—after they have permanently deteriorated to a condition which they consider personally undignified and intolerable. If that is your main concern, Sections III through VIII below give you a chance to define the conditions which, for you, would be intolerable.

II. A Terminal Condition

In my post-competence state, if I face an incurable condition which, according to medical judgment, will cause my death with or without medical intervention, I want life-sustaining care to cease, as follows:

    _____ when I have less than a year to survive

    _____ when I have less than six months to survive

    _____ when I have less than a month to survive

_____ when I have less than a week to survive

_____ none of the above; I want all life-sustaining care to be continued

_____ none of the above; I want my treatment to depend on my condition, not the remaining life span

III. Pain and Suffering

In my post-competence state, I am concerned about extreme pain to the following extent: (check one)

_____ intolerable; I prefer death

_____ a very negative factor, to be weighed with other factors in de-termining my best interests

_____ unimportant

My attitude toward pain which can be controlled only by substances which leave me drowsy and confused most of the time:

_____ intolerable

_____ a very negative factor, to be weighed with other factors in de-termining my best interests

_____ unimportant

IV. Mental Incapacity

In my post-competence state, I am concerned about the level of my mental deterioration to the following extent: (check one)

_____ a very critical factor

_____ important yet not determinative by itself, a factor to be weighed with other factors in determining my best interests

_____ unimportant

My attitude toward a permanently unconscious state, confirmed by up-to-date medical tests, showing no hope of ever regaining consciousness:

_____ intolerable; I prefer death

_____ tolerable

_____ tolerable, so long as insurance or

other nonfamily sources are paying the bills

My reaction to profound dementia to the point where I can no longer recognize
and interact with my loved ones:

    _____ intolerable, I prefer death
    _____ a very negative factor, to be
weighed with other factors in determining my best interests
    _____ tolerable

My reaction to dementia to the point where I can no longer read and understand
written material:

    _____ intolerable, I prefer death
    _____ a very negative factor, to be
weighed with other factors in determining my best interests
    _____ tolerable

V. Physical Immobility

In my post-competence state, I am concerned about physical immobility to
the following extent:

    _____ important
    _____ unimportant

My reaction to being permanently bedridden:

    _____ intolerable; I prefer death
    _____ a very negative factor, to be
weighed with other factors in determining my best interests
    _____ tolerable

My reaction to being nonambulatory, meaning I can leave my bed but can
only move around in a wheelchair:

    _____ intolerable; I prefer death
    _____ a very negative factor, to be
weighed with other factors in determining my best interests
    _____ tolerable

VI. Physical Helplessness

In my post-competence state, I am concerned about my independence and my ability to tend to my own physical needs to the following extent:

_____ a very critical factor
_____ important yet not determinative by itself, a factor to be weighed in determining my best interests
_____ unimportant

My reaction to being incapable of feeding myself:

_____ intolerable; I prefer death
_____ a very negative factor, to be weighed with other factors in determining my best interests
_____ a somewhat negative factor
_____ unimportant

My reaction to being incapable of dressing myself:

_____ intolerable; I prefer death
_____ a very negative factor, to be weighed with other factors in determining my best interests
_____ a somewhat negative factor
_____ unimportant

My reaction to being incontinent:

_____ intolerable; I prefer death
_____ a very negative factor, to be weighed with other factors in determining my best interests
_____ a somewhat negative factor
_____ unimportant

VII. Interests of Loved Ones

In my post-competence state, the emotional and financial burdens imposed on my loved ones are of concern to the following extent:

_____ a critical factor
_____ an important factor, depending on degree of burden
_____ unimportant

My reaction to emotional strain posed for my spouse or other loved ones surrounding me during my incompetency:

_____ an important factor
_____ a somewhat important factor
_____ irrelevant; they owe it to me

My reaction to a financial burden being imposed on my spouse or other loved ones:

_____ an important factor
_____ a somewhat important factor
_____ irrelevant; they can afford it
_____ irrelevant; my life is the critical factor

My reaction to my assets being depleted by heavy medical expenses being used for my care:

_____ an important factor
_____ somewhat important
_____ irrelevant; I earned it

VIII. Living Arrangements

I would find any of the following living arrangements intolerable so that, if there were no alternative, I would prefer cessation or withdrawal of life-sustaining medical care:

_____ living at home, but with need for full-time help
_____ living permanently in the home of one of my children or other relative
_____ living permanently in a nursing home or other long-term care facility
_____ being confined to a hospital with little or no hope of ever leaving

Notes

Introduction

1. See James F. Fries, "Aging, Natural Death, and the Compression of Morbidity," 303 New Eng. J. Med. 130 (1980). There are some predictions that medical science will ultimately prevail and conquer even degenerative ailments. See Silverstein, *The Conquest of Death* 13 (1979); Ellis, "Immortality Made Easy: A Short Guide to Longevity," in *Omni's Future Medical Almanac* 130 (Teresi & Adcroft eds., 1987). The likelihood, however, is that periods of chronic disability will be postponed and compressed, not eliminated entirely as factors in causing death. See Edward L. Schneider & Jacob A. Brody, "Aging, Natural Death, and the Compression of Morbidity: Another View," 309 New Eng. J. Med. 854 (1983); Binstock, "Health Care of the Aging: Trends, Dilemmas, and Prospects for the Year 2,000," in *Aging 2000: Our Health Care Destiny* (Gaity & Samorajski eds., 1985). Dying is unlikely to become outmoded.

2. Congressional Summary, "Losing a Million Minds: Confronting the Tragedy of Alzheimer's Disease and Other Dementias" 16–21 (Office of Technology Assessment 1987).

3. "The ultimate horror [is not] death but the possibility of being maintained in limbo, in a sterile room, by machines controlled by a stranger." In re *Torres*, 357 N.W. 2d 332, 340 (Minn. 1984).

4. See, e.g., John E. Ruark et al., "Initiating and Withdrawing Life Support," 318 New Eng. J. Med. 25, 27 (1988); Sidney H. Wanzer et al., "The Physician's Responsibility Toward Hopelessly Ill Patients," 320 New Eng. J. Med. 844 (1989); Charles L. Sprung, "Changing Attitudes and Practices in Forgoing Life-Sustaining Treatments," 263 JAMA 2211 (1990). Between 85% and 90% of critical-care health professionals acknowledge withholding life-sustaining treatment from patients deemed to have irreversible and terminal disease; see id. at 2213.

5. Appointment of a health-care agent is commonly accomplished by signing a durable power of attorney, pursuant either to a state law relating generally to durable powers of attorney or to a state law specifically providing for a durable power of attorney for health care (DPOA-HC). In this book I will treat a written designation of a health-care agent as a form of advance directive. This is done both because the designation is aimed at controlling post-competence medical handling and because it is frequently accompanied by substantive instructions to the designated agent.

1. The Bounds of Autonomy for Competent Medical Patients

1. Chapter 2 discusses the concept of prospective autonomy and describes the respect it has been accorded.

2. In re *Farrell*, 529 A.2d 404 (N.J. 1987); *State v. McAfee*, 385 S.E.2d 651 (Ga. 1989); *Satz v. Perlmutter*, 362 So. 2d 160 (Fla. Dist. Ct. App. 1978), aff'd, 379 So. 2d 359 (Fla. 1980); *Norwood Hosp. v. Munoz*, 564 N.E.2d 1017 (Mass. 1991); *Fosmire v. Nicoleau*, 551 N.E.2d 77 (N.Y. 1990); *McKay v. Bergstedt*, 801 P.2d 617 (Nev. 1990).

3. See *Farrell*, 529 A.2d at 412; Nancy S. Jecker & Donnie J. Self, "Medical Ethics in

the 21st Century: Respect for Autonomy in Care of the Elderly Patient," 6 J. Crit. Care 46, 46–51 (1991).

4. See Edmund D. Pellegrino & David C. Thomasma, "The Conflict Between Autonomy and Beneficence in Medical Ethics: Proposals for a Resolution," 3 J. Contemp. Health L. & Pol'y 23, 24 (1987); see also Jay Katz, *The Silent World of Doctor and Patient* (1984).

5. See *Schloendorff v. Society of New York Hosp.*, 105 N.E. 92, 93 (N.Y. 1914).

6. See, e.g., *Gray v. Romeo*, 697 F. Supp. 580, 588 (D.R.I. 1988); In re *Estate of Longeway*, 549 N.E.2d 292 (Ill. 1989); *Farrell*, 529 A.2d at 410; In re *Guardianship of Browning*, 568 So. 2d 4 (Fla. 1990); Thomas C. Marks, Jr., & Rebecca C. Morgan, "The Right of the Dying to Refuse Life Prolonging Medical Procedures: the Evolving Importance of State Constitutions," 18 Ohio N.U.L. Rev. 467 (1992).

7. Justice O'Connor raises this possibility in her concurring opinion in *Cruzan v. Director, Missouri Dep't of Health*, 110 S. Ct. 2841, 2858–59 (1990).

8. This last assertion—that an agent would enjoy the same range of decision-making power as a competent patient—is not intuitively self-evident. It is conceivable that a state would have to respect the appointment of an agent and accord that agent decision-making authority but would not have to give the agent as much choice as the competent patient would have. That is, it is conceivable that a state could impose its parens patriae authority (to protect helpless individuals) in order to limit the substantive choices which an agent or proxy can make. This is so because prospective autonomy (as reflected in advance directives) is not precisely the same thing as contemporaneous autonomy. The divergence is discussed in chapters 2 and 6.

9. *Cruzan*, 110 S. Ct. at 2841.

10. The parents' assertion was that even in the absence of autonomous choice by the now incompetent patient, the parents or some other guardian would be constitutionally entitled to make the same decision regarding terminal care that the patient would make if competent. In that fashion, the parents would be exercising Nancy's own constitutional interests. The attribution of autonomy-based rights to an unconscious patient (who has never issued prior, clear-cut instructions) raises fascinating and important constitutional questions. Those questions are beyond the scope of this book. This book treats situations where patients have issued advance instructions and have thereby exercised their autonomy interests.

11. *Cruzan*, 110 S. Ct. at 2852.

12. John A. Robertson, "Cruzan and the Constitutional Status of Nontreatment Decisions For Incompetent Patients," 25 Ga. L. Rev. 1139 (1991); Yale Kamisar, "When Is There a Constitutional "Right to Live?" 25 Ga. L. Rev. 1203 (1991); Thomas A. Eaton & Edward J. Larson, "Experimenting With the "Right to Die" in the Laboratory of the States," 25 Ga. L. Rev. 1253 (1991); James Bopp, Jr., & Daniel Avila, "The Due Process 'Right to Life' in *Cruzan* and its Impact on 'Right-to-Die' Law," 53 U. Pitt. L. Rev. 193 (1991).

13. There are scores of such decisions. See, e.g., the cases cited in note 6; see also Marks & Morgan, supra note 6, at 474.

14. *Cruzan*, 110 S. Ct. at 2852. For pre-Cruzan surveys of the relevant Supreme Court authorities, see Patricia Lerwick, Note, "Withdrawal of Life-Saving Treatment; Patients' Rights—Privacy Rights," 42 Me. L. Rev. 193, 199–208 (1990); Thomas Wm. Mayo, "Constitutionalizing the Right to Die", 49 Md. L. Rev. 1033, 112–25 (1990); Stewart G. Pollock, "Life and Death Decisions: Who Makes Them and By What Standards?" 41 Rutgers L. Rev. 505 (1989).

15. *Cruzan*, 110 S. Ct. at 2857.

16. *Snyder v. Massachusetts*, 291 U.S. 97, 105 (1934).

17. See *Moore v. City of East Cleveland*, 431 U.S. 494, 503 (1977); *Bowers v. Hardwick*, 478 U.S. 186, 192 (1986). See generally Susan R. Martyn & Henry J. Bourguignon, "Coming

to Terms with Death: The *Cruzan* Case," 42 Hastings L.J. 817, 848–50 (1991), regarding the role of history and tradition in defining fundamental liberty interests.

18. *Cruzan*, 110 S. Ct. at 2885. Justice Stevens speaks in terms of a "freedom to conform choices about death to individual conscience." *Id.* Arguably, this language might be read to embrace other forms of choosing death (such as assisted suicide or active euthanasia). I doubt that Justice Stevens intended such an expansive notion. The traditional freedom of conscience in dying to which he refers encompassed rejection of unwanted medical intervention and freedom to withdraw entirely from medical supervision and to die at home. The traditional freedom did not encompass active intervention to shorten natural dying processes. The distinction between a right to reject medical intervention and a right to die is discussed in detail later in this chapter.

19. *Cruzan*, 110 S. Ct. at 2890.

20. *Cruzan*, 110 S. Ct. at 2856–57.

21. For example, see the dissenting opinion of Justice Lynch in *Brophy v. New England Sinai Hosp., Inc.*, 497 N.E.2d 626, 642–44 (Mass. 1986).

22. See Philip G. Peters, Jr., "The State's Interest in the Preservation of Life: From Quinlan to Cruzan," 50 Ohio St. L.J. 891, 897 (1989); Martha A. Matthews, Note, "Suicidal Competence and the Patient's Right to Refuse Lifesaving Treatment," 75 Cal. L. Rev. 707, 719 (1987).

23. "[W]orse than the pain itself, is the frustration, bodily insult and the humiliation of having a stranger or some authority decide contrary to one's own wishes the quality, the nature, the form and the manner of one's own future life." In re *Farrell*, 514 A.2d 1342, 1346 (N.J. Super. Ct. Ch. Div. 1986), aff'd, 529 A.2d 404 (N.J. 1987).

24. See *Satz v. Perlmutter*, 362 So. 2d at 160; *Bouvia v. Superior Court*, 225 Cal. Rptr. 297, 305, 179 Cal. App. 3d 1127 (1986) (speaking to the "ignominy, embarrassment, humiliation, and dehumanizing aspects" felt by the patient in her helpless, debilitated state); see also In re *Conroy*, 486 A.2d 1209, 1249 (N.J. 1985) (Handler, J., concurring).

25. *Cruzan*, 110 S. Ct. at 2852–53.

26. *Cruzan*, 110 S. Ct. at 2855.

27. See, e.g., polls cited in Justice O'Connor's concurring opinion in *Cruzan*, 110 S. Ct. at 2857 n.1; Times Mirror Center for the People and the Press, *Reflections of the Times: The Right to Die* 6 (1990); Star-Ledger/Eagleton Poll, in the Newark Star-Ledger, Aug. 10, 1988, at Al.

28. See *Bowers v. Hardwick*, 478 U.S. at 190.

29. *Roe v. Wade*, 410 U.S. 113 (1973).

30. See *Planned Parenthood v. Casey*, 112 S. Ct. 2791 (1992).

31. In re *President and Directors of Georgetown College*, 331 F.2d 1010 (D.C. Cir.), cert. den., 377 U.S. 978 (1964) (dissenting opinion).

32. See *McKay v. Bergstedt*, 801 P.2d at 622–23; *Norwood Hosp. v. Munoz*, 564 N.E.2d at 1021; *Guardianship of Browning*, 568 So. 2d at 10; In re *Guardianship of L.W.*, 482 N.W.2d 60, 65 (Wis. 1992); *Guardianship of Doe*, 583 N.E.2d 1263,1267 (Mass. 1992). Other post-*Cruzan* decisions speak of a common-law right to reject life-preserving medical treatment. See *Estate of Longeway*, 549 N.E.2d at 297; *Mack v. Mack*, 618 A.2d 744, 755 (Md. 1993).

33. See, e.g., Leanne J. Fisher, Note, "The Suicide Trap: Bouvia v. Superior Court and the Right to Refuse Medical Treatment," 21 Loy. L.A. L. Rev. 219, 251–52 (1987); C. Everett Koop and Edward R. Grant, "The 'Small Beginnings' of Euthanasia: Examining the Erosion in Legal Prohibitions Against Mercy Killing," 2 Notre Dame J.L. Ethics & Pub. Pol'y 1585 (1986); Stanley S. Herr et al., "No Place to Go: Refusal of Life-Sustaining Treatment by Competent Persons with Physical Disabilities," 8 Issues in L. & Med. 3, 27–33 (1992).

34. *Conroy*, 486 A.2d at 1223. See also *McAfee*, 385 S.E.2d at 652; *Norwood Hosp. v. Munoz*, 564 N.E.2d at 1023; *McKay v. Bergstedt*, 801 P.2d at 623.

35. E.g., David C. Blake, "State Interests in Terminating Medical Treatment," 19:3 Hastings Cent. Rep. 5, 6–7 (May 1989).

36. Thus, government could insist that a patient receive full information about the consequences of a terminal decision, including information about the resources which might be available to ease the patient's plight if life-preserving medical intervention were accepted. See *McKay v. Bergstedt*, 801 P.2d at 621.

37. See, e.g., In re *Rodas*, No. 86PR139, slip op. at 28 (Mesa City Colo. Dist. Ct. 1987). But see Herr, supra note 33, at 4 (arguing that some judges undermine respect for disabled lives in endorsing terminal decisions).

38. See In re *Gardner*, 534 A.2d 947, 955 (Me. 1987); *Fosmire v. Nicoleau*, 551 N.E.2d at 80; *Saunders v. State*, 492 N.Y.S.2d 510, 517 (Sup. Ct. 1985); *Norwood Hosp. v. Munoz*, 564 N.E.2d at 1023.

39. In re *Requena*, 517 A.2d 886, 891 (N.J. Ch. Div.), aff'd, 517 A.2d 869 (App. Div. 1986). Note also Justice Stevens's remark in *Cruzan*, 110 S. Ct. at 2885, that a patient's choice to reject life-preserving medical intervention "presupposes no abandonment of the desire for life."

40. *Farrell*, 529 A.2d at 411.

41. See *Satz v. Perlmutter*, 362 So. 2d at 162; *Superintendent of Belchertown State School v. Saikewicz*, 370 N.E.2d 417, 425–26 (Mass. 1977); In re *Quinlan*, 355 A.2d 647, 663–64 (N.J. 1976); Pollock, supra note 14, at 516.

42. The issue is particularly important in light of statutory measures in some states which ostensibly confine the effect of "living wills" or powers of attorney to situations where an incompetent patient's death is "imminent." It is conceivable that such measures are unconstitutional. The nature and effect of such statutory measures will be addressed in chapter 3.

43. I specify "a naturally occurring dying process" in order to avoid connotations of suicide. The relevance of suicide to rejection of life-preserving medical intervention is discussed in the next subsection.

44. See *Fosmire v. Nicoleau*, 551 N.E.2d at 82–83; In re *Peter*, 529 A.2d 419, 423 (N.J. 1987); *Bartling v. Superior Court*, 209 Cal. Rptr. 200, 224 (Ct. App. 1984).

45. See *McKay v. Bergstedt*, 801 P.2d at 624–25.

46. Id. See also *Bartling*, 209 Cal. Rptr. at 224; *McAfee*, 385 S.E.2d at 652.

47. The whole concept of "terminal" conditions is somewhat problematic. The dividing line between terminal illness and chronic, degenerative illness may be difficult to define and may or may not be relevant, depending on the context. See Sandra H. Johnson, "From Medicalization to Legalization to Politicization: O'Connor, Cruzan, and Refusal of Treatment in the 1990's," 21 Conn. L. Rev. 685, 704 (1989). Further discussion is devoted in chapter 3 to the meaning of terminal illness in the context of living wills and other advance directives.

48. See *Guardianship of Browning*, 568 So. 2d at 9–10; *McConnell v. Beverly Enterprises*, 553 A.2d 596, 609 (Conn. 1989) (Healy, J., concurring); Developments, "Medical Technology and the Law," 103 Harv. L. Rev. 1519, 1667 (1990); see also *Guardianship of L.W.*, 482 N.W.2d at 60, 74 (suggesting that state interests in preserving life weaken as a patient's chance of recovery wanes).

49. See James F. Childress, *Who should Decide? Paternalism in Health Care* 164–65 (1982).

50. There are commentators who read *McKay v. Bergstedt*, 801 P.2d at 617, 630–31, as endorsing the possible judicial override of a nonterminal patient's determination to reject life-preserving medical care. See Thomas A. Eaton & Edward J. Larson, "Experimenting With the Right to Die in the Laboratory of the States," 25 Ga. L. Rev. 1253, 1274–75 (1991); M. Lisa Wilson-Clayton & Mark Clayton, "Two Steps Forward, One Step Back: *McKay v. Bergstedt*," 12 Whittier L. Rev. 439, 456 (1991). That seems to me to be an erroneous interpretation of

Bergstedt. McKay v. Bergstedt, 801 P.2d at 621, does talk about a separate state interest in encouraging humane care of incapacitated persons whose lives can be significantly extended. The opinion explains that the state interest requires a careful effort to inform a patient about all rehabilitative opportunities before acquiescing in the patient's decision to reject continued life support; see id. at 625, 627, 630. This emphasis on providing information to a patient does not undermine judicial recognition of the patient's ultimate entitlement to determine his or her own medical fate.

51. See, e.g., *Public Health Trust of Dade County v. Wons*, 541 So. 2d 96, 97–98 (Fla. 1989); In re *Milton*, 505 N.E.2d 255 (Ohio 1987); In re *E. G.*, 549 N.E.2d 322, 327 (Ill. 1989); In re *Estate of Brooks*, 205 N.E.2d 435 (Ill. 1965); Charlotte K. Goldberg, "Choosing Life After Death: Respecting Religious Beliefs and Moral Convictions in Near Death Decisions," 39 Syracuse L. Rev. 1197 (1988).

52. *Norwood Hosp. v. Munoz*, 564 N.E.2d at 1021.

53. See *Fosmire v. Nicoleau*, 551 N.E.2d at 77; cf. *Peter*, 529 A.2d at 423.

54. All this is not to say that nonreligious patients who are salvageable to a healthful existence will widely seek to invoke a prerogative to reject lifesaving medical intervention. Most salvageable patients desire lifesaving treatment. Resistance from nonreligious patients comes primarily when the preservable existence is highly debilitated and therefore distasteful to the patient.

55. See, e.g., *McAfee*, 385 S.E.2d at 652; *McKay v. Bergstedt*, 801 P.2d at 624; *Bouvia v. Superior Court*, 225 Cal. Rptr. at 300; *Lane v. Candura*, 376 N.E.2d 1232 (Mass. App. Ct. 1978).

56. See Laurence H. Tribe, *American Constitutional Law*, § 15-11, at 1367–68 (2d ed. 1988); Peters, supra note 22, at 932.

57. See *Georgetown College*, 331 F.2d at 1008–09; *John F. Kennedy Hospital v. Heston*, 279 A.2d 670 (N.J. 1971), overruled by *Conroy*, 486 A.2d at 1209.

58. *Cruzan*, 110 S. Ct. at 2859.

59. See, e.g., *Fosmire v. Nicoleau*, 551 N.E.2d at 82; *Brophy*, 497 N.E.2d at 635; *Rasmussen v. Fleming*, 741 P.2d 674, 685 (Ariz. 1987). For more detailed discussion of the relation between suicide and rejection of medical treatment, see Norman L. Cantor, *Legal Frontiers of Death and Dying* 46–51 (1987); Robert F. Weir, *Abating Treatment with Critically Ill Patients* 295–98 (1989); Matthews, supra note 22, at 729–43; Fisher, supra note 33, at 244–50; Sanford H. Kadish, "Letting Patients Die: Legal and Moral Reflections," 80 Cal. L. Rev. 857, 864–68 (1992).

60. "It is possible for a patient to refuse treatment precisely because she ignores or denies the intrinsic value of her own life." Blake, supra note 35, at 8. See also Mathews, supra note 22, at 732, 738–41. For an example of a refusal of care grounded on the conviction that the patient's existence has become too painful or frustrating, see *Bouvia*, 225 Cal. Rptr. at 297, 304.

61. See New Jersey Commission on Legal and Ethical Problems in the Delivery of Health Care, *Problems and Approaches in Health Care Decisionmaking* 56 (1990); *McKay v. Bergstedt*, 801 P.2d at 625.

62. This distinction may blur where the patient has had some role in causing the fatal condition precipitating a decision to resist life-preserving treatment. For example, a patient who launches a hunger strike, or who causes a fatal condition by intentionally neglecting himself or herself, is not simply "letting nature take its course." Such a patient is behaving like a suicide. For discussion of hunger strikers, see Cantor, supra note 59, at 51–53.

63. See *Cruzan*, 110 S. Ct. at 2851–52; *Fosmire v. Nicoleau*, 551 N.E.2d at 80–81; In re *Greenspan*, 558 N.E.2d 1194, 1201 (Ill. 1990).

64. "Asserting the right to refuse medical treatment is not tantamount to committing suicide." *Rasmussen v. Fleming*, 741 P.2d at 685. See also *Bouvia*, 225 Cal. Rptr. at 306.

65. *Norwood Hosp. v. Munoz*, 564 N.E.2d at 1022 n.5.

66. See Richard J. Bonnie, "The Dignity of the Condemned," 74 Va. L. Rev. 1363, 1375–77, 1389–90 (1988).

67. See *Bouvia*, 225 Cal. Rptr at 301–02; *McKay v. Bergstedt*, 801 P.2d at 631; *McAfee*, 385 S.E.2d at 652.

68. See also *Farrell*, 529 A.2d at 411; *Requena*, 517 A.2d at 870; *Rodas*, No. 86PR139, slip op. at 28.

69. *McKay v. Bergstedt*, 801 P.2d at 617.

70. Id. at 634.

71. See, e.g., *By No Extraordinary Means: The Choice to Forgo Life-Sustaining Food & Water* (Joanne Lynn ed., 1986); Johnson, supra note 47, at 700–01; Kamisar, supra note 12, at 1220–24.

72. See Developments, supra note 48, at 1662 n.142. For discussion of the idea that a "fundamental" societal value may be viewed at different levels of abstraction, see Wojciech Sadurski, "Conventional Morality and Judicial Standards," 73 Va. L. Rev. 339, 377–79 (1987).

73. For a discussion of the artificial nutrition issue in the context of permanently unconscious patients, see Norman L. Cantor, "The Permanently Unconscious Patient, Non-Feeding, and Euthanasia," 15 Am. J.L. & Med. 381, 384–98 (1989).

74. See, e.g., Bonnie Steinbock, "The Removal of Mr. Herbert's Feeding Tube," 13:5 Hastings Cent. Rep. (Oct. 1983), 13–14; William E. May et al., "Feeding and Hydrating the Permanently Unconscious and Other Vulnerable Persons," 3 Issues in L. & Med. 203 (1987).

75. See *Requena*, 517 A.2d at 888; *McConnell*, 553 A.2d at 608–09.

76. For an analysis of causation parallel to the one presented here, see *Rodas*, No. 86PR139, slip op. at 26–27. *Rodas* involved a 34 year old man who was permanently paralysed from the neck down and afflicted by a "locked-in" syndrome. The court upheld the competent patient's right to order withdrawal of artificial nutrition maintaining his existence, and it viewed the trauma to the brainstem which had ended the swallowing reflex as the determinative cause of death.

77. See, e.g., Daniel Callahan, "On Feeding the Dying," 13:5 Hastings Cent. Rep. 22 (Oct. 1983).

78. See Robertson, supra note 12, at 1156.

79. See Charles L. Sprung, "Changing Attitudes and Practices in Forgoing Life-Sustaining Treatments," 263 JAMA 2211, 2212 (1990).

80. See *Barber v. Superior Court*, 195 Cal. Rptr 484, 490, 147, Cal. App. 3d 1006 (1983); *Conroy*, 486 A.2d at 1226.

81. *Brophy*, 497 N.E.2d at 641 n.2.

82. Ronald E. Cranford, "Neurological Syndromes and Prolonged Survival: When Can Artificial Nutrition and Hydration Be Forgone?" 19 Law, Med. & Health Care 13, 18 (1991); Joanne Lynn & Glover, "Ethical Decision Making in Enteral Nutrition," in *Enteral and Tube Feeding* 577 (Rombeau & Caldwell eds., 2d ed. 1990); see also Evan R. Collins, Jr., and Doran Weber, *The Complete Guide to Living Wills*, 51, 56 (1991).

83. Cranford, supra note 82, at 18.

84. Current Opinions of the Council on Ethical and Judicial Affairs of the A.M.A. § 2.18 (1986). For citation to other medical bodies which have adopted a similar posture, see *Peter*, 529 A.2d at 428.

85. President's Commission for the Study of Ethical Problems in Medicine and Biomedical and Behavioral Research, *Deciding to Forego Life-Sustaining Treatment*, 88–90 (1983); The Hastings Center Task Force on Death and Dying, *Guidelines on the Termination of Life-Sustaining Treatment and the Care of the Dying* 57–62 (1987).

86. E.g., *Guardianship of L.W.*, 482 N.W.2d at 66–67. See Martyn & Bourguignon, supra note 17, at 826 n.50, for a list of relevant cases. Only the Washington State Supreme Court

has been equivocal with regard to equating artificial nutrition with customary medical treatment; see *Farnum v. Crista Ministries*, 807 P.2d 830, 842–44 (Wash. 1991) (Dore, C.J., dissenting).

87. Robert I. Simon, "Silent Suicide in the Elderly," 17:1 Bull. Am. Acad. Psychiatric Law 83, 86 (1989).

88. *Estate of Longeway*, 549 N.E.2d at 296.

89. There are commentators who do argue that a patient does have a right to reject manual feeding. See Robertson, supra note 12, at 1175. Professor Yale Kamisar sees a possible dividing line between artificial nutrition and "natural" feeding, but he doubts whether courts will adhere to that line; see Kamisar, supra note 12, at 1224–27.

90. *Cruzan* 110 S. Ct. at 2852.

91. See In re *Caulk*, 480 A.2d 93, 96–97 (N.H. 1984); Contra *Zant v. Prevatte*, 286 S.E.2d 715 (Ga. 1982). For discussion of hunger strikers, see Cantor, supra note 59, at 26–30.

92. See *Department of Public Welfare v. Kallinger*, 580 A.2d 887, 892 (Pa. Common. Ct. 1990); *Von Holden v. Chapman*, 450 N.Y.S.2d 623, 624–25 (App. Div. 1982).

93. See In re *Plaza Health and Rehabilitation Center*, order dated Feb. 2, 1984 (N.Y. Sup. Ct., Onondaga County); In re *Brooks, and Good Samaritan Nursing Home*, decision dated June 9, 1987 (N.Y. Sup. Ct., Albany County). See also *A.B. v. C.*, 477 N.Y.S.2d 282, 284 (Sup. Ct. 1984) (dictum in petition of a severely incapacitated person whose petition was dismissed as being prematurely filed).

94. But see *Bouvia v. Superior Court* (*Bouvia I*), No. 159780 (Calif. Super. Ct., Riverside County, 1983), referred to in *Bouvia v. Superior Court*, 225 Cal. Rptr. 297, 300 (Ct. App. 1986).

95. See Justice O'Connor's concurring opinion in *Cruzan*, 110 S. Ct. at 2856; In re *Hier*, 464 N.E.2d 959, 964 (Mass. App. Ct. 1984); George J. Annas, "Foreclosing the Use of Force: A.C. Reversed," 20:4 Hastings Cent. Rep. 27, 29 (July 1990); B. Lo, "The Clinical Use of Advance Directives," in *Medical Ethics: A Guide for Health Professionals* 210 (J. Monagle ed., 1988).

96. For example, in In re *Storar*, 420 N.E.2d 64 (N.Y.), cert. den. 454 U.S. 858 (1981), the court authorized blood transfusions for a mentally disabled leukemia patient even though the patient had to be physically restrained; likewise, the result in *Conroy*, 486 A.2d at 1209, was to suggest maintenance of artificial nutrition for the incompetent, debilitated patient despite the patient's resistance. See also *Bouvia I*, supra note 94.

97. See Robert J. Moss & John LaPuma, "The Ethics of Mechanical Restraints," 21:1 Hastings Cent. Rep. 22 (Jan. 1991).

98. See, e.g., George P. Smith, II, "All's Well that Ends Well: Toward a Policy of Assisted Rational Suicide or Merely Enlightened Self-Determination?" 22 U.C. Davis L. Rev. 275 (1989); Steven J. Wolhandles, Note, "Voluntary Active Euthanasia for the Terminally Ill and the Constitutional Right to Privacy," 69 Cornell L. Rev. 363 (1984); Linda Carl, Note, "The Right to Voluntary Euthanasia," 10 Whittier L. Rev. 489 (1988); Kadish, supra note 59, at 864–68.

99. *Donaldson v. Vandekamp*, 4 Cal. Rptr. 2d 59, 64 (Ct. App. 1992).

2. Advance Directives and Problems of Prospective Autonomy

1. For perceptive discussions of the difficulties of future-oriented decisions, see Allen E. Buchanan & Dan W. Brock, *Deciding for Others* 101–07 (1989); Donald L. Beschle, "Autonomous Decisionmaking and Social Choice: Examining the Right to Die," 77 Ky. L.J. 319, 335–45 (1988–89); Sanford H. Kadish, "Letting Patients Die: Legal and Moral Reflections," 80 Cal. L. Rev. 857, 873–76 (1982).

2. See President's Commission for the Study of Ethical Problems in Medicine and Biomedical and Behavioral Research, *Deciding to Forego Life-sustaining Treatment* 140 (1983); David S. Rosettenstein, "Living Wills in the United States: The Role of the Family," 4 Conn.

Prob. L.J. 27, 32 (1988); Stuart J. Eisendrath & Albert R. Jonsen, "The Living Will: Help or Hindrance?" 249 JAMA 2054, 2055 (1983).

3. See *John F. Kennedy Hosp. v. Heston*, 279 A.2d 670 (N.J. 1971), overruled by In re *Conroy*, 486 A.2d 1209 (N.J. 1985); In re *President and Directors of Georgetown College*, 331 F.2d 1000 (D.C. Cir.), cert den., 377 U.S. 978 (1964); *United States v. George*, 239 F. Supp. 752 (D. Conn. 1965); *Powell v. Columbian Presbyterian Medical Center*, 267 N.Y.S.2d 450 (Sup. Ct. 1965); cf. *Holmes v. Silver Cross Hosp.*, 340 F. Supp. 125 (N.D. Ill. 1972).

4. See generally George J. Annas & Leonard H. Glantz, "The Right of Elderly Patients to Refuse Life-Sustaining Treatment," 64 Milbank Q. Supp. 2, at 95 (1986); Martha A. Matthews, Note, "Suicidal Competence and the Patient's Right to Refuse Lifesaving Treatment," 75 Cal. L. Rev. 707, 724–28 (1987); Edmund D. Pellegrino & David C. Thomasma, *For the Patient's Good* 148–62 (1988).

5. See In re *Westchester County Medical Center*, 531 N.E.2d 607, 613, 534 N.Y.S.2d 886, 892 (N.Y. 1988); Nancy M.P. King, *Making Sense of Advance Directives* 65–67 (1991).

6. The limited scope of a person's predictive capacity might become a factor influencing the interpretation of advance directives. In that context, limited predictive capacity serves as a reason to afford flexibility to the agent ultimately charged with administration of an advance directive. But limitations of predictive capacity ought not preclude enforcement of advance directives, especially if the directive is clearly expressed and the product of deliberation.

7. For perceptive discussion of the difficulties of future-oriented decisions, see Beschle, supra note 1, at 335–45; Buchanan & Brock, supra note 1, at 106–07.

8. Buchanan & Brock, supra note 1, at 107, 153.

9. See Rebecca S. Dresser & John A. Robertson, "Quality of Life and Non-Treatment Decisions for Incompetent Patients: A Critique of the Orthodox Approach," 17 Law, Med. & Health Care 234, 236 (1989); John A. Robertson, "Cruzan and the Constitutional Status of Nontreatment Decisions for Incompetent Patients," 25 Ga. L. Rev. 1139, 1180–82, 1185 (1991).

10. See John A. Robertson, "Second Thoughts on Living Wills," 21:6 Hastings Cent. Rep. 7 (1991); Bernard Lo, "Caring for Incompetent Patients: Is There a Physician on the Case?" 17 Law, Med. & Health Care 214, 215–16 (1989).

11. Dan W. Brock, "Trumping Advance Directives," 21:5 Hastings Cent. Rep. S5 (1991).

12. See, e.g., John A. Robertson, "Prior Agreements for Disposition of Frozen Embryos," 51 Ohio St. L.J. 407, 421 (1990).

13. Many commentators note the practical obstacles to advance directives but favor them as the best way to honor self-determination in the death-and-dying context. See Laurence A. Tribe, *American Constitutional Law*, § 16-31, at 1599 n.29 (2d ed. 1988); Robert M. Veatch, *The Patient as Partner* 59 (1987); Philip G. Peters, Jr., "The State's Interest in the Preservation of Life: From Quinlan to Cruzan," 50 Ohio St. L.J. 891, 936 (1989); Susan M. Wolf, "Nancy Beth Cruzan: In No Voice at All," 20:1 Hastings Cent. Rep. 39 (Jan. 1990)

14. "Patients who feel secure that their wishes will be respected are relieved of anxiety and are more likely to seek medical advice in a timely and open manner." Hackler, Mosely, & Vawter, *Advance Directives in Medicine* 4 (1989). See also Peters, supra note 13, at 938.

Professor Robert A. Burt laments people's lack of confidence in terminal care and in the "nurturant potential in our common social life." He analogizes the nurturant aspects of terminal care to positive "images of childhood and infancy." See Burt, "Withholding Nutrition and Mistrusting Nurturance: The Vocabulary of In re *Conroy*," 2 Issues in L. & Med. 317, 320–21 (1987). Unfortunately, most people don't want to complete their life cycle by returning to an infant's status, even if the care process carries with it certain symbolic value.

15. See Special Committee on Aging, U.S. Senate, *A Matter of Choice: Planning Ahead for Health Care Decisions* 4 (1989).

16. Kent W. Davidson et al., "Physicians' Attitudes on Advance Directives," 262 JAMA 2415, 2417 (1989).

17. Thomas Wm. Mayo, "Constitutionalizing the Right to Die", 49 Md. L. Rev. 103, 146 (1990); Developments, "Medical Technology and the Law," 103 Harv. L. Rev. 1519, 1164–65 (1990).

18. See In re *Estate of Longeway*, 549 N.E.2d 292, 303 (Ill. 1990) (Ward, J., dissenting).

19. See, e.g., Beschle, supra note 1, at 360; Rebecca Dresser, "Life, Death, and Incompetent Patients: Conceptual Infirmities and Hidden Values in the Law," 28 Ariz. L. Rev. 373, 389 (1986); Rebecca Dresser, "Relitigating Life and Death," 51 Ohio St. L.J. 425 (1990).

20. Concerning the deep Anglo-American respect for personal choice, see Bruce J. Winick, "Competency to Consent to Treatment: The Distinction Between Assent and Objection," 28 Hous. L. Rev. 15, 36–37 (1992); Gerald Dworkin, *The Theory and Practice of Autonomy* (1988).

21. Justices Brennan and Stevens, in their dissenting opinions in *Cruzan v. Director, Missouri Dep't of Health*, 110 S. Ct., were sensitive to people's legitimate concern about the images and recollections to be left with loved ones. They saw this element as a critical reason to respect people's death and dying choices. Id. at 2868 (Brennan, J., dissenting); id. at 2883–84 (Stevens, J., dissenting).

22. In re *Conroy*, 486 A.2d 1209, 1229 (N.J. 1985); *Brophy v. New England Sinai Hosp.*, 497 N.E.2d 626, 633–34 (Mass. 1986); *John F. Kennedy Memorial Hosp., Inc. v. Bludworth*, 452 So. 2d 921, 923 (Fla. 1984); In re *Guardianship of L.W.*, 482 N.W.2d 60, 65 (Wis. 1992); see George J. Alexander, "Death by Directive," 28 Santa Clara L. Rev. 67, 79 (1988); Jeffrey J. Delaney, Note, "Specific Intent, Substituted Judgment and Best Interests: A Nationwide Analysis of an Individual's Right to Die," 11 Pace L. Rev. 565, 571–89 (1991).

23. See In re *Spring*, 405 N.E.2d 115, 119 (Mass. 1980); *Superintendent of Belchertown State School v. Saikewicz*, 370 N.E.2d 417, 431 (Mass. 1977); Delaney, supra note 22, at 592–616.

24. See *Kennedy Hosp. v. Bludworth*, 452 So. 2d at 926; James F. Childress, "Dying Patients: Who's in Control?" 17 Law, Med. & Health Care 227, 229 (1989); Sandra H. Johnson, "From Medicalization to Legalization to Politicization: O'Connor, Cruzan and Refusal of Treatment in the 1990's," 21 Conn. L. Rev. 685, 692–93 (1989).

25. See, e.g., *Gray v. Romeo*, 697 F. Supp. 580, 587 (D.R.I. 1988); In re *Guardianship of Browning*, 543 So. 2d 258, 267 (Fla. Dist. Ct. App. 1989), aff'd, 568 So. 2d 4 (Fla. 1990); In re *Peter*, 529 A.2d 419, 423 (N.J. 1987).

26. *Thompson v. Oklahoma*, 108 S. Ct. 2687, 2693 n.23 (1988).

27. See *Conroy*, 486 A.2d at 1231: "[I]n the absence of adequate proof of the patient's wishes, it is naive to pretend that the right of self-determination serves as the basis for substituted decision-making." See also *Guardianship of Browning*, 543 So. 2d at 267, 269, 272–73.

28. "[T]he state must recognize the dignity and worth of such a person [a PVS patient] and afford to that person the same panoply of rights and choices it recognizes in competent persons." *Brophy*, 497 N.E.2d at 634. See also Tracy L. Merrit, "Equality for the Elderly Incompetent: A Proposal for Dignified Death," 39 Stan. L. Rev. 689, 704 (1987).

29. See *Youngberg v. Romeo*, 457 U.S. 307, 317 (1982).

3. Choosing the Best Format in Light of the Statutory Framework for Advance Directives

1. A helpful state-by-state summary is provided in Evan R. Collins, Jr., & Doron Weber, *The Complete Guide to Living Wills* (1991), a paperback published by the Society for the Right

to Die (now known as Choice in Dying). That same organization also publishes a compendium of state advance directive legislation, under the title *Refusal of Treatment Legislation*.

2. For citations to living-will type laws in 43 states, see George J. Alexander, "Time for a New Law on Health Care Advance Directives," 42 Hastings L.J. 755, 758 nn.14–15 (1991). For a chronicle of the development of living-will laws, see Marguerite A. Chapman, "The Uniform Rights of the Terminally Ill Act: Too Little, Too Late?" 42 Ark. L. Rev. 319, 322–49 (1989).

3. Concerning the forms often contained in living-will laws, see Craig P. Goldman, "Revising Iowa's Life-Sustaining Procedures Act: Creating a Practical Guide to Living Wills in Iowa," 76 Iowa L. Rev. 1137, 1153–54 (1991).

4. See generally Pat M. McCarrick, Scope Note No. 2, "Living Wills and Durable Powers of Attorney: Advance Directive Legislation and Issues," Kennedy Institute of Ethics (1990); Nancy M. P. King, *Making Sense of Advance Directives* (1991); Evan R. Collins & Doron Weber, *The Complete Guide to Living Wills* (1991); Alan Meisel, *The Right to Die* §§ 12.1 to .10 (1989); Elizabeth D. McLean, Note, "Living Will Statutes In Light of *Cruzan v. Director, Missouri Department of Health*: Ensuring That a Patient's Wishes Will Prevail," 40 Emory L.J. 1305 (1991); Craig K. Van Ess, Note, "Living Wills and Alternatives to Living Wills: A Proposal—The Supreme Trust," 26 Val. U. L. Rev. 567 (1992).

5. See White, "Living Will Statutes: Good Public Policy?" in *Advance Directives in Medicine* 46–47 (Andrew Hackler et al., eds., 1989); Sandra H. Johnson, "Sequential Domination, Autonomy and Living Wills," 9 W. New Eng. L. Rev. 113, 120–22 (1987).

6. See David Orentlicher, "Advance Medical Directives," 263 JAMA 2365, 2367 (1990) (reporting about a 1988 survey conducted for the A.M.A.); Times Mirror Center for the People and the Press, *Reflections of the Times: The Right to Die* 19 (June 1990) (reporting on a poll indicating that 14% of all adults and 24% of people over 64 had a living will); Gene C. Anderson et al., "Living Wills: Do Nurses and Physicians Have Them?" 86 Am. J. Nursing 271 (1986). A December 1991 report indicated that somewhere between 4% and 24% of adults have signed living wills. Susan M. Wolf et al., "Sources of Concern About the Patient Self-Determination Act," 325 New Eng. J. Med. 1666, 1667 (1991).

7. Alexander M. Capron, "The Burden of Decision," 20:3 Hastings Cent. Rep. 36 (June 1990).

8. A 1990 poll of 1,213 adults nationwide showed that 28% think that little or no attention is ultimately paid to a patient's prior instructions. See Times Mirror Center, supra note 6, at 1.

9. Joel M. Zinberg, "Decisions for the Dying: An Empirical Study of Physicians' Responses to Advance Directives," 13 Vt. L. Rev. 445, 475, 477–79, 491 (1989); David A. Peters, "Advance Medical Directives: The Case for the Durable Power of Attorney for Health Care," 8:3 J. Leg. Med. 437, 460 (1987); Elizabeth G. Patterson, "Planning for Health Care Using Living Wills and Durable Powers of Attorney," 42 S.C. L. Rev. 525, 549 (1991).

10. Concerning physicians' fear of liability as an influence on extending life-preserving medical intervention, see Lawrence J. Nelson & Ronald E. Cranford, "Legal Advice, Moral Paralysis, and the Death of Samuel Linares," 17 Law, Med. & Health Care 316 (1989); B. D. Colen, *The Essential Guide to a Living Will* 14–16 (1991).

11. See James F. Childress, "Ethical Criteria for Procuring and Distributing Organs for Transplantation," in *Organ Transplantation Policy* 91–92 (James Blumstein & Frank Sloan eds., 1989).

12. Patient Self-Determination Act of 1990 (PSDA), Pub. L. No. 101-508 § 4206, codified at 42 U.S.C.A. § 1395cc (West 1992).

13. See generally Kelly C. Mulholland, Note, "Protecting the Right to Die: The Patient Self-Determination Act of 1990," 28 Harv. J. on Legis. 609 (1991); Susan Wolf et al., supra note 6.

14. Living-will statutes tend to be "riddled with restrictions presumably attributable to excessive caution and lack of experience." Alexander, supra note 2, at 766. See also Marni J. Lerner, Note, "State Natural Death Acts: Illusory Protection of Individuals' Life-Sustaining Treatment Decisions," 29 Harv. J. on Legis. 175 (1992).

15. See Meisel, supra note 4, § 11.12; Gregory Gelfand, "Living Will Statutes: The First Decade," 1987 Wis. L. Rev. 737, 740–44; Lerner, supra note 14, at 188–97.

16. Robert M. Veatch, *Death, Dying and the Biological Revolution* 159 (2d ed. 1990).

17. See Idaho Code § 39-4503 (3) (1991); Md. Health-Gen. Code Ann. 5-601 (g) (1990); Tenn. Code Ann. § 32-11-103 (g) (Michie Supp. 1991); Lerner, supra note 14, at 189; Susan R. Martyn & Lynn B. Jacobs, "Legislating Advance Directives for the Terminally Ill: The Living Will and Durable Powers of Attorney," 63 Neb. L. Rev. 779, 779–91 (1984). The wording is sometimes "incurable or irreversible," but the terms are read conjunctively. See N.D. Cent. Code § 23-06.4-02 (7) (1991); cf. Uniform Rights of the Terminally Ill Act § 1 (9), 9B U.L.A. 612 (1987 & Supp. 1992) [hereinafter URTIA].

18. See In re *Spring*, 405 N.E.2d 115, 118 (Mass. 1980); In re *Lydia E. Hall Hosp.*, 455 N.Y.S. 706, 708 (Sup. Ct. 1982).

19. In a number of jurisdictions, the living-will statutes have been amended to include permanent unconsciousness as a point at which life sustaining care may be withdrawn. But this does not help patients with chronic debilitated conditions and degenerative diseases.

20. Many commentators have recognized this truism. See, e.g., Meisel, supra note 4, at § 11.12. A few states have amended their living-will statutes to clarify that a condition is "terminal" if it would cause death in the absence of the disputed medical intervention. See Mont. Code Ann. § 50-9-102 (14) (1991); Ohio Rev. Code Ann. § 2133.01 (AA) (Anderson Supp. 1991); Iowa Code Ann. § 144A.2 (8) (West 1989); S.C. Code Ann. § 44-77-20 (4) (Law Co-op Supp. 1991).

21. In re *Greenspan*, 558 N.E.2d 1194, 1203–04 (Ill. 1990).

22. Id. See also In re *Guardianship of Browning*, 568 So. 2d 4, 17 (Fla. 1990) (interpreting Florida's living-will statute in a similar fashion).

23. See, e.g., Iowa Code Annn. § 144A.2 (8) (West 1989); Tex. Health & Safety Code Ann. § 672.002 (6) (West Pamph. 1992); Ohio Rev. Code. Ann. § 2133.01 (AA) (Anderson Supp. 1991); Mo. Ann. Stat. § 459.010 (3), (6) (Vernon Supp. 1992); URTIA, supra note 17, § 1 (9) (Supp. 1992); Daniel D. King et al., "Where Death Begins While Life Continues," 31 So. Tex. L. Rev. 145, 180–81 (1990); Lerner, supra note 14, at 191–94. See also *Guardianship of Browning*, 568 So. 2d at 17 (achieving a similar result by judicial interpretation).

24. Collins & Weber, supra note 1, at 7.

25. See In re *Peter*, 529 A.2d 419, 425 (N.J. 1987).

26. See *Satz v. Perlmutter*, 362 So. 2d 160 (Fla. Dist. Ct. App. 1978), aff'd, 379 So. 2d 359 (Fla. 1980).

27. See generally Philip G. Peters Jr., "The State's Interest in the Preservation of Life: From *Quinlan* to *Cruzan*," 50 Ohio St. L.J. 891 (1989).

28. See Yale Kamisar, "When Is There a Constitutional "Right to Die"? When Is There No Constitutional "Right to Live"?" 25 Ga. L. Rev., 1203, 1211–12 (1991); Lerner, supra note 14, at 186.

29. See White, supra note 5, at 46–47. Johnson, supra note 5, at 120–22.

30. Ariz. Rev. Stat. Ann. § 36-3201 (4) (Supp. 1991); Wyo. Stat. § 35-22-101 (a)(iii) (1991); Wis. Stat. Ann. § 154.03 (Interim Supp. 1992) (allowing for withdrawal of artificial nutrition and hydration); Me. Rev. Stat. Ann. tit 18A, § 5-701 (b)(4) (West Supp. 1991).

31. Tenn. Code Ann. § 32-11-103 (5) (Michie Supp. 1991); Okla. Stat. Ann. tit. 63, § 3103 (West Supp. 1992); N.H. Rev. Stat. Ann. § 137-H:3 (Supp. 1991); Colo. Rev. Stat. Ann. § 15-18-104 (2.5)(A) (West Supp. 1991); Idaho Code § 39-4504 (Supp. 1991); Fl.

Stat. Ann. § 765.075 (1)(a) (West Supp. 1991); Haw. Rev. Stat. Ann. § 327 D-4 (Michie 1991); Md. Health-Gen. Code § 5-605 (Michie 1990) as interpreted by 73 Op. Att'y Gen. (Oct. 17 1988); S.C. Code Ann. § 44-77-20 (2) (Law Co-op Supp. 1991); Ore. Rev. Stat. Ann. § 127.580 (1990) (elective provision is in DPOA-HC law).

32. Ga. Code Ann. § 31-32-2 (5)(A) (Michie 1991); Mo. Ann. Stat. § 459.010 (3) (Vernon Supp. 1992); Ind. Code Ann. § 16-8-11-4 (West 1992); Iowa Code Ann. § 144A.2 (5) (West 1989); Utah Code Ann. § 75-2-1103 (6) (b) (Michie Supp. 1991); Ky. Rev. Stat. Ann. § 311.624 (5)(b) (Michie Supp. 1990). Another statute is silent as to whether artificial nutrition and hydration can be foregone, but it places on the physician the responsibility to provide any nutrition and hydration needed to alleviate pain; see Mont. Code Ann. § 50-9-202 (2) (Michie 1991).

33. Ill. Rev. Stat., ch. 110 1/2, para. 702 (d) (Smith-Hurd Supp. 1992).

34. N.D. Cent. Code § 23-06.4-07 (3) (1991). For assessment of the living-will laws regarding nutrition, see Lerner, supra note 14, at 199–204.

35. E.g., Colo. Rev. Stat. Ann. § 15-18-103 (7) (West Supp. 1991); R.I. Gen. Laws § 23-4.11-2 (d) (Supp. 1991); Tex. Health & Safety Code Ann. § 672.002 (6) (West Pamph. 1992).

36. See, e.g., Va. Code Ann. § 54.1-2982, 2984 (Michie 1991); Fla. Stat. Ann. § 765.05 (1) (West Supp. 1992); R.I. Gen. Laws § 23-4.11-2 (d), (3) (Supp. 1991); S.C. Code. Ann. § 44-77-50 (Law. Co-op Supp. 1991); URTIA, supra note 17, §§ 1 (4), 2 (B) (Supp. 1992).

37. This language has been criticized as delegating uninformed discretion to those ultimately in charge of terminal care for an incompetent patient. See Thomas J. Marzen, "The Uniform Rights of the Terminally Ill Act: A Critical Analysis," 1 Issues in L. & Med. 441, 459, 470 (1986); C. Everett Koop and Edward R. Grant, "The "Small Beginnings" of Euthanasia: Examining The Erosion of Legal Prohibitions Against Mercy-Killing," 2 Notre Dame J.L. Ethics & Pub. Pol'y 585, 609, 615 (1986). See also Chapman, supra note 2, at 388; George J. Annas & Leonard H. Glantz, "The Right of Elderly Patients to Refuse Life-Sustaining Treatment," 64 Milbank Q. Supp. 2, at 95, 142–43 (1986) (contending that the formulation has no practical application because it would only forbid treatment which would be medically inappropriate anyway).

38. See Molly C. Dyke, Note, "A Matter of Life and Death: Pregnancy Clauses in Living Will Statutes," 70 B.U. L. Rev. 867 (1990); Goldman, supra note 3, at 1157–59.

39. See Alexander, supra note 2, at 764.

40. See Fla. Stat. Ann. § 765.06 (West 1986); R.I. Gen. Laws § 23-4.11-4 (a) (Supp. 1991); Iowa Code Ann. § 144A.4 (1) (West 1989).

41. Annas & Glantz, supra note 37, at 143; see also Goldman, supra note 3, at 1161–62.

42. New Jersey Commission on Legal and Ethical Problems in the Delivery of Health Care, *Problems and Approaches in Health Care Decision Making* 106 (1990) [hereinafter Report of the New Jersey Bioethics Commission]; David S. Rosettenstein, "Living Wills in the U.S.: The Role of the Family," 4 Conn. Prob. L.J. 27, 38–39 (1988).

43. See Chapman, supra note 2, at 357.

44. See, e.g., Utah Code Ann. § 75-2-1108 (Michie Supp. 1991); cf. N.Y. Pub. Health Law § 2985 (1) (Consol. Supp. 1992).

45. The issue of how to relate to the expressions of incompetent patients is considered further in chapter 5 on administration and interpretation of advance directives.

46. Capron, supra note 7, at 41.

47. See California Medical Association, Committee on Evolving Trends in Society Affecting Life, "What Health Care Providers Should Know About Foregoing Life-sustaining Treatment," Calif. Physician, Nov. 1989, at 67; Report of the New Jersey Bioethics Commission, supra note 42, at 89–90.

48. See Peters, supra note 9, at 451. The advocacy role of a health-care agent is considered in more depth in chapter 7, which deals with enforcement of advance directives.

49. See sources cited supra note 9; see also New York State Task Force on Life and the Law, *Life-Sustaining Treatment: Making Decisions and Appointing a Health Care Agent* 77 (1987).

50. See Orentlicher, supra note 6, at 2365, 2366; Patterson, supra note 9, at 571.

51. Ben A. Rich, "The Values History: A New Standard of Care," 40 Emory L.J. 1009, 119 n.38 (1991) (provides citations for 34 DPOA-HC laws); see also Cathaleen A. Roach, "Paradox and Pandora's Box: The Tragedy of Current Right-to-Die Jurisprudence," 25 U. Mich. J. Law Reform 133, 162 (1991).

52. See *Guardianship of Browning*, 568 So. 2d at 4; In re *Westchester County Medical Center*, 531 N.E.2d 607, 612 n.2 (N.Y. 1988); *Peter*, 529 A.2d at 426.

53. See, e.g., Cal. Civ. Code § 2430 (b) (West Supp. 1992); Idaho Code 39-4505 (Supp. 1991); Kan. Stat. Ann. § 58-629 (Supp. 1991); Nev. Rev. Stat. Ann. § 449.830 (Michie 1991); Tex. Civ. Prac. & Remedies § 135.002 (a) (West Supp. 1992).

54. N.Y. Pub. Health Law § 2982 (1) (Consol. Supp. 1992).

55. Ohio Rev. Code Ann. § 1337.13 (B)(1), (E) (Anderson Supp. 1991); Ore. Rev. Stat. §§ 127.540, .580 (1990); Tenn. Code Ann. § 34-6-204 (d) (1991); Fla. Stat. Ann. § 765.05 (2) (West 1986).

56. Ky. Rev. Stat. Ann. § 311.978 (1) (Michie Supp. 1990).

57. See, e.g., Md. Health-General Code Ann. § 20-107 (d)(1) (Supp. 1991); Utah Code Ann. § 75-2-1105 (2) (Supp. 1991); Va. Code Ann. § 37.1-134.4 (1991); Nev. Rev. Stat. Ann. § 449.626 (2) (1991); Veatch, supra note 16, at 163–64. See Judith Areen, "Advance Directives Under State Law and Judicial Decisions," 19 Law, Med. & Health Care 91, 97–98 (1991); David M. Schultz, Note, "Procedures and Limitations for Removal of Life-Sustaining Treatment from Incompetent Patients," 34 St. Louis U. L.J. 277, 279–80 (1990).

58. See Conn. Gen. Stat. § 19a-571 (West Supp. 1991); Fla. Stat. Ann. § 765.07 (West 1986 & Supp. 1992); Iowa Code § 144A.7 (West 1989); Me. Rev. Stat. Ann. tit. 18A, § 5-707 (West Supp. 1991); Nev. Rev. Stat. Ann. § 449.626 (Michie 1991).

59. Richard F. Uhlmann et al. "Physicians' and Spouses' Predictions of Elderly Patients' Resuscitation Preferences," 43 J. Gerontology: Medical Sciences M115, M117–20 (1988). The study analyzed the wishes of 258 elderly, chronically ill persons compared to the assumptions of surrounding physicians and family. The results suggested that "surrogate resuscitation decisions for elderly patients would often not approximate patients' wishes, even when surrogate decisionmakers appear to know the patients well and believe they are exercising substituted judgment." Id. at M120.

60. See King, supra note 4, at 91.

61. Susan J. Nanovic, Note, "The Living Will: Preservation of the Right-to-Die Demands Clarity and Consistency," 95 Dick. L. Rev. 209, 229 (1990).

62. The possibility of justifiable deviations from the substantive terms of an advance directive is addressed in chapter 5 dealing with administration of an advance directive.

63. Ill. Ann. Stat., ch. 110 1/2, para. 804-11 (Smith-Hurd Supp. 1992).

64. The only deviation from this pattern comes in a few states whose living-will laws do not give conclusive effect to the declarant's instructions. See Conn. Gen. Stat. Ann. § 199-571 (West Supp. 1992); Nev. Rev. Stat. Ann. § 449-640 (1) (Michie 1991): N.D. Cent. Code § 23-06.4-04 (Michie 1990); Ind. Code Ann. § 16-8-11-11 (6) (West 1992).

65. Even a health-care provider with conscientious objections to the declarant's wishes must either implement the living will or seek transfer of the patient to another provider. The impact of health-care providers' scruples will be discussed in chapter 5, which deals with administration of advance directives.

66. Not long ago, I published a suggested advance directive. See Norman L. Cantor, "My Annotated Living Will," 18 Law, Med. & Health Care 114 (1990). In that publication, I called the document a *living will*. I've changed my mind, at least with regard to jurisdictions with significant statutory limitations on the scope of living wills. In such instances, I would now recommend labeling the document a *nonstatutory advance directive* or *instruction directive*, unless the limitations contained in the relevant living-will law do not interfere with the particular declarant's wishes.

67. For endorsement of the idea of nonstatutory instruction directives, see King, supra note 4, at 9–10, 17, 97–98; Patterson, supra note 9, at 538–40.

68. Idaho Code § 39-4508 (1985); Iowa Code Ann. § 144A.11 (5)(1989); Fla. Stat. Ann. § 765.15 (West 1986); Cal. Health and Safety Code § 7195.5 (d) (West Supp. 1992); Gelfand, supra note 15, at 784 n.202; see also Lerner, supra note 14, at 191 n.72.

69. Chapters 1 and 2 already explained the great extent to which American jurisprudence has embraced self-determination in the context of shaping medical intervention in the dying process.

70. In re *Finsterbach* (N.Y. Sup. Ct., Oneida County 1990).

71. See In re *Gardner*, 534 A.2d 947, 952 n.3 (Me. 1987); *Camp v. White*, 510 So. 2d 166, 169–70; and cases cited in Tribe, *American Constitutional Law* § 15-12, at 1370 (2d Ed. 1988). Cf. *Bouvia v. Superior Court*, 179 Cal. App. 3d 1127, 1139–40, 225 Cal. Rptr. 297, 302–03 (1986) (regarding the import of a preservation of rights provision in a living-will law).

72. For comments supporting such a possible interpretation of legislative intent, see Report of the New Jersey Bioethics Commission, supra note 42, at 112–13; Prefatory Note and Comments to Section 2 of URTIA, supra note 17, § 2 (noting that the Act does not in any way affect authority under existing law). See also In re *Guardianship of Browning*, 543 So. 2d 258, 265 (Fla. App. 1989), aff'd 568 So. 2d 4 (Fla. 1990).

73. See Collins & Weber, supra note 1, at 45–46, 66, 87; King, supra note 4, at 102–03.

74. *Cruzan v. Harmon*, 760 S. W.2d 408, 419–20 (Mo. 1988), aff'd sub. nom., *Cruzan v. Director, Missouri Dept. of Health*, 110 S. Ct. 2841 (1990).

75. *Cruzan v. Harmon*, 760 S. W.2d at 420, 426. In December 1990, though, a Missouri trial court approved the removal of artificial nutrition from Ms. Cruzan. Missouri had adopted a DPOA-HC law permitting the removal of artificial nutrition in some circumstances.

76. *Couture v. Couture*, 549 N.E.2d 571 (Ohio Ct. App. 1989).

77. Ohio Rev. Code 1337.13 (B)(3) (1989).

78. *Couture*, 541 N.E.2d at 576. The same argument was accepted by the dissenting opinion in In re *Estate of Longeway*, 549 N.E.2d 292, 307–14 (Ill. 1989). In Illinois, however, the supposed public policy was more murky, since the DPOA-HC authorized cessation of nutrition while the living-will law did not. See *Greenspan*, 558 N.E.2d at 1200–04, and In re *Lawrance*, 579 N.E.2d 32, 40 (Ind. 1991). There have been post-Couture developments in Ohio. See *Anderson v. St. Francis Hosp.*, slip op. at 6 (Ohio Ct. Common Pleas 1989).

79. In my estimation, a careful analysis of the U.S. Supreme Court's 1990 Cruzan decision does not undercut that judicial trend. But see James Bopp, Jr., & Daniel Avila, "The Due Process 'Right to Life' in *Cruzan* and its Impact on 'Right-to-Die Law'," 53 Pitt. L. Rev. 193 (1991).

80. See Lerner, supra note 14, at 205–06.

81. See *Guardianship of Browning*, 568 So. 2d at 4; *Rasmussen v. Fleming*, 741 P.2d 674 (Ariz. 1987); In re *Crabtree*, No. 86-0031 (Haw. Fam. Ct., 1st Cir., April 26, 1990).

82. E.g., In re *Conroy*, 486 A.2d 1209, 1229 (N.J. 1985); *Brophy v. New England Sinai Hosp.*, 497 N.E.2d 626, 633 (Mass. 1986).

83. See *Guardianship of Browning*, 568 So. 2d at 9; *State v. McAfee*, 385 S.E.2d 651, 652 (Ga. 1989); In re *Drabick*, 245 Cal. Rptr. 840, 860 (Dist. Ct. App. 1988), cert. denied, 488 U.S. 958 (1989).

4. Drafting Advance Instructions

1. Charles P. Sabatino, *Health Care Powers of Attorney* 3 (A.B.A. pamphlet 1990) (distributed by the American Association of Retired Persons) [hereinafter *ABA Power of Attorney*]. The formula is offered in the A.B.A. document as an option, not as a recommended provision.

2. Concerning the multiplicity of factors which might influence the preparation of an advance directive, see, e.g., New Jersey Commission on Legal and Ethical Problems in the Delivery of Health Care, *Problems and Approaches in Health Care Decisionmaking* 87–88 (1990); Nancy R. Zweibel, "Measuring Quality of Life Near the End of Life," 260 JAMA 839, 840 (1988); Stuart J. Eisendrath & Albert R. Jonsen, "The Living Will; Help or Hindrance," 249 JAMA 2054 (1983); Linda L. Emanuel & Ezekiel J. Emanuel, "The Medical Directive: A New Comprehensive Advance Care Document," 261 JAMA 3288 (1989).

3. Joanne Lynn, "Why I Don't Have a Living Will," 19 Law, Med. & Health Care 101 (1991).

4. Id. at 101–04.

5. Letter from Ellen Friedland, Esq., December 1991.

6. See Robert S. Olick, "Approximating Informed Consent and Fostering Communication: The Anatomy of an Advance Directive," 2 J. Clinical Ethics 181, 185 (1991). Olick describes there how Professor George Annas recommends that the health-care agent receive a private letter from the principal, a letter to be disclosed and used only if necessary to convince health-care providers to cooperate with the agent.

7. Even Dr. Lynn advises that written instructions might be useful if the declarant's wishes deviate from what common medical approaches would normally dictate. Lynn, supra note 4, at 104.

8. See generally, Nancy M.P. King, *Making Sense of Advance Directives* 67, 112–13 (1991).

9. Concern for Dying recently merged with the Society for the Right to Die to form an organization known as Choice in Dying.

10. Quoted in Eisendrath & Jonsen, supra note 2, at 2055.

11. See Leflar, "A Framework for Legal Analysis of Advance Directives in Health Care," in *Advance Directives in Medicine* 60 (Andrew Hackler et al. eds., 1989)

12. See supra note 9.

13. An identical form appears in Pat M. McCarrick, "Living Wills & Durable Powers of Attorney: Advance Directive Legislation and Issues," Scope Note No. 2 (Kennedy Institute of Ethics 1990).

14. For criticism of the vagueness of many short-form living wills, see, e.g., King, supra note 8, at 10–11; Robert M. Veatch, *Death, Dying and the Biological Revolution* 149–52 (rev. ed. 1989); Olick, supra note 6, at 183.

15. See, e.g., Va. Code Ann. § 54.1-2984 (Michie 1991); Ariz. Rev. Stat. Ann. § 36-32-2 (Supp. 1991); Idaho Code § 39-4504 (Supp. 1991).

16. See, e.g., Me. Rev. Stat. Ann. tit. 18-A, § 5-702 (b) (West Supp. 1991); Uniform Rights of the Terminally Ill Act § 2(b), in 9B U.L.A. Supp. 1992, at 101.

17. Veatch, supra note 14, at 154–55.

18. *ABA Power of Attorney*, supra note 1, at 3.

19. *Evans v. Bellevue Hosp.* (N.Y. Sup. Ct. 1987), reported in N.Y.L.J., July 28, 1987, at 1, 11.

20. King, supra note 8, at 139–40; B. D. Colen, *The Essential Guide to a Living Will* 26, 117 (1991); Evan R. Collins, Jr., & Doron Weber, *The Complete Guide to Living Wills* 76

(1991); Ben A. Rich, "The Values History: A New Standard of Care," 40 Emory L.J. 1109, 1121–22 (1991).

21. Colen recommends a videotape as an additional index of the declarant's seriousness and determination. Colen, supra note 20, at 131–37.

22. See Collins & Weber, supra note 20, at 22; Elizabeth G. Patterson, "Planning for Health Care Using Living Wills and Durable Powers of Attorney: A Guide for the South Carolina Attorney," 42 S.C. L. Rev. 525, 579 (1991). Veatch, supra note 14, at 152.

23. For another commentary explaining why it is usually pointless to specify types of medical intervention in an advance directive, see Allan S. Brett, "Limitations of Listing Specific Medical Interventions in Advance Directives," 266 JAMA 825, 826–27 (1991).

24. See Colen, supra note 20, at 128–29. Ms. Colen explains that writing, playing guitar, and photography are the pursuits which make life worthwhile for her, so that permanent loss of mental acuity would be personally intolerable.

25. See Collins & Weber, supra note 20, at 64.

26. New Jersey Commission on Legal and Ethical Problems in Medicine, *Advance Directives for Health Care: Planning Ahead for Important Health Care Decisions* (1991); see also Appendix C.

27. Norman L. Cantor, "My Annotated Living Will," 18 Law, Med. & Health Care 114 (1990).

28. Upon reflection, I might add a sentence indicating that the directive is aimed at binding any ultimate decision maker on my behalf, in the event that neither designated agent were available. Such a provision ought to be unnecessary, for its content ought to be self-evident; but it might be added out of an excess of caution.

29. For a more detailed enumeration of a health-care agent's powers, see the sample power of attorney for health care drafted by Charles Sabatino, *ABA Power of Attorney*, supra note 1, at 1–2. A version of that useful sample document is provided as Appendix B.

30. See Ronald E. Cranford, "Neurological Syndromes and Prolonged Survival: When Can Artificial Nutrition and Hydration be Forgone?" 19 Law, Med. & Health Care 13, 19–20 (1991); Eric J. Cassell, "Recognizing Suffering," 21:3 Hastings Cent. Rep. 24, 26–27 (May 1991).

31. See Brett, supra note 23, at 826; Alan B. Handler, "Individual Worth," 17 Hofstra L. Rev. 493 (1989).

32. In an earlier version of my advance directive, I included a sentence providing a "standard of proof" for my designated agent. I stated: "In line with my normal preference and respect for life, any such terminal decision should be made only when that decision is *clearly* in my best interests." Upon further reflection, I've dispensed with that admonition. I am apprehensive that the word "clearly" would inhibit my agent in sound administration of the document. The substantive terms of my advance directive indicate that life-preserving treatment is to be withheld only when I have reached a status of extreme debilitation. Good-faith implementation of those instructions should foreclose any premature withdrawal of life support. Good-faith implementation is the minimum standard that the law would demand in any event, and I see no need to specify any further standard of proof.

33. See A.M.A. Council on Scientific Affairs and the Council on Ethical and Judicial Affairs, "Persistent Vegetative State and the Decision to Withdraw or Withhold Life Support," 263 JAMA 426 (1990); Ronald E. Cranford "The Persistent Vegetative State: The Medical Reality," 18:1 Hastings Cent. Rep. 27 (Feb. 1988).

34. Nonlife-extending palliative care should always be provided. Sometimes, though, a preventive medical measure may itself diminish a patient's self-defined dignity. For example, a tracheotomy designed to prevent choking in a patient who has lost a gag reflex can have negative consequences for the communication abilities of the patient. See Eisendrath & Jonsen, supra note 2, at 2056.

35. Alan Lieberson, letter to the editor, New York Times, Dec. 21, 1991, at A18.

36. King, supra note 8, at 90; Olick, supra note 6, at 183; Linda Emanuel, "PSDA in the Clinic," 21:5 Hastings Cent. Rep. S6 (Oct. 1991).

37. After an advance directive is prepared, further discussion must ensue. That is, the declarant ought to discuss the contents of his or her directive both with any agent designated in the document and with any physician likely to be attending during a subsequent dying process.

38. See Rich, supra note 20, at 1141–43, 1155–58; Olick, supra note 6, at 182–83.

39. Pam Lambert et al., "The Values History: An Innovation in Surrogate Medical Decision Making," 18 Law, Med. & Health Care 202 (1990); see also David J. Doukas & Laurence B. McCullough, "Assessing the Values History of the Elderly Patient Regarding Critical and Chronic Care," in Handbook of Geriatric Assessment 111–25 (J. Gallo et al. eds., 1988).

40. Not surprisingly, the compilers of the values history recommend preparation of a separate advance directive. They view their values history merely as an informational tool to assist future interpretation of a separate advance directive. Lambert, supra note 39, at 210; see also Collins & Weber, supra note 20, at 104–05.

41. Emanuel & Emanuel, supra note 2, at 3288, 3290.

42. Id. at 3290.

43. See Ezekiel J. Emanuel & Linda L. Emanuel, "Living wills: Past, Present, and Future," 1 J. Clinical Ethics 9 (1990).

44. Veatch, supra note 14, at 152.

45. See Collins & Weber, supra note 20, at 52; see also Appendix B.

46. See, e.g., Ala. Code § 22-8A-7 (1990); Ark. Code Ann. § 20-17-208 (Michie 1991); Iowa Code Ann. § 144A.9 (2) (West 1989).

47. Colen, supra note 20, at 130.

5. Interpretation and Administration of Advance Directives

1. These include living-will forms distributed by various right-to-die organizations as well as documents circulated as either required or suggested forms pursuant to living-will statutes.

2. Allan S. Brett, "Limitations of Listing Specific Medical Interventions in Advance Directives," 266 JAMA 825, 826 (1991).

3. An assessment of suffering is itself a herculean task. See Eric J. Cassell, "Recognizing Suffering," 21:3 Hastings Cent. Rep. 24 (May-June 1991).

4. See Nancy M.P. King, Making Sense of Advance Directives 58–60 (1991) (rejecting any heightened standard of capacity for the making of an advance directive).

5. This does not mean that compliance with the declarant's wishes is the exclusive guideline. There are a few jurisdictions which indicate that the administrator of a living will need only "consider" or "give great weight" to the declarant's wishes. See Nev. Rev. Stat. Ann. § 449.640 (1) (Michie 1991) (immunity to physicians who "give great weight to the declaration" but "consider other factors. . . . "); Conn. Gen. Stat. Ann. § 19a-571 (a) (West Supp. 1992) (immunity to physicians who used "best medical judgment [and] . . . considered the patient's wishes"); Ind. Code Ann. § 16-8-11 (f) (West 1992); N.D. Cent. Code § 23-06.4-04 (1991).

6. Haw. Rev. Stat. § 327D-19 (1991) (family court may be petitioned for appointment of a guardian for declarant whose living will is not being followed); Del. Code Ann. tit. 16, § 2506 (a) (1983); Me. Rev. Stat. Ann. tit. 18-A, § 5-707 (f) (West Supp. 1992).

7. See, e.g., Brophy v. New England Sinai Hosp., Inc., 497 N.E.2d 626, 639 (Mass. 1986); In re Gardner, 534 A.2d 947 (Me. 1987).

8. See, e.g., Elizabeth D. McLean, Note, "Living Will Statutes in Light of Cruzan v. Director, Missouri Department of Health: Ensuring That a Patient's Wishes Will Prevail," 40 Emory L.J. 1305, 1316–17 (1991).

9. See, e.g., Cal. Civ. Code § 2433 (a) (West Supp. 1992); Idaho Code § 39-4505 (Supp. 1991); N.Y. Pub. Health Law § 2982 (2) (Supp. 1992); Miss. Code Ann. § 41-41-163 (Supp. 1992); Ore. Rev. Stat. Ann. § 127.550 (1)(b) (1990); R.I. Gen. Laws § 23-4.10-2 (1989); Nev. Rev. Stat. Ann. § 449.830 (Michie 1991). Not all DPOA-HC laws confer such expansive authority on an appointed agent. For example, West Virginia confines the agent's authority to withdraw life-sustaining care to situations where medical intervention offers "no medical hope of benefit." W. Va. Code § 16-30A-4 (c)(6) (1991).

10. See Michael P. Kane, "The Application of the Substitution of Judgment Doctrine in Planning an Incompetent's Estate," 16 Vill. L. Rev. 132, 133 (1970); In re *Turner*, 305 N.Y.S.2d 387, 389 (Sup. Ct. 1969).

11. In re *Peter*, 529 A.2d 419, 426 (N.J. 1987); In re *Guardianship of L.W.*, 482 N.W.2d 60, 70 (Wis. 1992); See Craig K. Van Ess, Note, "Living Wills and Alternatives to Living Wills: A Proposal—The Supreme Trust," 26 Val. U.L. Rev. 567, 584 (1992).

12. Robert S. Olick, "Approximating Informed Consent and Fostering Communication: The Anatomy of an Advance Directive," 2:3 J. Clinical Ethics 181, 186 (1991).

13. See Mich. Stat. Ann. § 27.5496 (7)(f), (9) (Callaghan 1992); Van Ess, supra note 11, at 588 n.125; N.J. Stat. Ann. §§ 26:2H-63(d), -64(b) (West Supp. 1992).

14. Several jurisdictions beside Missouri impose a clear and convincing evidence standard when an incompetent patient's life-sustaining care is withdrawn in reliance on the patient's prior instructions. See In re *Westchester County Medical Center*, 531 N.E.2d 607, 613 (N.Y. 1988); *Gardner*, 534 A.2d at 952; In re *Longeway*, 549 N.E.2d 292, 300 (Ill. 1989). It's not clear, though, that these jurisdictions demand clear-cut prior instructions as the exclusive predicate for withdrawal of life support. Neither *Longeway* nor *Gardner*, for example, determines whether a patient's best interests might be used as a rationale for withdrawing life support in the absence of prior instructions. See *Longeway*, 549 N.E.2d at 300; *Gardner*, 534 A.2d at 952. And none of the above three cases involves action by an appointed health-care agent. A DPOA-HC type statute might well have changed the result in New York and Illinois. See N.Y. Pub. Health Law § 2982 (2) (McKinney Supp. 1992) (1990 law allowing agent to make all decisions without clear-cut evidence, except withholding of artificial nutrition and hydration).

15. *Browning v. Herbert*, 568 So. 2d 4 (Fla. 1990).

16. See In re *Conroy*, 486 A.2d 1209, 1230–31 (N.J. 1985); Allen E. Buchanan & Dan W. Brock, *Deciding for Others* 119–22 (1989).

17. See N.J. Stat. Ann. § 26:2H-57(b)(1) (West Supp. 1992).

18. Expressions inconsistent with an advance directive's contents might also be uttered *after* the declarant has become incompetent. The appropriate status of such post-competence expressions is considered later in this chapter.

19. See, e.g., Louise Harmon, "Falling Off the Vine: Legal Fictions and the Doctrine of Substituted Judgment," 100 Yale L.J. 1, 38 (1990); Larry R. Churchill, "Trust, Autonomy, and Advance Directives," 28 J. Religion and Health 175 (1989).

20. However, evidence of a patient's altruism must be used with caution. Arguably, the interests of others (family, friends, or health care providers) should be weighed in terminal care decisions only if so provided by the declarant. See Norman L. Cantor, "*Conroy*, Best Interests, and the Handling of Dying Patients," 37 Rutgers L. Rev. 543, 576–77 (1985).

21. This language was used by a declarant in *Saunders v. State*, 492 N.Y.S.2d 510, 512 (Sup. Ct. 1985).

22. Cf. Ohio Rev. Code Ann. § 1337.13 (f) (Anderson Supp. 1991).

23. For consideration of this issue relating to family members' interests, see Lawrence J. Schneiderman & Roger C. Spragg, "Ethical Decisions in Discontinuing Mechanical Ventilation," 318 New Eng. J. Med. 984, 987 (1988); Bernard Lo, "Caring for Incompetent Patients: Is There a Physician on the Case?" 17:3 Law, Med. & Health Care 214 (1989).

24. President's Commission for the Study of Ethical Problems in Medicine and Biomedical and Behavioral Research, *Deciding to Forego Life-Sustaining Treatment* 137 (1983) [hereinafter President's Commission].

25. New Jersey Commission on Legal and Ethical Problems in the Delivery of Health Care, *Problems and Approaches in Health Care Decisionmaking* 103, 155 (1990) [hereinafter Report of the New Jersey Bioethics Commission].

26. Marion Danis et al., "Patients' and Families' Preferences for Medical Intensive Care," 260 JAMA 797, 802 (1988).

27. See John A. Robertson, "Second Thoughts on Living Wills," 21:6 Hastings Cent. Rep. 6 (Nov. 1991).

28. See In re *Estate of Greenspan*, 558 N.E.2d 1194, 1197 (Ill. 1990) (patient repeatedly said he would rather die than live in a nursing home); Newark Star Ledger, Feb. 8, 1992, at 17 (letter to Ann Landers describing a living will dictating that no medical intervention be provided if the declarant "must enter a nursing home").

29. Surveys disclose that many persons wish to avoid future medical maintenance in a state of total and permanent dependence on others. Times Mirror Center for the People and the Press, *Reflections of the Times: The Right to Die* 6 (1990).

30. For a more complete explanation of my views, see Norman L. Cantor, "Prospective Autonomy—On the Limits of Shaping One's Post-Competence Medical Fate," 8 J. Contemp. Health L. & Pol'y 13 (1992).

31. For another view condemning use of a standard demanding "appropriate" or adequate contemplation of a directive's consequences on the part of a declarant, see King, supra note 4, at 57–59, 67–68.

32. Discussion of this issue is continued in chapter 6.

33. Uniform Rights of Terminally Ill Act 1989 § 4 (a), 9B U.L.A. 106 (Supp. 1992) [hereinafter URTIA]; Del. Code Ann. tit. 16, § 2504 (a) (1983); Me. Rev. Stat. Ann. tit. 18-A, § 5-704 (a) (West Supp. 1991). See Thomas A. Eaton & Edward J. Larson, "Experimenting with the "Right to Die" in the Laboratory of the States," 25 Ga. L. Rev. 1253, 1305 (1991). Not every state so readily accepts a revocation. In South Carolina, for example, a revocation must be "clearly expressed" in order to be effective. See Elizabeth G. Patterson, "Planning for Health Care Using Living Wills and Durable Powers of Attorney: A Guide for the South Carolina Attorney," 42 S.C. L. Rev. 525, 579 (1991).

34. See Norman L. Cantor, *Legal Frontiers of Death & Dying* 68–82 (1987); Jeffrey J. Delaney, Note, "Specific Intent, Substituted Judgment and Best Interests: A Nationwide Analysis of an Individual's Right to Die," 11 Pace L. Rev. 565, 591, 617–23 (1991) (concerning the legal standards generally applicable to the handling of incompetent patients who have left no clear instructions).

35. See Marguerite A. Chapman, "The Uniform Rights of the Terminally Ill Act: Too Little, Too Late?" 42 Ark. L. Rev. 319, 356 (1989); George J. Annas & Leonard H. Glantz, "The Right of Elderly Patients to Refuse Life-Sustaining Treatment," 64 Milbank Q. Supp. 2, at 95, 107 (1986).

36. A gravely incapacitated patient may fluctuate in resolve or give contradictory signals. See In re *O'Brien*, 517 N.Y.S.2d 346, 348 (Sup. Ct. 1986).

37. *Kurzweil v. Harrison*, No. 14810/91, slip op. at 3 (N.Y. Sup. Ct., N.Y. County).

38. See President's Commission, supra note 24, at 152.

39. See George J. Annas, *Judging Medicine* 255–56 (1988); Annas & Glantz, supra note 35, at 107. Both these sources criticize In re *Hier*, 464 N.E.2d 959 (Mass. App. 1984). See also Rebecca S. Dresser & John A. Robertson, "Quality of Life and Non-Treatment Decisions for Incompetent Patients: A Critique of the Orthodox Approach," 17:3 Law, Med. & Health Care 234, 238–39 (1989).

40. In In re *O'Brien*, 517 N.Y.S.2d 346 (Sup. Ct. 1986), the 83-year-old victim of a severe stroke had attempted 15 times to remove a nasogastric feeding tube. The court nonetheless refused to authorize detachment of the life-preserving device. The opinion commented: "This court is not prepared to order discontinuance of this life support based upon gestures of irritation or annoyance." Id. at 348. See also *Conroy*, 486 A.2d at 1243, where the court essentially disregarded a patient's moaning and attempts to remove a feeding tube because it was not clear whether the conduct was intentional or reflexive.

41. For a provision requiring a health-care agent to discuss treatment options with a now incompetent principal and to "take the patient's expressed wishes into account in the decision-making process," see N.J. Stat. Ann. § 26:2H-63(b) (West Supp. 1992).

42. Consultation with the incompetent person and consideration of that person's wishes and feelings do not compel adherence to those incompetent wishes. If an incompetent but comprehending minor were involved, it would be evident that the patient ought to be consulted even though the patient's substantive wishes would not necessarily be followed. Cf. Charles R. Tremper, "Respect for Human Dignity and Minors: What the Constitution Requires," 39 Syracuse L. Rev. 1293, 1314 (1988); John H. Garvey, "Freedom and Choice in Constitutional Law," 94 Harv. L. Rev. 1756, 1784 n.30 (1981).

43. Concerning the significance of "assent" from an incompetent person, see Annas & Glantz, supra note 35, at 119; Nancy L. Dubler, "Refusals of Medical Care in the Home Setting," 18:3 Law, Med. & Health Care 227, 231–32 (1990); Bruce J. Winick, "Competency to Consent to Treatment: The Distinction Between Assent and Objection," 28 Hous. L. Rev. 15, 37–42 (1991). Cf. Robert M. Veatch, *The Patient as Partner* 58–60 (1987). See also Sanford H. Kadish, "Letting Patients Die: Legal and Moral Reflections," 80 Cal. L. Rev. 857, 874–76 (1992).

44. In addition, there is always some chance that the consultation with the patient might yield surprising responses which reflect a level of function beyond that previously attributed to the patient. This would be a basis to reassess the patient's mental status.

45. Report of the New Jersey Bioethics Commission, supra note 25, at 104, 161. In In re *Clark*, 510 A.2d 136, 138 (N.J. Super. Ct. Ch. Div. 1986), in deciding that the burdens of the patient's continued existence did not outweigh the benefits, the court noted that the incompetent patient had answered "yes" when asked if she was happy. In In re *Storar*, 420 N.E.2d 64 (N.Y., 1981), cert. den., 454 U.S. 858 (1981), the lower court interpreted the incompetent patient's resistance to blood transfusions as expressing pain and anxiety, which furnished a basis for withholding further intervention. The New York Court of Appeals, however, refused to permit termination of life support in the absence of clear-cut prior expressions by the now incompetent patient. See also In re *Hier*, 464 N.E.2d 959 (Mass. App. 1984).

46. See In re *Guardianship of Grant*, 747 P.2d 445, 457 (Wash. 1987), amended by 757 P.2d 534 (Wash. 1988); In re *Guardianship of Ingram*, 689 P.2d 1363, 1370 (Wash. 1984).

47. *Ingram*, 689 P.2d at 1370.

48. Courts frequently solicit the views of an incompetent patient when the issue is sterilization or abortion. See In re *C.D.M.*, 627 P.2d 607, 612–13 (Alaska 1981); In re *A.W.*, 637 P.2d 366, 375 (Colo. 1981); In re *Hayes*, 608 P.2d 635, 641 (Wash. 1980). In those instances, the courts acknowledge that the weight to be given to the incompetent patient's pronouncements depend on the patient's understanding of the procedure being contemplated.

49. Perhaps this is what the New Jersey Bioethics Commission had in mind when it prescribed, in draft legislation, that a "clearly expressed" wish by an incompetent patient to continue treatment should take precedence over a contrary advance directive. See Report of the New Jersey Bioethics Commission, supra note 25, at 43–44.

50. See sources cited in chapter 3, note 9.

51. See Current Opinions of the Council on Ethical and Judicial affairs of the A.M.A. § 2.19 (1986) [hereinafter Current Opinions of the AMA Council] (indicating that aggressive intervention should ordinarily be maintained for an incompetent patient who is neither terminally ill nor irreversibly comatose).

52. King, supra note 4, at 39.

53. Ben A. Rich, "The Values History: A New Standard of Care," 40 Emory L.J. 1109, 1145–56 (1991).

54. See *Rust v. Sullivan*, 111 S. Ct. 1759, 1171–72 (1991). The disputed federal rules have been discontinued in the Clinton administration.

55. See, e.g., George J. Annas et al., *American Health Law* 657 (2d ed. 1990).

56. *Conroy*, 486 A.2d at 1225; see also Alexander Capron, "The Burden of Decision," 20:3 Hastings Cent. Rep. 37 (June 1990).

57. See, e.g., *Brophy*, 497 N.E.2d at 639; *Gray v. Romeo*, 697 F. Supp. 580, 591 (D.R.I. 1988).

58. Chapter 2 addressed the way in which principles of autonomy have been respected in the context of advance medical instructions.

59. See, e.g., S.D. Codified Laws Ann. § 59-7-2.5 (Supp. 1991); URTIA, supra note 33, § 9 (b); Chapman, supra note 35, at 387.

60. URTIA, supra note 33, § 9 (b); see also Alaska Stat. § 18.12.060 (1991); Ark. Code Ann. § 20-17-208 (b) (Michie 1991); Cal. Health & Safety Code § 7190.5 (West Supp. 1992); Iowa Code Ann. § 144A.9 (2) (West 1989).

61. Conn. Gen. Stat. Ann. § 19A-571 (West Supp. 1992).

62. Del. Code Ann. tit. 16, § 2505 (1983).

63. As will be discussed a few pages hence, this is almost certainly true when the practitioner's reluctance to comply with a patient's wishes is based on a claim of personal conscience—a deeply felt moral position. The conflict between a patient's wishes and practitioner's conscience will be resolved by transfer of the patient, if feasible. A similar framework probably applies where the practitioner's reluctance is based on a claim of professional judgment or sound medical practice. See American Hospital Association, *Patient's Choice of Treatment Options* (Feb. 1985).

64. See Mont. Code Ann. § 50-20-111 (1) (1991); Mass. Ann. Laws ch. 112, § 12 I (Law Co-op 1991); *Swanson v. St. John's Lutheran Hosp.*, 597 P.2d 702, 709–10 (Mont. 1979); Bruce G. Davis, "Defining the Employment Rights of Medical Personnel Within the Parameters of Personal Conscience," 1986 Det. C. L. Rev. 847, 862–85.

65. See *Conservatorship of Morrison*, 253 Cal. Rptr. 530, 534 (Ct. App. 1988); In re *Farrell*, 529 A.2d 404, 412 (N.J. 1987).

66. Approximately 10 jurisdictions say that, in the event of conscientious objection to implementing a living will, the physician "shall promptly transfer" responsibility to another physician. Ariz. Rev. Stat. Ann. § 36-3204 (c) (1991); Van Ess, supra note 11, at 577. Approximately 20 jurisdictions require only that the physician take "reasonable steps" to effect transfer. Iowa Code Ann. § 144 A.8 (1) (West 1989); Craig P. Goldman, "Revising Iowa's Life-Sustaining Procedures Act: Creating a Practical Guide to Living Wills in Iowa," 76 Iowa L. Rev. 1137, 1160 (1991); URTIA, supra note 33, § 8.

Not all states place responsibility upon a physician to arrange a transfer. For example, Alabama "permits" transfer of the patient but doesn't require the physician to arrange it. Ala. Code § 22-8A-8 (a) (1990). Kentucky simply provides that a physician shall not impede a transfer. Ky. Rev. Stat. Ann. § 311.634 (Michie Supp. 1990).

67. See John B. Boyle, "Religious Employers and Gender Employment Discrimination," 4 Law & Ineq. J. 637, 646–51 (1986); Davis, supra note 64, at 853–54.

68. See *Warthen v. Toms River Community Memorial Hosp.*, 488 A.2d 229, 233–34 (N.J. Super. Ct. App. Div.), cert. den., 501 A.2d 926 (N.J. 1985); *Pierce v. Ortho Pharmaceutical Corp.*, 417 A.2d 505, 514 (N.J. 1980).

69. In re *Requena*, 517 A.2d 886 (N.J. Super. Ct. Ch. Div.), aff'd, 517 A.2d 869 (N.J. Super. Ct. App. Div. 1986).

70. See In re *Jobes*, 529 A.2d 434, 450 (N.J. 1987) (institution estopped by lack of having given prior notice of its conscientious policy; discomfort of individual providers acknowledged but apparently overridden).

71. See *Bartling v. Superior Court*, 209 Cal. Rptr. 220, 225 n.7 (Ct. App. 1984). But see In re *Bayer*, No. 4131, slip op. at 8–9 (Burleigh County Ct., N.D., Dec. 11 1987). After 200 physicians refused to accommodate the patient's wishes, the court refused to compel the attending physician to violate his conscience; the patient was permitted to die at home.

72. See Robert M. Veatch & Carol M. Spicer, "Medically Futile Care: The Role of the Physician in Setting Limits," 18 Am. J.L. & Med. 15, 27–28 (1992).

73. It might be argued that a patient's request for continued medical intervention (deemed futile by the physician) is distinguishable from a request for withdrawal of medical intervention. In the latter event, the patient is invoking an interest in bodily integrity and asking that the medical invasion of that integrity be withdrawn. By contrast, a patient seeking continued intervention is asking the physician to affirmatively introduce medical measures into the body (contrary to the professional judgment of the physician). The patient's interest in bodily integrity may not include the prerogative to introduce substances or medical instrumentalities into the body. Yet, even in the absence of full-blown bodily integrity, the patient's interest in continued medical attention ought to be recognized. The patient is still asserting a self-determination interest in attaining life-preserving medical intervention. That self-determination interest is legitimate and cognizable.

74. See, e.g., Allan S. Brett & Laurence B. McCullough, "When Patients Request Specific Interventions," 315 New Eng. J. Med. 1347, 1349 (1986); Linda L. Emanuel & Ezekiel J. Emanuel, "The Medical Directive: A New Comprehensive Advance Care Document," 261 JAMA 3288, 3292 (1989); Schneiderman and Spragg, supra note 23, at 984; Nancy Jecker, "Knowing When to Stop: The Limits of Medicine," 21:3 Hastings Cent. Rep. 5, 7 (May–June 1991).

75. The best discussion of this issue which I have seen is found in Veatch & Spicer, supra note 72, at 17–18.

76. This point is made by numerous sources. See, e.g., Felicia Ackerman, "The Significance of a Wish," 21:4 Hastings Cent. Rep. 27, 28 (July–Aug. 1991); Daniel Callahan, "Medical Futility, Medical Necessity: The Problem-Without-a-Name," 21:4 Hastings Cent. Rep. 30, 32 (July–Aug. 1991); Ronald E. Cranford, "Helga Wanglie's Ventilator," 21:4 Hastings Cent. Rep. 23, 23–24 (July–Aug. 1991).

77. Yale Kamisar, "Who Should Live—Or Die? Who Should Decide?" Trial, December 1991, at 24.

78. 18:12 Report of the Society for Critical Care Medicine 1435–39 (1990); see Michael A. Rie, "The Limits of a Wish," 21:4 Hastings Cent. Rep. 24, 25 (July–Aug. 1991).

79. In re *Conservatorship of Wanglie*, PX-91-283, slip op. (Minn. Prob. Ct. 1991).

80. Lisa Belkin, "As Family Protests, Hospital Seeks an End to Woman's Life Support," New York Times, Jan. 10, 1991, at A1, D22.

81. In point of fact, there was considerable dispute about what the patient had previously said or indicated. See Cranford, supra note 76, at 23.

82. "Those vested by society with a licensed monopoly of skill to preserve life have a duty to provide that life preservation as long as it is believed to be a benefit by the patient. . . . " Veatch & Spicer, supra note 72, at 31.

83. For another interesting clash between prior instructions of incompetent patients and professional preferences, see Alexander Gold et al., "Is There a Right to Futile Treatment? The Case of a Dying Patient With AIDS," 1 J. Clinical Ethics 19 (1990). There, the authors conclude that if health-care providers regard the patient's advance instructions as calling for futile medical treatment which they are unwilling to furnish, those providers ought to make their position known in advance so that the patient or the patient's representative can seek care from other sources; see id. at 22. I go further and suggest an affirmative obligation of the providers to assist in arranging alternative care.

84. "Life should be cherished despite disability and handicaps, except when the prolongation would be inhumane and unconscionable." Current Opinions of the AMA. Council, supra note 51, § 2.16. This quote is from a section dealing with incompetent patients who have not articulated their wishes, but it seems relevant to the context of advance directives as well.

85. Andrew H. Malcolm, "Missouri Family Renews Battle over Right to Die," New York Times, Nov. 2, 1990, at A14.

86. See Judith W. Ross, "The Puzzle of the Permanently Unconscious," 22:3 Hastings Cent. Rep. 2 (May–June 1992).

87. See, e.g., *Conroy*, 489 A.2d at 1231; *Rasmussen v. Fleming*, 741 P.2d 674, 688–89 (Ariz. 1987); Jeffrey J. Delaney, Note, "Specific Intent, Substituted Judgment and Best Interests: A Nationwide Analysis of an Individual's Right to Die," 11 Pace L. Rev. 565, 617–23 (1991).

88. See, e.g., In re *Lawrance*, 579 N.E.2d 32, 34 (Ind. 1991); In re *Moorhouse*, 593 A.2d 1256 (N.J. App. Div. 1991); In re *Crum*, 580 N.E.2d 876, 882 (Ohio Prob. Ct. 1991). Notice also that a number of states have amended their living-will laws to permit persons to prospectively reject life support in a permanently unconscious state.

89. For a more expansive statement of my views on treatment of PVS patients, see Norman L. Cantor, "The Permanently Unconscious Patient, Non-Feeding and Euthanasia," 15 Am. J.L. & Med. 384 (1989).

90. The judge in *Wanglie* refused to remove the husband as guardian; see *Conservatorship of Wanglie*, supra note 79.

91. See Rie, supra note 78, at 25; Alexander M. Capron, "In re Helga Wanglie," 21:5 Hastings Cent. Rep. 26, 27 (Sept.–Oct. 1991).

92. See Veatch & Spicer, supra note 72, at 29.

93. See, e.g., *Gray v. Romeo*, 697 F. Supp. at 583.

94. George J. Annas, "Transferring the Ethical Hot Potato," 17:1 Hastings Cent. Rep. 20, 21 (Feb. 1987); Robert Schwaneberg, Medical Ethics Panel Proposes Giving Legal Recognition to "Living Wills," The Star Ledger, Feb. 11, 1988, at 17.

95. Steven H. Miles et al., "Conflicts Between Patients' Wishes to Forego Treatment and the Policies of Health Care Facilities," 321 New Eng. J. Med. 48 (1989); James F. Childress, "Dying Patients: Who's in Control?" 17 Law, Med. & Health Care 227, 230 (1989).

96. On the meaning of "conscience," see James F. Childress, "Appeals to Conscience," 89 Ethics 315, 318–22 (1979).

97. Many state legislatures and the U.S. Congress adopted laws exempting private institutions from performing abortions in violation of institutional scruples. See, e.g., 42 U.S.C. § 300a-7 (d) (1989); Alaska Stat. § 18.16.010 (b) (1991); Colo. Rev. Stat. Ann. § 18-6-104 (West 1990). For an example of accommodation in the public sector, see *Poelker v. Doe*, 432 U.S. 519, 520–21 (1977).

98. See *Planned Parenthood Ass'n v. Ashcroft*, 655 F.2d 848 (8th Cir. 1981); *Greco v. Orange Memorial Hosp.*, 513 F.2d 873 (5th Cir. 1975); *Chrisman v. Sisters of St. Joseph*, 506 F.2d 308 (9th Cir. 1974).

99. *Brophy*, 497 N.E.2d at 639; *Grace Plaza of Great Neck v. Elbaum*, 1992 N.Y. App.

Div. LEXIS 10728 (App. Div., Sept. 21, 1992); *Gray v. Romeo*, 697 F. Supp. at 591; *Morrison*, 253 Cal. Rptr. at 534.

100. See, e.g., *Jobes*, 529 A.2d at 450.

6. The Moral Boundaries of Shaping Post-Competence Medical Care

1. While analgesics can relieve the vast majority of pain, there are still some kinds of terminal conditions which are accompanied by unrelievable pain. Alternatively, the directive itself might preclude palliatives or analgesics because either they might violate the patient's religious precept that suffering has important redemptive value or the patient might wish to remain as lucid as possible.

2. See Allen E. Buchanan & Dan W. Brock, *Deciding for Others: The Ethics of Surrogate Decision Making* 185 (1989).

3. By future "persona" I mean the changed, incompetent version of the previously competent person who propounded an advance directive.

4. On the various interests underlying autonomy in the context of advance medical directives, see New Jersey Commission on Legal and Ethical Problems in the Delivery of Health Care, *Problems and Approaches in Health Care Decisionmaking* 86 (1990); Buchanan & Brock, supra note 2, at 91–92; Philip G. Peters, "The State's Interest in the Preservation of Life: From *Quinlan* to *Cruzan*," 50 Ohio St. L.J. 891, 930–31 (1989).

5. See, e.g., *Brophy v. New England Sinai Hosp., Inc.*, 497 N.E.2d 626, 635 (Mass. 1986); In re *Gardner*, 534 A.2d 947, 953 (Me. 1987).

6. See In re *Guardianship of Browning*, 568 So. 2d 4, 13 (Fla. 1990); In re *Estate of Greenspan*, 558 N.E.2d 1194, 1202 (Ill. 1990); In re *Peter*, 529 A.2d 419, 425 (N.J. 1987).

7. Implicit in this statement is the judgment that prolongation of life is not always in the best interests of a moribund patient.

8. Such measures commonly instruct a health-care agent to implement the wishes of the principal as gleaned from the advance directive or elsewhere. "Best interests" of the incompetent patient must guide the agent when the patient's wishes cannot be determined. See, e.g., Cal. Civ. Code § 2500 (West Supp. 1992); Idaho Code § 39-4505 (Supp. 1991); Miss. Code Ann. § 41-41-163 (Supp. 1991); N.Y. Pub. Health Law § 2982 (2) (McKinney Supp. 1992); R.I. Gen. Laws § 23-4.10-2 (1989).

9. See Buchanan & Brock, supra note 2, at 154–59; Rebecca Dresser, "Relitigating Life and Death," 51 Ohio St. L.J. 425, 432 (1990).

10. Professor Dresser's initial analysis was presented in Rebecca Dresser, "Life, Death, and Incompetent Patients: Conceptual Infirmities and Hidden Values in the Law," 28 Ariz. L. Rev. 373 (1986). A more developed explication of her position is presented in Rebecca Dresser, "Relitigating Life and Death," supra note 9. A joint presentation with Professor Robertson is found in Rebecca S. Dresser & John A. Robertson, "Quality of Life and Non-Treatment Decisions for Incompetent Patients: A Critique of the Orthodox Approach," 17 Law, Med. & Health Care 234 (1989). For Professor Robertson's separately stated position, see John A. Robertson, "*Cruzan* and the Constitutional Status of Nontreatment Decisions for Incompetent Patients," 25 Ga. L. Rev. 1139 (1991) [hereinafter Robertson, "Constitutional Status"]; John A. Robertson, "Second Thoughts on Living Wills," 21:6 Hastings Cent. Rep. 7 (Nov. 1992).

11. Dresser & Robertson, supra note 10, at 238; Dresser, supra note 9, at 430–31; see Robertson, "Constitutional Status," supra note 10, at 1158–59.

12. Such miraculous choice would reflect the patient's "current and future interests as incompetent individuals, not their past preferences." Dresser & Robertson, supra note 10, at 236.

13. Robertson, "Constitutional Status," supra note 10, at 1143, 1162, 1167.

14. This is not to say that an advance instruction must prevail against all countervailing

interests. For example, allocation of a scarce medical resource to another critically ill patient might necessitate overriding a patient's choice. The point is that the patient's interest in having a prior choice respected is affected in a meaningful fashion even if the plaintiff cannot sense the violation.

15. Professor Robertson suggests that the distaste experienced by observers, rather than the dignity interests of unsensing patients, accounts for any proscription of the practices involved. Robertson, "Constitutional Status," supra note 10, at 1162 n.94. For an unusual case in which a court suggested that an anencephalic neonate's nonvital organs could be harvested for the benefit of others, see "Organ Donations Barred by Judge," New York Times, March 28, 1992, at A7.

16. See Nancy K. Rhoden, "The Limits of Legal Objectivity," 68 N. C. L. Rev. 845, 864 (1990) [hereinafter Rhoden, "Legal Objectivity"]; Rhoden, "Litigating Life and Death," 102 Harv. L. Rev. 375, 417–18 (1988); Rhoden, "How Should We View the Incompetent?" 17 Law. Med. & Health Care 264, 266 (1989).

17. Rhoden, "Legal Objectivity," supra note 16, at 858.

18. Id. at 864. See also Peters, supra note 4, at 935–36.

19. James F. Childress, "Dying Patients: Who's in Control?" 17 Law, Med. & Health Care 227, 228 (1989).

20. The Dresser-Robertson position—that once incompetent, a person cannot experience the previously feared indignity associated with a grossly deteriorated status—is a shaky premise. I suggest that some patients, in some phases of mental incapacity, can be aware of, and suffer from, grossly reduced functioning. That is, the frustration, embarrassment, or humiliation originally feared by the patient may in fact materialize and inflict emotional suffering on some incompetent patients. Admittedly, it is difficult to identify and measure these phenomena in severely compromised patients. But there will be some such patients whose overall distress will be apparent. And there will be some less mentally deteriorated patients whose particular distress relating to indignity can be discerned (e.g., a senile incontinent patient, once proud, independent, and punctilious about personal hygiene, who now weeps each time that a diaper must be changed). In such instances as these, the patient's prior expressions, directives, or values may help observers understand the nature of the apparent distress. At stages in which the incompetent patient is still aware of the environment, loss of prior faculties can prompt real emotional consequences.

21. Ronald Dworkin, "Autonomy and the Demented Self," 64 Milbank Q. Supp. 2, at 4, 11 (1986). See also Buchanan & Brock, supra note 2, at 100 (acknowledging the legitimacy of future-oriented interests to individuals as well as their families).

22. In our culture, we attach great importance to the "embodiment" of our beings, whether that embodiment is competent, incompetent, or even dead. "We only know of our selves and each other in and through our bodies. . . . " Thomas H. Murray, "Are We Morally Obligated to Make Gifts of Our Bodies?" 1 Health Matrix 19, 24 (1991).

23. *Cruzan v. Director, Missouri Dept. of Health*, 110 S. Ct. at 2841, 2885–86; see also id. at 2892.

24. See, e.g., *Gardner*, 534 A.2d at 953; *Delio v. Westchester County Medical Center*, 516 N.Y.S.2d 677, 691 (App. Div. 1987).

25. See Buchanan & Brock, supra note 2, at 99–100; Ronald E. Cranford, "Going Out in Style, The American Way, 1987," 17 Law, Med. & Health Care 208, 208 (1989).

26. *Cruzan*, 110 S. Ct. at 2869.

27. Times Mirror Center For the People and the Press, *Reflections of the Times: The Right to Die* 10 (June 1990).

28. See Buchanan & Brock, supra note 2, at 164.

29. See H. Frankfort, *The Importance of What We Care About* 83, 91 (1988).

30. My late stepbrother's will prescribed that a Dixieland band play at his wake and that the mourning family wear white. It was obvious to me that fulfillment of his wishes gave expression to his character and that to dishonor his instruction would have been an offense to his memory.

31. Recent court decisions indicate that a parent is entitled to reject life-preserving treatment so long as the minor is not totally abandoned (i.e., so long as a spouse or relative can care for the minor). Presence of emotional harm to the minor is not a basis to override the parent's medical decision. See *Norwood Hosp. v. Munoz*, 564 N.E.2d 1017, 1024 (Mass. 1991). At least one court has indicated that the parent's autonomy interest would be upheld even if the dependent minor would be totally abandoned; see *Fosmire v. Nicoleau*, 551 N.E.2d 77, 83 (N.Y. 1990).

32. This is not to say that a competent person who neglects his or her body and precipitates subsequent hardship during the post-competence stage of existence forfeits the moral prerogative of prospective control.

33. See generally James F. Childress, "Ethical Criteria for Procuring and Distributing Organs for Transplantation," in *Organ Transplantation Policy* 87 (James F. Blumstein & Frank A. Sloan, eds., 1989) (describing the effect of the Uniform Anatomical Gift Act); Erik S. Jaffe, Note, " 'She's Got Bette Davis['s] Eyes:' Assessing the Nonconsensual Removal of Cadaver Organs Under the Takings and Due Process Clauses," 90 Colum. L. Rev. 528 (1990) (discussing the substantive rights existing relative to the body and the family's disposition of the cadaver).

34. Dresser & Robertson, supra note 10, at 237.

35. See Rhoden, "Legal Objectivity," supra note 16, at 859.

36. See Dan W. Brock, "Trumping Advance Directives," 21:5 Hastings Cent. Rep. S5 (Sept. 1991); Dresser, supra note 9, at 432; Buchanan & Brock, supra note 2, at 154–59. For discussion of the personal identity issue, see Ben A. Rich, "The Values History: A New Standard of Care," 40 Emory L.J. 1109, 1122–32 (1991); Nancy M. P. King, *Making Sense of Advance Directives* 73–74 (1991).

37. See Robertson, "Constitutional Status," supra note 10, at 1157.

38. Buchanan & Brock, supra note 2, at 160–61.

39. Id. at 160, 185. Even in situations in which Buchanan and Brock consider personal identity to be unchanged, they wrestle with the conflict between a person's autonomy interests and the contemporaneous interests of the incompetent patient. To them, it would be immoral to accomplish the demise of an incompetent persona possessing clear capacity for net pleasure or satisfaction in life; see *id.* at 160. See also Sanford H. Kadish, "Letting Patients Die: Legal and Moral Reflections," 80 Cal. L. Rev. 857, 876–78 (1992).

40. Rich, supra note 36, at 1123.

41. Dworkin, supra note 21, at 5.

42. Rhoden, "Legal Objectivity," supra note 16, at 860.

43. For examples of judicial willingness to follow the perceptible best interests of a patient when the patient's prior contrary instructions were not clear-cut, see In re *Estate of Dorone*, 534 A.2d 452, 455 (Pa. 1987); *University of Cincinnati Hosp. v. Edmond*, 506 N.E.2d 299, 302 (Ohio Comm. Pleas 1986). See also Mo. Ann. Stat. §§ 459.025, .045 (Vernon Supp. 1992) (authorizing health-care providers to treat a patient in contravention of prior expressions if the treatment would be consistent with the best interests of the patient).

44. See Sean M. Dunphy & John H. Cross, "Medical Decision Making for Incompetent Persons: The Massachusetts Substituted Judgment Model," 9 W. New Eng. L. Rev. 153, 156 (1987); David A. Peters, "Advance Medical Directives: The Case for the Durable Power of Attorney for Health Care," 8 J. Leg. Med. 437, 454 (1987).

45. Dresser, supra note 9, at 433.

46. Buchanan & Brock, supra note 2, at 111, 188–89. See also Rhoden, "Legal Objectivity," supra note 16, at 859–60; King, supra note 36, at 75; Kadish, supra note 39, at 876–78.

47. See Bruce J. Winick, "Competency to Consent to Treatment: The Distinction Between Assent and Objection," 28 Hous. L. Rev. 15 (1991).

48. If the vitalist patient's advance directive is overridden, it must be based on some other rationale such as the moral impropriety of extending the suffering of a helpless, incompetent person on the basis of prior instructions. Such a sweeping rationale that an unambiguous advance directive must always yield to a patient's contemporaneous interests is difficult to accept.

49. See Irene P. Loftus, Note, "I have a Conscience Too: The Plight of Medical Personnel Confronting the Right to Die," 65 Notre Dame L. Rev. 699, 712 (1990); Anne L. Rubin & Mary E. Scrupski, Note, "When Ethics Collide: Enforcement of Institutional Policies of Non-Participation in the Termination of LIfe-Sustaining Treatment," 41 Rutgers L. Rev. 399, 425 (1988).

50. Buchanan & Brock sympathize with this position; see Buchanan & Brock, supra note 2, at 98. It's not clear, however, how this can be reconciled with their position that advance directives might not be permitted to dictate withdrawal of life-preserving care for an ostensibly happy incompetent; see id. at 186–89. Perhaps they are suggesting that a person should be able to dictate post-competence medical care by instructions in accord with the interests of an incompetent patient who is clearly enjoying his or her incompetency.

51. Gerald Dworkin, *The Theory and Practice of Autonomy* 98 (1988).

52. Restraints are often used to prevent institutionalized patients from harming themselves or others. Such restraints are not per se inhumane, although they may become inhumane, depending on their nature and duration.

7. Enforcing Advance Directives

1. See note 9 in chapter 3. See also Felicia Ackerman, "The Significance of a Wish," 21:4 Hastings Cent. Rep. 23, 29 n.1 (July 1991).

2. The PSDA requires all health-care institutions receiving federal funds (which includes the vast majority of health-care enterprises) to educate their staff and patients about advance directives and about the relevant state law applicable to advance directives; see Patient Self-Determination Act of 1990 (PSDA), Pub. L. No. 101-508, § 4206 (a), codified at 42 U.S.C.A. § 1395cc (f)(1)(E) (West 1992). See generally Kelly C. Mulholland, "Protecting the Right to Die: The Patient Self-Determination Act of 1990," 28 Harv. J. on Legis. 609 (1991); "Practicing the PSDA: A Hastings Center Report Special Supplement," 21:5 Hastings Cent. Rep. S1–S16 (Sept. 1991).

3. See Nancy M. P. King, *Making Sense of Advance Directives* 141 (1991).

4. Usually, medical staff will be the key factor. If a responsible relative had been available, the declarant would probably have designated that relative as health-care agent. So in many instances there will be no close family or friends surrounding a declarant's dying process. Of course, the picture may be complicated by the presence of relatives who are not sympathetic to implementation of the patient's advance directive.

5. See Willard H. Pedrick, "Dignified Death and the Law of Torts," 28 San Diego L. Rev. 387, 399 (1991); Richard P. Dooling, "Damage Actions for Nonconsensual Life-Sustaining Medical Treatment," 30 St. Louis L.J. 895, 917 (1986); M. Rose Gasner, "Financial Penalties for Failing to Honor Patient Wishes to Refuse Treatment," 11 St. Louis U. L. Rev. 499, 512–15 (1992).

6. See *Elbaum v. Grace Plaza*, 544 N.Y.S. 840, 847 (App. Div. 1989). In *Elbaum*, the trial court upheld a refusal to pay for medical care rendered by a hospital after the comatose patient's husband had requested cessation of treatment. The husband had sought withdrawal of

treatment on the ground that his wife would have wanted that course. The trial court's decision as to liability for medical care was recently overturned. *Grace Plaza of Great Neck v. Elbaum*, 1992 N.Y. App. Div. LEXIS 10728 (App. Div., Sept. 21, 1992). However, this latest decision does not vitiate the notion that payment can be withheld for unwanted medical services. The appellate court relied on its reading of New York law as requiring (in the absence of a proxy directive) a judicial determination that the now incompetent patient had previously given clear-cut instructions about withdrawal of life support. The hospital would be denied compensation for "unwanted" care only after such a judicial determination. New York's law on decision making for incompetent patients is particularly narrow. See also Alaska Stat. § 18.12.070 (a) (1991).

7. Norman Paradis, "Making a Living Off the Dying", New York Times, April 25, 1992, at 23.

8. For example, the New Jersey Division of Health Facilities requires that hospitals and other health facilities comply with the state's advance directive act. N.J. Admin. Code tit. 8, § 39-4.1 (a) (1992).

9. PSDA, Pub. L. No. 101-508, § 4206 (a), codified at 42 U.S.C.A. § 1395cc (f) (1)(D) (West 1992).

10. See Colo. Rev. Stat. Ann. § 15-18-113 (5) (West 1989); Kan. Stat. Ann. § 65-28, 107(a) (1985); Utah Code Ann. § 75-2-1112 (3) (Supp. 1991); Craig P. Goldman, "Revising Iowa's Life-Sustaining Procedures Act: Creating a Practical Guide to Living Wills in Iowa," 76 Iowa L. Rev. 1137, 1160 (1991). Technically, these statutory measures apply only to failure to abide by living wills conforming to statutory requirements (such as terminal condition limitations). However, because of constitutional and common-law mandates to respect an incompetent patient's prior instructions, the same kind of professional obligations exist with regard to nonstatutory advance directives (as discussed in chapter 3).

11. So long as the attending physician did not have a conscientious objection to the desired medical course, an order to comply with the advance directive would be plausible. In the event of personal or professional scruples, the order might be directed at compelling transfer of care to a more amenable professional.

12. See B. D. Colen, *The Essential Guide to a Living Will* 14–16 (1991).

13. See Alan Meisel, "Refusing Treatment, Refusing to Talk, and Refusing to Let Go: On Whose Terms Will Death Occur?" 17:3 Law, Med. & Health Care 221, 223 (1989) (indicating that litigation is more likely to flow from nonadherence to a living will than from implementation).

14. For an examination of the role of institutional ethics committees in the terminal decision making process see Maureen Cushing et al., "The Role of Hospital Ethics Committees in Decisions to Terminate Treatment," 29:2 Boston Bar J. 22 (March–April 1985).

15. See David C. Blake, "The Hospital Ethics Committee: Health Care's Moral Conscience or White Elephant?" 22:1 Hastings Cent. Rep. 6, 9 (Jan. 1992).

16. Paradis, supra note 7, at 23.

17. Concerning the possibility of health-care providers' liability for nonadherence to an advance directive, see, e.g., President's Commission for the Study of Ethical Problems in Medicine and Biomedical and Behavioral Research, *Deciding to Forego Life-Sustaining Treatment* 141 (1983); William C. Knapp and Fred Hamilton, " 'Wrongful Living': Resuscitation as Tortious Interference With a Patient's Right to Give Informed Consent," 19 N. Ky. L. Rev. 253, 261 (1992); Pedrick, supra note 5, at 396; Dooling, supra note 5, at 895; Gasner, supra note 5, at 504–12; *Estate of Leach v. Shapiro*, 469 N.E.2d 1047, 1054–55 (Ohio App. 1984).

18. While pain-and-suffering damages are not ordinarily awarded as a contract remedy, the situation is different with regard to an intimate matter such as physicians' services.

19. See Tenn. Code Ann. § 32-11-108 (a) (Supp. 1991); Md. Health-Gen. Code § 5-607 (a) (1990); R.I. Gen. Laws §23-4.11-9 (e) (Supp. 1991); Alaska Stat. § 18-12-.070 (1986).

20. A clear exception is Alaska, which specifies the civil liability involved. There, the offending physician may be liable for a civil penalty not to exceed $1,000—plus any costs associated with the unwanted medical treatment; see Alaska Stat. § 18.12.070 (a) (1991). New Jersey provides that a noncooperating institution is subject to a civil fine of up to $1,000 for each offense; see N.J. Stat. Ann. § 26:2H-78(b) (West Supp. 1992).

21. See James Moskop, "Advance Directives in Medicine: Choosing Among the Alternatives," in *Advance Directives in Medicine* 15 (Andrew Hackler et al. eds., 1989).

22. Id. Concerning the absence of enforcement machinery in living-will type statutes, see Ben A. Rich, "The Values History: A New Standard of Care," 40 Emory L.J. 1009, 1117 (1991); Susan R. Martyn & Lynn B. Jacobs, "Legislating Advance Directives for the Terminally Ill: The Living Will and Durable Power of Attorney," 63 Neb. L. Rev. 779, 794 (1984).

23. But see *Foster v. Tourtellotte*, 704 F.2d 1109, 1113 (9th Cir. 1983) (denying liability because of a lack of precedent indicating the scope of a patient's constitutional rights in this area). More recent cases seem to provide the authority *Foster* found lacking. See *Gray v. Romeo*, 697 F. Supp. 580, 587–88 (D.R.I. 1988) (patient's constitutional right to refuse life-sustaining treatment could be exercised based on evidence of conversations patient had with husband and sister); *Tune v. Walter Reed Army Hosp.*, 602 F. Supp. 1452 (D.D.C. 1985) (ruling that a patient does have a constitutional right to reject treatment and that it can be exercised via an advance directive). See also Gasner, supra note 5, at 506–08.

24. Many living-will type statutes accord immunity to physicians who conform to reasonable medical standards. See Marguerite A. Chapman, "The Uniform Rights of the Terminally Ill Act: Too Little, Too Late?" 42 Ark. L. Rev. 319, 387 (1989). I previously argued that professional preferences as to terminal treatment must yield to patient autonomy. But the issue is sufficiently open so that counsel for the health-care providers will be making the argument that physicians can rely on sound medical practice. A few states' advance directive laws give special support to the physicians' defenses. For example, Connecticut permits the attending physician to use "best medical judgment" and mandates only that the physician "consider" the patient's wishes; see Conn. Gen. Stat. Ann. § 19a-571 (West Supp. 1992). Also, a couple of states explicitly excuse a physician from liability for ignoring an advance directive. See Cal. Civ. Code § 2438 (c) (West Supp. 1992); Ohio Rev. Code Ann. § 1337.15 (b) (Anderson Supp. 1991)

25. In chapter 3, I noted the restrictions posed by some living-will type statutes. I advised there that declarants use a nonstatutory directive in order to try and avoid these statutory constraints.

26. Of course, I would argue that if reasonable efforts to transfer the patient are unavailing, the health-care providers should be required to fulfill the patient's advance instructions.

27. In *Bartling v. Glendale Adventist Medical Center*, 228 Cal. Rptr. 847 (Ct. App. 1986), where a hospital and physicians had resisted a competent patient's rejection of life-sustaining care, the defendants paid $160,000 in attorneys' fees. See Evan R. Collins, Jr. and Doron Weber, *The Complete Guide to Living Wills* 94 (1991). See also Gasner, supra note 5, at 515–16 (concerning the availability of attorneys' fees).

28. See *Estate of Leach v. Shapiro*, 469 N.E.2d at 1052; Pedrick, supra note 5, at 396; Rich, supra note 22, at 1160–67.

29. One lower court judge recently commented: "Ohio's public policy . . . disfavors imposing liability upon a health care provider who allegedly saved or sustained a human life," in *Anderson v. St. Francis Hosp.*, No. 8910187, slip op. at 6 (Ohio Ct. Common Pleas 1991). See also Knapp & Hamilton, supra note 17, at 266 n.72; Gasner, supra note 5, at 517–19.

30. For criticism of the judicial hesitance to award damages for "wrongful life," see Rich, supra note 20, at 1167. In some jurisdictions, an additional obstacle exists. A number of states say that a person's cause of action for mental suffering does not survive the person's death. See W. Page Keeton et al., *Prosser and Keeton on The Law of Torts* 949 (5th ed. 1984); Gasner, supra note 5, at 517.

8. New Jersey's Model Legislation

1. New Jersey Advance Directives for Health Care Act, N.J. Stat. Ann. §§ 26:2H-53 to -78 (West Supp. 1992).

2. Cf. George J. Alexander, "Time for a New Law on Health Care Advance Directives," 42 Hastings L.J. 755 (1991) (urging that provisions dealing with advance directives be combined in a single statute).

3. New Jersey Commission on Legal and Ethical Problems in the Delivery of Health Care, *Advance Directives for Health Care: Planning Ahead for Important Health Care Decisions* (1991) [hereinafter Booklet of the New Jersey Bioethics Commission].

4. In Massachusetts, Michigan, and New York, a DPOA-HC type statute is the sole legislative enactment concerning advance medical directives. See Mass. Ann. Laws ch. 201D, §§ 1–17 (Law Co-op Supp. 1991); Mich. Stat. Ann. § 27.5496 (Callaghan Supp. 1991); N.Y. Pub. Health Law §§ 2980–2994 (McKinney Supp. 1992).

5. N.Y. Pub. Health Law § 2982 (1) (McKinney 1992).

6. See Tracy E. Miller, "Public Policy in the Wake of *Cruzan*: A Case Study of New York's Health Care Proxy Law," 18 Law, Med. & Health Care 360, 362 (1990).

7. See New York State Task Force on Life and the Law, *Life Sustaining Treatment: Making Decisions and Appointing a Health Care Agent* 75–83 (1987) [hereinafter New York State Task Force].

8. Id. at 82–83; Miller, supra note 6, at 362.

9. New York State Task Force, supra note 7, at 78; Miller, supra note 6, at 362. This claim seems spurious. An advance substantive directive can be geared to the general conditions of an incompetent patient rather than to specific maladies. See chapter 4, which deals with the drafting of an advance directive.

10. N.J. Stat. Ann. § 26:2H-64 (West Supp. 1992). This provision governs so long as an instruction directive offers some discernible guidance as to the particular medical decision being faced. If the directive does not provide any guidance as to the wishes of the incompetent patient under the circumstances at hand, then the A.D. Act is not applicable and New Jersey's common law of death and dying governs. See New Jersey Commission on Legal and Ethical Problems in the Delivery of Health Care, *Problems and Approaches in Health Care Decisionmaking: The New Jersey Experience* 163–64 (1990) [hereinafter Report of the New Jersey Bioethics Commission].

11. N.J. Stat. Ann. § 26:2H-67(a)(2)–(4) (West Supp. 1992).

12. N.J. Stat. Ann. § 26:2H-55 (West Supp. 1992).

13. See Report of the N.J. Bioethics Commission, supra note 10, at 140 (rejecting a fixed life expectancy limitation as "artificial and unrealistic"); see also id. at 170 (criticizing a terminal condition limitation as "overly restrictive" of patients' rights and "contrary to widely held societal values").

14. In defining the best-interests test applicable to an incompetent patient who has not left clear-cut prior instructions, the New Jersey Supreme Court has thus far confined "burdens" to physical pain or suffering. In re *Conroy*, 486 A.2d 1209, 1232 (N.J. 1985). See also In re *Peter*, 529 A.2d 419 n.5 (N.J. 1987) (reserving decision on whether the burdens associated with the best-interests test should include interests other than physical pain and suffering).

15. The comment to this section in the report confirms that a health-care agent is intended to have "broad authority to make the same kinds of health-care decisions the patient would have the right to make on his or her own behalf." Report of the New Jersey Bioethics Commission, supra note 10, at 155.

16. See id. at 80, 85–87, 98, 104, 106.

17. Id. at 80.

18. N.J. Stat. Ann. § 26:2H-63(d), (e) (West Supp. 1992); See Report of the New Jersey Bioethics Commission, supra note 10, at 106.

19. Report of the New Jersey Bioethics Commission, supra note 10, at 104. Many sources recognize that an incompetent patient's best interests should be defined in terms of the patient's own values and preferences. See Gerald Dworkin, The *Theory and Practice of Autonomy* 98 (1988).

20. Report of the New Jersey Bioethics Commission, supra note 10, at 87.

21. In re *Peter*, 529 A.2d 419, 425 (N.J. 1987).

22. In re *Farrell*, 529 A.2d 404 (N.J. 1987), indicates that a New Jersey patient's right to decline life-sustaining medical treatment is grounded in the judicially developed common law, in the state constitution, and in the federal constitution; see id. at 410. I also contend that the United States Supreme Court's *Cruzan* decision in July 1990 reinforces the conclusion that constitutionally based autonomy rights include the prospective decision to decline life-preserving medical intervention, even if the incompetent patient is preservable for an indefinite period; see chapter 2.

23. In re *Conroy*, 486 A.2d 1209, 1229 (N.J. 1985). State courts in several other jurisdictions have taken a similar posture. See *Brophy v. New England Sinai Hosp.*, 497 N.E.2d 626 (Mass. 1986); *John F. Kennedy Hosp. v. Bludworth*, 452 So. 2d 921 (Fla. 1984).

24. See *Farrell*, 529 A.2d at 410; *Fosmire v. Nicoleau*, 551 N.E.2d 77 (N.Y. 1990); *Bartling v. Superior Court*, 209 Cal. Rptr. 220 (Ct. App. 1984); *State v. McAfee*, 385 S.E.2d 651 (Ga. 1989).

25. See *Peter*, 529 A.2d at 419, 425 (N.J. 1987); John D. Arras, "The Severely Demented, Minimally Functional Patient: An Ethical Analysis," 36 J. Am. Geriatric Soc'y 938, 939–41 (1988); Yale Kamisar, "When Is There a Constitutional "Right to Die"? When Is There No Constitutional "Right to Live"?" 25 Ga. L. Rev. 1203 (1991); Nancy K. Rhoden, "The Limits of Legal Objectivity," 68 N. C. L. Rev. 845, 849–52 (1990).

26. See "Combined Advance Directive for Health Care" (sample form), in Booklet of the New Jersey Bioethics Commission, supra note 3, at 3.

27. Id.

28. See also the option in the DPOA form prepared by Charles P. Sabatino and printed by the A.B.A. Commission on Legal Problems of the Elderly, *Health Care Powers of Attorney* 3 (1990). One option there instructs the agent to consider "relief of suffering, the expense involved, and the quality as well as the possible extension" of life.

29. S.1211, 204th Leg., 1st Sess. (1990).

30. Id. at § 16. The patient would also have to be in a situation where the burdens of continued therapy would likely outweigh the benefits of continued existence. The meaning of burdens in that context was not perfectly clear, as prior discussion has indicated. Section 16 explicitly permitted removal of artificial nutrition from a patient in a permanently unconscious state. *Id.*

31. Report of the New Jersey Bioethics Commission, supra note 10, at 173.

32. Id. at 236. Twelve of the Commission's 25 members filed a separate statement disagreeing with the bill's differentiation of artificial nutrition from conventional medical technology.

33. President's Commission for the Study of Ethical Problems in Medicine and Biomedical

and Behavioral Research, *Deciding to Forego Life-Sustaining Treatment* 87–90 (1983); New York Task Force, supra note 7, at 38–40; Hastings Center Task Force on Death and Dying, *Hastings Center Guidelines on the Termination of Life-Sustaining Treatment and the Care of the Dying* 57–62 (1987).

34. N.J. Stat. Ann. §§ 26:2H-64(a), -61(f) (West Supp. 1992).

35. N.J. Stat. Ann. §§ 26:2H-61(f), -63(e) (West Supp. 1992).

36. Report of the New Jersey Bioethics Commission, supra note 10, at 104 n.1; see also id. at 87, 98, 162.

37. N.J. Stat. Ann. § 26:2H-67(a)(4) (West Supp. 1992).

38. Report of the New Jersey Bioethics Commission, supra note 10, at 107.

39. Id. at 89.

40. Report of the New Jersey Bioethics Commission, supra note 10, at 103.

41. N.J. Stat. Ann. § 26:2H-63(c) (West Supp. 1992).

42. Id. See also Report of the New Jersey Bioethics Commission, supra note 10, at 162.

43. N.J. Stat. Ann. § 26:2H-64(b) (West Supp. 1992).

44. N.J. Stat. Ann. § 26:2H-61(f) (West Supp. 1992).

45. Report of the New Jersey Bioethics Commission, supra note 10, at 103, 155.

46. See also N.J. Stat. Ann. § 26:2H-64(b) (West Supp. 1992), which anticipates some possible deviations from the terms of an advance directive.

47. See Report of the New Jersey Bioethics Commission, supra note 10, at 161 (ascribing the statutory language to "a commitment to the preservation of life"); see also id. at 106.

48. Section 62(b) of the Act clearly states that a physician may not "abandon" a patient by declining to participate in the withholding or withdrawal of measures to sustain life. N.J. Stat. Ann. § 26:2H-62(b) (West Supp. 1992).

49. Report of the New Jersey Bioethics Commission, supra note 10, at 158.

50. N.J. Stat. Ann. § 26:2H-65(b) (West Supp. 1992). An objecting religiously affiliated institution is required to take "all reasonable steps" to effect the transfer of the patient to another facility; see N.J. Stat. Ann. § 26:2H-65(a)(4), (b) (West Supp. 1992).

51. Report of the New Jersey Bioethics Commission, supra note 10 at 117, 167.

52. See id.

53. *Doe v. Bridgeton Hospital*, 366 A.2d 641 (N.J. 1976), cert. denied, 433 U.S. 914 (1976).

54. "Moral concepts cannot be the basis of a [charitable] hospital's regulations where that hospital is holding out the use of its facilities to the general public." Id. at 647. The court specifically refrained from deciding whether religiously affiliated institutions could refuse to perform elective abortions. *Id.* The opinion, however, interpreted the New Jersey legislation protecting institutional conscience as applicable only to sectarian institutions. *Id.*

55. N.Y. Pub. Health Law § 2984 (3) (Consol. Supp. 1990).

56. Id. at § 2984 (3)(b). See also Miller, supra note 6, at 364.

Index

Abortion: federal government regulations limiting counseling in clinics receiving federal funding, 88; state statutes concerning physicians' conscientious objections to, 91; recognition of institutional conscience by courts and legislatures, 96; New Jersey Supreme Court and differentiation between religiously affiliated and nonsectarian health-care institutions, 145

Adequacy of contemplation standard: justifications for deviations from terms of advance directives, 81–82

Administration, advance directives: justified and unjustified deviations from terms of, 77–86; third-party opposition to, 86–97; New Jersey Advance Directive Act and guidance on, 142–46; example of form for health-care power of attorney, 157

Advance directives: definition of, viii, 23; confinement of right to reject medical intervention to terminal patients, 10–14; problems in formulating, 24; practical difficulties affecting prospective autonomy, 25–29; enactment of living-will type legislation, 33–35; statutory constraints in living-will type laws, 35–41; designation of health-care agent, 41–43; choice of format for, 43–53; objectives of, 54–55; "no written directive" option, 55–57; short-form option, 57–59; option of sketching out intolerable debilitation, 59–61; Cantor option, 61–67; values-profile option, 67–69; miscellaneous optional provisions for, 69–71; generalized standards of interpretation, 72–74; declarant's wishes as basic guideline to interpretation, 74–77, deviations from terms of, 77–86; third-party opposition to administration of, 86–97; incompetency and conflicts with contemporaneous best interests, 98–102, 112–21; defining of interests of incompetent patients, 102–109; personal identity and status of incompetent persona, 109–12; mechanisms for enforcement, 122–26; internal institutional routes to enforcement, 126–30; litigation and enforcement, 130–34; New Jersey legislation as model, 135–46; im-

portance of legal and medical resolution of barriers to, 146–47; examples of, 149–53, 159–65

Advance Directives for Health Care Act (A.D. Act): as model for new or reform legislation, 135–47

Advocacy: role of health-care agent, 41–42, 123

Agent. *See* Health-care agent

American Medical Association Council on Ethical and Judicial Affairs: on withdrawal of artificial nutrition, 19

Anxiety: emotional benefits of advance directives, 28–29

Appeals: litigation and enforcement of advance directives, 132

Assent: incompetent patients and consultation on course of medical treatment, 84. *See also* Informed consent

Authority: health-care agents and opposition from health-care providers, 44; written instructions as check against agent's abuse of, 46–47

Autonomy, patient: legal and medical consensus about, 1–2; common-law sources of, 2; and state interest in sanctity of life, 8–10; confinement of rights to terminal patients, 10–14; right to relinquish existence preservable for extended period versus society's antipathy toward suicide, 14–17; competent patient and rejection of artificial nutrition, 17–21; accomplishment of death by means other than rejection of medical intervention, 21–22; incompetency and moral stature of future-oriented, 98–101. *See also* Prospective autonomy

Battery, doctrine of: common-law sources of patient autonomy, 2

Behavior: interpretation of advance directives, 77

Benefit: customary meaning of term and drafting of advance directives, 63

Best interests: inclusion of values and preferences of principal, 75; justifications for deviations from advance directives, 79–82; incompetency and conflicts of advance directives with con-

203

NORMAN L. CANTOR is Professor of Law, as well as Justice Nathan L. Jacobs Scholar, at Rutgers University School of Law, Newark. He was also a member of the faculty of law at Tel Aviv University. He has served as an advisor to counsel in the Karen Ann Quinlan case and as advisor to the New Jersey Bioethics Commission. He is author of *Legal Frontiers of Death and Dying*.

ipating the major problems likely to confront administrators of such directives, and discusses possible channels for enforcement of directives when health-care providers balk at implementation. Finally, he considers the moral foundation and the moral limits of future-oriented autonomy.

This book will be an important resource for any person involved in the design or application of an advance medical directive—physicians, nurses, hospital social workers, administrators of health-care institutions, lawyers, clergy, and lay people seriously concerned about exercising control over the dying process in today's high-tech medical environment.

NORMAN L. CANTOR is Professor of Law and Justice Nathan L. Jacobs Scholar at Rutgers University School of Law, Newark, and is also a member of the Faculty of Law at Tel Aviv University. He served as an advisor to counsel in the Karen Ann Quinlan case and as advisor to the New Jersey Bioethics Commission. He is author of *Legal Frontiers of Death and Dying* and numerous law journal articles covering legal aspects of death and dying.

THE ARTS AND
THEIR INTERRELATIONS

THE ARTS

AND THEIR

INTERRELATIONS

by Thomas Munro

Cleveland
THE PRESS OF WESTERN RESERVE UNIVERSITY
1967

700
M 92 a

64016

December, 1968

FOREWORD

This book is a general survey of the arts and of ideas about them. It includes a detailed comparison of the arts, to show their similarities and differences; the ways in which they cooperate and work for similar effects; the ways in which they diverge along separate lines. It provides an outline map of the field of the arts, indicating its main divisions and how they have arisen. This involves a description of the various mediums or materials used in the arts; of their principal techniques and processes; of the distinctive types of form produced in each.

Special attention is paid throughout to problems of definition and classification, not in a merely verbal, pedantic spirit, but as a necessary step to clear understanding of the facts themselves. This involves an examination of the nature of art in general, as distinguished from science, industry, and other activities; the nature of each of the principal arts, and of various groups of arts, such as fine and useful, major and minor, visual and auditory, combined arts, theater arts, industrial arts, and handicrafts. The ancient arts of sculpture and dance are compared with the newest, such as film and lumia. A critical survey is made of the chief attempts by philosophers to classify the arts, and to arrange them in some form of diagram or systematic table, according to their basic similarities and differences.

To show that these problems are of practical as well as theoretical importance, the discussion ranges over several widely separated fields of administration in which classifications of the arts are used—in particular, those of curriculum organization, library science, and personnel or occupational management. The effects of faulty, obsolete conceptions of the arts in these fields are pointed out and suggestions made for their correction.

It is sometimes assumed that the nature and interrelations of the arts are common knowledge by this time; that we can take these fundamentals for granted, and go on to more concrete problems. Those who think so will be surprised to discover how little has been written about such fundamentals in English, or in any language except German. They will be surprised to find what vague, conflicting ideas on the subject are current among influential writers today.

The history of ideas about the arts and their interrelations is an important and neglected thread in cultural history, and in the history of philosophy. It is a revealing indication of the different world-views

v

and social orders, from ancient Greece to the present day, in which these ideas have flourished. Beginning with the present situation in theories about the arts, we shall look backward from time to time at earlier beliefs from which our own have been derived.

This is not a book on art appreciation or on the history of the arts. If it were, it would be full of concrete examples of works of art for analysis and of references to particular artists. It does not describe in detail the history of relations between the arts in different periods. There are many such books, and this one has a different purpose. It is concerned more directly with theories about the arts, as expressed by philosophers, critics, and psychologists, than with particular works of art. The historical sections of the book emphasize the development of these ideas rather than the history of art itself. However, it is impossible to separate the two completely. Frequent mention is made of the great variety of styles which have arisen in each art at different times. This shows how hard it is to define the scope of a particular art. New experiments by artists themselves are constantly breaking down the artificial walls which theorists have tried to set up in order to determine the rightful "province" of each art.

An understanding of these theoretical issues can help in the understanding and appreciation of the arts themselves. We often hear that a certain work is bad because it goes outside the proper limits of its art. If it is a painting or a piece of music, it is said to do things which can be done only in literature, and should not be tried anywhere else. Such dubious assumptions, which we shall examine, directly influence judgments of art value. Chapter IX of this book is especially relevant to appreciation. It outlines a method for analyzing form in any art, and for comparing works of art as to form and style.

Much of the book is philosophical in scope and purpose. Present terms and theories about the arts are largely derived from *aesthetics*—a branch of philosophy which is now struggling toward scientific status. But we shall not confine ourselves, as many philosophers have done, to highly abstract questions of beauty and value. We shall go far outside the traditional limits of philosophy, in studying the nature of the particular arts.

Little is said about aesthetic value, and no theory is advanced about what is good or beautiful in art. Our aim is an objective, factual account of the arts, and of words and concepts used in talking about them. The general approach is that of philosophic naturalism, based on natural science; as such it will not seem adequate to mystics, supernaturalists and transcendentalists, who have their own theories about art.

Suggestions are made for improvements in the present terminology and conceptual apparatus for scientific study of the arts. These are made on a pragmatic or instrumentalist basis. It is assumed that words, definitions, and systems of classification are man-made things; that no one set of them is eternally right and true, and that they need to be constantly sharpened up to make them more effective tools of thought and discussion. The terminology of aesthetics and art criticism is now, to a large extent, confusingly ambiguous and loaded with misleading associations.

The chapters which follow touch upon many special fields and subjects in which art is studied or actively dealt with. They bring together many different approaches to art, and show many ways in which ideas about art are applied in practice. Suggestions are made for improvements along many of these lines. The book thus aims to be of use to readers interested in the following subjects:

1. Aesthetics; the philosophy and criticism of the arts.
2. The psychology of art; creation, appreciation; aesthetic experience.
3. The history of philosophy; cultural history; the history of ideas.
4. Semantics; the nature of words and meanings; the logic and psychology of conception, definition, and classification.
5. Art education, including education in music and literature.
6. The place of the arts and humanities in general education and in curriculum organization.
7. Library science; systems of classification as applied to books on the arts.
8. Art museum administration.
9. Encyclopedias; the place of the arts in the organization of knowledge as a whole.
10. Job analysis; occupational studies in relation to the arts.

T. M.

THE CLEVELAND MUSEUM OF ART
March, 1949

ACKNOWLEDGMENTS

Cordial thanks are extended to many former teachers, students, and colleagues, for aid and instruction in ways too numerous to itemize; to the trustees of the Cleveland Museum of Art for their encouragement of education and scholarship, and for the great resources of that institution; for recent help in connection with this book, to the following: William M. Milliken, director of the Cleveland Museum of Art, for many opportunities and kindnesses; George Boas, Ruth Bowman, Katharine Gilbert, Lucile Munro, Wolfgang Stechow, and Frederick S. Wight, for reading the manuscript and giving valuable suggestions; Houston Peterson and Herbert W. Schneider, for other friendly help; Prudence Myer, Beatrice Bowman, and Laura Gnagi, for careful lecture notes from my courses at Western Reserve University, on which this book is based; also for preparation of the manuscript.

Of the many definitions given, some are original, some are quoted from the *Oxford Dictionary,* and some are from other sources credited in the text. Otherwise, the definitions used in this book are reprinted by permission of the publishers of *Webster's New International Dictionary,* Second Edition, Copyright, 1934, by G. and C. Merriam Company. They are indicated by the word "Webster." Special thanks are extended to the Oxford University Press and to G. and C. Merriam Company for permission to quote this material.

Special acknowledgment is also made to the following publishers for permission to quote copyrighted material: *The Encyclopaedia Britannica;* The Philosophical Library, for quotations from the *Encyclopedia of the Arts;* the Columbia University Press, for quotations from *The Columbia Encyclopedia;* also to the many publishers named in footnotes, who gave permission for the quotations indicated, especially the following: Appleton-Century Co., Inc.; Cambridge University Press; Columbia University Press; Chatto & Windus; E. P. Dutton & Co.; Ernest Flammarion; Forest Press, Inc.; George Allen & Unwin, Ltd.; Harcourt, Brace & Co., Inc.; Harvard University Press; Henry Holt & Co.; Alfred A. Knopf; Lake Placid Club Education Foundation; Macmillan Co.; McGraw-Hill Book Co.; Methuen & Co.; W. W. Norton; Oxford University Press; Philosophical Library; Princeton University Press; G. P. Putnam's Sons; Stanford University Press; University of Chicago Press; University of Toronto Press; and Yale University Press.

T. M.

PREFACE TO THE SECOND EDITION

Since this book first appeared there has been a notable trend in education and scholarship toward a more broadly humanistic study of the arts, including comparative aesthetics. This trend has included a more objective approach in the spirit of empirical science, without exaggerated claims to scientific exactness or certainty. It has emphasized more careful observation and descriptive analysis of the work of art as a kind of cultural phenomenon. Since one of the chief aims of *The Arts and Their Interrelations* was to advocate these developments and to help lay a theoretical foundation for them, a persistent demand for the book has led to this new edition.

In revising it to meet the present situation, I have corrected a few typographical errors and clarified several statements, but have made no substantial cuts in the text. The only major change has been the addition of a final chapter entitled "Four Hundred Arts and Types of Art: A Systematic Classification." This was published in the *Journal of Aesthetics and Art Criticism* after the book appeared. The first edition of the book explained the need for a combined, many-purpose classification of the arts for theoretical and practical purposes, but did not provide one. The new final chapter does so. It also demonstrates in some detail a thesis maintained throughout the book, that far more arts exist in the modern world than the few which are commonly discussed in aesthetics and art history. The aim of the new final chapter is, not merely to enumerate or fit them into pigeon-holes, but to help explain their nature and interrelations.

T. M.

Cleveland Museum of Art, 1966

TABLE OF CONTENTS

PART ONE

THE NATURE OF THE ARTS

I. THE NEED FOR CLEAR THINKING ABOUT THE ARTS

II. THE CONCEPT OF FINE ARTS: ITS HISTORICAL BACKGROUND

III. THE MEANINGS OF ART

xi

Part Three

INDIVIDUAL CHARACTERISTICS OF THE ARTS

X. HOW CAN AN ART BE DEFINED?

Part One

THE NATURE OF THE ARTS

I

The Need for Clear Thinking about the Arts

1. Persistent problems and conflicting answers

What is art? As a type of human activity and product, what are its main, distinctive characteristics? As a field of phenomena for aesthetics and art history to examine, what does it include? What are the arts, as specific parts of this field, as distinctive pursuits and types of product? How are they related, as to similarities and differences, common and divergent aims and methods? How can they best be grouped and divided for study and teaching?

These and similar questions have been answered in many different ways during the past two hundred years. The arts change, and so do ideas about them. Some old arts, like mosaic and tapestry, have declined. New ones, like the motion picture, have grown extensively. Old arts are combined in new forms, as in the sound film made from "animated" paintings, with synchronized music and speech. New uses are made of old arts, in industry, commerce, and political propaganda. Applied science and machine industry have altered the methods, materials, and products of all the arts. Styles and standards are changed by revivals and exotic importations, such as the present strong influence of oriental and primitive arts. Trends in social organization and theory, in religion, philosophy, and ethics, alter men's views about the functions and values of art and about the relative importance of past artists and their works.

There is no final answer to the question "what are the arts?" or to the question "what should the arts become?" New answers must be made by each generation from the standpoint of its own beliefs and standards of value. These answers, of course, need not and should not be entirely new; but old conceptions must be constantly revised in the light of recent experience, for present situations and uses.

The field of phenomena studied by aesthetics is made up, to a large extent, of the arts and related types of experience. The particular arts are main divisions within this field. A general idea of their nature and interrelations, if correct, can provide the student with a preliminary survey of the field, and help him to direct his special studies within it.

Comparisons between the arts are always a popular subject of discussion between persons of artistic interests. One dogmatic assertion is countered by another *ad infinitum,* when artists in different fields meet and talk about their respective crafts, the peculiar difficulties and potentialities of each, and what an artist in each field should aim to do. Opinions range from one extreme to the other: from the view that the arts are utterly different, so that no comparison is possible, to the view that all the arts are fundamentally one, and their apparent differences merely superficial. Works in one art are often characterized in terms drawn from another: for example, that a piece of music is "dramatic" or "colorful." A painting is in "a low key" or "a harmony of muted tones." Analogies are drawn between line in painting and melody in music; between visual color and musical "tone-color." Bach's fugues are likened to Gothic cathedrals for their complex and rigorous design. But the specialized worker in a given art is usually impatient with such comparisons. He feels that his own craft and its problems are quite different from those of other artists.

Such arguments seldom arrive at any definite conclusion; partly because the persons who engage in them usually lack the patience for clear, systematic study. Artists and students often prefer an endless interchange of excited affirmations and denials, and feel that they are saying something new, profound, and penetrating. They fail to realize how often their thoughts revolve in ancient grooves and circles. Even the meanings of technical terms such as "art," "form," and "harmony," are treated as subjects for personal pronouncement, as in the familiar expression, "this is what it means to me."

Any systematic study of relations between the arts must deal, directly or indirectly, with problems of definition and classification. What is the distinctive, essential nature of painting as an art? Of poetry? Of music? Can the arts be grouped under various headings, such as "space arts" and "time arts," so as to bring out their basic connections and divergences? In the eighteenth and nineteenth centuries, these problems were attacked with enthusiasm, and many elaborate answers were produced. None of them is quite satisfactory in the twentieth century. But no adequate substitutes have been provided.

There has been little concern in recent years with classifications of the arts, by scholars in aesthetics. Some philosophers have condemned all attempts to work them out, as useless and foredoomed to failure. The arts, they say, are too intangible and changing to be defined or classified. There is much to be said for these objections. They provide a valuable warning against the grandiose, unrealistic theorizing which has been done in the past. But that is not the whole story. We shall not be satisfied with the negative conclusion that there is no use in further thinking about the matter.

Many artists and art-lovers have a hearty dislike for all definitions and classifications. All such talk is dull and boring, they say. Let us deal with art itself; with concrete works of art, and the flesh-and-blood artists who make them—not with endless verbal hair-splitting. Again, there is much to be said for this attitude. It is partly a question of personal likes and dislikes. Many persons are impatient with all theoretical studies of art: with all historical scholarship, and all attempts to understand the psychology of art and artists. Such studies, including the whole subject of aesthetics, are not for them. Even philosophers and aestheticians are often impatient with definition and classification. These are mere preliminaries, they feel; mere verbal A B C's, which any advanced scholar can take for granted. They, too, are anxious to get on to the concrete realities of art.

Unfortunately, one cannot always solve problems by ignoring them, or escape the consequences of ignoring them. In modern aesthetics and art criticism, a great deal of confusion arises from ambiguity in the meaning of basic terms, and from antiquated assumptions about the nature of the arts, which survive from previous centuries because they have never been replaced. However one may wish to come to grips with art itself, and avoid mere verbal issues, one has to use words in writing or talking about art; and there the trouble begins. The most up-to-date writers on ultra-modern art find themselves using the same old terms and concepts, for the lack of better ones. They take it for granted that everyone knows what the "fine arts" are, and what poetry is; never stopping to realize the astonishing variety of ways in which nearly all the basic terms of aesthetics are understood today.

Current criticism of the arts is permeated with traditional assumptions about the proper aims and limits of each art. What kind of effects and values should each one try to achieve? What kinds should it avoid, for fear of trespassing on the field of some other art? Should painting try to tell a story? Should music try to describe a scene? Or is this an encroachment on the field of literature and a confusion of values? Should sculpture employ colors or leave such effects to painting? Can poetry dispense with meaning and rely on the musical effects of word-sounds? Does a combined art, such as opera, preserve the values of all the arts within it and achieve the highest form of art? Or is music at its best when it specializes on its own distinctive effects, as pure music? The answers made to such questions often assume that each art has definite, proper limits, and is at its best when it stays within them. A work of art, old or new, is appraised as good or bad on the basis of such assumptions. We owe them especially to the eighteenth-century philosopher Lessing. Few contemporary critics are acquainted in detail with the "systems of the arts" produced by Kant, Hegel, and their followers; but these ideas still influence current thinking. Unconsciously, one inherits certain conceptions of the arts, produced mainly by German philosophers of a century or two ago. These conceptions one rarely stops to analyze; some of them would appear very dubious in the light of modern knowledge.

Definition and classification can be quite as interesting as any other phase in the general theory of art. They are a necessary part of the effort to think clearly about the facts of art as we know them, and to summarize our conceptions in an orderly way. Every subject, in progressing out of vague emotionalism and personal impressions toward scientific status, has to work out a set of definitions for its basic terms. It has to describe the main types of phenomena within its field, whether these are triangles, kinds of matter, species of animal life, or kinds of art. It has to investigate how these various types are interrelated; which are included in which; what types are broad and what ones are narrow. In aesthetics, too, such definition and classification are unavoidable, if we are to have clear thinking at all, and gradual advance toward science. As long as we ignore them, our thinking remains inevitably muddled in certain fundamental ways, and our attempts to deal with more advanced problems are impeded.

It is a mistake to think of definition and classification as "mere preliminaries," coming at an early stage in investigation. They come also at the end and in the middle, in fact, all along the line. Those made in the early stages of a subject always have to be revised later on, in the light of increasing knowledge. The ones we make now must be recognized as tentative hypotheses, sure to need further change in a few years' time. But we can summarize in them the results of our latest discoveries up to the present moment, and use them in turn as instruments in further inquiry.

The confusion begins with the basic terms "art" and "arts." The full extent of their ambiguity is not commonly realized. In the first place, the word "art" is applied to certain kinds of skill or technique, and also to the products of these skills—that is, to works of art. It is sometimes applied broadly to all kinds of useful skill, including medicine and agriculture; sometimes restricted to skill in certain media such as painting, or to skills aimed at producing "aesthetic pleasure." (This last term is itself a vague and controversial one.) The word "art" is sometimes used in a laudatory way, to imply high aesthetic quality in the product; sometimes in a neutral, indiscriminate way, as applied to all production and performance in certain fields.

Many of the terms used to classify the arts into various groups, such as "fine and useful arts," "major and minor arts," "decorative arts," and "arts of design," are also very differently understood. For example, music and literature are sometimes classed as fine arts. At other times, that term is restricted to a few visual arts, such as painting and sculpture. Thus our present nomenclature of the arts, though adequate for casual use, is far from being precise or standardized for technical discussion.

We imply a partial classification of the arts whenever we use such a term as "fine arts," "useful arts," "theater arts," "graphic arts," or "handicrafts." Several other terms, such as "space and time arts," "plastic arts," "imitative and non-imitative arts" are also used. Inclusive arts such as literature are divided into subclasses such as prose and poetry, drama and fiction. Some arts are closely connected, with much in common—for example, the pictorial arts of drawing, painting, and etching. Others, such as music and sculpture, seem farther apart, and it is harder to see what they have in common, or to group them under a single heading.

2. The need for clear definitions, as shown in the Brancusi case

What constitutes a work of art, and in particular, a piece of sculpture? What qualifies a man to call himself a sculptor? These were no academic questions a few years ago, when United States customs officials pondered whether to admit as art and as sculpture a work by the Rumanian modernist, Constantin Brancusi.[1] The case well illustrates how problems of philosophic theory can take on practical importance, and how the conduct of affairs—here legal and commercial—can be impeded by vague, confused thinking or by the conflicting views of supposed experts. It brings in several different ideas about the nature of art.

The object which aroused this celebrated and often amusing lawsuit was a bronze entitled *Bird in Flight,* which had been purchased by the American artist Edward Steichen. It was entered as a work of art in the form of a sculpture, with the claim that it was therefore entitled to entry free of duty. However, the New York collector of customs assessed it at 40% ad valorem as a manufacture of metal. He had been advised by certain artists, members of the National Academy and National Sculpture Society, that it was not art and not sculpture. When the case, *Brancusi vs. The United States,* was tried in the United States Customs Court, Robert Aitken was the main witness for the government. For the plaintiff, witnesses included Edward Steichen, owner of *Bird in Flight,* Jacob Epstein, Frank Crowninshield, Henry McBride, William H. Fox (Director of the Brooklyn Museum), and Forbes Watson (Editor of *The Arts*). The decision of three judges, rendered by Justice Waite, ruled that the object "is the original production of a professional sculptor and is in fact a piece of sculpture and a work of art," and as such entitled to free entry.

In this decision, which was hailed by *The Arts* as just, liberal, and intelligent, Justice Waite referred to an earlier court decision (1916) on the definition of sculpture. It had been cited by government counsel in the Brancusi case, in support of their contention that *Bird in Flight* was not sculpture. That earlier decision, which in its turn had referred for authority to both the *Standard Dictionary* and *Century Dictionary,* had said: "Sculpture as an art is that branch of the free fine arts which chisels or carves out of stone or other solid material or models in clay or other plastic substance for subsequent reproduction by carving or casting, imitations of natural objects in their true proportions of length, breadth, and thickness, or of length and breadth only." Justice Waite conceded that, although the piece

[1] Details of the case are given in *The Arts* for June and December, 1928 (XIII, No. 5, 327; and XIV, No. 6, 337).

had been characterized as a bird, "Without the exercise of rather a vivid imagination it bears no resemblance to a bird except, perchance, with such imagination it may be likened to the shape of the body of a bird. It has neither head nor feet nor feathers portrayed in the piece." Accordingly, he believed that "under the earlier decisions this importation would have been rejected as a work of art or, to be more accurate, as a work within the classification of high art."

However, he went on to say that "Under the influence of the modern schools of art the opinion previously held has been modified with reference to what is necessary to constitute art. . . . In the meanwhile there has been developing a so-called new school of art, whose exponents attempt to portray abstract ideas rather than to imitate natural objects. Whether or not we are in sympathy with these newer ideas and the schools which represent them, we think the fact of their existence and their influence upon the art world as recognized by the courts must be considered. The object now under consideration is shown to be for purely ornamental purposes, its use being the same as that of any piece of sculpture of the old masters. It is beautiful and symmetrical in outline, and while some difficulty might be encountered in associating it with a bird, it is nevertheless pleasing to look at and highly ornamental."

In effect, the decision held that the accepted meaning of "sculpture" and of "art" had changed since 1916; that to qualify as such an object no longer had to "imitate natural objects," or even to bear a definite resemblance to any natural object. What, then, did qualify *Bird in Flight* as sculptural art? In the first place, no one contested that it was made from solid material "in clay or other plastic substance for subsequent reproduction by carving or casting." Secondly, it was "for purely ornamental purposes." This was necessary in view of paragraph 1704 of the Tariff Act of 1922, which had stated that "the words 'painting' and 'sculpture' and 'statuary' as used in this paragraph shall not be understood to include any articles of utility." Justice Waite pointed out that certain court decisions had classed "drawings or sketches, designs for wall paper and textiles" as works of art, "although they were intended for an utilitarian purpose." No one had argued that *Bird in Flight* was useful and therefore disqualified as art. However, it was relevant to describe it as "for purely ornamental purposes." The court also undertook, without fear of the many theoretical difficulties involved, to decide that it was "beautiful," "pleasing," and "highly ornamental." No doubt the more conservative sculptors, called as witnesses for the government, remained unconvinced on this point.

As Forbes Watson, editor of *The Arts*, remarked before the trial, "There is no scientific proof that a work is or is not a work of art. Mr. Brancusi says that Mr. Aitken is not a sculptor and Mr. Aitken says that Mr. Brancusi is not a sculptor. These opinions are equally sincere and equally meaningless—except to those who enjoy the same artistic predilections." Obviously, the words "art" and "sculptor" are being used here with evaluative implications. "Art" is being restricted to products of high aesthetic worth. "Sculptor" does not include anyone who carves, casts, or models; but only those who do so with results considered valuable and meritorious, according to the standards one accepts.

"You cannot prove," continued Watson, "that a work of art is, but you can prove that it is a work of art to someone. If it can be proved that the intention of Brancusi was to create a piece of sculpture and that he was successful to the point of conveying his sculptural idea to others the purpose of the Tariff Act would be met, even if a hundred predisposed academicians should sincerely deny that the work was sculpture." This argument shifts the issue to the more objective, factual questions of (a) the artist's intentions, and (b) the likings and opinions of others. The object is to be regarded as art from the legal standpoint, according to this argument, if the artist intended it to be such, and if other persons (especially experts) regard it as such. Whether or not Brancusi is a sculptor would likewise be decided, not on evaluative grounds, but again on the basis of easily established facts—whether he had studied and practiced sculpture professionally. Watson and others brought evidence to show that *Bird in Flight* and its creator did qualify on these grounds. The judges were impressed by it, for Justice Waite's decision stressed the points that (a) Brancusi had been shown to be a professional sculptor of established reputation, (b) the work was original, (c) some, though not all, of the "persons competent to judge upon that subject" regarded it as art and sculpture. It was not expressly stated that beauty or aesthetic value is a matter of individual taste, or that anything is good art if a considerable number of reputable experts like it; but this was the general tone of the prevailing arguments. There was a strong desire, at the same time, to put aside the whole question of values—not to decide how good the object and its maker were, but to establish new, non-evaluative definitions of art and sculpture.[2] According to these, anyone would be a sculptor who had received professional training in sculptural techniques and was practicing them professionally. Anything would be a work of art which was intended as such by a professional artist, and regarded as such by experts of established reputation in the field.

Among other things, the Brancusi case illustrates the fact that art today is not a remote and trivial affair, of penniless Bohemians in garrets. The making and selling of "art goods" is an industry, or a group of industries, running into vast annual sums. Copyrights of the stories, tunes, and jingles used in radio and advertising, rights to motion picture scenarios, phonograph records and popular color-print reproductions, run into figures that arouse frequent legal dispute, with sharp legal talent on both sides. Questions of the nature and inter-relation of the arts are no longer allowed to remain in the placid backwaters of philosophy, but are dragged into court and marketplace, with impatient calls for some definite ruling on the meaning of terms.

3. Classification of the arts for practical purposes

Far from being a merely theoretical problem, the way in which arts are defined and classified—whether rightly or wrongly—affects the practical organization and conduct of the arts themselves. It is bound up with educational administration, and helps to determine how the arts shall be taught; what shall be the curricula of art academies, music institutes, and liberal arts colleges. Within each of these schools, separate departments and courses are usually set up, such as "Fine Arts," "Industrial Arts," "Musical Arts," and the like; each implying a partial classification and a theory—often not clearly realized—on what a certain group should cover. The training of prospective artists and scholars in all these fields is correspondingly specialized, and their subsequent outlook is influenced. New schools

---

[2] The argument over what is and what is not sculpture goes merrily on. For example, see the article on Alexander Calder's "mobiles" in the *Art Digest*, XXII, No. 6 (Dec., 1947), 17, entitled "It May Not Be Sculpture—But It's Vital." The French aesthetician E. Souriau prefers to call abstract, non-representative sculpture a kind of architecture (*La correspondance des arts*, Paris, 1947).

and faculties are organized, researches are planned and published, technical journals are edited, books on the arts are classified in libraries and publishers' lists.

Artists in various mediums, teachers and scholars, museum officials, band themselves into professional organizations, and sometimes into craft unions, on the basis of current distinctions among the arts. Whenever a government census bureau or a labor union works out a list of occupations in the field of art, it has to classify the arts. It divides them into occupational groups, such as architects, musicians, and graphic artists (including draughtsmen, lithographers, etc.), along with garment designers, scene painters, and others. Playwrights and musicians organize themselves into leagues of authors, composers, and performers. For legal and administrative reasons involving large sums of money, the definition of a certain art or type of artist and his services or products must be made as clear and true to fact as possible. Admission to certain craft unions, such as the motion picture photographers', is greatly sought after; hence the question of what constitutes an artist in these fields is no matter of idle hair-splitting.

Library science has dealt directly and systematically with the problem of classifying books on the arts. It has evolved not one but several systems of headings and subheadings, with the aim of arranging books and filing cards so that librarians can easily decide where to put a new book, and so that readers can easily find it.

Art museums face the problem of classifying many different products under convenient headings, such as paintings, prints, textiles; classical art, oriental art, and decorative arts. Original works of art, photographs, lantern slides, record cards, and the like must be somehow grouped and subdivided for arrangement into galleries or filing cabinets, and for the assignment of specially trained personnel to care for them. Such an arrangement must not be merely arbitrary or casual; it must somehow express the nature of the facts themselves, so that people can find a thing where it ought to be. It must sometimes be adapted to the various ways in which the objects are to be used. For example, lantern slides will be used by artists who wish to find examples of a certain medium or technique such as enamelling, or various portrayals of a certain subject, such as birds or trees. Some teachers wish to select materials on a chronological basis; others on a geographical basis, or on one of abstract types such as classic and romantic. In such a context as this, verbal systems of classification emerge out of practical experience, becoming more extensive and precise as needs determine. They usually begin with traditional terminology, but change and augment it as time goes on.

Such practical systems of classification usually have the merit of close touch with concrete phenomena. They are functional, and seldom rigid or artificial. They are flexible, adaptable to change, so that new arts or branches of art can be admitted. We shall consider them in more detail later on. However, all of them have limitations and difficulties of their own. None is perfect or adaptable to all uses. Hence the need remains for aesthetics to compare and criticize them from a broader, philosophical standpoint, and to survey the whole problem without restriction to any one special use.

All these practical modes of organization have been thought out and directed, to a large extent, in terms of traditional names and classifications. The distinctions made therein, as we shall see, are sometimes false and misleading. By imposing arbitrary, sharp distinctions between certain arts in theory, they help to place wide gulfs between them as actual careers and courses of study. For example, music, painting, and literature are so widely separated on the higher levels of education that it is hard for a student to see their interrelations or to study them in close combination. The artist's range of creative work is narrowed by the traditional belief that each art has certain necessary "limits" beyond which he cannot go without violating aesthetic laws. Thus the tremendous modern pressure toward specialization is aggravated by excessively compartmental theories of the arts.

Educators whose minds do not comfortably dwell in such tight compartments protest, calling for "integration" and "orientation." As one phase of this reaction, there has been a new emphasis in recent years on the active interrelation of the arts. Should visual art be taught as a separate subject or somehow "integrated" with history, literature, music, and other subjects? What is its own proper content of history, appreciation, and technical skills? Specialists in a certain art sometimes object strongly to so-called "integration," and with some reason, on the ground that it tends to lose or overwhelm the essentials of that particular art, through subordinating it unduly to some other subject. Thus teachers of painting and art appreciation rightly object when their part in a school curriculum is relegated to the making of posters on safety or hygiene for "social studies" and other school activities.

But what are the essentials of painting as a fine art, in technique and appreciation? How are they related to the various practical uses which society, in school and out, now requires of its artists? Can painting, literature, music, and acting be harmoniously merged in theater art "projects," as a way to study the history of a certain period?

Such educational questions raise anew the problem of how the arts are and should be interrelated; what are the main concerns of each, and how they can best cooperate. They call for a thorough reconsideration of inherited concepts, in the light of present needs and artistic tendencies.

To be sure, neither artists nor teachers are bound to follow past aesthetic theories or use traditional concepts. Consciously, they often strive to be original. Sometimes they work out new conceptions, which aesthetics itself later adopts. Few artists, and not many educators, have ever read a book on the classification of the arts, or would feel bound by its conclusions if they did. But it is not easy to escape from the grooves of thought and action marked out by past authorities. It is not easy for an individual worker to establish a new terminology, a new set of theoretical distinctions in a complex field, or to make others understand them. The terms and meanings which have been stamped with authority by such a philosopher as Aristotle sift down through innumerable cultural channels to help determine, unconsciously, the attitudes and mental processes of modern artists, writers, and teachers. Conservative writers and university professors cling to venerable concepts and resist innovations. In spite of all this, basic concepts do change, in fields where active theoretical progress is going on, as in psychology and the social sciences. Interest and active discussion, on the part of those concerned with aesthetic theory, can gradually sharpen up our traditional and somewhat obsolete terminology.

4. *Classification of the arts as a problem of philosophy and science*

The attempt to group all the arts systematically, under one consistent set of headings and subheadings, is known as "classification of the arts," "division of the arts," or "system of the arts." (There are slight differences in meaning between these terms, which we shall notice later.)

The task of working out a systematic classification or division of the arts has been a recognized problem of aesthetics since the eighteenth century. It has challenged the ingenuity of philosophers, especially in Germany, up to the present time. The aim is not a merely superficial grouping, as in classifying things alphabetically or chronologically, but one based on fundamental resemblances and differences among the facts themselves, as in biological classifications of plants and animals. At the same time, attempts are made to define the individual arts in terms of their supposed aims and limits, their methods and types of product. An important place has been assigned by German philosophers to the problem of classifying the arts. This is illustrated by Max Schasler's remark that "the classification of the arts must be regarded as the real touchstone, the real differential test of the scientific value of an aesthetic system; for on this point all theoretical questions are concentrated and crowd together to find a concrete solution." [3]

In English, one of the latest attempts at a large-scale, systematic theory of the arts is that of Sydney Colvin, whose articles on "Art" and "Fine Arts" were published in the eleventh edition of the *Encyclopaedia Britannica* in 1910. As we shall see, it is open to serious objection, but it is still influential and often followed. Many notable studies have appeared in German since that time, some of which we shall examine. But English-speaking scholars have not been drawn to improve on Colvin, to any great extent.

Some of the classifications worked out by early philosophers were based on dubious, evaluative criteria, as in the theory of "liberal" and "servile" arts, which implied an aristocratic prejudice against the practical, useful, and manual. Later on, highly absolutistic, rigid systems of classification were proposed, which failed to allow for the changing, intermingled character of the arts.

In protest, other philosophers (notably Croce and Dewey) have denounced the whole effort to classify the arts systematically, as mistaken and useless. This has helped to throw it into some disfavor as a subject for discussion in aesthetics. The most extreme view is that of Croce, who asserts that "any attempt at an aesthetic classification of the arts is absurd. If they be without limits, they are not exactly determinable, and consequently cannot be philosophically classified. All the books dealing with classifications and systems of

---

[3] *Das System der Künste* (Leipzig-Berlin), p. 47. *Cf.* B. Croce, *Aesthetic*, New York: The Macmillan Co., 1922, p. 456.

the arts could be burned without any loss whatever." [4] In a more moderate tone, John Dewey also takes a negative attitude. "If art is an intrinsic quality of activity," he warns, "we cannot divide and subdivide it. . . . Rigid classifications are inept (if they are taken seriously) because they distract attention from that which is esthetically basic—the qualitatively unique and integral character of experience of an art product. . . . They inevitably neglect transitional and connecting links." [5]

There has been a tendency among philosophers, especially those outside of Germany, to jump from one extreme to the other on the subject of classifying the arts. It was once the fashion to construct vast, compartmental systems of the arts, with a claim to eternal rightness and completeness. The Platonic idealist, believing in the independent reality of universals or general concepts, found it easy to infer that each *art* was a fixed, transcendent realm of Being. To define an art, then, was to state the eternal limits of that realm; and to classify the arts was to show how all were eternally fitted together as a logical structure in the cosmic mind. In the traditional, Aristotelian logic, a definition stated the "essence" of what was defined. Definition was not of mere names or words, but of *things* of a certain sort. Everything had a determinate essence, and there was only one definition appropriate to it: that which expressed the essence. [6] So long as there was a belief in the fixity of organic species, each species (of animals, arts, or other things) was thought to have an essence which must be stated in the definition.

Romantic philosophers will have none of this fixity in regard to the arts. All is in flux, at least in the world of sensory experience. The romanticist revels in the uniqueness and constant change of all phenomena, including works of art. He prefers to think of art as a process of creating and experiencing, rather than of the finished work of art as a static form. But individual works of art, in all their sensory fullness, seem much more real and significant than any scientific generalizations about art. Each is unique, and each moment in which

---

[4] Croce, *op. cit.*, p. 114.

[5] *Art as Experience* (New York, 1934), pp. 214-217.

[6] *Cf.* L. S. Stebbing, *A Modern Introduction to Logic* (London: Methuen, 1933), p. 432. *Cf.* B. C. Heyl, *New Bearings in Esthetics and Art Criticism* (New Haven: Yale U. Press, 1943), p. 20, on "real definitions" of art.

it is experienced is unique. These are the aspects of art to be cherished; why bother with abstract concepts of types and species, which never fit the changing facts? Classifications are anathema to the romanticist, because they seem to threaten a harnessing of the infinite variety of art by some repressive, conceptual framework. Dewey mentions with approval how "William James remarked on the tediousness of elaborate classification of things that merge and vary as do human emotions. Attempts at precise and systematic classification of fine arts seem to me to share this tediousness." [7]

Those romanticists who incline toward mystic transcendentalism, such as Emerson, tend to oppose all attempts to study the arts from the standpoint of natural science. Such an approach, they assert, loses sight of the inward, spiritual values of art. The cosmic mind, some of them believe, is gradually externalizing itself through art and nature. Thus the philosopher tries to look through the individual work of art to something ineffable and purely spiritual, to the inward vision of the artist, in which there is something divinely creative. He feels strongly the "oneness" of all the arts, and resents attempts to distinguish systematically between them. Most of the differences between the arts seem concerned with external, superficial matters of medium and technique. To describe them may be of some practical utility, but can provide no basis for a genuine scientific classification of the arts. Says Croce, "The collection of technical knowledge at the service of artists desirous of externalizing their expressions, can be divided into groups, which may be entitled *theories of the arts*." Thus arise theories of architecture, sculpture, painting, oratory, and music. "It should be evident that such empirical collections are not reducible to science. They are composed of notions, taken from various sciences and disciplines, and their philosophical and scientific principles are to be found in the latter. To propose to construct a scientific theory of the different arts would be to wish to reduce to the single and homogeneous what is by nature multiple and heterogeneous." [8]

The romantic antipathy toward natural science goes far beyond the limited issue of classifying the arts, and beyond aesthetics itself.

[7] *Ibid.*, p. 217.

[8] *Op. cit.*, p. 112. For criticism of Croce's views on classification in art, see "Classification, Literary," by C. LaDrière, in *Dictionary of World Literature.* New York, 1943.

The resentment expressed by James and Dewey toward attempts at classifying arts or emotions could be extended toward all recent psychology and biology, with their attempts at describing the subtle mysteries of mind, personality, and life in terms of an abstract, conceptual framework. In fact, similar attacks have been made on these sciences by Bergson and by various modern mystics.

No doubt, all classification is somewhat tedious; and so is much of the slow, detailed observation and inference of scientific method in every field. That is, it is tedious to those who prefer to practice the arts or to generalize about them in an informal, literary way. Others find it absorbing, and it is certainly an integral part of all progress along the lines of natural science. If the naturalistic assumption is correct, the arts are not fundamentally different from other kinds of natural phenomena, though perhaps more subtle, complex and variable. The difficulty in aesthetics with regard to classification and other rational processes is different only in degree from that which exists in any science dealing with the merging, shifting phenomena of life and mind. These processes may have to go ahead more slowly and cautiously in aesthetics, but are not barred entirely by the nature of things.

In biology, the effect of evolutionism was to destroy the notion of fixed organic species. As Dewey has well explained, that effect has spread through every field of thought including philosophy.[9] But it has not deterred biologists in the least from working out detailed and increasingly systematic classifications in their own field. The fact that their phenomena were now seen to be in constant change (some slowly and some rapidly) was no bar to describing and classifying whatever temporary configurations might appear in organic life. The fact that some early, pre-evolutionary classifications of organic species were excessively sharp and rigid is not held up as a bogy, to frighten off all attempts at a better one. Quite the contrary, it is a spur to continued effort. Some of the groups or classes which biology classifies are ephemeral variants; others, like the conservative clam, last for millions of years—long enough to justify a name and definition. It

---

[9] John Dewey, *The Influence of Darwin on Philosophy.* New York, 1910. In *Reconstruction in Philosophy* (New York, 1920, p. 152 f.), Dewey recognizes the value of special classifications in science, as guides to thought and action. See also his Introduction to H. E. Bliss's *The Organization of Knowledge and the System of the Sciences,* New York, 1929.

is taken for granted that all such concepts are flexible and subject to change in the light of new facts or new knowledge.

In every science, the steady improvement of nomenclature, definition, and classification is an essential phase of advance. Biology did not achieve scientific status until after Linnaeus had established a system of classifying plants, with definite names for species and subspecies.[10] This opened the door to countless other lines of research, including the study of evolution. Biological classifications have had to be changed many times since Linnaeus' crude system based on the stamens and pistils of plants. Taxonomy, in which various systems of classification are studied and improved, is an active and important branch of biology today.

Aesthetics should follow its example, in systematizing its concepts as much as the facts will permit. Like those of biology, some types of art change less rapidly than others, and assume more clear-cut form while they last. These can be named and described more definitely by the scientist. Such types as painting and sculpture, though not eternal, are as old as human civilization. There are intermediate types, such as painted reliefs, but there are also examples which belong definitely under one or the other. The *Mona Lisa* is definitely a painting, and Michelangelo's *David* is a piece of sculpture. The Greek orders of architecture have remained alive as persistent styles for more than two millennia, in spite of many adaptive modifications. It is misleading, therefore, to overstress the change and merging of aesthetic phenomena, as if all were in a state of chaotic, bewildering flux. On the whole, they change faster than biological species do, but not without many highly stable configurations. These can be taken as the basis for a systematic classification of types.

At the same time, it should henceforth be taken for granted that no aesthetic system can be absolutely clearcut or permanent. However defined, the various arts do overlap to such an extent that no sharp boundaries can be drawn between them. Proceeding from a naturalistic, relativistic point of view in philosophy, one must assume that art in general and all the particular arts are evolutionary types in process of constant change, as parts of the larger process of cultural evolution. Any modern attempt to define and classify them must frankly disown

[10] On the work of Linnaeus, his predecessors and successors, see E. Nordenskiöld, *The History of Biology* (New York, 1928), pp. 190-219.

any claim to absolute validity on a metaphysical, psychological, or other basis. It must aim instead at more limited, temporary usefulness as a set of intellectual tools for dealing with the past and present phenomena of art.

5. The need for flexible concepts and methods

In a broad sense, definition and classification are basic mental processes, common to all intelligent thinking. Definition, in this sense, is only trying to make plain what we mean by a word. Classification, fundamentally, is the process of grouping and separating various phenomena on a basis of likeness and difference. All language and all perception involve classification. It involves comparison and abstraction, in perceiving certain qualities of an individual or group apart from others. It involves the forming of concepts of these various groups, individuals, and qualities, with verbal names or signs to record them and communicate them to others. In this broad sense, no reasonable person could object to definition and classification, or try to avoid them. Every philosopher, whatever his views, practices them constantly.

Like other phases of reasoning, however, they have been developed by formal logic into highly specialized, technical processes, each with its own rules, and with high standards of scientific precision. In a narrow sense, classification is restricted to the process of arranging individuals into groups according to their degrees of likeness, and combining these groups into still larger groups or one all-inclusive group. The opposite procedure is then called "division." Here a single group is divided and subdivided according to some quality possessed or not possessed by some of the individuals it contains.

Strictly speaking, the process of dividing the group called "art" into smaller and smaller subgroups is often referred to as "division of the arts"; but "classification" is commonly employed to cover both phases of the process. The final scheme, or "system of the arts," also includes both grouping and dividing, according to whether one works up to the broadest or down to the narrowest class. A system of the arts usually undertakes to do more than classify them: it is a philosophic theory of their basic interrelations, and perhaps of their past evolution and relative values. To outline such a system may involve a good deal more than simple classification and division. It may introduce several bases of division, and show how the results are inter-related. It thus combines several different, briefer classifications, and attempts to explain them in a thorough way.

Formal logic set up ideally precise rules of correct definition and classification, which can be fully achieved only in the exact sciences; perhaps only in mathematics and formal logic itself, and not always there. As we have seen, traditional logicians thought of "defining" a concept as setting precise limits to it, marking it off sharply from all others. This led to the erroneous notion (so strongly resented by Croce and Dewey) that "defining" an art meant setting definite limits to it, permanent limits based on the eternal nature of things, limits in the sense of walls and prohibitions beyond which an artist should not go in trying for effects which are "proper" to some other art. Such a concept, as we have seen, is pre-evolutionary, and has long since been abandoned in natural science. Most certainly, it has no place in modern aesthetics.

To define a concept now is, primarily, to define the meaning of a *word,* as determined by current human usage—not by the objective nature of things. Concepts, of course, are intended to correspond in certain ways with objective reality or at least with perceptual experi-ence—just how, is a difficult problem of epistemology. Most concepts and their meanings are not constructed in a purely arbitrary, fanciful way, as products of human imagination. Definition is in part, then, a process of adjusting words and meanings to the requirements of intel-lectual and practical experience in dealing with our environments. But there is nothing sacred or irrevocably determined for all time about the definition of a word. It is a human product, a tool of thought and communication. What any word shall mean—for example, the English word "art" or "poetry"—is something for people to decide on the basis of expediency in discussion.[11]

The meaning or definition of most words has no precise limits, in reality or in human thought. Each concept marks off an approximate area of connotation and denotation which is fairly clear at the center, but shades off gradually into others toward the margin, which is never clearly defined. For example, everyone will agree that the Parthenon is art, and that an ordinary heap of builders' refuse—scattered bits of brick and mortar—is not art. But in between are many borderline,

[11] *Cf.* B. C. Heyl, *op. cit.,* Ch. I, on various types of definition from a stand-point of semantics.

debatable examples, and no possible definition of "art" can draw a completely satisfactory, sharp line between them.

The formal rules of logical classification, which are quoted in textbooks on library science and elsewhere, are harmless enough, and sometimes useful as remote ideals, if not applied too rigidly. It is well to remember that "characteristics must be used consistently at each step of the division." If we use such a term as "fine," "applied," or "decorative" to distinguish one group of arts from another, we should not use it elsewhere in the same classification, in another sense. In dividing a class into subclasses, we should if possible use one basis of division only, within that step of the process. Even where no great precision is sought, clear thinking demands a certain consistency in the arrangement of ideas.

On the other hand, to insist that "co-ordinate classes must be mutually exclusive," and that "division must be exhaustive," is to call for a standard of precision which is unattainable in aesthetics at present. It can be dangerous when it leads a theorist to distort the facts in order to achieve what he thinks is necessary for a correct, logical system of classification. It is not incorrect or illogical to violate these traditional rules to some extent, in dealing with natural phenomena, especially those of life, mind, and art. In fact, it is impossible to live up to them, not only in aesthetics, but in all other natural sciences. Says Stebbing:

No scientific classification achieves the ideal of logical division. Natural species are not demarcated one from another in a way analogous to the division of classes (by formal logic). . . . One species is connected with another by intermediate links. . . . This being the case, it follows that a biological classification cannot strictly conform to the rule that classes should not overlap. Nor can it secure an exhaustive division, since there are many gaps in the series of living organisms. . . . But though the mode of classification has been profoundly affected by the thoroughgoing acceptance of the principle of continuity of descent, the aim of classification remains unaffected, namely, so to arrange classes that their relations may be exhibited in accordance with the principles of hierarchical order.[12]

In short, what Dewey and others object to as "rigid classification" is only one kind of scientific classification, and one which is largely

---

[12] Stebbing, *A Modern Introduction to Logic* (London: Methuen), p. 438.

obsolete in natural science generally. A far more flexible type, which takes account of the merging and changing character of natural phenomena, is highly developed in fields other than aesthetics. It can and will be worked out there also, in due course of time. Any workable classification in aesthetics must give up all hope of neat, mathematical precision. It must be content to group phenomena roughly and approximately, under headings which will indicate important similarities and differences, thus providing useful bases for generalization.

To leave out all grouping and subgrouping is to lose the great value of classification in organizing data. Nor is a mere alphabetical or other superficial grouping enough for scientific purposes; it must bring out important inner relationships. Dewey concedes that "an enumerative classification is convenient and for purposes of easy reference indispensable. But a cataloguing like painting, statuary, poetry, drama, dancing, landscape gardening, architecture, singing, musical instrumentation, etc., etc., makes no pretense to throwing any light on the intrinsic nature of things listed. It leaves that illumination to come from the only place it can come from—individual works of art." [13] True, the illumination must come primarily from observing individual works of art, but that is only part of the story. Illumination, in the form of recognizing important likenesses and differences, important recurring types within the phenomena of art, needs to be expressed and recorded in the form of general concepts, names of groups and classes, under which examples can be variously marshalled.

Between the old absolutistic classification which Dewey attacks and the mere enumerative listing which he tolerates, there is a middle ground of flexible, tentative systematization. Here, as in the older natural sciences, lies an open road for theoretical advance in aesthetics. The dangers of absolutism have now been so amply pointed out in aesthetics, and so thoroughly outgrown in other fields, that there seems to be little reason for dwelling further on a negative, cautionary attitude. The warning has been salutary, for outworn conceptions have a way of surviving in aesthetics long after they have been superseded elsewhere. Absolutism has had a long lease of life in aesthetics, and is still far from dead. But it is hardly seductive enough to lure astray every student who attempts an aesthetic classification.

The problem of classifying the arts is closely related to that of

[13] *Ibid.*, p. 217.

defining particular arts, and of defining art in general. All definition is related to classification, in that one of the best ways of defining a thing is to locate it within a larger class (its "genus") and then to show how it differs from other members of that class (its "differentia"). Thus we may define "art" as a kind of skill, which differs in certain respects from other kinds of skill. Classification, on the other hand, cannot go far without defining the various headings and subheadings it employs—unless, indeed, the classification is a very superficial one, on an alphabetical or other external basis, which makes no attempt at bringing out the inner likenesses and differences of things. "A classification of species," says Stebbing, "enables us to obtain easily a definition of any species. . . . The two processes proceed *pari passu*. . . . We must know the properties of a species before we can know with what species it can be co-ordinated and under what genus. On the other hand, we may reach more determinate knowledge of the characteristics of the species through the process of comparing and contrasting it with the other species entering into the classification." [14]

In trying to classify the arts significantly, one necessarily defines them, at least roughly and partially, by giving some idea of the genus and differentiae of each—the broader art or group of arts which includes it, and the narrower ones which it includes. Thus poetry may be classified as a type of literature which includes epic, lyric, and dramatic poetry. One may define a single art in comparative isolation, mentioning only the class immediately larger, and some of its own direct subdivisions. In other words, one can define poetry without trying to show its relation to music or architecture. One can even give separate definitions of all the known arts, as in a dictionary, without attempting to show their mutual relations systematically. On the other hand, one can classify the arts in a merely topical, schematic way, by arranging their names in some brief table of headings and subheadings, and yet give no explicit definition of any one art.

In short, the two problems can be separately studied; but it is more advantageous to study them together, for each leads to the other when carefully pursued. We shall study both in the following pages, with the emphasis on systematic, extensive classifications which attempt to bring in all or most of the arts, and to explain as clearly as possible the nature of each as well as its relations to others.

[14] *Op. cit.*, p. 437.

The problem of classification in aesthetics is not limited to classifying whole *arts* as such. Works of art can be classified in many different ways: under various abstract types of form and style, according to chronological, geographical, or national origin, and so on. The skills and processes involved in art production and performance can be grouped for study on psychological grounds, or from an ethnological or sociological standpoint, as parts of a culture-pattern. In the following pages, we shall consider some difficulties which arise in the attempt to classify whole arts in any single system. But it is one important way of organizing the phenomena of aesthetics, and as such deserves attention.

II

The Concept of Fine Arts: Its Historical Background

1. The origin of the English term "fine arts" in the eighteenth century

The aesthetic sense of the word "art," says R. G. Collingwood, is recent in origin. *Ars* in ancient Latin means a craft or specialized form of skill, like carpentry or smithying or surgery. *Ars* in medieval Latin meant any special form of book-learning, such as grammar or logic, magic or astrology. That is still its meaning in the time of Shakespeare. But the Renaissance, first in Italy and then elsewhere, re-established the old meaning; and the Renaissance artists, like those of the ancient world, did actually think of themselves as craftsmen. It was not until the seventeenth century that the problems and conceptions of aesthetic began to be disentangled from those of technic or the philosophy of art. In the late eighteenth century the disentanglement had gone so far as to establish a distinction between the fine arts and the useful arts; where "fine" arts meant, not delicate or highly skilled arts, but "beautiful" arts. In the nineteenth century, this phrase, abbreviated by leaving out the epithet and generalized by substituting the singular for the distributive plural, became "art." [1]

The English term "fine art" is a product of the eighteenth century. The *Oxford Dictionary* states that it was originally used in the plural as a translation of the French *beaux-arts,* and that "fine" as an adjective meaning "beautiful" is often used as equivalent to *beau.* "Fine art," then, means "In plural, the arts which are concerned with 'the beautiful,' or which appeal to the faculty of taste; in the widest use including poetry, eloquence, music, etc., but often applied in a more restricted sense to the arts of design, as painting, sculpture,

---

[1] *The Principles of Art* (Oxford U. Press, 1938), pp. 5-6. On the meaning of "art" in Shakespeare, see for example *The Tempest*, Act V. Scene i: "Graves at my command / Have wak'd their sleepers, op'd, and let 'em forth / By my so potent art."

and architecture. Hence in singular one of these arts." The earliest examples which the *Oxford Dictionary* cites are as follows: "1767 Fordyce, *Serm. Yng. Wom.* I. vi 250. They . . . wanted instruction in the principles of the Fine Arts. 1785 Reid, *Int. Powers.* VI. vi. The fine arts are very properly called the arts of taste."

Samuel Johnson's *Dictionary of the English Language,* in its 1773 edition, makes no reference to "fine art" as a technical term. It does list, among the meanings of "fine" as an adjective: "elegant, beautiful in thought or language, accomplished, elegant of manners, showy, splendid." The last two are illustrated with Pope's words, "It is with a fine genius as with a fine fashion; all those are displeased at it who are not able to follow it." The six senses of "art" which Johnson lists include none which is definitely aesthetic or "fine." First comes the broad technical sense: "The power of doing something not taught by nature and instinct, as, to walk is natural, to dance is an art." Dancing is an art, then, not because it is beautiful but because it is an artificial, acquired skill. South is quoted as saying, "Art is properly an habitual knowledge of certain rules and maxims, by which a man is governed and directed in his actions." Johnson's other definitions of "art" are: "A science; as, the liberal arts; a trade ('This observation is afforded us by the art of making sugar'); artfulness, skill, dexterity; cunning, speculation."

In 1769, when Sir Joshua Reynolds opened the Royal Academy of Arts, the term "fine arts" was apparently not in common use. He speaks rather uncertainly, in the first pages of the *Discourses,* of the arts which the Academy is to foster as the "Polite Arts," the "Arts of Design," and the "arts of elegance, those arts by which manufactures are embellished, and science is refined." The first act of the new Academy was to establish schools for painters, sculptors, and architects,[2] which shows the scope of its interests.

Reynolds's mention of politeness and elegance recalls the traditional, aristocratic conception of liberal arts, and the question of whether painting and sculpture belonged among them. Alongside it, the new conception was growing up of fine arts as concerned with beauty and pleasure. Liberal and fine arts were not clearly distinguished. In 1790, R. A. Bromley published in London *A Philosophical and Critical History of the Fine Arts, Painting, Sculpture, and Architecture, with Occasional Observations on the Progress of Engraving.*

[2] *Encyc. Brit.,* 14th ed., "Academy, Royal."

J. G. Sulzer's German encyclopedia, called *General Theory of the Fine Arts*,[3] refers to an anonymous English work entitled *The Polite Arts, or a Dissertation on Poetry, Painting, Music, Architecture and Eloquence*, London, 1749. "Polite" meant, in those days, "highly civilized, cultivated, refined." The scope of the concept was evidently elastic even then, since music and speech arts are explicitly included, and sculpture left out.

As early as 1623, Francis Bacon, in *De Augmentis Scientiarum*,[4] had spoken of music, painting, and other "arts of the eye and ear" as "arts voluptuary" or "arts of sensual pleasure" *(Artes Voluptariae)*. Poesy was placed elsewhere, along with history. But this hedonistic attitude toward music and the visual arts was a remarkable anticipation of the eighteenth century. Bacon thought of them also as "liberal": "Of all these arts those which belong to the eye and ear are esteemed the most liberal; for these two senses are the purest; and the sciences thereof are the most learned, as having mathematics like a handmaid in their train."

For Bacon, as for modern usage, the term "voluptuary arts" suggested primarily the refinements of erotic and festive pleasure rather than the arts now called "fine." In *The Advancement of Learning* (1605), an earlier, briefer version of the *De Augmentis*, Bacon does not include painting and music as "voluptuary" arts. His reference to Tacitus, *Annals* xvi, 18, indicates that he was thinking of the gaieties directed for Nero by Petronius, a man whom Tacitus describes as *eruditus luxu* (educated or refined in luxury), and *scientia voluptatum potior* (more expert in the science of pleasure). "For arts of pleasure sensual," says Bacon in the earlier essay, "the chief deficience in them is of laws to repress them." Between 1605 and 1623, Bacon realized the error of omitting music and the visual arts from the branches of human learning. But he still found no better place to classify them than as arts concerned with the good of the body, along with medicine, cosmetic, and athletic. Like many seventeenth century moralists, he was severe also toward the art of painting the face.

The English concept of "fine arts" can thus be traced back a considerable distance, to somewhat similar meanings under different

---

[3] *Allgemeine Theorie der schönen Künste*, 2d ed. (Leipzig, 1792), I, 49.

[4] Bk. IV, Ch. 2.

English names, such as "polite," "elegant," and "voluptuary" arts. Under any name, however, this idea was rare in English until the late eighteenth century. The main stem of its ancestry goes back rather to France and Italy.

2. The concept of "beaux arts" in France and Germany

The term *beaux arts* was current in the seventeenth century, and, in 1690, it was used by Charles Perrault in the title of a book.[5] In French literature, it occurs as early as La Fontaine's *Songe de Vaux* (1657-61).

The Royal Academy was patterned after the Académie royale des beaux arts, to which we must turn for the French ancestry of the concept of fine arts. It was founded by Louis XIV in 1648. At first limited to painting and sculpture, it was later unified with the Académie d'architecture, founded 1671. "It is composed of painters, sculptors, architects, engravers and musical composers. From among the members of the society who are painters, is chosen the director of the French *Académie des beaux arts* at Rome, also instituted by Louis XIV in 1677. . . . The *Académie nationale de musique* is the official and administrative name given in France to the grand opera." [6] Thus music in general has come to be included in the realm of *beaux-arts,* even though a separate academy was nominally created for it. In 1661, Louis XIV opened the *Académie de danse,* to debate once a month on measures for improving conditions and standards in that art.[7] The sciences received their academy in 1666. All these academies were in turn patterned after the *Académie française,* established in 1635 for discussions of literature. The revolutionary convention abolished them in 1795, and organized, instead, an *Institut National* with three classes: physical and mathematical science, moral and political science, literature and the fine arts. Later, the third class was divided into French language and literature, ancient history and literature, and fine arts.

It is worth while noticing these institutional divisions, because

---

[5] *Le Cabinet des beaux-arts,* etc. See A. P. McMahon, *Preface to an American Philosophy of Art* (Chicago, 1945), pp. 24, 181.

[6] *Encyc. Brit.,* 14th ed., "Academies."

[7] N. Pevsner, *Academies of Art, Past and Present* (Cambridge, 1940), p. 17.

they have had great influence on the meaning of the names assigned. They were inspired to some extent by theories about the nature of the arts, but to a greater extent by existing professional alignments. This partition of culture among the various academies, including the realm assigned to the *Académie des beaux-arts,* did much to determine what arts should be considered *beaux-arts* or "fine arts." The emphasis on visual arts in both the French and British Academies is partly responsible for the conception of the fine arts as visual, and as distinct from music and literature.

There has been persistent disagreement as to whether music and literature should be included. Tolstoy remarks that Winckelmann (who wrote before 1767) "makes external beauty the aim of art, and even limits it to visible beauty." [8] But many eighteenth century writers explicitly included music and literature as fine arts, notably J. G. Sulzer in his widely read *General Theory of the Fine Arts.* [9] This was consistent with the French and Italian emphasis on similarities between poetry and painting. Thus McMahon points out that the term *beaux-arts* had been devised to cover both "art" and literature, as well as other techniques which Aristotle had classed as imitation; but that the name came to be applied chiefly to the so-called "arts of design." [10] As we shall see, the claim of music and poetry to be classed as fine arts is far more ancient than that of the visual arts, going back to the Greek idea of "arts of the Muses."

3. Beautiful and liberal arts in the Italian Renaissance

The modern history of the concept of fine art leads us back from Baroque France to Renaissance Italy, and to earlier academies. There were academies in Italy, including one for architecture in Milan in 1380; but they were smaller and more specific. To divide up the empire of culture into a few vast realms, each chartered by the king and regally supervised through his patronage, was a grandiose and typically baroque idea. The countless literary and scientific academies in Renaissance Italy are remarkable for their whimsical names and

---

[8] *What is Art?* Ch. III.

[9] *Allgemeine Theorie der schönen Künste.* First ed., 1777.

[10] A. P. McMahon, *op. cit.,* p. 27. See all of his Ch. II for further historical details regarding the idea of *beaux arts.*

their lack of interrelation. There was no systematic apportionment of the arts among supervisory bodies; there was no national government to have undertaken it.

The Italian academies were successors to the medieval guilds as institutions for training young artists. The latter had become repressive by the fifteenth century, and the academies at first allowed individual competition. (Later on, they also became repressive.) The earliest academy concerned with painting is said to have been the *Accademia del Disegno,* founded by Vasari in Florence in 1562. Vasari used the expression "most beautiful arts," as applied to the arts of design.[11] The essential difference between the guilds and the academies, says Anthony Blunt,[12] was that "the latter treated the arts as scientific subjects to be taught theoretically as well as practically, whereas the guilds had mainly aimed at fixing a technical tradition."

L. Venturi thus describes the transition from Italy to France: "Even the terms which comprehend painting, sculpture, and architecture are changed. Vasari had called them arts of design, attributing to design their unity. Likewise he had spoken of 'the finest arts,' and Baldinucci of 'fine arts in which design is adopted,' and Scamozzi of 'fine arts.' But it is only in the milieu of the Academy of France that the term 'beaux-arts' is in general use, and the term then remained. For unity of design is substituted that of the ideal of beauty." [13]

Emphasis on the scientific, theoretical approach to painting was an important phase in the struggle of painting, sculpture, and architecture to raise their status. This struggle, whose crucial phase was enacted in Renaissance Italy, is summarized by Blunt as follows:

The upshot of all these disputes was that the painter, sculptor, and architect obtained recognition as educated men, as members of Humanist society. Painting, sculpture, and architecture were accepted as liberal arts, and are now grouped together as activities closely allied to each other and all differing fundamentally from the manual crafts. The idea of the "Fine Arts" comes into existence this way, though a single phrase is not attached to them till the middle of the

[11] McMahon, *op. cit.,* p. 26.

[12] A. Blunt, *Artistic Theory in Italy, 1450-1600* (Oxford: Oxford U. Press, 1940), p. 57. *Cf.* N. Pevsner, *op. cit.,* pp. 42, 46.

[13] *The History of Art Criticism* (New York: E. P. Dutton, 1936), p. 126.

sixteenth century, when they come to be known as the *Arti di disegno*.[14] At the same time critics begin to have the idea of a *work of art* as something distinct from an object of practical utility, as something which is justified simply by its beauty and which is a luxury product.[15]

The public respect for artists, especially architects, had increased considerably during the early fifteenth century, but there was still theoretical opposition to the inclusion of painting and sculpture as liberal arts. A fifteenth-century list by Lorenzo Valla and a later one by Cardanus left them out as mechanical, and Pinturicchio left them out in his frescoes of the liberal arts in the Vatican, painted in the late fifteenth century. A duel was fought between an Italian and a French nobleman, says Blunt, "because the latter accused the Florentine nobles of practising manual arts in that they took an active interest in painting and sculpture."[16]

The chief argument of the artists, led by Leonardo da Vinci, was to show that painting demanded a knowledge of mathematics, especially in perspective, and of other sciences as well. They demanded equality with poetry, on the ground that painting could achieve a moral end through showing human action by gesture and facial expression. Its representation of action could thus be more complete than in poetry. Painting is less mechanical in execution than sculpture, and achieves the illusion of solidity by intellectual means. The ignoble quality of manual labor was still assumed, as it had been in the middle ages, and the defense was to point out how the intellectual element in painting outweighed the manual. "You writers," says Leonardo, "also set down manually with the pen what is devised in

[14] According to the *Oxford Dictionary*, article "Design," "In 16th c. It. *disegno* had the senses, 'purpose, designe, draught; model, plot, picture, pourtrait' (Florio)." In modern aesthetics, "design" has much wider implications than "drawing," so that literature and music are in a sense "arts of design." Hence it is confusing to translate *disegno* as design, or to call painting, sculpture, and architecture the "arts of design." (*Cf. Oxford*, "Design," def. 8.) F. P. Chambers treats *disegno* as equivalent to "drawing." "During the Renaissance," he says, "the common denominator of painting and sculpture, so to speak, was drawing, 'il bon disegno,' and their avowed aim was the representation of natural objects." "As late as the eighteenth century, the Italians were still describing the fine arts as 'le belle arti del disegno.'" (*The History of Taste*, New York, 1932, p. 41; *cf.* p. 72). *Cf.* McMahon, *op. cit.*, p. 32.

[15] *Op. cit.*, p. 55, and all of Ch. IV on "The Social Position of the Artists."

[16] *Op. cit.*, p. 48.

your mind." [17] The sculptor is at a disadvantage in this dispute, because of the strenuous, dusty labor of his calling; whereas the painter, as Leonardo complacently remarks, "sits in great comfort before his work, well dressed, and wields his light brush loaded with lovely colors. He can be dressed as well as he pleases, and his house can be clean and filled with beautiful paintings." Through such arguments did painting advance to the status of fine art.

In Renaissance Italy, there was a revival of the aesthetic attitude toward art which had arisen late in Greek and Roman culture—an attitude prerequisite for the modern conception of *beaux-arts*. It was the attitude of the *dilettante* and the connoisseur of art values; of the gentleman of means who appreciated art for its beauty and pleasantness; for its illusion of reality or its richness of ornament rather than for its religious or moral teachings. Says F. P. Chambers:

In so far as the arts and literature were concerned, the Renaissance was the revival of the aesthetic consciousness, which had existed in Graeco-Roman times, but which had been suppressed or ignored in the revolutions of early Christianity. The essence of the Renaissance was the conception of "fine art"; it was the accident of the Renaissance that fine art should be Roman. The Renaissance was not the discovery of the ancient classics, long since buried in darkest ignorance, but the discovery that the ancient classics were beautiful. . . . The Renaissance upset the old distinction between the liberal and the servile arts. Had not Pliny the Elder written of painting and sculpture and recorded the tributes paid to those arts by the ancients? In the Middle Ages painting and sculpture were no nobler than carpentry or cobbling. The idea of the Fine Arts, or as they were first called *le arti del disegno,* was slowly infused into the European mind and superseded the degrading distinctions of the Middle Ages. Noblemen like Alberti were flattered to own the name of artist.[18]

Early discussions of the arts are largely evaluative, often from an educational standpoint. They deal with the question of what skills are worthy of a freeman or a gentleman, and hence with what should be taught to the well-born youth. Also, they ask more searching moral and religious questions, as to the values and dangers of practicing various arts. These are answered differently, according to the religious

[17] J. P. Richter, *The Literary Works of Leonardo da Vinci* (London, 1880), Vol. I, ¶ 654. Blunt, *op. cit.,* pp. 52, 55. Pevsner, *op. cit.,* p. 30.

[18] Chambers, *The History of Taste.* New York: Columbia University Press.

and moral principles assumed, and with different verdicts about which arts are worthy to be taught the superior man.

In Castiglione's *Book of the Courtier* (1528), Count Ludovico da Canossa praises painting as a genteel subject, worthy for the courtier to study. It is useful, he observes, as well as noble:

> And do not marvel that I desire this art, which today may seem to savour of the artisan and little to befit a gentleman; for I remember having read that the ancients, especially throughout Greece, had their boys of gentle birth study painting in school as an honourable and necessary thing, and it was admitted to the first rank of liberal arts; while by public edict they forbade that it be taught to slaves. Among the Romans too, it was held in highest honour, and the very noble family of the Fabii took their name from it; for the first Fabius was given the name *Pictor*. . . . Nor is there lack of many other men of illustrious family, celebrated in this art; which besides being very noble and worthy in itself, is of great utility, and especially in war for drawing places, sites, rivers, bridges, rocks, fortresses, and the like; since however well we may keep them in memory (which is very difficult), we cannot show them to others.[19]

From the standpoint of aristocratic, secular education, the important criterion for classing an art as "liberal," "polite," or "elegant" was that it be recognized as genteel and honorable.[20] For this recognition, the approval of ancient aristocrats was of greater weight than the beauty or intellectuality of the product. Many beautiful and pleasant things, such as chairs and garments, were made by humble artisans, and hence were not "fine" in the sense of elegant, noble, or superior.

4. *Ancient and medieval conceptions of the liberal arts*

The idea of liberal as distinguished from servile or mechanical arts has been traced back as far as Solon (6th c. B.C.), Plato (*Repub.* VII, 522b), and Aristotle (*Pol.* VIII, ii). At various times in Greek, Roman, and medieval history, the basic program of literary and mathematic studies has been regarded as instrumental to elegant oratory, philosophical knowledge, the truth of faith, and interpretation

[19] Bk. I; ¶ 49.

[20] *Liberal:* "Befitting, or worthy of, a man of free birth; free; not servile" (Webster).

of the sacred text.[21] The "Seven Liberal Arts" of the Middle Ages were strongly intellectual in tone, and largely devoted to what we should call sciences: to grammar, dialectic, and rhetoric (the *trivium* or literary group), arithmetic, geometry, music, and astronomy (the *quadrivium* or mathematical group). They were intellectual instruments or apparatus for more advanced studies, especially philosophy. They involved little manual skill or pursuit of sensuous beauty. Music, says Bird, was strictly theoretical, having for its object the proportions of numbers.[22]

Even literature, in the modern sense of *belles lettres,* was not an integral part of the Seven Liberal Arts. Hugo of St. Victor, in the twelfth century, classed it as a *supplement* of the arts:

There are two kinds of writings, first those which are termed the *artes* proper; secondly, those which are the supplements *(appendentia)* of the *artes*. *Artes* comprise the works grouped under philosophy, those which contain some fixed and determined matter of philosophy, as grammar, dialectic, and the like. *Appendentia artium* are those writings which touch philosophy less nearly and are occupied with some subject apart from it; and yet sometimes offer flotsam and jetsam from the *artes,* or simply as narratives smooth the road to philosophy. All the songs of poets are such—tragedies, comedies, satires, heroics, and lyrics too, and iambics, besides certain didactic works; tales likewise, and histories. . . . One should first of all devote himself to the *artes,* which are so fundamental, and to the aforesaid seven above all, which are the means and instruments of all philosophy. Then let the rest be read, if one has leisure, since sometimes the playful mingled with the serious especially delights us, and we are apt to remember a moral found in a tale.[23]

As to the "arts of design" and other visual arts, they were arts in the broad technical sense of skill in making and doing. Their first purpose was usefulness: that of the building arts, says Chambers, was "strength and shelter; the usefulness of the figurative art was the illustration of moral doctrine and sacred history. Architecture was

[21] O. Bird, "Arts, The Seven Liberal." In *Dictionary of World Literature.* Philosophical Library, New York, 1943.

[22] *Ibid.* However, H. O. Taylor mentions that "Fulbert and his scholars did much to advance the music of the liturgy, composing texts and airs for organ chanting." His cathedral school at Chartres taught the Seven Liberal Arts in the eleventh century. (*The Medieval Mind.* New York, 1919. Vol. I, p. 301).

[23] *Didascalion,* iii, 4. H. O. Taylor, *op. cit.,* vol. ii, p. 137.

admired for being well and skillfully built; painting and sculpture were admired because they bore some semblance of reality. . . . Ornament for its own sake was the conception of a later time." [24] Their artists were not genteel: "The 'mechanic' arts were low in the scale of labor, and masons and painters at the best of times were classed as 'mechanic' artisans." [25]

All through the fourteenth century, says Coulton, "The artist is still a mere artisan, the architect is a master-mason, and the musician is a minstrel. From the time of King John (d. 1364) . . . the artists enter royal households side by side with the lower attendants— spicers, tailors, etc. . . . Under Pius II, the first pope who represents every side of the Renaissance, Paolo Romano was admitted to the great dining-hall, while master Giovanni (who bore the title of 'Sculptor of the Apostolic Palace') was relegated to the second hall, with the tailors, cooks, porters, couriers, grooms, sweepers, muleteers, water-carriers, and so forth." [26] "The medieval craftsman," Coulton adds, "was, according to modern ideas, very poorly paid. We must bear in mind, to begin with, that scholastic philosophers, following Aristotle, drew only one main distinction in art, between the 'liberal' and the 'mechanical.' The former included all the 'humanities,' the latter included everything manual. There was, therefore, no essential distinction between the cobbler or tailor on the one hand, and Giotto or the Della Robbias on the other; indeed, in more than one place we find that the painters' gild was a mere branch of the saddlers', through the accident that the heavy wooden medieval saddles were often elaborately painted." [27] When Dante mentioned in the *Commedia* two brilliant miniaturists, Oderisi and Franco, some contemporaries marvelled that he should thus immortalize "men of unknown name and low occupation" (*homines ignoti nominis et bassae artis*).[28]

Slight rises and falls in the status of the visual arts and their artists are recorded in Greek and Roman history. Plutarch tells of Aemilius Paulus, a Roman aristocrat of the second century B.C.,

---

[24] Chambers, *op. cit.,* p. 10.

[25] *Ibid.,* p. 9.

[26] G. G. Coulton, *Art and the Reformation* (New York: A. Knopf, 1928), p. 523. (Partly quoted from Renan.)

[27] G. G. Coulton, *Medieval Panorama* (Cambridge: Cambridge U. Press, 1938), p. 567.

[28] *Ibid.,* p. 566.

who—like Castiglione's Count—dared to approve of painting and sculpture as genteel studies. In teaching his children the discipline of ancient Greece, he "not only procured masters to teach them grammar, logic, and rhetoric, but had for them also preceptors in modelling and drawing, managers of horses and dogs, and instructors in field sports, all from Greece." Such occasional comments of the ancients, favorable to the visual arts, were often quoted in the Renaissance. But on the whole, the practice of the visual arts held a lowly social status in Greece and Rome, as in the Middle Ages, with the stigma of being manual and mechanical. Isocrates (436-338 B.C.) had urged that Phidias, Zeuxis, and Parrhasius should not be classed with vase-painters and doll-makers. As McMahon points out, this shows that most artists were actually so regarded.[29] And who was there to defend the vase-painters? In the time of Augustus, Vitruvius still had to defend the dignity of architecture. It was, he said, not only manual craftsmanship, but also an intellectual science, involving mathematics, optics, history, philosophy, music, medicine, and astronomy. Its aims were convenience, beauty, and strength.[30]

Pliny the Elder, writing in the middle of the first century A.D., refers to painting as a "dying art" (artis morientis).[31] About that time, some of the finest works of Hellenistic painting were being made at Pompeii and Herculaneum, near the spot where Pliny was to meet his death. He traces a long history of progressive achievements by Greek and Roman artists in silver chasing, bronze sculpture, painting, clay modeling, and marble sculpture, with emphasis on realistic effects and technical devices. Among the Romans, he says, the art of painting was honored in early times (about 304 B.C.), "seeing indeed that so distinguished a family as the Fabii drew from it the name of Pictor (Painter). . . . Since that time, however, the profession of painter has received no honor at the hands of men of good birth, unless we except in our own time Turpilius, a Roman knight from Venetia, whose excellent pictures are still to be seen at Verona." [32] A certain governor of praetorian rank, he continues, "was proud of the little pictures that he painted . . . yet his art only brought him ridicule

[29] Isocrates, De Permutatione 2. McMahon, op. cit., p. 20.

[30] De Architectura. Loeb ed., Bk. I, c. 1, pp. 7-9; also p. 173.

[31] Nat. Hist. XXXV, I, 29. Cf. K. Jex-Blake, The Elder Pliny's Chapters on the History of Art (London, 1896), p. 95.

[32] Loc. cit., I, 19. Tr. by Jex-Blake, p. 89.

and scorn." Pamphilos the Macedonian, teacher of Apelles in 367 B.C., "was the first painter who was thoroughly trained in every branch of learning, more particularly in arithmetic and geometry; without which, so he held, art could not be perfect." "It was owing to his influence," says Pliny, "that first at Sikyon, and afterwards throughout Greece, drawing (*graphicen*) or rather painting (*picturam*), on tablets of boxwood, was the earliest subject taught to free-born boys, and that this art was accepted as the preliminary step towards a liberal education (*in primum gradum liberalium*). It was at any rate had in such honor that at all times the freeborn, and later on persons of distinction practiced it, while by a standing prohibition no slaves might ever acquire it, and this is why neither in painting nor in statuary are there any celebrated works by artists who had been slaves." [33] As we have seen, Leonardo da Vinci was to repeat, long afterwards, this claim of painting to respect as an intellectual, scientific subject, rather than a mere handicraft.

As to the status of an art at a particular time, there is much more to be considered than whether well-born citizens practiced it. At all times, they have patronized and encouraged many arts which they would not condescend to practice. The visual arts, as well as theater and music, enjoyed this kind of favor throughout the flourishing days of Greek, Roman, and Medieval civilization. As Pliny shows, Roman aristocrats paid well for pictures and statues. As a result, large numbers of self-respecting artisans could gain an honest living by making them. This is very different from a period when a certain art is forbidden, despised, or deprived of financial support, as representational painting and sculpture were during much Hebrew and Islamic history. (Also, for example, the theater in Puritan England.)

5. The arts of the Muses in Greece

The Greek word *technē* and the Latin word *ars* both implied useful skill in general. Under the general concept of *technē*, a certain type of art was recognized in Greece: namely, *mousikē technē* (μουσική τέχνη) or art of the Muses. This is sometimes translated as "fine art," and the particular arts included are sometimes called "fine arts." The word *technē* was often omitted in Greek, and *mousikē* alone meant "art of the Muses." According to Liddell and

[33] *Loc. cit.*, I, 76. Jex-Blake, p. 119.

Scott's *Greek-English Lexicon, mousikē* included "any art over which the Muses presided, esp. music or lyric poetry set and sung to music— one of the three branches of Athenian education, the other two being *grammata, gymnastikē;* generally, arts, letters, accomplishments." When it is said that Athenian education was based on music, grammar, and gymnastic, it should be made clear that "music" included poetry and sometimes the other arts of the Muses, as well as the specialized auditory art which we call by that name. If "music" were still understood to mean "art of the Muses" or "fine arts," then "musicology" could mean the scientific study of the fine arts, or aesthetics in general. However, the narrower sense of "music" is now established. On the other hand, a "museum" (*mouseion*) is now devoted mainly to visual exhibits, although it formerly meant "a temple of the Muses; a school of arts and learning."

Mousikos (μουσικός) is translated as "of the Muses, or the fine arts devoted to the Muses." The arts presided over by Apollo and the Muses were history, lyric poetry, comedy, tragedy, dance, erotic and mimic poetry, sublime hymns, and astronomy. A related Greek term is *philómousos* (φιλόμουσος), which Liddell and Scott translate as "loving music and the arts." F. P. Chambers translates it as "dilettante," in a quotation from Menander which, he says, is the earliest reference to that idea in Greece: " 'That he is a great dilettante and forever nurtured on sensuous music.' " [34] "Art-lover" would be a closer equivalent, since "dilettante" now often suggests superficiality.

There appears to be no clear conception in Greek or Roman thought of a group of "fine arts," distinguished from other arts by their devotion to beauty and aesthetic pleasure, rather than to practical use. Certainly, no group of visual arts, such as painting, sculpture, and architecture, is so set apart. The "arts of the Muses" were "fine" in being distinguished from the humbly utilitarian, manual skills, but were also regarded as useful from a moral and educational standpoint. They were not regarded (at least by Plato and Aristotle) as devoted mainly to pleasure and sensuous beauty.

The "arts of the Muses" were mainly literary and musical, with a dash of early science. They gave no place to the visual arts of painting and sculpture, which are today regarded as fine arts *par excellence.* The arts of song, speech, and gesture were set apart from those of

[34] *Cycles of Taste* (Cambridge, Harvard U. Press, 1928), p. 30.

making things with the hands. But Greek mythology reveals an ideal conception of the union of craftsmanship with beauty. In the *Iliad* (Book XVIII), the wife of Hephaestus, god of fire and crafts, was Charis, one of the Graces. In Hesiod, she was Aglaia, youngest of the Graces. In the *Odyssey*, Aphrodite was his wife. "Architecture, sculpture, and painting belonged to no Muse," says Chambers, "but were protected possibly by such deities as Athena or Hephaestus, who turned these arts to profitable and honorable purposes in life. It was wisdom which was made the aim of Muses of poetry." [35] The concept of Fine Art, purged of all moral content, and the concept of art as the externalization of beauty, "did not find a consistent exponent until Plotinus," in whom "the doctrine of Fine Art as the expression of an absolute value, Beauty, is consistently developed." [36]

No doubt the Epicurean philosophers came nearer than Plato and Aristotle did to a hedonistic attitude toward the arts, justifying the sensuous enjoyment of beauty as an end in itself. But few of their works have come down to us in full, or even in comprehensive summaries. These tend to praise the simple life, avoidance of luxury (in which visual art was often classed), freedom from fear, and the pleasures of friendship and meditation. Epicurus is quoted by Diogenes Laertius as writing, "I know not how to conceive the good, apart from the pleasures of taste, sexual pleasures, the pleasures of sound (ἀκροαμάτων), and the pleasures of beautiful form (μορφῆς)." [37] Such fragmentary hints are not enough to let us infer the existence of a hedonistic theory of art in ancient Greece. But the very insistence with which Plato argues for a moral and intellectual conception of beauty is a sign that hedonistic views were current and influential. They would have been especially liable to ecclesiastical censorship during the middle ages, or at least to neglect. This may help explain why so few expressions of them now survive.

[35] *Ibid.*, p. 24.

[36] *Ibid.*, pp. 24, 49.

[37] *Lives of Eminent Philosophers.* R. D. Hicks, tr., "Loeb Classical Library." 1931. Vol. II, p. 535. The translator comments, "The last words have been taken to refer especially to the pleasures afforded by music and again by painting and the plastic arts. But perhaps Epicurus is merely citing typical examples of intense pleasures under the heads of the four senses: taste, touch, hearing, seeing." Even so, it suggests that Epicurus may have said more about aesthetic psychology than is now extant.

It is undoubtedly true that no clear conception of fine art existed in Greece, which is identical with any of those in modern definitions. However, many of the ideas included in those definitions did exist in Greece, under various names and in various associations. So it is not correct to suppose that the concept of fine art is entirely modern. After all, modern thinkers disagree on which arts are "fine," and on the relative importance of beauty, pleasure, and utility in them. We can find similar disagreement in Greece. Moreover, Greek thinkers developed the notion of liberal arts as those befitting an educated, free citizen. This, as we have seen, deeply influenced medieval and modern theories of the arts.

Plato distinguishes between the necessities and the luxuries of life, classing music and painting among the latter. In describing the development of a state, he tells first of the basic crafts providing food, shelter, and clothing; then of commerce; then of comforts, conveniences and luxuries:

Many will not be satisfied with the simpler way of life. They will be for adding couches, and tables, and other furniture; also dainties, and perfumes, and incense, and courtesans, and cakes, all these not of one sort only, but in every variety; we must go beyond the necessaries of which I was at first speaking, such as houses, and clothes, and shoes: the arts of the painter and the embroiderer will have to be set in motion, and gold and ivory and all sorts of materials must be procured. . . . Now will the city have to fill and swell with a multitude of callings which are not required by any natural want; such as the whole class of hunters, and all who practise imitative arts, including many who use forms and colors, and many who use music, poets also, and their attendant train of rhapsodists, players, dancers, contractors; also makers of divers kinds of articles, including women's dresses.[38]

The fact that Plato disapproved of a great part of this "luxury" on moral grounds does not alter the fact that he made a fairly clear distinction in theory between two sets of arts: one which satisfied basic human needs, and another which provided sensuous pleasure.

[38] *Republic*, II, 373f. Lucretius makes a similar distinction in describing the origins of civilization: "Ships and the tilling of the land, walls, laws, weapons, roads, dress, and all things of this kind, all the prizes, and the luxuries of life, songs and pictures, and the polishing of quaintly-wrought statues, practice and the experience of the eager mind taught them little by little, as they went forward step by step . . . until they reached the topmost pinnacle" (*On the Nature of Things*, V, 1448).

This is one important element in the modern distinction between useful and fine arts. He was, however, more interested in another distinction, between what were later called the liberal and the illiberal or servile arts. The useful arts were put in the latter class: "All the useful arts, I believe, we thought degrading." [39] Most of the "luxuries" also were put there by implication; at least, in so far as they were merely pleasant. Music, including literature, had been classed as a luxury; but Plato went on to approve certain kinds of it as beneficial to the soul. Thus a portion of music and literature—that which has the desired moral and spiritual effect—was accepted as one of the basic divisions of the guardians' education, along with gymnastic. It was an art suited for the voluntary studies of the "freeborn man," who might, in case of special ability, go on to study arithmetic, plane and solid geometry, astronomy, theoretical harmony, and dialectics.[40]

Plato has praise for other arts, again in a selective way: that is, when gracefulness, rhythm, and harmony enter into them. All life is full of these qualities, "as well as every creative and constructive art; the art of painting, weaving and embroidery, and building, and the manufacture of vessels, as well as the frames of animals and of plants; in all of them there is grace or the absence of grace." [41] This recognition that there is an element of beauty and worth in the minor useful arts as well as in painting and architecture, apart from their practical functions, is an important first step toward their full recognition as "fine arts" many centuries later. The right way to deal with all arts is to learn to understand the intellectual principles of beauty and harmony in them; not merely to enjoy them sensuously as particular objects. In other words, Plato refuses to class the whole arts of music, painting, poetry, or the useful arts as liberal, but he does see liberal elements in them, and liberal approaches to them.

Plato himself is of course a literary artist of high degree. As a teller of dramatic dialogues and myths, he might be called a representative or "imitative" artist. But his aim and emphasis in these works are always symbolic and expository rather than imitative: the expressing of general principles. The weight of his metaphysical system is against painting, sculpture, and poetry as "imitative arts." Since particular objects are imperfect copies of the eternal ideas, a represen-

[39] *Ibid.*, VII, 522-3.
[40] *Ibid.*, VII, 536f.
[41] *Ibid.*, III, 401.

tation of a particular object is a mere imitation of an imitation, far from the source of all beauty, truth, and goodness.[42] The poet and the imitative artist are placed, in the *Phaedrus,* at the sixth stage away from the truth. The first stage is shared by the philosopher with the "lover of beauty, or one of a musical or loving nature." [43] The true artist always creates in accordance with an idea or eternal prototype, which generates inspiration in him and ensures beauty in his product; he never merely imitates a particular object.[44]

Plato shows little sign of realizing how much the painting, and especially the sculpture, of Greece contained besides mere imitation. His scorn of the painter as an ignorant imitator was a serious blow from a high authority. "The painter will paint a shoemaker, a carpenter, or any other craftsman, without knowing anything about their trades; and notwithstanding this ignorance on his part, let him be but a good painter, and if he paints a carpenter and displays his painting at a distance he will deceive children and silly people by making them think that it really is a carpenter." [45] This passage presented the Renaissance defenders of painting with a hard task of rebuttal. Cellini had to argue that a sculptor must know about the art of war and be brave himself, to make a good statue of a brave man; and that he must know about music and rhetoric to represent a musician or an orator.[46]

In the *Philebus,* Plato seems to be on the verge of a modern conception of pure design: a theory that abstract lines, shapes, masses, especially definite geometrical forms, are beautiful in themselves. At least, they would be direct imitations of the eternal forms, and not imitations of imitations, as in representative art. The same would be true of musical patterns. Plato, of course, would not admire abstract patterns of line, color, or sound for their sensuous charm, as would the modern lover of post-impressionism. He would value them somewhat as he would the diagrams in a geometrical treatise—intellectually,

---

[42] *Repub.* 596-8.

[43] 248D. H. N. Fowler trans. "Loeb Classical Library." New York, 1913, p. 479. Jowett errs in translating φιλοκάλου ἢ μουσικοῦ τινὸς καὶ ἐρωτικοῦ as "artist, or musician, or lover." The craftsman (δημιουργικὸς) is at the seventh stage.

[44] *Cf.* C. Ritter, *The Essence of Plato's Philosophy* (New York, 1933), p. 367.

[45] *Republic.* X, 598b.

[46] *Cf.* Blunt, *op. cit.,* p. 51.

but for their beauty also, and not in a coldly specialized, scientific way.

In his latest writings, Plato apparently became more tolerant of visual art: of public works which are both "useful and ornamental," as "pleasing amusement"; of palaces which "put together different stones, varying the pattern to please the eye, and to be an innate source of delight." [47]

Aristotle, in the *Politics*, resumes the discussion of which arts are suitable for the education of freeborn children:

There can be no doubt that children should be taught those useful things which are really necessary, but not all useful things; for occupations are divided into liberal and illiberal; and to young children should be imparted only such kinds of knowledge as will be useful to them without vulgarizing them. And any occupation, art, or science, which makes the body or soul or mind of a freeman less fit for the practice or exercise of virtue, is vulgar; wherefore we call those arts vulgar which tend to deform the body, and likewise all paid employments, for they absorb and degrade the mind. There are also some liberal arts quite proper for a freeman to acquire, but only in a certain degree, and if he attend to them too closely, in order to attain perfection in them, the same evil effects will follow.[48]

The customary branches of education, says Aristotle, are reading and writing, gymnastics, music, and sometimes drawing. No one doubts the usefulness of these studies, except perhaps that of music. But this is not enough to qualify them as liberal arts. "To be always seeking after the useful does not become free and exalted souls." They must then be appraised on other grounds. Aristotle's viewpoint on the values of drawing is that of the art collector and connoisseur. Drawing gives one a correct judgment of the works of artists, so as to prevent one from mistaken purchases. (This seems to him a kind of utility.) A more important value is that it makes one a judge of the beauty of the human form. Aristotle seems to recognize the possibility of an aesthetic attitude toward art, for its beauty alone: "If any one delights in the sight of a statue for its beauty only, it necessarily follows that the sight of the original will be pleasant to him." The moral effect of painting and sculpture, figures and colors, is slight; but in so far as there is any, young men should be taught to admire such artists as Polygnotus, who express moral ideas.

[47] *Laws*, VI 761. *Critias*, 115-6. *Cf.* Chambers, *Cycles of Taste*, pp. 26-8.
[48] VIII, 2 *et seq.*

Music has a more powerful effect on character, through the effects of the various modes. Plato was right, says Aristotle, in saying that certain kinds of music should be a part of education. Even skill in performing certain instruments is worthy, although the freeman will not attempt marvels of execution or play professionally. Music is of value for education, purging the emotions, intellectual enjoyment, relaxation, and recreation after exertion. Even "perverted, highly strung and unnaturally colored melodies" have their place, for professional musicians should be allowed to practice this lower sort of music before "a vulgar crowd of mechanics, laborers, and the like," while the "free and educated" listen elsewhere to good music.

Leisure-time amusements are not to be condemned. "Leisure is better than occupation and its end; . . . it gives pleasure and happiness and enjoyment of life," and music is one of the best ways of enjoying leisure. Homer is right when he says "there is no better way of passing life than when men's hearts are merry and 'the banqueters in the hall, sitting in order, hear the voice of the minstrel.' " [49] The visual arts, for similar purposes, are not stressed by Aristotle. Yet Aristophanes thus advises the banqueter: "Extend your knees and let yourself with practised ease subside along the cushions; then praise some piece of plate, inspect the ceiling, admire the woven hangings of the hall." [50]

The treatise *Mechanica*, which is included among Aristotle's minor works, takes on an attitude of respect and interest toward practical skill and manual work. For this reason, some scholars attribute it, not to Aristotle directly, but to one of his followers. It conceives of art in the broad technical sense, and anticipates the development of applied physical science which began so propitiously in the Alexandrian era. "When we have to do something contrary to nature, the difficulty of it causes us perplexity and art has to be called to our aid. The kind of art which helps us in such perplexities we call Mechanical Skill." Had such utilitarian art developed steadily in antiquity, it would no doubt have led to a correspondingly clear conception of the fine arts as aesthetic and non-utilitarian.

[49] *Politics*, VIII, 3.

[50] *Wasps*, 1212; *cf.* Chambers, *Cycles of Taste*, p. 26. Athenaeus, in *The Deipnosophists*, often mentions the luxurious equipment of banquets, as well as the food, drink, music, and other amusements.

6. Summary. Present status of the fine arts

We have seen that the term "liberal arts" covered a group of skills or subjects, variously conceived in the Greek and medieval periods, but always distinguished as (a) genteel, noble, aristocratic, befitting a freeman or member of the upper class, and thus opposed to "servile" arts; (b) involving mental rather than crude manual or mechanical work and ability, hence manifesting a higher type of mental development; (c) tending to elevate the mind of the artist and those whom he serves rather than merely providing physical necessities and comforts.

In the seventeenth and eighteenth centuries the conception of art became more hedonistic in tone, less intellectual and moralistic. It marked off a certain group of arts as aiming to provide aesthetic pleasure, by producing beautiful forms for sensuous perception. This type of arts came to be called "beaux-arts" or "fine arts." However, it had much in common with the older conception of liberal arts, in that the fine arts also were regarded as (a) genteel, befitting one of the upper classes; (b) involving mental rather than crude physical ability (even though some fine arts did use physical tools and materials); and (c) tending to refine and elevate the mind.

The term "fine arts" came to be associated mainly with certain visual arts. These were separately grouped for practice and instruction. In Italy, they were called "the beautiful arts of design," and had their own academy. Later, in France, control of the visual arts was assigned to a separate academy, which bore the title "Académie des beaux-arts."

To the extent that the modern "fine arts" are successors to the Greek "liberal arts," we have the strange spectacle of the visual arts being, first, excluded from the select list as too manual; second, admitted to the list through a rise in social and intellectual status; third, so dominating the list that music and poetry, though original members, are often omitted from it.

However, such an account would somewhat oversimplify the story. We still have a concept of "liberal arts" or "humanities," which (in some of its meanings, at least) is distinct from that of "fine arts." It is the concept used in higher education, to designate the "liberal arts" curriculum, and to justify the degree of "Bachelor of Arts." This concept retains the literary and intellectual denotation which it inherited from the middle ages. It has changed in specific content, but still leans toward language and social studies rather than toward the visual arts. Indeed, the visual arts still have a precarious and far from universal place in liberal education on the higher levels. As subjects for technical training, they are still opposed on the ancient ground of being too practical and manual for a "liberal" curriculum. At the same time, both practice and appreciation of the visual arts are attacked on the opposite ground: that they are mere frills, mere leisure-time amusements for women, children, or the idle rich; hence out of place in the new "liberal education" as interpreted by a practical age.

There has been a partial democratization in the concepts of both liberal arts and fine arts. Students from lower economic and social levels are not excluded from them, and free or low-cost public education makes it easier for any one to enter them professionally. Students from higher levels are less concerned about the degrees of social prestige attached to various occupations. Little or no stigma is now attached to use of the hands or to occupations which satisfy man's physical needs, as in farming, commerce, building, and engineering. The fact that one art requires use of the hands while another does not has little or no bearing on social prestige. In so far as prestige is determined by success in money and fame, persons who achieve it either with or without manual work are respected; while poorly paid workers in any field are often regarded with condescension. But again, this oversimplifies the situation. There is still a lingering aura of prestige about the "liberal arts" curriculum in the educational field, about intellectual occupations such as teaching and librarianship, and about creative work in literature, music, and painting, which attracts many to practice them in spite of small financial return. There is still a noticeable stigma, or lack of prestige, in occupations which are crudely physical and dirty without the redeeming factor of mental, technical skill or administrative ability. It is not held against Thomas Edison that he used his hands; but this does not raise all manual occupations to the same social level as mental ones. In short, there is still a distinction between types of occupation, as to which are more suited for persons of the upper classes, even though the distinction is more vague and flexible than it used to be; less rigid along hereditary lines, and less sharply dualistic in contrasting "mental" with "physical" skills.

The fine or aesthetic arts have continued on the whole to rise in social status, ever since the Renaissance. Little remains of the Puritanical antipathy toward them as immoral, although this still operates to censor the subject-matter of art. Dangerous ideas and images in art are opposed, but not art in general, for conservatives recognize the value of approved types of art for their own side. The chief antagonism to the fine arts in general, especially in education, springs from the belief that they are impractical and precarious financially; a frivolous waste of time which could be devoted to more useful work and more assured ways of gaining a livelihood. If a boy wants to enter the arts, the first question asked at home will probably be, "How are you going to make a living that way?"

III

The Meanings of Art

1. Dictionary definitions, based on the concept of skill

The question "what is art?" is difficult to answer directly. The only correct, short answer is that art is many different things. Art is a name which is applied to many different kinds of human product and activity. No one kind has clear and undisputed possession of the title. To this verbal symbol, and its equivalents in other languages, have been attached a variety of meanings: some old, some new; some obsolete, some current. Dictionaries list many, as equally correct. Even in the realm of aesthetics and art criticism, several are current. There is no *a priori* basis for deciding which is the real or true meaning of "art." Where authorities disagree on the meaning of a term, and lexicographers offer various alternatives, the individual writer or teacher must choose a meaning, consciously or unconsciously. The choice is not a "merely verbal" matter. It expresses one's interests and beliefs, and affects the course of one's subsequent thinking about the facts concerned.

The word "art," as we have seen, is derived from the Latin *ars* (plural *artes*), and retains some of the meanings of that Latin word. Its nearest equivalent in Greek is *technē* (τέχνη), but it now differs considerably in meaning from both of these ancient words. The English word "art" has approximate equivalents in all civilized languages, such as *Kunst* in German,[1] which have undergone somewhat similar changes in meaning. These changes are not merely verbal, but expressions of underlying cultural movements. Hence they are significant for aesthetic theory.

The chief current meanings of art, as recognized by leading dictionaries, can be grouped under five headings. They differ from one another in degree of breadth, and are here arranged from broadest to narrowest, by the addition of more specific limitations. All are based on the concept of *skill*. The first and broadest sense is also the

[1] Said to be derived from a primitive *Ich kann*, and to suggest both *können* (to be able) and *kennen* (to know). *Cf.* "Art," in *Encyc. Brit.*, 11th ed., by S. Colvin.

oldest: useful skill in general. There has been a tendency to narrow down the extension of the term "art," to make it cover a smaller and smaller field, fewer and fewer types of skill. The narrowest extreme is to identify art with skill in painting alone; but that meaning has not been generally accepted, and one of moderate breadth is now favored. However, all the meanings discussed in this section are accepted by standard reference works. Most contemporary usage of the words "art" and "arts" conforms approximately to one of these definitions. As stated here, each definition is a composite or consensus of slightly different wordings by various reference books, in which the same basic meaning is expressed. They have been rearranged to bring out theoretical connections and distinctions more clearly than the dictionaries do. No new definitions are included in this section of the chapter.

In addition, many individual writers have proposed their own definitions of art. Some of these will be examined in later sections of this chapter. On the basis of this discussion, a revised definition will be recommended.

DEFINITION 1. *Art is useful skill, or the product of such skill; especially, a skill which is developed and transmitted socially, as a tested set of methods for adapting means to purposeful ends.* In this sense, art means "any kind of skill in adapting nature for human uses." [2] It is contrasted with nature itself, as in describing how the wildness of nature has been subdued by human art. (Some philosophers object to this dualism, pointing out that man and his arts are a part of nature, if nature is broadly conceived.) Art in this sense is also opposed to theory, following the Greek distinction between *technē* as art or practical skill and *epistēmē* as knowledge or science. It is not restricted to the "fine arts" (which we shall consider later) or to the making of beautiful things; it includes all skillful making and doing. On the other hand, it does not exclude the making of beautiful things. This meaning dates from an early period, when such distinctions had not yet been made.

Even activities of the lower animals are sometimes included, if

[2] *Oxford Dictionary*, Vol. I, 1888, "art," definitions I, 1, 2, 3; II, 7, 8, 9, 11a. "Artists," definitions I, II. *Webster*, "Art," definitions 2, 5. *Cf.* S. Colvin, "Art," in *Encyc. Brit.*, 11th ed.: Art is "every regulated operation or dexterity by which organized beings pursue ends which they know beforehand, together with the rules and the result of every such operation or dexterity."

they are finely coordinated and useful to the animals themselves. Thus reference is made to the beaver's "art" in building dams, or the spider's in spinning webs. Usually, however, some intelligent planning is considered a requisite of art. A slightly more restricted form of Definition 1 thus specifies *developed, organized* skill, beyond the reach of any lower animal. Art is then conceived as accumulated, tested experience about the best ways of doing things, leading to a body of rules, principles, techniques, or systematic procedures, which serve to facilitate action. It is socially established and culturally transmitted skill rather than an isolated, trivial knack which some individual acquires by himself, for a short time. Even so, it is broad enough to include, not only the "fine arts" of painting, sculpture, and music, but also all applied science, industry, and manufacture. It includes as particular arts all building (whether beautiful or not) and the arts of war, agriculture, and navigation. This sense of "art" we shall call the *broad technical sense.*[3]

The products of such skilled activity are also called "art." In other words, art can mean a process of making or doing, and also its products. The term "artist" used to be applied to a skilled practitioner in any technical field, but that usage is now obsolete. To avoid confusion with works of "fine art," the products of art in this broad sense are often called "artifacts" or "manufactures." These terms cover all human products, whether intended to be beautiful or not.

"Art" in this broad sense is closest to the Greek *technē,* which is also translated as skill, craft, cunning, or regular method of making a thing. From the Greek term we derive "technique," "technics," and "technical." These are now applied to the fine arts, but in a restricted way. They do not always cover the whole of art, especially the essentials of imagination and expression which make a work of art unique or inspired, but rather the more mechanical skills and applied knowledge which are used in executing it. "Technology" now refers mainly to industry, engineering, and applied science, excluding the fine arts. The Greek conception of *technē* made no such distinction. Like the

---

[3] United States patents are granted to devices within the following classes: art, machine, manufacture, composition of matter, and new varieties of plants. "The term 'art' by interpretation of court has substantially the same meaning as the word 'method' or 'process.' Examples of 'arts' that have been patented are methods of centrifugal casting and methods of manufacturing chemicals" (J. H. Byers, "Criteria of Patentability," *Scientific Monthly,* 1945, p. 435).

broad sense of "art" which we are considering, it included skill in making either useful or beautiful things, or things combining the two qualities. The conception of art as useful skill is still taken to include both fine and useful arts, all being considered useful in a broad sense. The word "technics" is also used with this broad meaning, especially in the social sciences.[4]

If we sought a name derived from the Greek for the modern subject which studies art scientifically, "technology" might seem to be the nearest equivalent. By etymology, it can be defined as the science or theory of art. But it has been pre-empted by industry and applied science for their own kinds of skill, and is not often applied to the modern fine arts. German scholars use the word *Kunstwissenschaft* (science of art), but in English *aesthetics* (derived from the Greek word for perception) is commonly used to cover theoretical study of the fine arts.

The broad sense of "art" is still used rather loosely, as in the expression "medical arts." But in precise discussion, this early meaning is now obsolescent, having split into (a) technology or applied science on the one hand, aimed mainly at usefulness; and (b) the various concepts we are about to examine, all regarded as more or less antithetical to usefulness. Important innovation in technology is called "invention" or "discovery," whereas in fine art it is called "creation" or "original composition."

DEFINITION 2. *Art is skill in intellectual and cultural pursuits, or a branch of learning conducive to that skill.* (Usually in plural, with "liberal.") "Arts" in this sense means "liberal arts." This sense is also comparatively old, and is now used mainly in regard to education. One speaks of an "arts" course, curriculum, or college as one devoted to the "liberal arts." It is contrasted with a vocational, technical, or professional course. The former type of curriculum, aimed at broad cultural development, is sometimes called "general education," in contrast with the greater specialization of a technical curriculum.

Webster gives the following definition: *"Liberal arts.* (Trans. of *artes liberales,* the higher arts, which, among the Romans, only freemen (*liberi*) were permitted to pursue.) In the Middle Ages, the seven branches of learning: grammar, logic, rhetoric, arithmetic, geometry, music, and astronomy. In modern times the liberal arts

---

[4] E.g., by Lewis Mumford in *Technics and Civilization,* New York, 1934.

include the languages, sciences, philosophy, history, etc., which compose the curriculum of academic or collegiate education, as distinguished from technical or professional education. The abbreviated term *arts* is also used, as in the designation of certain degrees granted by colleges and universities, as master and bachelor of *arts*."

This sense of "arts" is narrower than the broad technical sense, in that it excludes specialized technical training. If one takes an intensive curriculum in the techniques of any art—whether a "useful" art such as medicine, or a "fine" art such as painting—one is not taking an "arts" curriculum in the sense of liberal arts. One is taking a technical or professional curriculum. The content of a liberal arts curriculum varies considerably today, and in some colleges a student is allowed to take a moderate amount of technical training as part of his preparation for the B.A. or M.A. degree. But this is usually restricted, and a fairly wide range of subjects is required, especially in the early years of college work.

The history and appreciation of painting, sculpture, and architecture are sometimes included as part of a liberal arts curriculum, at least as elective subjects. They are seldom required, and are often omitted entirely. Only literature, among the fine or aesthetic arts, is always included. Courses in "English" and foreign languages often stress grammar and verbal technique rather than literary art. These facts make the degree, Bachelor or Master of *Arts,* seem a misnomer to those who understand "art" in an aesthetic sense; for students can secure these degrees and know little or nothing about art in this sense. "Liberal arts" is still understood in the medieval way, in so far as it includes some amount of science. Today an "arts" curriculum usually involves some work in mathematics, and a basic acquaintance with several other sciences; not in itself enough to make one a professional scientist, but (supposedly) enough to make one aware of their cultural contribution.

This is not, then, a definitely aesthetic sense of the word "art," for it includes a considerable amount of science, and may include nothing in the "fine arts" except literature. We shall call it the *broad intellectual* sense of "art."

The term "humanities" is sometimes used instead of "liberal arts," with similar meaning. Webster defines it as follows: *"Humanities.* The branches of polite learning regarded as primarily conducive to culture; esp., the ancient classics and belles-lettres; sometimes,

secular, as distinguished from theological, learning." Broadly interpreted, a curriculum in humanities is sometimes made to include some
work in physical science, and certainly in the social sciences, history,
languages, and literature. More narrowly, it may indicate a range of
choice within the general "liberal arts" curriculum, with emphasis
on language and literature. It may include work in the visual arts
and music; but that is not always implied.[5] In short, "humanities"
may be a synonym for "liberal arts" and for "arts" in this sense; but
all of these terms are variously construed to include more or less of
science, more or less "fine art." More and more, the "humanities" are
understood as distinct from physical or natural science and mathematics; as the study of human nature, society, and culture. Psychology
and sociology are sometimes included, but often the humanities are
regarded as antithetical to all science, and restricted to scholarship
of a literary and aesthetic sort.

The old connotation of *skill* as essential to any form of art is
somewhat obscured today by the contrast between "liberal arts" and
"technical" courses. It is sometimes supposed that only the latter aim
at any kind of skill or training for practice, and that liberal arts
courses are studied only because they are worth while in themselves.
If instrumental at all, the arts courses are supposed to fit one for a
good life in general, and for such comprehensive ends as civic usefulness, leadership, ability to associate with educated people, ability to
enjoy and to carry on intellectual activities. The utilitarian emphasis
of technical courses leads to a corresponding emphasis on the non-
utilitarian aspects of "liberal education."

In this, there is some survival of the old aristocratic idea of a
gentleman's education as opposed to an artisan's: the former mental
and refined, the latter manual and menial. Bailey's English Dictionary
(London, 1745) defines "art" first in the broad technical sense, as "all
that which is performed by the Wit and Industry of a Man." It then

----

[5] See, however, discussion of the term in L. Dudley and A. Faricy, *The
Humanities: Applied Aesthetics*, New York: McGraw-Hill, 1940, p. 3. "It now
indicates all the subjects of learning except the sciences . . . includes religion as
well as the arts . . . We shall take the province of the humanities to include
principally five arts: literature, music, architecture, painting, and sculpture."
(Quoted by permission of the publishers.) Such emphasis on the visual arts in
defining "humanities" is new and still somewhat exceptional, as is the exclusion
of social science. It makes "humanities" equivalent to "arts" in the general
aesthetic sense, to be considered next.

makes the following contrast: *"Liberal Arts and Sciences,* such as are Noble and Genteel, viz. Grammar, Rhetorick, Musick, Physick, Mathematicks, etc. *Mechanick* Arts, are such as require more the Labour of the Hand and Body than of the Mind; as Carpentry, Carving." The contrast of an "arts" curriculum with a "technical" or professional one is thus in part a survival of the old contrast of "liberal arts" (befitting a freeman or a gentleman) with "mechanical" or servile arts (befitting an artisan or a servant). The latter, as transformed into applied science, are of course elevated in social status today, and have lost the stigma of servility. They are recognized, also, as involving work of the mind as well as the hand. (The more manual, less mental and creative skills are sometimes called "trades." [6] The arts curriculum does retain a little of its ancient social prestige, as intended for those who have the means, the leisure, and the intellectual ability to study subjects instrumental to general culture rather than to a specific gainful occupation.

These changing attitudes help to make the terms "useful" and "utilitarian" somewhat ambiguous today, especially as applied to certain arts. They can be given a narrow and rather derogatory meaning, as restricted to comparatively menial, physical uses. In this sense, useful or mechanical arts are contrasted with "liberal arts" and with "fine arts." It is often claimed that study of the liberal arts is an intrinsic good, a pursuit worth while in itself. From this standpoint, it would be less distinctly and specifically utilitarian than a technical course. But "usefulness" can also be broadly conceived as including intellectual, moral, religious, and aesthetic uses; as equivalent to "instrumental" or "functional." In this sense, a book or a picture can be useful in liberating or elevating the mind, or in giving pleasure. It has always been recognized that the liberal arts are useful in an intellectual way, as prerequisite to advanced studies in many fields, including the technical.

It was in this sense that the Seven Liberal Arts of the Middle Ages were classed as "arts." Under the general definition of "art" as "anything wherein skill may be attained or displayed," the *Oxford Dictionary* lists the following:

[6] (Webster): *trade.* "A pursuit requiring manual or mechanical training and dexterity. . . . Trade applies to any of the mechanical employments or handicrafts, except those connected with agriculture; *craft* is often interchangeable with *trade,* but denotes esp. a trade requiring skilled workmanship."

7. Chiefly in plural. Certain branches of learning which are of the nature of intellectual instruments or apparatus for more advanced studies, or for the work of life; their main principles having been already investigated and established, they are in the position of subjects requiring only to be acquired and practiced. Applied in the Middle Ages to the *trivium* and *quadrivium,* a course of seven sciences.

The main contrast between liberal arts or humanities and technical or professional studies is now coming to be made on other grounds than usefulness or lack of usefulness. One is that the liberal arts are more generalized, wide and balanced in range; the technical studies specialized and intensive. Another is that liberal arts include more attention to literature and perhaps to other fine arts, while the latter usually stress applied science. The second contrast would hardly be true of present technical training in musical performance or in painting; but it is increasingly true of architecture, ceramics, and certain other "fine arts."

DEFINITION 3. a. *Art is skill in producing beauty or that which arouses aesthetic pleasure, or the product of such skill.* (In this sense, "art" is an evaluative, eulogistic term, implying superior aesthetic worth.)

b. *Art is the practice of any of the fine or aesthetic arts (including music and literature as well as certain visual arts), or the product of such practice.* (In this sense "art" is a non-evaluative term. It is a name for a certain group of occupations, without any implication as to how well they are practiced or how good the products are.)

These definitions are intermediate in breadth. The first defines "art" primarily as "the application of skill to the production of what is beautiful, or of what arouses aesthetic pleasure; to the gratification of aesthetic taste; to production according to aesthetic principles." [7] We shall call it the *broad aesthetic* sense of the term. Again, the products as well as the activities are called "art," or "works of art," as in saying that Paris excels "in the production of art."

This definition further narrows down the extension of "art" by excluding not only the purely "useful arts" and applied sciences, but the intellectual skill in letters, philosophy, and pure science which the "liberal arts" undertook to give. It is still moderately broad in that it includes skill in music and poetry, as well as in certain visual arts,

---

[7] See *Oxford,* "Art," defs. I, 5; II, 10; "artist," def. III, 7. *Webster,* "art," def. 9.

such as painting and sculpture. Only a product of these particular arts is a "work of art," according to the present definition, and only a practitioner of one of these arts would be an "artist."

"Art" in this sense is sometimes called "fine art." However, the prefix is often omitted, especially in aesthetics. Thus architecture, painting, sculpture, music, poetry, and the decorative arts are sometimes grouped as "the fine arts," and sometimes as "the arts," "the particular arts," or "the several arts." "Fine" is sometimes added when it is necessary to distinguish this group from the so-called "useful arts," and from engineering and applied science. The latter, however, have tended to drop the name "art" entirely, using "technology" instead. This leaves the name "art" in fuller possession of the aesthetic field, and with less need of the prefix "fine."

With or without "fine," the word "art" in this sense includes music and poetry. With or without "fine," it is also used in a narrow sense, restricted to the visual arts. The former is the one we are now considering. Some of the definitions of "fine art" are synonymous with this sense of "art," and will be considered along with it.

Use of the word "art" alone in this sense is comparatively modern. The prefix "fine" or "beautiful" used to be thought necessary because of the very broad meaning of "art" in general. Now that this very broad meaning is dying out, the prefix is less necessary. Even without it, "art" is commonly understood in an aesthetic sense, while most of the old "useful arts" have been transformed into branches of engineering, technology, and applied science, and are so designated.

"Art" in sense 3a does not ordinarily include the beauties of nature; only those made by human skill. Close association between the ideas of "art" and "beauty" has led a few writers to speak of "art in nature," meaning "beauty in nature," as in sunsets, flowers, and bird-songs. This tends to lose sight of the basic, original concept of art as skill. But that concept may return when a religious writer speaks of the Divine Artist who has made these natural beauties.

Sydney Colvin, in his influential articles on "Art" and "Fine Arts," in the *Encyclopaedia Britannica*,[8] distinguished the fine arts in general as "those among the arts of man which spring from his impulse to do or make certain things in certain ways for the sake, first, of a special kind of pleasure, independent of direct utility, which it gives

---

[8] 11th ed., 1911. The 14th edition treats the subjects in more cursory fashion, without further development in theory.

him so to do or make them, and next for the sake of the kindred pleasure which he derives from witnessing or contemplating them when they are so done or made by others." On the same basis, the *Oxford Dictionary* defines an "artist" (def. III, in sense of a fine artist) as "One who pursues an art which has as its aim to please. . . . One who cultivates one of the fine arts in which the object is mainly to gratify the aesthetic emotions by perfection of execution, whether in creation or representation." Colvin goes on to list the particular arts which he regards as "fine"—"the five greater arts of architecture, sculpture, painting, music, and poetry, with a number of minor or subsidiary arts, of which dancing and the drama are among the most ancient and universal."

To define art as skill in producing "beauty" or "aesthetic pleasure" leaves considerable room for different interpretation. The same ambiguity arises in defining art as production "according to aesthetic principles." All these terms raise disputed issues of aesthetic value. If we use them in defining art, how can we decide whether a particular case is one of art or not? The decision will rest on our standards of value. Hence the term "art" itself will be one of eulogy, not one of objective description. Any attempt to use it in marking off a field of phenomena for scientific study will be confused by evaluative issues.

In actual usage, two alternatives are followed. One, which we may call the *eulogistic* sense of "art," lays emphasis upon the term's evaluative specifications. Only those activities and products which fulfill them are recognized as art. To call a thing "art" in this sense is to praise it as beautiful, worthy, or pleasant. By definition, then, there is no such thing as ugly, unskillful, or unpleasant art. We say of the painting we do not like, "Is that supposed to be art?" We say of the painter, "I don't consider him a real artist." Those who purchase things for art museums often have the question raised, especially in regard to primitive or unconventional modern work, "Is it really art?" Sometimes it will be decided that a primitive statue does not belong in an art museum, but in one of archeology or ethnology. Thus "art" is used as a restricted term of evaluation, even within such a field as sculpture or painting. Being a statue or an oil-painting is not enough to constitute an object a work of art; it must also have beauty and be made according to "aesthetic principles," whatever these are.

The second alternative is to interpret "art" and "fine art" in a neutrally *descriptive, non-evaluative sense.* This lays stress upon the general nature of the *occupation or métier and its products,* rather than upon their beauty or merit. Since painting, sculpture, and other particular arts are classed *in toto* under the general headings of "art" and "fine art," then any example of one of these arts is necessarily an example of "art" and "fine art" in general. It is so classed on the basis of its technique, material, and general form. To class it thus implies no evaluation of it one way or the other. In this sense, art can be beautiful or ugly, pleasant or unpleasant, and a man can be a very bad artist. In this sense, we speak of "children's art," or "the art of the insane," meaning to include any kind of drawing by such persons, whether or not it is considered skillful or beautiful.

From the census standpoint, anyone who practices art for a living is an artist, whether good or bad; the necessary modicum of skill is taken for granted. A fire insurance inventory will list any oil painting or piece of sculpture as an "object of art," without quibbling as to its aesthetic merits. This non-evaluative point of view is usually taken by ethnologists, in speaking of the arts and art products of a certain cultural group. This usage does not bar the door to explicit evaluation in other terms: one can say that the arts of people A are debased and crude, while those of people B achieve refined technique and beauty of form.

To leave room for these two varieties of meaning, definition 3 has been divided into two senses. The first implies a favorable evaluation: (a) "art is skill in producing beauty, or the product of that skill." The second is non-evaluative: (b) "The practice of any of the fine or aesthetic arts, or the product of such practice." Any poem or musical composition, however inferior, is a work of art and of fine art, in this latter sense. We shall call it the *broad aesthetic non-evaluative* meaning of "art." It is widely used in aesthetics, psychology, and the social sciences today, as an objective name for certain types of phenomena.

The connection between these two variants is easy to see. The essential characteristic of art or fine art is conceived as its devotion to the aim of beauty or aesthetic pleasure. Certain arts, such as painting and music, are classed as being usually devoted to this aim; hence as fine arts. Loosely, then, anyone who practices one of these arts comes to be regarded as an artist, and any of its products is accepted as a work of art. The emphasis is placed on the nature of the techniques or occupations in themselves, and the requirement of high quality or success in producing beauty is dropped.

The distinction is only relative. There is bound to be a hint of evaluation in any reference to art or skill. The latter word implies expertness, competency, ability to use one's knowledge readily and effectively—that is, to do something well. But many kinds of skill are objectively measurable, as in speed and accuracy of typewriting or shooting at a target. Their appraisal does not involve debatable moral or aesthetic standards. The results need not be valuable or useful in a general, social way. Black magic and necromancy were regarded as arts; picking pockets is an art of limited and questionable value. In this broad, loose sense anyone who practices an occupation at all is assumed to have some skill. The element of evaluation becomes emphatic and problematic when "art" is made to imply a high degree of ability in producing beauty or aesthetic value, as in Definition 3a.

The same two interpretations—eulogistic and non-evaluative—apply also to definitions 4 and 5, below. Hence these also are given the two wordings. Definitions 4 and 5 differ from 3 in including a narrower range of particular arts.

DEFINITION 4. a. *Art is skill in producing beauty in visible form, or the product of that skill.* b. *Art is the practice of one of the visual aesthetic arts* ("fine arts" in this restricted sense), *or the product of such practice.*

DEFINITION 5. a. *Art is skill in producing beauty in visible form in painting, or the product of that skill.* b. *Art is painting, or a product of it.*

The fourth type of definition restricts the concepts of "art" and "fine art" to those arts which produce *visible* beauty. We shall call this the *visual aesthetic* sense of both concepts. Again, "art" or "fine art" in this sense can mean the product rather than the activity, as in speaking of a museum of art.

In the fifth definition, "art" is restricted to the single activity of *painting*, and its products. This is the *pictorial aesthetic* sense of "art."

In the *Oxford Dictionary*, sense I, 6, art is "the application of skill to the arts of imitation and design, Painting, Engraving, Sculpture, Architecture; the cultivation of these in its principles, practice, and results; the skillful production of the beautiful in visible forms. (This is the most usual modern sense of art, when used without any qualification. It does not occur in any English Dictionary before 1880, and seems to have been chiefly used by painters and writers on painting, until the present century.)" Accordingly, an artist (*Oxford,* sense III, 8) is "one who practices the arts of design; one who seeks to express the beautiful in visible form. In this sense sometimes taken to include sculptors, engravers, and architects; but popularly, and in the most current acceptation of the word, restricted to: One who cultivates the art of painting as a profession."

Thus the idea of art is restricted, not only to the so-called "arts of imitation and design," but to a particular one of these: the art of painting. This last is the narrowest definition of art, in which a concept which once covered the whole domain of human skill is limited to the single activity of painting pictures. It has not achieved much currency in technical aesthetics or art criticism.

The slightly broader meaning, covering several visual arts, is very common today, in both technical and popular discussion. One might speak of "studying art" and mean painting in particular; but it is expected that an art school, an art museum, or a history of art will deal with other visual arts besides painting. Thus Webster, after defining "art" as fine art in general, continues: "Specif., such application [of skill and taste] to the production of beauty in plastic materials by imitation or design, as in painting and sculpture; as, he prefers art to literature." Also, says Webster, the meaning of "fine art" is sometimes restricted to painting, drawing, architecture, and sculpture.

The visual aesthetic meaning of "art" is well established in educational administration. Here the term "art" or "fine art" marks off a restricted area of study with peculiar types of material and activity; one distinct from music and literature, and more or less coordinate with them. "Art, Music, and English (literature)" are understood to mean three separate subjects of the curriculum, three departments of the faculty, three different groups of courses—even though the three may occasionally cooperate on a joint project. Libraries follow the same principle in classifying their books.

Theoretically, this definition presents several new problems for elucidation. In general, what is "visible form" in art, and what arts produce such forms? What does it mean to call certain arts "the arts of imitation and design"? In particular, what arts are included? Painting is always mentioned; sculpture and architecture usually; drawing and engraving occasionally. Numerous other arts devoted to visual form are usually omitted. Architecture, although mentioned in many lists, is usually taught as a separate subject and department in universities, at least as a profession to be practiced. "Art" and "Architecture" are then regarded as distinct and coordinate fields. At the same time, "art histories" usually give a prominent place to the history of architecture, and it is studied along with other visual arts from the standpoint of knowledge and appreciation.

SUMMARY: *five definitions based on the concept of skill; comprising about eighteen different meanings.*

1. *Broad technical sense.* Art is useful skill or the product of that skill; especially, a skill which is developed and transmitted socially, as a tested set of methods for adapting means to purposeful ends.

2. *Broad intellectual sense.* Art is skill in intellectual and cultural pursuits, or a branch of learning conducive to that skill.

3. *Broad aesthetic senses, eulogistic and non-evaluative. a.* Art is skill in producing beauty or that which arouses aesthetic pleasure, or the product of that skill. *b.* Art is the practice of any of the fine or aesthetic arts (including music and literature as well as certain visual arts), or the product of such practice.

4. *Visual aesthetic senses, eulogistic and non-evaluative. a.* Art is skill in producing beauty in visible form, or the product of that skill. *b.* Art is the practice of one of the visual aesthetic arts ("fine arts" in this restricted sense), or the product of such practice.

5. *Pictorial aesthetic senses, eulogistic and non-evaluative. a.* Art is skill in producing beauty in visual form in painting, or the product of that skill. *b.* Art is painting, or a product of it.

2. Definitions and theories of art by individual writers

We have just examined those definitions of "art" which have gained sufficient currency to be recognized and listed by standard reference works, such as the *Oxford Dictionary, Webster's Dictionary* and the *Encyclopaedia Britannica*. This is not to say that they are right and all others wrong. Our premise here is that there is no such thing as a definition which is right or wrong by the eternal nature of things. There are various ideas and groups of phenomena, each important in its own way, to which the name "art" has become attached. When a writer speaks of "art," it tends to suggest one or more of these ideas, with some help from the context to indicate which is meant. If an individual writer uses the word in still another, radically different sense, he runs the risk of being misunderstood, and he further aggravates an already confusing situation. The burden of proof is upon him to show why this is advisable; but even so, his new definition will not become established or "correct" from a standpoint of lexicography unless and until it wins fairly widespread, authoritative usage. Then it may be listed in future dictionaries.

Some writers on aesthetics accept one of the current, dictionary definitions of "art," and then present their ideas about the nature and values of art as so defined. Any of the definitions just listed allows great latitude in that regard. Other writers prefer to concentrate their attack upon the current definitions, and to express their views in terms of a new, basic definition of the term. Consequently, the field of aesthetics abounds in individual definitions of art, most of which are never used by anyone but their authors. Some of the older ones have been accepted, and are now included with more or less revision in the dictionary lists of meanings. It would take a great deal of space to quote all the recent individual definitions of art, and the results would not justify it. However, there have been several useful surveys and summaries of them.

Summaries of definitions by individual philosophers have been made by Külpe,[9] Listowel,[10] Rader,[11] Heyl,[12] Parker,[13] and others. One of the latest and shortest is that of Parker, who states that "Three general conceptions of art have dominated the history of aesthetics: *imitation, imagination,* and *expression* or *language.*" There is no contradiction between the conceptions of art as language and as imagination, says Parker; and he cites as the best short definition of art Shelley's—"the expression of the imagination." His account is incomplete and oversimplified, in that it neglects the original, basic concept

[9] O. Külpe, "The Conception and Classification of Art from a Psychological Standpoint." *Univ. of Toronto Studies,* "Psychological Series," 1907, II, 1-23.

[10] Earl of Listowel, *A Critical History of Modern Aesthetics.* London, 1933.

[11] M. M. Rader, *A Modern Book of Esthetics.* An Anthology. New York, 1935.

[12] B. C. Heyl, *New Bearings in Esthetics and Art Criticism.* New Haven, 1943. With a valuable discussion of the logical and semantic problems involved in defining art.

[13] DeWitt Parker, "Aesthetics." *Encyclopedia of the Arts,* New York, 1946.

of art as skill, and also the great emphasis later placed on its relation to beauty, pleasure, and aesthetic experience. His own definition of art as opaque, plurally suggestive, lyrical language, departs widely from the current usage of the term. Later on we shall return to this general way of defining art in terms of *expression or communication.*

The great novelist Leo Tolstoy, in *What is Art?* [14] includes a historical survey of definitions of art. It leads up to his own definition, following Véron, of art as "expression and communication of emotion." Tolstoy reviews the chief writers who have been responsible for the association of "art" with "beauty." Beginning with Winckelmann, for whom "the law and aim of all art is beauty only," he attributes a similar view to Lessing, Herder, Goethe, and others up to Kant. Beauty, he adds, was understood as "a something existing absolutely and more or less intermingled with Goodness." Several English and French writers (Kames, Batteux, Diderot, Voltaire, d'Alembert) then argued, says Tolstoy, that taste decides what is beautiful, that pleasure or enjoyment is the aim of art, and that the laws of taste can not be settled. According to Schiller, "the aim of art is, as with Kant, beauty, the source of which is pleasure without practical advantage." Tolstoy then reviews the rise of German metaphysical idealism, with its theory that art and beauty express the divine, cosmic spirit. He continues:

The latest and most comprehensible definitions of art, apart from the conception of beauty, are the following:—(1) *a.* Art is an activity arising even in the animal kingdom, and springing from sexual desire and the propensity to play (Schiller, Darwin, Spencer), and *b.* accompanied by a pleasurable excitement of the nervous system (Grant Allen). This is the physiological-evolutionary definition. (2) Art is the external manifestation, by means of lines, colours, movements, sounds, or words, of emotions felt by man (Véron). This is the experimental definition. According to the very latest definition (Sully), (3) Art is "the production of some permanent object or passing action which is fitted not only to supply an active enjoyment to the producer, but to convey a pleasurable impression to a number of spectators or listeners, quite apart from any personal advantage to be derived from it."

[14] Aylmer Maude, *Tolstoy on Art,* Boston (Small, Maynard & Co.), 1924. This is a collection of essays containing, as Part XIII, "What is Art?"; also "On Art" and other notes and essays on the subject. Tolstoy draws heavily for his historical information on M. Schasler's *Kritische Geschichte der Aesthetik* (1872) "What is Art?" was first published in 1898.

How are these theories related to our currently accepted, dictionary definitions of art? Definition 3a in that group is a partial residue of this chain of theorizing from Winckelmann to Sully. What the lexicographers have done is to leave out the more controversial details of these theories, the peculiarly individual elements in them, and preserve as a common denominator the idea that "Art is skill in producing beauty or that which arouses aesthetic pleasure, or the product of such skill." They have left out, and avoided committing themselves, as to whether beauty *or* pleasure is more important; both are allowed. They have left out the controversial metaphysical notions of German transcendentalism, and the whole question of whether beauty is absolute or relative, subjective or objective. They have left out many incidental theories, such as the kinship of art with play. In short, the attempt has been to produce a concept which could be used as a neutral medium of exchange by persons of many shades of opinion. This definition is nothing like a complete theory of the nature of art, beauty, and pleasure, but it is a brief starting-point from which many kinds of theory on that subject can be developed. As such, it will not satisfy anyone who wishes a definition to include a complete, specific theory of the nature of art and beauty which will coincide with his own views. But it is a fairly workable tool of discussion, because it can be used by a great many people who share the same basic belief that art is the production of beauty and/or aesthetic pleasure.

However, it is not a completely neutral, uncontroversial definition, in spite of the lexicographers' efforts. It could not be so, without being so abstract as to be almost meaningless. Special associations from the theories which gave it birth still hover around it, making it seem to imply these theories, and hence offend anyone who does not accept them. Defining art in terms of beauty and pleasure simply passes the question on, as all definitions and all theories have to do: explaining concept A in terms of B and C, we have to explain B and C, until we reach some concepts that seem familiar and obvious enough to be taken for granted, or until the author is tired. Tolstoy understands both "beauty" and "pleasure" as implying certain beliefs which he objects to; hence he objects to defining "art" in terms of them. We shall return to this question shortly, and to Tolstoy's own theory of art as expression.

Rader, in his anthology of quotations, classifies recent theories of art under the following list of headings: play (Lange, Groos); **will** to power or wish fulfillment (Nietzsche, Freud, Parker); expression and communication of emotion (Véron, Tolstoy, Hirn); pleasure (Marshall, Santayana); intuition, technique (Croce, Bergson, Bosanquet); intellect (Maritain, Fernandez); form (Parker, Bell, Fry, Carpenter); empathy (Lipps, Lee); psychological detachment (Bullough, Ortega y Gasset); isolation and equilibrium (Münsterberg, Puffer, Ogden, Richards, and Wood); cultural influence (Spengler, Mumford); instrumentality (Morris, Dewey, Whitehead). Nearly all, he says, unite in support of this one principle: that a work of art is not a mere imitation or reproduction of facts, and not a mere manipulation of matter; it is a "projection of the artist's inspiration, his emotions, preferences, or sense of values." [15]

Not all of these theories are explicitly offered as *definitions* of art. Some of them are, and others are more indefinitely worded as theories about art and its values, or about the processes of making and experiencing art. Some of the surveys and anthologies of quotations call them, quite interchangeably, definitions, theories, doctrines, views, ideas, or conceptions of art. Such vagueness is characteristic of aesthetics in general, and especially of this phase of it. Too many art critics and aestheticians have no clear understanding of what a definition is and should be: that is, a brief statement of the meaning of a word as a medium of communication.[16] Consequently, they phrase all sorts of assertion about the nature of art, its origins, values, processes, etc., as if they were new definitions of the word "art" itself. One finds innumerable sentences beginning "Art is . . ." or "The fundamental nature of art consists in . . . " etc., with little clue to whether they are intended as basic definitions of the term. The same writer will make several such statements, very different since they apply to

[15] *Op. cit.*, p. XV.

[16] Heyl (*op. cit.*, p. 10) points out the fallacy of what semanticists call "real" or "metaphysically realistic" or "quasi" definitions, in regard to art. These are definitions, he says, "which pretend to reveal the 'true nature,' 'ultimate characteristic,' 'whatness,' 'Essence,' or 'Reality' of their referents." Volitional definitions, he continues, "in contrast to propositions (or to statements and judgments), are about language; they define words, not things; they do not assert facts and hence do not raise issues of truth and falsehood." He cites I. A. Richards for the warning that "the great snare of language" is confusion between a definition and a statement that is not about the use of words.

of experience related to them, are recognized as forming the central, principal field of phenomena with which aesthetics deals.[18]

No other name than "arts" is currently available to indicate this field. Some others, such as "technique," have been proposed by exceptional theorists who wish to use "art" in a different sense.[19] But "technique" is inadequate to cover all aspects of the arts. It is commonly used in a much narrower sense, referring only to certain phases of art. We say, "he has lots of technique, but not much imagination or expression."

There is some advantage in starting thus with the term's extension, and not (as is usually done) with its intension, abstract meaning, or connotation. In the latter approach, one usually begins by asserting that the "essential meaning" of art is beauty, or pleasure, or expression, or some other general concept. One then goes on to interpret this general concept in a certain way. Thereafter, it is hard to tell what the concrete extension of the term will be. According to one's views on what is or is not beautiful, or expressive, one may end up by including the whole universe, or the Cosmic Mind, or all intuitions, or only a narrow range of painting and music that one happens to like. By deciding first on a certain field of extension, we at least raise a fairly definite problem: "what are the distinguishing characteristics of this particular field?"

Before we decide on it, however, let us look for a moment at the other current definitions of "art," and at the extension of each. Definition 5, in which "art" means only painting, is perhaps satisfactory for persons who deal with painting only. As long as they talk only with other painters, and with students, teachers, and historians of painting, they can call it "art" without being misunderstood. But as soon as they come out of this little domain, and talk with sculptors and architects, they will discover that people in those fields also refer to them as "arts." If they say "art" when they mean only "painting," they will

[18] DeWitt Parker goes so far as to say that "The purpose of aesthetics is to discover the generic characteristics of fine or beautiful art, and to determine the relation of art to other phases of culture, such as science, industry, morality, philosophy, and religion." ("Aesthetics," in *Encyclopedia of the Arts,* New York, 1946, p. 14). The beautiful in life and nature, he adds, may also be included, but art is preëminent.

[19] E.g., McMahon, *op. cit.,* pp. 155-6.

be not only misunderstood but a little resented, as arrogating to themselves a title to which others also have a right.

The same can be said of Definition 4, in which "art" means only certain visual arts: painting, sculpture, architecture, and the so-called "decorative arts." This usage is followed in speaking of an "art school" or an "art museum," and there is a venerable tradition behind it.[20] To the many scholars and other workers whose field is the visual arts but not music or literature, it may seem quite correct and unobjectionable to call them, simply, "the arts" or "the fine arts." But again, when they come to exchange ideas with people interested in music and literature, they will find that the latter also regard their fields as "arts," and have a long tradition to support them in that claim. (Indeed, much longer than that of the visual artists, for it goes back to the Greek "arts of the Muses," as we saw in Chapter II.) Aside from "arts," there is no adequate name to cover all these fields at once. Hence it is expedient here to use the term "art" in its broader extension, as in Definition 3—the *broad aesthetic* sense of "art"—which is also sanctioned by a long and honorable tradition.

Why not, then, choose Definition 1, the broadest of all, and the original meaning of "art"? This course necessitates using the prefix "fine," "aesthetic," or "beaux" to distinguish the arts which are of special concern to aesthetics. George Santayana, in *Reason in Art,*[21] uses "art" in the broad technical sense. "Art is plastic instinct conscious of its aim," and "if the birds in building nests felt the utility of what they do, they would be practicing an art." "Art is that element in the Life of Reason which consists in modifying its environment the better to attain its end." The fine arts, including dance, music, and eloquence as well as architecture, sculpture, and painting, emerge out of utility and automatism. "Productions in which an aesthetic value is supposed to be prominent take the name of fine art. . . . " Sydney Colvin, also, in the *Encyclopaedia Britannica*

---

[20] See A. P. McMahon, *Preface to an American Philosophy of Art*, Chicago, 1945, p. 155. He favors redefining "art," as *beaux-arts*, in the sense of "arts of design," which Winckelmann reduced to the one word "art." The term's extension would then cover "products of the techniques of architecture, painting, sculpture, and the minor arts," but not music, dancing, or poetry. The qualities we call "aesthetic," he adds, are not limited to works of art or even to products of technique in general, but occur in any object. He joins in attacking the definition of "art" in terms of beauty.

[21] New York: Ch. Scribner's Sons, 1905, pp. 4, 15, 36.

definitions cited above, follows this usage.[22] "Art," he says, is "every regulated operation or dexterity by which organized beings pursue ends which they know beforehand, together with the rules and the result of every such operation or dexterity." He distinguishes the fine arts, chiefly on a basis of aesthetic pleasure.

This extremely broad definition of art has two disadvantages. In the first place, the term "fine arts" or "beaux arts," which we then have to use for the chief subject-matter of aesthetics, is itself extremely ambiguous, as we have seen. It also is commonly understood to mean only certain visual arts. It has many controversial associations, from the old antithesis between "fine" or "liberal" and "useful" or "servile," which are unnecessarily confusing. As a prefix, the word "fine" does not help much in clarifying the meaning of "art." In the second place, the term "art" is less and less frequently used in the broad technical sense, in aesthetics or elsewhere. When people mean to include the more utilitarian and less aesthetic skills, such as war, engineering, and medicine, they now tend to say "technology," "technics," [23] or "applied sciences." These are called "arts" only in a rather loose and popular way, as in "Medical Arts Building." The aesthetic associations of the word "art" are so strong that other names are increasingly used when these associations are not intended, and "art" is left in more unquestioned possession of the aesthetic field. This tendency has progressed far since Colvin and Santayana wrote, early in the twentieth century. Using "art" to cover all technics now has a somewhat archaistic, poetical flavor. It would seldom be used today by a writer more concerned with the non-aesthetic technics: e.g., in a history of modern engineering methods. We conclude that the broad technical sense of "art" is not expedient in aesthetics today.

By elimination, we thus come back to a field of medium size as most thoroughly established, and most convenient, for the term "art" within the subject of aesthetics. Definition 3 comes nearest to covering this field, of all the dictionary definitions listed above. In respect to its extension, then, Definition 3 appears so far to be the most advantageous. We shall call this the "broad aesthetic extension" of art. The most established and convenient name for this field, or exten-

[22] Eleventh ed., 1910, articles on "Art" and "Fine Art." The discussion of "Fine Art" in the 14th ed., by E. S. Prior, is briefer on theoretical points, and acknowledges indebtedness to Colvin.

[23] As in *Technics and Civilization*, by Lewis Mumford, New York, 1934.

sion, we have also seen, is "art" or "the arts," instead of "fine art" or "fine arts." When there is need to distinguish it explicitly from the non-aesthetic, utilitarian technics, we can say "aesthetic arts"; but the prefix is usually unnecessary.[24]

5. What are the distinguishing characteristics of this field?

What distinguishes a work of art, an artistic activity or skill, from other types of product, activity, and skill? The answer, in terms of abstract genus and differentiae, will provide the *intension* or connotation of the term "art" in this sense. Is Definition 3 the most acceptable in this respect also?

Many of the theories quoted by Rader and others do not even attempt to single out the distinctive characteristics of this field of phenomena. For example, Nietzsche in speaking of the "will to power," and Freud in speaking of "wish fulfillment," do not assert that these mechanisms are peculiar to art. On the contrary, they expressly show them to be operative in almost every human activity—in personal relations, war, politics, religion, commerce, and elsewhere. Such theories, if true, may enlighten us as to the nature of art by showing what it has in common with other human activities. Like science, it involves the intellect, and it produces significant forms; it is subject to cultural influences; it produces useful, instrumental objects. But for definition, we need to find rather the characteristics which differentiate art from science, religion, technology, personal relations, and other fields.

This does not imply that the field of art is quite distinct from these other fields. They overlap and interpenetrate. Art and science, art and religion, art and human relations, have much in common. But there are also differences between them, and they should be defined so as to bring out the characteristics peculiar to art.

The ordinary man, says Tolstoy, if asked "what is art?", will reply "Art is architecture, sculpture, painting, music, and poetry." [25] This would be to define art in terms of its extension only. It is close to the dictionary definition which we have numbered 3b: "Art is the practice of any of the fine or aesthetic arts (including music and literature as well as certain visual arts), or the product of such practice."

---

[24] John Dewey refers to "the vexed problem of the relation of esthetic or fine art to other modes of production also called art" (*Art as Experience,* p. 80).

[25] Maude, *op. cit.,* Ch. II, p. 133.

As we noticed above, this is a non-evaluative definition, taking in all activities and products within the field, whether good or bad. But Tolstoy is not satisfied with it. Wherein lies the characteristic sign of a work of art, he asks, which will distinguish works of art from (a) practically useful things, and (b) unsuccessful attempts at art? By insisting that "art" be restricted to the successful, important, and truly worthy examples within each field, he demands an evaluative, eulogistic definition.

Whether or not the differentia of art should be evaluative, Tolstoy is right that some abstract differentia is needed. It is not enough to say, with Definition 3b, that art is any example of certain particular arts. That leaves us still wondering why these particular fields, techniques, or types of product are brought together under one heading. What have they in common, that makes us call them "arts" in the aesthetic sense?

To find the distinctive characteristics of art, it would seem that the obvious way is to compare the products of the various arts with each other—sonatas, paintings, statues, poems, and all the rest; to find some common characteristics in all of them, occurring in all styles and periods. Of these characteristics, we should eliminate the ones which art has in common with the products of science and other related activities, leaving only those peculiar to art. The same should be done for the processes of art, to distinguish them from scientific and other activities.

Some theories about the distinguishing characteristics of art are irrelevant to our present investigation, because they start with a different extension for the term "art." Hence they are describing a different group of phenomena from the one we are trying to describe. Some propose differentiae which are too broad, in that they occur in many other phenomena besides those of art. To say merely that "art is expression" is of this sort; it fails to distinguish art from science, conversation, and many other things. Some proposed differentiae are too narrow, in that they characterize only certain kinds of art. Lange's definition is of this sort. "Art," he says, "is the . . . capacity of man to give to himself and others a pleasure based upon illusion and free from any conscious aim except the immediate enjoyment." [26] Some types of art are based on illusion and some are not. Some are

[26] Rader, *op. cit.*, p. 9.

made only for immediate enjoyment and some are not. The selection of actual differentiae, common to all art and absent or very minor elsewhere, requires much careful comparison.

In comparing two groups of phenomena, such as art and science, we have the double problem of generalizing correctly about both of them. Many attempts to distinguish art from science [27] make dubious statements about the latter. Is science, as Bergson and Croce would have us believe, always a summary of the general, while art is a vision of the unique? Does not science deal with unique events and make unique products? Does not some art contain generalizations about the universe? Some alleged contrasts between art and science are so vague as to be hard to verify: for example, Véron's statement that "Art consists essentially in the predominance of subjectivity over objectivity; it is the chief distinction between it and science."

We shall go on in later chapters to compare the arts with each other, as to their products, processes, and mediums. Something along this line is necessary in any comprehensive account of the arts and their interrelations. But it is a task of great difficulty, for various reasons. Scholars are just learning how to describe and compare works of art in a fairly objective way. Hitherto, most attempts at "describing" them and picking out distinctive characteristics have been permeated with expressions of personal preference and evaluation; of the describer's own emotional reactions to art. Also, the differences between works of various arts are so tremendous—e.g., between a statue and a symphony—that it is hard to find any objective traits of form which exist in common between them. A start is now being made at methods of form-analysis in various arts.

The processes of art creation, performance, and appreciation are also hard to analyze and compare. So far, they have been largely inaccessible to psychological observation. Here again, a good start is being made toward finding what is common and distinct in the processes of art. Some light is being thrown by psychoanalysis. But the results are still too unclear and controversial to serve in a brief definition for general use. Tolstoy's own definition is an attempt along this

[27] See the summary in Rader, *op. cit.*, p. xxiv. Rader's own theory is that "art is the expression of values, isolated, unique, and ideal." This, he says, "provides us with a clear distinction between art and science," and between art and practical affairs.

line, stressing the artist's desire to "express his feeling" and the way this expression is communicated to others. We shall consider it shortly.

Various attempts have been made to define art on the basis of some type of form, supposedly peculiar to works of art. One which has been widely quoted is Clive Bell's theory of "Significant Form." [28] He defines significant form as "arrangements and combinations [of lines, colors, etc.] that move us in a particular way." "Lines and colors combined in a particular way, certain forms and relations of forms, stir our aesthetic emotions. These relations and combinations of lines and colors, these aesthetically moving forms, I call 'Significant Form'; and 'Significant Form' is the one quality common to all works of visual art." But he fails to distinguish these types of form other than by their power to "move us aesthetically." In other words, the differentia is once more shifted back to a kind of emotional effect produced on the observer. Likewise T. M. Greene defines "a work of art" as "an intrinsically satisfying and, at the same time, a meaningful organization of some appropriate medium." [29]

A long tradition in aesthetics favors choosing this power to satisfy aesthetically as the main differentia of art. Let us return for a closer look at it.

6. Objections to beauty and pleasure as distinguishing characteristics of art

Definition 3a involves a certain intension as well as an extension: it gives, abstractly, a certain genus and set of differentiae. The genus (or genera) is "skill, or the product of that skill." The differentia is "in producing beauty or that which arouses aesthetic pleasure." "Beauty" and "pleasure" may be regarded as two alternative differentiae, or as roughly equivalent according to the hedonist interpretation of beauty as objectified pleasure.

Are these adequate differentiae for the field of art? One serious objection is that they limit art to the *actual, successful* production of beauty or pleasantness. By implication, then, "real" art does not include examples of painting, sculpture, music, and poetry which are not beautiful or pleasant. They are not really art, in this eulogistic

[28] *Art*. New York: F. A. Stokes, 1914.

[29] *The Arts and the Art of Criticism*. Princeton U. Press, 1940, p. 11.

sense, although they resemble works of art in many ways—as to general form, medium, technique, etc., so that even experts often disagree on which ones are really "art" and which are not. In other words, the implied extension of definition 3a is not what it appeared to be at first sight. It does not take in the whole of painting, of sculpture, of music, etc., but only the successful examples in each of these fields. This intension of "art" cannot be accepted if we wish to make art cover the whole of these fields.

As Tolstoy and many other writers have pointed out, this definition is unworkable in practice. It fails to mark off a definite field of phenomena to be studied in aesthetics. There will be constant doubt and disagreement on whether a thing really is a work of art, and hence the sort of thing on which we can base our generalizations about art. "All attempts to define absolute beauty in itself," says Tolstoy, "whether as an imitation of nature, or as suitability to its object, or as a correspondence of parts, or as symmetry, or as harmony, or as unity in variety, and so forth—either define nothing at all, or define only some traits of some artistic productions and are far from including all that everybody has always held and still holds to be art. There is no objective definition of beauty." And nothing is gained, he adds, by translating "beauty" into "pleasure." Different people are pleased by different things. Again, we have no objective criterion for deciding what is art and what is not.

Tolstoy has another objection to the use of beauty and pleasure as the differentiae of art. He understands them as referring specifically to certain kinds of art, which he dislikes and disapproves. The word "pleasure" he associates with frivolous, irreligious desire for personal enjoyment on the part of the wealthy upper classes. Restricting "art" to what is pleasant implies, for him, the assumption that art should be amusing, light, gay, novel, sophisticated, clever, and often erotic or pornographic in its emphasis on sex. It implies a glorification of what he calls "counterfeit art." Even technical skill he suspects, along with all art-school training, as tending to glorify such counterfeit art, and train successive generations of students to produce it. Hence he avoids emphasizing even the concept of skill, which, as we have seen, is the original meaning of "art," and the genus in most later definitions.

There is much to be said for these negative criticisms of Tolstoy's. True, the kind of art which he praised for its morality, and contrasted with the art of beauty and pleasure, has not won favor among critics. (He would accuse them of preferring "counterfeit art".) Most critics today would not go as far as he went in denouncing aristocratic art—e.g., the rococo style. They concede it a legitimate place in the history of art. But they would at least agree that such art is not the only good kind, and that gay, sensuous amusement is not the only valuable kind of experience to be had from art. Art should certainly not be defined in terms which apply only to certain styles of art. That would again restrict the extension of art, to cover only some poems, some paintings, etc.

As an artist, with unusual powers of self-analysis, Tolstoy was interested in the role of the individual artist in creating art. In conceiving and defining art itself, he tended to do so from the standpoint of the artist: one who feels something strongly, desires to express it and to make others feel the same way. He was interested primarily in verbal expression, as in fiction, and this also tended to make him stress the kinship of art with language. Many philosophers have a similar tendency, because they express themselves in words, and are less at home in other arts. Like Croce and Parker, they try to define art in terms of "general linguistic" or of linguistic signs and meanings. This works fairly well for literature, but encounters difficulties in music and visual decoration, where the linguistic aspects, the signs and meanings, are less clear.

Philosophers who approach art from the standpoint of metaphysical idealism, in the tradition of Hegel, also tend to stress the role of the artist and of the creative mind in art. They conceive of art, and of all life and civilization, as a process of "self-expression" by the Cosmic Mind. The thoughts in an individual artist's mind, his concept of the picture before it is painted, are all parts of this process of divine expression. Croce affirms that "art is vision or intuition," and not a physical fact of any kind, since "physical facts do not possess reality." [30] Some form of outward expression is necessary for full intuition, he concedes. But his emphasis is on the idea in the artist's mind; not on the statue or painting as a visible form, or the symphony as an arrangement of sounds. He constantly minimizes the importance of differences in medium and technique, as merely superficial and apparent.

Thus each point of view, each set of interests in art, tends to

[30] *The Breviary of Aesthetic.* Cf. Rader, p. 159.

motivate a certain way of defining art. The emphasis on beauty and pleasure as characteristics of art expresses to a large extent the viewpoint of the connoisseur and historian of art, like Winckelmann, and that of the collector and dilettante, like the eighteenth century aristocrat in London or Paris. Each of these approaches can be fruitful in increasing our understanding of art and its place in human life.

7. Art as expression and communication

Now, what of Tolstoy's own substitute definition: that art is the expression and communication of remembered emotion? It was based on the theory of Eugene Véron, that "art is the manifestation of emotion, obtaining external interpretation, now by expressive arrangements of line, form, or color, now by a series of gestures, sounds, or words governed by particular rhythmical cadence." [31] Tolstoy added the point that communication or "infection" is indispensable to art; and also that art transmits remembered emotion, as distinct from spontaneous expressions such as laughing or weeping. "If only the spectators or auditors are infected by the feelings which the author has felt, it is art. To evoke in oneself a feeling one has experienced, and having evoked it in oneself, then, by means of words, so to transmit that feeling that others may experience the same feeling—this is the activity of art. Art is a human activity, consisting in this, that one man consciously, by means of certain external signs, hands on to others feelings he has lived through, and that other people are infected by these feelings, and also experience them." [32]

Although this definition has not yet found its way into most dictionaries, it has been influential in aesthetic theory, and has been highly praised. Roger Fry comments on its revolutionary effect in the following words:

In my youth all speculations on aesthetic had revolved with wearisome persistence around the question of the nature of beauty. Like our predecessors, we sought for the criteria of the beautiful, whether in art or in nature. And always this search led to a tangle of contradictions or else to metaphysical ideas so vague as to be inapplicable to concrete cases. It was Tolstoy's genius that delivered us

[31] *L'Esthétique*, 1878. There are many older anticipations of the theory that art is expression.

[32] Maude, *Tolstoy on Art*, p. 173.

from this *impasse,* and I think that one may date from the appearance
of "What is Art?" the beginning of fruitful speculation in aesthetic.
. . . Tolstoy saw that the essence of art was that it was a means of
communication between human beings. He conceived it to be par
excellence the language of emotion.[33]

J. A. Symonds, too, is close to Tolstoy in asserting that "art is
expression or presentation of the feeling or thought of man." [34] C. J.
Ducasse declares that "art is essentially a form of language—namely,
the language of feeling, mood, sentiment, and emotional attitude." [35]

Unfortunately, Tolstoy's definition also encounters difficulties,
the minute we attempt to apply it specifically. "If only the spectators
or auditors are infected by the feelings which the author has felt, it
is art." But, as in the case of pleasure and enjoyment, there is great
individual variation in such effects. A work which will succeed in
communicating the artist's feelings to one individual will not succeed
in doing so to another. How is one to tell, by inspecting a picture or
poem, whether it is the kind which will communicate the artist's feelings to the spectator? How can one tell what the artist's feelings were,
and how much they resemble the spectator's feelings? How can one
tell whether the artist actually experienced, and now remembers, the
emotion which the work of art arouses in others?

The full significance of a definition or any abstract principle never
becomes clear until we see how it is applied by the one who makes or
uses it, or, in other words, what its concrete extension is for him. At
first sight, it would appear that Tolstoy accepts the usual extension of
art in the broad aesthetic sense, as consisting of the so-called fine arts.
The feelings which an artist communicates to others, he writes, are
various: patriotism or religious devotion expressed in a drama, "rap-
tures of lovers described in a novel, feelings of voluptuousness
expressed in a picture, courage expressed in a triumphal march, merri-
ment evoked by a dance, humor evoked by a funny story, the feeling
of quietness transmitted by an evening landscape or by a lullaby, or
the feeling of admiration evoked by a beautiful arabesque—it is all
art."

[33] From "Retrospect," in *Vision and Design.* London: Chatto and Windus,
1920.

[34] *Op cit.,* p. 124

[35] *Art, the Critics, and You* (New York: Oskar Piest, 1944), p. 52. See his
discussion of Tolstoy and Véron, *ibid.,* pp. 52-60.

But later we find that art has both a much broader and a much narrower extension for Tolstoy. "What we hear and see in theatres, concerts, and exhibitions, together with buildings, statues, poems, novels . . . is but the smallest part of the art by which we communicate with each other in life. All human life is filled with works of art of every kind—from cradle-song, jest, mimicry, the ornamentation of houses, dress, and utensils, to church services, buildings, monuments, and triumphal processions. It is all artistic activity."

On the other hand, art "in the full meaning of the word" is *not* all human activity transmitting feelings, "but only that part which we for some reason select from it and to which we attach special importance. This special importance has always been given by all men to that part of this activity which transmits feelings flowing from their religious perception, and this small part they have specifically called art, attaching to it the full meaning of the word."

This is extremely convenient and pleasing to the unscientific reader. To the large number of people who distrust technical skill and knowledge, who think that any peasant boy, if "sincere," can be as good as a highly trained, mature artist, Tolstoy offers his all-embracing conception: that art is not confined to the formal products of urban civilization; it takes in the humblest mother's lullaby. On the other hand, he offers to severely moral and religious persons his very strict concept: that the only kind of art which is *really* art, in the full meaning of the word, is the kind which these people (including Tolstoy himself) like and approve. The rest is mere "counterfeit art."

It turns out, then, that Tolstoy is far from holding consistently to the simple formula, that art is expression and communication of remembered emotion. The sensuous art of the selfish, pleasure-loving aristocrats is also expression and communication of emotion, but of a certain kind which Tolstoy does not like. Modern art, he says, transmits chiefly three "base emotions": pride, sexual desire, and discontent with life. Like all vague and ambiguous concepts, this one is highly elastic, and can be interpreted in practice as the user wishes. Tolstoy's strict conception of art is definitely evaluative, and hence quite as controversial as the beauty-pleasure conception. To produce a "real work of art," he says, it is necessary that a man "should stand on the level of the highest life-conception of his time." Without this, a man may be talented in producing poems, paintings, or complex symphonies, and yet these will not be "works of art"—only "the counterfeits of art which pass for art in our society and are well paid for." Obviously this merely shifts the problem of evaluation to another issue: what is the highest life-conception of each age? It leaves us again with no objective, consistent criterion for marking off a field of phenomena to be studied in aesthetics.

Tolstoy's broad and narrow concepts of art both imply a radical departure from the extension which is commonly given the word in aesthetics. In the broad sense, art would include not only all the traditional fine arts, good and bad, but all cases where remembered emotion is expressed and communicated. It would include, as he says, the case of a boy relating his encounter with a wolf, and "infecting" his hearers with his fear. In the narrow sense, it would exclude, as Tolstoy explicitly tells us, Wagner's *Ring,* Beethoven's *Sonata Opus 101,* and the works of Baudelaire, Verlaine, Ibsen, Monet, Manet, and Puvis de Chavannes.

Now there is nothing wrong in Tolstoy's disliking and disapproving these artists, or attacking them as violently as he wishes. There is nothing wrong in his praising the obscure but edifying artists who qualify as great according to his standards. Such vehement evaluations are the life-blood of art criticism. Our problem here is a different one: a matter of logic and the choice of words. All of Tolstoy's evaluations could be expressed, quite as forcibly, without these radical shifts in the extension of the word "art." He might easily have retained the more neutral, non-evaluative extension of art as covering *all* painting, *all* literature, etc., and then have gone on to say that some art is good and some bad. He seems to concede this in speaking of "real art" and "counterfeit art." Are they not both, then, types of art? But elsewhere he speaks of mere "counterfeits of art," which would suggest that they are not art at all. Tolstoy is driven to this vagueness and shiftiness of meaning by his desire to make the definition of art fit his own peculiar tastes in art. His own formula, the expression and communication of remembered emotion, will not conform to these tastes without being twisted and turned to do so.

Suppose we apply this formula to the field of the arts in a broad aesthetic, non-evaluative sense: to *all* works of painting, music, poetry, etc.—that is, to the whole range of these arts. Is it true, then, that all art involves the expression and communication of remembered emotion? Secondly, is such expression and communication peculiar to art? The answer to both questions is "no." As to the second, the expression and communication of remembered emotion occurs constantly in ordinary conversation. It occurs every time we tell someone how pleased, bored, irritated, or amused we were on a previous occasion, with enough vivacity to arouse a sympathetic response. True, art arises out of life and is continuous with it; there is no radical difference in kind between literary art and such ordinary conversation. But there are differences in degree, which are socially regarded as very important: as to the extent of selection, emphasis, organization, embodiment in a lasting form and medium, etc. The basic, original connotation of art is *skill*, and all subsequent usage retains a little of that connotation, in restricting the term to comparatively skillful, controlled manipulation of a medium. We do speak very broadly of "children's art" in drawing pictures without special skill; but even there some detachment from the context of experience occurs, so that a distinct linear form is produced. Only by stretching the traditional extension of art beyond all customary limits can it be made to cover all expression and communication of remembered emotion.

On the other hand, it is not true that all art (in the broad aesthetic, non-evaluative sense) involves expression and communication of emotion. Tolstoy concedes this in part by admitting that an artist need not have had an emotion "in reality," in order to communicate it. He may have had it only "in imagination." This would cover, for example, the case of a writer who vividly describes or dramatizes the dying agonies of some character, even though he has never seen, and certainly never felt, anything of the kind. But we must go still farther. It is quite possible for a skillful artist to arouse feelings of any desired kind, in a suitable percipient, without having such feelings himself to any considerable extent, even in imagination. He often can do so, simply by presenting the images and types of form which he knows by experience to be emotive: to be "sure-fire" wit and humor, or conventional "tear-jerking" pathos. No doubt the artist must have experienced some emotions of the sort, at some previous time in his life, in order to present the stimuli effectively; but the real experience may be very remote indeed. He can be in a sour and cynical frame of mind, and still draw smiling, pretty faces, which "express happiness." It would be less misleading to say that they "suggest happiness," through culturally established bonds between a certain sign—the upturned mouth, etc.—and certain meanings—

inward happiness. In that way, we would not be assuming that the picture is an actual putting out of the artist's own state of mind.

Moreover, the observer's experience is not necessarily a repetition of the artist's, in spite of the common assumption to that effect. We constantly respond to art in ways very different from those of the artist: for example, when we appreciate a work of primitive or exotic religious art for its decorative design. A connoisseur may look at a smiling face in a painting, and be moved to any one of a number of feelings, none of which may happen to coincide with those which the artist had when he painted it.

Tolstoy explicitly recognizes these facts, in going on to denounce the skilled technicians who can turn out "counterfeits of art" even without having "the essence of art, that is, feeling wherewith to infect others." They may have "a talent for some branch of art" and to know the "definite rules or recipes" which exist in each branch of art. "So the talented man, having assimilated them, may produce such works *à froid,* cold-drawn, without feeling." [36]

Again, one can sympathize very cordially with Tolstoy's attitude; with what he approves and what he disapproves in art. But all this can be said quite as easily and clearly in other words. One can say that works produced *à froid* are usually bad art, insincere, artificial, and so on; without denying that they are, in a neutral and generic sense, works of art.[37] One can believe that the *right* way to appreciate art is to repeat the emotional experience of the artist, and that all other ways are superficial, missing the real essence, etc. At the same time, one can recognize that this is not the only way to experience art; that responses to art often do not involve any "infection" or communication of a specific emotion from artist to observer.

The advantage of this way of stating the facts is that it retains a fairly definite, objective extension for the term "art." It marks off a central field of phenomena for aesthetics, consisting of *all* products of certain recognized techniques and mediums; *all* examples of certain

[36] Maude, p. 237. (Ch. XI of *What is Art?*)

[37] Cf. Dewey, *Art as Experience,* p. 68, on "Why certain works of art offend us." The cause, says Dewey, is likely to be "that there is no personally felt emotion guiding the selecting and assembling of the materials presented." But he uses "art" in the evaluative sense in adding that "Without emotion, there may be craftsmanship, but not art" (p. 69).

typical forms, such as pictures, poems, statues, symphonies, etc. The whole problem of evaluation—of what are the best kinds of art, the best ways of creating and experiencing art—is set apart for separate consideration in its own right.

From this point of view, one would have to say that some but not all art involves the expression and communication of remembered emotion; also that such expression and communication often occur outside the realm of art, in ordinary life and conversation.

Again, Tolstoy recognizes this fact in saying that "Many conditions must be fulfilled to enable a man to produce a real work of art. It is necessary that he should . . . experience feeling and have the desire and capacity to transmit it, and that he should moreover have a talent for some one of the forms of art." [38] In other words the production of art, in Tolstoy's strict sense, requires some skill in the use of a medium. So he comes around, indirectly, to accepting the traditional conception of art as a kind of skill—as skill in expressing emotion so that it will infect others.

We must insist, however, that it is not always necessary for the artist to have the emotion himself; that he may only arrange and present the stimuli which are capable of arousing it in others. In other words, art does not always *express* the emotion of the artist. It would be more accurate to say, then, that art is *skill in arousing emotions in others,* through the use of an appropriate medium. No doubt, it helps the artist to do so if he feels the emotion to some extent himself; too much may decrease his power to control the medium. But in any case, having the emotion is not essential to the process or the product of art, in the non-evaluative sense.

When so revised and interpreted, Tolstoy's definition turns out to be not as far from the hedonist definition as at first appeared. According to the latter, art is skill in arousing pleasure or pleasurable feeling. The hedonist would ask of Tolstoy, whether most of the feelings which an artist seeks to arouse are not agreeable or acceptable— pleasant, in a broad sense. At least, people welcome and enjoy them, to a large extent; if they did not, they would avoid them.

From the standpoint of present-day psychology it appears, however, that both Tolstoy and the hedonists laid too exclusive stress on emotion or feeling. This is, after all, only one element in experience. Why not say that art communicates the results of social and individual

[38] Maude, p. 237.

experience, including perceptions, beliefs, concepts, desires, attitudes, folkways—all the accumulated cultural heritage? [39] Tolstoy recognized this in an earlier essay, entitled "On Art." [40] "Artistic (or scientific) creation," he said, "is such mental activity as brings dimly-perceived feelings (or thoughts) to such a degree of clearness that these feelings (or thoughts) are transmitted to other people." The artist tries to communicate to others "what he has seen, felt, or understood," and it is in trying to make this clear that the activity of an artist consists. "What was formerly unperceived, unfelt, and uncomprehended, by them is by intensity of feeling brought to such a degree of clearness that it becomes acceptable to all, and the production is a work of art."

It was in the later essay, *What is Art?*, that Tolstoy restated his position as more sharply antithetical to the usual hedonist one. In so doing, he exaggerated and oversimplified it. A thorough reading of both texts discloses that his understanding of the facts of art was extensive and discerning, as one might expect from a great artist. But the verbal definition he proposed is far from adequate to cover these facts, or to distinguish art as an objective field for aesthetic investigation.

8. Combining the hedonist and expressionist concepts of art

There is nothing radically inconsistent between the definition of art in terms of pleasure and the various other definitions which have been opposed to it. The difference is largely one of interpretation and emphasis. As Tolstoy himself says, "The satisfaction of the intense feeling of the artist who has achieved his aim gives pleasure to him." [41] No one denies that the contemplation of art often gives pleasure to people, and is often intended to do so. If it were not in some way satisfying or enjoyable, people would be likely to avoid it instead of seeking and welcoming it as much as they do. To this extent, hedonist psychology is not obsolete, but amply sustained by that of the present day. Even the metaphysical idealist and the religious mystic, who radically oppose the hedonist attitude in general, have to agree that their own ways of experiencing art are to a large extent directly satisfying, as well as contributing to more important ends.

[39] Cf. Dewey, *Art as Experience;* esp. p. 270 on *"expression of experience."*
[40] Published in *Tolstoy on Art,* by A. Maude, pp. 75, 80.
[41] "On Art." Maude, *op. cit.,* p. 82.

St. Thomas Aquinas defines beauty as *Id cuius ipsa apprehensio placet.*[42] The crucial issues are two: (a) what "pleasing" or "pleasure" specifically implies; and (b) whether pleasure is the ultimate aim and highest value in art, or only an incidental by-product.

Contemporary psychologists and aestheticians tend to avoid the word "pleasure" for much the same reason that Tolstoy avoids it: because it has been interpreted in a narrow sense, with false psychological implications. If pleasure is understood as a specific emotion or feeling-tone associated with sensuous gratification, joy, happiness, mirth, amusement, and the like, then it is untrue to say (as some early hedonists did) that everyone seeks his own pleasure. People often choose pain and sadness, as in war and religious sacrifice. Art, especially tragedy and serious religious art, is full of these graver, more negative feelings.

"Beauty" also has been conceived narrowly, as a particular kind of form or appearance, characterized by smoothness, grace, harmony, refinement of finish, restraint, regular proportions, etc.—the qualities which Winckelmann discerned in classical sculpture. If it means this, it is not an adequate differentia of art in general, for much that is now accepted and admired as art lacks these characteristics. A great deal of primitive, oriental, and modern art is quite the opposite: with rough, irregular forms, distorted representations of human anatomy, sordid realism, etc.

There are various ways out of this difficulty. One, that of Tolstoy, is to abandon "beauty" and "pleasure" entirely, and define art in some other terms. Another is to redefine "pleasure" more broadly, so as to include other kinds of art. "Pleasure" or "the pleasant" is then construed as covering all sorts of experience which people welcome, accept, and desire in life, including pain and grief at times. Psychoanalysis has somewhat strengthened this solution, by showing us how many and devious are the ways in which people satisfy desires and pursue pleasures, including the willing acceptance of pain and privation to soothe an unconscious sense of guilt or inferiority. By this definition, the feelings aroused by contemplating tragic or painful art can be pleasant, just as religious and moral art of the kind Tolstoy admires give their own kind of serious pleasure.

Whether all pleasant art is *beautiful* is again a question of definition. Sydney Colvin, in his article on "Fine Art," accepts the narrower

[42] *Summa,* 1 a, 2 ae, *quaest.* 27, art. 1.

meaning of "beauty," as excluding caricature and the grotesque. Hence devotion to beauty is not a sufficient criterion of fine art for him. "Even the terrible, the painful, the squalid, the degraded . . . can be brought within the province of fine art"—if so handled as to give aesthetic pleasure. Devotion to such pleasure, then, is for him the essential differentia of fine art.

However, "beauty" itself can be given a broader definition, to include certain kinds of "ugliness," or of art and life which used to be considered ugly. By this definition the sordid and deformed, the rough, uncouth and irregular, images of pain and wickedness, can all be beautiful, especially when conveyed in artistic form. Anything which affords aesthetic satisfaction, which people enjoy looking at, listening to, or reading about for its own sake would thus be "beautiful" for them. Beauty, according to this definition, is not a purely objective trait which things can have in themselves, apart from people's responses to them. It is a name for those responses themselves, when they are projected upon the object and regarded as qualities of the object. Such a definition of beauty is in the tradition from Kames, Kant, and Thomas Brown through Santayana,[43] who once defined beauty as "pleasure objectified," or "pleasure regarded as the quality of a thing."

Sydney Colvin's definition of fine art has a Victorian flavor today, but it avoids many of the faults of other formulas:

The fine arts are those among the arts of man which spring from his impulse to do or make certain things in certain ways for the sake, first, of a special kind of pleasure, independent of direct utility, which it gives him so to do or make them, and next for the sake of the kindred pleasure which he derives from witnessing or contemplating them when they are done or made by others. . . . Fine art is everything which man does or makes in one way rather than another, freely and with premeditation, in order to express and arouse emotion, in obedience to laws of rhythmic movement or utterance or regulated design, and with results independent of direct utility and capable of affording to many permanent and disinterested delight.[44]

[43] *The Sense of Beauty* (New York, 1890), p. 52. *Cf.* A. L. Jones, "A Note on Dr. Thomas Brown's Contribution to Esthetics," *Studies in the History of Ideas* (New York: Columbia University Press, 1918), Vol. I, p. 216.

[44] "Fine Arts." *Encyc. Brit.*, 11th ed., 1910. As mentioned above, he uses "art" alone in the broad technical sense, and therefore has to use the prefix "fine" for the aesthetic sense.

The end of the fine arts "is not use but pleasure, or pleasure before use, or at least pleasure and use conjointly." They minister, not primarily to man's material necessities or conveniences, but to his love of beauty; "and if any art fulfills both these purposes at once, still as fulfilling the latter only is it called a fine art."

This statement is questionable in several ways, in addition to its reliance on the concept of pleasure. To say that the pleasures of art are "independent of direct utility" now seems exaggerated, in view of later emphasis on the intermingling of aesthetic and practical values. Colvin's reference to the "laws of rhythmic movement," etc., also raises doubts as to the existence of such laws. But in certain respects his wording is useful and suggestive.

In the first place, Colvin does *not* say, "Fine art is the production of what *is* beautiful, or of what *gives* pleasure." That, as we have seen, makes it impossible to decide whether a product is "fine art" without evaluating it, and thus parting company with objective, scientific description. Colvin, instead, merely says that fine art is produced *for the sake of* a certain kind of pleasure. It is done or made *in order to* express and arouse emotion. Its *end* is pleasure, and *it ministers to* the love of beauty. Its results are capable of affording delight "to many"—not necessarily to all, or to any particular kind of person. This is not a slight verbal distinction. It makes the whole statement much more cautious and objective. There may be endless dispute over whether a certain painting actually is beautiful or pleasant, and none whatever about the fact that its artist intended it to be so. It is an established fact of social culture and history that artists often— perhaps not always, but with characteristic frequency—*try* to make their products beautiful and pleasant to observe, in addition to serving other purposes. It is a little misleading to say that the "end" of art is pleasure, for that suggests some fixed, prior entelechy or final cause; the aims of art can be anything that people choose to make them. It is always somewhat doubtful what the aims, conscious or unconscious, of a particular artist were in a particular case. They vary tremendously, and one cannot be sure that the artist intended to give aesthetic pleasure, just because we find his work pleasing. In the case of a whole art or the so-called fine arts as a group, it is safer to say that the desire to produce a favorable aesthetic effect has usually, and on the whole, been a characteristic aim—not the only aim, and often not the chief one, but at least *a* persistent aim. This is by no means restricted to the eighteenth century, when the emphasis on beauty and pleasure was carried to an extreme. Such a persistent motivation or intention is an objective cultural phenomenon, which can be inferred not only from the works of art themselves, but from critical appraisals of them by contemporaries; from instructions to artists to paint a beautiful altar-piece; from boasts of kings about the splendor of the the temples they have built, and so on.

It would be even safer, perhaps, to speak in terms of the *functions* which the arts have carried on, and not of conscious aims or intentions. The arts have many utilitarian functions in common with non-aesthetic technology; those functions cannot be regarded as distinguishing characteristics of the aesthetic arts. They have political and religious functions in certain cultures. Some of these are intended to operate through and by means of aesthetic charm: e.g., by pleasing the gods, or the ruling class, or by impressing subject masses with the glamor and power of the rulers. Many of the functions of art, in other words, are aesthetic and utilitarian at the same time. The two are combined; but it is the aesthetic element in their operation or attempted operation which distinguishes the arts from other attempts to gain analogous ends. Religious *art* is distinguished from other types of religious activity and product by its use of forms having an aesthetic appeal.

Not all the functions of art can be reduced to the producing of a pleasant aesthetic effect on the observer, however broadly "pleasant" is defined. This would oversimplify the problem by assuming the observer's or consumer's point of view exclusively—by assuming that art is always made for his gratification.[45] Art also has the psychological function of providing the artist with an outlet for his pent-up psychic energies—a means by which he can achieve outward, symbolic expression for his emotional conflicts and unsatisfied desires. He is pushed from behind, as it were, to translate his own personal drama, conscious and unconscious, into symbolic visual, musical, or verbal form; a personal drama which is never purely individual, but influenced by the psychic tensions of his cultural group and of the human race. By

[45] George Boas distinguishes between the artist's point of view and the observer's, as to the end of art: the former stressing expression, the latter self-revelation, stimulation of an emotion, communication of an idea, or transfer of impressions. (*A Primer for Critics*, Baltimore, 1937, p. 88). *Cf.* C. J. Ducasse on the creator's and consumer's viewpoints in art. (*Art, the Critics, and You*, p. 71).

producing a form in which these tensions are symbolized and partly resolved, or at least stated in a more universal way, the artist achieves release and satisfaction for himself, as well as helping others to it. In the process of production, or looking back upon it, he often feels that he is doing it just because he wants to, or has to; as if he were pregnant with something which had to be brought forth. He may feel quite indifferent to its possible effects on the public, or even wish to shock and irritate them. On the other hand, he may wish to reform their conduct, ridicule their faults, or create new ideal values for their spiritual benefit.

For such reasons, any variation of the hedonist definition of art may seem false and misleading to an artist, or to anyone who sympathetically presents his point of view. So far as he is concerned, he will insist he does not produce art in order to make something beautiful or pleasing to anyone, or to produce any kind of aesthetic effect on the observer; he produces it because he has to express himself in that way. This seems to be its essential nature and function, and any possible effect it has on the observer seems incidental. As a rule, he hopes also for a sympathetic, cordial response from discriminating appreciators, and is willing to adapt his product somewhat, so as to help them understand and share his feelings. But, he may say, he is not trying to please them but to make them feel as he does about things: angry, horrified, disgusted, at what deserves to be so regarded. He is seldom as indifferent to public sympathy as he thinks he is; he feels lonely without it, and warmed by the sense of renewed solidarity with his group if he can succeed in communicating his feelings to others.

Being made by a theorist who is also an artist, Tolstoy's definition does justice to this frequent attitude of artists toward their art. It is also confirmed to some extent by psychoanalysis, in regard to the motivation and creative process of the artist. To say that art is the expression of an artist's feeling, and an attempt to communicate that feeling to others, is not a completely adequate definition of art for all purposes; but it does bring to light one aspect of art which is overlooked in the hedonist approach. It is not a contradiction of the hedonist approach, but a supplement to it. On the whole, as we have seen, the hedonist definition expresses the viewpoint of the consumer and appreciator. But the difference between the two is not radical. Unless the artist pleases some influential part of the public, he is not encouraged to continue. Many artists take a strongly hedonist attitude toward their art; they are simply and frankly trying to please the public, by providing it with beautiful and agreeable things to look at, read, and listen to. For them, the hedonist definition of art is adequate.

From the consumer's standpoint, also, the hedonist and expressionist definitions of art can be regarded as supplementary. The former emphasizes a certain kind of feeling-tone or general quality in the aesthetic response, vaguely described as pleasantness or agreeableness. This quality, it asserts, is commonly sought in and through experience of the arts, and in many cases achieved. To stimulate it is one of the distinctive functions of the arts. The expressionist definition, on the other hand, points to one of the principal ways in which an agreeable feeling-tone is achieved in the aesthetic response: namely, by the artist's expressing his own emotion strongly and skillfully enough to arouse an echo of it in the percipient.

We have been taking Colvin's definition as a point of departure, and will now return to it. His statement incorporates several ways of defining art: it is, one might say, a double-barrelled or a triple-barrelled definition. He tries to do justice to both the producer's and the consumer's viewpoint, in saying that fine art springs from man's impulse "to do or make certain things in certain ways for the sake, first, of a special kind of pleasure . . . which it gives him so to do or make them, and next for the sake of the kindred pleasure which he derives from witnessing or contemplating them when they are done or made by others." He includes the Tolstoyan viewpoint in saying that "Fine art is everything which man does or makes in one way rather than another . . . in order to express and arouse emotion." He thus attempts a synthesis of the hedonist and expressionist conceptions of art.

Is this merely a loose, catch-all method of definition, which tries to satisfy everybody by including all opposed theories? Is it merely an evasion of the task of selecting one basic differentia? There is a fascination, rather specious, about extremely brief, concise definitions. They are striking and easy to remember; they impress us with their ease and neatness in disposing of old problems. Croce excels at this kind of deceptively simple definition, which is usually a mere statement that two conceptions are synonymous or identical. "As to what is art—I will say at once, in the simplest manner, that art is *vision* or *intui-*

tion." [46] This is startling and plausible until one remembers that, after all, these are three different concepts, each with specific connotations, and not exactly synonymous. If art is *one kind* of vision or intuition, what are its differentiae? How does it differ from other kinds of vision or intuition? But this begins to complicate the definition; to make it a little more laborious and hard to remember.

As a matter of fact, it is comparatively seldom that one can adequately define, in a simple phrase or sentence, any major cultural concept.[47] Unlike mathematical concepts, those in the humanities are packed with a multitude of accumulated connotations, which demand to be included if the definition is to give a true account of the concept's functioning. To some extent, these different meanings can be sorted out under different numbers, each for a different realm of discourse.

It is not necessarily a fault in a definition of art, then, if it gives *two or more differentiae of art:* if it states that art usually has, among other functions, that of stimulating pleasant or favorable aesthetic experience; and also that it usually involves the expression and communication by the artist of remembered emotion and other types of experience. This is simply to distinguish art in various ways from other kinds of activity or product: e.g., from science and utilitarian technology. Future study may point out still other important differentiae. The problem will then be how to indicate as many important distinguishing features of art as possible, without making the definition too complicated for easy use.

9. Art as a means to aesthetic experience

As we have observed, the terms "beauty" and "pleasure" are both extremely ambiguous, and made to imply various beliefs which are unacceptable today. So deeply fixed are these misleading associations that it seems almost hopeless to try to prune them away, and to redefine "beauty" and "pleasure" in a manner acceptable to the modern critic and psychologist. However carefully one defines them,

---

[46] *The Breviary of Aesthetic,* quoted in Rader, p. 159. He also identifies art with language, etc. R. G. Collingwood, English follower of Croce, strings together a similar list of alleged synonyms. *Cf.* Listowel, *op. cit.,* p. 16.

[47] On the dangers of oversimplification in defining "art," see Carl Thurston, "Major Hazards in Defining Art." *Journal of Philosophy,* Feb. 27, 1947, p. 130.

and disowns the undesired associations, readers will misunderstand.

Many current writers on aesthetics, accordingly, choose instead some partial synonym, such as "aesthetically valuable," "delightful," "agreeable," "satisfying," "gratifying," "consummatory," or the like. Listowel defines art as "those material products of the hand and brain that afford delight in contemplation, by reason either of their formal structure or of their spiritual content or both in combination." [48] Such substitutes often have a more up-to-date sound, and avoid a few misleading suggestions. But they still leave the task of defining the new words in a clear and specific way; a task too often neglected.

In such a loose, preliminary definition, there is no great harm in including such words as "beauty" and "pleasure," without attempting to define them precisely, and with full recognition that they may be interpreted in various ways. They should be mentioned in a fairly neutral, objective way, which will not commit the definition prematurely to any special, controversial interpretation. It can be said, for example, that one of the actual functions of art—one of the services commonly required of it—is to make things which are felt and considered as beautiful. This leaves room for different opinions on what beauty actually is, and how important it is among the various functions of art. It is an undeniable fact that some artists do aim at beauty, and that some critics appraise it on that basis. We can also say that one of the functions of art is to arouse pleasant aesthetic experience. This leaves open the question whether beauty is a kind of pleasure, and how important either is among the functions of art. In thus mentioning beauty and pleasure, it will be well to list also a few alternative words, which some theorists prefer.

Instead of "beauty" and "pleasure," a number of recent writers stress "aesthetic experience" as the distinctive aim and function of art. Richard Müller-Freienfels adopts the following definition: "I call art every activity and its products which may, and sometimes should, produce aesthetic effects, although this effect need not be the only criterion." [49] Such definitions belong in the general hedonist tradition although they avoid the word "pleasure," since they find the differentia of art in its power to produce a certain kind of intrinsically desirable experience in the individual observer. However, Müller-

[48] *Op. cit.*, p. 210.
[49] *Psychologie der Kunst,* Berlin, Munich, 1923-33. Vol. III, p. 3.

Freienfels points out that such an aesthetic effect is not necessarily the only aim of art.[50] He continues:

> In order to regard a work of human accomplishment as art, we demand that it *can*, at least, be aesthetically effective even if it may, originally, have been created for non-aesthetic purposes. We speak of the *arts* of riding horseback, gymnastics, and cooking only in those cases where aesthetic values are attained beyond the practical goals of such activities. . . . Enjoying art is widely regarded as the purest type of aesthetic experience; on the other hand, that kind [of human accomplishment] which aims at aesthetic experience is considered art in the particular sense.

Also, he insists, the original connotation of art as a kind of skill or ability (*können*) must not be abandoned. It is a mistake, he says, to limit art too narrowly to the beautiful or aesthetic, as Lipps and Witasek have done, in defining it as "intentional production of the beautiful" or "human activity aiming at the creation of objects of favorable aesthetic effect." On the other hand, any definition neglecting the aesthetic element in art (as Vierkandt and Hegel have done, he asserts) is "too wide." The recent tendency to emphasize the social character of art should not be carried, he thinks, so far as to ignore the role of the individual as producing and enjoying. In psychology as a descriptive science, the drawings of a child or the dance of an Australian primitive must be considered as art.

As always, the choice of a new term to indicate the differentia of art places on the theorist an obligation, sooner or later, to define that term as well. What is aesthetic experience, aesthetic effect, or aesthetic response? It is usually described much as Kant and the English hedonists described the sense of beauty, or the pleasure of enjoying fine art, with an emphasis on its freedom from the practical, utilitarian considerations. This idea, as we have seen, goes far back in history, through the aristocratic theory of "liberal arts." Detachment from the practical as a criterion of the aesthetic attitude was elaborated psychologically by Bullough in his influential paper on " 'Psychical Distance' as a Factor in Art and an Aesthetic Principle." [51]

On the other hand, John Dewey protests against too sharp a sepa-

[50] *Ibid.*, vol. I, pp. 11-15.

[51] *British Journal of Psychology*, June, 1912.

ration between the aesthetic and the practical, and insists that the former should not be limited to experience of the so-called fine arts, or to mere passive enjoyment. "The word 'esthetic' refers," says Dewey, ". . . to experience as appreciative, perceiving, and enjoying. It denotes the consumer's rather than the producer's standpoint."[52] "That which distinguishes an experience as esthetic is conversion of resistance and tensions, of excitations that in themselves are temptations to diversion, into a movement toward an inclusive and fulfilling close."[53] "A measure of artistic products is their capacity to attract and retain observation with satisfaction under whatever conditions they are approached. . . . Any activity that is productive of objects whose perception is an immediate good, and whose operation is a continual source of enjoyable perception of other events exhibits fineness of art."[54] Thus for Dewey, who attacks hedonism in many respects, art and aesthetic experience are still defined with the help of words like "enjoying" and "objects whose perception is an immediate good." An aesthetic object, he points out, is "not exclusively consummatory," but "indefinitely instrumental to new satisfying events." He does not deny, however, that certain types of product which we call "art" or "fine art" are specially planned and often specially fitted to arouse such "consummatory experience" and "immediately enjoyable perception." Like other aestheticians, he recognizes this fact in devoting special attention to the fine arts as sources of aesthetic experience.

A common mistake has been to speak of "the aesthetic sense" or "the sense of beauty," as if there existed in the human organism a separate, specialized psychological mechanism for that purpose. This idea is reflected in definitions of fine art, for example, as "the creation of things which appeal directly to the aesthetic sense."[55] Aesthetic experience is now seen to be, rather, a certain configuration or way of combining and directing the same basic functions of perception, imagination, etc., which occur in other types of experience.

Torossian describes the aesthetic experience as "free from our practical needs, divorced from our active desires, so that we have no

[52] *Art as Experience*, p. 47.

[53] *Ibid.*, p. 56.

[54] *Experience and Nature* (New York: W. W. Norton and Co., 1930), p. 365.

[55] "Art," in *The Modern Encyclopedia*. New York, 1935.

motor impulse toward it." [56] This is very questionable. Is our experience of a delicate porcelain bowl or a piece of silk velvet any the less aesthetic when we desire to touch it? Is our enjoyment of a dance less aesthetic when we feel impelled to move in sympathy with its rhythms? "Practical" is not the same as "motor." We are on safer ground when we distinguish aesthetic experience as lacking, or comparatively lacking, in the element of active problem-solving, of thinking out means to ends which we personally desire. Even there, the distinction is subtle, since we try to solve imaginary practical problems in reading a detective or mystery story. The essential point is that in responding aesthetically to an object, one pays more exclusive attention to its nature as a perceptual form, or as a form suggested to one's imagination; and less to thinking about how the object might be used, altered, or avoided so as to achieve one's own desires. It is not aesthetic experience of a picture to scheme how one may purchase it at a bargain price, though some aesthetic experience may have preceded the scheming, and even now tinge it to some extent.

We are seldom or never "purely aesthetic" in attitude or experience. Innumerable mixed and intermediate types exist: e.g., where practical reasoning is present but subordinate. Comparatively speaking, an aesthetic experience is one containing little or no active effort to solve practical or theoretical problems—one in which the ordinary processes of scheming and planning, weighing evidence, adapting means to ends and testing hypotheses are suspended. In this type of experience, attention is directed (a) toward the directly perceptible aspects of an outer stimulus, such as the colors and shapes in a picture, the melodies and rhythms in a piece of music; or (b) toward suggested images and meanings, as in a realistic picture or a set of printed words; or (c) toward both at once, or alternately. There is a comparatively undistracted effort to apperceive intensely and thoroughly, and to savor the emotional qualities aroused by the images and meanings. Aesthetic experience may emphasize direct sense perception or imagination and interpretation of meanings. It may change from one to the other. Aesthetic experience is distinct from dreams and free-flowing reveries in being controlled to some extent by a set of outer stimuli, such as words in a book or the details in a visible

[56] A. Torossian, *A Guide to Aesthetics* (Stanford Univ. Press, Calif., 1937), pp. 15, 25.

object or scene.[57] It may be a single, momentary response or a sustained attitude, as in listening to a symphony. It may be a confirmed habit, as in the aesthetic type of personality as contrasted with the practical or intellectual. It often involves suspension and quiescence of motor-muscular activities, except those required in active perceiving. Selected perceptual and mental functions tend to be hyperactive; so it is incorrect to call aesthetic experience "passive" without qualification.

The aesthetic attitude, and the aesthetic type of experience should be distinguished from the *artistic*, with which they are frequently confused. An artist often assumes an aesthetic attitude, as in contemplating a natural scene or a work of art. But much of his activity consists in solving problems, especially in devising means for effective expression, construction, and execution of his plans. The processes of art contain a large element of practical thinking, in addition to aesthetic experience.

Traditional aesthetics is justified in assuming that certain arts, called "fine" or "aesthetic," are specially contrived and adapted to stimulate and sustain aesthetic experience. On the other hand, those like Dewey who prefer to emphasize the continuity of art with life are correct in insisting that aesthetic experience can also be aroused by other kinds of object and situation; by nature, utilitarian forms, and things encountered in everyday life. They are correct in insisting that experience can take on aesthetic quality without being as "pure" and extreme as the kind just described; without being as highly specialized in its devotion to aesthetic contemplation, or as completely detached from practical thinking and acting. We can enjoy a cup aesthetically while raising it to our lips; a garment while wearing it. We can use and think about it practically, while contemplating it aesthetically. The aesthetic functions of a work of art are not necessarily detached from its useful functions. Various attitudes, various responses, can be merged in the flexible human organism. There is no reason for calling any of them *the* right or best way to respond to art. But one can say that specialized development of an aesthetic attitude and response is furthered by conditions which make it unnecessary

[57] Pleasant fantasies stimulated by a drug or other internal agent are not aesthetic experiences. In stimulating them the drug does not qualify as a work of art. The stimulus must be an external object, acting on and through sense perception. However, a drug or other internal agent or condition may heighten or diminish aesthetic sensitivity to outside stimuli.

for the individual to scheme and plan: e.g., a comfortable seat in a theater after the day's work is over, or a comfortable bank-account and station in life which makes it unnecessary to worry about one's future.

Although the arts are on the whole intended and adapted to stimulate satisfactory aesthetic experience, along with other functions, their success in doing so is extremely variable. It depends to a great extent on the training and conditioning of the percipient, not only in the necessary skills of perceiving and understanding complex forms, but on the tastes or habitual attitudes of preference necessary to approve and like a certain type of art.

Although they are characteristically used as stimuli to aesthetic experience, works of art can be treated in many other ways. A practical man can treat them as means to his ends: e.g., in advertising or political propaganda. A man of intellectual, theoretical interests can treat them as data for the problems of aesthetics, history, sociology, or psychology.

A contemporary psychologist of art, A. R. Chandler, asserts that "The aesthetic experience may be defined as satisfaction in contemplation or as a satisfying intuition. When I enjoy a beautiful sunset I am satisfied to contemplate it. My intellectual curiosity is put to sleep—I do not care just then about the physical causes of clouds and light. My practical interests are suspended—I do not care just then whether such a sky foretells dry weather, though my garden may need rain. I am satisfied to contemplate the sunset. The object contemplated may be real and present, like the sunset or a musical performance; then we call the process perception. . . . When the object contemplated is absent or unreal we call the process imagination. . . . It is convenient to have a general term for perception, memory, and imagination; either contemplation or intuition may be used in this broad sense." [58] Chandler avoids the word "pleasure." He continues—

The word *satisfaction* in my definition may be defined indirectly as the state of mind which is indicated by the willingness to prolong or repeat the experience in question. . . . The term *satisfaction* is better than *pleasure,* because satisfaction is the broader term. The harrowing excitement aroused by a melodrama is scarcely a pleasure,

[58] *Beauty and Human Nature: Elements of Psychological Aesthetics* (New York: Appleton-Century, 1934), p. 9.

but it is undoubtedly a satisfaction, since people seek to prolong or repeat it. The same may be said of pathos in music or poetry. It may reduce us to tears, but our experience is nevertheless a satisfying one.

Defining the term "satisfaction," as Chandler does, in behavioristic terms, as "willingness to prolong or repeat the experience" evades one central issue: whether there is any specific feeling-tone, called "pleasure" or "pleasantness" (for want of a better name), which occurs as an element in the total experience when we are willing to prolong or repeat it, and even helps to make us willing.[59] Anyone who has eaten a piece of candy, or watched a child doing so, knows that there is a positive, affective quality in his experience, a joy in tasting the candy, which operates in motivating him to continue. When it is lacking, or an opposite feeling-tone of disgust or nausea is present, he will fight against continuing. This is the "subjective" or inwardly felt aspect of what appears from the outside as willingness or unwillingness to continue an experience. Because of its inaccessibility to view, except introspectively, the behavioristic school of psychology has frightened many aestheticians into ignoring its existence, lest they be charged with all the crudities of eighteenth-century hedonist psychology. In so doing, they ignore a phenomenon whose existence, though hard to describe, is a universal datum of human experience. Feeling happy, pleased, or interested in contemplating an object is *not* the same as mere "welcoming behavior" toward it. The latter is manifested by amoebas and even by fly-devouring plants toward their prey, as well as by hungry humans. The power to feel subtle and varied emotion toward something, even while doing nothing but observe it, is apparently limited to animals with a complex nervous system, and especially to man.

Aesthetics cannot get very far if it dodges the issue of explaining the emotional aspects of aesthetic experience. The eighteenth century hedonists met this issue boldly, in psychology, aesthetics, and ethics, using "pleasure" as the best available name for a certain universally felt and recognized kind of experience. Contemporary aesthetic psychology must take up the problem where they left off, using a different name for the phenomenon if necessary, but studying it nevertheless.

There is some doubt and disagreement as to whether aesthetic

[59] In later chapters, Chandler does not hesitate to use the word "pleasantness," and describes many experiments in relation to it.

experience is necessarily pleasant, agreeable, or satisfactory. Some writers apparently assume that it is, and use "aesthetic experience" interchangeably with "aesthetic enjoyment." Others—e.g., Witasek, in the quotation by Müller-Freienfels—specify *favorable* aesthetic effect." This would coincide with the view that aesthetic experience can be unpleasant or disagreeable, as in listening to music one finds harsh and irritating. Aesthetic experience would not be synonymous with "experience of beauty," for it would include experiences of the ugly, painful, and repulsive as well. Psychologically, these are certainly ways in which people respond to art, for its direct perceptual qualities and apart from all practical considerations. Thus the old hedonistic problem reappears, as to whether or not the kind of aesthetic effect sought in art is one involving a pleasant feeling-tone. The problem is by no means solved by vague references to "aesthetic effect" without further psychological specifications.

It is evident that "aesthetic experience" now has implications somewhat different from "pleasure," in the older hedonist systems. It usually lacks the special associations with sensuous luxury and gay amusement, which have so offended Tolstoy and other moralists.[60] It covers direct sensory perception of art, as in listening to music, and imaginative contemplation, as in reading poetry. It covers the sympathetic response to an artist's religious or moral feelings as expressed in art, which would further placate many anti-hedonists. It is not sharply antithetical to the practical and useful, since one may experience it (a) in the course of one's daily tasks, and (b) in admiring useful objects such as chairs and dishes for their form and design.

Modern aesthetics should not be too quick to surrender all vestiges of the eighteenth century concept of pleasure as an aim of art. All the theoretical assaults on hedonism have not disposed of pleasure, happiness, enjoyment, or something of the sort, as one of the things which make life worth living and art worth cultivating. It is easy enough to avoid the errors and exaggerations of eighteenth century hedonism without losing its permanently valid elements as well. The modern aesthetician does not need to avoid and conceal all traces of hedonism, as if it were not only wicked but entirely disproven and obsolete. In the field of aesthetics, there are always

---

[60] J. S. Mill and other nineteenth century hedonists tried to avoid this difficulty by distinguishing between "higher" and "lower" pleasures, the former including those of art. (Mill, *Utilitarianism*, Ch. II).

sad-faced Puritans and angry partisans in the social struggle, who are quick to reprove any suggestion that art has a right to be pleasant at all. They are entitled to their own grim view of life and art, but need not frighten others from including the essentials of hedonism in a healthy, naturalistic philosophy of art. Hedonism has no necessary connection with aristocracy or selfish exploitation of the poor; the masses can find pleasure in art, as well as the privileged few. Even "pleasure of the senses" need not be rejected as bad, even though we no longer accept it as the whole or highest good of life. "The artist," said Whistler in his memorable "Ten O'Clock" lecture, "is glad, and laughs aloud, and is happy in his strength, and is merry at the pompous pretension—the solemn silliness that surrounds him. For Art and Joy go together, with bold openness, and high head, and ready hand—fearing naught, and dreading no exposure."

10. Avoiding religious, moral, and political prejudice in the conception of art

Much confusion about the meaning of "aesthetic" still persists. Not infrequently, someone refers to the "purely aesthetic" element in art as if it were entirely distinct from the "meaning" of art; from the intellectual, religious, and ethical significance of art. Thus the "aesthetic" aspects of art are confusingly narrowed down again to the purely sensory, decorative, and formal. By the same token, "aesthetic experience" is regarded as a narrow, crude kind of purely sensual pleasure, like that of a child sucking a piece of candy. Any definition of art as devoted (even in part) to aesthetic ends is branded as crudely hedonistic. So the perennial attack of transcendentalists and ascetic moralists on the aesthetics of naturalism is shifted from its eighteenth-century targets—beauty and pleasure—to the new one of "aesthetic experience." Their strategy is to make it appear that any naturalistic conception of art and its values wallows in the same old "Epicurean" sty—in which, of course, even the scholarly Epicurus himself never set foot.

This attack has recently gained new reinforcements from the standpoint of oriental mysticism. It repeats the familiar charge of Hindu lecturers, admiringly applauded by American audiences, that modern western civilization is crassly materialistic, thinking only of dollars and cheap excitements, while the orient is deeply spiritual. A straw man is set up for drubbing, a caricature of the modern western concepts of fine art and aesthetic experience. It is falsely asserted that these concepts reduce art to the crudely sensual, and to the superficial imitation of external appearances.

This dualism, of course, is false on both counts. The orient is not free from the cruder forms of greed and sensuality. It also contains refined and erudite connoisseurs of art who can enjoy a piece of fine jade or porcelain in much the same aesthetic way that western connoisseurs enjoy it. For the educated taste in both east and west, aesthetic enjoyment includes attention to the cultural meanings of art as well as to sensory qualities; it includes appreciation of how skillfully these meanings—e.g., the religious symbolism in a statue of Siva—are set forth in and by the visible form. By pointing out these symbolic meanings, oriental scholars have greatly increased our ability to enjoy eastern art aesthetically as well as to understand it intellectually. But there is nothing radically foreign to the western view of art in the belief that such meanings are important. The aesthetic form of a work of art includes its culturally established meanings in addition to its sensory qualities. The aesthetic attitude toward a work of art, on the part of an educated person, may include careful attention to its intellectual and spiritual meanings, as a source of pleasure and delight. To say that aesthetic enjoyment is one of the functions of art does not, then, imply any derogation or ignoring of spiritual meanings and values, whatever these are believed to be.

Aesthetic experience and pleasure are not inconsistent with religious belief and austere conduct. All but the most severely ascetic worshippers permit themselves occasionally to admire the beauty of a simple church edifice, the sound of its bell or the words and music of a hymn. To change from an attitude of worship to one of aesthetic admiration is not necessarily to deny or disparage the former. The two can be combined as integral parts of the same experience, as in contemplating the object's beauty, utility, and religious significance at the same time. But, on the other hand, a highly religious person may *at times* wish to concentrate his attention on the qualities which, in his opinion, make the object beautiful. He may even, as an artist, critic, or teacher, specialize professionally on the technical problems involved in making religious art beautiful.

The opponents of naturalistic aesthetics often fail to distinguish between frivolous sensuality and the deliberate specialization of scholars on problems of aesthetic form which has occurred in recent decades, especially in regard to painting and sculpture of the late nineteenth and twentieth centuries. This confusion is understandable, since the latter trend was associated, in the minds of some nineteenth-century "decadent" artists, with sensuous hedonism, diabolism, and various other forms of revolt against conventional morality. The emphasis on form and design in visual art, as opposed to over-reliance on stories, moral lessons, and other suggested meanings, has been carried on in a serious, almost scientifically experimental spirit by many later artists, as a study of the potentialities of various types of visual form, and the extent to which visual art can emulate music in stressing non-representative design. Their attitude toward abstract and non-objective art has sometimes, as in the case of Kandinsky, been mystical and moralistic rather than frivolous. Even Whistler, whose "Ten O'Clock" lecture in 1885 was a notable expression of the new emphasis on aesthetic form, did not carry it to extremes. He protested against another extreme which then prevailed: that of judging painting only from a literary point of view, as telling a story, or for the virtues of the subject represented; the extreme of ignoring (as "mere execution") the painter's own kind of "poetry"—"the amazing invention, that shall have put form and color into such perfect harmony, that exquisiteness is the result—the nobility of thought, that shall have given the artist's dignity to the whole, says to him absolutely nothing." The result of Whistler's protest, and that of other impressionists and post-impressionists, has been on the whole positive and constructive. It has enriched art with countless new harmonies of shape and color, and it has enriched the technique of art appreciation by teaching people to look in painting for something more than the narrative, sentimental, and moral associations: to look directly, and see what is there in front of their eyes.

In any movement, of course, there are some who carry it to absurd extremes. There are critics who insist that any attention to the "subject-matter" of a picture is wrong, and that real aesthetic appreciation is limited to "pure form"—i.e., to the visible aspects only. But these are a negligible minority. The moderate and general view in aesthetics today is that *both* visible form and meanings are important; that art is at its best when it works out a harmonious synthesis of them, and that aesthetic experience is at its best when it discerns and enjoys this synthesis. But those who would maintain a moderate, balanced attitude must constantly be warding off attempts to push them toward one extreme or the other, or to caricature their attitude in some extreme form which can be easily denounced.

We must reject the caricature of modern, western aesthetics which would place it in radical opposition to the oriental and medieval views, as a glorification of idle luxury and crude sensuality. At the same time, this does not imply that the modern western view of art is exactly like those of the orient and medieval Europe. The rise of modern naturalistic science in the west has had profound repercussions on the nature of art, and of people's attitudes toward art. We have seen how the development of scientific technology has tended to remove the more purely utilitarian pursuits from the field of "art," as commonly conceived; and how the field of art has consequently been left with a more specialized emphasis on aesthetic functions. The development of pure science and philosophical explanations based on science has also tended to deprive the arts—poetry, painting, sculpture, etc.—of the need to deal so much with intellectual problems, or to describe the facts of the universe for the benefit of the young. The secular trend of much western science, philosophy, and education has gone along with a secular trend in the arts. Undoubtedly, there is less definitely religious expression in recent western art than in that of medieval Europe or India.

Antagonism toward any conception of art which emphasizes its aesthetic and pleasure-giving functions is not limited to conservative religious philosophers or to metaphysical idealists. At the opposite extreme, in some respects, is Communism of the Russian, Marxist variety, whose ideological background is atheistic and materialistic. But there too, after the first flush of revolutionary modernism in art, during the early 1920's, the official attitude has been to condemn "formalism"— i.e., an emphasis on aesthetic form and design—as bourgeois decadence. Art must be easily intelligible to the masses, and must teach an approved political or economic doctrine. On this basis, the famous composers Prokofieff and Shostakovich were given official censure for dangerous formalistic tendencies. Art is conceived primarily as an instrument of propaganda and indoctrination. Thus the outcome is similar, whether the lesson is one of orthodox Christianity or Marxist Communism. Both extremes unite to condemn the artist who emphasizes form in art—even in so traditionally formal and abstract an art as music—and to condemn as well the public which enjoys such art and the theorist who justifies it. Hitler and his Nazi philosophers preached the same attitude toward modern art as decadent. This, too, is the attitude of the ordinary Philistine or practical citizen (including many influential persons in this country) who boast of their hostility toward all but the most conventional art, unless it serves some obvious purpose of a religious, patriotic, commercial, or other approved kind.

The definition of art advocated in this chapter is no more anti-religious than anti-communist, but is neutral and adaptable for use by persons of different views. It does not imply that one should be neutral in general, in all one's thinking and acting, but simply that the basic definition of "art" should not be loaded in advance with a special set of assumptions, which would unfit it for use by persons with a different point of view.

11. A revised definition of art

As we have seen, it is impossible and undesirable to reduce the many meanings of art to a single, brief, formula. After the most confusing senses have been put aside, to be called by other names, there still remains a group of closely related, alternative senses which are mutually consistent and supplementary. All are useful in different connections, to emphasize different aspects of approximately the same phenomena. All the definitions are drawn from current usage; no entirely new meanings are proposed. The reason for most of the wordings will be apparent from the foregoing discussion; for others, it will be explained in later chapters.

In the first definition, or group of definitions, art refers to certain related types of skill; in the second to a type of product; in the third, to an area of social culture; in the fourth, to a division of this area. Definition 1a expresses on the whole the consumer's point of view; 1b, that of the artist or producer; 1c, a sociological interest in various types of occupation.

1a. *Art is skill in making or doing that which is used or intended as a stimulus to satisfactory aesthetic experience, often along with other ends or functions; especially in such a way that the perceived stimulus, the meanings it suggests, or both, are felt as beautiful, pleasant, interesting, emotionally moving, or otherwise valuable as objects of direct experience, in addition to any instrumental values they may have.*

b. *Art is skill in expressing and communicating past emotional and other experience, individual and social, in a perceptible medium. c. Especially, that phase in such skill or activity which is concerned with designing, composing, or performing with personal interpretation, as distinguished from routine execution or mechanical reproduction.*

2. Also, a product of such skill, or products collectively; works of art. Broadly, this includes every product of the arts commonly recognized as having an aesthetic function, such as architecture and music, whether or not that particular product is considered to be beautiful or otherwise meritorious.

3. Art, as a main division of human culture and a group of social phenomena, includes all skills, activities, and products covered by the above definition. As such, it is comparable in extent to religion and science; but these divisions overlap in part.

4. An art, such as music, is a particular division of the total field of art, comprising certain distinctive kinds of skill, activity, medium, or product. Especially, a division regarded as comparatively large, important, or distinctive; others being often classed as branches or subdivisions of an art.

The core conception, favored by contemporary scientific usage, is in *1a*. Where brevity is needed, it can be reduced to the following: *Art is skill in providing stimuli to satisfactory aesthetic experience.* However, in making it so brief, one loses several important distinctions, which help to avoid misunderstanding and to convey the special implications of the word in current usage.

"Making or doing" covers performing, as of sounds or gestures; also the manufacture of lasting objects such as statues. It includes designing or planning as well as final execution, when this is formulated in observable sketches, musical scores, or verbal directions. Later on, we shall see why the term "art" is sometimes restricted to the designing or composing phase.

"Used or intended as . . . ." This puts the definition in behavioristic, objective terms. To qualify as art, the product does not need to *be* beautiful or aesthetically satisfying; only to be used or adapted for an aesthetic function, by the producer or consumer. It is not even required that the object be *intended* as beautiful or pleasant; room is left for other types of aesthetic function and for products which fulfill aesthetic functions unintentionally.

"Along with other ends or functions . . . ." This avoids saying that aesthetic experience is the sole or even the most important function of art. Ordinarily, art has other functions also; but it is unnecessary to specify them in the definition. The aesthetic function is emphasized because it differentiates art from the more purely utilitarian and scientific skills.

"Expressing and communicating" is of course intended to recognize the conception of art advanced by Tolstoy and others. Instead of "feeling" or "emotion," the broader term "experience" is used. It covers not only feeling and emotion, but also perception, cognition, conation, beliefs and attitudes toward the world, etc., all of which are communicated in art. But art is recognized as especially concerned with emotional experience.

"Stimulate" is used in a psychological sense. It does not imply that the percipient is passive in relation to the work of art or the artist. The work of art is a stimulus and an object of apperception, helping to arouse psychosomatic responses in the percipient, and receiving some share of his attention. Through light-waves, sound-waves, or other physical means, it stimulates his sense-organs, nervous system, and related mental apparatus to certain kinds of activity, whose nature is determined also by his character, conditioning, attitudes, present moods and anticipations.

A work of art, such as a picture or symphony, is an arrangement of stimuli in space, time, or both, consisting of lines, color-areas, etc., in visual art, or of sounds in auditory art. It is called an "aesthetic object," which implies that it can become the object of attention and interested contemplation. Natural forms or objects, such as sunsets and flowers, can also become aesthetic objects; but in art we deal with man-made products. All aesthetic stimuli must be presented first to one or more sense-organs, in order to arouse later responses of interpretive, imaginative, cognitive, emotional, or other nature. The emphasis here on appeal to the senses (as in music and visual decoration) and to the imagination (as in literature) helps to distinguish art from science and other fields.

Art does not always stimulate perception and imagination to an equal degree, but it tends to stimulate both to some extent. A novel is addressed through the eyes to the imagination; a sonata is addressed more directly to sense perception. There is little if any perception without some experience of suggested images.

IV

Different Kinds of Art

1. Fine and useful arts: recent attacks on this antithesis

One source of disagreement over the meaning of art arises from the old problem of the relation between "fine" and "useful." When art is defined in the broad technical sense, as by Colvin, it includes both "fine" and "useful" arts; all branches of applied science and technology. When art is defined in the broad aesthetic sense, as recommended in this book, the question still remains: does it include the "useful arts," or only those supposedly devoted to aesthetic ends? How much of technology is covered by the word "art"? How much is left out?

In some extreme interpretations, the hedonist theory is said to imply a sharp separation between beauty and aesthetic pleasure on the one hand, utility on the other; between the "fine" and "useful" arts, supposedly devoted to these different ends; between the aesthetic and the practical attitudes. The latter in each case has been identified narrowly with what Colvin calls "ministering to man's material necessities and conveniences."

This antithesis has been repeatedly attacked as too extreme. No one today would venture to uphold it in that form, and writers who state the antithesis at all usually hasten to add that it is not intended sharply; that there is much overlapping between fine and useful arts, and that the latter are not necessarily inferior. The sharp separation in theory, it is now insisted, proceeds from an unhealthy, undemocratic social condition, in which a lower class does most of the useful work and an upper, exploiting class most of the enjoying. "Arts that are merely useful," says Dewey, "are not arts but routines; and arts that are merely final are not arts but passive amusements and distraction, different from other indulgent dissipations only in dependence upon a certain acquired refinement or 'cultivation.' " [1] "The division between

---

[1] *Experience and Nature* (Chicago: The Open Court Publishing Co., 1925), p. 361. Ed. 1929 published by W. W. Norton and Co., New York.

fine and useful," says Edman, "produces on the one hand, a practical
civilization in which there is no interest in sensuous charm or imaginative grace," and on the other "the decorative trifling of the piddling
little exquisites, the soft luxuriance of the aesthete whose dainty
creations and enjoyments have no connection with the rest of life." [2]
Torossian declares that "the less we emphasize the difference between
these two types of art work, the better it will be for the arts; for they
all have one aim and purpose." [3] He subscribes to Anatole France's
unqualified disapproval: "Let us blot out these unintelligent distinctions! Let us break down this destructive barrier, and consider the
inseparable unity of art in its endless manifestations. No! there are
not two branches of art; 'industrial' and 'fine' are without meaning!
There is only one art, which is at once workmanlike and beautiful;
which devotes itself to the worthy task of charming life by multiplying
beautiful forms that shall surround us, by expressing beautiful
thoughts." [4]

The attack is levelled at both parts of the antithesis; each being
charged with narrowness. In the first place, the so-called "fine" arts
are, or should be, useful also. In the second place, the so-called "useful" arts have, or should have, their aesthetic and immediately satisfying aspects, including the production of beauty. They are, or should
be, quite as noble and worthy as the "fine" ones. Thus the word
"fine," implying a claim to superior quality, is unjustified and misleading.

On the first of these points, Dewey argues that fine art is useful,
in a broad sense. "We reach a conclusion regarding the relations of instrumental and fine art which is precisely the opposite of that intended
by seclusive estheticians; namely, that fine art consciously undertaken
as such is peculiarly instrumental in quality. It is a device in experimentation carried on for the sake of education. It exists for the sake
of a specialized use, use being a new training of modes of perception."
"The fine arts as well as the industrial technologies are affairs of
practice." [5] The terms "use" and "practice" are thus interpreted

[2] I. Edman, *Arts and the Man* (New York: W. W. Norton & Co., 1939), pp.
42-3.

[3] *Op. cit.*, p. 41.

[4] A. France, "On the Unity of Art," *Journal of American Institute of Architects*, January, 1914, p. 18.

[5] *Experience and Nature*, pp. 392, 355.

broadly, as including much more than material necessities and conveniences.

Dewey presses the second line of attack with equal vigor. "Objects of industrial arts have form—that adapted to their special uses. These objects take on esthetic form, whether they are rugs, urns, or baskets, when the material is so arranged and adapted that it serves immediately the enrichment of the immediate experience of the one whose attentive perception is directed to it." [6]

It is widely recognized today that artistic impulses can be expressed in many other channels than the established arts, fine or useful. Aesthetic experience can be derived from contemplating any kind of human activity or product. In a cultural analysis of Plainville, a small American town, Abram Kardiner remarks that the women "like pretty dresses, are interested in hairdos, and sometimes take an aesthetic pleasure in the labeling and arrangement of glass jars of canned fruit. Men who farm admire a straight furrow better than anything else in the world." [7]

The conclusion that fine and useful arts overlap and have much in common is so widely accepted today that one would have a hard time finding an upholder of the sharp separation between them. Colvin, whose theory is attacked by Dewey,[8] makes no sharp distinction between "fine" and "useful." Architecture, he says, exists primarily for service:

In so far as it provides shelter and accommodation, it is one of the useful or mechanical arts, and one of the fine arts only in so far as its structures impress or give pleasure by the aspect of strength, fitness, harmony and proportion of parts, by disposition and contrast of light and shade, by colour and enrichment, by variety and relation of contours, surfaces and intervals.[9]

In other words, the whole art of architecture is not placed in any ironclad compartment. Some of its aspects are fine or aesthetic; others useful. He says much the same of the minor serviceable or useful arts.

[6] *Art as Experience*, p. 116. *Cf.* discussion of Dewey's position by M. M. Rader, *op. cit.*, p. xxx.

[7] *The Psychological Frontiers of Society* (New York: Columbia U. Press, 1945), p. 307.

[8] *Art as Experience*, p. 218.

[9] Article on "Fine Arts," *Encyc. Brit.*, 11th ed., vol. 10, pp. 370, 355.

They are, in fact, a "division of fine arts," not a separate class, because—like architecture—"they all yield products capable of being practically useful and beautiful at the same time."

On the other hand, as Colvin points out, the fine arts are not devoid of utility. Didactic poetry aims at practice and utility. Hortatory and patriotic lyrics "belong to a phase of fine art which aims directly at one of the highest utilities, the stimulation of patriotic feeling and self-devotion. So may the strains of music which accompany such poetry." Such divisions are not eternal and in the nature of things, but changing historically. "Most of what we now call fine arts served in the beginning to fulfil the practical needs of individual and social life. . . ."

The overlapping of "fine" and "useful" is no new discovery. Since the concept of fine arts came into use in the eighteenth century, it has almost always been defined so as to include some sort of use as well as beauty. Kant explicitly includes many useful arts as fine or *schöne Künste*. There is a clear statement on this point by J. G. Sulzer, in his *Allgemeine Theorie der schönen Künste*.[10] "He who first gave these arts the name of 'fine arts,'" he says, "seems to have perceived that their nature consists in the interweaving of the pleasing and the useful, or in the beautifying of the things which are made by ordinary art."

Since practically all aestheticians recognize that fine and useful art interweave and should interweave, the issue resolves itself largely into one of emphasis and terminology. Shall the differences in degree between the fine and useful arts be emphasized, or the similarities? Are the differences so slight that the whole antithesis should be abandoned, for fear of conveying harmful implications? In the heat of polemics against an exaggerated distinction, one is tempted to exclaim, "Throw it out entirely! Never mention it again." Later on, when the false implications have been corrected to some extent, one may find it hard to get along without the old distinction, or something very much like it. Throwing out all old distinctions which have been exaggerated would leave few general concepts in aesthetics, or in the rest of philosophy. It would incur the new risk of obscuring certain real and important differences among phenomena; differences in degree only, perhaps, and hard to describe, but worth analyzing further. That there is a difference of some sort between two groups of skills, roughly

[10] 2nd ed., Leipzig, 1793, III, 72. The first edition appeared in 1771-74.

expressed in the distinction between fine and useful arts, is attested by the persistence of this distinction in spite of all attacks upon it.

2. *Aesthetic and utilitarian functions of art; emphasis on one or the other*

Part of the difficulty centers in the meaning of "useful" and "utilitarian." When narrowly restricted to "material necessities and conveniences," they seem to exclude most poetry, music, painting, and sculpture. If these arts are not "useful" in a material sense, must they be called "useless"? Are they merely for immediate pleasure? Of course not. They have many kinds of use or function. Some of these are educational, some political, some religious, some moral, and so on. The stimulation of aesthetic experience is itself a function of art. It is one way of using art: as an object of contemplation, and a means to satisfactory aesthetic experience.

In springing to the defense of "useless art," as against those who insisted that art should always have some obvious practical or moral use, the "art for art's sake" group were rightly calling attention to the aesthetic functions of art, and urging that they be not overlooked.[11] Such functions are not limited to the giving of pleasure or direct enjoyment, important as this is in a suffering world, for all but the dour ascetic. There are other values to be derived from the intensive study and experience of art, such as the development of powers of perception and imagination; the enlargement of mental horizons and the refinement of emotional sensitivity; in short, the development of personality. These are social values, worth cultivating in education; not narrowly individualistic. To achieve them without distraction, one must experience art directly, paying close attention to its inner nature and diversity of form, without constantly looking away from art to ask how it can serve this or that ulterior end. Fine art is functional and in a broad sense useful, not in addition to being aesthetic, but in the very fact of being aesthetic.

In denouncing "art for art's sake" so violently today, and urging that the antithesis between "fine" and "useful" be cast aside, we should not forget that a moderate amount of specialization is valuable and necessary for progress in all fields. It is well that art should some-

---

[11] On the theories of Pater, Whistler, and Moore, see H. Ladd, *With Eyes of the Past* (New York, 1928), Ch. V, "For Art's Sake."

times be observed, enjoyed, and studied in and for itself, aside from all question as to what it can do to serve the state or public morals. It is well that some artists should experiment along specialized lines: to see what can be done with new arrangements of colors or of musical tones, to interest and move the observer in new ways, as artists in the past have experimented with fugues and arabesques. Since many skills and industries specialize upon utilitarian functions, it is well that some should specialize upon the aesthetic; not exclusively or permanently, but to a moderate extent at certain times. The partial separation of "fine" from "useful" arts, though much condemned today, has definite advantages which should not be overlooked in a hasty reaction against old-fashioned hedonism. Some focusing of interest upon aesthetic form and aesthetic experience, by the artist, the connoisseur, and the critic, should be encouraged and not frowned upon. It is not necessarily effete, trivial, precious, or piddling. It has no connection today with idle wealth or luxury, with aristocracy or democracy; it implies no disparagement of practical, utilitarian pursuits. It does *not* imply that art is best when devoid of utility, or when devoid of religious, moral, or intellectual content; it does not imply that "pure design" or abstract, non-representative art is better than realism, or that "subject-matter" should be ignored, or that architecture should stress appearance rather than function. It *does* imply that there is room in art and in civilization for many kinds of art, and many ways of experiencing art; that it is worth while to specialize at times on the aesthetic kind, at other times on the practical, and at still others on the relation between the two. Specialization must of course be supplemented by integration, and kept within reasonable bounds; but there is little danger, in these times of stress, of overemphasis upon the aesthetic.

The old antithesis between fine and useful arts is so loaded with confusing associations today, that it is just as well to give it up and think in other terms. It is more illuminating to contrast the arts, not as "fine and useful" or as "useful and useless," but as commonly emphasizing different kinds of function.

The *aesthetic* functions of art, we have just seen, are those which operate in and through the direct aesthetic contemplation of a work of art. They operate through its ability to serve as an object and stimulus for aesthetic experience. They include, not only the stimulation of satisfactory emotion, but all the diverse psychological processes which may enter into the total aesthetic response. These shade off gradually into the subsequent, indirect effects of the work of art—e.g., in inducing a lasting belief, attitude, or predisposition toward some kind of action.

Some works of art have at the same time aesthetic and non-aesthetic functions. A house can be admired for its appearance while it is being used to keep the rain out; a knife while it is being used to cut with. These are works of "utilitarian" art, because they combine aesthetic and utilitarian functions. Their utilitarian functions are not adventitious and occasional, but established, and manifested to some extent in their materials, forms, and methods of construction.

On the other hand, there are some skills and products which are not used at all, or at least not in any regular way, to stimulate aesthetic experience. They are sometimes called "purely utilitarian." We have been abundantly cautioned, in recent years, not to assume that such products are totally unaesthetic or lacking in beauty. Machines and grain elevators, though not made to be beautiful, can appear so to the aesthetic eye. But this is another question. Clocks and electric refrigerators are made to be seen and to look well, in addition to serving other purposes. They are judged and chosen partly on this basis. Aesthetic quality or "eye appeal" is one of their definite, intended functions. Hence they are works of utilitarian *art*. Some other devices (e.g., sewer-pipes) are not intended to be seen, and aesthetic appeal is not one of their functions; hence the skill and activity of making them is not an art. The making of machines, tools, utensils, and buildings is sometimes an art and sometimes a utilitarian technic. The line between the two is often hard to draw, but in extreme forms and on the whole it is fairly clear. Coal-mining is an extreme example of a *non-aesthetic, utilitarian technic*. Granting all that has been said about the possibility of aesthetic joy in one's daily work, and all that can be said about the beauty of coal or its delightful warmth when burned, the fact remains that coal is not mined to be contemplated aesthetically. That is not one of its regular, socially established functions. Coal-mining is not a "useful art," because it is not an art at all.

Many utilitarian technics today are conducted scientifically, and have become branches of applied science; e.g., scientific agriculture and mining engineering. Farming in a primitive tribe is a utilitarian technic, but not an applied science. Some arts, such as architecture, are conducted with the aid of science, and are branches of technology. The field of applied science, or scientific technology, thus overlaps that of art, where such methods are used directly for products or performances with an aesthetic aim. This is true today in the motion picture "industry," which is also regarded as an art.

Painting, sculpture, music, and poetry are traditionally classed as "fine" or aesthetic arts, in contrast with furniture and pottery as "useful" arts. In a broad sense, all the fine arts have utilitarian functions, as in the case of painting used for advertising purposes. The distinction can best be made in terms of degree: between arts which are *more,* and those which are *less,* utilitarian. This does not imply that the former have a greater usefulness in general, but that they emphasize utilitarian functions more frequently, along with the aesthetic, and tend to adapt their products more obviously to some non-aesthetic use. If we continue to speak of "the useful arts" for the sake of brevity, it should be in this relative sense.

We must be careful even in making a relative contrast. This statement, by H. E. Bliss,[12] is much too simple: "The arts in which utility is a secondary consideration to beauty and pleasure are distinguished as the Fine Arts, or Aesthetic Arts." Even if we substitute the broader term "aesthetic experience" for "beauty and pleasure," it is not true that utility is always a secondary aim in the fine or aesthetic arts. Architecture is traditionally classed as a fine art, and utilitarian aims often dominate there.

The more accurate contrast would be as follows: within the general class of "arts" (which are all by definition fine or aesthetic), there are some which customarily emphasize utilitarian functions more than others do. These, including architecture, furniture, and pottery, can be described as "more utilitarian." They are "less aesthetic," not in being less beautiful or valuable aesthetically, but in being less specialized along aesthetic lines; less exclusively devoted to providing objects for aesthetic contemplation. On the other hand, there are some like music, painting, sculpture, and poetry, which customarily emphasize aesthetic functions more than utilitarian; they can be called "less utilitarian" or "more strongly aesthetic" arts. They do have important functions over and above giving pleasure; but these (e.g., educational) are mostly exerted in and through aesthetic contemplation, as in reading a story which informs one about foreign customs and international problems.

[12] *The Organization of Knowledge and the System of the Sciences* (New York: Henry Holt and Co., 1929), p. 304.

One way of interpreting "utilitarian" is in terms of fitness for use in some activity involving general bodily movement. Aesthetic contemplation is never quite passive; it always involves activity of the sense organs, as well as of the inner nervous system. But it can be inactive otherwise, as in looking at a picture or listening to music. Many works of painting, sculpture, music, and poetry are made *only* to be contemplated, observed and thought about. They are not adapted to any active bodily use. On the other hand, a cup or a sword is so adapted. Its possibilities are not exhausted in quiet observation; it is suited to be handled, drunk from or wielded. A house is suited to live and move in; a coat to be worn. The active use which makes a thing utilitarian does not, from this point of view, have to serve man's basic physical needs. It may be for amusement, as in equipment for a game or sport, or as an instrument in performing a work of art; e.g., a paintbrush or a violin. Again, it is hard to generalize about a whole art. Music is used in action when we dance to it. A picture may be used as a map or diagram, to guide travel or manufacture. In short, we must be cautious even in saying that one art is "more utilitarian" than another, in any sense of that word, since there is great variation within each art from one period to another, and one style to another.

In saying that music, painting, and poetry are on the whole "less utilitarian" or "more purely aesthetic" than architecture and furniture, we do not imply that beauty or pleasure is always their "primary aim." We do not imply that their main emphasis is or should be on "pure design" or abstract decorative form. The functions and types of form covered by the term "aesthetic" are extremely diverse. They include not only decoration and design, but representation, as in painting and drama; and symbolic exposition, as in allegorical religious art. They are aesthetic in that the work of art can exert these functions through serving as an object for apperception or aesthetic contemplation; through being looked at or listened to, and thought about. No active bodily movement is required except what is necessary for perceiving: e.g., turning the pages of a book, or walking around a statue or house to see it from different points of view, or touching one's fingers to a velvet cloth. Utilitarian objects, on the other hand, function more actively in our daily life, work, and play, in countless different ways.

In discussing fine and useful arts, we are already entering the subject of classification of the arts. That subject will be examined later in its own right. Here it is relevant only that we may understand the extension of the word "art" according to the proposed definition. We have just seen that it does include the useful *arts,* which are also aesthetic technics; but not the non-aesthetic, most purely utilitarian technics. These should no longer be called "useful arts."

One other way in which the aesthetic and utilitarian functions of art interweave is as follows. The understanding of how a thing works can itself become part of a total aesthetic response to that thing. In admiring a house, cup, or sword, which is ornamented and also functionally effective, we do not necessarily admire it for the ornamentation alone, or for its purely visual design alone. Even when the object lies in a glass case, so that we cannot handle it, our knowledge of similar objects may suffice to show us that it would be well balanced, easy to grasp and wield, effective in doing its work, if one did handle it. This realization, perhaps along with a fantasy of using it, can become an integral phase in aesthetic apperception. Associations based on actual or possible use and fitness for use become part of the object's total meaning, thus making it more significant and potentially interesting as an aesthetic stimulus.

Those who attack the aristocratic, narrowly hedonistic view of art can find a good argument here, even on aesthetic grounds. Scorn for the useful and practical extended not only to purely utilitarian objects, but to the utilitarian aspects of the decorative arts. It was fashionable to admire a house or chair, not for how well it fulfilled its utilitarian functions, but for its surface ornamentation and other purely visual aspects of its form. Functional excellence was likely to be ignored, beyond minimum requirements. Such standards of appraisal encouraged the artist to neglect functional problems, and to concentrate on obvious surface decoration, often to the point where it overpowered and conflicted with strength, convenience, and efficiency.

Very often a particular skill, technic, or occupation has an aesthetic phase (which may be called an "art") and a non-aesthetic one. The former is sometimes indicated by the prefix "decorative," as in "decorative ironwork." This would mark it off as an art from the many kinds of ironwork which have no aesthetic aim. Sometimes the artistic phase receives a special name, as when artistic carpentry is called "cabinet-making." In France, a man may be called an *artiste-peintre,* to distinguish him from a house-painter. A great many fields or occupations fall only in part within the realm of aesthetic art. The line is often vague and easily crossed. A particular worker and his skill (e.g., in engraving or photography) may be devoted to aesthetic aims at one moment, and hence be "artistic," "pictorial," or "decorative." The next moment, they may leave the realm of art entirely, as when the photographer is employed by a science laboratory or police court. Thus in one respect after another, the boundaries of art and of each particular art are shifting and arbitrary.

3. Functional arts, applied arts, decorative arts, minor arts, handicrafts

A number of expressions are now current, with meanings close to the concept of useful arts. They are often preferred because of the older term's ambiguity. Each of them has certain peculiar associations. None has yet found universal acceptance, and present discussion is hampered by an oversupply of almost synonymous terms, used in a vaguely interchangeable way, with slightly different meanings.

Many writers on art are impatient with attempts to find the right generic term, and brush the question aside as do Faulkner, Ziegfeld, and Hill. Their book, they say, deals with "those arts of form and color with which we come in contact every day. Sometimes they are referred to as the Fine and Industrial Arts, the Fine and Applied (or Allied) Arts, or the Plastic and Graphic Arts. Whatever the name, the field comprises city planning, architecture (including the furnishing of interiors), painting, printing and the graphic arts, sculpture, and the arts of industry and commerce. . . . The distinction between the Fine and Applied Arts is hardly defensible, for . . . if a product is not 'Fine,' it is not art." [13] Colvin speaks of "the lesser or auxiliary manual arts (commonly called 'industrial' or 'applied' arts)" as including pottery, embroidery, and goldsmith's work. Modern usage, he adds, "has adopted the phrase 'arts and crafts' as a convenient general name for their pursuits."

Functional arts. Dudley and Faricy, in *The Humanities,* have a section entitled "Functional and Nonfunctional Arts." In that book, they explain, "the word *function* will be reserved for such definite, practical, and utilitarian meanings" as being a salt cellar or a double boiler for cooking. "We shall not say that it is the function of a poem

[13] Faulkner, Ziegfeld and Hill, *Art Today.* New York: Henry Holt and Co., 1941.

to teach a lesson, the function of a painting to be beautiful, or the function of a play to be entertaining." [14] This restricted sense of the word "function" is implied in speaking of "functionalism" as an aim or trend of architecture. It means that the utilitarian purposes of a building should determine its form, and be apparent in its visible appearance; not concealed by superficial ornamentation. People ask, about some part of a house or piece of furniture, "is it functional?"— meaning, "does it do something useful, or is it merely decorative?" This is a narrow use of "function." Some word should be reserved for the other kinds of service—in education, entertainment, therapy, etc.—which art carries on. "Utilitarian" has long possessed the more narrow, physically practical connotation. [15] There is something to be said for retaining "functional" in the broader sense. Psychologically, the human functions include perceiving, imagining, desiring, and enjoying. Anything which serves or stimulates them aesthetically is in a way functional. To class music, poetry, and painting as "nonfunctional" is to run the risk of obscuring their definite and important psychological and social uses. The choice of terms is somewhat arbitrary, but we shall retain "functional" in the broader sense, and "utilitarian" in the narrower.

Applied arts. This term is analogous to "applied science." In that connection, says Webster, "applied" means "put to use; pursued for some end outside of its own domain, whether in a distinctly utilitarian way, or as an aid to some other science; as, applied mechanics, chemistry, mathematics, psychology;—distinguished from 'pure.'" If it means "applied to some useful end," it is equivalent to "useful," and there is not much gained in substituting it. Sometimes "applied art" is used as equivalent to "practice of art"—that is, to production or performance as contrasted with history or theory. That sense is confusing and should be avoided.

"Applied" also suggests "arts in which decoration has been applied to a utilitarian basis." This suggests a superficial kind of decoration, as in pasting or painting scenes, flowers, etc., on a table or lamp-shade. The concept of "applied art" is much less clear than "applied science." The latter is definitely contrasted with "pure science," and implies the application of scientific knowledge to practical

---

[14] *Op. cit.,* p. 59.

[15] Not always, however. J. S. Mill uses it much more broadly in his essay *Utilitarianism.*

ends. To make a similar distinction in art suggests a very dubious theory: that such a thing as "pure art" exists by itself, apart from all practical uses, and that useful arts merely apply it to this or that practical function. The term "applied art" is not objectionable if such interpretations are avoided.

A more serious difficulty arises from the fact that architecture is usually excluded from the class of "applied arts." According to Dudley and Faricy, "The applied arts are almost entirely functional. In fact, they are called applied arts because they have function. Rugs, blankets, clothes, jewelry, cups and saucers, plates, teapots, sugar bowls, baskets —one need only name examples to realize that each is made for some definite and specific use. Architecture is even more entirely functional than the applied arts, for we do have examples of the applied arts that are not functional." [16] Why, then, is not architecture one of the applied arts? There is no logical reason. Its exclusion follows the custom of listing architecture with the "fine arts" instead of the "useful arts," for honorific reasons. Since architecture is obviously "applied" or "functional," any list of applied arts which leaves it out should be qualified in some way.

The term "decorative arts" is widely employed instead of "useful arts," especially in art museums. Paris has a separate *Musée des arts décoratifs*. Many of the objects classed as "decorative" are also "useful" in one way or another; at least as accessories of dress or interior furnishing. In calling them "decorative" rather than "useful," we are choosing to emphasize the former aspect of their double nature. In an art museum, it is the decorative quality of a cup or chair—not its usefulness—which admits it to the galleries as art.

"Decorative" has a broad and a narrow sense. Broadly, it is almost synonymous with "aesthetic" or "beautiful." It means, says Webster, "pleasing or intended to please by harmonious adaptation of pattern, line, color, rhythm, etc., to imposed restrictions, such as space, position, length, etc." This would apply to most painting and sculpture; even music and literature are sometimes called decorative. But in the narrower sense, "decorative" is opposed to representative: "distinguished (continues Webster) from realistic, representative, and expressive; as, the decorative character of Gothic sculpture." But painting and sculpture can be decorative and, at the same time, realistic, representative, and expressive, as in the works of Tintoretto

[16] *Op. cit.*, p. 59.

and Donatello. These categories are all overlapping. Pictures and statues are most likely to be classed under "decorative arts" in a museum when they are small and made of materials possessing intrinsically decorative properties, such as gold, silver, enamel, jade, crystal, ivory, or silk; especially when the emphasis in style is on design rather than on representation. Medieval manuscript illuminations and tapestries are often so classed, and likewise small, sculptured figures in wood or gilt bronze. In other words, if the object possesses marked decorative qualities, it can be placed in this class regardless of whether it is also representative or utilitarian.

Architecture is commonly excluded, aside from occasional small, detached bits such as capitals of columns and ornamental friezes. This, in spite of the fact that it is obviously decorative in both the broad and narrow senses. By no definition of "decorative" can furniture be consistently included and architecture not. Once more, the exclusion is due to no theoretical reasoning, but is made on grounds of custom and convenience. "Decorative arts" really means, in practice, "minor decorative arts," and is often worded so.

Major and minor, greater and lesser arts. What is meant by calling architecture a major art, and pottery or jewelry a minor art? Buildings are usually large; cups and necklaces small. This is an important factor in museum classification, since few original works of architecture can be brought into the galleries. Hence they are treated apart from other decorative arts.

But there is more than this to the concept of major and minor. Songs, poems, and pictures are not especially large, but music, poetry, and painting are traditionally "major arts." In Renaissance Italy, the arts were divided into *maggiore* and *minore,* these terms being applied to the guilds or corporations which carried on the various industries.[17] The antithesis between major and minor came to imply a difference in rank or importance among the arts from a standpoint of aesthetic value.[18] Colvin defines "fine art" as consisting of "the five greater arts of architecture, sculpture, painting, music, and poetry, with a number of minor or subsidiary arts, of which dancing and the drama are among the most ancient and universal." This evidently implies an evaluation of the arts as to their relative importance. It is a way of

[17] *Cf.* Colvin, "Art," *loc. cit.*

[18] *Major:* "Greater in dignity, rank, or importance; superior in quality or position; as, major poets" (Webster).

eulogizing certain arts as grand and noble, and disparaging others as trivial by comparison.

Such an attitude is one more survival of the ancient, aristocratic prejudice in favor of certain arts and against others. It is reinforced by professional snobbishness today, so that teachers and connoisseurs of painting and sculpture often look down upon the "minor decorative arts," and relegate them to a humble place in the aesthetic hierarchy. It has harmful effects in education, in that students have been led to overcrowd the fields of painting and sculpture, overstress them in studying art history, admire mediocre examples of them, and correspondingly neglect the values of useful or decorative art. Wholesale grouping of the useful arts as "minor" leads to the quite erroneous assumption that no chair or cup, however good, can possibly be as "great art" as an oil painting. Dubious arguments have been brought forward to show that the "minor arts" are incapable of lofty intellectual and spiritual content; but these will not stand scrutiny. The Orient and medieval Europe expressed some of their loftiest symbolism in bronze utensils, stained glass, wood-carving, goldwork, enameling, and other mediums which we call "minor." [19] What is "minor" to us today may have been "major" in some other age or culture, and vice versa. How can we call stained glass a minor art in the middle ages, or mosaic in the Byzantine period? Architecture is a minor art for the nomadic Persian tribe, and rug-weaving a major one. As a rule, such judgments should be limited to specific cultural contexts. To be sure, against a background of world history, architecture looms up as a mighty art, and so do sculpture, painting, music, and poetry. But to disparage dancing and the drama is to reveal a failure to appreciate their own tremendous roles in cultural history; their power to express important human ideas and aspirations.

In short, to call certain arts "greater" or "major," and other "minor," is ambiguous and full of dubious implications. It should not be done in a wholesale, absolutistic way, as if certain arts were intrinsically and permanently better than others. Such terms can

[19] A. Coomaraswamy points out that, in Indian aesthetic theory, no distinction of kind was made as between fine and decorative, free or servile art. Lists of arts "embrace every kind of skilled activity, from music, painting, and weaving to horsemanship, cookery, and the practice of magic, without distinction of rank, all being equally of angelic origin." (*The Transformation of Nature in Art*. Cambridge: Harvard U. Press, 1934, p. 9.)

properly be used to imply that works of certain arts are (a) physically smaller, or (b) less important in a particular culture-pattern. The meaning intended should be clearly shown.[20]

Crafts; handicrafts; arts and crafts. These terms are all used at present as roughly equivalent to "minor useful and decorative arts" with additional stress on the fact of hand manufacture as opposed to large-scale, machine production. There are borderline cases: a piece of realistic sculpture, such as a small wood-carving, may be classed as "craftwork" simply because it is small, and whittled crudely by a rural or provincial artist. But most handicrafts are expected to produce small useful articles, such as rugs, quilts, baskets, pottery, metal trays, etc.

Thus the handicrafts are distinct from the industrial arts, in so far as the latter involve machine methods. However, through the merging and shifting of modern technics, the line between them is melting away. Craftsmen come to use complex machines adapted for individual operation, such as electric lathes, drills, sewing machines, and kilns. Objects of handicraft, such as bowls and textiles, are adopted as designs for mass production. The term "crafts" is a little broader than "handicrafts," avoiding the issue of how much machinery is used.

"Arts and crafts" is defined by Webster as "The arts of decorative design and handicraft, as bookbinding, weaving, and needlework, which are concerned with objects of use;—from the Arts and Crafts Exhibition Society founded in London in 1888." Thus these three words together mark off an area which is much smaller than that of "arts" alone.

4. Industrial arts. Art and mechanical reproduction. The artistic phases in production and performance

The term "industrial arts" has long been employed as synonymous with "useful arts" and "servile arts." In this sense it is traditionally contrasted with "fine arts." Santayana uses it thus in discussing "The Rationality of Industrial Art," [21] pointing out that "all industry contains an element of fine art and all fine art an element of industry."

---

[20] Santayana speaks of "the smaller plastic arts." (*Reason in Art,* p. 122.)
[21] *Reason in Art,* Ch. II, esp. p. 33.

Edman follows this usage in distinguishing between "the fine arts and the merely useful or industrial." [22]

"Industrial arts" is also used with special reference to engineering and applied science. It then implies not only a utilitarian emphasis but also the use of modern scientific technology. *The Industrial Arts Index, a Cumulative Subject Index to Engineering, Trade, and Business Periodicals,* has been published in New York since 1914. Typical of the many publications indexed therein are the *Harvard Business Review,* the *American Gas Journal, American Petroleum Institute Proceedings,* and *Review of Scientific Instruments.* Few if any of these periodicals emphasize the aesthetic aspects of the products concerned. The extension of "industrial arts" is definitely non-aesthetic in this case. Such a meaning is confusing, because of the strongly aesthetic associations which the word "art" has taken on. Instead of "industrial arts," it would be better to say "industrial technics" (or technology), "applied science," "engineering and business administration," or something equivalent.

Also, there seems to be no great advantage in using "industrial arts" in Santayana's sense, as equivalent to "useful arts." The latter term is more established, in the broad sense which includes handicrafts as well as machine production.

A new and preferable usage of the term "industrial arts" is now becoming current. It refers to a specific idea, different from those so far considered. This is the large-scale, machine production of useful articles with some claim to aesthetic value or "eye appeal." Art schools now have courses on designing for industrial art, emphasizing beauty along with use. Modern, good-looking stoves, refrigerators, radio cabinets, automobiles, bicycles, dishes, cutlery, etc., are in this category.[23] "Industrial arts" are not the same as "industries"; the former term implies an aesthetic aim. Industrial art is a type of aesthetic art, distinguished from handicraft in that it involves mechanized, mass production.

The word "industries" does not always imply "mechanical," but

[22] *Op. cit.,* pp. 38-40.

[23] The Museum of Modern Art in New York has exhibited such products under the title of "Machine Art." Also, some machine-made objects such as wheels, springs and bearings were included, which seemed beautiful to the modern critic even though not made with that intention.

it does suggest mass production. We speak of pottery-making, brewing, and weaving as industries of the ancient Egyptians. Their products were turned out on a fairly large scale without machinery. But machinery has enormously increased the amount of industrial production, in proportion to the amount of labor expended.

For a while after the industrial revolution, and through much of the nineteenth century, large-scale machine methods were applied mostly to utilitarian products (except for certain items like cheap, figured cotton textiles). Expensive things intended to be beautiful were mostly made by hand, as before. Hence it was supposed that only handmade things could really be "art." Now, machine methods are spreading through the field of artistic production. Realizing the commercial value of attractive appearance in selling products, manufacturers employ artist-designers to collaborate with engineers and production managers. Thus beauty and utility are combined again as joint aims in certain branches of large-scale, machine production, as they have long been in the handmade, useful arts. These branches are the industrial "arts," art manufactures, or art industries.

The spread of large-scale, machine methods through the realm of art is so rapid that no one knows where it will stop, and there are many borderline fields with a slight amount of mechanization. At present, for example, machine-made reproductions of painting and sculpture (color-prints and plaster casts) are not usually classed as works of industrial art. But the processes of mechanical reproduction—photo-engraving, color-printing, etc.—have become highly industrialized. In fact, there is no single art, if considered in the large as the whole process of making a certain kind of product, into which machine industry has not already entered. Paintings are reproduced by more or less mechanical devices; musical performances are reproduced on records and films; poems are printed in newspapers and magazines, and so on. Literature was the first art to be revolutionized by machine methods of reproduction and distribution, through the printing press in the fifteenth century.

In these cases, the creative phase of designing or composing is fairly distinct from the mechanical phase of reproduction, and only the former is usually classed as "art." In other cases, such as the motion-picture industry, the two are almost inextricably blended. Mechanical devices are used all along the line, and creative modifications are contributed all along the line, even in final cutting and editing of the film. There is no distinct process of individual, handmade creation, followed by another of mechanical reproduction.

Where, then, does "art" end and "industry" begin? Does "art" include the whole process of making or performing something with aesthetic functions? Yes, according to the first part of our definition, and in a very broad extension of the term "art." Are all its workers to be classed as "artists"? Yes, if we apply the definition literally. Even the operator of an automatic motion-picture projector or a phonograph record is performing something with an aesthetic function. The mechanical printing of color-print reproductions is a technic whose products function aesthetically, and are therefore works of art. As to the attractively finished stove or refrigerator, there is usually no such thing as an original. All are reproductions, the first one off the assembly line being identical with the five-hundredth. The whole process aims at a beautiful product; hence the whole process can be broadly included as an art.

On the whole, however, present usage stops short of this extreme of consistency. It refuses to recognize as art the whole process of making or reproducing works of art in mass quantity, by machinery. It refuses to recognize all the workers in it as artists. It tries instead to single out within the industrial process those phases concerned with designing or working out the plan. These only are creative; these only are "art," and only those who perform this phase are artists. As we have seen, the distinction is often hard to make, but it nevertheless exists in theory. It is followed out as far as possible in occupational classifications, where designers and artists of various sorts are distinguished from machine operators, sales managers, and others involved in the total process.[24] The term "art" is usually restricted to certain phases of the process, with the inference that many workers who are not artists can take part in the production of art. The basis of distinction here applies as well to hand methods as to machine industry. It existed in the atelier of Rubens, where the master sketched the plan of the picture, executed a few important details, and left the more easy, "mechanical" parts to be painted in by students and apprentices. Only the former was art, in a strict sense, and the latter was artisanship, craftsmanship, or skilled assistance. In the theater,

[24] This will be considered more fully in Ch. VIII.

the performance as a whole is a work of art, but not every stagehand is an artist.

Does this mean that we are once more introducing an evaluative, eulogistic requirement into the definition of art? Is only the good, highly skilled producer of really beautiful things an artist? No; the essential difference is one which may be objectively described, in terms of the kind of work done. One phase, and perhaps one group of specialized workers, is concerned especially with designing, planning, and directing; another with executing in accordance with plans received. True, the two phases overlap; which is to say that no sharp line exists between the artistic and the non-artistic. But the concept of art remains non-evaluative, in that nothing is said about the quality of the designs or plans, or about the actual beauty of the final product.

In large-scale industry, such related activities are formally organized, with large departments or groups of individuals looking after each. In large or small-scale production, it is sometimes necessary to specify that only part of the total activity concerned is to be called "art." This part, by general agreement, is the creative, designing, or inventive phase. We sometimes distinguish between an art and an industry or business by the same name, connected with that art. For example, a man can be "in the music business" if he sells sheet music, or runs a concert engagement bureau. Architecture is an art, a science, and an industry, from the standpoint of different workers in it. In other words, the artistic phase of architecture is only one part of architecture as a total field or area of human culture.

As to performance also, a problem is raised by our example of the operator of an automatic phonograph or motion-picture projector. Is he an artist and is his occupation a kind of art? Again we must answer, "in a broad and literal sense, yes." But current usage favors a stricter sense which would exclude him. His work is largely mechanical, concerned with making a complex machine run smoothly in a fixed, routine way. How does he differ from a concert singer or dancer who is called an artist? Once again, it may seem at first that the distinction is evaluative, and that "artist" is a term of praise. But this is not necessarily so. In the neutral sense employed by scientific occupational surveys, a person is an artist merely by virtue of engaging in a certain occupation. He may be a very bad singer and yet an artist. The motion-picture operator may be an excellent mechanic, and yet not an artist.

What is the general distinction between types of occupation classed as art, and others? Several are used, as we shall see when that subject is examined in detail. One is the element of more or less creative, *personal interpretation.* Work as an artist is expected to involve this, even if it does not in every case. If a machine for producing music or motion pictures is not entirely automatic, and must be adjusted frequently to produce desired nuances of tone, light, tempo, etc., then the operation of it will be said to require some artistic training, musical ability, etc. Such an operator may have less ability in mechanics, and be helpless at repairing a machine. It is not a question of which man or kind of work is better, but simply of a different kind of work, only one of which is classed as "art."

In our general definition of art, such considerations make it advisable to include the clause: "especially that phase of such activity which is concerned with designing, composing, or performing with personal interpretation."

Returning to the concept of "industrial" art, how does it differ from "art" in general? We have seen that the arts so classed now have two distinguishing characteristics. (a) *Large-scale, machine processes* are used in turning out the product. However, not all of these processes are included as industrial "art." This term implies especially the creating of designs, sketches, or ideas, usually in consultation with engineers and production men, to be produced by machinery. (b) Most of the products so made and classed as industrial arts, are *useful* arts—furniture, vehicles, utensils, etc. However, as we have seen, the less utilitarian arts, such as painting, music, and literature, are gradually being affected by large-scale, machine methods; primarily in regard to reproduction and distribution of their products, but also in regard to the nature of these products and of the creative process. The tendency, then, is for the so-called fine arts, as well as the useful arts, to become partly industrialized. At present, the "industrial arts" are mainly a subdivision of "useful arts"—the portion involving mechanized mass production. But they will probably not remain so.

As to machine-made products and performances, there is some disagreement on whether to class them as art, however beautiful they may be. In some opinions, only the handmade, original sketch is a work of art. According to our definition, the machine-made industrial product, the machine-made reproduction of a painting or statue, and the automatic performance of music or drama by phonograph records or films, are all works of art in so far as they have aesthetic functions: i.e., are adapted to stimulate favorable aesthetic experience. This is not inconsistent with the fact that some non-artistic processes go into their making or performance.

The use of machinery and other automatic or partly automatic means for producing works of art is still in its infancy. We do not realize their aesthetic capabilities, and should not assume that their present limitations are necessarily permanent. According to Lewis Mumford,[25] the characteristic mark of production of the automatic machine is absence of any trace of hand work. Each unit is identical, he says, completely objective, and divorced from human hand or hand-directed tool. But it is quite possible—easy, in fact—to reproduce in the machine product any desired trace of hand work, such as a slight irregularity of surface texture. The phonograph record or film sound track reproduces with great fidelity any desired trait of personal performance, such as a facial expression or tone of voice. When desired, a machine can be set to make products which are not identical, but each one slightly different. At present, public taste favors certain kinds of machine product in which many units are identical and smoothly geometrical in form—e.g., in automobiles and refrigerators. If there is a revival of the romantic taste for unique and slightly irregular forms, as in the rough-hewn board or hand-shaped vase, machines will turn them out with any specified individual peculiarities. They may be more expensive than identical units, but less expensive than ones laboriously made by hand.

With increasing ease of automatic production and reproduction in all the arts, we may expect a further decline of the belief that works of art are necessarily handmade, or that original, handmade products are necessarily better and more beautiful than machine-made. In so far as the reproduction approaches perfect fidelity, the premium placed upon the original will decline, or at least be recognized as based upon associations and not on intrinsic qualities. Some persons will still be proud of owning the original, signed sketch or model from which the reproductions were made. They will enjoy the realization that they are seeing and hearing a singer in person, however perfect television and radio become. But we shall probably be surrounded to an increasing extent by architecture, home furnishings, pictures, music, and

[25] *Technics and Civilization,* pp. 358-9.

clothing in which no unit is absolutely unique, though all give aesthetic satisfaction. We shall enjoy their beauty and serviceability, their cheapness and disposability when worn out, as we now enjoy our automobiles and motion picture films, with no sense of loss because other people are enjoying identical objects or performances elsewhere. Some of our visible decorations will be extremely evanescent and illusory, as in the images of distant paintings placed upon our wall by television. We enjoy the beauty of flowers and sunsets even though no single example of them lasts very long. No single flower is unique and indispensable, unless for sentimental reasons.

At the same time, other outlets will have to be found for the persistent human craving for unique, individual expressions of taste and personality. Direct art production and performance will always be valued for this characteristic. As at present, most individuals— even those who make no claim to being artists—will desire some small field for such expression in the choice and arrangement of their clothing, furniture, and personal belongings. These arrangements will be, or will seem to their owners, unique and individual, even though all the units within them are products of large-scale, mass production.

5. Fine arts and visual arts

In the list of dictionary meanings, at the beginning of the last chapter, we noticed that both "art" and "fine art" are sometimes used in a narrow sense, excluding music and poetry. As the *Oxford Dictionary* says of "fine art," it is "often applied in a more restricted sense to the arts of design, as painting, sculpture, and architecture." The term "art" alone can also be used in this sense, according to the *Oxford:* "The application of skill to the arts of imitation and design, Painting, Engraving, Sculpture, Architecture; the skillful production of the beautiful in visible forms." This we have called the "visual aesthetic" sense of "art" and "fine art."

The term "art" alone is popular in this sense because of its brevity, as in "art school," "art museum," and "art history." College art departments like it because it puts their subject at the head of alphabetical lists. However, we have found it unwise to use "art" alone in this narrow sense, at least in technical discussion. In popular usage, it does no great harm, and the context usually shows what is meant.

Shall we use "fine art," then, with this extension? There are numerous college departments and professors of "fine arts." The term has a pleasantly genteel and superior sound.

We have already noted the peculiar historical changes which led up to this conception. Whereas the visual arts were largely excluded from the select Greek list of "arts of the Muses," as being too manual, they came in time not only to secure admission as fine arts, but (like the camel in the tent) to push out the original occupants. Now, music and literature must endure the slight disparagement of hearing another group of arts call itself *"the* fine arts."

So honorific a title is not likely to be abandoned without a struggle by any college faculty or museum which has once adopted it. The arts excluded are not complaining violently. Nevertheless, the situation operates to confuse still further the mix-up in terminology which we have been attempting to correct in this chapter. The restriction of the concept of "fine art" to a few visual arts is a historical accident. Its literal implications are not taken seriously. Even the most ardent admirer of painting, sculpture, and architecture would hardly maintain that they are actually finer, more beautiful, noble, or pleasant in general than music and poetry. Indeed, architecture involves to a conspicuous degree the trait of utility; hence its theoretical right to be considered "fine" at all has always needed some adroit defending.

The concept of "fine art" in this narrow, visual sense involves the same difficulties which it has in the broader sense. Is it to be considered as antithetical to the "useful arts," and if so to which ones? If architecture is to be included, what right have we to keep out furniture, pottery, and textiles? Is "fine arts" really intended to mean "major fine arts"? In any case, to omit them is to imply a disparagement of pottery and the rest, as necessarily less great and fine. Admirers of Greek and Chinese vases have a right to protest, when they see the inferior quality of many paintings and statues.

Gladstone, the liberal statesman, is quoted by the *Oxford* as summing up the situation in 1869: "By the term Art, I understand the production of beauty in material forms palpable; whether associated with industrial purposes or not." By "material" and "palpable," he shuts out music and poetry; but he does let in the useful arts.

As we have seen, fine art is often defined so as to exclude the so-called minor useful arts. However, many authoritative sources now include them without argument under the general heading of "fine art." "The Institute of Fine Arts," a part of New York University, gives no general definition of the term "fine" in its *Announcement of Lectures*. But it does include a course on "Furniture and the Decorative Arts," and one on "Chinese Minor Arts," including pottery, mirrors, and belt buckles. By implication, these are all "fine arts." But music is a separate heading in the University *Bulletin*,[26] and literature is also separated under the usual linguistic headings. This illustrates how questions of general definition or intension are sometimes passed over, while the actual meaning of a term is determined by the extension given it. To include belt buckles under "fine arts" implies a certain conception of fine arts, whether explicitly stated or not.

The advisable solution here is to use the term "visual arts" instead of "fine arts," in the sense under discussion. This term is coming into technical use in aesthetics,[27] and should be generally adopted as a substitute for "fine arts." It should also be used instead of "art" alone when "visual art" is meant, as in college catalogues. To restrict the term "art" to visual arts involves an undesirably sharp separation from music and literature. It is preferable to use "art" in a more generic sense, as including all aesthetic skills; then to subdivide it into "visual arts," "musical arts," etc. Dudley and Faricy, in their treatise on *The Humanities*, have chapters on "The Mediums of the Visual Arts," "The Elements of the Visual Arts," and "Plan in the Visual Arts." The visual arts here are made coordinate with music, literature, and the "combined arts" (dance, theater, opera, cinema, radio and phonograph).

The term "visual arts" was not quite specific enough when "arts" was used in its old, broad, technical sense; for visual arts would then include purely utilitarian buildings, tools, and machines. They are as visible as pictures and statues, though not necessarily made to be seen. But if we understand that art means *aesthetic art*, then "visual art" is by definition restricted to products having some aesthetic func-

---

[26] Vol. XLV, No. 26, May 25, 1945. The Graduate School of Arts and Sciences lists several groups of subjects, among which "Fine Arts and Music" are bracketed as Group VI.

[27] For example, R. M. Ogden uses "visual art" as one of three major fields of art, along with music and poetry (*The Psychology of Art*, New York, 1938, p. 26). Blunt also speaks of "the visual arts" becoming liberal (*Op. cit.*, p. 53). Cf. *The Visual Arts in General Education*, report of a committee of the Progressive Education Association (New York: Appleton-Century, 1940).

tion. Their visibility is no mere incidental, but an essential character-istic; power to attract and interest through the eyes is one of their principal aims. There is need for a term which definitely groups them together, as apart from music and literature. They are taught and writ-ten about as a group, in art schools, art histories, and courses on art appreciation. When it becomes necessary to contrast them with other aesthetic arts, such as music and literature, an explicit prefix is needed. "Fine arts" is not the best possible term, because of its other current meanings. "Visual arts" is fairly neutral and objective.

One advantage of calling them "visual" rather than "fine" is that it avoids the old contrast with "useful." There is no theoretical diffi-culty in including chairs or belt buckles as visual art. The whole basis of classification is shifted from the difficult and controversial one of "useful or not useful" to a more objective, psychological one: that of *which sense is primarily addressed.*

The term "fine arts," like the term "beauty," has become so loaded with confusing associations that it is difficult to use in any technical sense. One must keep repeating the sense intended, to avoid misunderstanding. In such cases, it is often best to avoid the term entirely, if a less ambiguous substitute can be found. This course is recommended now. For its broad aesthetic sense, one can use "art" alone; for its visual aesthetic sense, the term "visual arts" is sug-gested. For the sense opposed to "useful arts," one may speak of "less utilitarian" or "more purely aesthetic" arts; but even this rela-tive antithesis, as we have seen, involves many controversial points.

Questions arise also in the meaning of "visual arts." What arts are or should be covered by it? Literature is visual in some ways: it is often read with the eyes, and it suggests visual images. Music also can suggest visual images, and is read from printed scores. But such visible means of recording and presenting are not usually considered integral, necessary factors in a work of musical or literary art. Are dance, theater, and film visual arts? To some extent, but they are also auditory, when they involve music. This is usually covered by calling them "combined," "mixed," or "audio-visual" arts.

To group certain arts as "visual" does not imply that this is their only, or necessarily their most important characteristic in all respects. It is not necessarily the only way in which they are presented to the senses. In some arts called "visual," there is also an intentional appeal to the senses of touch and hearing. Clothing is required to be pleasant to the touch; furniture must give us a kinesthetic effect of balance and security; clocks are heard. Their classification as visual is a matter of convenience, to facilitate certain lines of investigation. In calling painting or sculpture visual arts, we do not imply that they should restrict themselves to "purely visual" effects; that they should avoid "story interest" and leave representation to literature. That would be to perpetuate Lessing's erroneous theory of the fixed limits of the arts.[28]

For study and teaching, we often wish to indicate painting, sculpture, architecture, and the "minor useful" arts as a group by themselves, leaving out dance and theater. This group is also vaguely designated as "the arts" or "the fine arts." How should they be called, to distinguish them from dance and theater, which are also visual, at least in part? One way is to call them "static" visual arts, as distinct from "mobile"; or "space arts," as distinct from "time arts." They are also called "arts of design," from the fact that drawing *(disegno* in Italian, and *dessin* in French) is used in them. This also is hardly satisfactory, since drawing is used in dance and theater, as in sketching costume and scene design. The word "design" also has other meanings, some of which apply even to music and literature.

6. Lower-sense arts

According to the definition of art recommended here, products and services appealing aesthetically to the lower senses are included. The terms "art of perfume," "art of cooking," etc., are in common use. They imply an aesthetic appeal to the senses of smell and taste. Tactile qualities, as we have just seen, are a recognized part of the total appeal of many visual arts, such as clothing, utensils, and furniture. A tactile "art of love," *ars amatoria,* has been elaborately worked out in theory and practice by Greek and Roman, Renaissance, and Oriental writers.

The exclusion of lower-sense products and pleasures from the categories of "art" and "fine art" is largely a result of ascetic Christian morality. Its radical dualism of good and evil, spirit and body, has operated to condemn all physical pleasures, especially those connected with sex, and especially those of the so-called "lower senses," which are regarded as more crudely physical. The very expres-

[28] *Cf.* G. Boas, "Classification of the Arts and Criticism," *Journal of Aesthetics,* June, 1947, p. 270.

sion "lower" implies this moral disparagement. Severe disapproval of lower-sense pleasures has subsided, but has often been succeeded by a condescending attitude, in which they are treated as trivial and ridiculous, unworthy of serious consideration. The change to a more naturalistic attitude in aesthetics and ethics now requires a thorough reconsideration of the problem.

It is an obvious and recognized fact that lower-sense stimuli *can* be enjoyed for their own sake, and not as instrumental values. There would be little point in all the ascetic denunciation of sensuality, Epicureanism, and the like, if this were not true. Those aestheticians who have wished to exclude lower-sense products from the categories of art and aesthetic experience have not found very cogent arguments to justify it. Kant's influence has set a strong precedent against including them as fine arts, and the question is often ignored. Colvin's argument is typical: that lower-sense products are too much bound up with the "private, personal utilities" of eating, drinking, etc. It will stand little scrutiny. Are eating and drinking purely private, or often highly sociable? Are they more bound up with utility than clothing and shelter? And even if they are, being "bound up with utility" is no longer held to disqualify a thing as artistic and aesthetic—provided it stimulates aesthetic experience also.

A. R. Chandler asserts that "Aesthetic satisfaction must be contrasted with various practical and intellectual satisfactions. Bodily pleasures must be classed as practical rather than aesthetic satisfactions. In these your attention is focused upon the state of your own body rather than upon any object which you may perceive. The experience of sitting by a fire after coming in from a cold drive is indeed a satisfying one; but in it you are thinking about your body, not about the fire. The same is true of eating when you are hungry. The important thing is the satisfaction of the bodily craving, not an interest in the taste or texture of the food." [29] Surely this is untrue as a universal psychological principle. It describes rather an individual and cultural type. Some persons do, and others do not, take an aesthetic attitude toward food, drink, or other bodily satisfactions. There is nothing necessarily impossible or even difficult about paying attention to a fire, or a glass of wine, rather than to one's own skin or throat, while

[29] *Beauty and Human Nature*, p. 11. *Cf.* Souriau, *La correspondance des arts,* pp. 79-83; F. W. Herring, "Touch—the Neglected Sense," *Journal of Aesthetics,* March, 1949.

enjoying it. Nor must one be thinking only about its utility, its effects on health, or its nourishing qualities. One can wear a hat, and be conscious either of its appearance or its use in protecting the head, or both at once; and the same is true of food. Perfume has very little practical value, except indirectly through sexual selection, and is enjoyed for its immediate sensuous effect.

Two arguments against the inclusion of lower-sense products in art have some validity, but less than is often assumed. It is said that the lower senses are cruder, less capable of perceiving complex and subtle forms; also that lower-sense products are less capable of expressing intellectual and spiritual meanings. Both these arguments are true to a large extent, as principles of general psychology. But they are considerably more true in the practical culture of the west, with its ascetic traditions, than in the rest of the world. The weakness, crudity, and insignificance of lower-sense experience have been aggravated by disuse and inhibition. Thus the argument involves a vicious circle. In the culture of India, lower-sense images, including the erotic, are more richly endowed with cultural associations, including religious and ethical symbolism.

The lower senses have degenerated to a large extent in the human, as compared with other animals; and some biologists think they may continue to do so. To that extent, it will be impossible for humans to produce or to enjoy complex and subtle forms addressed to the lower senses. If our definition of a work of art were to specify that it has to be complex and subtle, most lower-sense products would be excluded. But no such requirement is made. There is considerable variation in this respect, even in visual art. Lower-sense forms can be complicated to some extent, as in the succession of foods and drinks in a banquet.

Tolstoy, whose attitude toward art is Puritanical on the whole, quotes with some approval the German aesthetician Kralik and the French Guyau.[30] The former, he points out, recognizes five types of art: the aesthetic treatment of the five senses. The latter speaks of touch, taste, and smell as capable of giving aesthetic pleasures, and even an effect of beauty. "If the sense of touch lacks color," says Guyau, "it gives us on the other hand a notion which the eye cannot

[30] Richard Kralik, *Weltschönheit:Versuch einer allgemeinen Aesthetik.* Guyau, *Les problèmes de l'esthétique contemporaine.* See Maude, *Tolstoy on Art,* p. 134.

afford, and one of considerable aesthetic value, namely, that of softness, silkiness, polish. The beauty of velvet is characterized not less by its softness than by its lustre. In the idea we form of a woman's beauty, the softness of her skin enters as an essential element."

Interest in the lower senses, as sources of aesthetic experience, has been too exclusively associated with the decadent school of writers exemplified by J. K. Huysmans and his novel, *Against the Grain*. No such association is necessary. Such an interest is quite compatible with a healthy naturalism, and indispensable to a fully naturalistic aesthetics.

7. One hundred visual and auditory arts

The following list illustrates the extension of the concept of art, as defined in the previous chapter, by naming some of the realms included in it. Only arts primarily addressed to sight, hearing or both are listed, and the list is incomplete in other ways. Many of the arts are named on a basis of material used, such as ironwork and lacquerwork; these could be multiplied indefinitely.

Even so, the list will seem excessively long to those accustomed to thinking only of the "five major arts." Some of those included are considered by scholars in the "fine arts" (if considered at all) as extremely humble and trivial; absurdly unworthy of mention in a serious list of arts. No attempt has been made to indicate relative importance. It is not implied that acrobatics or decorative animal-breeding is as great or valuable aesthetically as architecture, merely because they are listed without discrimination in an alphabetical list. The list is intended as a rough, unclassified list of fields deserving some attention by aesthetics, but not necessarily the same amount of attention. They all involve some claim to an aesthetic function; but their appraisal as "major" or "minor," more or less capable of becoming vehicles for high cultural values, is a complex problem in its own right.

Readers who have studied the history of the arts in other cultures will find some items less strange than will those who know only our own culture. For example, embalming and the making of funerary monuments were important arts in ancient Egypt. Tattooing, featherwork, and symbolic string figures are important in some Polynesian cultures. Flower arrangement, tray landscapes, and decorative cord-work are recognized arts in Japan; the first of these is coming into prominence here. Even in our own culture, scholars in the "major arts" are not always aware of the progress that is being made in other skills, once of humble status, to justify noticing them in aesthetics. For example, taxidermy and the making of habitat groups are no longer merely "stuffing animals." A sculptural figure is now made, showing the animal in a realistic, animated posture; the habitat setting usually contains a painted landscape background and a clever blending of solid objects with it. The combined effect can be of artistic as well as scientific interest. The use of some mediums is in a rudimentary, infantile stage, without rich cultural associations or extensive use by artists of high standing. The decorative use of electric lights, including neon and other gas-filled tubes, is emerging from this category. Commercial art uses many tricky effects to catch attention and sell products, with mobile electric signs, smoke and vapor displays, and the like; these may sometime be given more serious uses. Lumia is an art of electric light and color which is already used for serious works of art, but not extensively.

No attempt is made at classification, except alphabetically. The interrelations between these arts will be discussed in later chapters. There is much overlapping among them; hence this is not a list of one hundred different arts. Some are broad and inclusive, such as literature; some are included in them, such as poetry and prose. Some (e.g., industrial design) are groups of arts rather than single ones. Some are important as contributing factors in a complex combined art, as cosmetics (make-up) and coiffure are in drama and films. Some, whose omission may be noted, are covered under other names. In short, the list is merely tentative and preliminary.

1. Acrobatics
2. Acting, dramatic
3. Animal-breeding, decorative (goldfish, birds, etc.)
4. Architecture
5. Armor
6. Athletics, gymnastics (esp. theatrical); incl. diving, swimming, figure skating, skiing
7. Ballet
8. Basketry
9. Beadwork
10. Book designing and manufacturing
11. Brickwork, esp. decorative
12. Bronze-casting, sculptural and ornamental
13. Calligraphy
14. Ceramics

15. Circuses
16. City planning; community planning
17. Cloth designing, other than weaving; batik, tie - die, block printing, stencilling, etc.
18. Coiffure; hairdressing
19. Collage and montage
20. Cooking; visual, decorative aspects of, as in cakes and confections
21. Copper and brasswork
22. Cordwork; knotting, braiding, tasseling (esp. decorative)
23. Cosmetics
24. Costume; clothing and accessories; incl. millinery, tailoring, etc.
25. Dance
26. Dioramas; three-dimensional scenes
27. Displays; advertising, shop window, exposition, etc.
28. Doll making
29. Drawing
30. Electric lighting, decorative, architectural, representative; static, mobile
31. Embalming; mortuary and funerary arts
32. Enameling
33. Engraving
34. Etching
35. Expositions, fairs, amusement parks
36. Featherwork; quillwork
37. Festivals; carnivals
38. Fireworks; pyrotechnic displays
39. Flower arrangement
40. Furniture
41. Glass making
42. Goldsmithing and silversmithing
43. Horticulture; garden art; decorative flower and plant breeding and cultivating
44. Industrial designing
45. Interior decoration and design
46. Ironwork
47. Ivory carving
48. Jewelry; gem - cutting and mounting; costume jewelry
49. Knitting and crocheting
50. Lace making
51. Lacquerwork
52. Landscape design and architecture
53. Leatherwork; incl. bookbinding and saddlery
54. Literature; belles lettres
55. Lithography
56. Lumia; mobile color
57. Marionettes; puppets; shadowplays
58. Metalry
59. Monument making
60. Mosaic
61. Motion pictures; film; cinema
62. Music
63. Musical instrument-making
64. Opera
65. Oratory; speech, diction, eloquence, elocution, recitation
66. Packaging
67. Pageantry, parades, floats, ceremonial processions
68. Painting
69. Pantomime; mimicry
70. Paperwork, decorative; incl. wallpaper
71. Photography
72. Plastics, decorative and representative uses of
73. Poetry; verse
74. Pottery

75. Printing; typography; advertising and other layouts
76. Prose literature
77. Regional planning; geoarchitecture
78. Rituals; religious, as in the Christian mass; secular, as in Japanese tea ceremony and some children's games
79. Sand painting
80. Sculpture
81. Silk-screen printing
82. Smoke and vapor designing
83. Stage designing; incl. lighting
84. Stonework; masonry; architectural and decorative
85. String figures (esp. representative and symbolic)
86. Table setting and decoration
87. Tableaux vivants
88. Tattooing
89. Taxidermy; habitat groups
90. Textile designing; weaving
91. Theater arts; dramatic enactment; incl. stage and play direction
92. Tilework
93. Tool and machine designing; decorative aspects of
94. Toy making
95. Tray landscapes
96. Transportation design, incl. vehicles, ships, aircraft
97. Utensil design
98. Weapon making (swords, etc.)
99. Water-designing, decorative, as in fountains and cascades
100. Woodworking; carpentry; woodcarving.

8. Branches of an art; types of form in art

Long as it is, this list omits a great number of skills, activities, and products which are sometimes called arts. It omits, not only the non-aesthetic skills, but such aesthetic ones as "the art of the fugue," "the art of portraiture," "the art of arabesque," and "the art of short story writing." There is no harm in such expressions when used informally, for brevity; but in formal classification of the arts it is advisable to regard them as branches or subdivisions of an art, or as types of product. The fugue is a type of form produced in music; not an independent art. The short story has a similar status in prose fiction, which in turn is a division of literature. Portraiture occurs in painting, graphic arts, photography, sculpture, and other arts—even, by extension of the term, in literature. Arabesque, or non-representative linear design, is a type of form produced in drawing, painting, engraving, sculptural relief, and many other mediums.[31]

All these skills, activities, and products qualify as art under our

[31] It is, however, classed as one of fourteen principal arts by E. Souriau in *La Correspondance des Arts*, Paris, 1947, p. 97.

general definition. But this is not to say that each of them is *an art* in itself. In theoretical classifications, it is well to distinguish between classes or divisions of different size. We no longer call all types of animal "species," but reserve that name for classes intermediate between a "genus" and a "variety." Likewise, it will help in classifying aesthetic phenomena if we reserve the concept of "an art" or "a particular art" for one of the main divisions of the total realm of art. It would multiply our list of arts indefinitely if we tried to include all the specific skills, activities, and types of product within the vast realm of art.

There is, of course, great room for difference of opinion on what specific types or branches within the realm of art are large, important, or independent enough to be classed as arts in this sense. One might say, for example, that beadwork, ironwork, lacquerwork, and various other skills, bound up with a certain physical medium, do not deserve to be classed as arts in their own right. Perhaps they should be listed rather as branches or subdivisions of some wider class, such as "decorative arts" or "minor useful arts." In listing them separately, we are stressing the importance of differences in medium, as a basis for marking off particular arts from each other.

The foregoing list is a rough, arbitrary one, which could have been much longer or much shorter if differently classified. It is intended for further analysis, and to give the reader a broader conception of the total realm of art than is implied by traditional lists of the five or seven fine arts.

9. Some fields which border on the arts

Aesthetics abounds in overly sharp antitheses between art and other fields. We are told, for example, that art is subjective and science objective; that art is concrete and particular, science abstract and general, and so on. Striking and plausible at first sight, these statements usually prove unsound when carefully examined. Art is not a sharply specialized activity which can be placed at the opposite pole from any other kind of activity. It is highly diversified, full of oppositions within its own domain, ranging widely from one extreme to another. It overlaps and interpenetrates every other major field of human enterprise.

This condition is partly responsible for the difficulty of defining art, and of deciding what special fields should be included as arts. If we adopt a narrow definition, we find ourselves shutting out important fields which are often considered as arts, or have a claim to be. If we are too broad and lenient, our concept of art expands to take in all human skill and expression. It becomes vaguely identical with science, religion, and all human culture. This is detrimental to clear thinking. To be most useful, a concept of art should have some limits, however indefinite, and recognize some basic differences between art and other fields.

Where no definite boundaries exist and there is much overlapping, concepts can still be distinguished from one another. The best way to do so is to stress the central, most distinctive area of each, and not their marginal, overlapping regions. There is a borderline area where things may be called either art or science, or both; either art or religion, or both. There are also more specialized, distinctive areas where a clearer contrast is possible; kinds of art which are not scientific and not religious.

No question of value is raised here. We should be careful not to assume that art is at its best when religious or when not religious; when most different from science, or most infused by a scientific spirit. All such questions should be dealt with separately. We are now concerned only with an objective, though rough and tentative, distinction between overlapping classes of phenomena.

The overlapping between art and other major realms of culture becomes most obvious when we go backward in the evolutionary process; when we encounter relatively primitive cultures, at an earlier period in history and in retarded areas today. There we find no specialized realm called "science," conscious of its aims and methods, working along its own distinctive lines. We find the beginnings of science combined with poetry and visual art. This is true, not only of extremely primitive cultures, but down to modern times, and even at present outside the centers of Western urban civilization. The works of Plato, Lucretius, and Dante are works of literary art and also works of philosophical, prescientific reasoning. It is often pointed out by critics of our time, now as a virtue and now as a fault, that religion penetrated the lives and arts of ancient peoples more than it penetrates ours. At least, the divergence has occurred, and religion tends to be more segregated, more shut out from state affairs and public education, than it used to be.

The emergence of art as a specialized realm, with its own aims and values such as the giving of aesthetic pleasure, has also been praised and denounced. We have considered several aspects of this problem, especially in relation to the contrast between "fine" and "useful." Once again, let us put aside the issue of whether art *ought* to be divorced from religion, morals, useful skill, and everyday life. The facts are that art has become thus divorced in some of its phases, though not in all. It has developed certain artists, schools of art, critics, and public clienteles which do treat art as a separate field with its own values, its own aims and methods. These people resent being told that they ought to subordinate their work to criteria used in other fields: to make it patriotic, or useful, or moral. "Art for art's sake" is not only an aim and standard, but a factual description of how certain types of art are made and valued. There are also contrary movements, as we have seen, where the divorce is bitterly protested; where older ideals are reasserted, and the artist tries to recombine aesthetic values with those of other fields. On the whole, the trend toward specialization has predominated since the Renaissance. As a result, we can say that modern Western art is more distinct from science, religion, and other neighboring fields than is the case in other cultural epochs.

With reference to the modern situation, it is thus comparatively easy to define art in a way which marks it off from other concepts. But most definitions of art do not specify a particular epoch or stage of evolution; they speak as if art were, by the nature of things, a fixed and eternal realm in itself. This, of course, was the pre-evolutionary view. Modern definitions of art, as of other cultural phenomena, should recognize that art is in process of change, internally and in relation to other fields. A definition of art should not try to mark it off from neighboring fields in an absolute, timeless way. It should either be flexible enough to cover the facts at different times and places, or specify some particular cultural context. Our definition in the previous chapter is of the former type, broad and flexible enough to characterize both primitive and modern art. It applies to the stage in which art, science, religion, and other types of activity are undifferentiated, indistinguishable. It also covers the modern stage in which they have partly diverged along different paths. A basic definition need not be explicit on all such points, but it is well for us to think about them now.

Art is in its most distinctive form, most different from all other activities, when devoted exclusively to the stimulation of agreeable aesthetic experience. One can go that far with eighteenth century hedonist aesthetics, without in the least conceding that art is at its best when so highly specialized. On the contrary, one may feel that it loses precious values, and becomes corrupt or attenuated to the point of triviality. But in a secular poem, a sonata, a painted landscape, or a decorative fabric, made purely to delight the observer, we are dealing with phenomena which cannot easily be classed as science, technology, religion, or anything outside of art in the aesthetic sense. To do so would be to strain these other categories in a far-fetched way.

On the other hand, art coincides with religion in many of its phases. It does so in the painting and sculpturing of divinities, in the building of temples and churches, in impressive rituals and pageants, in hymns of worship, and in prayers, sermons, and mystical writing where the wording takes on poetic quality. Religion, in its turn, often parts company with art. Many sermons are too prosaic in thought and wording to be classed as literature. The administration of churches and monastic orders involves financial and practical considerations far removed from art.

Pure science also coincides with art at times, and diverges at others. The models, diagrams, and illustrations used by scientists to explain a principle sometimes take on pictorial and decorative quality, whether by accident or because the scientist is also a man with aesthetic interests. Even modern, specialized scientific writing can at times lay claim to literary style. On the other hand, the artist sometimes undertakes to set forth general principles; to describe and explain the universe. He seldom if ever attempts fully scientific form in respect to logical reasoning and measurement. But literature and visual art are full of prescientific intuitions, especially as to the human mind and personality, which may form the basis of future science. Oedipus and Hamlet are psychological as well as literary types of character.

Applied science and utilitarian technology are more obviously akin to art, in that they produce concrete, individual forms, such as tools, machines and houses. As we have seen, these are often decorative, by intention or otherwise. Art is hard to mark off from applied science in these cases, since the two overlap, and the object can be classed in both realms at once. Architecture, ceramics, etc., are defined as arts and also as applied sciences or branches of engineering.

As we come to understand aesthetic psychology, we also learn how to control people's aesthetic responses and experiences. We learn the probable effects of various stimuli on persons of different ages, sexes, and personality types. We discover how to use art to produce calmness, agitation, pleasure, grief, or indignation. This phase of scientific technology is still in its infancy; but it will embrace more and more of art as time goes on.

In a list of arts, such as that in the previous section, it is hard indeed to know where to stop. For example, cosmetics and costume are included by common consent, because they have to do with beautifying the body. But if so, why not include nutrition and fresh-air sports? They also can beautify the body, perhaps more thoroughly than paint and powder can. Dentists and plastic surgeons, who are seldom classed as artists, have to think very definitely about the aesthetic appearance of the face. Through eugenics, we may breed a more beautiful race of humans, as science has done with horses, birds, and goldfish. It would be far-fetched to include as arts every modern skill which has slight or occasional aesthetic functions; but it is worth realizing that such borderline fields exist in great number, and that art in the broad aesthetic sense is by no means limited to the traditional fine and decorative arts.

An interesting problem in this connection is presented by *games* and *sports*. Not only do they sometimes beautify the players by making them strong and healthy; they are also watched as spectacles by thousands of people—far more than those who go to symphony concerts. The experience of watching a football game or a track meet is in many ways similar to that of watching a play or ballet. In some systems of classification (e.g., in libraries and occupational surveys) they are all bracketed together under the heading of "amusements; entertainments." This offends the serious devotee of art who is impressed by its serious side; but it has an element of truth. In so far as modern art has become specialized away from religion and philosophy, toward the giving of aesthetic pleasure, it does invite being bracketed with other amusements and entertainments. Perhaps this is less derogatory than Puritanical philosophers believe it to be. Amusements and leisure-time recreations are now seen to have many values, not only as direct contributions to the joy of living, but as easing psychic tensions in the individual and group. Sports redirect much competitive, combative zeal into harmless channels. But again, the question of value should be put aside for the present, so that we can see what actual similarities and differences exist between art on the one hand, games and sports on the other.

The psychology of games and sports is a complex subject in itself, of more cultural importance than is generally recognized. There is great difference between the role of the active participant and that of the more or less quiet onlooker. In cultures smaller and simpler than ours, it was common for every able-bodied person—or the males at least—to take part in active physical sports or ceremonies, in which a religious, civic, and military spirit was often infused. Not only has athletics been increasingly divorced from these other interests, but the roles of onlooker and participant have been increasingly separated from each other. As in ancient Rome, and in the Spanish bullfight arenas, thousands cram the stadium seats to watch a few highly trained gladiators or toreros struggle. Much the same thing can be said about the arts. In both, in spite of partial counter-trends, the tendency has been for vast crowds of non-participating but appreciative, critical observers to look or listen while a few experts perform. This has led, in aesthetics, to increasing emphasis on the nature of aesthetic experience rather than artistic experience—on works of art from the standpoint of observers and appraisers, not from that of makers and performers.

The audience at an athletic spectacle behaves in much the same way as the audience at a dramatic or musical spectacle, applauding its favorite stars for their successes. The type of attitude and experience involved is apparently similar in many respects. In both cases, there is pleasure (often mixed with displeasure) in seeing and hearing an organized sequence of actions, performed with skill. That athletic feats can be felt as beautiful is evidenced by the countless artists—from Minoan times and earlier—who have painted and sculptured athletes. Sports and artistic performances are alike hard work for the participants, whether or not they are play for the audience.

The word "game" is now usually applied to activities in which there is a contest of some sort, according to prearranged rules. (The contest may be imaginary, as in playing solitaire.) But not all games are definitely competitive. Some are ritualistic, especially children's games like "Farmer in the Dell" and "London Bridge is Falling Down." These are often survivals of primitive religious and secular rites, whose origin under other names is lost in antiquity. They are modern survivals of that early undifferentiated art from which drama developed: an art combining rhythmic gestures and movements with rhythmic words and chanting.

The term "sport" loosely covers all athletic games and also many outdoor, recreational activities which are not necessarily competitive. Swimming, skating, horseback-riding, boating, fishing, shooting, boxing, fencing, and similar sports may be organized into contests, with rules for fair play, or may be practiced merely "for the fun of it," in groups or alone. Even when non-competitive they require skill, and are often watched with interest. In this they resemble art. The most enduring and popular of them are survivals of activities once used for practical purposes in the struggle for existence. Their practice as sports by the tired city-dweller is a playful, controlled regression to earlier cultural levels for the sake of mental and nervous relaxation and muscular exercise. The arts and handicrafts, likewise, are often practiced "for the fun of it," by amateurs with no great technical skill and no great need of the products.

Competitive sports and contests have one important difference from most works of art: the outcome is not decided in advance, if the game is fair and honest. The game as a temporal form is not completely predetermined. As to the general framework pattern, it is determinate; but there is room all along and at the end for either side to gain the victory. In games of chance, the outcome is likewise uncertain, but due in less degree to skill. Where the contest is between representatives of a school, a city, or a nation (as in the Olympic games), it becomes a kind of symbolic warfare, and a substitute for wars and duels to the death. As a result, there is suspense, tension, in both the players and the audience. The latter, if interested in the outcome, tend to identify themselves with one side. With strong feelings of empathy, they project themselves into the contest, vicariously striving, hoping, fearing, exulting or desponding. To some extent we do this also in watching a play or reading a novel whose plot involves strong conflict, and which arouses our sympathy for one of the protagonists. If we know how the story comes out, our suspense is less; we observe the fixed march of events without real hope or fear of unexpected outcomes. In music there is some surprise on first hearing a composition, but less and less as we rehear it. In painting, sculpture, and architecture, the whole thing is finished, and spread out before us.

The fact that most art lacks the suspense and thrills of uncertain conflict is partly responsible for its frequent lack of appeal to active youth. It seems tame and dead by comparison with games and sports, partly because it is all worked out in advance, with nothing for the onlooker to do but contemplate the finished product. He can not participate actively, and in many kinds of art he cannot even cheer for his favorite team or hero, thus achieving in fantasy a sense of union with the group, and a share in victory or defeat. Even active practice of the arts does not necessarily give this particular kind of thrill; e.g., to an active boy who is made to practice the piano.

Art itself sometimes becomes competitive, and like a game. It was so in Greek times, when prizes were given for winning the pentathlon and also for writing the best ode or tragedy. It is so in *The Mastersingers of Nuremberg,* for the best original song. Some educators object to giving prizes for students' art products, on the ground that it interferes with the pure love of creating; but there is much to be said on both sides. The rules of the game and the fairness of the victory are usually not clear in artistic competitions.

The modern *amusement park,* in or near a large city, is a large, elaborate, permanent carnival or fair; a miscellaneous assemblage of devices for giving pleasant thrills to holiday crowds, old and young. It appeals to sight and hearing with glaring, noisy stimuli; to taste with candies and sweet drinks; to the kinesthetic sense of active youth with agreeably frightening rides and slides. The experiences offered are mostly juvenile in mental level; yet advanced engineering skill and ingenuity are devoted to building their fantastic machinery. There is little order, little differentiation; the flood of heterogeneous stimuli is barbaric and exuberant, at the opposite pole from the restrained simplicity and intellectual seriousness of classical, adult art. Nevertheless, much of the experience thus aroused is aesthetic in a broad sense of that word, and at least on the periphery of art.

10. Ways of classifying the arts: a preliminary view

In discussing other problems, we have had to give some incidental consideration to the classification of the arts. We have noticed several bases of classification, criteria by which various skills are marked off into groups or types, each with a name of its own. None of these groupings is completely false; each expresses the discernment of certain likenesses and differences among human activities, as they have existed at some time in the history of society. Each expresses certain interests and ideals, certain standards of excellence, ways of subdividing human activities for practical administration and theoretical understanding. Each contains an element of truth and validity. But in time some of them become obsolete, perhaps because they express attitudes based on social conditions which no longer exist, such as feudalism. As interpreted in accompanying theory, some of them oversimplify the facts, suggesting oversharp separations and contrasts, ignoring borderline and other additional types. New demarcations are made, with old names often transferred to them, so that the old names become increasingly ambiguous. New demarcations must be made, to deal intellectually with newly perceived similarities and differences; new specializations and combinations in the practice and teaching of the arts.

The earliest basis examined was a complex of ideas expressing the aristocratic point of view of Europe from the Greek period through the eighteenth century. It divided skills primarily on the basis of the *kind of process* involved: *manual* or *non-manual* (the latter implied mental or spiritual). Another basis was assumed to be correlated: the intended *nature of the product;* its principal *aim or emphasis:* whether that of *utility* (in ministering to man's material needs and comforts) or *mental and spiritual elevation.* The non-manual arts, aiming at mental and spiritual elevation, were regarded as noble, genteel, liberal, or fine; the others as ignoble or servile. The former came to be known as fine arts; the latter as useful arts.

Later, especially during the eighteenth century, a slight change was made in the basis of division concerned with aim and nature of the product: instead of mental and spiritual elevation, or along with it, *beauty and aesthetic pleasure* came to be stressed as aims of the fine or non-manual, non-useful arts.

In the Renaissance and afterward, the prejudice against the manual diminished, and less emphasis was placed on the basis of division—"manual or non-manual." The aristocratic distinction between noble and ignoble still persisted, however; and it continued to be associated with that between "fine" (aesthetic, non-utilitarian) and "useful."

Still later, in the late nineteenth and twentieth centuries, another change occurred, through the rise of democratic ideas and the rising power of the middle and lower classes. The basis of distinction "noble, ignoble" no longer seemed important. "Manual and non-manual," "fine and useful," seemed much less important than before. However, theorists tried to preserve some objective distinction out of the old complex of ideas. They pointed out that the contrast between "fine or aesthetic" and "useful" was only a matter of degree, but preserved it nevertheless in theoretical classifications.

Through the industrial revolution and the rise of applied science, many skills and industries became highly developed along specialized, utilitarian lines, with little or no aesthetic aim. They gradually ceased to be called "arts" or "useful arts," thus leaving the term "art" for those skills which did have an aesthetic aim or function, perhaps along with others, as in architecture. The principal basis of division was still that of "aim and emphasis" or "intended nature of the product." Another distinction on this basis now came into use: the arts previously called "useful" were sometimes called "decorative" instead, because this aspect of their double nature now seemed more important from the aesthetic point of view. However, terms emphasizing their usefulness were also current, such as "applied" and "functional."

During the late nineteeenth and especially the twentieth century, a trend occurred which may be described either as the spread of industrialism into the aesthetic realm—into the making of beautiful products—or as the revival of aesthetic aims in machine industry. In any case, products with aesthetic aims now came to be made and reproduced by mechanized, mass processes. This led to a revival in theory of an old basis of division: that of the *kind of process* involved. On this basis, however, the important distinction no longer seemed to be *manual or non-manual,* but *handmade or machine-made.* Handmade methods had dominated the aesthetic realm so long that it was sometimes doubted whether there could be such a thing as machine-made art. But the strong emphasis on attractive appearance or "eye appeal" in some machine products led to a new category within the realm of art: that of industrial arts, or mechanized, mass-produced, aesthetic arts. However, only part of the process of manufacture was usually included as art: the designing, inventive phase.

Since the establishment of the French academies, there had been a tendency to divide the arts into three or more groups, partly because of existing professional alignments. Music was one; literature was another; architecture, painting, sculpture, and the useful decorative arts formed a third. Opera and dancing, as combined theater arts, sometimes formed a fourth. These main groups have often split into smaller ones. For example, architecture often parts company with painting and sculpture in setting up separate educational institutions. Literature has tended to split into linguistic sections: English, French, Latin, etc., with occasional reintegration as "comparative literature." But architecture, painting, sculpture, and the useful decorative arts are treated as one field in books and courses on art history and appreciation, and in college art departments. Sometimes the old name "fine arts" is transferred to this field, thus leaving out music and literature. Sometimes "art" alone is used. But the name "visual arts" has begun to replace it in this connection, being more objectively descriptive, less ambiguous and controversial. Such a name implies still another basis of division: that of *which sense is primarily addressed*.

Part Two

RELATIONS BETWEEN THE ARTS

V

Philosophical Classifications of the Arts

1. In philosophy before 1700

The concept of fine or aesthetic arts being largely a product of the eighteenth century, no attempts were made before that time to classify such arts in a systematic way. During and since the eighteenth century, a great many theories have been proposed, involving classification of the arts under various headings.

The more philosophical of these go far beyond mere verbal classification, seeking to explain the basic similarities and differences between the arts; to point out the underlying factors—metaphysical, psychological, social, and others—which connect and differentiate the arts; and thus to show the place of each art in the total scheme of world history and culture. Some also appraise the relative values of the arts, and arrange them in a hierarchy of ascending importance. Such philosophical theories are called "systems" of the arts, in contrast with superficially classified lists. Most of them have constituted sections in larger philosophical systems, intended by their authors to set forth fundamental truths about the universe in general: the nature of reality, of mind, of moral values, of man's place in the universe. As such, they often form a part of some general theory of aesthetics— of beauty, aesthetic value, and the nature of aesthetic experience. Some have fitted into vast empirical surveys of human knowledge— schemes for classifying all the branches of science and technology, within which the fine arts are shown to have a place. In more recent years, since the problem of classifying the arts has come to be a recognized task of aesthetics, many separate articles have been written on the subject.

Like all other problems of aesthetics, this also can be traced back to ancient philosophy. Aristotle, for example, seems to be on the verge of a system of arts and sciences when he distinguishes "productive philosophy" from theoretical and practical philosophy, as that

157

which terminates in the origination of permanent products.[1] This might well have led him to a theory of the arts. "Poetics," in a broad sense, means "making" or "doing," and is applicable to all the arts, useful and fine. But Aristotle's *Poetics* deals mainly with one of the "imitative" arts, which we now call "poetry." Some scholars have supposed that Aristotle intended to give a theory of all the arts, and that the *Poetics* is only one surviving fragment of this. It begins with a brief comparison between epic poetry, tragedy, comedy, dithyrambic poetry, and the music of the flute and lyre. All are said to be modes of imitation, but to differ in respect to medium, objects, and manner of imitation. All these arts are contrasted with the imitation or representation of objects through the medium of color and shape. They are said to produce imitation through rhythm, language, and harmony. In flute and lyre music, harmony and rhythm alone are employed, while dancing uses rhythmical movement without harmony. There is another art, says Aristotle, which has no name (today, we call it "literature"), and which imitates by means of language alone.[2] This is a clear start toward distinguishing the arts, including the visual arts and music, on a basis of medium. It is unfortunate that the *Poetics* in its present form does not pursue this broad approach, which was not carried out thoroughly until modern times.

We have already looked at the early history of the concept of fine arts, at its relation to "liberal" and "useful" arts, and at the varying list of arts which were considered "fine" at different times. There is little between Aristotle and the seventeenth century which bears directly on the classification of the fine arts. One may cull from many writers, here and there, an isolated reference which now seems related to that problem. But the problem of classification itself is not systematically followed up.

To choose but one example: St. Augustine (354-430 A.D.) is led to begin a grouping of the arts on a basis of sense addressed, when he undertakes to list the ways in which the beauties of the sensory world have tempted him. He agrees with the eighteenth century hedonist in

[1] *Metaphysica*, Bk. XI, Ch. vii, sec. 1064a. See Robert Flint, *Philosophy as Scientia Scientiarum and History of Classifications of the Sciences* (New York, 1904), p. 79. *Cf.* H. E. Bliss, *The Organization of Knowledge and the System of the Sciences* (New York, 1929), p. 310.

[2] *On the Art of Poetry*, ch. i (Butcher's tr.) [Ed. "Little Library of Liberal Arts," p. 3]. *Cf.* W. H. Fyfe, *Aristotle's Art of Poetry* (Oxford, 1940), p. 4.

regarding what we now call the fine arts as devoted largely to sense pleasure, while differing radically in condemning rather than praising that result. The pleasures of taste allure him; those of smell not much. "The delights of the ear," he writes,[3] "had more firmly entangled and subdued me, but Thou didst loosen and free me." He fears lest the "whole melody of sweet music which is used to David's Psalter" may become too attractive. "There remains the pleasure of these eyes of my flesh. . . . The eyes love fair and varied forms, and bright and soft colors. . . . What innumerable toys, made by divers arts and manufactures, in our apparel, shoes, utensils, and all sorts of works, in pictures also and divers images . . . have men added to tempt their own eyes withal." This contrast of arts on the basis of sense addressed is so obvious and fundamental that it was in common use for centuries before aestheticians thought of building it into a formal theory.

Francis Bacon (1561-1626) wrote two epoch-making surveys of human knowledge and scientific activity: *The Advancement of Learning* (later enlarged in Latin, as *De Augmentis Scientiarum*), and *The New Atlantis*. The former is a systematic classification of the sciences or branches of learning, together with an analysis of their aims and shortcomings, and advice as to their progress. His approach is on the whole fresh and individual, breaking away from the traditional "liberal arts" as basic categories. Bacon stresses the importance of studying nature, and defends the dignity of manual and mechanical activities in scientific discovery and invention. He makes occasional, penetrating comments on the aesthetic arts,[4] but he shows nothing like the understanding which Leonardo expressed in his notebooks, over a century earlier, of the close connection between the scientific and the artistic study of nature.

Bacon does not grasp the kinship of poetry as an aesthetic art to music and painting, but regards it as "feigned history." His division of human learning is "derived from the three faculties of the rational

---

[3] *Confessions*, Bk. X, sections 49, 51.

[4] Especially in his essays "Of Beauty" and "Of Building." In *The Advancement of Learning*, he asks, "Is not the trope of music, to avoid or slide from the close or cadence, common with the trope of rhetoric, of deceiving expectation? Is not the delight of the quavering upon a stop in music, the same with the playing of light upon the water?" In *The New Atlantis*, he looks forward to synthetic perfumes and flavors; also to imitating "motions of living creatures by images of men, beasts, birds, fishes, and serpents."

soul, which is the seat of learning. History has reference to the Memory, poesy to the Imagination, and philosophy to the Reason. And by poesy here I mean nothing else than feigned history or fables; for verse is but a character of style, and belongs to the arts of speech, whereof I will treat in its proper place."[5] Poesy is divided into Narrative, Dramatic, and Parabolical (that is, symbolic or allegorical, as in parables). The sound, meter, and accent of words in poesy are mentioned briefly in a later book, along with grammar.

We have already noticed how Bacon anticipates the eighteenth-century, hedonistic conception of fine art in regarding music and painting as "voluptuary arts" or "arts of sense pleasure." His discussion of this point in the *De Augmentis*[6] is worth considering here, as an example of classifying the arts. The basis employed is that of sense addressed:

Lastly I come to Arts of Pleasure Sensual (*Artes Voluptarias*), which are divided according to the senses themselves. The pleasure of the eyes is chiefly Painting, with a number of other arts (pertaining to magnificence) which respect houses, gardens, vestments, vases, cups, gems, and the like. The pleasure of the ears is Music, with its various apparatus of voices, wind, and strings: water instruments, once regarded as the leaders of this art, are now almost out of use. Of all these arts those which belong to the eye and ear are esteemed the most liberal; for these two senses are the purest;[7] and the sciences thereof are the most learned, as having mathematics like a handmaid in their train. The one also has some reference to memory and demonstrations, the other to morality and the passions of the mind. The pleasures of the other senses, and the arts relating to them, are less esteemed; as being more allied to luxury than magnificence. For unguents, odours, the dainties and pleasures of the table, and most of all the stimulants of lust, need rather laws to repress than arts to teach them. It has been well observed by some that military arts flourish at the birth and rise of states; liberal arts when states are settled and at their height; and voluptuary arts when they are turning to decline and ruin. And I fear that this our age of the world, as being somewhat upon the descent of the wheel, inclines to arts voluptuary.[8] Wherefore let these things pass. With arts voluptuary I couple

[5] *De Augmentis Scientiarum*, Bk. II, Ch. 1 (Spedding tr.), *Works*, vol. IV, London, 1875.

[6] Bk. IV, Ch. 2, p. 395.

[7] *Casti*, which can also be translated "chaste" or "disinterested."

[8] This pessimistic attitude of Bacon toward the arts, in his old age, is quite unlike his persistently hopeful attitude toward the progress of the sciences.

arts jocular; for the deceiving of the senses is one of the pleasures of the senses.

As we have seen, this reference to music and the visual arts does not occur in the early version of the essay, written some eighteen years before; and even here, it has the appearance of an afterthought, rather superficially inserted. Music and the visual arts are grouped with sleight of hand and lower-sense delights as "voluptuary arts." These are one of the four kinds of art which aim at the good of man's body; the others being medicine, cosmetic, and athletic. This narrowly materialistic, sensualistic way of classifying music and the visual arts shows little appreciation of their mental values, even though their claims to learning and morality are briefly acknowledged. The fact that poesy is treated elsewhere, under two separate headings, shows that Bacon had not clearly conceived of the aesthetic arts as a distinctive group concerned with beauty, or thought out the problem of relating them systematically to the sciences. He might, for example, have consistently pointed out the connection of painting with the scientific observation and inductive study of nature, following the lead of Leonardo da Vinci.

2. *From 1700 to 1790*

Several other philosophers attempted systems of the sciences during the late seventeenth and early eighteenth centuries: notably, John Henry Alsted, Comenius, Weigel, Hobbes, Locke, Leibniz, Vico, and Wolff.[9] Christian Wolff made a basic distinction between metaphysics and practical philosophy, the latter including ethics, economics, and politics.

"His follower Baumgarten," says Flint, "did good service by vindicating the right of aesthetics to a place by the side of ethics." By this move, the fine arts themselves did not at once gain a recognized place in the system of human knowledge; but a step was made in that direction by giving a place in that system to aesthetics as the science or branch of philosophy dealing with sensuous ideas, beauty, and the liberal arts. "*Noeta,*" said Baumgarten in 1735, "as what can be known by the higher faculty of knowledge, are the object of logic;

---

[9] *Cf.* Flint, *op. cit.*, pp. 113-131.

aistheta belong to the aesthetical science or to aesthetic." [10] Fifteen
years later, in the *Aesthetics* (sec. 1), he added that "Aesthetics (the
theory of the fine arts, the theory of the lower kind of knowledge, the
art of thinking beautifully, the art of analogical reasoning) is the
science of sensuous knowledge."

G. E. Lessing's *Laocoon* (1766) was subtitled, *On the Limits
(Grenzen) of Painting and Poetry*. It protested against the French
academic doctrine that painting and poetry had much the same functions. This doctrine, as McMahon points out,[11] was based on a misinterpretation of Horace's words, *ut pictura poesis,* to the effect that
poetry should present vivid verbal descriptions, while painting should
give parallel visual portrayals. Not only had the similarity between
these arts been exaggerated, but each had been conceived in a narrow
way, as merely doing the same thing by different means. Lessing's
insistence on their basic difference of function had a liberating effect
at the time, in encouraging both arts to go their separate ways. It
directed the attention of artists and critics away from the mere representation of subject-matter to basic types of æsthetic form.

Later on, the notion that each art had necessary limits or boundaries became repressive in its turn, when interpreted to mean that
each art should avoid effects deemed proper to another. This notion
is far from dead today. It is often invoked, for example, by critics who
argue that painting should avoid "story-telling," because that is a
"literary value." [12] The history of the arts is full of overlapping between them, as well as of divergences. Various types of effect are
constantly being taken over from one medium to another, with appropriate adaptations. The adventurous artist is not likely to be deterred
from doing so by theoretical prohibitions.

Lessing distinguished between painting and poetry on the basis
of the nature of the medium *(Mittel)* or type of sign *(Zeichen)*
employed. Painting uses figures *(Figuren)* and colors in space, while
poetry uses articulated sounds *(Töne)* in time. Bodies *(Körper)* with
their visible properties are the peculiar subjects of painting, while

---

[10] *Philosophical Thoughts on Matters Connected with Poetry,* Sec. 116. *Cf.*
McMahon, *op. cit.,* pp. 29-31, for a fuller discussion of Baumgarten.

[11] McMahon, *op. cit.,* p. 23.

[12] *Cf.* A. Torossian, *A Guide to Aesthetics,* p. 164.

actions *(Handlungen)* are the peculiar subjects of poetry.[13] Painting can directly imitate visible bodies, and indirectly suggest actions through showing a single moment, from which preceding and subsequent moments can be inferred. Poetry deals primarily with actions, but can depict bodies too, by suggestions conveyed through actions. Such classification on the basis of medium, and into arts of *space* and *time,* has since been extensively applied to other arts. Much of what Lessing says about painting is intended to apply to sculpture also, and to the plastic arts *(bildende Künste)* generally, as he states in the Preface.

Lessing's conception of painting is limited by current academic standards, in regard to the propriety of representing two or more moments of time in the same picture. That had been common in the middle ages and in oriental art, but had declined during the Renaissance in favor of the single moment. Says Lessing:

> To introduce two necessarily distant points of time into one and the same painting, as Fr. Mazzuoli has the rape of the Sabine women and their subsequent reconciliation of their husbands and relations, or as Titian has the whole history of the prodigal son, his disorderly life, his misery, and his repentance, is an encroachment by the painter upon the sphere *(Gebiete)* of the poet which good taste could never approve.[14]

Twentieth century art has again become tolerant toward free experiments with time and space in any medium, including the portrayal of successive moments in the same picture. Hence Lessing's dictum, "succession of time is the department of the poet, as space is that of the painter," is no longer accepted without qualification. Indeed, painting has achieved complex temporal development through film "animation." Moreover, Lessing wrongly assumed that the Laocoon group, which he had never seen in the original, lacked agonized expression and signs of outcry. He accounted for this by the theory that expressions of extreme suffering, legitimate in poetry, were prohibited by the law of beauty in the plastic arts, in that crying

---

[13] Ch. XVI. Abbé Dubos, Baumgarten, Burke, and Kames anticipated certain elements in Lessing's theory. *Cf.* Bosanquet, *History of Aesthetic,* p. 225; B. Croce, *Aesthetic,* p. 449; H. Kuhn, "Philosophy of Art," in *Encyclopedia of the Arts,* New York, 1946, p. 744.

[14] Ch. XVIII.

would disfigure the face with a wide-open mouth. Lessing's theory, declares Margarete Bieber, "would make, in contrast to poetry, the rendering of movement, action, truth, and character forever inaccessible to figurative art. This thesis, by the way, is refuted by the entire art of the Greeks." [15]

Had Lessing's theory of what was proper in the visual arts been actually followed in those arts, the effect would have been repressive in the extreme. The theory has a kernel of truth, in that sequences of action are much easier to represent in literature than in static painting or sculpture, and that static portrayals of violent passion tend to lose their effectiveness when looked at frequently. Moreover, painting can usually give a more vivid sensory image of a scene than verbal description can. But these sound generalizations are exaggerated by Lessing into a rigid system of boundaries and prohibitions. This illustrates a failing which has weakened many later systems: that alleged "fundamental differences" between the arts are often based on inadequate knowledge of the variety of styles that have actually been produced in each art, and on dogmatic prejudices—resulting from this limited experience—as to what each art "has a right" to do. When the actual history of the arts is better understood, many supposed differences between them turn out to be less radical than was first believed, and tastes change accordingly, as to what is allowable and beautiful.

Johann George Sulzer (1720-79) was a Swiss writer whose contribution to aesthetics was greater than is commonly recognized. His *Allgemeine Theorie der schönen Künste* ("General Theory of the Fine Arts") was published in 1771-74, shortly after Baumgarten had added aesthetics to the list of the sciences. "A scarcely less honor," says Robert Flint, "seems to have been due to Sulzer, as his work apparently was the first in which there was given a comprehensive view of the fine arts (literary included) in their various relationships. For more than half a century he was considered in Germany the chief authority in aesthetics." [16] He also wrote a "Short Summary of all the Sciences," and showed the relation between these and the arts. Thus he had a place in the line of those who have tried to systematize all human knowledge, and was the first to give detailed recognition to the fine arts in such a system. Flint is right in taking Bosanquet to

[15] *Laocoon: the Influence of the Group since its Rediscovery* (New York: Columbia U. Press, 1942), p. 10. *Cf.* Bosanquet, *op. cit.*, p. 221.

[16] *Op. cit.*, p. 136. *Cf.* Bliss, *op. cit.*, p. 330.

task for omitting Sulzer's name entirely from the *History of Aesthetic*. Perhaps one reason for this neglect is the fact that Sulzer's encyclopedic survey is arranged in alphabetical order of topics, so that its underlying system of ideas is hard to piece together. There are articles on general topics such as aesthetics, fine arts, form, and taste; on separate arts such as painting, music, sculpture, poetry, drama, dancing, architecture and garden art; on technical factors in the arts, such as color, versification, and harmony; and on historical periods. Extensive bibliographies are given under each important topic. Without pretense to metaphysical profundity, it carries aesthetics as *Kunstwissenschaft* a long way toward comprehensive, rational organization. Unfortunately, the broad highway of advance thus indicated was soon forsaken by the post-Kantian romantic philosophers, in favor of cloudy speculations on "art as expression of the Universal Mind." Sulzer's discussions are, on the whole, much more in the spirit of twentieth-century aesthetic form-analysis than is the bulk of nineteenth-century German aesthetics.

He divides the arts primarily according to medium or "means of representation"—color, body, tone, and words. Here is his definition of *bildende Künste,* a most important term in classifying the arts:

With this general name one designates all arts which represent visible *(sichtbare)* objects, not only through drawing and colors, especially in true bodily form. These are sculpture *(Bildhauerkunst),* gem-carving *(Steinschneiderkunst),* stamp-cutting *(Stempelschneiderkunst),* and stucco-work *(Stukkaturkunst).* . . . . These approach and climb to perfection together, and decline again.

The art of medal-making *(Schaumünzen)* is also listed here by Sulzer. The *bildende Künste,* then, are arts of visual representation, especially those in which the third dimension is actually developed through carving or otherwise. There is no article on *Plastik,* the term later preferred in that connection. Architecture and painting are not listed as *bildende Künste.*

"Aesthetics" is defined as "the philosophy of the fine arts, or the science which derives both general theory and the rules of the fine arts from the nature of taste." In other words, he does not separate aesthetics, as the abstract study of beauty, from *Kunstwissenschaft* as the science of art.

Among other contemporaries of Kant, the French writer, Charles

Batteux [17] (1713-1780), and the German, J. G. Herder (1744-1803),
should be briefly noted for their reference to the senses as a basis
for dividing the arts. Herder asserted that each of the three chief senses
(vision, hearing, and touch) gave rise to a kind of art: painting,
music, and sculpture.[18] He defended painting as a distinct art, which
Lessing in his desire to mark off the *bildende Künste* from poetry and
music had not distinguished clearly from sculpture. Painting, said
Herder, was less real than sculpture, because lacking the third dimension, and it allowed greater freedom of treatment. He helped to
establish aesthetics as a science by distinguishing more clearly than
Baumgarten had done between aesthetics and art. The study of beautiful objects, he said, is not itself necessarily beautiful. Herder assigned
to aesthetics a place within the field of anthropology.

3. Kant's theory of the arts

Immanuel Kant's brief but influential contribution to the subject
is contained in his *Critique of Judgment*.[19] Art in general *(Kunst)* is
first conceived in the broad technical sense as human skill *(Geschick-
lichkeit)*, and is distinguished from nature and from science *(Wis-
senschaft)*.[20] It is then distinguished from handicraft, trade, or
artisanship *(Handwerk)*, as being free, while the latter is paid or
mercenary *(Lohnkunst)*. That is, art can only succeed when done as
play, as agreeable in itself, whereas *Handwerk* is disagreeable drudgery
in itself and is attractive only for the pay or other compensation.[21]
Thus art is human skill which is practiced freely, as play, or as an
occupation which is agreeable in itself. However, the soul's freedom
in such art is somewhat restricted by such necessary mechanisms as
prosody and meter.

[17] *Les Beaux-arts réduits à un même principe* (1746).

[18] *Cf.* H. Kuhn, "Philosophy of Art" in *Encyclopedia of the Arts*, p. 744.
Gilbert and Kuhn, *A History of Esthetics* (New York, 1939), p. 433.

[19] Published 1790; vol. IV in Rosenkrantz's edition of the *Works*. Tr. by
J. C. Meredith, Oxford, 1911; and by J. H. Bernard, Macmillan, London, 1914.

[20] Part I, Bk. II, sec. 43.

[21] Meredith's translation of *Handwerk* as "industrial art" is misleading. Kant
does not imply the modern connotations of the latter term, as we have noted
them in the previous chapter. His distinction between art and *Handwerk* is a
very dubious one. Actually, any kind of skill may be practiced for pay or for its
own sake; either may at times be "play" or drudgery.

Art is divided into the "mechanical" [22] and the "aesthetic"; the latter has the feeling of pleasure *(Lust)* as its immediate aim. Aesthetic art is further divided into "agreeable" *(angenehme)* and "beautiful" *(schöne)* art.[23] The former have mere sensuous enjoyment as their aim, as in arranging a table for enjoyment, in entertaining narrative, in sprightly conversation, or in dinner-music *(Tafelmusik)* to whose composition one does not pay close attention. Beautiful art is to be experienced in a more cognitive way; it advances mental culture in the interest of social communication, although it is pursued for its own sake rather than for an ulterior end. "Hence aesthetic art, as art which is beautiful, is one having for its standard the reflective judgment and not organic sensation."

Here Kant underestimates the extent to which a cognitive, reflective element enters into the arts which he regards as merely agreeable. All perceptual experience, especially that of mature, educated persons, necessarily contains some cognitive interpretation. There is no such thing as "purely sensuous pleasure," even in the enjoyment of foods and perfumes; for associated meanings, trains of thought, and evaluative judgments are sure to enter in some degree. There is often a considerable amount of organized form in a table-arrangement (for example, in the elaborate feasts of Chinese, Roman and Renaissance palaces), as well as in entertaining stories and jests. Any kind of music can be used as dinner-music, and what is used often has complex form, although simpler forms are usually felt to be more appropriate. The essential difference lies not in the art itself, but in the attitude taken toward it by the observer. Kant is right in recognizing a difference between the highly thoughtful, alert attitude which is called for (though not always given) toward serious products of the major arts, and the casual attitude we often take toward other enjoyable productions. No sharp and permanent line can be drawn on this basis, between the arts which Kant includes as "beautiful" and those which he depreciates as merely "agreeable." An art such as that of perfume may be endowed with little intellectual meaning in one culture (for example, in American frontier life), while elsewhere (for example, in the Orient)

---

[22] "Art merely seeking to actualize a possible object to the cognition of which it is adequate . . . is mechanical" (Meredith tr.).

[23] Sec. 44. Bernard gives this literal translation of *schön*, while Meredith calls it "fine" or "elegant." Bernard translates *angenehm* as "pleasant."

it is developed into much more complex forms in respect to sensory qualities and symbolic meanings.

In the previous chapter, we adopted a definition of "art" or "aesthetic art" which is close to Kant's conception of aesthetic art, except that his is stated in more exclusively hedonistic terms. We shall not follow Kant in restricting the aesthetic concept of art to the few established "beautiful arts" which he recognizes, but shall also include what he calls the "merely agreeable" ones.

Whether stimuli addressed to the lower senses are to be called "beautiful" or "ugly" is another question; certainly these evaluative terms are usually restricted to visual and auditory stimuli. Beautiful or not, they can arouse aesthetic experience of a complex and meaningful type. They deserve careful study by scientific aesthetics, in comparison with forms addressed to the higher senses. Kant's narrow conception of "beautiful arts" also leaves out many types of visual and auditory form which deserve attention in aesthetics; not as a group condescendingly set apart from the major beautiful arts, but as closely related to them. Our understanding of the so-called major arts themselves, and of their cultural settings, has much to gain from a wider range of data for comparison. Whatever real differences exist between them and the less recognized or less developed arts can be pointed out later on, in detail.

Kant goes on to subdivide the beautiful or fine arts into three types: "arts of speech" (redende Künste), "plastic or shaping arts" (bildende Künste), and "arts of the beautiful play of sensations" (Künste des schönen Spiels der Empfindungen). This division (Einteilung) is based on an analogy with the three modes of expression which, according to Kant, enter into spoken communication: namely, word, gesture, and tone, or articulation, gesticulation, and modulation.

The word bildend presents a problem for the translator. Meredith and Bernard both translate it as "formative." The dictionaries allow "formative," "plastic," or "graphic." [24] "Plastic," however, is more

[24] Muret-Sanders, Encyclopaedic German-English Dictionary (16th ed., 1910), p. 196. The trouble with "visual," as with "formative," is that both apply also to several arts which Kant excludes from the bildende group. He excludes the fine art of color (Farbenkunst) and the agreeable art of table-arrangement, both of which produce organized visual forms. Dancing is visual but not bildend. The arts he includes are those which produce mainly static forms. The difficulty is not only in the English translation, but in Kant's own application of his concept. We shall return to this problem in Chapter VIII.

exactly equivalent to the German *Plastik,* which Kant restricts to sculpture and architecture, and "plastic" is commonly so used in English. It is hard to make it cover painting, as some writers try to do. The trouble with "formative" is that *all* arts are formative; music and literature included. "Art," as Goethe said, "is but formgiving." It is misleading, therefore, to restrict "formative" to a single group of visual arts. Kant himself says, "in all beautiful art the essential thing is the form *(Form),* which is suitable for observation and judgment." [25] The word *Bild* refers primarily to visual shapes, especially pictorial and sculptural images. The German words *Form* and *Gestalt* are nearer to our conception of form in a broad sense, although *bildend* can also be so used. As a name for the group of arts which Kant includes, *bildend* is perhaps too broad even in German. "Visual arts," as suggested in the previous chapter, is in some ways a preferable name for them, although it is not an exact translation of *bildende Kunst.* J. A. Symonds [26] prefers the term "figurative arts" for sculpture and painting, and this is sometimes used for *bildende Kunst.* However, Symonds does not include architecture as a figurative art, while Kant does include it as *bildende Kunst.* "Figurative" relates "to the representation of form or figure by drawing, carving, etc." (Webster). Colvin translates *bildend* as "shaping" and *redend* as "speaking." [27] He includes architecture, as Kant does, although it is not "figurative" in the sense of "representative." There is much to be said for this translation, if "shaping" is understood to mean "visual shaping."

The "arts of speech" are subdivided into "eloquence" or "rhetoric" ("the art of transacting a serious business of the understanding as if it were a free play of the imagination") and "poetry" ("that of conducting a free play of the imagination as if it were a serious business of the understanding"). The *bildende Künste* are "those for the expression of ideas in sensuous intuition (not by means of representations of mere imagination that are excited by words)." They are sub-

[25] Section 52 (Bernard tr.).

[26] "The Provinces of the Several Arts," in *Essays Speculative and Suggestive* (London, 1890), vol. I, p. 133. *Cf.* K. Gilbert and H. Kuhn, *A History of Esthetics* (New York, 1939), p. 433.

[27] "Fine Arts," in *Encyc. Brit.* (11th ed.), X, 362. "Architecture, sculpture, and painting are arts which give shape to things in space, or, more briefly, shaping arts."

divided into "plastic" art *(Plastik)* and "painting" *(Malerei)*. Both use figures in space to express ideas; but plastic art has sensuous truth in that its figures are actually given in bodily extension, and are discernible to touch as well as to sight, although touch is irrelevant to their beauty. Painting has sensuous semblance, in giving figures as they appear when projected on a flat surface. Once more, plastic art is subdivided into "sculpture" *(Bildhauerkunst)* and "architecture" *(Baukunst)*. Sculpture presents concepts of things corporeally, as they might exist in nature; it is an imitation of nature (men, gods, animals, etc.) in which regard is paid for aesthetic ideas. Architecture presents concepts of things which are possible only through art. It includes furniture and household utensils *(Hausgeräte)* along with other things meant to be used *(Dinge zum Gebrauche)*. "The adaptation of the product to a particular use is the essential element in a work of architecture."

It will be noted that Kant sees no difficulty in classing architecture, along with the making of furniture and other useful things, as fine or beautiful art. Their utilitarian functions are not seen as a bar to such classification; there is no sharp antithesis between "beauty" and "use," or fine and useful art. In this respect, Kant is comparatively free from ancient prejudice against the useful and manual, with which so much earlier discussion of the arts is concerned. A trace of the old way of thinking survives in the notion (later developed by Schiller) that art is essentially like play—done freely, for its own sake [28]— rather than for an outside purpose. This has strengthened the misconception that art is mainly a leisure-time avocation or recreation for the wealthy, remote from the serious business of life; also that it is less fine and noble when done for a living. As a matter of fact, any skill or occupation—including art, science, war, and commerce—can be practiced for its own sake, or for pay, or for other ulterior purposes. The difference in motivation is not necessarily correlated with any difference in the medium or occupation itself, or in the type of product.

Coordinate with plastic art, in Kant's classification, is *painting*. He divides it into (a) "painting proper" (the beautiful portrayal of nature), (b) "landscape gardening" *(Lustgärtnerei,* the beautiful arrangement of nature's products), and (c) those types of interior

---

[28] There are other implications of "play." See B. Bosanquet, *History of Aesthetic* (London: George Allen and Unwin, 1922), pp. 281, 294, on the concept as used by Kant and Schiller.

decoration, furniture, and "tasteful dressing" whose "sole function is to be looked at." Kant's limited understanding of the possibilities of painting and sculpture leads him to regard both as necessarily concerned with the representation of nature, thus ignoring abstract or non-representative types of form in both arts. His inclusion of landscape gardening, interior decoration, and costume under "painting" involves an extreme and confusing inflation of the concept of painting. He might better have listed them as coordinate with painting under *bildende Kunst*.[29] Also, it is confusing to list furniture under both architecture and painting, according to whether it is useful or merely ornamental.

The third division of fine or beautiful art is "the art of the beautiful play of sensations." This includes *music*[30] and the art of *color (Farbenkunst)*, as artistic play with sensations of hearing and of sight. Both arts are conceived as essentially abstract or non-representational, and there is no specification here of the medium through which colors are to be shown. What distinguishes these arts as fine or beautiful, rather than as merely agreeable, is the extent to which they involve perception of *form* in the play of sensations: for example, in estimating color-contrasts, time-intervals, and mathematical relations between sounds.[31]

The beautiful arts, Kant adds, can be combined *(verbunden)* in one and the same product, as in drama, song, opera, dance, and oratorio. The expression "combined arts" is still in common use for these types.

Kant's system of the arts can be diagrammed as follows:

(see next page)

---

[29] Bosanquet (p. 280) makes a weak objection to including oratory and landscape gardening under fine arts at all. One is too "practical"; the other "does not deal with a true expressive material." Here Kant's judgment is more sound. However, he too has a low opinion of oratory. (*Crit. Judg.*, Pt. I, § 53). He rates poetry most highly, music next.

[30] That is, music as a fine art, as distinguished from "merely agreeable" *Tafelmusik* ("dinner music").

[31] *Cf.* section 14: "In painting, sculpture, and in all the formative arts—in architecture, and horticulture *(Gartenkunst)*, so far as they are beautiful arts—the delineation is the essential thing; and here it is not what gratifies in sensation but what pleases by means of its form which is fundamental to taste" (Bernard tr.).

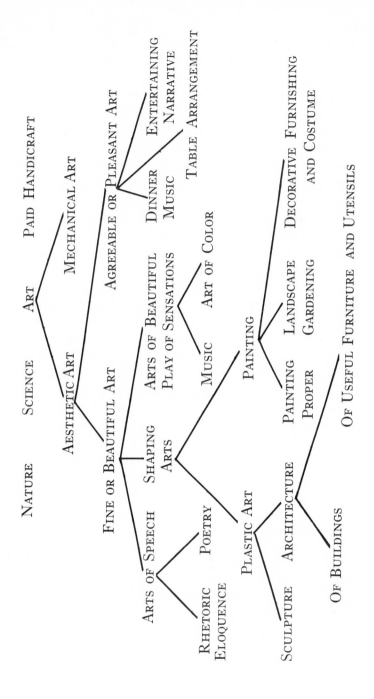

KANT'S SYSTEM OF THE ARTS

Nature

Science

Art — Paid Handicraft
 — Aesthetic Art — Mechanical Art
          — Agreeable or Pleasant Art — Dinner Music
                                      — Entertaining Narrative
                                      — Table Arrangement
          — Fine or Beautiful Art
                — Arts of Speech — Rhetoric Eloquence
                                 — Poetry
                — Shaping Arts — Plastic Art — Sculpture
                                             — Architecture — Of Buildings
                                                            — Of Useful Furniture and Utensils
                              — Painting — Painting Proper
                                         — Landscape Gardening
                                         — Decorative Furnishing and Costume
                — Arts of Beautiful Play of Sensations — Music
                                                        — Art of Color

4. Some nineteenth-century German theories

Kant's classification contains much that is dubious and cumbersome, and many of his groupings are not followed today. Nevertheless, it is fairly factual, and based in large part on observable resemblances and differences in the field of art. It is concise, modest, and tentative. Unfortunately, many of his nineteenth-century followers sidetracked the discussion into mazes of metaphysical idealism, subjectivism and dogmatic evaluation. Much of Kant's classification can be accepted independently of his other philosophical theories. Later German attempts, until recent years, have been for the most part inextricably bound up with metaphysical idealism, and of little use or plausibility to anyone who does not share that belief.

Bosanquet's *History of Aesthetic,* long the only detailed history in English, is itself a product of the same philosophy. Says Bosanquet: "The objectivity and necessary historical continuity of the sense of beauty as a supreme expression of the absolute or divine reality as uttering itself through man, has become an axiom of philosophy." [32] Philosophers who accepted such "axioms" naturally approached the subject of the arts from that point of view. What they had to say about the different ways in which the various arts "expressed the cosmic mind" has little importance for contemporary, naturalistic aesthetics. In nineteenth-century German philosophy, it became tediously verbose and artificial. Bosanquet's *History* provides a useful summary of this mass of material, but it is naturally colored by its author's idealistic sympathies.

Schelling, at the beginning of the nineteenth century, is credited by Bosanquet with the "axiom" just quoted, and also with having made the first thorough-going attempt at a systematic classification of the arts. [33] His classification is based on Kant's distinction between the arts of speech and those of shaping *(bildend)*, which he develops into an elaborate contrast of two parallel series of arts. The former belong to the "ideal" series, the latter to the "real." Those of the real series are "embodiments of the Infinite in the Finite—the principle of beauty in general, and more especially of antique beauty. Those of the ideal

[32] *Op. cit.,* p. 333.

[33] K. F. A. Schelling, *Philosophie der Kunst* (*Werke,* Vol. V, from lectures given in 1802-3).

series are cases of the subordination of the Finite to the Infinite." [34]
Modern art belongs mainly to the ideal series; ancient art to the real
series; sculpture is typically antique and painting typically modern.
Each group and series is divided and redivided on the basis of the
relative predominance of *real* or *ideal*. In the realm of mind (an ideal
unity) the real predominates in art, the ideal in philosophy. Within
each series of arts, each particular art is characterized in the same way.
For example, "in the real series the real *par excellence* is music, the
relatively ideal is painting, and the synthesis of the two is sculpture."
In his speech "On the Relation of the Plastic Arts to Nature," [35]
Schelling follows Herder in stressing the difference between painting
and sculpture. The former is less material, using light and color as its
medium, and expressing the higher passions of the soul.

All this appears today as far indeed from the realities of art.
Bosanquet himself considers it notable mainly as the first attempt at
an extensive, systematic survey of the arts.

Hegel's classification of the arts is incorporated in an elaborate
theory of the evolution of the arts.[36] This evolution is explained as part
of a larger, world process in which the Idea—the cosmic mind or world
spirit—gradually particularizes itself, and reveals itself in sensory
forms. The evolution of the Ideal, or world of imagined beauty and
concrete fancy, has three successive but cumulative stages, determined
by the progress of the human mind. These stages constitute three
main types of art: *symbolic, classical,* and *romantic.* Hegel is concerned with *evaluating* these types, and the arts which embody them,
as higher or lower in a hierarchy of values.

The first or symbolic type, exemplified by Egyptian, Chinese, and
Indian art, is "rather a mere search after plastic configuration than a
power of genuine representation." It manifests struggle, aspiration,
disquiet, and often sublimity. "Classical" art, especially Greek, attains
"free and adequate embodiment of the Idea in the shape that, according to its conception, is peculiarly appropriate to the Idea itself." It

[34] Bosanquet, *op. cit.,* p. 330. *Cf.* Gilbert and Kuhn, *op. cit.,* p. 433.

[35] *The German Classics,* V, 129 (New York, 1913).

[36] 1770-1831. The *Aesthetik,* published in 1835, was translated as *Philosophy
of Fine Art,* by F. P. B. Osmaston, 4 vols., London, 1920. *Cf.* Bosanquet, *op. cit.,*
pp. 336f; Gilbert and Kuhn, *op. cit.,* pp. 438f. Quotations are from Hegel's
"Introduction" to the *Aesthetik,* translated by Bosanquet, and included as Appendix
I of the *History of Aesthetic,* pp. 471f. In Osmaston's tr., vol. I, pp. 103f.

affords "creation and vision of the complete Ideal," and establishes it as a realized fact. The shape with which the Idea invests itself when manifested temporally, is the human form, as in anthropomorphic art, which is suited to reveal mind to sense. Modern "romantic" art "annuls the completed union of the Idea and its reality, and recurs, if on a higher plane, to that difference and opposition of two aspects which was left unovercome in symbolic art." Classical art had a defect which is fundamental in all art; it tried to objectify Mind, which is infinite concrete universality, in the shape of sensuous concreteness. It set up a perfect amalgamation of spiritual and sensuous existence. But Mind cannot be adequately represented thus, being infinitely subjective and incapable of finding free expansion when transposed into a bodily medium. Romantic art seeks to escape from such a condition, dissolving the classical unity. It seeks free intellectual being, addressing itself to the inner mind rather than to sensuous perception. However, it needs an external vehicle of expression, and finds it in the display of feelings. It represents the sensuous externality of concrete form, as well as individual characters and actions, as transient and fugitive. It achieves a higher perfection in that it "withdraws itself from any adequate union with the external element, inasmuch as it can seek and achieve its true reality nowhere but in itself." Thus the three types of art "consist in the aspiration after, the attainment and the transcendence of, the Ideal as the true Idea of Beauty."

Hegel goes on to show how these general types of art, or stages in art history, reveal themselves in the several arts. Different sensuous materials make the general types of art separate into particular arts. Each general type finds its most complete application and realization in some one particular art or group of arts. For each general type or stage, some one particular art or group of arts is most adequate for complete, characteristic realization: *architecture* for the symbolic type; *sculpture* for the classical; *painting, music,* and *poetry*—especially music—for the romantic. However, the other principal arts also recur within each stage in a subordinate way, to satisfy recurrent needs for expression in modes which are not in accord with the dominant spirit of the age. Each particular art thus has a symbolic, a classical, and a romantic stage; in only one of which it achieves pre-eminence as expressing the dominant spirit. "There is a romantic and classical type of architecture, though the art is primarily symbolic."

Bosanquet discusses the question why Hegel touched so briefly on the two common bases for classification—the sensuous medium and the relation to space and time—and then let them drop. These were the principal bases in use before Hegel, and for some time after him. Lessing had emphasized space and time. Kant and Schelling had divided the arts of form from the art of speech. Hegel points out that this is based on the division according to sense organs, except that music should be distinguished from speech; the former only being the art of sound, while poetry is the art of the imagination. (Hegel was apparently rather insensitive to the auditory aspects of poetry, and inclined to disregard them as parts of its essential nature.) Hartmann, later on, was to divide the arts as those of the eye, those of the ear, and those of the fancy.

Hegel's theory of art history has certain undeniably factual elements, such as the relative importance of sculpture in classical times, and the suitability of music to express romantic feeling. It was a pioneer attempt at viewing the history of the arts in the large, and at showing a comprehensive pattern therein, with successive stages causally interrelated. It opened new paths in seeking for a few basic types of art which occur in all particular arts, whatever the medium, function, or subject. It was an ambitious attempt to reconcile classicism and romanticism by showing the place of both in the scheme of things. Some of its evolutionary principles, such as the tendency toward differentiation and individuation, or the increasingly rational self-consciousness of art and civilization, can be defended apart from a transcendentalist metaphysic. But in the light of present historical knowledge, Hegel's account of the events of art history appears distorted and oversimplified, even aside from the question of their metaphysical interpretation. It exaggerates the extent of correlation between certain arts, certain periods, and certain types or styles. The history of art now appears much more diversified and irregular.

Logical classification of the arts is obscured in Hegel's work by the historical approach, and by the emphasis on general types which cut across all the arts. He begins by dividing the realm of fine art *(das Kunstschöne oder das Ideal),* not into particular arts, but into abstract types of art. He does not arrive, as most classifications do, with each particular art under one heading and only one. However, his main ideas on this subject can be summarized in schematic form for comparison with other systems.

First, fine art is divided into symbolic, classical, and romantic.

This is a division on the double basis of historic stage and general type; the two being held to coincide on the whole, since each main stage is dominated by a certain type. *Secondly,* each main type is divided into two subtypes: (a) materials and techniques which are most adequate for complete, characteristic realization of that type; (b) materials and techniques which are not adequate, or are less adequate. *Thirdly,* each of these subtypes is shown to include one or more particular arts. Steps two and three are not clearly distinguished, but made together. The resulting system can be diagrammed as follows: (see next page)

Since each art occurs under all three types, one could divide each art into the same three types or stages: symbolic, classic, and romantic.[37] This would produce the following division:

I. FINE ART
   A. Architecture
      1. Symbolic stage or type
      2. Classical stage or type
      3. Romantic stage or type
   B. Sculpture
      1. Symbolic
      2. Classical
      3. Romantic
   C. Painting; and so on.

However, this would not correspond with Hegel's main emphasis, which is upon the three historic types as the primary basis of division.

Schopenhauer (1788-1860) presents a systematic view of the arts which, like Hegel's, is less a direct attempt at classification than a theory of evolutionary stages and of relative excellence.[38] Instead of Hegel's "Idea" with its somewhat intellectual connotations, Schopenhauer relies on an underlying cosmic Will, which seeks to objectify itself in the external types of specific existence. Every art exhibits opposing forces. Arts vary from the crudely heavy to the finely spiritual, according to the stage of advancement of the Will which they

---

[37] *Cf.* Bosanquet, *op. cit.,* p. 349.

[38] *The World as Will and Idea.* Trans. by Haldane and Kemp. 3 vols.; London, 1883-6. The first German edition was published with the date of 1819, thus antedating Hegel's *Aesthetik. Cf.* T. Whittaker, *Schopenhauer,* pp. 7, 49f; Gilbert and Kuhn, *op. cit.,* pp. 464f; Bosanquet, p. 366.

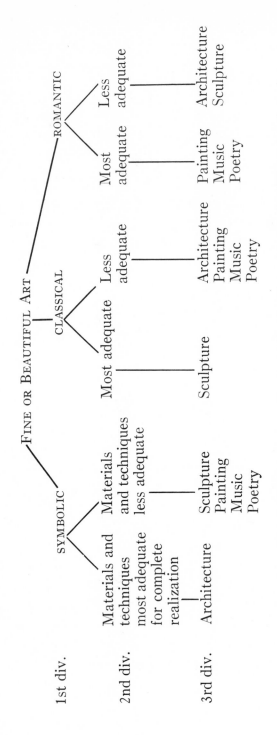

FINE OR BEAUTIFUL ART

	SYMBOLIC	CLASSICAL	ROMANTIC

1st div. Materials and techniques most adequate for complete realization — Materials and techniques less adequate

2nd div. Most adequate — Less adequate | Most adequate — Less adequate

3rd div. Architecture — Sculpture Painting Music Poetry | Sculpture — Architecture Painting Music Poetry | Painting Music Poetry — Architecture Sculpture

The following diagram would allow distributing the arts in different categories:

FINE OR BEAUTIFUL ART

Art most adequate for the *symbolic* type: architecture.

Art most adequate for the *classical* type: sculpture.

Art most adequate for the *romantic* type: painting, music, poetry.

HEGEL'S SYSTEM OF THE ARTS

express, and are correspondingly low or high in the scale of values. Architecture is the lowest of the arts in this respect; its function is to show the relation of gravity to rigidity, and also the nature of light upon or within a building. Landscape gardening and landscape painting strive to reveal the essential nature of the plant as a combination of stillness and growth. Sculpture and painting can reveal the essence of animal nature, but their highest task is the representation of man. Painting can go farther than sculpture in exhibiting man's psychological permutations, and in setting forth general types by concrete examples. Poetry, especially tragic, can illuminate the resource and strength of the human will. As an art, it helps one to escape the entanglement of the Will, and to achieve philosophical resignation. Music "stands alone, quite cut off from the other arts. . . . It is by no means like the other arts, the copy of the Ideas, but the copy of the Will itself, whose objectivity the Ideas are. This is why the effect of music is so much more powerful and penetrating than that of the other arts, for they speak only of shadows, but it speaks of the thing itself. . . . In the melody, in the high, singing, principal voice . . . I recognize the highest grade of the objectification of Will, the intellectual life and effort of man." [39]

J. F. Herbart (1776-1841) offers an unconvincing classification, which Bosanquet rightly dismisses in a few words. It divides the arts into two groups on a basis, says Bosanquet,[40] which is intended to correspond to the distinction between classical and romantic, or complete and incomplete presentation. One group is supposed to consist of arts which can be "looked at on all sides" like sculpture; the others "keeping in soft twilight and admitting of no complete critical exploration." The former includes architecture, sculpture, church music, and classical poetry; the latter, landscape gardening, painting, entertaining music, and romantic poetry.

F. T. Vischer (1807-87) published a Hegelian system of aesthetics in six huge volumes between 1846 and 1857. He divided the arts according to three forms of the imagination: constructive, receptive or sensitive, and poetic. The first of these gives rise to architecture, sculpture, and painting; the second to music, and the third to poetry.

The division made by Carriere distinguishes three arts: of form,

[39] *Op. cit.*, I, 330f.

[40] *Op. cit.*, p. 371. Herbart's *Werke*, I, 171.

of music, and of poetry.[41] These are, respectively, (a) coexisting in space, (b) successive in time, and (c) combining coexistence and succession. In the art of form, "architecture corresponds to inorganic matter, sculpture to organic individual shape, and painting to the combination of the two in individual life. Music is divided as instrumental, vocal, and the combination of the two; poetry into epic, lyric and dramatic." [42] These subdivisions of music and poetry are supposed to rest on differences of "inner perception," according as the object of the art is mind in general, personality as a whole, or personality in its particular relations with other persons.

German theorists of this period take special pains to work out a system which will be neatly divided into two main categories (for example, space and time or eye and ear), or into three, as into Hegel's three types. They are delighted if they can incorporate both kinds of division at once—into twos and into threes—and still more if some plausible analogy or correspondence can be pointed out between opposite items in different columns. This all seems to indicate a perfection of form which must be founded on higher truth. Any "gap" in a system is an "awkward blot." Thus, Max Schasler points out,

if we arrange the arts according to their means of presentation and organs of perception, and designate one group as "arts of the eye" (architecture, sculpture, painting), and the other group as "arts of the ear" (music, poetry), it is possible to coordinate the two series, so that music corresponds to architecture, and poetry to painting; but then there seems to be no kind of art on the other side corresponding to sculpture and comparable with it. This fatal gap was an awkward blot in the system, the true articulation of which was otherwise plain.[43]

The difficulty, of course, was an entirely artificial one, produced by the traditional selection of a list of five "major" arts out of the many which actually exist. Adding a sixth, such as "mimic dancing," seemed to solve the problem cleverly, by allowing a symmetrical division into two columns, of three arts each. It was quite uncongenial to the spirit of the times—still pervaded by scholastic rationalism, in spite of all the talk about evolution—to remain content with a lop-

---

[41] *Aesthetik* (1859), I, 625. Bosanquet, *op. cit.*, p. 411.

[42] Bosanquet, p. 412.

[43] *Critical History of Aesthetic* (1869), I, XXV.

sided, irregular system; or to recognize that this is not the sort of world which can be correctly described in a rigid, symmetrical diagram. Up to the present day, the real problem of showing how the arts are interrelated has been hampered by the over-anxiety of philosophers to produce a symmetrical pattern of some sort, on which all the arts can be evenly placed—whether in parallel columns, in a circle, or otherwise. Such obsession by neat intellectual patterns, and by the fascination of balancing groups of two, three, or four is a sign of unconscious motivation which future scientists will no doubt psycho-analyze. In vain had Lessing warned in 1766, "We Germans have in general no want of systematic books. At deducing everything we wish, in the most beautiful order, from a few assumed definitions of words, we are the most complete adepts of any nation in the world." [44]

Schasler is frankly proud of the following division: [45]

Arts of simultaneous perception	*Arts of successive perception*
1. Architecture	1. Music (productive); virtuosity (reproductive or auxiliary)
2. Sculpture	2. Mimic dancing (prod.); mimic performance (reprod.)
3. Painting	3. Poetry
a. Landscape painting	a. Lyric (prod.); declamation (reprod.)
b. Genre painting	b. Epic (prod.); rhapsodic (reprod.)
c. Historical painting	c. Dramatic (prod.); acting; theatre art (reprod.)

The basic antithesis between "simultaneous" and "successive" per-ception, which underlies this division, is supposed to be reducible to "rest and motion," and to correspond also with "matter and mind," "material and form," and "space and time." (Bosanquet rightly pro-tests against this excessive identification.) In each column, the arts are said to differ in relative predominance of material and idea, the latter increasing as one goes down the list. The left-hand series is supposed to be visual, the right-hand auditory; but, as Bosanquet points out, this breaks down in the case of mimic dancing. Other

[44] Preface to *Laocoon* (Beasley tr.).

[45] *System der Künste* (1885), p. 124. *Cf.* Bosanquet, *op. cit.*, p. 419.

analogies which Schasler alleges, between corresponding items in the two columns, are denounced by Bosanquet as "wild." These include a far-fetched correlation of landscape, genre and historical painting with lyric, epic, and dramatic poetry; also an attempt to distinguish some of these as "subjective," others as "objective."

Bosanquet is on weaker ground, however, in attacking the right of dancing, acting, and landscape gardening to figure at all in a list of major arts, on the ground that "organisms and individuals are bad material for the artist to work with," imposing their own individuality on the artist and "refusing to be cast in the spirituality of his mood." Bosanquet also rejects a distinction by Schasler between the *material* of art (for example, marble or paint) and the *means* or *medium* (for example, perceived form or color). The two, it is said, all but coincide in music and poetry. Bosanquet's objection is that the artist's feeling for his material is an important basis for distinguishing the arts, as in metalry, and even in musical instrumentation and poetry. This is true; but we need not go so far as to call it "the only true analogy for the classification of the 'higher' arts." In observing and comparing the finished product, the sense-quality is often more important than the physical material, and it is more useful to describe in terms of red and blue, light and dark, smooth and rough, than in terms of oil and marble. Many later students of aesthetic form prefer, with Schasler, to stress "medium" rather than "material."

Eduard von Hartmann achieves,[46] by a different juggling of concepts, a pattern much like that of Schasler:

Arts of perception	*Arts of fantasy* (poetic art)
Formative art	Epic poetry
Music	Lyric poetry
Mimic art (acting and mimic dance)	Dramatic poetry

The successful combination of twos and threes pleases him as much as it did Schasler:

The lover of abstract designations will be glad to find in the primary dichotomy of arts of perception and arts of fancy the truth of Schelling's division into a real and an ideal series, and the friends of dialectic triads will recognize to their satisfaction, in the secondary

[46] *Aesthetik* (1887), II, 625. Bosanquet, *op. cit.*, p. 436.

triple division of the two groups, the triad of objective, subjective, and subjective-objective. . . . In both groups or series, the secondary triple division represents the predominance of perception, of feeling, and the equilibrium of the two. It is obvious at first sight that the epos, intended for recitation, is in its plastic and colored vividness just as analogous to formative art as the song, which is meant to be sung, is to music, and the drama, which is meant to be played, to "Mimik."

He adds, complacently, "These analogies and parallelisms have so often been noted and insisted on in detail, that it is absolutely incomprehensible how it has been left for me finally to combine them."

This gratifying result is achieved, however, only by some rather violent measures. Architecture and the minor arts are omitted entirely from the list, as "unfree." The branches of poetry are elevated to a rank coordinate with all the other "free" arts: they "transcend and absorb" the arts of perception. Under Wagner's influence, the "quaternary complex arts," with opera as their culmination, are given highest aesthetic value. Bosanquet aptly remarks at this point that architecture is the true type of a complex art, although Hartmann accords it a low place in his system.

5. Recent philosophical and psychological systems of the arts

During the late nineteenth and early twentieth centuries, numerous German philosophers worked out systems of the arts, based on the ones we have been considering. It became the accepted procedure to include a chapter on the subject in any comprehensive treatise or textbook on aesthetics. Many of these expressed the traditional idealistic metaphysics.

For example, Max Diez praises Friedrich Vischer's distinction between three kinds of fantasy, one organized for the eye, one for the hearing, and one for the imaginative faculty, from which plastic art, music, and poetry are respectively derived.[47] He goes on to describe fantasy as an organ of the self-materializing mind, which materializes itself on three levels: the direct and natural as sound, the indirect and natural as objects, and the artificial as speech. This leads to three kinds of art, since the mind can appear impersonally as mood, personally as real mind in its body, and ideally in the configurations and actions of life. "In the first case the mind remains in the subject; it

[47] *Allgemeine Aesthetik* (Berlin, 1922), pp. 154-166.

is our own mood which we attribute to inanimate objects like clay and stone. In the second, we are aware of the mind only through the medium of a mind which has become materialized. In the third, we feel the individual mind only as an expression of the general mind." This leads to a distinction between (a) architecture and music, as arts the essence of which lies in harmony, which use natural, unorganized materials; (b) sculpture and painting, as arts which do not permit the mind to make itself thoroughly at home in the form itself, but only through the mediation of life or the feeling of life; and (c) poetry, which succeeds in expressing the universal or ideal mind. Its three subdivisions (notice the constant recurrence of the mystic number three) are lyric, epic, and dramatic, which express subjective, objective, and absolute beauty.

Oswald Külpe's approach, on the other hand, is psychological and naturalistic.[48] It avoids metaphysical entanglements, and is content to rest on the simple, concrete, and obvious basis of *sense addressed.* Such a division is scorned as superficial by the Hegelians, and it does ignore many important aesthetic problems as to the nature and interrelation of the arts. But, as far as it goes, it is one of the least controversial and most useful modes of classification. For practical purposes, it is more easily applied than those which depend on vague and debatable theories about art's inner nature. For theoretical purposes, it is always possible to take up the deeper questions elsewhere in aesthetics, leaving the classification itself less profound but more generally acceptable.

R. F. Piper is right in calling this one of the schemes which "succeed best in displaying the range, interrelations, and differences of the fine arts." In his article on "Classification of the Arts," [49] Piper quotes Külpe's outline, with supplements of his own enclosed in brackets. These are useful, and are included here in what we may call the Külpe-Piper system:

I. Optic arts (appealing to the sense of sight):

A. Surface arts, producing works on surfaces:

1. Uncolored or monochrome: Drawing [Graphic Arts, Photography];

---

[48] "The Conception and Classification of the Arts from a Psychological Standpoint." *University of Toronto Studies, Psychological Series* (1907), II, pp. 1-23.

[49] *Encyclopedia of the Arts* (New York: Philosophical Library, 1946), p. 229.

2. Polychrome: Painting, Tapestry, [Stained Glass, Mosaic];
[3. With motion: Kinematic Arts: Silent Cinema, Lumia].

B. Solid [or three-dimensional] arts, producing plastic works:

1. Semi-solid: Relief and Intaglio;
2. Completely solid: Sculpture, [Ceramic Arts];
[3. With motion: Pantomime, Eurhythmics, Fireworks].

C. Aggregate arts: combining surface and solid effects:

1. Tectonic Arts;
2. Architecture, [Monuments, Landscape Design, Interior Decoration, Flower Art].

II. Acoustic arts (appealing to the sense of hearing):

A. Of tones: Music;
B. Of words: Poetry, [all Literature, Speech Arts];
C. Aggregate arts: of tones and words: Song, Melodrama (recitation with music).

III. Optic-acoustic arts, appealing to both the higher senses: [often with costumes and architectural settings]:

A. Of gestures and tones: Choreographic Art (dance with music);
B. Of gestures, words, scenery: Drama, [Puppetry];
C. Of gestures, words, tones, scenery: [Pageants], Opera.

Külpe's division is made on several bases. The first is that of sense addressed, and on it the arts are divided into optic, acoustic, and optic-acoustic, which is equivalent to visual, auditory, and audio-visual (now the more usual terms).[50] The optic arts are subdivided as to how the third dimension is developed, into surface, semi-solid, solid, and mixed or aggregate arts. These again are subdivided in terms of coloring and motion. The acoustic and optic-acoustic groups

[50] R. M. Ogden's classification of the arts is similar to Külpe's in being based on the senses addressed. But he adds a class of lower-sense arts, to make four main classes. These are (1) *auditory-rhythmical* arts (music, poetry, and their combinations); (2) *visual arts* (drawing, painting, sculpture, tectonics—for example, architecture and crafts); (3) *combinations* of 1 and 2 (choreography, drama, opera); (4) *"lesser arts of taste, smell, touch, and movement"* (cookery, perfumery, gymnastics, dance, etc.)—*The Psychology of Art* (New York: Charles Scribner's Sons, 1938), p. 26.

are subdivided in terms of medium: tones, words, or gestures. Further differentiation, says Külpe, can be made in terms of technical procedure in production.

In addition to this outline, Külpe sketches the history of classifications of the arts, as follows:

In the history of aesthetics, five points of view have chiefly been adopted for the primary division of the conception of art: (1) The *senses,* which mediate the perception of the work of art—Batteux, Herder, Hegel, Vischer; (2) The *means of representation* (word, tone, color, etc.)—Mendelssohn, Sulzer, Kant; (3) The *spatial and temporal form of the phenomenon*—Köstlin, Schasler, Fechner; (4) The *subjects of representation* (the ideas)—Schopenhauer; (5) The *relation of idea to appearance*—Dubos, Home, Schelling, Hegel.

He rightly stresses the importance of the *primary* basis of division, and inquires which of these five bases should be so used. In the "aesthetic impression" made by the work of art on the observer, he distinguishes two factors: (a) the direct or sensational, and (b) the associative. The first three of the bases involve the direct or sensational factor; the fourth involves the associative; and the fifth, the relation between the two factors. The associative factor, he continues, cannot well be taken as a basis, because of the great variety of individual associations and of subjects represented, whose classification does not correspond with that of the arts. The direct or sensational factor "is the only applicable principle of classification, because it alone presents the objective mediation between the artist and the appreciator, viz., those contents of the work of art which are approximately equal for everybody." It is "the basis and starting-point for all presentative activity, and a ground of agreement for all differences of opinion." This explains why it has comparatively often played the decisive role in classification.

Of the three bases which involve the direct factor in impression, says Külpe, the first is the best—that of the senses. But we should not extend it, as Herder did, to include the sense of touch in relation to sculpture, or the imagination as an inner sense or receptive faculty (Hegel, Vischer). Poetry acts only through one of the senses; and imagination is stimulated in all the arts. The division into spatial and temporal, or simultaneous and successive, or rest and motion, can not be made all through the list of arts. All the acoustic arts are successive, and also arts of motion, in that the moment of the spatial process is essential.

The second of the five bases—means or medium of representation—can be well employed to differentiate sense impressions. Külpe continues:

What differentiates painting from sculpture, in the optic, and music from poetry in the acoustic arts, is precisely that which separates, respectively, surfaces from bodies and tones from words, as individual, optic and acoustic contents. Here also occurs the difference between the simple and the mixed, and correspondingly the difference between indivisible and aggregate arts. Thus, every form of art within the third division of each of the three chief groups deals with a combination of the means of expression which serve the other two.

By "aggregate arts," Külpe does not mean a combination of arts, as of surface and solid arts in architecture, but "that the means of expression of the two kinds are made to serve a new form of art, which is a unity in itself, and not a combination of other arts." Opera is an aggregate art but not a mere fusion of individual arts. Music, poetry, scenery, etc., though independently treated and combined, "form rather the constituents of a comprehensive whole, in which the direct factor assumes a considerably more manifold aspect."

The article by Sydney Colvin, mentioned several times in previous chapters,[51] is one of the few detailed, systematic attempts in English at a classification of the arts. Colvin's approach is naturalistic and empirical; not based on metaphysical idealism. It follows German sources on the whole, but is fairly relativistic, avoiding rigid patterns:

It is possible in thought to group these five arts (architecture, sculpture, painting, music, poetry) in as many different orders as there are among them different kinds of relation or affinity. One thinker fixes his attention upon one kind of relations as the most important, and arranges his group accordingly; another upon another; and each, when he has done so, is very prone to claim for his arrangement the virtue of being the sole essentially and fundamentally true. . . . The relations between the several fine arts are much too complex for any single classification to bear this character. Every classification of the fine arts must necessarily be provisional, according to the particular class of relations which it keeps in view. And for practical purposes it is requisite to bear in mind not one classification but several.

[51] "Fine Arts," *Encyclopaedia Britannica* (11th ed., 1910), X, 361.

Colvin proposes three principal modes of classification, which can be summarized as follows:

FIRST MODE OF DIVISION:

SHAPING ARTS	MOVING ARTS	SPEAKING ARTS
(Stationary, Manual, Space Arts)	*(Space and Time Arts; midway between stationary and transitory)*	*(Transitory, Vocal, Time Arts)*
Architecture	Acting	
Sculpture	Dancing	Music
Painting	Eloquence	Poetry

SECOND MODE OF DIVISION:

IMITATIVE ARTS	NON-IMITATIVE ARTS
Sculpture	Music
Painting	Architecture
Poetry	

THIRD MODE OF DIVISION:

SERVICEABLE ARTS	NON-SERVICEABLE ARTS
Architecture	Sculpture
Lesser shaping arts	Painting
(weaving, joining,	Music
pottery, etc.)	Poetry

Colvin makes no attempt to force these three modes of division into coinciding, so as to make a single, regular pattern. In that, his system is more flexible and factual than many of the German ones. It is most open to criticism in minimizing the exceptions and borderline cases which occur in each category. It is not enough, for example, to concede that music sometimes makes an "excursion" toward representation or utility, and then class it definitely as "non-imitative" and "non-serviceable." In many important ways, on the other hand, painting is not an imitative art. The radical dichotomy implied by such headings tends to obscure and deny a diversity of effects within each art which are more than mere aberrations or trifling exceptions. As long as he keeps assuring us that such contrasts are merely relative, our protests are subdued. But in practice, it would give a false conception of the arts if these extreme dichotomies were accepted as fundamental headings for classification. The effect of such grouping is never merely nominal; if accepted, it tends to influence thought and action.

Many separate articles on the system of the arts have been published in the *Zeitschrift für Ästhetik* since its founding in 1906. We shall not have to pay special attention to each of these, for there is a good deal of resemblance among them, and they are taken into account by the few recent writers whom we shall now consider.[52]

A comparatively cautious, empirical system is that of Johannes Volkelt.[53] He avoids at least a few of the pitfalls which have trapped some of his predecessors and contemporaries. On the one hand, he attacks the sweeping, indiscriminate scepticism which Croce and Lotze displayed toward all attempts at systematic division of the arts. On the other, he denounces the passion for regular formulas which led Schasler and von Hartmann astray, and which (as we shall see) still influenced German theorists up to the Second World War:

The search for regularity has often led aestheticians to believe that every quartering produced by the schematic crossing of two principles of division must also correspond to an actual art. So Zeising established in advance that the number of arts must come to nine because he had two principles of division, each of which had three branches. It did not occur to him to ask whether or not the combination of two branches might in one case or another prove internally impossible in the nature of things.[54]

He sees the need for using several different bases of division, remarking that "the exaggerated tendency toward unity of human

[52] Volkelt (in the book to be cited) criticizes the theories of Friedrich Vischer, Schmarsow, Zeising, H. Dinger, and Dessoir, as well as those of Hartmann and Wagner. Dessoir comments on those of Schmarsow, Horne, Lange, and Urries y Azara; Urries y Azara discusses Dessoir, Schmarsow, Wize, Mila, Spitzer, and Volkelt. Bosanquet's account goes no farther than Hartmann, while Gilbert and Kuhn have little to say about recent systems of the arts.

[53] *System der Aesthetik* (Munich, 1925), Vol. III, Ch. 12: "System of the Arts."

[54] *Op. cit.,* p. 393n.

thought leads here, as in so many other cases, to emptiness and super-ficiality." [55] He notes as a common fault in systems of the arts the tendency to confuse various viewpoints, such as the ontogenetic or developmental, the teleological or evaluative, etc.[56]

Volkelt proposes six bases of division; none of them strictly new, but restated and applied.

The *first* is the type of *sensory perception* by which representa-tional and emotional content is conveyed, with corresponding type of sensory form. Accordingly, the arts are divided (as by Külpe) into *optic, acoustic,* and *optic-acoustic.* At this point Volkelt departs from the strict question of which sense is primarily addressed by the work of art in direct perception, and begins to speak of "imaginary sense perception"—in other words, of suggested sensory images. This shift, necessary in order to account for poetry, makes possible another sub-division on the first basis, and we now have (a) optic, (b) acoustic, (c) optic-acoustic, (d) imaginative, with words as acoustic or visual tokens. Obviously, logical consistency suffers a little by this shift in basis of division from presented to suggested sensory images, which Volkelt had previously refused to make in regard to the tactile sug-gestions of sculpture.

The *second* basis of division is that of the type of *psychic con-tent*—that is, the kind of representation and emotion conveyed. This separates the arts into *objective* and *non-objective.* The former, includ-ing sculpture, painting, graphic arts, poetry, and drama, can convey precise, individualized, specific representations of things, persons, scenes, actions, and events. Movements, moods, emotions, can be referred to a specific object. The latter, including music, dance, archi-tecture, and all branches of applied or industrial art, are non-objec-tive in that no specific things, events, or actions are represented; sug-gested images and emotions remain vague, general, not referred to individual objects. Here, it would seem, Volkelt again oversimplifies the situation.

Now the first two bases of division must be connected with each other. Auditory art can be only non-objective, for "through tones as such no things, events, or actions are represented, but only movements of moods, emotions, and affects." (Is this true?) In imaginary art, on the contrary, there can be no non-objective art. Poetry, says Volkelt,

[55] P. 400.
[56] P. 385.

is always objective. So is visual-acoustic art, as in combining dance and music. Some visual arts, however, are objective and others non-objective, as in the list above.

The *third* basis of division is the *degree to which the material to be worked by the artist already possesses form*. There are two subdivisions. In some arts, the materials show comparatively little form, as in plaster, paint, wood, and silk threads. These are *arts with formation of the first order*. In others, the material already has a complete form in itself. The dance uses living human bodies; the garden uses plants. These are arts with *formation of the second order*. Acoustic art, using tones, is of the first order; visual-acoustic, as in the drama, is of the second. Poetry, using words which already possess form, is also of the second.

Another basis of division which Volkelt includes under this one, is the extent to which *movement* or *rest* is characteristic of the arts—characteristic, he specifies, of their sensory existence, for all arts may suggest either movement or rest. Arts using the living human body are *arts of movement;* the plastic arts, such as architecture and applied arts, are *arts of rest*. Thus, in the visual and visual-acoustic fields the "arts of formation of the first order" are arts of rest; those of the second order are arts of movement. Music is an art of movement, and so is poetry. At this point, Volkelt resorts to some highly dubious generalizations in order to show that arts using unformed materials must be arts of rest. Apparent exceptions, such as marionettes and the cinema, are said to be very minor. Marionettes, he argues, are comical in their artificiality; the film tends toward harshness and distortion, destroys organic development, and prevents artistic balance and composure. A moving house would be absurd. (What of cars, ships, and airplanes?) Alas, like the rival theorists whom he criticizes, Volkelt is irresistably drawn toward the same error. He must produce a self-consistent system, wherein all the different bases of division harmonize, with whole arts and groups of arts put neatly into compartments. Negative instances are ignored or minimized.

The *fourth* basis of division is the extent to which *utilitarian purpose* was of decisive importance when the work of art was formed. Here the customary distinction is followed, into *fine* or non-utilitarian and *utilitarian* or non-fine. Utilitarian arts are not to be disparaged as mere minor appendages of pure art; they are true arts in their own right. Only the non-objective visual arts (architecture, garden art, and applied arts) are utilitarian. Apparent exceptions are explained away. Works of objective fine art, such as pictures and statues, may occasionally be used for utilitarian purposes, but such applications are super-imposed, incidental, and fortuitous. This is the case, too, when music is applied to a useful purpose. Non-objective visual arts which are not useful, like fireworks and kaleidoscopic play of colors, are regarded as very minor because of their slight powers of expression. Many useful or entertaining activities, such as interior decoration, laying tables, arranging shop-windows, dress and coiffure, circuses and variety shows, may partake of artistic quality, but "are not really arts." Photography, he says, is too mechanical to be an art, and oratory is a special use of an art rather than an art in itself.

The *fifth* and *sixth* bases of division are of narrower scope, applying only to "objective visual arts of the first formation"—that is, to sculpture, painting, and graphic art. Volkelt inquires just how they materialize their objective visual content. Two distinctions are made: one as to how effects of *solidity or depth* are conveyed; the other as to how realistically *colors* are used. By the former criterion, he distinguishes sculpture as the *really solid* art; painting and drawing as *apparently solid* arts. In sculpture, there is a predominance of spatial form over colors; in the apparently solid arts, color is freed from its restrictions to develop in cooperation with illusions of space. It may develop there in two main ways; hence apparently solid art has two subdivisions—painting, with imitative use of colors; prints and drawings, with non-imitative use of colors. He ignores the fact that color in painting may be non-realistic. Volkelt's chapter on the system of the arts concludes with a discussion of the characteristic *values* of the various groups of arts which he has distinguished. For example, the sensory abundance of the world is presented in most variety, strength, inclusiveness and penetration by the visual and visual-acoustic arts; least so by poetry.

In conclusion, he claims to have distinguished the individual arts and their values "by combining and crossing a long list of bases of division." In truth, this multiple cross-reference, which makes his theory a "system" rather than a mere "classification" of the arts, does have the effect of reinforcing the groupings and demarcations which he seeks to emphasize. But every step is achieved, as usual, through drastic over-simplification.

Max Dessoir founded the *Zeitschrift für Ästhetik und allgemeine*

Kunstwissenschaft in 1906, and edited it for many years. His generalizations about the arts and aesthetic experience, based on wide observation and comparatively free from dogmatic prejudices, are summarized in a book of similar title.[57] It contains the usual section on *Das System der Künste,* devoted partly to the origin of the arts and partly to their classification. On the latter problem, his brief and simple system is condensed into the accompanying diagram.

DESSOIR'S SYSTEM OF THE ARTS

Space Arts (Arts of rest and of coexistence)	Time Arts (Arts of movement and of succession)	Arts of imitation, of definite associations, of real forms (*reale Formen*)
Sculpture	Mimicry	
Painting	Poetry	
Architecture	Music	Free arts of indefinite associations and unreal forms *(irreale Formen)*
Plastic Arts (Affective means: spatial image)	Poetic Arts (Affective means: audible gesture) *(Laut-Gebärde)*	

Dessoir wisely concedes:

There seems to be no system which satisfies all demands. . . . Every one of our arts is so blended with other arts in some of its subspecies that classification is difficult, and the difficulty is heightened by the aestheticians' fondness for discovering highly intellectual analogies between the different fields and, by refined analysis, reducing the apparent similarity to dissimilarity. The practice of our time also makes it very easy to increase the means of expression of one art with auxiliaries from another.[58]

Rejecting many proposed bases of division, he retains the following: space or time; rest or movement; imitative or "free" (that is, not bound by the need of representing reality); definite or indefinite associations; concrete or abstract forms (as to the content of repre-

[57] *Aesthetik und allgemeine Kunstwissenschaft* (Stuttgart: Enke, 1923), Ch. VI, sec. 4.

[58] *Op. cit.*, p. 260.

sentation); use of spatial images or tones and gestures. The last of these, the "means of expression," he considers most fundamental in determining the individuality of an art: "In gestures, tones, words, abstract spatial forms and images, we have the languages in which art speaks." In other words, he considers the medium of an art to be most important in determining its nature. This is a return to the simple, obvious basis of division which had been scorned as superficial by many German philosophers. It rejects as unsound many of the bases for which metaphysical profundity had been claimed, especially by the Hegelian school.

As briefly diagrammed, even the distinctions which Dessoir accepts oversimplify the facts. One must again insist that painting, sculpture, and poetry are not always imitative or representative, and that music and architecture sometimes are. Poetry is often abstract and indefinite in its associations. But Dessoir makes it clear that his system is subject to many exceptions.

In a two-dimensional diagram or table such as Dessoir's and the two which follow, there is no one primary basis of division. The bases of division are not applied successively, first one and then another, but simultaneously. The vertical and horizontal columns are coordinate. One basis is used in dividing the arts into vertical columns: "space arts" and "time arts." Another divides them horizontally into "imitative" and "free." Such divisions are supposed to cooperate in marking off a definite field or compartment for each art or group of arts to occupy. More than two bases of division are used, but they are combined into two composite bases. It is assumed that the division into (a) "space arts" and "time arts" will correspond with that into (b) "arts of rest" and "arts of movement," and (c) with that into "arts of coexistence and succession." "Imitative" is supposed to coincide with "definite," and "free" with "indefinite." This is fallacious. The divisions thus produced do not actually coincide.

Dessoir is evidently impressed by the more complex system devised in Spanish by J. J. de Urries y Azara, which he had already translated and published in the *Zeitschrift*.[59] He reproduces the diagram again, with the comment that it is more finely worked out, but more difficult to grasp. The Spanish writer pays tribute to Volkelt for abundant and detailed observations. He reproves Dessoir for omit-

[59] *Über das System der Künste. Z. f. A.,* XV, 456-459.

ting the space-time arts, for treating "mimic art" as imitative, which is not true of dance, for putting "imitative" with "concrete," and for failing to distinguish between lyric, epic, and drama. He commends an earlier division by Wize[60] into "arts of sound, plastic arts, and arts of movement. Arts of sound and arts of movement divide, according to whether they rouse determinate or indeterminate images, into poetry and music on the one side, pantomime and dance on the other.

His own system (see chart) involves, he says, four principles of classification. "First: works of art are created as imitation or freely out of the consciousness. Naturally the one does not include the other, and Jean Paul is quite right when he observes that poetry has grown more and more subjective. . . . Second: concrete and abstract arts. This distinction is often the same as the first, but not altogether: the (objective) engraving, for example, becomes abstract when it caricatures a person, and the (subjective) lyric is as a rule concrete in its expression." The third principle is space and time. The fourth distinguishes plastic from musical arts, including under the latter "the rhythmic arts which in ancient times were combined, and which we might call, according to Spitzer's proposal, Dionysiac. Under the first heading (plastic) are united the arts which are intended for the eye, and which affect it with plane surfaces and masses—also, according to Schmarsow's proposition, with presence or absence of enclosed space. Under musical arts are those of performance *(ejecución)*, which are directed at the two higher senses and certainly form a transition from the plastic arts to the word arts. They are arranged, according to their claim on the senses, in three groups; according to space and time, in two groups." Urries y Azara then continues:

Hence it follows that we can no longer speak simply of six arts (architecture without enclosed space), the kinds of music, the distinction between epic and lyric, etc. The connection of several arts with each other, as in music drama, . . . is expressed in our chart as having independent value. Notice the three-fold division of music drama, the double division of vocal music, and finally the large type sometimes used. By such small means the relations of the arts are shown as distinctly as possible (the decorative arts are shown in parentheses because of their dependence). It seems to me that nothing vital is omitted in this summary.

[60] Z. f. A., II, 178.

URRIES Y AZARA'S SYSTEM OF THE ARTS

	PLASTIC ARTS		MUSICAL ARTS			
	Two-dimensional	Three-dimensional	of performance			of words
		with inside space / solid bodies	optical	optical-acoustic	acoustic	
Objective (imitative) — Concrete in their expression	PAINTING	SCULPTURE	Pantomime	Drama-	Dra- ma musi- cal	tic Epic / *POETRY* / Lyric
	Graphics		MIMIC ARTS		*MUSIC*	
Subjective (free) — Abstract in their expression	(Surface decoration) / ARCHITECTURE	Plastic decoration / Monumental arts / Smaller arts	Dance		Vocal Music / Absolute music	
	SPACE ARTS		TIME-SPACE ARTS		TIME ARTS	

It can not be denied that Urries y Azara's chart is on the whole in accord with facts, aside from a few important faults, some of which we have repeatedly noted in regard to other systems.[61] It is remarkably clever in indicating on a two-dimensional table, by vertical and horizontal divisions, a large number of recurrent similarities and divergences among the arts. By spreading certain arts, such as drama, over two or three columns, he suggests some of the diversity which may exist within a single art. Being complex, his chart avoids some of the false simplicity of others. For example, his vertical columns are under two main headings at the top (plastic and musical) and under three at the bottom (space, time-space, and time). Thus he avoids the mistaken tendency to group all musical arts as temporal only, in order to have two main headings throughout.

The question is, how far it is possible or desirable to compress into a single diagram, or a brief verbal formula, the tremendous diversity of traits and tendencies among the arts. As modern theorists break away from the specious simplicity of early, *a priori* schemes and learn more about the variety of actual styles in art, they react in different ways. Some of them, as we have seen, give up the whole task of systematizing the arts, as impossible and undesirable. Some of them, like Külpe and Dessoir, are content with a simple and rather superficial classification for purposes of convenience in dividing up the subject for discussion. They do not try to cover detailed distinctions of form and content in the scheme of classification itself, but treat these problems elsewhere.[62] Still others try to pack more and more bases of division, more and more subdivisions and cross-references, into a single formula. To reduce the whole story (apparently) to a single, ultra-complex diagram is a *tour de force* in which they take great pride. Such a formula takes on for them almost the glamor of a mystic symbol, a mandala for contemplation, as an epitome and microcosm of the artistic world. From an educational standpoint, one may question whether so complex a diagram is more enlightening or confusing to the student, suggesting as it does a conception of the arts which is

---

[61] For instance, it would be hard to place Disney's "animated cartoon" films on this chart. They belong under "Painting" (at left) and also under "Time Arts, with words" (at right). Sculpture also becomes a time art, in marionettes.

[62] Richard Müller-Freienfels, who succeeded Dessoir as editor of the *Zeitschrift für Ästhetik*, takes the same attitude in *Psychologie der Kunst* (Munich; Reinhardt, 1933), Vol. III, Introduction, sec. 7.

falsely regular and symmetrical in spite of all efforts to the contrary. When complicated beyond a certain point, a scheme of classification is likely to lose its practical value as a tool for organizing materials to be studied; it is too fixed, inflexible, and unwieldly. Moreover, there is a constant danger that the theorist, introducing more and more kinds of division into his formula, will not be adapting it to show the actual diversity of the facts, but on the contrary building up an artificial pattern of concepts, less and less true to fact as it becomes more fascinatingly symmetrical.

Such a diagram is that of Leo Adler, which is contained in another *Zeitschrift* article,[63] and which is certainly the most complex up to date. (See diagram). In addition to dividing and contrasting the present-day arts on several familiar bases, plus one or two unfamiliar ones, he contrives to bring in a scheme of their supposed historical genesis as well. The result is impressive, but dubious on close analysis.

The basis which Adler stresses most is that of the use or non-use of *tools* or limb-projections. The arts are divided into *direct* and *indirect;* the former creating without the use of tools, and including mimicry, music and poetry, while the indirect or tool-using arts are architecture, sculpture, and painting. He continues:

The direct arts need for their production only the natural materials of man as an organic living being: the body—mimicry; the voice—song (music); speech—poetry. In these natural materials—speech and movement, words and performance—the realm of the musical or direct arts is revealed. The indirect arts, on the other hand, are formed of non-human materials—stone and earth, wood and clay, etc. . . . In the realm of indirect or plastic art the work is thus not bound to the existence of the creator. A separate existence, free from the personality of the artist, is the essence of plastic art, in contrast to musical works of art which only achieve independent existence through something brought in from outside, not characteristic of them; that is, through writing them down. Oral transmission, which binds them to a human individual, is primary and essential to musical works.

As to all this, the obvious question is, "what about musical instruments? Are they not tools? And what about phonographs, radios,

---

[63] "On the System of the Arts." Z. *f. A.*, XVII (1923), No. 3, pp. 258-261. This is the second of the two systems which, according to R. F. Piper, "succeed best."

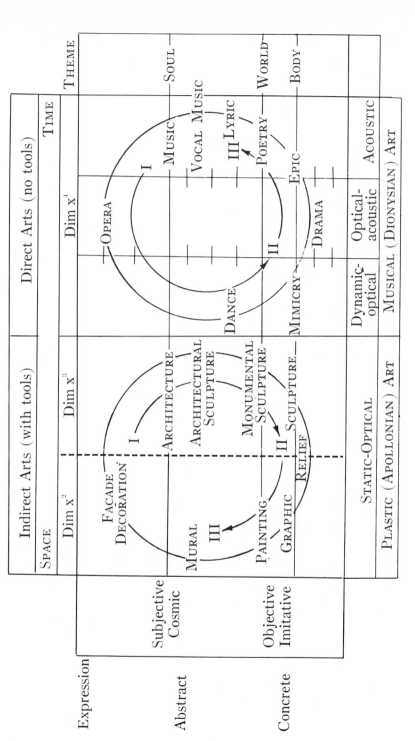

L. ADLER'S SYSTEM OF THE ARTS

paper and pencil for writing words or music? Why limit music to the vocal? Why is writing not characteristic of literature? On the other hand, there are plastic or visual arts which are "bound to a human individual"—namely, tattooing, dress, and cosmetics.

Putting "indirect" and "direct" at the heads of two vertical columns, Adler adds a horizontal division on the familiar basis of *abstract or subjective* vs. *concrete or objective.* "Architecture and music are abstract, cosmic, subjective art; sculpture, mimicry, painting, and poetry are concrete, imitative, objective art." We have already questioned this division elsewhere. For example, poetry is often abstract and subjective. And how is architecture more "cosmic" than poetry? To speak of "mimicry" instead of "dance," and to list it as an objective, imitative art, ignores the important fact of non-mimetic dancing.

"We can further coordinate these pairs," he goes on, "as to their aesthetic themes: . . . (1) the soul—the subjective pair of architecture and music; (2) the body—the objective pair of sculpture and mimicry; (3) the world, synthesis of body and soul—the objective pair of painting and poetry." This adds another neat little pattern of concepts—body, soul, and their synthesis. But does it mean much as a basis for dividing the arts? Does architecture really represent or express the soul more than sculpture and mimetic dancing do? Of course, bodies are obviously present in most sculpture and dancing; and of course painting and poetry deal with the world, souls and bodies included. But what of it? This gives no real insight into the "themes" of the various arts. It is high-sounding, empty verbalization—always the curse of aesthetic theory.

Now as to *dimensions:* music, mimicry, and poetry are fourth-dimensional (temporal); architecture and sculpture three-dimensional (spatial); painting has two spatial dimensions; there is no one-dimensional art. The following table results:

Dim. a^4:   Music—Mimicry—Poetry
Dim. a^3:   Architecture—Sculpture
Dim. a^2:   Painting
Dim. a^1:   —

So far so good. We are now presented with this very scientific-looking formula (and a scientific formula in aesthetics is a notable achievement): "The number of arts (k) coordinated to a dimension is always equal to the index of the dimension less one.

$$\text{A dimension } a^x \text{ equals } (x-1)k."$$

There is a kernel of obvious truth in this algebra, which is worth stating if stated more modestly. Naturally, when art is given more dimensions in which to build, there will tend to be more opportunities for different ways of building, and perhaps for more different arts, though these will not necessarily appear at any particular time. Four dimensions give a good deal of latitude, three somewhat less, and two still less. But the pretense at mathematical exactness is pure mumbo-jumbo. The formula results from the fact that Adler has begun with an arbitrarily selected, incomplete list of six arts, arranged in a certain way. It would be immediately invalidated if one were to add, for example, textile design to the list of two-dimensional arts, or prose drama to the temporal arts. Furthermore, to put music along with mimic dancing obscures the fact that the latter is actually developed and presented in four dimensions (three spatial and one temporal), while music has little if any spatial development. It may be fourth-dimensional, but is not four-dimensional as ballet and dramatic acting are.

The "historical" element in Adler's system is diagrammed as follows:

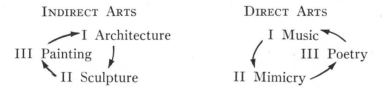

INDIRECT ARTS   DIRECT ARTS

The arrows and the Roman numerals are supposed to indicate the order in which the various arts developed. The position of the various arts on the table (left and right, up and down) has already been assigned through the bases of classification just discussed. Now it appears that the left-hand group has developed in a clockwise order; the right-hand anti-clockwise. Remarkably, "the two cycles are reverse duplicates (mirror images) of each other." Again, a fascinating symmetry in the conceptual pattern, which must indicate profound truth.

The trouble, of course, is with the premises. Did architecture and music originate first, then sculpture and mimicry, then painting and poetry? Perhaps, but mural paintings and statuettes are among the earliest works of art yet found. Adler's argument is vague on this point: "Painting and poetry begin, to be sure, at a very early cultural stage, but they are undoubtedly first typical of a more advanced period, so that the sequence, as expressed in the chart, seems correct."

One more shaky foundation to this house of cards is added in the assertion (quite unsupported here) that the indirect, plastic arts are "Apollonian," and the direct, musical arts "Dionysian." This dualism, derived from Nietzsche's *Birth of Tragedy*, is usually taken as referring to certain recurrent types in all the arts. Its use to divide the arts themselves into opposing camps is extremely questionable. Is not painting often Dionysian, and poetry Apollonian?

It is strange, in view of France's eminent position in the arts, that so little has been written in that country, in a systematic way, on the subject of their interrelations. One of the few exceptions is *La correspondance des arts*, by Etienne Souriau. This was the first important book on the subject in any language, after World War II.[64]

Instead of the rectangular diagrams favored by the Germans, Souriau offers a wheel-shaped one; (see next page).

The numbers within the innermost circle refer to what Souriau calls *qualia sensibles* or *sensibles propres*. Each stands for a particular kind of perceptible data *(donnée spécifique)* or a scale *(gamme)* of qualities. Each of these which is capable of artistic use gives birth, he says, to two arts, one of the first degree and one of the second. Arts of the second degree (in the outside circle) are representative; those of the first degree are non-representative, and are placed in the middle concentric circle. Thus *line* gives rise to the non-representative art of arabesque and the representative art of drawing. *Volume* produces the non-representative art of architecture and the representative art of sculpture, and so on. The cyclical arrangement allows one to

[64] Paris: E. Flammarion, 1947. In an earlier book (*L'avenir de l'esthétique*, Paris, 1929, p. 168) he comments briefly on classification of the arts, referring to Dessoir and other German writers. An earlier French treatise was *Système des beaux-arts*, by Emile Chartier ("Alain"), Paris, 1926.

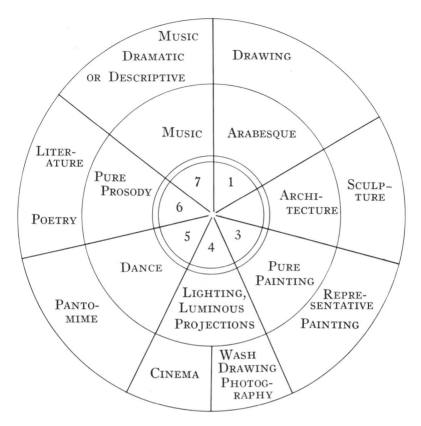

1, LINES; 2, VOLUMES; 3, COLORS; 4, LUMINOSITIES; 5, MOVEMENTS;
6, ARTICULATED SOUNDS; 7, MUSICAL SOUNDS.

juxtapose the arts which have most affinity with each other, says the
author. We can move from representative painting, by way of cinema,
to pantomime, poetry, and then dramatic music. From music, we can
move along the circle of the first degree to arabesque and then to
architecture.

In comparison with Dessoir's system, which he considers one of
the best proposed, Souriau claims "an enormous gain in simplicity and
clear ordering" through the cyclical arrangement of the corresponding arts of both degrees. Its architectonic clarity is a guarantee, he
declares, of having well considered the essentials of the situation
(p. 105). This feeling, that the facts about the arts must be somehow
clear, distinct, and regular, and that symmetrical clarity in a diagram

is a sign of its truth, is evidently not limited to German philosophers. As always, this clarity and simplicity, this reduction to the mystic number seven, are secured at the cost of drastic alterations in the usual conception of the arts and their respective fields.

The list of arts is reduced, the author points out, to those which are simple and pure, "devoted to a unique play of *qualia sensibles*." It omits all the "minor useful arts." It omits most of the "synthetic arts," in which several types of *qualia* cooperate, but it does include the cinema. On the other hand, several fields which are commonly regarded as mere branches or abstract types of art are elevated here as separate, major arts in their own right, so as to fill the available spaces. "Pure prosody" is separated from "poetry," as one of the fourteen fine arts. "Music" is made to appear as a separate art from "dramatic or descriptive music." [65] "Pure painting" is a separate art from "representative painting." At the same time, Souriau refuses to concede a separate place to "pure" or non-representative sculpture. There are indeed non-representative, three-dimensional forms, he says, such as those produced by Lipchitz; but they are really examples of architecture, broadly considered. They are "small, free architectures (that is, independent of all practical utility . . .). Their principle is none the less architectural." "Wash drawing" *(lavis)*, which one might suppose to have a close affinity with drawing *(dessin)* and with painting *(peinture representative)* is grouped with cinema as an art of luminosity—"that element which gives birth to all the arts of which chiaroscuro *(clair-obscur)* is the principal medium."

Souriau's seven *qualia* or groups of perceptible qualities thus correspond roughly to what are sometimes called the "elements" or "means" of art.[66] "Articulated sounds" and "musical sounds" are sometimes placed by other theorists among the *media* of art. Souriau's theory is open to question, in trying to pin down each pair of closely related arts to a single element or medium. Drawing and arabesque are said to be the arts of line; dance and pantomime, the arts of movement, and so on. He does not deny that other elements cooperate, but

[65] Souriau reveals later that he is quite aware of the artificiality of this diagram. For example, he remarks that "essentially representative music" and "literature without meanings" are almost non-existent as distinct arts; and that pure and representative music are not separate but continuous (pp. 130, 139).

[66] In the present book, the word "components" is used instead.

insists that the one selected in each case is *the* preponderant, "hegemonic" one.

Here again, one may ask whether a violent over-simplification has not been necessary, in order to produce this neat array of elements—a different one for each pair of arts. Empirically, it would seem that each of these elements or components occurs in more than one art: color, for example, in sculpture, architecture, dance, photography, cinema, lighting, arabesque, and many others in addition to painting. Which element predominates is largely a matter of style. Some kinds of painting are highly coloristic—the late Venetian, and still more the impressionist; some are highly linear—for example, that of Botticelli, Ingres, and others. Drawing, in the usual sense, is sometimes highly linear, and sometimes emphasizes textures or softly blended lights and shadows. Movement is important in cinema as well as in dance and pantomime. Some sculpture emphasizes volume and some, especially that in relief, emphasizes lines, surface shapes, or textures.

But these are details. Again and again, the reader accustomed to a more pluralistic view of the world is moved to wonder, why this persistent craving for a simple, regular formula? How can it still tempt philosophers—even those like Souriau, whose empirical acquaintance with the arts is wide and sensitive—to force these empirical facts into an arbitrary, inadequate pattern?

On the other hand, the Souriau system deserves credit for having emphasized an important fact, often ignored—that within each realm of art, and in the use of every major medium or component in art, there is a place for non-representative as well as representative forms. Too many people assume that a painting must be a representation of something. By giving a major place in his scheme to "pure painting," Souriau underlines the fact that non-representative painting is a legitimate kind of art, and not a mere aberration. His scheme makes it easy to see how, in each main sector of the circle, one can encounter types of form which use the medium for representing things which exist in an imaginary world outside the work of art, and other types which invite attention more exclusively to the work of art itself.

Souriau is especially interested in correspondences between the elements or *qualia* used in different arts. For example, to what extent is line in visual art analogous to melody in music? Color in painting to harmony in music? Others have speculated on these correspondences, but Souriau has analyzed them in minute detail. He recalls the common tendency of critics to speak metaphorically about one art in terms derived from another: to say that a wintry landscape is "a symphony in white major"; to speak of the architecture of a sonata, the rhythm of a building, or the arabesque of a sonnet. Not content with these vague metaphors, he has gone on to inquire what specific analogies exist between the linear curves of an arabesque and the melodic lines of a musical composition. An ordinary musical score, he points out, gives a distorted representation of the actual curves in a melodic line. Accordingly, by ingenious mathematical calculation, he proposes a more exact way of representing melodic lines in the form of visible graphs, in order to show their similarity to the patterns of Arabic ornamentation. Harmony in music, he continues, is analogous to color in the decorative arts. A musician varies his melodic themes by stating them in different keys and chord progressions, just as the visual designer treats the same linear motif in different color combinations. Pursuing the analogy, Souriau raises anew the question whether there are any laws of color harmony like those which have been laid down for musical harmony. There are, he says, mathematical ratios between the physical light-waves of different colors, as there are between different sound-waves; one can build arbitrary color-chords upon them. But are such chords actually found in visual art, spontaneously chosen for aesthetic reasons? The answer, on the whole, is negative. There is a real analogy, he asserts, between musical chords and color-chords, but one based on "aesthetic functions" rather than on physical ratios. This leads into complex problems of aesthetic aim and style.

There are two great dangers in such theorizing about correspondences between the arts. One is to overstress far-fetched, slight analogies and ignore important differences. The other is to assume that there is a definite, predictable relation between physical phenomena— for example, ratios among sound or light waves—and aesthetic effects. The latter are psychological, and many variable factors enter into them. The fact that two things are physically similar does not mean that they will appear so in artistic contexts, or produce similar emotional effects. Souriau is aware of these dangers, but many other aestheticians are not. The attempt of eighteenth and nineteenth-century musical theorists to erect a set of "laws of harmony," based on the physics of sound, is a flagrant example.

6. Some general comments

A century and a half of theorizing on the relations between the arts have brought us to a renewal of the stubborn attempt to find some regular conceptual pattern in this relationship. The result may not tell us anything conclusive about the arts, but it does indicate some persistent drives in modern philosophy.

Systems of the arts frequently ignore the negative instance, one of the common errors against which Francis Bacon warned. They are also subject to another of these common errors—that of spinning grandiose philosophical systems, based on traditional doctrines and methods. The negative instances which they ignore are, for the most part, stylistic variations within a given art which do not conform to the supposed "basic characteristics" of that art, as the theorist believes them to be. In the time of Lessing and Kant, ignorance of most exotic and primitive styles in the arts was understandable and pardonable, along with the consequent basing of generalizations on the few familiar styles. For example, sculpture was mainly late Greek and Roman sculpture, hence devoted to realistic representation of the human body. But now our horizon of the arts, past and present, is enormously wider. Recent tendencies in the arts have violated many of the traditional conceptions of what each art should do and be. For example, we must alter our conception of painting, now that painting has been set in motion through the animated cartoon film. Today, it is less pardonable to advance oversimplified generalizations, ignoring important types of art, in order to make a pretty theory stand up. It is less and less convincing to brush exceptions aside as mere aberrations, minor departures from the basic, eternal nature and limits of an art. In future, theorists who attempt a system of the arts will have to reckon with the fact of tremendous diversity, far beyond anything dreamed of in the early nineteenth century. They will have to expand the list of arts, far beyond the traditional half dozen or so on which the systematizers have based their formulas. They will have to recognize that many effects or functions, formerly considered peculiar to certain arts and absent in others, really occur in all to some extent. Hence division of the arts on such bases will become increasingly difficult.

As we discover the many kinds and degrees of value which different arts have in different cultures, it will seem less possible to grade them in any single, universal hierarchy of values. Increasing relativism and naturalism in value-theory have made aestheticians wary about using, for this purpose, any single standard of value such as Hegel's "expression of the cosmic Mind." A vestige of such evaluation persists in the conventional, widely accepted distinction between "major" and "minor" arts. The tendency today is to attribute much greater value and importance to the so-called "minor" arts and crafts than heretofore, and less unquestioning veneration to poetry as the "supreme" art.

However, to say that German systems of the arts have been oversimplified and overregularized is not to say that they are completely false. There is a good deal of truth in them; there are many generalizations which are valid over a limited range, and these can serve as hypotheses for future study. It is useful to show, as they have done, how the various characteristics of the arts are interrelated, cutting across each other and dividing up the total field in different ways. The progress of aesthetic knowledge requires that the task be pursued, though more cautiously and perhaps with a different way of expressing the results.

It is unlikely that many future theorists will try to outdo Adler in cramming all the principal types of art, stages and sequences in art history, into one small diagram. A diagram is itself a form of expression, if not of art, and there are limits to what can be done with it in the way of symbolizing the distribution and change of many complex, variable factors. It may at least seem advisable to use several different diagrams to show different relationships, and sometimes to forego diagrams entirely, relying on the less graphic medium of words.

VI

Practical Classification of the Arts, in Art Museums, Education, and Library Science

1. How art museums classify their collections and activities

The classifications examined in the previous chapter were devised, on the whole, for philosophical reasons; to satisfy a desire for intellectual order rather than to meet a practical need. Such classifications tend to be carefully logical and systematic. At the same time, they often become artificial and remote from the concrete facts of art. People who deal directly with these facts sometimes have to work out classifications of their own, for some practical purpose. They have to group and divide a particular set of art products or activities, in order to manage them in some particular way. Classifications of this type are more incomplete and casual. Often they are not thought out very carefully from a theoretical standpoint, and violate logical rules. They tend to use concepts and distinctions worked out in an earlier day, without examining them critically. As a rule, they do not state explicitly what concepts are being used as bases of division, or define important terms. In spite of these faults, continued use and revision tend to make them express not only theories about the arts but various ways of dealing with the arts.

Examples of this practical, informal type of classification are to be found in the field of museum administration.[1] Every large museum of art has to divide up its field into departments. Each department is normally under the direction of a curator, with one or more assistants, and has charge of certain galleries and types of art. It is largely a problem of classification to mark off such departments within a museum staff, and assign to each the care of a certain group of objects, or the performance of a certain kind of service.

Some museums use the term "fine arts" to designate their total field. The Boston Museum of Fine Arts does so, and so do the museums

---

[1] *Cf.* T. Munro, "Aesthetics and the Art Museum," *College Art Journal,* VI (Spring, 1947), 173-188. Reprinted in *Toward Science in Aesthetics* (New York: Liberal Arts Press; Bobbs-Merrill Co., 1956).

of Columbus, Ohio, and Syracuse, New York. The term "art" alone is more common, as in the Metropolitan Museum of Art, the Fogg Art Museum, and the Art Institute of Chicago. The Minneapolis Institute of Arts uses the plural. In all these cases, the visual aesthetic arts are considered as the main province of the museum, although it is not unusual to have musical and dramatic performances take place there. These are considered more or less relevant to its ancient function as a "temple of the Muses" (from which the word *museum* is derived), and to its traditional concern with all the arts of beauty. Hence we find, occasionally, departments of music and dancing in an art museum. But the main division is within the field of visual arts.

Let us notice briefly the departments in existence at a few leading museums. The British Museum, which is not limited to aesthetic arts, lists the following departments:

> British and mediaeval antiquities and ethnography
> Ceramics and ethnography
> Coins and medals
> Egyptian and Assyrian antiquities
> Greek and Roman antiquities
> Manuscripts
> Printed books
> Prints and drawings
> Scientific and industrial research
> Oriental printed books and manuscripts
> Oriental antiquities and ethnography

> The Victoria and Albert Museum, in London, lists the following:

> Engraving, illustration and design
> Architecture and sculpture
> Ceramics
> Paintings
> Metalwork
> Textiles
> Woodwork
> India Museum
> Circulation

> The Metropolitan Museum of Art, New York, has these departments:

> Egyptian art
> Greek and Roman art

Near Eastern art
Far Eastern art
Renaissance and Modern art
American wing
Paintings
Armor
Education and museum extension
Library

Special departments:

Musical instruments
Benjamin Altman collection
Music
Conservation and technical research

The Cleveland Museum of Art has these:

Decorative arts
Textiles
Far Eastern art
Near Eastern art
Paintings
Prints
Musical arts
Education (including circulating exhibits)
Library

The Museum of Modern Art, New York, departs most radically from the traditional list. It groups its departments as "Curatorial" and "Program":

Curatorial

Research in Painting and Sculpture
Architecture
Dance and Theatre Design
Film Library
Industrial Design
Manual Industry
Painting and Sculpture
Photography

Program

Exhibitions
Publications
Circulating Exhibitions

Educational Program
Library
Docent Staff

In addition, all museums have still other departments or staff divisions, not in charge of any particular field of art, such as that of buildings and grounds, comptroller, registrar, etc.

One interesting thing about museum classification is the number of different bases which are used in it. Departments are marked off, not only in terms of a particular art, but in terms of periods, regions, and ethnic groups. This falls short of strict logical correctness, when the departments are coordinate and independent; it involves the use of more than one basis of division in the same step. To set up departments of Painting, Sculpture, Textiles, and Ceramics is to divide on the basis of medium and technique. To set up departments of Egyptian Art, Greek and Roman Art, Renaissance, and Modern Art is to divide on the basis of nationality and period. To set up a department of Far Eastern Art is to divide on the basis of geography, with implied racial and cultural specifications.

To divide the field on so many different bases at once produces great overlapping,[2] as if one were to divide "flowers" into

Red flowers
Large flowers
Fragrant flowers
Flowers imported from Japan.

Theoretically, such a division is incorrect. In practice, it may raise disputes over what department should have charge of a certain object. Does a Chinese painting belong under "Painting" or under "Far Eastern Art"? Each museum has its traditional policies in such matters: for example, that "Painting" is understood to mean only modern, occidental painting. Thus a Hellenistic painting would be assigned to "Greek and Roman Art." Japanese prints may be stored with European prints, for convenience, yet remain under the control of the oriental department. If real disputes arise, they can be settled more or less arbitrarily; perhaps by the director, or perhaps because the donor of the object wishes it placed in a certain setting. Such vagueness in

[2] In Ch. IV, § 3, we noticed the overlapping between "decorative arts," "representative arts," "painting," "sculpture," and other fields.

theoretical classification makes comparatively little trouble in practice, disturbing as it may be to the aesthetician.

On the other hand, most of the philosophical classifications of the arts which we have been considering would not work very well as applied to museum collections. From the practical standpoint, different factors have to be considered. In the museum, one is not concerned primarily with arts in general, or with modes of production, or with abstract qualities of the medium. One has to classify, not "arts," but a collection of concrete objects; works of art. One has to group them for effective management in regard to display, labelling, preservation, and repair. Hence there is a tendency to group all textiles together, under one curator, because they require similar methods of storage, display, care, and mending. The type of expert available is another factor to be considered. What special ability and training are required for expertness in a certain field? For taste and knowledge of values in selecting new purchases? For labelling and interpreting to the public? Oriental art, for example, takes a special kind of training in languages and cultural history. No one person is likely to be a great expert in both oriental and occidental art. Thus there is a tendency to have one curator responsible for all oriental art, or at least for all far eastern art. Questions of jurisdiction are sure to result. Should a Persian rug be assigned to "Textiles" because of its medium, technique, and form, or to "Near Eastern Art" because of its origin? Theoretically either would be correct, and the question must be decided on practical grounds. Still another factor enters when a diversified art collection is presented to the museum on the understanding that it be kept intact. Then we may have a group of objects marked off on the basis of who gave them, as in the Benjamin Altman Collection at the Metropolitan. Museums usually prefer to break up such collections and rearrange them in combination with other objects.

As a rule, practical classifications are not carefully thought out in advance. If a new museum is established, a few traditional departments may be set up at once, such as "Painting" and "Sculpture." Afterwards, departments are created and curators appointed when enough important objects of a certain kind arrive to make them necessary. The unexpected gift of a great collection of coins and medals, or a fund for buying and caring for them, may lead to the establishment of a major Department of Coins and Medals (as in the British Museum), under its own curator. If the gift is smaller, it may be placed under "Decorative Arts," or be set aside as a minor, "Special Department", as in the case of Musical Instruments at the Metropolitan.

The need to consider so many different factors leads to an informal, compound sort of grouping. A certain field of art will be marked off for several reasons at once. It will be given a brief title which serves well enough to indicate it, but does not reveal the many considerations determining what shall be assigned to it.

Similar problems arise in the classification of lantern slides and photographs, which may run up into many thousands in a large museum. They are kept in filing cabinets, and classified on a variety of bases. Some are grouped according to technique (for example, textiles), and some according to material (ironwork, silver). Some are grouped according to period, region, or cultural stage (Egyptian, South American, Primitive). Some are grouped according to the age or type of artist (Children's Drawings; Soldiers' Drawings). As a result, one who is unacquainted with a particular slide collection will have difficulty in knowing where to look for particular items. Will a certain silver bowl be under "Silver," under "Persian Art," or under "Decorative Arts"? There is no one right way of performing such classification. In practice, it is usually a compromise between traditional theories of classification and the way in which public demand expresses itself. For example, if many teachers and students ask for slides on "Egyptian Art" or on "Portraits," and few ask for "Religious Symbolism" or "Pictorial Realism," then the headings should be adapted in some degree to the ways of thinking of those who use it. Later on, a different educational emphasis may require changes in classification.

New ways of thinking, new demands and functions give rise to new conceptual devices for expressing them. For example, there is a growing demand for educational services by the art museum, and for traveling exhibits to be circulated by it. These are expressed in the Museum of Modern Art's list of "Program" departments, as distinct from "Curatorial." Some museums now have a department of education under a "curator," by analogy with other departments, even though it has no particular works of art to care for.

If the names and groupings are too vague and inconsistent, they will work badly, creating friction within the institution, and obstructing public understanding of its exhibits and services. Philosophic systems are of use in helping to rationalize practice, by suggesting relevant names and distinctions. But these should be used with great freedom to select and adapt.

Sensitivity to changing facts and needs will produce a conceptual apparatus with its own kind of pragmatic logic. Current museum practices in classification are theoretically significant in several ways. More faithfully than philosophic systems, they reflect the great variety of interests and activities concerned with the visual arts today. The aestheticians oversimplify in reducing everything to "creation" and "appreciation." There are countless ways of dealing with art, some old and some new; some with a claim to consideration as arts in themselves. Arranging pictures on a wall, or porcelain vases in a display case, demands a good deal of artistic creativeness. Judicious collecting, labelling, installing, lighting, interpreting and explaining to different kinds of students—all these are important activities in the field of art. Each leads to a distinctive way of grouping and separating works of art; hence to a kind of classification. For example, some works of art need special conditions of humidity and temperature. Some profit by spot-lighting; others by a diffused or changing light. From the standpoint of those actually concerned, such groupings are quite as valid as the traditional one of "Fine Arts" and "Useful Arts," and are perhaps more productive under present conditions.

2. Encyclopedias and the organization of knowledge

The word "encyclopedia" in Greek meant instruction in the whole circle or system of arts and sciences. In 1538, Thomas Elyot defined it as "that lernynge whiche comprehendeth all lyberall science and studies." [3] Many encyclopedias have been organized as systematic classifications of the arts and sciences; for example, that of Schmid in Jena (1810). [4] In this sense, Bacon's *Advancement of Learning* is encyclopedic. Modern encyclopedias have ceased to be so in their final form, through adopting alphabetical order. That order is purely arbitrary and superficial, but it is most convenient in encyclopedias and dictionaries because it is easily understood. One requires no understanding of the complex interrelation of subjects in order to find an item so arranged. Early encyclopedias were not alphabetical, but arranged in some supposedly rational order. For example, in the middle

---

[3] *Encyclopaedia Britannica*, 14th ed., article "Encyclopaedia."
[4] *Allgemeine Encyklopädie und Methodologie der Wissenschaften.*

ages it was customary to begin with God and the angels, as most important. Later on, there were so many different theories of the best way to systematize knowledge that every encyclopedia was different, and it was hard for the reader to find a given topic. After 1700, attempts at methodical arrangement were gradually abandoned in favor of the alphabetical.

However, some conception of the structure of knowledge is usually implicit in the way an encyclopedia distributes its articles. The board of editors has to subdivide the branches of learning, in order to assign topics to different writers, and in order to insure a balanced survey of the whole field of knowledge. For example, the Managing Editor of the *World Book Encyclopedia*,[5] J. Morris Jones, prepared a detailed outline of this sort for the guidance of writers and departmental editors, although the outline was not intended to appear in the books themselves. In such ways as these, theories of the organization of arts and sciences have a practical use, even when they are not explicitly stated. They can be combined with alphabetical, chronological, and other modes of arrangement, so as to organize the content of social experience in various ways for various purposes.

Too much reliance on alphabetical order, ignoring the logical or theoretical, tends to produce a scattered, fragmentary kind of survey, with many unintentional gaps. When the editors of an encyclopedia go ahead with no philosophic grasp of the organization of knowledge, the result is likely to be a capricious overemphasis on trivial topics, with underemphasis on important ones, and lack of unifying cross-references. For the reader's benefit, synoptic tables showing the interrelation of topics can well be placed in an appendix. All too often, "study guides" at the end of encyclopedias are also alphabetical in arrangement, thus again ignoring the interrelation of subjects. As to the arts, such a survey can be "encyclopedic" in the present sense, while providing only isolated facts, with no clue to the interrelation of the arts. Some of our leading current encyclopedias are very faulty in this respect.

3. Library classifications; their relation to philosophic systems

The simplest way of classifying books is in alphabetical order of authors' names and of titles. This method is followed in card index

[5] For young readers. Field Enterprises, Chicago, Ill.

files, which are much used in libraries. It is most useful when one knows the exact name of the author or book desired; less so when one wants to see what is available on a general subject. Also, there are many books by unknown authors or groups of authors, or with long, cumbersome titles. So it is also helpful to classify books according to subject and general approach, such as "Painting: history of." So grouped on a shelf or in a bibliography, one can explore them without knowing particular names in advance.

A library classification is a systematic arrangement of the different kinds of books, mostly in terms of their subject-matter. The classes are divided and subdivided minutely, and each is given a distinctive symbol, usually consisting of letters and numbers. Its aim is to help the librarian arrange and label books and index cards, so that a reader can easily find the book or kind of book he wants.

Since books now cover the whole range of human experience, the physical universe and all realms of thought, any system for classifying books must be of great scope and diversity. To develop a system which will do so in a logical, organic way, so as to bring out main differences and connections of subject-matter, is a task requiring philosophic breadth and insight. Naturally, systems of library classification have been influenced by philosophic systems, especially those like Francis Bacon's *Advancement of Learning,* which attempt a comprehensive description of the branches of human thought and activity. Library scientists do not, as a rule, try to work out original philosophical systems, or invent new names for types of book and realms of thought; that would defeat the aim of being readily understandable. They try not to base their classifications on special, controversial theories, but rather to follow authoritative current usage on the names and grouping of subjects. But a good deal of adaptation is necessary to organize current philosophical, scientific, and scholarly conceptions into a usable, consistent scheme.

"A classification of books," John Dewey once remarked, "to be effective must correspond to the relationships of subject-matters, and this correspondence can be secured only as the intellectual, or conceptual organization is based upon the order inherent in the fields of knowledge, which in turn mirrors the order of nature." [6] Of course, conceptions of the order of nature vary widely from one period and

[6] Introduction to H. E. Bliss, *The Organization of Knowledge and the System of the Sciences* (New York: Henry Holt & Co., 1929), p. viii.

cultural setting to another; and even today, individual philosophers disagree about it. If libraries follow some special, controversial theory of the orders inherent in knowledge and nature, their methods will not fit the thinking of most readers. Many difficulties face the task, and no perfect classification has ever been devised. The subjects of books, and ways of describing them, are in process of constant change, with new ones appearing every year. The system must be flexible, to admit books of new and unusual kinds. Yet the names and symbols of classes should be comparatively stable, for it involves tremendous labor and expense to relabel and rearrange a large library, and it takes time for readers and librarians to learn a new system. Hence there is a tendency to hold on to the existing system, even though faulty. The situation is not as simple as it would be if one could begin from the ground up in each generation; to a large extent one must accept defective systems just because they are established, as one accepts antiquated systems of measurement. But one can at least try to see the faults, so that improvements can be made if and when they become practicable.

Since all subjects overlap, and a single book can deal with many at once, it is always possible to place a book in any of several different categories. The reader may often question whether it has been put in the best place. But, for the sake of convenience, it is usually necessary to assign it arbitrarily to some one class, and then mention it elsewhere by cross-reference.

Since many books have been written on the arts, all library systems have had to make a place for them, and to classify them in various ways. They are grouped according to arts and kinds of art, such as design; also according to the book's approach, as historical, theoretical, etc., and according to the nationality and period of artists. Grouping according to arts and kinds of art involves many of the same problems here that it does in aesthetic theory. There is less need for profound explanations, and the grouping is made more arbitrarily, with less defense or consideration of possible alternatives.

American ingenuity, which has not been much attracted to aesthetic theory, has taken a leading part in the task of devising library systems. It has thus been drawn to the problem of classifying the arts, in a practical rather than a philosophical spirit. Theoretical difficulties could not be avoided, however, and all the current library systems are faulty in their ways of classifying the arts. Of the Dewey system, an

English librarian writes, "Several sections of the scheme, notably divisions of 700 Fine Arts, have remained undeveloped through many editions, but it is hoped that the next edition will, as promised, remedy those faults." [7]

4. The Dewey and Library of Congress systems; how they classify books on the arts

The widely used library system of Melvil Dewey was constructed in 1876 on the basis of Bacon's system, in addition to those of Battezati, (a modern Italian), and W. T. Harris, of St. Louis (1870). The systems of Harris and Dewey have been described as "inverted Baconian" schemes.[8] Bacon assumed three human faculties of memory, imagination, and reason, which produced three main branches of learning: History, Poesy, and Philosophy. Inverting the order, we have Philosophy, Poesy, and History. Harris and Melvil Dewey both follow and expand this list.

The Dewey system divides knowledge into nine classes.[9] Works too general for inclusion in any of these, such as encyclopedias and periodicals, form a tenth class. The list is as follows:

0 General works
1 Filosofy
2 Religion
3 Social Sciences
4 Filology
5 Pure Science
6 Useful Arts. Applied Science
7 Fine Arts. Recreation
8 Literature. Belles-lettres
9 History

Each class is divided into nine divisions, with highly general works belonging to no division, having 0 as division number. Divisions are

[7] W. H. Phillips, *A Primer of Book Classification* (London, 1938), p. 71.

[8] W. C. Berwick Sayers, *A Manual of Classification for Librarians and Bibliographers* (London, 1926), p. 137.

[9] Melvil Dewey, *Decimal Classification and Relativ Index*. Edition 14, vol. I: *Tables*. Lake Placid, N. Y.: Forest Press, Inc., 1942. (Quotations are printed with permission of Lake Placid Club Education Foundation, Lake Placid Club, New York, owners of copyright. Simplified spelling is quoted as in text.)

divided into nine sections, and these into sub-sections and sub-subsections. After three figures a decimal point is introduced to aid the eye, and by adding figures any class is capable of indefinite subdivision.

The Library of Congress system was originated by H. Putnam, and is also widely used. It has a longer list of main classes, which are given capital letters:

A	General works
B	Philosophy. Religion
C	History—auxiliary sciences
D	History and Topography (excluding America)
E-F	America
G	Geography. Anthropology
H	Social sciences (Statistics, Economics, Sociology)
J	Political science
K	Law
L	Education
M	Music
N	Fine Arts
P	Language and Literature. Literary History
Q	Science
R	Medicine
S	Agriculture. Plant and animal industry
T	Technology
U	Military Science
V	Naval Science
Z	Bibliography and Library Science.

The order here is somewhat arbitrary, and admittedly not based on any scientific conception of the logical or evolutionary order of subjects.[10] Several letters have not yet been used, so that new main classes can be added. Since the list of main classes is not limited to ten, as in the Dewey system, it is easier to promote a class to the main level. There are twenty-six letters of the alphabet to use separately, and in addition such combinations as BL Religion and HM Sociology are sometimes regarded as main classes. Each class is subdivided by additional numbers and letters; again, not necessarily into ten parts, but into as many as desired. There is less distinction between the levels of division, and less clarity as to which group is coordinate with others.

Neither list of main classes is entirely satisfactory today, when

---

[10] Cf. B. Sayers, op. cit., p. 168; W. H. Phillips, op. cit., p. 88.

considered as a list of what subjects or groups of books are most important, most worthy to rank as primary divisions of human thought. Subjects which are minor, embryonic, and hardly recognized in one generation, can blossom into full-fledged major sciences a generation or two later. This has happened with regard to psychology, which is placed in both systems as a division of philosophy—a relationship which was true a century ago, but not today. Economics and sociology are at first mere divisions of Social Science in the Library of Congress system; and religion is a division of Philosophy. But as HB, HM, and BL, they can gradually rise to the status of main classes.

The Dewey system of division by tens appears at first sight to be more scientific, and to have the advantage of regularity which all decimal division possesses, as in the metric system. But this is partly outweighed by its rigidity in limiting division to tens on any one level. Thus it is hard if not impossible to promote any newly developed subject to the level of a main division, or from sectional to divisional status. The Library of Congress method is more arbitrary and more flexible in this regard. In fact, the Dewey system has to some extent the same fault that we have noticed in German systems of the arts: domination by a neatly regular but repressive pattern, which is hard to adapt to changing facts and ideas. What seems in one generation to be "scientific" is often an obsolete formula in the next, and an obstacle to growth if authoritatively imposed.

In any classification, as we have seen, the order of steps in division is highly important. This includes, not only the order in which different bases of division are used, but also the relative status given to any particular group, as a main class or a product of some later subdivision. Library classifications are theoretically neutral on the question of relative values; it is not implied that a main class is necessarily more important than a small subdivision. Presumably, main classes comprise a larger number of books. But in practice, it works to the advantage of a subject to be placed high up in the system, as a main class or division. This is one way of recognizing its prestige as an established discipline, about which many books are written. Whether intended or not, the suggestion is obvious that a subject which appears far down the list of divisions, or is scattered into several categories, has a less established status. Moreover, a subject which is placed as a subdivision of another seems to be regarded as a "mere branch" of that other, as if all its data, activities, and functions were comprised within that larger subject. To keep psychology as a division of philosophy, as is done in both systems, tends to obscure the new status of psychology as an experimental science in its own right, no longer limited by the methods and traditional problems of philosophy. Keeping psychology as a branch of philosophy, while "Science" (Library of Congress) or "Natural Science" (Dewey) is a separate main class, tends to obscure the new affiliations of psychology with the sciences of biology, sociology, and anthropology; also its claim to be considered as a natural science itself.

Let us grant again that mere library classification has no coercive power over people's reading or thinking. Putting books on a subject in a certain category does not force us to think about it only within that category. If it did, the situation would be more dangerous. But at the same time, classifications do have a subtle effect on habits of thinking, writing, reading, and publishing. They help to determine the kinds of book which a publisher will print; the way in which library materials are presented to authors, students, and teachers; the way in which bibliographies are grouped for reference. Library classifiers are under some pressure to follow current ways of thinking; to group books as readers group them, in asking for books on a certain subject. But such a grouping may be irrational and temporary, as in classing books on psychoanalysis as "occult," because they deal with dreams, which books on fortune-telling also do. To recognize such a grouping tends to perpetuate it, whereas a more rational, modern grouping would influence people to think accordingly.

The makers of library systems have done rightly in choosing a list of main classes as well as they could at the time, with the advice of scientists and philosophers. No such list will suit succeeding generations. Hence the system should be, if possible, flexible as regards the relative status of subjects or types of book, so that some can rise and others fall; so that some can join together from scattered sources into a new, unified, main division, and others do the opposite. Where the library system itself cannot well do this, there is correspondingly greater need for supplementary bibliographies and systematic charts of the fields of knowledge, to bring out revised conceptions of the order inherent in them and in nature.[11] This is a task which philosophers

---

[11] Cf. H. M. Kallen, "A Discussion of the Unity of Science," *Philosophy and Phenomenological Research*, VI, No. 4, pp. 493f.

could well be called upon to do, in collaboration with library scientists and educators.

How do library systems classify the *arts,* and relate them to other subjects? Both the Dewey and Library of Congress systems employ the confusing, ambiguous term "Fine Arts," but they use it in different senses. Both separate it from literature, but the Dewey system makes it include Music, while the other has Music as a separate main class. In other words, "Fine Arts" in the Library of Congress system covers only the visual arts, which is one recognized extension of the term. It is well to have them as a separate main class, although "Visual Arts" would now be a preferable name for it. There is little precedent for the Dewey system's inclusion of music but not literature. Dewey also preserves the other ambiguous, traditional term "Useful Arts," which the Library of Congress abandons. No single class takes its place in the latter system; it is split into several, including Medicine, Agriculture, Technology (in a narrow sense), Military, Naval, and Library Science. Both systems recognize without argument a distinction which philosophers have disputed: that there is a real difference between the "Fine Art" or aesthetic point of view toward certain products and the "Useful Art" or technological point of view. Many arts, such as textiles, ceramics, furniture, clock making, metalwork, and house building, are listed under both main classes: under "Useful Arts" in the Dewey system, from the standpoint of manufacturing techniques and non-aesthetic functions; and under "Fine Arts" when regarded aesthetically. Whether or not the two points of view should be separated, they evidently are to a great extent, in the actual writing of books. On the other hand, many books combine both approaches just as the arts themselves do, and there is room in the "Fine Arts" category for discussion of utilitarian techniques and functions.

The Dewey system fails to recognize aesthetics as a definite subject, or even as a branch of philosophy. The Library of Congress lists it as one of the main divisions of philosophy (BH), along with logic, metaphysics, and ethics. Both systems recognize it as applied to special fields of art: as the aesthetics of fine (visual) arts, of music, or of literature. But this is not enough; clear recognition should be given to the broader approach to aesthetics, which deals with all arts. When no main class or division or aesthetics exists, books on it are likely to be placed under "Fine Arts," which separates them unduly from

literature and perhaps from music. Even recognition as a branch of
philosophy is increasingly unsatisfactory, as aesthetics follows the lead
of psychology in becoming a separate, descriptive science.

As a major division of Philosophy in the Library of Congress
system, aesthetics (BH, Esthetics) is subdivided minutely as follows: [12]

1-8 Periodicals
11-18 Societies
19 Congresses
21-28 Collections

Theory, scope, relations

39 General
41 Special
     Theory of fine arts, see N61-79
     Theory of literature, see PN51-75

Study and teaching

61 General works
63 Particular schools, A-Z

History and systems

81 General

Antiquity

91 General
101-2 Orient
108-9 Greece
115-6 Rome

Middle Ages

131 General
136 Special

Modern

151 General
160-8 16th century
170-8 17th century
180-8 18th century
191-8 19th century
201-8 20th century

[12] Library of Congress, *Classification. Class B, Part I. B-BJ Philosophy.*
Washington, D. C., 1910.

In addition, each of the main classes "Fine Arts," "Music," and "Language and Literature" begins with a "general" division, covering problems of aesthetics, technique, criticism, etc., relevant to that special realm of art.

The Dewey system not only lacks a main division on aesthetics under "Filosofy," but relegates it under "Fine Arts" to a small subdivision, narrowly conceived. Under general works on Fine Arts, one subdivision is "701 Philosofy, Theory." Under this, "Esthetics" is 701.17, and is explained as dealing with "beauty, sublimity, grace, proportion, symmetry, rithm, pictureskness, groteskness, ugliness, taste, etc." It is made coordinate with "psicology of art, stile, tecnical methods, and art criticism," instead of covering the broader aspects of all these subjects, as in fact it does today. Under "Music" and "Literature," place is given for the aesthetics or philosophy of these subjects, but always in a relatively specialized way. In short, the place given to books on aesthetics by the Dewey system is extremely inadequate. It assumes that such books must be of narrow scope, and provides no adequate way of grouping books which deal with the subject in a broad, comparative way, including music and literature as well as the visual arts.

Concepts of great importance in general aesthetics, and in the criticism of all the arts, are mentioned as minute subdivisions under one art, then omitted elsewhere. For example, under "740 Drawing, Decoration, Design," we find

741 Freehand drawing. Illustration. Caricatures. Cartoons
    .4   Tecnic
    .41 General questions. Elements, fundamentals. Good taste, appropriate medium, mood and character of subject to be exprest.
    .43 Composition
    .432 Balance, proportion, symmetry
    .433 Sequence. Rithm
    .45 Light and shade. Chiaroscuro

"Design," which applies to all arts, appears chiefly as a subdivision of "Arts and crafts." These are explained as the arts which, "in association with the mother craft of building, go to making of the house beautiful." Little is said about the design factor in other arts, such as painting.

Fine Arts are coupled with Recreation as the heading of class 7.

This makes some strange bedfellows, and some strange omissions. The divisions of this class are as follows:

700 Fine Arts [in general]
710 Landscape and civic art
720 Architecture
730 Sculpture. Plastic arts
740 Drawing. Decoration. Design
750 Painting
760 Engraving
770 Photografy
780 Music
790 Amusements

Theater arts, dancing, and motion pictures do not appear in this divisional list. Under "Amusements," however, the following sections appear:

791 Public entertainment
792 Theater; stage; dramatic art. Theater lighting
793 Indoor entertainment; parties
794 Games of skil
795 Games of chance
796 Athletic and outdoor sports and games
797 Boating and other water sports; aerostation
798 Horsemanship, racing
799 Fishing; hunting; target shooting

All theater art is thus coordinate with a small section under Engraving, such as Line Stipple and Relief Engraving—an odd scale of relative importance, necessitated perhaps by the fact that only nine main divisions could be made under Fine Arts. Motion pictures, unknown when the Dewey system was devised, appear still farther down the ladder of subdivision. Under "791 Public entertainment," we find the following:

.1 Traveling shows
.2 Concerts. Floral games
.3 Circuses. Rodeos
.4 Panoramas. Magic lanterns. Moving pictures. Radio. (Class here general works on moving pictures as entertainment. For fotoplays see 792 Theater)
.5 Waxworks

.6 Public fêtes
.7 Public games and sports
.8 Menageries; trained animals
.9 Other

Under "792 Theater," photoplays are mentioned in a note. But they do not appear in the list of subheadings:

.1 Serious drama. Tragedy. Passion plays, miracle plays. Morality plays
.2 Comedy. Vaudeville
.3 Farce. Pantomime
.4 Opera. Lyric drama
.5 Comic opera
.6 Operetta and musical comedy
.7 Music halls
.8 Ballet. Fairy scenes. Choreografy
.9 Other

The Dewey system, it appears, is elastic at the bottom, or in allowing addition of new topics as minor decimal sub-subdivisions; but not at the top or near it, on the first few levels. The list of main branches of human culture is rigidly frozen, in a form which must have seemed dubious even when first proposed. Thus topics which do not seem of first importance appear at a high level—for example, Mausoleums, Bricabrac, Fanciwork, Photozincografy; while Serious drama, Opera, Ballet, and Artistic Dancing are tucked away in obscure, tiny pigeon-holes.

Under "793 Indoor entertainment. Parties," we come at last to "Artistic dancing":

.3 Dancing
    .32 Artistic dancing
.4 Games of action
    Blindman's buff, hot cockles, hunt the slipper
.5 Forfeit and trick games.

This may have expressed Melvil Dewey's opinion of the relative importance of opera and dancing; but is hardly adequate for so influential a means of organizing ideas as a library system.

The Library of Congress system is likewise far from perfect in

its classification of the arts. It also contains anachronisms, such as
"8600-8605 Pyrography," as a main division of "Art Applied to Industry." But its very lack of definite pattern makes it easier to revise. The
only arts now listed as main divisions of class N, Fine Arts, are

NA Architecture
NB Sculpture and related arts
NC Graphic arts in general. Drawing and design
ND Painting
NE Engraving
NK Art applied to industry. Decoration and Ornament
     Photography: see TR (under Technology)

This is a scanty list, which needs bringing up to date. Engraving
could well be placed under graphic arts. "Fine Arts" should be changed
to "Visual Arts," and several new main divisions added. Such arts as
interior design, furniture, textiles, ceramics, stage design, motion
pictures, city planning, landscape architecture, and several others
deserve to be main divisions, rather than subdivisions of "Art applied
to industry," or under some other vague heading. Photography has
many books discussing it from the aesthetic standpoint, and should not
be relegated entirely to technology. Landscape gardening appears
along with "General plant culture, including field crops; pests and
diseases," under class S, Agriculture, Plant and Animal Industry. But
it is not enough to place it in a technological context only, when it has
important aesthetic or "fine art" aspects also. That results in an
incomplete collection of books on the visual fine arts, on the shelves
devoted to them. The student must be guided far afield, into alien
technological contexts, to find some of them. All important visual skills
which have recognized aesthetic quality should at least be mentioned
under visual arts with the necessary cross-references, until the number
of books about their aesthetic quality justifies a more important
heading.

Many bases of division are used in both library systems, in classifying the arts. These are usually implicit, rather than clearly stated.
There is little consistency; different arts are subdivided on different
bases, without explanation. The Dewey system subdivides Painting,
mainly on the basis of subject represented; Literature, mainly on the
basis of language and nationality; Music, mainly on the basis of
instrument used. Some sections under Drawing and Decoration indicate

the technique or material ("Freehand, Crayon"); some indicate types of product ("Iridescent glass"); some indicate factors in pictorial form ("Perspective"). Architecture is divided according to period ("Ancient, Medieval"), and according to function ("Public, Ecclesiastical, Educational, etc.").

Doubtless the choice of a basis in each case indicates a feeling that books are actually written and called for on that basis preeminently, even though other bases might be theoretically possible. This is the practical way to proceed; but it would help if the choice of basis were explicitly explained, and other bases mentioned as also in use there. From one generation to another, different bases or organizing concepts are emphasized. In painting, there is less emphasis now on subjects represented than there was when the Dewey system first appeared.

In all complex, detailed classifications of the arts, much the same bases recur. All of them have to divide, at one time or another, in terms of medium, technique, function, form of product, etc. The important differences between systems depend on the *order* in which the various bases are used: whether as a primary or secondary basis, to determine the main classes and divisions, or on a much lower level, to distinguish minor subdivisions only. The former are applied consistently to the whole field or a large part of it; the latter are often applied only in one small area, while other, coordinate small areas are divided upon a different basis. In the Dewey system, the concept of style appears under Fine Arts as "701.16 Stile: general characteristics of Stile in art; special stiles:—impressionist, surrealist, etc." Such a concept could be a major, primary basis for classifying all books on the arts: for example, books on polyphonic music, romantic music, rococo architecture, rococo painting and textiles, etc. That would probably be unwise, because most people do not at present organize their books and reading on a basis of styles. But the fact that "style" is used as a subordinate basis of division in literature, while "language" is used as a primary basis, helps to distinguish one sytem of classification from another. The choice of a certain sequence of bases, in dividing a certain field, should be explicitly defended by the system-makers, and changed when advisable. No particular sequence can please everybody, since different people will always organize the same field in different ways. But the system should be consciously aimed at suiting a majority of readers in that field, or at some other defined objective, such as convenience in scientific research.

5. The Bliss system; its philosophical basis

Another American library scientist, Henry E. Bliss, has produced a system which is in many ways the best in existence.[13] It has been used in certain libraries since 1902, and is highly praised by other experts in the field.[14] But the tremendous task of reclassifying all the books in existence makes it hard to secure general acceptance of any new system. Features especially praised in the Bliss classification are its scholarship, which renders its groupings acceptable to specialized users; its flexibility and adaptability, shown in the large number of alternative places provided without the risk of confusion; its brevity of symbols, which are allocated in proportion to present-day bulk and importance of the literature available; and the many bases for systematic subdivision.

Bliss's classification of the arts is not highly original or wholly satisfactory. His list of main, lettered classes includes

> U Arts; Useful and Industrial
> V Fine Arts and Arts of expression (Including Indoor Recreations and Pastimes)

He thus follows the Dewey system in combining fine arts with recreation and amusement, a grouping which ignores the serious intention and content—intellectual, social, religious, and moral—of many of the arts included.[15] True, fine art has qualities in common with recreation, in that both are often regarded as leisure-time enjoyments; but the differences are enough to warrant separate main classes. Certain arts should be listed under both headings: dancing is sometimes a trivial amusement, and sometimes a serious, religious ceremonial.

[13] Bliss's philosophical approach was contained in *The Organization of Knowledge and the System of the Sciences* (New York, 1929), with a laudatory introduction by John Dewey. More practical developments followed, in *Organization of Knowledge in Libraries*, 1933; *A System of Bibliographical Classification*, 1935, 1936.

[14] For example, by the English librarian W. H. Phillips, in *A Primer of Book Classification* (London, 1938), pp. 128-137.

[15] *Cf. The Organization of Knowledge*, p. 297.

Bliss follows ancient usage in giving "Art" its broad technical meaning, as—

a method of doing or making or producing something that does not exist as such in nature.[16] . . . From the useful arts it is customary to distinguish the fine arts, in which utility is less regarded than beauty, or some kindred aesthetic quality. The fine arts deal with perceptual objects and perceptual media of expression, but also with conceptual meanings, ideals, symbols, and imaginative elements, and especially with human interests, affections, and emotions. That they are pleasurable, cultural, educative, and edifying are among their most important values. . . . As the main division, the *tectonic* arts, including Architecture, Ceramics, and other constructive arts combining aesthetic with utilitarian qualities, may be distinguished from the *Representative, Imitative,* or *Expressive* Arts, which represent, or express, the things of nature and of life, whether realistically or symbolically, with some intellectual, emotional, or aesthetic quality, and with little regard for mere utility in a physical or economic sense. . . . The term *Expressive* Arts is applied especially to Music and to Poetry and Drama, and more broadly also to all language and literature. . . . The word, or the sound, has its mental or conceptual correlate. In music this mental correlate is vague, tho still *expressional.* In painting, sculpture, and architecture, and especially in their symbolical elements, the meanings are hardly less vague and are merely *impressional* or *suggestive.* In language and literature, however, the expression is comparatively definite and precise. . . .

Objection can be made to "expressive arts" as a special division of the fine arts. All arts are expressive, in the sense of suggesting meanings, desires, emotions, concepts, and other types of experience. The statement that the meanings of painting, sculpture, and architecture are "vague, impressional, and suggestive" is far from convincing.

Bliss's more important theoretical contribution is in placing the arts within a comprehensive outline of human knowledge. He reviews the principal systems of the sciences and arts from Plato and Aristotle through Bacon, Comte, Spencer, and other moderns; then proposes one of his own, in which the "main divisions, fundamental sciences, and derivative studies" are outlined, each in relation to a branch of philosophy. The author works primarily from a set of concrete data— printed books; and toward a practical purpose—library classification; which helps to keep his feet on the ground. The divisions in the system, he says, imply conceptual distinctions but not permanent

[16] *Ibid.,* p. 295.

separations in the order of nature. As knowledge progresses, more specialized sciences will be absorbed in more general ones. Subjects are graded from the more general to the more special.

The outline or "synoptic table of the classification of knowledge" [17] is arranged in four vertical columns, headed Philosophy, Science, History, and Applied Sciences. Under Philosophy is a list of its branches, as follows:

Principles
Ontology (Reality)
Epistemology
Philosophy of Nature; Cosmology
Philosophy of Life
Philosophy of Human Life
Philosophy of Religion
Theology
Ethics
Political Philosophy; Philosophy of Law
Aesthetics; Philosophy of Art

Moving horizontally toward the right from each of these topics, we encounter first a group of sciences which investigate that realm. (For example, the "philosophy of human life" leads to a group of anthropological sciences, including anthropology, psychology, and sociology.) Farther to the right are the related historical studies; then the technologies and applied sciences, such as hygiene, medical science, applied psychology, psychiatry, and education.

The last level is as follows:

Aesthetics; Philosophy of Art	History of Arts	Technology of Arts
		Technic of Fine Arts
Philology; Linguistics		
	History of Languages and of Literatures	Grammar, Rhetoric, Oratory, and Criticism
		Dramatics

To the right of "Aesthetics," there is a blank space, indicating that no sciences yet exist in that realm, except Philology and Linguis-

[17] *Ibid.,* p. 302.

tics, which deal only with the literary arts. This is substantially true; there is no full-fledged science of aesthetics which deals with music and the visual arts. But aesthetics itself is in process of becoming such a science rather than a branch of philosophy; scientific knowledge is gradually being developed in regard to all the arts, as in the psychology of art production and appreciation, and in the physical aspects of musical and color harmony.

"Technology of Arts" and "Technic of Fine Arts" are both put under "Applied Sciences." This will arouse protest from the mystics and romantics who believe that art production is something entirely different from science—a matter of intuitive genius and inspiration. At the present time, the painter, sculptor, or composer can get along with little scientific knowledge; the architect and pottery glazer need more. But all benefit from scientific technology: for example, through improved chemical paints, tools, and instruments. Applied psychology, teaching the artist how to control human emotions, will contribute further toward making the "technic of fine arts" a kind of applied science.

Recent philosophers, in reacting away from the grandiose systems of Hegel, Herbert Spencer, and others, have tended to avoid all extensive organizations of thought; all attempts to cover the whole universe in one connected theory. On the whole, they have preferred to express their ideas in more fragmentary, specialized essays and treatises. It is interesting to note here an American exception to the rule. The scope of Bliss's outline is all-inclusive, but his aim is specific and practical. The fabric is well-knit as far as it goes, but it makes no pretense to solve underlying, metaphysical problems. Like Bacon, he is content to map the various realms of human thought, and to provide a few improved instruments for future discovery.

6. The arts in curriculum organization

Schools and colleges undertake to impart to the young the cultural heritage of arts and sciences, and of accumulated skills and wisdom in using them. Their work is divided into courses and curricula—a curriculum being traditionally defined as "the whole body of courses offered in an educational institution, or by a department thereof." One might expect, then, to find in the curricula of schools and colleges an application of the organized system of sciences and arts, as worked

out by philosophers. At least, one might expect to find a partial, simplified version of such a system, especially in schools devoted to a
general or "liberal arts" education. Specialized vocational schools and
academies, of course, would take in a relatively small area of the
system. In so far as the faculty of a school is divided into departments
such as mathematics, history, music, and the courses of study likewise,
one would expect to find the organization of teachers and courses
mirroring the division of culture into sciences and arts.

In discussing the organization of the sciences and arts, Bliss
considers various ways of arranging them. One is the "natural" or
"logical" order, in which they are graded from the more general (such
as logic and mathematics) to the more special (such as economics and
philology). Another is the "developmental" or historical order, in
which the sciences have arisen chronologically. There is some correspondence between this and the logical order, but they are not the
same. A third is the "pedagogic" order, in which the individual mind
tends to acquire knowledge. Here again, Bliss believes that there is
partial but not exact correspondence with the logical order. Primary
instruction begins with the learning of simple facts determined by the
child's early interests. "The secondary curriculum and the higher
education closely follow the logical order of the sciences and the
gradation by speciality, from mathematics to physics, to chemistry,
to biology, to psychology, and to sociology; from history to civics,
to ethics, to politics, and to economics; from languages to literatures,
and from arts to technologies." [18] However, he concedes that this
logical sequence is greatly altered in education, by the need of having
primary courses in a variety of subjects (including some highly
"special" ones such as civics), then secondary, and finally advanced
courses in the same wide range. In other words, one does not wait
until college to begin the "special" subjects. On the contrary, some
of the general ones such as logic, though simple in one sense, are not
suited to young students.

Until recently, it was taken for granted that the curriculum of
liberal education should follow on the whole the logical organization
of sciences and arts. At different times, there were different conceptions of this order, such as the "seven liberal arts" and later the
Baconian scheme, which long influenced education in the natural
sciences and humanities. As to the lower grades, it was assumed that

[18] *The Organization of Knowledge,* p. 228.

they should be devoted, not to children's present needs and interests, but to acquiring as speedily as possible the necessary tools and rudiments of adult knowledge. Thus the pedagogic order was actually shaped, to a considerable extent, in accordance with the supposed logical order.

Modern theories of the organization of knowledge have changed greatly during the last century, through the influence of Comte, Spencer, Bain, Karl Pearson, Wundt, and other philosophers discussed by Flint and Bliss. These theories have influenced curriculum organization, often without any explicit realization of the fact among educators. To a large extent, they still determine the organization of departments and courses in schools and universities.

A strong reaction has developed in recent years, however, against this influence and the whole assumption that curricula should follow a logical order of subjects. In recent textbooks on curriculum construction, there is little reference to the logical interrelation of sciences and arts. The emphasis has shifted to a more *psychological* and *functional* approach, which tries to adapt the sequence of learning experiences to the child's development, and which tries to organize teaching in less highly specialized forms.

A representative textbook of this sort, intended for prospective educational administrators, is *Curriculum Development,* by H. L. Caswell and D. S. Campbell.[19] These authors recognize "logically organized subject matter" as one of the influences which actually influence the curriculum. It results, they say, in the subdivision of broad areas of logically organized knowledge into smaller and smaller units in the family of knowledge. But educators have been trying to reduce the domination of this approach by developing fusion courses in the social studies (for example, history and geography combined), by organizing courses around specific objectives, by organizing activity curricula, and by basing courses of study on "unit" organization. All these newer approaches tend to disregard subject divisions in the sciences and arts, and to build up new units or activities, each of which may involve elements drawn from several of the traditional sciences and arts. For example, instead of teaching history by itself, geography by itself, and painting by itself, a class may embark on a project of making decorative maps and murals incorporating historical and geographic data.

[19] New York: American Book Co., 1935 (p. 38).

This is sometimes called "integration" or "correlation," but it involves more than a recombination of old subjects. The new approach involves the organization of studies from an entirely different point of view, in which the influence of John Dewey has been paramount. Instead of stressing logical organization of subjects, it stresses the growth and needs of the individual child, the present social situation, and the vocational objectives of students. It does not present whole subjects as such in any definite order. The concept of a curriculum is redefined: it should be "a series of guided experiences so related and so arranged that what is learned in one experience serves to enrich and make more valuable the experiences that follow." [20] Subject matter is to be selected for each age level, not only for its significance to an organized field of knowledge, but for its significance in understanding contemporary life, for adult use, and for the interest and use of the child.[21]

The traditional organization of subject matter on a logical basis, "in terms of relationships inherent between the facts and principles involved," comes to be regarded as a "malefic influence on instructional organization," killing the vitality of the modern curriculum with its "fatal disconnection." [22] It breaks vital knowledge into fragments, says J. H. Robinson, and acts as a barrier to the cultivation of a really scientific frame of mind. Too strict adherence to it produces educational confusion, says John Dewey, especially in a situation where the skills or arts and the subject matter of knowledge have become interwoven and interdependent.[23] However, it is conceded a place in education, especially for advanced research workers.[24] It reveals places in which knowledge is lacking or uncertain; it is useful in finding knowledge, as a library catalogue is useful. Most students are not ready to think in terms of specialized subjects before late adolescence; hence the curriculum should not be so broken down before the middle of college.[25]

[20] G. D. Strayer, *Report of the Survey of the Schools of Chicago, Illinois,* 1932.

[21] Caswell and Campbell, *op. cit.,* p. 255.

[22] *Ibid.,* pp. 275-6, quoting A. N. Whitehead.

[23] *The Way Out of Educational Confusion* (Cambridge: Harvard U. Press, 1931), p. 17.

[24] Caswell and Campbell, *op. cit.,* p. 277.

[25] *Ibid.,* p. 279.

The modern curriculum expert, then, does not recommend special courses on painting, sculpture, or "fine arts" in the lower stages of general education. Instead, he recommends lists of "pupil activities," many of which involve the visual arts: for example, making posters and wall hangings; diagramming and charting; making plaster of Paris plaques and molds; making friezes; making motion pictures; making peep shows and miniature scenes; giving shadow plays, puppet shows, and marionette performances; beautifying home and school environment.[26] In this form and not as a special subject, a great deal more visual art has recently been introduced into the public school curriculum, all along the line, than ordinarily existed there before. Under the old subject curriculum, it was crowded out by the emphasis on supposed "basic" subjects, such as mathematics and languages.

The traditional subject division persists in various aspects of curriculum construction and administration, however. It persists in assigning bibliographies for prospective teachers, on Art, Music, Industrial Arts, and Language Arts (English language and literature, handwriting, reading, spelling).[27] It persists in the list of subjects required of prospective teachers by state boards of education, and in the classification of specialized teachers of art, music, etc., in the higher grades. Large school systems have directors and supervisors of art, music, English, etc., to look out for special courses in these subjects, and for the proper incorporation of these subjects in fusion courses and cooperative projects. In addition, many of the more conservative schools and school systems are still organized on a frankly traditional, subject basis.[28]

The higher one goes on the ladder of age-levels, the more one is likely to encounter subject division into particular sciences and arts. In the first two years of college, comprehensive "orientation courses" often cut across subject lines; but for the last two years, the student is always allowed to specialize in terms of subjects. Hence the curriculum offers him a list of recognized subjects to choose from. When curricu-

[26] *Ibid.*, quoting *Tentative Course of Study for Virginia Elementary Schools*, State Board of Education, 1934.

[27] *Ibid.*, p. 523.

[28] The struggle between various theories of curriculum construction in secondary, general education is summarized in "U. S. High School," *Life*, April 22, 1946. The "Harvard Plan" and the "National Education Association Plan" are contrasted.

lum-planners undertake to give a balanced, diversified acquaintance with human culture, they encounter the problem of its main divisions. This is one statement of objectives: "At the terminal point of his college career, in addition to accomplishment in his chosen field, the student should have a reasonable acquaintance with the subject matter and skill, together with interest and appreciation, with respect to: the world in which we live, including both organic and inorganic, animate and inanimate; the realm of personal and social relationships; the literary, linguistic and artistic products by our civilization; and the tools necessarily involved in the acquisition of these." [29] Students should be acquainted with "the major resources for intellectual and aesthetic enjoyment, that they may know nature, literature, music and the fine arts sufficiently to choose superior to inferior enjoyments." They should acquire "knowledge of fundamentals in each of the four following fields: Natural Science; Social Science; Language and Literature; Fine Arts." [30]

Such reference to main fields in culture implies awareness of the organized interrelation of sciences and arts. Any attempt to discuss the arts in detail, however, soon becomes entangled in problems of terminology and grouping. Hitherto, the visual arts have played so slight a part in the liberal college curriculum that there has been little need for subdivision. One course on "The History and Appreciation of Art" has often sufficed, and even this is often lacking. College art instruction is now developing rapidly, and this is raising the question of how best to subdivide and organize it: whether on a historical, a creative, a critical, or some other basis. Also, it raises questions as to the relation between visual and other arts.

In the Harvard Report on *General Education in a Free Society*,[31] Chapter IV deals with "Areas of General Education; the Secondary Schools." Three principal areas are listed: "The Humanities," "The Social Studies," "Science and Mathematics." The Humanities are made to include English and "The Arts." "By the arts," say the authors, "we mean chiefly music, painting, drawing, and modeling. We do not of course deny the value of the dance, architecture, and the rest of the arts; but we are now concerned with general education in

[29] Rollins College: *Report of the Curriculum Conference* (Winter Park, Fla., 1931), p. 11.

[30] *Ibid.*, p. 37.

[31] Cambridge: Harvard U. Press (1945), p. 103 (by P. H. Buck and others).

the schools and with what has been and can be usually taught there. . . . The happiness of . . . people will be enhanced or diminished by the presence or absence of aesthetic sensitivity to music and the fine arts, as well as to literature." Thus music and literature are arts, but not "fine arts." The term "fine arts" is used interchangeably with "visual arts." In "General Education in Harvard College" (Ch. V), a prominent place is again given to "The Humanities." They are again distinguished from the social studies and science. (In an earlier day, as we have seen, the humanities included sciences dealing with man and nature, as distinguished from theology). The humanities now are to include, not only English, but "Great Texts of Literature," comparative literature, philosophy, the fine arts, and music. "The claim for the fine arts in general education rests on several assumptions: first, that the function of education is to develop our faculties of perception and understanding; second, that works experienced visually (architecture, sculpture, and painting) are a significant part of human culture." [32] Few students "have ever been exposed to the visual arts"; hence the college should acquaint "as many students as possible with the visual arts through a systematic introduction in the classroom."

Concepts implying classification of the arts, and the relation of arts to sciences, are thus still active in discussions of the college and secondary school curriculum, in spite of the tendency to disregard "logical subject organization" on lower levels of the curriculum.

Even where the curriculum is planned mainly in terms of activities and experiences, it is well for the educational planner to have an understanding of "logical subject organization" in the back of his head, so as to be aware of what is going into the melting pot of fusion courses and compound units. The subjects as such may not appear in the resultant curriculum, but the educator should be aware of them as a classified list of possible ingredients, and as another way of organizing experience on advanced intellectual levels. In this way, aesthetics may contribute indirectly to the subject of curriculum construction, by offering the educator an improved logical system of the arts and sciences. The latter may refer to it for his own intellectual clarification, without following it directly in subdividing instruction. Without such clear understanding of relationships inherent in the arts as adult activities and products, the educator is more likely to err in

[32] *Ibid.*, p. 211.

omitting important areas, and in neglecting important ways of integrating artistic with other factors in a diversified experience.

The "experiences" and "activities" which are built up and managed by the modern teacher in collaboration with his students are not altogether new in kind. They are returns from the highly specialized attitudes of modern adults toward art and sciences to something more simple and undifferentiated, resembling in some ways the condition of the arts and sciences themselves in an earlier day. This regression is on the whole a wise and invigorating step, bringing the experiences of art closer to the interests and abilities of young students. But it should not be too sharply opposed to the logical organization of arts and sciences, which can also be made realistic and functional for other realms of activity. When teachers and curriculum builders think too exclusively in terms of activities and units, regulated only by such shifting frames of reference as "child interests" and "social situations," they are in danger of reacting to the opposite extreme from academic discipline. They risk a new kind of confusion, by substituting detached episodes for systematic progress in a subject, erratic versatility for habits of perseverance and rational synthesis. Both extremes can be avoided, if the "activity" approach is made to lead gradually toward a more intellectual grasp in terms of logical relationships and systematic techniques, for students capable of learning them.

"Progressive education" is sometimes charged with neglecting content or subject matter, through excessive concern with classroom methods and the child's personality. This is usually untrue, but happens in extreme cases. When facts and skills are acquired in a series of diverse experiences, they may lack continuity in the student's mind, never achieving the logical organization which gives them stability and broad significance. They may acquire only a personal, episodic sort of organization, in terms of one immediate situation after another. More stable, generalized ways of integrating facts and skills are demanded on a higher intellectual level, including logical, chronological, and geographical orders. Their acquirement, as modes of integrating successive experiences, should not be too long delayed. Also, the natural desire of capable students for intensive, specialized progress in a single subject should not be always sacrificed to the "enrichment" or diversification of present activities.

A desirable curriculum on the higher levels of general education is one which follows to some extent the logical organization of subject matter; which gives the student some opportunity to grasp the interrelation of arts and sciences in modern culture, and to specialize somewhat along subject lines. This is not the only principle which should be followed in curriculum organization, but it is one of them. It should be flexibly combined with other approaches to contemporary life, thus cutting across subject lines. Even in the "orientation" courses, which avoid and correct excessive specialization, the logical organization of subjects can be presented. One kind of orientation course attempts to give the student a comprehensive picture of the interrelations between the arts and sciences. Another approaches contemporary civilization historically. A third selects certain major conditions and problems of the modern world, such as those encountered in city planning, and analyzes them without regard to traditional subject barriers.

This compromise and adjustment of approaches is now being worked out in the curricula of modern universities. They follow subject divisions to some extent, in the arts and elsewhere, but not exclusively. A glance at the titles of particular courses in a large university will reveal several bases of division and classification. The following examples are drawn from Columbia University *Bulletins of Information,* including those of Barnard and Teachers Colleges.

Theoretical classifications of the arts are expressed in titles of departments such as Fine Arts and Archaeology; Drama; Music. Architecture has its own entire professional school. Music is combined with Fine Arts and Archaeology to make a university division, an administrative unit larger than a department. Distinction between arts or groups of arts is not the only basis. In combining Archaeology with Fine Arts, the university adds a historical science, and indicates that the approach of this combined department is to a considerable extent historical. Teachers College combines "Fine and Industrial Arts," and treats "Music and Music Education" as a separate department.

In regard to literature, divisions between the arts are usually subordinated to divisions between languages—the specific mediums of literary art. There is rarely a college department of poetry, or even a course on poetry in general. (Philosophy, at Barnard, includes a course on "The Aesthetics of Poetry and Prose.") The primary division is usually made on the basis of the language employed, as English, French or Romance Languages, German or Germanic Languages

and Literatures, Greek and Latin or Classical Languages and Literatures, etc. This splits the art of literature into widely separate fields.
A counter-trend is the development of departments and courses in
Comparative Literature, using translated texts. In these, the courses
may be divided according to art or type of form (Drama, Epics, etc.),
or according to period and culture (Oriental Literature, Renaissance
Literature, etc.).

Subdivision into particular courses within a department is made
on many different bases, of which these are the most frequent:

(a) *Historical; chronological; biographical:* For example, Ancient
Art; Islamic Art; Chaucer and his Times; Medieval Fiction; Baroque
Music.

(b) *Theoretical; types of form or design in a certain art; principles; criticism and appreciation:* For example, Fundamentals of
Design (in Fine Arts); Design and Style in Music; Music in General Culture; The Reading and Criticism of Literature.

(c) *Techniques; methods of production and performance; practice of the arts:* For example, Harmony; Composition; Orchestration
(in Music); [33] Elementary Piano; Water Color Painting; Weaving;
Acting; Creative Writing; Radio Workshop.

(d) *Teaching the arts; educational methods on various age
levels:* For example, Teaching and Supervision of Instrumental Music;
Teaching of Art in the Elementary School; Teaching of English Composition in Secondary Schools.

The educational problem of subdividing instruction in the arts
is thus complicated by several factors which do not arise in the
theoretical classification of the arts. In addition to grouping and dividing the arts themselves, according to medium, technique, form, etc.,
the educator must organize them according to *different approaches and
age levels.* He must distinguish between the teaching of music or English composition on the elementary level and that on the secondary
or college level. There are also courses for prospective teachers, on
how to teach a particular art to a particular age group of students.

[33] Such studies in music are commonly classed as "theory," in contrast with
instrumental or vocal practice. But they are usually taught as part of the technique
of composition; not as "pure theory," for the sake of understanding and appreciation.

The educator must mark off some courses on a historical basis, and some on a theoretical or practical basis, in dealing with the same art or group of arts. The choice of bases is determined by the dominant aim of the school and the interests of teachers and students; for example, in a professional art or music academy, practice courses will dominate. In a liberal arts college, history and appreciation usually dominate. These aims and interests determine not only the division of subject matter into courses, but the organization and emphasis within each course. Since there are many such bases to be considered in education, no one of them is often carried very far. Subdivision of the arts now tends to be rather vague and rough, without clear definition of class names or indication of the basis on which division is being made. As instruction in the arts develops, more careful study will have to be given to the question of how they can best be subdivided into courses, groups, and sequences of courses.[34]

[34] Instruction in the arts on various levels is discussed more fully in the author's *Art Education: Its Philosophy and Psychology* (New York: Liberal Arts Press; Bobbs-Merrill Co., 1956).

Comparing the Arts as to Material or Medium

1. Bases of classification

Having traced in historical sequence the principal philosophical systems of the arts, let us now look more carefully at the concepts which are used to build such systems, and to compare the arts in less systematic ways. These are called *bases* or *principles* of classification and division.[1]

What is a "basis" for classifying the arts? It is some highly general kind of characteristic, which is said to occur in all or many arts, and in regard to which the arts are said to resemble or differ from each other. Just as animals are contrasted in terms of their circulatory system, food, habitat, etc., arts are contrasted in terms of medium, process of manufacture, sense addressed, etc.

At the end of Chapter IV, we began the survey of bases used in classifying the arts. The study of "fine" and "useful" arts led us there to observe three bases frequently used: (a) the nature and intended functions of the product; (b) the sense primarily addressed; (c) the process involved in production or performance. We saw that these bases could be used in different orders, resulting in different schemes of classification. More extensive study of German systems of the arts has provided us with several additional bases, and with some understanding of how they have been used.

---

[1] The reader is reminded that these terms are slightly different in meaning. "Classification" refers to the grouping of particulars and small groups under larger headings; "division" to separating large groups into smaller groups and particulars. "Division" is more accurate to describe the process by which art or fine art is broken down into various subdivisions, and it is used more by German theorists. "Classification of the arts" is more familiar in English, and we shall continue to use it. The outcome of both processes may be identical, and the same concepts are used as bases in both. R. F. Piper, in "Classification of the Arts," *Encyclopedia of the Arts* (New York, 1946), p. 229, calls them "principles of classification." We shall call them "bases," as closer to the logical term *fundamentum divisionis,* and as distinguishing them from the logical principles or rules of classification in general.

Our present aim in examining these bases systematically is to gain a clearer view of the possible ways of comparing the arts—the grounds on which resemblances and differences can be noted—and also to see the uses and limitations of each basis. No one is completely adequate by itself. Each can lead us a certain distance in bringing out important resemblances and differences; then it becomes less significant as a tool of comparison. Taking up another, we are led along another path of exploration through the arts, which also has its limits. Each has its practical as well as theoretical uses. Each expresses and results from a certain attitude toward the arts; a certain way of being interested in them. Each can be used by itself, to make a separate, brief classification of the arts. As a rule, several are used in combination, either (a) one after another in different steps of a topical outline, or (b) simultaneously as different coordinates, vertical and horizontal, of a chart such as that of Urries y Azara. We shall go on to consider the advantages and disadvantages of using each by itself, and of combining them in various ways.

In considering these concepts one after another, we shall often have to deny the claims which have been made for them; to deny that they are adequate for a systematic division of the arts. This will not imply a completely negative attitude toward them. Many of them serve very well to distinguish certain arts from each other, if not all arts. Many of them are suggestive as hypotheses along other lines. They may point out enlightening contrasts between various types of art, or various types of artist, if not between whole arts as such. Besides examining the bases already proposed, we shall attempt some further distinctions under each main heading.

2. The nature of the medium

This is one of the commonest bases for naming, defining and classifying the arts. It leads to such concepts of particular arts as "painting," "jewelry," "metalry," and "ceramics." It is seldom omitted in systematic classification, although some philosophers minimize it as superficial. Bosanquet, on the other hand, emphasizes physical material as powerful in determining the course of artistic creation. Through working in a certain medium, he says, the artist learns to love and cultivate its qualities, such as those of wood, clay, and iron.[2]

[2] *Three Lectures on Aesthetic,* p. 58.

In the definition of an art, its materials are usually mentioned. Thus J. A. Symonds says that "sculpture employs stone, wood, clay, the precious metals, to model forms, detached and independent, or raised upon a flat surface in relief." [3] "Each of the arts," he remarks in general, "employs a special medium, obeying the laws of beauty proper to that medium. The vehicles of the arts, roughly speaking, are solid substances (like ivory, stone, wood, metal), pigments, sounds, and words. The masterly handling of these vehicles and the realization of their characteristic types of beauty have come to be regarded as the craftsman's paramount concern."

This way of classifying the arts, and courses of instruction, books, equipment, lantern slides, etc., for studying them, is especially suited to the interests of the practicing artist and to those of the student and teacher of artistic techniques. It is important for them to learn, by direct handling as well as by information, the special properties of the materials they wish to control—what effects can be secured with them, and how; what obstacles and dangers occur; what effects are easiest, and what ones hard or impossible.

The mediums of art have been classified in different ways. Kant, as we have seen, began with the idea that three modes of expression enter into spoken communication: word, gesture, and tone. By analogy, he grouped the fine arts as arts of speech, plastic or shaping arts, and arts of the beautiful play of sensation. "Gesture," as applied to the shaping (bildenden) arts, includes the movements of a sculptor in carving or a painter in painting. Kant did not emphasize the directly exhibited gestures of dancing, but allowed for them in mentioning dance as a combined art. Dessoir concludes his chapter on the system of the arts by declaring, "In gestures, tones, words, abstract spatial forms and images, we have the languages in which art speaks. It is by these means of expression that its individuality is principally determined." [4] In his later chapters on particular arts, music, mimic dance, and theater arts are grouped together as using tone and gesture; the branches of literature are grouped under "word art"; architecture, sculpture, painting, and graphic arts under "space art" (Raumkunst) and "form" or "image art" (Bildkunst). This rough division is adequate to organize a survey, and Dessoir is quite aware of the many

[3] "The Provinces of the Several Arts," *Essays Speculative and Suggestive* (London: Chapman & Hall, 1890), I, 124f.

[4] *Aesthetik und allgemeine Kunstwissenschaft,* p. 261.

overlappings: for example, that space and solid shape enter into dance and theater as well as into "plastic art."

In applying this basis of classification, one soon encounters difficulties. There are several different interpretations of "medium" and "material," and each of them divides the arts in a different way. Are they to be understood in a strictly *physical* sense (as stone, pigment, etc.) or in a *psychological* sense as well? [5] Both are used in referring to the materials of art; in saying that sensory images, desires, and emotions are materials for poetry, we are using "materials" in a broad sense, including psychological data. Since the concept of "medium" is interpreted in several different ways, it covers several different bases of division.

3. Physical materials and instruments

Let us think for a moment of what happens if we interpret "medium" or "material" in a strictly physical sense, as the kind of matter out of which a work of art is made. It seems to work fairly well in distinguishing between some of the visual arts: for example, between ceramics (using clay), glass-making (glass), metalry (metals), goldsmithing (gold), etc. The art of painting is likewise divided into oil painting, water-color painting, and so on, in terms of physical materials. Light waves which a picture reflects to the eyes, and sound waves which a piano sends to the ears, are physical phenomena though not materials. As part of the physical medium, they help distinguish visual from auditory arts.

The term "raw materials" is applied to materials in a comparatively crude, unprocessed state, before the artist has organized them. Paint in tubes, pails, or lumps of pigment is a raw material in this sense, even though the paint manufacturer has given it a complex chemical form. The idea of "rawness" is always somewhat relative, expressing a contrast between the material as a particular artist begins

---

[5] "Medium" is defined by Webster (def. 3) as "That through or by which anything is accomplished, conveyed, or carried on; an intermediate means or channel; instrumentality; as, an advertising medium." "Material" is not necessarily physical matter; it can be "The substance or substances, or the parts, goods, stock, or the like, of which anything is composed or may be made; as, raw materials . . . Data of any sort, such as notes, documents, sketches, etc., which may be worked up into a more finished form; . . . The apparatus or implements necessary to the doing of anything; as, writing materials."

to use it, and as he finishes with it. In manufacturing, some materials are called "semi-processed." This too is relative, but useful to designate an intermediate stage. Spools of thread and bolts of cloth are semi-processed by comparison with bales of cotton, but they constitute raw materials for the dress-maker. Some artists deal with materials in various stages of processing. An interior designer may arrange finished or completely "processed" pieces of furniture, or may direct the building and upholstering of the furniture itself, from samples of textiles, wood, and metal.

Volkelt expressed this difference between the arts, with somewhat unnecessary elaborateness, by classifying them as "arts with formation of the first order" and "arts with formation of the second order." Sculpture and painting, using relatively unformed materials, illustrate the first type; while the dance and garden art, using human bodies and plants, illustrate the second. Poetry, using words, is of the second order, while music, using tonal material, is of the first order. (This last is debatable, since the musical tones which a composer arranges have been previously organized into scales, definite instrumental timbres, etc.) Volkelt's division into two distinct classes of arts on this basis is too simple and rigid; there are many intermediate gradations, and various practices within a given art. But it is significant to ask, in regard to a particular artist's work, in just what stage of development he received his materials, and in what stage he left them. Sometimes an author or composer—Shakespeare and Liszt, for example—takes existing tales or folksongs and reorganizes them. A city planner thinks in terms of complete houses and even districts. It is significant, by contrast, that painting, sculpture, and many crafts begin with physical materials in a very crude condition, and that one artist may carry them through to completion.

Besides raw and semi-processed materials, the concept of physical medium is often made to include *instruments and tools*. The sculptor's medium then includes his chisel as well as his marble. The musician's medium is his piano or violin, with the specific kind of tones that come from it, rather than "sound" or "tone" in general. Thus music has been described as "the scraping of horsehair on catgut." A composer is likely to write for piano, or orchestra, soprano voice, or some other particular medium. Performer and composer both have to learn to use this particular medium of expression. It is always physical in basis, whether violin or vocal cords, and it is usually a complex mechanism.

In this sense, the modern musician uses highly organized materials, such as a piano or a pipe organ. Some arts, such as motion pictures, use even more complex instruments. Some are variable and changing in this respect; the Indian potter still uses simple tools, while pottery as an urban art uses electric kilns and scientific measuring devices. Some instruments are peculiar to certain arts (as the violin is to music), while others are used in many arts—the voice in music and drama; the brush in painting and pottery; the mallet in sculpture and architecture.

Human bodies are indeed the principal physical medium of the dance, of song, and of dramatic acting. The appearance, manner, voice and personality of the performer are vital parts of the medium on which the composer, dramatist or choreographer has to depend. They are psychological as well as physical, and only partly subject to his control. In the theater, the stage director's art is more directly responsible for them. Animal breeding uses animal bodies as its medium, often with aesthetic aims, as in decorative birds and goldfish.

A distinction can sometimes be made, then, between arts which use simple physical materials and those which use complex ones; also between those which use only inanimate materials and those which use living plants, animals, or humans. In other cases the distinction is hard to make, because of the variety of materials and tools used within a given art, and the recurrence of certain ones in different arts.

Every art uses more than one physical material, even when it emphasizes one in particular and is named after it. Ceramics uses not only clay but glazes and other coloring materials. Some arts use a great number of materials: especially architecture, furniture, and costume. Many arts today are using new materials—plastics, synthetics, photographic film, fluorescent lights, etc. A classification of these arts on a basis of materials used would be short-lived as well as cumbersome.

Some materials have comparatively few different artistic uses— diamonds, for example. It is then more correct to speak of *the* art of diamond-cutting. In simple, primitive cultures, each material is used in comparatively few ways, so one can speak more correctly of the art of ceramics or pottery, the art of metalry, and so on. But today, each of a long list of materials is used in many different arts. Wood is used in sculptural wood-carving, architecture, furniture, utensils, violins, and in making wood engravings, block-printed textiles, and countless other products. There is thus no single art of wood-working. Paint, of course, is also used in many arts and manufactures. To speak of "the art of painting" or even "the art of oil painting" is ambiguous unless the context indicates some particular kind of product, such as the painting of pictures rather than houses.

To classify arts in terms of physical material tends to obscure the fact that similar types of product can be made in very different materials. There is a kinship, in terms of aesthetic form, between all sorts of pictorial representation, whether made in paints, ink, mosaic, tapestry, enamel, stained glass, colored sand, or photographic film. Dividing the arts on a basis of physical material widely separates these types of picture-making, in practice as well as in theory. It influences schools to teach them in separate courses of study, and museums to store examples of them in separate galleries, so that comparison between them is difficult, and each is regarded in a more isolated way.

In classifying the arts on a basis of medium, we sometimes change the meaning of "medium," almost unconsciously, to fit the facts. Because the specific material seems important in the case of painting, sculpture, and the crafts, we distinguish them on that basis. Because it seems less important or distinctive in the case of music and literature, we ignore the physical material and think of "medium" in a more psychological sense. Music is sometimes distinguished as the art which uses *tones,* and literature as that which uses *words.* Both of these concepts involve a psychological element. Musical tones are not merely sound-waves of a certain frequency, but sound-waves as humanly experienced, with qualities such as pitch and timbre.[6] Words are said to be the medium of literature; but words are not merely physical objects. The meaning of a word or a poem usually remains unchanged, regardless of the particular material in which it is written, engraved, or sounded. By social usage, the same or almost the same meaning is attached to several different symbols, which are different in sensory qualities as well as in material: to equivalent words in different languages, and to visible characters of different shapes. The art of literature is named in terms of one set of these symbols—letters; but they are not the only possible medium of literary art. Physical materials to give off light or sound waves have to be used in literature, as in any art, but the particular substance used is optional, variable, and

---

[6] "tone": "Vocal or musical sound, or esp. sound quality; a sound considered as of this or that character; as . . . a low, high, loud, soft, sweet, or harsh tone" (Webster).

of no significance in distinguishing literature as an art. When we shift to a psychological interpretation of "medium" in discussing literature and music, we are conforming to fact, but our basis of classification becomes somewhat inconsistent and illogical.

4. Medium as presented sensory images

To make the comparison more consistent, and rise above the overwhelming multiplicity of physical materials used, the attempt is sometimes made to put the whole concept of medium on a more abstract, psychological basis. Thus painting is said to use *color* rather than pigments; and sculpture *solid shape,* rather than marble or bronze. The concept of "color," like that of musical tone, implies a kind of sensory image, which may be produced by many different external agencies. In classifying the various arts according to medium, we can thus ignore physical material, and try to list instead various groups of abstract qualities with which each art is peculiarly concerned. Thus the medium of painting is said to include, not only color, but line, light and dark, and other visual qualities.[7] This leads us off on an entirely different line of thought, and results in a very different kind of classification. Aristotle's *Poetics* begins in this way, by distinguishing certain arts which represent "through the medium of color and form (σχήμασι), or by the voice," from those which use "rhythm, language, or harmony."

As experienced in art and elsewhere, sense qualities are usually "affect-laden," or mixed with emotional response. For example, a sound is experienced not only as high or low, but as harsh, melodious, or the like.[8] In seeking to analyze art form into its basic psychological elements, some theorists have tried to eliminate affects, and distinguish various types of sense image or percept. These are sometimes called "art elements," and sometimes "components in aesthetic form." [9]

As such, they are sometimes distinguished from the "medium" of an art (conceived as its physical material), and sometimes included under the heading of medium. T. M. Greene makes a distinction

[7] *Cf.* Schasler's distinction between material and means or medium. Also J. Dewey, *Art as Experience,* Chs. IX, X.

[8] Roger Fry calls rhythm, light, mass, color, etc., "emotional elements of design" (*Vision and Design.* London, 1920), p. 33.

[9] T. Munro, "Form in the Arts," *Journal of Aesthetics* (Fall, 1943), p. 11.

between "primary and secondary media," the former being the "partly or wholly sensuous medium which is directly manipulated by the artist." [10] "The primary medium of architecture," he says, "is three-dimensional solids and voids." "The sensuous medium of sculpture is a three-dimensional solid, that of painting, a two-dimensional surface. . . . The primary medium of literature is words in meaningful relation." The musical composer's primary artistic medium (as distinguished from his raw material, which is sound and silence) "consists of readily producible sounds organized into a system of musically related tones expressible in a scale." However, Greene goes on to list the primary sculptural mediums in terms of physical material: "various types of stone, metal, and wood, ivory, porcelain, stucco, etc."

The problem of analyzing all the forms of art into various types of sensory quality is a complicated one in itself, and no specific list has yet attained acceptance. There remains the problem of deciding which group of sense-qualities each art is most concerned with. Obviously, they overlap a good deal. Just as wood and stone occur in many arts, color and solid shape occur in many: in architecture, sculpture, and furniture, for example. Certain auditory qualities such as rhythm and timbre occur in both music and literature, especially when the latter is spoken aloud. Thus abstract sensory qualities do not provide any clear and simple basis for dividing the arts.

In seeking to classify the sensory qualities themselves, we naturally think in terms of the various sense organs which perceive them. We think of visual and auditory qualities or images, and of those derived from the "lower" senses: tactile, olfactory, and gustatory qualities. Color (including hue, value, and chroma), linear, surface, and solid shape, are recognized attributes of visual experience, or types of visual image. (Solid shape can also be perceived by touch, but we learn to perceive it visually through association and inference.) This approach leads to a widely used basis for classifying the arts—that of the *sense primarily addressed*. On this basis, as we have seen, the arts are grouped as visual (or optic), auditory (or acoustic), and audio-visual (or optic-acoustic). We shall consider this again later, in relation to the nature of the finished art product; as a question of how the work of art is presented to the observer. Here the names of the

[10] *The Arts and the Art of Criticism* (Princeton University Press, 1940), pp. 35f.

various senses come in as a way of classifying types of sense-quality; hence as helping to classify the arts in terms of medium. Visual arts are those in which directly perceived visual qualities such as color and line are emphasized; auditory arts are those in which pitch, rhythm, and other auditory qualities are emphasized, and so on. Within these groups, one can try to specify more exactly: for example, that architecture is concerned with solid shapes and voids or empty spaces; sculpture also with solids, but not so much with empty spaces, especially internal, enclosed ones.

At this point, literature again appears as a stumbling-block to the system-builder. In saying that painting and architecture are visual arts, and music auditory, we have been referring to *directly perceptible or presented* qualities. Line, light-and-dark, color, are directly visible in the picture, statue, and building; pitch and rhythm are directly audible in the symphony. They are not all perceptible in the raw, unformed physical material; line, for example, does not appear in the paint until it is shaped. But they do appear in the finished product in such elementary, widely distributed ways as to be considered qualities of the artistic medium itself; as basic means which the artist manipulates. Now, what of literature? It is sometimes called an auditory art, because it was at first entirely oral and is still often spoken aloud.[11] But it is now experienced visually to an increasing degree; much more than aurally, by educated people. Shall we then call it visual, or audio-visual? But no specific visual qualities are essential to literary form, in the same way that they are essential to painting. The letters may be in any color, and with much variation in visual shape, or even translated into Braille type for tactile perception, without substantially altering the literary product. When poetry is spoken aloud, its auditory qualities are directly presented to the hearer and perceived by him, as essential elements in the poem. Otherwise, they are *suggested* rather than directly presented; *imagined* rather than perceived by the reader. If, by "medium" we mean presented or directly perceptible qualities, then this concept does not work very well when we get to literature. We cannot say that any particular group of such qualities is characteristic of literature, as we have in regard to the other arts. We can only say that they are optional and extremely variable. This basis of division does not help us at all in

[11] *Cf.* Dewey, *Art as Experience,* p. 218.

distinguishing lyric, epic, and dramatic poetry from each other, and these branches of literature are often considered as separate arts.

To retain the concept of "medium" as a basis of division, one is tempted to shift its meaning again, so as to imply *suggested* as well as presented sensory qualities. Says Volkelt:

> Hitherto sensory perception has been regarded only as sensation; we must think of it also as imaginary sensory perception. There are also such things as imaginary seeing, imaginary hearing, imaginary tactile feeling. Artistic creation can lead representation and emotional content, not into sensory perception of sensation, but into imaginary sensory perception.[12]

We then find ourselves describing literature as an art of highly diversified sense imagery, including tactile, olfactory, and other types of image. And why stop there? Literature can also suggest emotions, desires, concepts, inferences, and every other type of experience. But what has happened to our concept of "medium"? It has now expanded to include all kinds of suggested meaning in the work of art, including objects and persons represented.

5. Medium as including suggested subject-matter

With this new conception of medium, we should now go back and reconsider what was said about the other arts. Is it correct to say that the medium of painting is visual, and that of music auditory? Painting can suggest a wide range of non-visual experiences; music can suggest visual scenes, emotions, conative attitudes, and so on.

This course is explicitly taken by T. M. Greene, in expanding the conception of medium to include what he calls the "secondary artistic medium." [13] This is "the subject-matter whose interpretation achieves artistic expression only indirectly through the organization of the primary medium." Consistently, he tries to characterize each of the arts on this basis. "The secondary medium or subject-matter of pure music is human emotion and conation." That of the non-mimetic dance, "like that of music, is human emotion and conation." Evidently, the concept of secondary medium does not serve to distinguish music from non-mimetic dancing. As to literature, its primary medium

[12] *Op. cit.,* p. 387.
[13] *Op. cit.,* pp. 35f.

includes "the meanings of words used singly and in combination." "The referential meanings of words refer us to 'objects' of one type or another which, in aggregate, constitute the potential subject-matter or secondary medium of literature. This medium is much more extensive and varied than that of any of the other arts. . . . The chief subject-matter of architecture is man's social activities which require to be housed. Sculpture lends itself best to the representation of the human body, and even painting can directly represent only the visible world of nature." But is this consistent, or fair to the visual arts? As to the dance, music, and literature, we were not restricting their subject-matter to what could be "directly represented," but including all sorts of indirect expression of "inner emotional states and attitudes." Now, if we are going to admit all these, painting and sculpture also have the right to enlarge their claims. Do the sculptures of Chartres Cathedral merely "represent the human body," or do they suggest a whole universe of medieval thought and feeling? Do the paintings of Giotto, Michelangelo, and Greco merely "represent the visible world of nature," or do they suggest a great deal more? Of course, the latter is true, and these arts are not so different from literature in range of subject-matter as Greene would have us believe. The suggestive or expressive range of architecture, too, can not fairly be limited to the social activities which it houses. Once again, the cathedral as an architectural form has an almost limitless diversity of expression.

When we look at the facts in this way, it appears that the greatly expanded conception of medium succeeds even less than the narrower conceptions, in distinguishing the major arts from each other. Each can, in one way or another, suggest so many different types of human experience that there is no ground for sharp distinction.[14]

6. Technological properties of the medium

There is always something lost in expanding a somewhat narrow, specific concept into a very inclusive one. When we enlarge the mean-

[14] Greene concedes (p. 44) that "each art can, in one way or another, treat of each of the generic types of subject-matter," but insists that "different types are basic to different arts." There is certainly a difference in emphasis; but Greene's "basic types" give too narrow a conception of the range of each art, as in saying that "the basic subject-matter of sculpture is the human body in motion and at rest."

ing of "medium" to include the whole range of ideas, desires, and emotions which an artist can suggest, we make the term less useful in its original context. Even with the qualifications "primary" and "secondary," so broad a conception of medium tends to obscure a valuable distinction contained in the term's usual, more restricted meaning. This is the difference between a medium as "that through which anything is conveyed" and the ideas or experiences which are conveyed by it. An Indian, for example, can convey a warning of danger through the medium of smoke-signals. There the medium or means and the message conveyed are quite distinct. There is also another useful distinction, between medium in the sense of raw material (for example, a block of marble) and the organized form which appears in the statue.[15]

The observer and critic of art does not have to deal with the "primary" medium or raw material of art apart from the finished form. From his point of view, the distinction may well seem unimportant. The medium now appears as an integral part of the form itself: the marble, the words, the tones, the colors, are not left behind, but have ceased to be mere means or raw materials, and are now experienced as essential parts of the total effect. He tends to forget about the qualities which the medium may have had *before* the artist dealt with it, and to stress the qualities which it takes on in the finished product. This attitude helps to motivate some of the changed conceptions of medium which we have just been considering: those which define a medium in terms of abstract sensory and other qualities, as experienced in the work of art or suggested by it. Paint is experienced as something colorful; marble as something dull white and solid; glass as something translucent, thin, and smooth. The aesthetic theorist, being usually an observer and critic first of all, and not an artist, tends to follow up this approach to the mediums of art: to analyze them psychologically into a long list of sensory and other qualities, experienced in the process of looking at or listening to a work of art. To him, these are the important things about a medium; and if the arts are to be classified, it should be in terms of such abstract qualities.

Carrying out this approach consistently, one may come to care less and less about the actual materials of which a work of art is made,

---

[15] No such distinctions are implied here as were often made in the old false antithesis between form and content, or form and subject-matter. *Cf.* McMahon, *op. cit.*, p. 167.

or the process by which it was made, so long as it presents the required sensory qualities. Aesthetically, it comes to be unimportant whether a work of art is actually made of marble, or gold, or oil paint, as long as it presents the appearance of that material so accurately that no difference is perceptible. Of course, many imitations of material are disappointingly unsuccessful to the trained eye, but scientific methods are overcoming this difficulty. Statues made of plaster or new synthetic materials are given a convincing patina of bronze or granite; color-prints take on a texture much like that of oil paint. In the auditory realm, the distinctive tones of violin, voice, and piano are reproduced with increasing fidelity by radio, film, and phonograph. From the standpoint of aesthetic experience, the actual physical nature of the external stimulus may come to seem irrelevant, and the psychologist can ignore it, concentrating instead on the problem of differentiating types of sense-quality from each other. Thus what has long been true of literature comes to be increasingly true of music and even of the plastic arts—that the nature of the physical material is irrelevant, non-essential; and that the nature of the art can not be defined in terms of the use of any particular materials.

In following up the observer's and critic's approach to art with greater and greater scientific refinement, we are likely to find ourselves farther and farther from that of the artist. Both are valid in their own right, and that of the artist should not necessarily dominate. It is a false and misleading notion that the appreciation of art should attempt to recapture the artist's complete experience, even if that were possible. They are two different kinds of experience, and each has its own justification. But it would be unfortunate if aesthetics should completely lose sight of the artist's attitude toward his art, instead of incorporating both in a comprehensive account.

The artist's attitude toward a medium resembles that of the observer in some respects, but not in others. The artist, too, is interested in the colors of the paints—but also in how they mix and spread; how brushes of different size and stiffness can lay them in streaks and patches. The former, the abstract qualities which the observer picks out as *the* distinctive traits of the medium, appear to him as important end results to be aimed at. But he is also interested in many other qualities of the medium, which the observer as such seldom learns to know. To the artist these also are important, and often much more in the focus of his attention. If he were to read the aesthetician's account of his medium, he would feel that the account was not adequate; that it left out many important things about the materials he has to deal with. This is least so in the case of literature, for there the artist and the aesthetician are using the same medium of words; the divergence is greater in the other arts.

Such qualities in the medium, which interest the artist as an artist, can be described as *technological*. They are properties of the medium which must be dealt with if the work of art is to carry out its intended functions: aesthetic, utilitarian, and otherwise. They determine whether the building, chair, or statue will stand up or collapse; whether the vase or stained glass window will crack or resist pressure, cold, heat, and moisture; whether the garment will shed water, wear well, and hold its color and shape. Such qualities and their opposites are described in terms like hardness and softness, strength and weakness, durability, toughness, malleability, elasticity, ductility, porosity, flexibility, brittleness, resistance to rust and corrosion, heat and cold resistance, moth and termite resistance, electrical conductivity, even-drying, non-fading, and so on. Some of them are mechanical, physical, and chemical properties, measured and estimated from a standpoint of practical control; as to how they can be used and developed or corrected and avoided.

The musical performer and composer are both interested in the properties of the instrument with which they are dealing: the human voice, the piano, violin, or orchestra. What effects can it be made to produce, in the way of fast tempo, high and low pitch, sustained and percussive tones? By what means, such as proper fingering or breath control, can these effects be produced? Which ones are impossible with this instrument? Some technological properties are thus biological: physiological, botanical, and other. The composer for ballet must understand the capabilities of the trained human body, in agility and endurance; the types of movement suited to male and to female anatomy—powerful and angular or gentle and flowing. The landscape gardener and horticulturist must consider, not only how certain plants will look, but which ones will thrive under the probable conditions of climate, sun, moisture, insect enemies, and so on.

Some properties or potential effects are psychological and social, as in the case of the writer's medium: words and their meanings. He must be able to predict and estimate, to some extent, what the effect of certain words and allusions would be on the type of person who will probably read or hear them. Such effects and tendencies are the result of cultural configurations. Which words will be easily understood and which will be too technical? Which may give offense, provoke ridicule, touch emotive associations in desired or undesired ways? Some words, phrases, tones of voice, and gestures are complimentary, some insulting; some derisive, some respectful; some exciting, some soothing. These are technological properties of words, speech, and gesture. They are used in literature, theater and elsewhere; sometimes with effective control, and sometimes with unintended results.

From the standpoint of the literary artist, the grammar and syntax of the language he is using, as well as its accepted pronunciation, spelling, and punctuation, are all technological properties of his medium. He must accept them as partly determining and limiting, as well as inspiring, the verbal forms which he is to produce. He must not depart too far from established usage if he is to be widely understood. Yet this usage is flexible, and can be moulded to some extent into the new patterns of word-sounds and meanings which he wishes to create.

Before the time of science, the artist learned to deal with such properties more or less successfully, by trial and error and by transmitted practical wisdom—"The life so short; the craft so long to learn." Now applied science aids greatly, but there is always an incalculable margin for personal judgment, because the ends in view and the particular conditions determining success or failure are constantly changing. On the whole, science lags behind the artist in discovering the technological properties of different mediums; he is the pioneer experimenter, and his results give clues to science.

Technological properties can not be investigated thoroughly apart from considerations of process and product. The technological properties of a medium—of some particular set of materials, tools, and devices—consist in how they function when treated in certain ways, as means to certain kinds of art product, and to the aesthetic and other effects intended. They are to be described in terms of fitness or unfitness for these techniques and goals; of cheapness or costliness; of easy or difficult adaptability; and of other, incidental effects or by-products which may or may not be desired. Only by using them in the work of producing or performing art can we learn what these potentialities are. But it is possible to record and organize such knowledge with special reference to each medium. That is, we can describe and evaluate such a medium as water-colors or violins in terms of the kinds of effect it can be made to produce when treated in certain ways.

The technological properties of a medium can be theoretically distinguished from its aesthetic properties, however. The latter are those which appear or function directly in the finished work of art—for example, the color of paint, the tone of a violin, the sound of words. The observer can perceive and appreciate them to some extent, without any knowledge of how the work of art was produced. In addition there are many technological properties of a medium which do not appear directly in the product, although an observer who knows the technical difficulties involved may infer that they have been dealt with, well or ill. The inner chemical composition of certain paints, of mosaic and well-glazed, well-fired porcelain does not appear to the observer; it is not an aesthetic quality; but it determines the ability of the object to hold its shape and color for centuries. The observer of a garden may not realize how certain plants have been chosen because of their ability to grow in dry soil and resist insect pests.

There is no sharp line between technological and aesthetic qualities; they overlap to a great extent. A technological quality may function aesthetically through suggestion and association. An observer who knows structural materials and engineering principles will be able to infer, in looking at a daring cantilever bridge, or an apparently unsupported platform out in space, that strong invisible supports and counter-balances have been used. This realization will contribute to his total understanding and enjoyment of the product, and the technological properties concerned may thus be said to exert an indirect aesthetic function. But many others are still more remote from observation in the product, being forgotten in the blueprints and calculations of the architect, and in the laboratory tests of those who made the building materials.

From a highly specialized aesthetic standpoint, it may seem that aesthetic qualities are the ends or intrinsic values of a work of art, and the technological qualities merely means to those ends. This is true to some extent. The chemical properties of a durable, unfading paint are means of ensuring that it will continue to present the same color and texture for a long time to come. But again there is no sharp distinction; either type of quality may appear as a goal to the artist, and either type as a means. The chemistry of paints is not part of the painter's job, today; but it is part of the architect's job to see that his building is strong and serviceable. To him, these are goals to be sought in their own right, and not merely means of preserving the visible appearance. On the other hand, all aesthetic qualities function as means or causal factors when the artist considers their effect on each other in producing the total aesthetic effect which is desired. A too bright red, a too loud tone, a too colloquial word, can destroy the intended quality of the whole. When aesthetic qualities cooperate, the observer is conscious of the total effect, but not (unless he is trained in form-analysis) of how each individual quality helps to bring this about.

We are not concerned at present with organized form, but it is impossible to separate medium entirely from organized form. The medium does not cease to be a medium when it is organized. Some aesthetic qualities it has in both the raw and the finished state: the whiteness of the sculptor's marble, for example. Some it loses in the process of production (for example, the rough, irregular shape of the block); some it acquires (for example, the smooth, curving surfaces). Some technological properties are in the raw material; others are imparted, as by firing, or by combining stones in the equilibrium of a buttressed arch.

There is need for the concept of medium, and for that of its technological qualities, even though the medium can never be clearly distinguished from the finished product, or technological qualities from aesthetic. The reason is to preserve in aesthetic theory the viewpoint of artists toward the arts, instead of substituting completely that of the observer and appreciator. Failure to do so in the past has often led to an artificial kind of aesthetic theory, of interest only to philosophers; one which seems unrealistic and bookish to the artist and all who share his point of view. He is interested in the arts, not only for their finished products and the abstract traits which these may reveal on analysis, but also in their raw materials and tools, and in the stages of production. In the medium, he is interested not only in its final aesthetic qualities, but also in those which must be controlled to achieve the final outcome: some to be used as means to ends; some to be eliminated; some to be fostered and developed.

Due attention to the technological aspects of medium has its effects on the classification of the arts. In distinguishing the different types of medium employed, one should pay more attention to their technological properties than is usually paid in aesthetics. It is not enough to distinguish them as "stone, wood, etc." or as "line, color, etc.," or as "visual and auditory." From the artist's standpoint, it sounds a little strange to hear architecture, sculpture, and pottery called "visual arts." To him, a building is not something which one merely looks at. One lives and moves in it, also. Its medium is tangible, consisting of wood to be sawed and hammered; of stones to be cut and laid; of plaster to be spread. To a sculptor, a block of marble is something to be drilled and chiseled with the hands. To a musician, music is not merely auditory, but a medium to be controlled by fingers on keys or strings, or by throat and lungs. It is not wrong to speak of visual and auditory mediums, but it does express the specialized point of view of an observer or listener, as in a museum or concert hall. Of course, there are different kinds of artists. Most architects work chiefly on paper, and seldom put their hands to coarser materials. But to the craftsman who handles materials directly, the most realistic distinction between the arts may well seem to be that of physical materials. He will think of himself as a painter, a glass-maker, or a wood-carver, rather than as a "visual artist."

7. Summary

There are different ways of defining "medium," each of which provides a different basis for comparing and classifying the arts. Each serves to distinguish some arts from each other in important ways; but when applied to other arts it serves less well. There the differences it points to seem trivial and non-essential—for example, the question of what physical materials are used for writing literature. In some cases, the difference in medium coincides with a difference between recognized arts; in others it does not, because the same art can use different mediums, and the same medium is used by different arts. A valid theory must take account of the fact that arts diverge and overlap in various ways; some diverging mainly on a basis of medium, while others diverge rather in respect to the process used, or the nature of the forms produced.

As to which meaning of "medium" is preferable, a legitimate difference of opinion may exist. Artists and those who share their point of view tend to emphasize the medium as a basis for distinguishing the arts, and also to stress raw or semi-processed materials, instruments, and technological properties in conceiving the nature of a particular medium. Those who share the artist's point of view include many who are not necessarily artists: for example, those who teach prospective artists, and organize educational courses for them; those who provide equipment and write books for them, and those who classify these books in libraries. This point of view deserves careful recognition in aesthetic theory.

Another point of view is also important: that of the observer, appreciator, and critic. It is inclined to minimize physical materials as such, and technological properties of the medium, stressing instead aesthetic qualities which occur in the finished work of art. Theorists with this point of view tend to define medium in terms of such aesthetic qualities. Sometimes they restrict these to direct perceptible sense qualities, such as color and solid shape; sometimes they include also suggested images, concepts, and emotions. In regard to literature, it is hard to avoid doing so, since there is little left of words as a medium if one eliminates their suggested meanings. In that case, the power of other mediums to suggest diverse meanings should also be given full recognition in systematic comparison of the arts.

On the whole, it is advisable not to expand the concept of "medium" to include too large a share of the finished work of art, or to analyze it entirely into aesthetic qualities, presented or suggested. It can well be regarded primarily from the artist's standpoint, with the emphasis on raw materials, instruments, and technological properties. The various types of image (presented and suggested) which occur in the finished product, the whole subject-matter of art and its modes of organization, can then be described in other terms: for example, as components in aesthetic form.

Under the general heading of medium, we have considered the following different bases of division. Each can be used for classifying arts and types of art, and each will lead to a different result:

a. Nature of the physical materials out of which a work of art is made: for example, stone, wood, metal, gold, oil paint.

b. Other physical phenomena used as stimuli to sense perception: for example, sound-waves, light-waves.

c. Physical tools and instruments: for example, chisels (steel, wood); violins and bows; vocal cords (living flesh).

d. Degree of complexity in the physical materials used by various arts; degree to which they have already been worked over by previous artists or manufacturers: for example, unformed, formed (according to Volkelt); raw, semi-processed, processed; simple (for example, marble); complex (for example, plants; human bodies, as in the dance).

e. Psychological qualities manifested by various mediums, as perceived: for example, color, solid shape, tone, pitch, rhythm.

f. Sensory types of such qualities, as classified on a basis of sense primarily addressed. Presented components in art: for example, visual, auditory, audio-visual.

g. Presented and suggested components: types of perceptible and auditory qualities involved in art; primary and secondary artistic medium (Greene): for example, emotion, conation, represented human figures, human activities.

h. Technological properties of the medium; physico-chemical: for example, flexibility, brittleness, rust-resisting; biological: for example, vocal register, muscular strength; psychological and social: for example, offensive or flattering words and gestures.

Most arts use a diversified array of these types of medium. They undertake to control many different technological properties. The chief possible grouping is on a basis of sense addressed, as into visual and auditory mediums; the former using light waves and pigments; the latter, sound-waves.

VIII

Comparing the Arts as to Process or Technique

1. Attitudes and interests expressed in this basis of comparison

The idea of skill in some process or technique is fundamental in the concept of art, and in that of each particular art. As we have seen, the word "art" is sometimes applied to the product rather than the skill or process of production, but the earlier meaning is never lost. It makes a good deal of difference in comparing and classifying the arts, whether we are thinking of them as groups of static products—pictures hanging in museums, books and musical scores in libraries—or as human activities. In one case we shall be likely to emphasize the characteristics of the finished forms as bases of comparison, while in the other we shall be looking for differences between artists' ways of doing things.

The emphasis on process or technique, like the emphasis on medium, tends to express the artist's point of view rather than that of the user and critic of art. The latter type of person may sometimes be curious about how works of art are produced, but often he is quite indifferent, as he is about the origin of most of the things which he wears, uses, eats, or glances at in the modern industrial world. As production becomes more complex and specialized, it tends to be more remote and impersonal from the standpoint of the ultimate consumer. Often he has no way of knowing who made a thing or how, and its present nature is all that interests him. He sometimes reacts from this extreme impersonality, and reads with interest about the life of some individual artist; but this is an exception to the general trend. The buyer of a work of art, for his own collection or a museum, has a special reason for wanting to know whether it was made by a famous artist or an imitator; whether it was individually made by hand and was thus comparatively unique, or was turned out by machinery as one of many identical, standardized mass products. But ordinarily we take the picture, poem or symphony for what it is, liking it or disliking it, but not troubling to find out much about the gradual, often intricate technical procedures by which it was made.

As to the process of *performance*, especially in music and theater, the consumer is more directly concerned. That process is not remote but directly before his attention, almost indistinguishable from the work of art itself. He often takes a more lively interest in the performance and in the individual performers than in the play or symphony itself. Their concrete appearance, in person or on the screen, helps to make up for that impersonality which hides the original author or composer from his view. But here again, it is the outcome which interests him especially—the quality of the performance rather than the technical means by which a skilled performer achieves his effects.

Since there are many kinds of person in the audience or reading public, one cannot generalize very sharply; many of them may share the artist's interest in technical procedures. An interest in the activities of art, sometimes more than in the finished product, is shared by many who are not artists. It is felt by psychologists, who want to know how the wheels go round inside the artist. It is felt by sociologists and ethnologists, who wish to see art as a dynamic phase of culture-patterns. It is shared by many teachers and students of art, who are concerned primarily with techniques from a vocational point of view. It is shared by economists, who see the artist as a producer of goods and services for economic reward.

The inner, psychic phases of artistic production are still comparatively unexplored by science. Speculative theories, philosophical and fanciful, abound as to the role of inspiration or divine madness, intuition, expression of the cosmic mind, and the like. Naturalistic psychology, including psychoanalysis, has now begun describing the processes of art production, conscious and unconscious, including the complex roles of perception, imagination, conation, emotion, reasoning, and other functions therein. The present chapter will not undertake a detailed account of these processes. It will point out a few resemblances and differences among the arts, as to the modes of production and performance they employ.

2. Skills, processes, and occupations

The concept of "skill," the basic and original meaning of "art," is broadly defined by Webster as "a power or habit of doing a particular thing competently; a developed or acquired aptitude or ability." The psychological meanings are given there in a narrower form: "a. Smoothness and good co-ordination in the execution of a learned motor performance. b. A motor performance that has become facile and well integrated as the result of practice."

Skill, then, is the ability to do something well, competently, easily, smoothly, as a result of learning and practice. It is an acquired ability, as distinguished from other abilities which may be due to inborn reflexes or instincts; for example, the newborn infant's sucking reflex is not a skill. The abilities of an adult are based on inborn capacities, potentialities, disposition, or endowment; they also involve acquired skills, through which these inborn capacities are brought toward realization. The word "technique" implies a comparatively high degree of organized method, as distinct from minor skills as in playing a child's game. Webster defines it as "Expert method in execution of the technical details of accomplishing something, especially in the creative arts; as, the technique of a master violinist; the formal elements collectively, of an art; as, the technique of versification; manner of performance with respect to mechanical features or formal requirements; as, a bad technique." The word "technique" suggests that a skill is mature, transmitted through formal education, and based to some extent on scientific or other theoretical principles.

The psychological definitions quoted above, which restrict "skill" to motor performance, are too narrow for our present purposes. We shall include also acquired mental abilities or techniques, such as versification. Later in this chapter, we shall distinguish between overt or motor skills and psychic, mental, or inward skills, both of which are involved in the processes of art. This is in accordance with the older, broader meaning of "skill."

A skill or technique can be manifested only through activity of some sort; through doing a specific kind of thing. Hence the idea of a particular skill is always bound up with the idea of some activity in which more or less skill can be shown. Skill is learned ability to perform some kind of task or process, or a group of them. Of course, the individual has the skill even when he is not exercising it; the skill is embodied in a structural configuration of his brain, nervous, and muscular system, which persists when not in use. But it differs from an undeveloped capacity in being ready for immediate activation under appropriate conditions.

An "aptitude" is potential ability or capacity to learn some particular kind of work or skill, for example, an aptitude for music or foreign languages. It is inferred in the child or student from rudimentary skills already learned, or from his ability to learn a simple, typical skill in the field concerned, with relative ease and speed under standardized conditions.

Although "skill" is defined in evaluative terms, as competence, good co-ordination, etc., it can often be appraised objectively. For example, the number of words typed per minute without error, on a standard machine, can be objectively measured. Here there is a definite, accepted criterion for measuring degree of success in standard units. In other types of skill, such as violin-playing and versification, the criteria are more vague, debatable, and hard to measure; hence appraisal is partly a matter of personal taste and judgment.

Skill being intimately bound up with a specific process, there are as many kinds of artistic skill as there are processes in art. Each process can be done more or less skillfully. To analyze the skills and other abilities required in art, we must analyze the processes involved. These vary from extremely simple to extremely complex; from extremely regular and mechanical to extremely variable, subtle, and intellectual.

An "occupation," job, *métier* or vocation, such as that of a painter or novelist, involves many different activities, each with its own skill. The person who carries it on is likely to be more skillful at some of them than at others; his total skill or ability in his occupation will be a joint result. The occupation and general skill of painting can be analyzed into constituent phases, steps, or tasks. We speak of the painter's skill or lack of skill in the use of his medium—for example, in mixing colors, underpainting, etc., or in producing some kind of pictorial form, as in drawing, perspective, figure composition, etc. Even the greatest artists are analyzed and appraised in this way—for example, that a certain one is strong in melody or line drawing; weak in harmony or coloring.

Each constituent process and skill may in turn be analyzed into more minute, elementary phases or steps. For example, musical harmony involves the control of chord structure, chord progression, modulation from key to key, relations to melody and counterpoint, etc. Each of these is complex and bound up with the others. In some complex motor skills, the constituent phases are easier to dissociate—for example, into the coating of a copper plate, the drawing of a picture with a needle, the bathing of the plate with acid, etc.

Some occupations in art are comparatively uniform and specialized, restricted to the performance of a few regular processes, as in tending a machine. Others are extremely diversified and variable, as in directing an opera company. The latter are hard to classify under any one heading. Such diversified occupations overlap greatly. Certain basic skills such as drawing occur in many of them. On the other hand, the elementary steps and skills are overwhelmingly numerous and varied. We shall look especially at the processes of intermediate complexity, which recur in different artistic occupations.

3. Techniques in various arts

Each phase in the production of art develops its own peculiar skills or techniques. The more each phase becomes specialized as a distinct occupation, carried on by a separate man or group, the more we come to recognize a distinct kind of "art" or skill in carrying it out successfully. Thus hundreds of "arts" or skills develop in the place of one: for example, that of a man who specializes on orchestration in a large music-publishing company, adapting vocal and piano pieces for a group of different instruments. Such specialization occurs in the designing phase as well as in others. In a furniture-factory, the oldtime versatile cabinet-maker is succeeded by a variety of skilled designers, upholsterers, and wood-polishers. The single architect is succeeded by a staff of specialists, capable of designing an office building or a chemical factory.

Along with these survive many all-round, versatile craftsmen of the old-fashioned type, just as relatively undifferentiated types persist in the plant and animal world.[1] Some arts, as we have seen, resist

---

[1] Herbert Spencer showed how the arts as professions conform to the general evolutionary trend of increasing differentiation (separating from each other, and subdividing within each art) and integration (for example, forming into professional organizations). They all develop, he maintains, out of the primitive "politico-ecclesiastical agency." Spencer's discussion of the subject in *Principles of Sociology* (Vol. II, Part VII, "Professional Institutions"; New York, 1897), is full of valuable suggestions, though needing some correction today. He notes that the differentiation of painting has been relatively slow. However, Spencer fails to notice here, as in biological evolution, how many undifferentiated types persist, and how some types even regress to less complex forms. Croce's scornful comment on Spencer's evolutionary approach to art (*Aesthetic*, p. 473) is unjustified, and merely an example of his hostility toward naturalistic, positivistic philosophy in general. He had apparently not read Spencer's full discussion, but only an 1860 prospectus.

the tendency to specialization and collectivization much more stubbornly than others. There has been little tendency to industrialize the writing of lyric poetry. However, no art is necessarily exempt: some large music-publishing firms turn out "lyrics" for popular songs, almost by mass-production methods. Where little industrialization has occurred, as in the writing of serious sonnets, it is usually a sign of comparatively little popular demand for the product. Where production remains undifferentiated, we tend to recognize only one "art" or "creative process." Often it combines a great many different phases in a rudimentary, indistinct way; most of them inner, mental processes which are hard to observe and describe. In such cases, we are more likely to think of the creative process as something mysterious and ineffable; an event of mysterious inspiration, quite different from ordinary production. A description of the obvious skills manifested— for example, penmanship and versification in writing sonnets—appears very superficial and external to the essentials of creation.

Innumerable specific techniques are used in the arts; a long list of complex, interrelated methods in each, whose description would require many volumes. To read a book on the techniques of pottery brings one down to a multiplicity of small details about preparing the clay, shaping a vase on the potter's wheel, mixing chemical colors, applying glazes, incising patterns, successive firings at various temperatures, gradual cooling, and so on. To a casual observer, the techniques of the various arts appear so different as to defy comparison; each is its own realm and speaks its own technical language, which the outsider cannot learn without a long course of instruction. For purposes of classification, we need to find some moderately general, basic characteristics which distinguish the techniques of various arts from each other.

Let us begin by considering those arts whose names imply a kind of technique: for example, drawing, etching, writing, dancing, singing, textiles (from the Latin *texere,* to weave), and sculpture (from the Latin *sculpere,* to carve). These are all names of activities, most of them in participial form. If all arts were so designated, each in terms of its most essential, distinctive technique, we should have a means of classification ready at hand. But many arts are not so named: there is little clue to process in the words "poetry" (from a Greek word meaning to "make"), "music" (from "art of the Muses"), and "architecture" (from the Greek for "chief artificer").

Even when a technique is indicated by the name, it is not always very specific or distinctive. There are many kinds of carving or cutting, and some of them occur in other arts than sculpture; for example, in making houses, furniture, and utensils. There are many kinds of weaving; they are used in making baskets and wire fences, as well as cloth. When we speak of the "art" of sculpture or weaving, we usually have in mind some particular kind of product: for example, the art of carving statues, or of weaving cloth. On the other hand, the art of sculpture includes many other techniques besides carving: stone is drilled and polished; clay shaped with the hands; bronze melted and cast. Thus the common names of arts are not a clear indication of distinctive techniques used in them.

Some arts, as we have seen, are named in terms of a kind of material, such as the art of metalry; of painting; of glass or glass-making; of silver or silversmithing. These give little clue to how the material is worked, made, or formed. Others are named in terms of a kind of product: for example, garden art, horticulture; the drama; the motion picture; the art of the novel. In this case, the process of making it is not clearly specified. It is hard to describe a process specifically without reference to the materials used and the kind of product formed. Otherwise the concept of process is very abstract, like "carving," "rubbing," or "drilling," and it applies to many different arts. Only the context can indicate that "painting" means the art of painting pictures, rather than the painting of houses or chairs.

There has been great and accelerating change in the techniques of many arts, especially those which are being mechanized. Those of architecture are very different in the age of steel and concrete from what they were in previous ages. In all arts, they change to some extent with the growth of science, and with the change of styles in the product, necessitating new techniques to fit them. To define or classify the arts in terms of any specific technique or set of techniques is sure to be rather ephemeral. The concepts of architecture and pottery have outlived many changes in technique.

From a genetic standpoint, the development of techniques in art and industry can be roughly described in various sequences. There has been on the whole a development from simple to complex, as from primitive chipping and scraping to modern machine production. This has involved increasing specialization and division of labor, along with the coordination of large groups of specialized workers in collective processes: the trend known as industrialization. Many individual workers therein perform simple, repetitive tasks. It is usually, though not always, combined with mechanization and applied science: the increasing use of complex, labor-saving machinery and technical processes based on physical, chemical, biological, and even psychological knowledge. This involves a change in the types of power utilized, from unaided human strength and dexterity to the use of fire, domesticated animals, wind, water, steam, electricity, molecular energy, and atomic energy.

To a large extent, the fine or aesthetic arts have lagged behind other human industry in adopting these more highly developed techniques. As we have seen, such techniques are gradually pervading certain phases of every art, especially those concerned with reproduction; with producing many identical examples of the same cup, book, or picture; also those concerned with communication, as in radio and television. In the original designing, more primitive techniques persist. We still draw and write with some pointed instrument—an automatic pencil or fountain pen, perhaps, but handled in much the same way as the drawing and writing tools of ancient Egypt. Painters use brushes, and sculptors use knives and chisels, whose technique is not radically different from those of ancient artists. Many of the primitive, elementary types of movement persist: the perennial cutting, boring, rubbing, daubing, pounding, kneading, and twisting which have always characterized the craftsman's work from a standpoint of bodily movement. These often persist along with scientific machinery, the machine merely extending the scope of their effects. The same ones are used in different arts, applied to different materials, so cannot well be used to distinguish them. The more scientific processes are on the whole adapted to specialized types of product; accordingly, the techniques of operating them within the field of art are more closely correlated with specific kinds of art. For example, making half-tone color-prints is very unlike operating an electric kiln. But even here, there is no definite correlation between different techniques and different "arts." A great number of scientific techniques, such as welding, electro-plating, and airbrush painting, are used in many arts.

Artistic techniques can be classified and described in various ways. One is in terms of the physical *medium, materials, and instruments* involved. In sculpture, for example, we can distinguish the use of clay, marble, bronze; the use of knives, chisels, and drills made from stone, copper, bronze, and iron; the act of carving, drilling, rubbing, etc. Many techniques are described in terms of certain tools or instruments, such as hammering, chiseling, sawing, drumming, trumpeting, violin-playing. We have already seen the difficulties involved in comparing the arts on this basis: such distinctions between techniques correspond only to a limited extent with traditional divisions between the arts. Still, such a classified list of materials, tools, and related techniques is well worth making. It is highly important for archeology and anthropology, in describing various cultures. In that case, it is advisable to forget our traditional names and definitions of "arts," major and minor, since they were formulated largely on the basis of modern European culture. The whole problem of "classifying the arts" then appears to be rather artificial and unnecessary. The primary need is for descriptions of specific tools, techniques, and materials used, and of how they were interrelated in a culture-pattern. One can, of course, take the same approach to modern civilization; but there the number and variety of materials, tools, and related skills becomes overwhelming. We find ourselves again in need of some system or classification of arts as a means of organizing the data.

Techniques can also be described and classified in terms of their goals or outcomes in some *characteristic of the product,* that is, in technological or aesthetic traits of the work of art produced. One can speak of the art of making glazed pottery, or of writing sonnets, or of composing fugues. This tells us comparatively little about the procedure itself. It can be further analyzed from the same point of view, in terms of producing specific factors of characteristics in the work of art. We speak, for example, of the art of melody-writing, or of counterpoint; of plot-construction; of color-harmony. To describe the technique of painting in detail, we must refer to certain factors in pictorial form, or ways of organizing details in a picture. The technique of modern western painting includes "perspective," the representation of how things appear in respect to their relative distance and positions. It includes learning how to represent various substances, and to arrange figures in a landscape. When different styles of product are aimed at, the techniques or means of producing them vary accordingly. Thus the techniques of art cannot be fully described apart from a consideration of the products or forms produced, which is the subject of the next chapter.

Techniques can also be described, to some extent, in terms of the *processes* which they involve. For this, we have some welcome assistance from experts outside the field of aesthetics.

4. Occupational classifications of the arts

Several of the problems which we have been considering, chiefly from the standpoint of general aesthetic theory, are now being approached in a more scientific and practical manner as problems of "occupational research" and "job analysis." The most thorough study in this field so far has been published by the United States Government, in a series of books called *Dictionary of Occupational Titles*.[2] Part I defines 17,452 separate jobs, many of them under more than one title, making a total of almost 30,000 titles defined and classified. Far from being restricted to the fine or aesthetic arts, it covers all recognized ways of making a living in this country, and the vast majority are in other fields. But the arts are included, in so far as they have become definite occupations.

Most important from our present standpoint, the arts are defined and classified as techniques or processes, not as abstract realms or types of product. The treatment is extremely realistic and empirical, being based on actual practice; on types of work actually being done, and on the names commonly applied to persons who do such work. Scientific study has come in to classify them systematically, and to define them concisely. Many occupations, including arts, have also been grouped by labor unions, for purposes of organization.[3] But the

---

[2] *Part I: Definitions of Titles,* and *Part II: Group Arrangement of Occupational Titles and Codes,* prepared by the Job Analysis and Information Section, Division of Standards and Research, U. S. Department of Labor; published by U. S. Government Printing Office in 1939. *Part IV: Entry Occupational Classification,* prepared by Division of Occupational Analysis, War Manpower Commission; revised edition, 1944. A similar but briefer study. called *Classified Index of Occupations,* was published by the U. S. Department of Commerce, Bureau of the Census, in 1940.

[3] See, for example, the list of craft unions affiliated with the American Federation of Labor, in the Federation's *Report of the Proceedings of the 64th Annual Convention,* 1944. Washington, D. C.: Ransdell, Inc. Several of these unions include workers in the arts, such as "Actors and Artists of America, Associated"; "Bookbinders, International Brotherhood of"; "Jewelry Workers' Union, International"; "Leather Workers' International Union"; "Musicians, American Federation of"; "Potters, National Brotherhood of Operative"; "Textile Workers' International Union"; and "Upholsterers' International Union."

government survey is more comprehensive and more carefully systematized. As compared with philosophical systems of the arts, it avoids a good deal of the fog which has been raised by vague, speculative generalization. It avoids the snobbish condescension with which admirers of the fine arts have traditionally regarded other skills, by giving factual, non-evaluative descriptions of all.

As a result, some venerable old arts are surprisingly juxtaposed with plebeian new ones, because they appear essentially similar when regarded objectively in terms of process. Nothing is said as to which are finer or better. Lofty "classical dancers" find themselves bracketed with humble chorus girls, as "entertainers" in the "amusement and recreation" industry. The traditional list of five or more "major arts" is gone; dissolved in the sea of thirty thousand modern, specialized occupations, so that one has to search out the traditional names. Most of them are still there, along with many new types of job which have sprung up within or around them. No distinction is made between "fine" and "useful" or "applied" arts. Apparently this distinction, so greatly emphasized in the past, is of little importance from the practical standpoint of job analysis. The aim here is to assist public employment offices and related services, including the classification and guidance of military personnel and students.

This is certainly the right approach for the practical aim in view, and it has some value for aesthetic theory. It gives a coldly realistic picture of the place of the arts among modern ways of making a living, which the young, prospective artist would do well to ponder. It shows how much can be done in the scientific classification of such fluid, overlapping phenomena as human activities, in spite of the philosophical quibbles which we noted in Chapter I. It also shows that there is a practical need for such attempts, however imperfect the results must always be. The bases of classification used have the strength of being derived from practice, and from observable resemblances and differences among occupations; not from *a priori* speculation.

At the same time, there is something lost in this approach. It is not, so far, sufficient as a classification of human occupations from the standpoint of aesthetics. The difference between skills which aim at aesthetic effects and those which do not, though hard to define and sometimes overstressed in the past, is psychologically and culturally important. If the aesthetic skills are not to be given a special place in occupational studies, they do deserve special attention from other points of view. Curious omissions and changes of perspective result from including only gainful occupations, by which one can make a living. For example, "psychologist" is listed, apparently because one can directly earn a living by practicing psychology. So are "poet" and "critic," however scanty a living such vocations may provide. But there is no place for "philosopher," "logician," "metaphysician," "moralist," or "aesthetician"—no doubt because there is no direct sale for their services. They must earn a living in some other way; perhaps as college professors. The point is not without significance as an index of cultural change; a century ago, one could not have made a living as a psychologist.

As in classification of the arts, the problem of what *bases* to use arises also in classifying all occupations. The authors of this research have seen the need of using many different bases, and they have combined them into a single system of classification which is workable, though not always logically neat. No attempt is made to force all modes of division into a correspondence which they do not actually possess; there is much cross-reference and duplicate listing of certain types of work under several headings.

Occupations are divided first into six "major occupational groups," as follows:[4]

> Professional, technical, and managerial work
> Clerical and sales work
> Service work
> Agricultural, marine, and forestry work
> Mechanical work
> Manual work

These groups are distinguished on the basis of (a) amount of knowledge, mental ability, and power to do independent or directive work; and (b) type of environment, as in grouping agricultural, marine, and forestry work with "other related outdoor activities." Throughout the subdivision, various bases are used, and the problem is discussed in an introduction, as follows:

[4] The terminology varies slightly in different volumes and editions. This is from Part IV: *Entry Occupational Classification.* The Census Bureau's list includes eleven similar groups; see its *Classified Index of Occupations*, p. 2.

Each job definition has been given an "industrial designation" for the purpose of indicating the type of economic activity with which the job is associated. . . . Several bases have been used for determining what the various industrial designations shall include, but in all cases they reflect the relationship of the jobs to each other. The relationship may be on the basis of similarity (1) in the *character of the services rendered,* as in the Amusement and Recreation Service; (2) in the *products manufactured,* as in the Ice Cream Industry; (3) in the *use of the products* manufactured, as in the Electrical Equipment Industry; (4) in the *raw materials* used, as in the Rubber Goods Industry; (5) in *primary processes* employed, as in Quarrying; (6) in the *type of occupation* engaged in, as in Clerical work; (7) or in the *type of activity* carried on, as Machine Shop work.[5]

In the classification of jobs—

No single criterion has been followed in determining what constitutes a job classification. For some, it is the duties of the jobs; for others, the industrial surroundings or circumstances in which the jobs exist. The determining factor in establishing a job classification on the basis of duties performed may be the machines operated, the articles produced, the material worked with, the machine attachments used, or other considerations. . . . Jobs that require the same experience, techniques, or abilities on the part of the worker are classified together.

The occupations which we have been considering as "arts" are scattered widely through the system. The first main heading, *Professional, Technical, and Managerial,* covers the composing, designing, and other supposedly "creative" phases of all the traditional major arts. Administrative directors in art production are placed here, and so are many types of artistic performance, under the category of "entertainment." Farther down the list, under *Mechanical Work,* we find many types of skilled craftsmanship, especially in the visual arts. The last main group, *Manual Work,* takes in those who do the cruder types of "elemental" and "manipulative" labor. Many of these are engaged in what we have broadly called "art production."

Let us look more carefully at these headings. *Professional, Technical, and Managerial Work* is defined as "work requiring the capacity to acquire and apply special knowledges involved in artistic creation, entertainment, social service work, teaching, scientific study, research,

[5] *Op. cit.,* pp. xx, xxi.

engineering, law, medicine, business relations, or management." [6] One's assignment to a major occupational group depends, then, more on general mental and educational level than on the difference between art, science, and management. Within this professional group, the main subheadings are:

(a) *Artistic Work:* defined as "involving artistic creation in the fields of fine or commercial arts as evidenced by active engagement in painting, sculpturing, drawing, and similar activities." The terms "art," "artistic," and "fine arts" are thus used in the visual aesthetic sense, excluding music and literature. "Artistic work" includes three main subdivisions: *Artistic Drawing and Related* ("involving the creation or reproduction of artistic designs on flat surfaces by hand, using such tools as brushes, pens, etching needles, pencils, or crayons"), *Artistic Shaping* ("the creation and shaping of artistic objects by modeling or carving by hand or hand tools, using such materials as plaster of Paris, clay, wax, wood or stone"), and *Artistic Arranging* ("the arrangement of objects or materials to achieve artistic or decorative effects for apparel, interiors, photographic composition, or other types of artistic creation"). Under "Artistic Drawing" are listed the following specific occupations: advertising lay-out man, art lay-out man, cartoonist, catalog illustrator, commercial artist, etcher, painter, bank-note designer, chargeman (motion pic.), cover designer, histological illustrator, industrial designer. Under "Artistic Shaping" are listed: sculptor, memorial designer (stonework), modeler (brick and tile).[7] "Artistic Arranging" includes: clothes designer, display man, floral designer, hat designer, interior decorator, window trimmer, art director

---

[6] Pt. IV: *Entry Occupational Classification,* p. 13. The Census Bureau's *Classified Index of Occupations,* p. 2, defines a professional worker as "(1) one who performs advisory, administrative, or research work which is based upon the established principles of a profession or science, and which requires professional, scientific, or technical training equivalent to that represented by graduation from a college or university of recognized standing; or (2) one who performs work which is based upon the established facts, or principles, or methods in a restricted field of science or art, and which work requires for its performance an acquaintance with these established facts, principles, or methods, gained through academic study or through extensive practical experience, one or both."

[7] Note that "shaping" is here understood in a very narrow sense, restricted to making static, solid shapes. In speaking previously of the "arts of visual shaping," we have included flat and mobile shapes also.

(motion pic.), photographer (commercial; portrait), stage scenery designer (amusement & recreation).

(b) *Musical Work:* "involving musical expression as evidenced by activities in composing, arranging, directing, singing, or playing a musical instrument." There are three subdivisions: *Musical Work, Creative* ("involving the composition, arrangement, or direction of instrumental or vocal music"), *Musical Work, Vocal* ("musical expression by means of the human voice"), and *Musical Work, Instrumental* ("musical expression by means of stringed, percussion, wind, or other musical instruments"). "Musical Work, Creative" includes: arranger, chorus master, composer, copyist, orchestra leader, orchestrator. (Note that copyists and orchestra leaders are classed as "creative," along with composers). "Vocal" includes: character singer, concert singer; both are given the industrial designation "amusement and recreation." Under "instrumental," accompanist, organist, and violinist are given the same designation.

(c) *Literary Work:* "involving written expression as evidenced by active engagement in such activity as writing plays, poetry, or narrative prose; critically evaluating the written work of others; translating from one language into another; and editing, compiling, or adapting written material." There are two subdivisions: *Creative Writing and Translating* ("the original writing, adaptation, or translation of prose, poetry, or other forms of written expression, excepting the writing of advertising copy or journalistic reporting") and *Copy Writing and Journalism* ("the writing of promotional material to induce a desired action, attitude, or opinion, or the reporting, editing, or interpretation of facts, events, or opinions of current interest"). "Creative Writing" includes: collaborator, continuity writer, literary writer, playwright, poet, scenario writer, script writer (radio), translator.

(d) *Entertainment Work:* "work which involves amusing, diverting, or informing the public as evidenced by active engagement in such activities as speaking, acting, dancing, dramatic reading, impersonating, or in other varied activities exclusive of the field of music." There are three subdivisions: *Entertainment Work Oral* ("primarily the use of spoken words to amuse, entertain, or inform others"), *Rhythmic* ("the use of such forms of rhythmic expression as ballet or ballroom dancing"), and *Not Elsewhere Classified* ("amusing, entertaining, or informing others by some physical demonstration such as juggling, riding, sleight-of-hand, or pantomime").

The performance phase of various arts is thus distributed through several categories: partly under "creative music" (orchestra directing); partly under "vocal and instrumental music," and partly under "entertainment."

Other occupations related to the arts are to be found in the three remaining subdivisions of *Professional, Technical, and Managerial:* "*e.* Public Service Work" includes instructive service, and hence teaching of the arts. "*f.* Technical Work" includes laboratory science, engineering, and drafting; hence it overlaps architecture, ceramics, and other industrial arts. It includes geographical work, which covers agriculture and forestry, thus overlapping landscape architecture. "*g.* Managerial Work" takes in supervisors and directors of all sorts, many of whom are engaged in various forms of art production.

Turning now to another major occupational group, that of *Mechanical Work,* we find that it involves ability "(1) to exercise independent judgment in determining the form, quality, and quantity of work, (2) to follow more complicated specifications and work to closer tolerances, making all necessary mathematical computations, and (3) to use tools and equipment skillfully." It is divided into *Machine Trades* and *Crafts,* the latter of which involves—

planning and performance of tasks that require skillful use of hands, hand tools, or equipment. Workers may also be required to control processes and to exercise judgment in maintaining standards of production. Machines may be used by the worker as aids in the accomplishment of tasks, but the worker is not normally required to maintain or repair them, nor to understand the mechanical principles upon which machines operate.[8]

Crafts are subdivided as follows: Machining, Mechanical Repairing, Complex Machine Operating, Electrical Repairing, Structural Crafts (including Assorted Materials, Wood, Metal, Stone or Glass, Plastic Materials, Welding, Excavating, etc.), Bench Crafts (Assorted Materials, Metal, Wood, Stone, Glass, or Jewels, Plastic Materials, Fabric, Leather and Related, Paper Products, Foods, Inspecting and Testing),

[8] *Cf.* the Census Bureau's *Index,* p. 3: "A craftsman is one engaged in a manual pursuit, usually not routine, for the pursuance of which a long period of training or an apprenticeship is usually necessary, and which in its pursuance calls for a high degree of judgment and of manual dexterity, and for ability to work with a minimum of supervision and to exercise responsibility for valuable product and equipment."

Graphic Art Work (including Art Work with Brush, Spray, Pen, or Stylus, Typesetting, and Photographic Work), and Processing (subdivided according to materials). In the "Bench Crafts," especially, are to be found the descendants of many types of old-time artist-craftsmen, such as cabinet-makers, clock-makers, jewelers, goldsmiths, silversmiths, basket-makers, violin-makers, stone-carvers, glass blowers, furniture decorators, picture frame ornamenters, hand weavers, tailors, upholsterers, and bookbinders. "Graphic Art Work" takes in many more, such as glass decorators, pottery painters, wallpaper sketch makers, engravers, lithographic artists, and photographic colorists. But no attention is paid to the fact that their work may have an aesthetic aim; the identity of "artist-craftsmen" as a type is lost among hundreds of other craftsmen whose function is mainly or wholly utilitarian, such as plumbers, steam-fitters, and electrical repairmen. Those who have an aesthetic aim and interest are here, and not in the "professional, artistic" group, because manual and mechanical skills are presumed to outweigh creative ability in their cases.

When we come to *Manual Work,* we find again several types of manipulative work (structural, bench assembling, etc.) which overlap the general field of art production. Workers here need "coordination and dexterity in the use of hands, arms, feet, or other parts of the body, usually in rapid performance of repetitive tasks." They may have to "feed a repeating machine." But they, too, had ancestors in the pre-mechanical era: the men, women, and apprentices who did some of the cruder, more menial tasks in a master-craftsman's studio. They are a grade above the "elemental workers" in having some coordination and dexterity.

The occupational classification makes no pretense to avoid overlapping, or to settle all debatable questions. Innumerable cases will occur to any reader, where a certain kind of art or of worker would fit equally well under several categories, as abstractly defined. Many individuals present unusual combinations of abilities and jobs. Some debatable areas are expressly mentioned, with an arbitrary decision indicated. For example, it is said that "band leaders whose abilities are adequately expressed in terms of a particular musical instrument should be classified only in terms of that instrument"—for example, not as orchestra leaders. Distinction is made between "informing the public" by radio commercials and by church ministerial work, the latter being placed under "public service." Much art of all kinds could of course be classed as "informing the public," or as "attempting to induce a desired attitude." But the important thing in such cases is to make some decision, so that thought and action can be released through definite channels, instead of being held up by ambiguities and hesitations.

From the standpoint of economics, employment, or the census, it is doubtless unnecessary to distinguish systematically between occupations with an aesthetic aim and those without, or to preserve the identity of the former—the traditional "fine arts"—as a group. It is also unwise to try to evaluate products and performances: to place the "classical dancer" on a different level from the "tap dancer." From the standpoint of aesthetics, such groupings and evaluations still seem highly important. Hence, in aesthetics, there is need for a different kind of occupational classification, in which all the workers and skills involved in producing the fine or aesthetic arts are described, so as to bring out the nature of their collaboration.

Taking a particular product such as the motion picture, it is worth while to study the various occupations that cooperate to produce it: on various levels of creativeness and responsibility; with various types of skill, applied to visual, musical, and verbal materials. Such an approach and classification would be primarily industrial, in terms of the type of product or the service rendered.[9] When we classify primarily in terms of particular jobs or of levels, from "managerial" down, we tend to miss the structure of the art or industry, since many of these jobs and levels can occur in different arts.

Types of labor organization in this country have tended to express these two approaches: craft and industrial. Theoretically, the former groups workers on a basis of similarity in craft or occupation, such as electricians; the latter on a basis of product or service, such as steel or railroads. In practice, both are usually combined to some extent. In aesthetics, one can also begin with a kind of product or performance, such as a play or symphony, and then trace the various kinds of skill which cooperate in its production. One will always find a

[9] A start is made toward this kind of classification in Part IV of the *Dictionary of Occupational Titles*, called *Entry Occupational Classification*. See pp 20-22 for a list of occupations on the professional level, concerned with Artistic Work, Musical Work, Literary Work, and Entertainment Work.

diversity of occupations, with certain ones recurring in different arts. But their interrelation, their way of combining, will be distinctive in each case.

In terms of process, the modern counterpart of the old-time art or handicraft is often to be found, not in any single, specialized occupation, but rather in a whole industry, such as the building, publishing, or motion picture industry. Its outlines are often shadowy, because of the interpenetration among all industries. Nevertheless, it will disclose some coherence of structure as a vast, diversified, teleological system, aimed at providing the public with a certain set of products or services. The analysis of such a dynamic structure will lead the aesthetician far afield into economic and technological realms. But it is necessary for a thorough understanding of the arts today, in terms of the processes involved.

In the type of occupational study we have been considering, a good deal of light is thrown on the kinds of thing which artists do, and what abilities they need to do them. Taking a long list of artistic occupations such as "architect" or "enameler," the government experts have made some progress in analyzing these into particular techniques and activities, and in classifying them under such headings as these:

(a). Level of mentality, education, and responsibility required: for example, professional or managerial; craftsman; laborer.

(b). Special skills, abilities, and aptitudes required: for example, ability to create a design, or to follow a design; to run and repair a machine.

(c). Type of medium or material: for example, stone, paint, words, violin music.

(d). Type of product, performance, or service rendered: for example, houses, pictures, essays, vaudeville entertainment.

(e). Conditions of work: for example, outdoor, studio, factory.

(f). Phases in work done: for example, tracing patterns in pencil; rendering them in watercolor.

Much further work is needed to follow up these leads in ways more relevant to the special problems of aesthetics. Little is said there about the more inward, mental phases of artistic work, and these we shall have to consider shortly. The meaning of "art" and "artist" used in these studies is too narrow for aesthetics, being limited to the visual realm. Also, there are serious disadvantages, from the standpoint of aesthetics, in breaking up a given art such as "furniture" into several main levels—the professional, mechanical, and manual types of worker. Here the professional or creative furniture designer is grouped with other professional and creative men in all fields, and his relation to other workers in his own field is obscured. In aesthetics, we need to group together all types of workers in a given art or realm of art, and to interrelate them in terms of what each contributes to the whole product or service.

5. Particular occupations in the arts

In addition to classifying occupations under various headings, the *Dictionary of Occupational Titles* gives a brief definition of each.[10] With the aid of accompanying tables, it is easy to select the principal ones in the arts. The occupations are listed alphabetically.

It is interesting to compare these definitions with each other and with the definitions of arts contained in ordinary dictionaries or in aesthetic treatises. Some are comparatively detailed and specific, bringing in much fresh observation of actual work being done. Some are extremely brief, vague, and conventional, throwing no new light on the nature of the process.

Those which are most specific about particular phases of the artist's work are, on the whole, those in the visual arts. They deal with occupations in which various types of bodily activity, in relation to tools and materials, can be easily observed and described from the outside. Thus we are given a fairly specific account of what it means to be an "Architect." He is—

a worker, trained in architectural methods, who plans and oversees the construction of buildings, marine projects, or other construction work; consults with client relative to specifications for project; prepares full-size detail drawings and specifications or supervises and coordinates work of preparing drawings and specifications; plans structural lay-outs; coordinates structural and architectural discrepancies and errors and makes any necessary adjustments and corrections to suit client; furnishes professional advice in connection with architectural problems or policies. Specifically designated according to type of architectural project on which he works, such as Architect, Building; Architect, Marine.[11]

[10] Part I: *Definitions of Titles* (June, 1939).
[11] *Ibid.*, p. 16.

Careful distinction is made between such closely related occupations as "Architect, Landscape," "Landscape Engineer," "Landscape
Gardener," and "Gardener." For example, a "Landscape Engineer"—

carries out the plans of Architect, Landscape; gathers together the
equipment and supplies needed, according to type of land being
landscaped and the extent of the plan; builds roads, bridges, dams,
buildings, and other structures; plants trees, shrubs, and flowers
according to specifications; covers land with topsoil, and sods lawns;
installs sprinkler systems, water supply and sewers.

A plain "Gardener," on the other hand, merely "keeps flowers, trees,
and premises about home in a healthy and attractive condition; plants,
transplants, fertilizes, sprays, waters, prunes, and otherwise tends to
the cultivation of flowers, bushes, fruit trees," etc.—that is, without
much general planning or designing. Certainly, it helps us understand
the nature of landscape and garden art in general to break it down in
this way into specific, interrelated tasks and operations.

Similar accounts are given of many other occupations in the visual
arts, such as "Art lay-out man" in printing and publishing, Embroiderer, Etcher, Interior Decorator, Painter, and Silversmith. A "Painter,"
on the professional level, is one who—

paints portraits, landscapes, still life, figure paintings in which imagination and taste control the execution on canvas or other background; sketches outline and applies various pigments as oils, paints,
and washes to bring out natural colors; applies varnish for a preserva-
tive; performs artistic or illustrative work involving prescribed or
standard methods, for purposes of publication, exhibition, and scientific record.

Such a list of kinds of work, recognized as belonging to a certain
occupation, is not merely academic; it has definite practical uses.
Especially in matters involving different trade unions, or prestige
among different types of worker, acrimonious disputes arise about
whether a man hired for a certain job should be asked to do a particular task. Of course, a house painter is not to do plastering. How
much gardening—that is, actual tending of plants after they are
installed—shall a landscape engineer be asked to do? In some cases,
the boundary is vague, and decision is up to the individual; but the
trend is toward clear specification of what a job entails. This is espe-

cially true in civil service and other government jobs, and in highly industrialized, unionized fields like motion pictures. It is especially true where different jobs are paid at different rates, and a criterion is sought to justify the difference. As in ancient and medieval times, each grade or class of worker is jealous of its own prestige and prerogatives, which entitle it to greater pay, better working conditions, and higher social status. This is quite as true under Communism as under Capitalism. Since the rewards are no longer determined by heredity, and since individuals can rise, fall, or change occupations more easily, it becomes increasingly important to have an up-to-date, neutral, accepted authority on the nature of each occupation.

In the older, undifferentiated, individualistic kind of art, such as poetry, there is less reason to draw the line so sharply. Accordingly, the definition of "Poet" gives us little information about how he goes to work. He is simply one who "writes poems, choosing his own subject matter or composing poem about a specific theme." That is, if he is employed by an advertising bureau, he may be asked to write laudatory verse about a certain advertised product.

Similar vague definitions are given for several other literary occupations, such as "Author," "Essayist," and "Literary Writer." There are probably several reasons for this vagueness. Not only is the job more elastic, more subject to individual regulation, but it is one with comparatively little overt activity which can be seen and described. The author may spend hours sitting at his desk and meditating, or scratching notes on a pad. He may be paid, as in motion pictures, merely for giving, by word of mouth, a story idea for others to write up.

A "Music Composer" is defined here as one who "conceives and writes musical compositions; translates into notes the melody and harmony." Again, this tells us little about the process, and for similar reasons. But one might expect more detail about "Singer" and "Violinist," because they involve overt performance; likewise, about "Dancer," "Ballet Dancer," and "Choreographer." A "Ballet Dancer" (under "Amusement and Recreation") is merely "A Dancer who performs artistic dances which suggest a theme or story, usually dressing in colorful costumes; practices systematically to become proficient and to develop new steps." Evidently, there is no practical reason for trying to analyze these occupations more specifically, for it would not be hard to do so.

Aesthetic theory, less bound by practical considerations, should certainly pursue these analyses further, in all important fields of art. It can profit by the start that has been made, toward conceiving of each occupation as a composite, variable activity or group of related, interlocking tasks, involving both physical and mental phases in varying proportion. To be sure, most occupations differ greatly from time to time and place to place, especially those left up to the individual artist's own discretion. There is a tendency to standardize many of them, and hence to formulate standard definitions of each, for the practical reasons just noted. But constant change in technology, in styles of art, and in social conditions, now prevents any crystallization like that of ancient and medieval times.

6. Artistic aptitudes and the problem of testing them

In an Appendix[12] to the *Entry Occupational Classification*, a start is made toward analyzing the various types of aptitude and ability which are believed to fit a person for entering the different occupational groups. These are listed for use in vocational and educational guidance, but are worth noting in aesthetics, as psychological hypotheses. Under "Special Talent Group," the following traits are selected:

For *artistic* (that is, visual art) work: creative imagination as applied to pictorial representation and design; aesthetic appreciation; visual memory; space perception; color discrimination; perception of form and design; dexterity and muscular control. Such traits, it is added, "may be estimated from samples of work, achievement in art or related courses, and scores on aptitude tests."

For *musical* work: creative imagination as applied to musical expression; tonal memory; relative or absolute pitch; voice quality; perception of musical intensity, rhythm, melody, and harmony; dexterity and muscular control.

For *literary* work: creative imagination as applied to the translation of ideas, events, and experiences into verbal forms; lucidity of expression; understanding of abstract ideas; interpretative or analytical attitude toward people and things; sense of rhythm and euphony; facility with language and knowledge of good usage; extensive vocabulary.

For *entertainment* work: creative imagination as applied to the portrayal of action and states of feeling through speech, facial expres-

[12] Section II: Classification Factors: Personal Traits, pp. 158f.

sion, and other physical motions; poise; showmanship; fluent use of language; pleasing, distinctive, or expressive speaking voice; exceptional stamina, energy, coordination, development, or personal appearance.

The introduction explains:

No objective techniques have been developed for distinguishing and evaluating all the personal traits listed on the following pages. Some traits can be distinguished fairly easily in the interviewing process, others through the administration of aptitude tests, and many are best evaluated when cumulative records of school grades, test records, and other personal history data are available.

Suggestive and useful in practice as such a list is, it is obviously full of vague conceptions, referring to abilities which are hard if not impossible to diagnose and measure. This is especially true when we are looking, in a young person, not for a fully developed power such as might exist in a famous adult artist, but for the aptitude or capacity to acquire such skill through education and experience. We are trying to estimate the probability of a future power which does not yet exist. This is largely a matter of inborn ability rather than acquired skill; yet it can be estimated only from objective demonstrations of partial or rudimentary skill, as in tests or school products. Hence it may be necessary to discount some individual differences in special training, opportunity, or personality type, which may have made one child forge ahead rapidly along a special line for reasons other than native talent, showing a precocious skill which will probably not continue to develop at the same rate. Great talents are often slow to manifest themselves in an individual, for personal or environmental reasons.

Some of the traits listed are objectively measurable to a large extent: for example, relative or absolute pitch; dexterity and muscular control; color discrimination; extensive vocabulary; exceptional stamina. Others are not; to estimate them is a matter of evaluation, requiring the use of standards which are usually debatable. Some involve complex and subtle inner processes which are not yet well understood, and whose nature or quality cannot well be inferred from scanty outward manifestations. It is not yet possible to measure, or even estimate with any exactness, powers of aesthetic appreciation or creative imagination. One can be fairly sure of the upper and lower ends of the curve of distribution: that student A shows great vitality and sensitivity along these lines, while student B is utterly dead and unresponsive. But in between are countless intermediate cases, where a little more or a little less facility in self-expression or use of a medium is not necessarily significant. Temporary lack of interest or energy may make a capable student seem inferior and perform badly on tests.

Even good performance on a test is misleading if the test itself is unsound. So far, most tests of aesthetic taste and judgment have been based on dubious assumptions about what actually is good or bad art; when a student prefers what the makers of the test prefer (or other judges chosen by them) he is given a high grade. This operates to put a premium on conventional taste, and on conformity to accepted academic standards at the time. Society is not always able to recognize genuine creative imagination even in the mature, professional artist. It is common knowledge that the real innovators are often scorned or neglected, while the purveyors of familiar, easy types of beauty are admired. How, then, can we expect to recognize the exceptional genius at an early age? Recognizing ordinary capability, or talent a little above the average, is another question. From the standpoint of everyday vocational guidance and educational administration, it is a much more urgent question.

In spite of the difficulties just noted, it is useful to work out and experiment with all manner of test devices for appraising artistic ability. The primary aim should be to induce the student to show what he can do in producing art, in criticizing it, or in other ways. He should do so if possible under standardized conditions giving equal opportunity to all who are being tested. The results will almost certainly be enlightening to the teacher and psychologist, even if it is not possible to appraise them with any accuracy. Even if no claim is made to accuracy, some kind of estimates have to be made in evaluating students' work for promotion to a higher grade, and in awarding scholarships and special opportunities. Though necessarily somewhat arbitrary and subjective, the appraisal of art abilities will become more intelligent if made with careful analysis of standards, and comparison of estimates with later school and professional achievement.[13]

The formulation of tests will be greatly aided by further theoreti-

---

[13] On tests of art ability, see A. R. Chandler, *Beauty and Human Nature* (New York, 1934), Ch. XV, "Talent and Genius." Also T. Munro, "Art Tests and Research in Art Education," *Western Arts Association Bulletin*, Vol. XVII, No. 6 (Dec. 1, 1933).

cal analysis of traits. "Art ability" or "creative ability" in general is too broad and vague a phenomenon to be effectively tested. These are names for extremely diversified and variable compound abilities. But as we analyze each of these broad abstractions into more specific, component abilities, we gradually approach the level of scientific observation and experiment.[14] We become able (a) to single out certain traits which can be objectively measured, and which may be indicators of the less accessible ones; (b) to narrow down the inaccessible ones to more specific phases, which can be investigated inductively. "Pictorial imagination" and "musical imagination" are vague ideas, but not quite as vague as "creative imagination" in general.

As we analyze artistic ability into its constituent phases, we discover that many of them are not peculiar to the aesthetic arts, but are important also in science, practical affairs, and all successful cultural achievement. General intelligence, some self-control, and the will to achieve are necessary for success in any of the channels which society esteems. In fact, they may well be more influential in determining the success of an artist than the specific skills and aptitudes, concerned with the use of his medium, which are emphasized in tests. Accordingly, predictions should not be based on tests of specific skill alone, apart from general personality diagnoses. But these general abilities and character traits may be directed in some way which fits the individual especially for a certain realm or type of activity. For instance, "general intelligence" is often estimated with special reference to verbal thinking, and measured by success in solving verbal or numerical problems. But some kinds of intelligence may be more successful in thinking musically, with auditory images and forms, or visually, with pictorial images and forms. So our conception of the supposed general, basic abilities and their measurement may have to be revised and enlarged in dealing with the arts.

Traits which bring success in one field often militate directly against success in another. Clear, cool, objective rationality is to be desired in science; but not necessarily in art. In so far as creative fantasy depends on unresolved, unconscious conflicts, or on desires and personality situations which are not clearly understood, the attempt to

[14] *Cf.* T. Munro, "Creative Ability in Art and its Educational Fostering," in *Art in American Life and Education* ("40th Yearbook of the National Society for the Study of Education, 1941"); reprinted in *Art Education: Its Philosophy and Psychology* (New York: Liberal Arts Press; Bobbs-Merrill Co., 1956), Ch. IV.

analyze and express them consciously in words may be disastrous. Illogical modes of thinking, false or distorted conceptions of reality, and the ego's relation to it, have apparently been instrumental in producing much of the world's great art. Hence it is not to be taken for granted that traits which psychologists regard as "desirable" in general, or conducive to mental health and social adjustment, are conducive to success in art. This does not imply the opposite view that genius is akin to insanity. It is simply a statement of our present ignorance on the subject, and a caution against unwarranted assumptions.

The aesthetic psychologist must try to decide, as open-mindedly as possible, what configuration of traits and abilities is prerequisite for success in each art, and each main type of art, as judged by prevailing cultural standards, or by other conceivable standards. He will certainly find much room for individual variation: a great range of possible differences among the various component abilities involved, which will lead to various kinds of achievement and success. Any single, definite standard for judging or predicting success is sure to become repressive and misleading, by discouraging individual variation.

7. The artist as free or bound

In the search for more profound, far-reaching distinctions between types of artistic process, let us now recall some of those which have been proposed by philosophers.

Divisions of the arts have been made on the basis of supposed differences in the artist's conative attitude. Kant distinguished art from handicraft, trade, or artisanship, as being free, while the latter was paid or mercenary. Art could succeed only when done as play, agreeable in itself, whereas *Handwerk* was disagreeable drudgery in itself, attractive only for the pay or other outside reward. This is a dubious distinction, as we have already observed, since either type of motivation may prevail in fine art, and also in trade or artisanship.

We have noticed several similar distinctions, made by later writers, between "free" arts and "bound" arts, or "free" arts and "imitative" arts. These antitheses are all related to each other and to certain main attitudes and concepts of the eighteenth and nineteenth centuries. Kant's own distinction was descended from the traditional concept of fine art as aristocratic, free from mercenary, practical, or narrowly utilitarian considerations. He partly democratized this, by admitting several useful arts such as architecture, furniture, and utensils within the class of fine art. Kant and Schiller (the latter in his theory of art as play) were both concerned with the psychology of the artist; they stressed the free play of his imagination and aesthetic vision; his delight in seeing for its own sake. If a man is motivated by the desire to make money, that limits his freedom to create or to enjoy beauty for its own sake. Carried to the extreme, this line of thought would lead one to conceive of fine art, at its best and purest, as free from *both* mercenary and utilitarian aims—a point to which Kant did not carry it. For many aestheticians before and after Kant, the archetype of a fine artist was a gentleman of independent means, composing music or poetry for no practical purpose.

The musician, especially, seemed free in another sense, wherein the poet and painter were restricted. He was said to be free from the need to "imitate" or represent nature; from the need to make his imaginings conform to the "laws" and facts of nature as to anatomy, perspective, etc.[15] Those who held this view failed to realize how often, and how easily, painting and poetry have escaped the requirements of naturalism. Obviously, post-impressionist and surrealist painting are not "bound" in this respect.

Other philosophers in the Romantic period, when raising the slogan of "freedom" for the artist, thought rather of freedom from the unnatural restraints and conventions of modern civilization. This attitude found its clearest expression in Rousseau. Still others revived in a new form the ancient dualism between spirit and flesh, soul and body, or soul and material world. The body is a tomb or prison, said the medieval ascetic, from which the soul tries to escape. The pursuit of beauty, said Plato and Plotinus, is one way of escape from the physical world into the realm of eternal ideas. Man, according to Spinoza, should also strive to be free from bondage to the emotions.

Many variations on this theme of freedom were played by nineteenth century aestheticians, with art in the role of liberator for the human spirit. All fine art could liberate, it was held, but some arts were freer and more liberating than others.

---

[15] Lotze groups the arts according to degrees of freedom from the necessity of either imitating nature or ministering to practical purposes. He places music highest in this respect. *Cf.* Colvin, "Fine Arts," p. 361. Note also Urries y Azara's contrast between "free" and "imitative" arts.

Toward the end of the nineteenth century, the "art for art's sake" school of critics praised certain types of art as a means of escape from the ugly, industrial world of modern factory towns. There was, in short, a persistent tendency to regard fine art (especially music) as free; but opinions differed as to what it was free from, and as to the kind of bondage from which it could liberate the spirit.

Today, less is said about the freedom of art, with these older implications. The prevailing attitude in aesthetics has changed from glorifying escape to praising the reintegration of art with practical life. Each art accepts certain functions and conditions; each artist accepts certain limitations, at least for a particular task. Such restraints are not necessarily evil, or a sign that the art is inferior to others.

At the same time, the artist today in many countries is facing a new kind of coercion, or an old one in a new form: that of dictatorship and totalitarian government. He is being told what to create and how to create it, in music, painting, and literature as well as in the useful arts. He is made to function as an instrument of propaganda, indoctrination, military strategy, or in some other way abhorrent to the spirit of liberalism. Romantic artists first hailed Napoleon as a child of the Revolution; then denounced him as a dictator. Many revolutionary movements of our own century have gone through a similar cycle, becoming anti-liberal in the arts as in politics.

In this present sense, the contrast between art as free or bound cuts across all the arts. Hence it is not a basis for contrasting the arts. In a totalitarian régime, no art and no artist is free.

From another point of view, modern psychology has something to say about the claims of any art to be free, even in the most liberal society. Is the apparently free artist really free, or is he unconsciously following out certain impulses, desires, and cultural trends? Heredity and environment make him what he is. Certain particular coercions may be present in one case, absent in others; but there are always some antecedent conditions determining an artist's procedure. The need to make a living and please one's public may act as a drag on an artist in any field. Traditional rules of form exist in all arts, including music. Often an apparent restriction acts as a stimulus and directive, while completely "free" people, with all the money and opportunity they need, never get started. Observation of nature can stimulate the imagination instead of confining it. An architect does not need to feel bound by the functional requirements of his building; today, he may feel them instead as an opportunity and a challenging problem. In all arts, an artist feels free when he is doing what he consciously wants to do. All arts give some scope to active imagination, and all can be pursued in passive obedience to some external authority.

8. Hand or machine production; use of tools

In a previous chapter, we noticed that the distinction between "handmade" and "machine-made" was emphasized especially in the realm of useful arts; but that it could also be applied in painting and sculpture, and to some extent in all arts. In all—including music and literature—mechanical devices are being used to an increasing extent, for purposes of reproduction and performance, and even by the creative artist himself.

At first sight, it seems far-fetched to talk about machine-made literature and music. What difference does it make whether the author or composer writes down his ideas by hand or by typewriter, or speaks, sings, or plays them into a recording device? In many cases, none at all; but the use of new tools has a way of subtly and gradually influencing the forms produced. For example, the novelist and playwright are affected by quick and easy typing, revision, and retyping of manuscripts. Cheap paper and printing bring out a mass of literature that would otherwise not be preserved. Young children and illiterate adults can express themselves directly in a phonographic device, without learning a difficult method of notation. Machinery often frees and facilitates expression, instead of enslaving it. This can be true in any art, where the machine is directed by a creative mind or minds. It would be possible to invent a machine which could automatically shuffle and recombine musical tones in various patterns of melody, harmony, and rhythm, as a kaleidoscope produces visual patterns. This would be truly mechanical art. But the mental phase of production can be hardly less mechanical in another sense, without the use of any machinery: that is, when it falls into a stereotyped routine of unthinking repetition, or obedience to set rules.

If it ever seemed possible to divide all the arts permanently on this basis, that hope is dwindling now that machine-techniques are invading all the arts. At most, one can compare in terms of degree. The creation of literature and music makes least use of mechanical devices at present; that of applied arts and architecture most; that of pictures and sculpture an intermediate degree, as in the graphic arts and bronze-casting.

Leo Adler, it will be remembered, proposed a division of the arts into "direct" and "indirect"—the one type requiring no tools, as in dancing and music; the other requiring them. We have already criticized this idea, on the ground that all arts use tools, instruments, or accessories of some sort. Dancing and music use masks, costumes, instruments; written literature uses writing tools. On the other hand, pottery can be made with no tools but the human hands. "Direct or indirect" does not distinguish many whole arts, but types or stages within the arts. Singing and spoken literature are notable exceptions, and it is well to point out their ability to dispense with all external instruments, materials, or body-extensions. Completely nude dancing might be added, but it has great limitations aside from all sex taboos, and has never received much development as an art, even among primitive peoples.

9. Solitary and cooperative production

This distinction has received comparatively little notice in systems of the arts.[16] It is related to the degree of mechanization and to the nature of the raw materials used. One type of artist creates in solitude: the traditional poet or painter, alone in his garret awaiting the Muse of inspiration. He needs only blank paper or canvas and simple writing or painting materials, to emerge with a finished product. Another type works in a group, performing a specialized task or coordinating a number of specialized workers; consulting, arguing, and aiding one another. Is this difference determined mainly by the nature of the art, or by the individual temperament of the artist, by the cultural environment, or by temporary styles and trends?

All these factors operate to some extent. An introverted, shut-in personality will be more likely to choose an art which can be solitary, such as poetry; one in which he will not have to brush up against other people. The sociable type will love a busy, crowded workshop. Some artists alternate between society and solitude. The Romantic move-

---

[16] Alain (Emile Chartier), in *Système des beaux-arts* (Paris, 1926), distinguished between "solitary" and "social" arts. He exaggerated the distinction, however. No art is entirely solitary. Many can be either.

ment glorified solitary brooding. Many primitive cultures do not foster or permit this type; art production is a more communal, socially regulated process. So it is in modern communist Russia. Some arts allow either type: painting was a more collective process in the medieval guild or in the studio of Rubens than in the lonely wanderings of Gauguin. Some assistants mixed the colors, others filled in minor parts of the picture, while the master made sketches, assigned tasks, and painted important parts himself. There is room in any art for some collaboration, and for the solitary worker who emerges once in a while with a sketch, a tune, or a story. But there is also a difference of degree among the arts in this respect. Architecture has always been a highly collaborative art, its magnitude and diversity preventing single-handed execution. In the medieval cathedral, many minds consulted on the sketches, and supervised various phases of the building. The theater has always been a noisy, crowded place, with much shouting of orders back and forth. The motion picture industry today is an extreme example of specialization and cooperation, often confused and often efficient.

Specialization and collaboration can occur in one simultaneous process, in the same room, as in the filming of a motion picture. They can also be detached in time and space, into many apparently separate processes one after the other. The total process by which an upholstered armchair is made from crude materials is highly specialized and subdivided. The fabric made to cover the chair was probably made in a factory quite separate from that which made the wooden frame. Springs, webbing, and varnish were likewise separate products. The fabric had its own creative, designing phase, in a textile mill which produced cloth for upholstery, drapery, garments, and other uses.

Modern industrialization is now affecting the production of popular fiction, special articles, plays, and biographies; also of popular music and verse for songs and musical shows. Large publishing and theatrical companies assign orders, buy products, alter and combine them in their own offices. Magazines and advertising agencies order specific pictures, to be painted in a certain way. More and more, the completely solitary artist is disappearing, although some intervals of privacy are still considered necessary for the creative individual. To offset the impersonality of such a process, individual names and "glamorized" personalities of authors, composers, and actors are publicized, which gives a false impression of their actual independence.

Many artists stubbornly maintain their creative isolation, but the rewards of collectivization are tempting.

It would seem, then, that no art is exempt from the collectivizing, industrializing process of the present age; but that some (such as poetry) resist it longer than others (such as architecture). At any particular time, the arts can be compared as to the degree to which their productive phase has become industrialized. But conditions change rapidly, and the result is not a permanent division of the arts. Reactions will doubtless occur, even in highly industrialized arts, toward a revival of solitary artistry.

Much theorizing about the artistic process has assumed that the solitary type is the only type, or the only important one. Both should be considered, and the process described accordingly.

10. Shaping, sounding, and verbalizing

Kant's distinction between *bildende* and *redende Künste* refers to kinds of activity. *Redend* is "speaking" or "speech," while *bildend*—a hard term to translate, as we have seen—is perhaps best rendered in this connection as *visual shaping*. As Kant used it, it is broader than *Plastik* or plastic arts, which are restricted to sculpture and architecture; the shaping arts include painting, gardening, furniture, and costume.

The concept of a group of arts concerned with visual shaping was not wholly clarified by Kant himself. He restricted it in a way which is open to debate, by leaving out "table arrangement" and other merely "agreeable or pleasant" arts which are also concerned with visual shaping. He also omitted the art of mobile color, leaving a place for it along with music, under "arts of the beautiful play of sensations." This is in spite of the fact that it also can involve visual shapes. (Witness the modern clavilux and "abstract" color films.) He was not clear about the dance, which also involves visual shape, as does the modern motion picture in general. His apparent restriction of *bildende Künste* to static arts or "arts of rest" has led a train of followers, down through Dessoir, to identify these two groups. This has the disadvantage of divorcing the dance, pantomime, dramatic acting, and motion pictures from the *bildende Künste,* and putting them under the time arts with music and poetry. It obscures their obvious kinship with painting and sculpture as arts of visual shape—a kinship evidenced by Isadora Duncan's use of Greek vases and statues, and by Disney's use of paintings in the animated cartoon film. From another point of view, of course, it is right to put them with music and poetry; that is, when we are listing the mobile or time arts. The mistake, which occurs again and again in German theory, comes from trying to make all these divisions coincide. The fact is that dancing and motion pictures belong with music in some respects; with painting and sculpture in others.

In short, Kant's conception of "arts of visual shaping" is a useful point of departure, provided we do not adhere too closely to its traditional interpretation. We shall find it useful as well as consistent to include in that group the mobile, temporal arts of visual shaping, as well as the static ones. It will thus take in architecture and city planning; painting and sculpture; the applied arts and crafts, including garden art, furniture and interior design; the dance and theater arts, including motion picture, lumia or mobile color, and a host of minor arts such as fireworks and table arrangement, which Kant ignored or looked upon with gentle condescension. It will take in all other arts in which there is an important factor of visual shaping, whether static or mobile, flat or solid.

What is shaped in these arts? A great range of physical, visible materials. In terms of sensory qualities or components: line, light and dark, color, texture, surfaces, and solids. All are given shape or spatial form, in two or three dimensions. In drawing, one shapes lines and areas of light and dark on a flat surface. In sculpture one shapes raw material into a more or less permanent, solid form. In dancing, one shapes one's own body into a series of transitory postures and gestures.

From the standpoint of the creative *process*, the "shaping" in all these arts is active, mobile, and temporal. The distinction between static and mobile, or rest and movement, applies only in dividing the arts on a basis of the type of *product*. The artist himself is not static in any of them.

How can dance and theater arts be included here, when they also include a musical factor; when they are usually classified as mixed or combined arts? There is nothing wrong with listing an art under two or more headings; it is often unavoidable, because of the many-sided nature of the arts. Theater is a visual art; it is also a musical and a speaking art. A great source of error in systems of the arts, as we have often seen, has been the insistence on putting each art in one compartment and only one. However, if one prefers, "arts of visual shaping" can be interpreted as "arts restricted to visual shaping," thus leaving out the dance and theater. This will necessitate the usual extra group of "combined arts," involving two or more such factors. Either method has advantages. At times, it is well to have a complete survey of the arts involving visual shape, so that our generalizations on visual shape in art can be based on adequate data. For this purpose, it is well to have a broad concept which can embrace them all, and not leave several important ones in a distant category, merely because they also bring in other factors.

Kant's third heading, "arts of the beautiful play of sensations," is a vague and cumbersome expression, which has found little acceptance. It is too broad, since all arts involve some kind of "beautiful play of sensations." It is rather belittling to music, stressing the sensory rather than the expressive factors therein. It has the disadvantage, for some purposes, of bringing in color together with music. Kant had little idea, in his day, of what mobile color might become; indeed, it is still in its infancy. But it is certainly becoming an art of visual forms, of color-areas arranged in organized groups and sequences, rather than of scattered sensations. Music, as an art of sounds directed to the hearing, is different enough from all the rest to deserve a class by itself, from the standpoint of process. Of course, if one is thinking of mobility and temporal development, the alignment is entirely different, with music placed beside theater, dance, and literature.

What are the basic types of process involved in music? Singing and playing; the latter word covers all instrumental music. "Sounding" covers both.[17] Not all kinds of sound are accepted as musical art; but not all kinds of visible shape are accepted as visual art. In both cases, selection and organization for aesthetic effect are taken for granted as a characteristic of all art. Just what kinds of sound are to be selected as musical is a matter of taste and style, which should not be too narrowly prescribed in an objective definition. The occidental regards much oriental and primitive music as mere noise, and vice versa. Musical sounds are sometimes called "tones," as we noted in connection with medium. But that word has no convenient verb form. Music

[17] "sound" (v. intrans.): "To make a noise or sound, as with the voice or with an instrument; to produce an audible effect; to make an impulse of the air affecting the organs of hearing. 'First taught speaking trumpets how to sound' (Dryden)" (Webster).

is not always restricted to tones having definite pitch; much primitive music consists wholly of organized drum-beats.

The "speaking" arts, according to Kant, are poetry and rhetoric or eloquence. Prose literature, including fiction and the essay, is ignored as by most theorists; the great age of the novel was just beginning. Drama is put elsewhere as a combined art. "Literature" is our accepted name for all the verbal arts. Are they all adequately covered, in terms of basic process, as "arts of speaking?" To speak is "to utter words or articulate sounds with the ordinary modulation of the voice, as opposed to singing; to express thoughts by spoken words" (Webster). The difficulty here, as we have often observed, is that literature is no longer a wholly spoken art; it is largely one of silent writing and silent reading, especially in fiction and the essay. As the name implies, it is an art of letters. "Verbalize" covers both the speaking and writing of words; it is a term in current psychological use, and is defined as follows: "to be skilled in wording; to express with emphasis upon the choice of words" (Webster). By analogy with shaping and sounding, verbalizing is the third basic process of the arts.

Obviously, these categories overlap. In certain respects, literature is an auditory art, in others a visual art. It has become so vast and important in itself, differing much from other visual and auditory arts, that it deserves to be a separate main category.

In so far as literature is spoken, it has characteristics in common with music. This is important especially in the analysis of poetry. In so far as literature is written, it becomes an art of visual shaping. This is important in regard to early cultures: for example, in tracing the development of written language and literature out of pictographs in China and Egypt; and in studying the relation of literature to calligraphy. In modern times, the visual shape of the letters has been detached from the essential structure of literary form, and developed as a separate technique. It often aims to be highly standardized, transparent, and without effect on meaning, except through the conventional symbolism of letters—that is, the exact shape and color of the letters does not alter the meaning of the poem. Literature has thus become essentially an art of arranging verbal meanings into forms.

On the other hand, verbalizing is a process which enters into both the shaping and the sounding arts. Calligraphy and typography are ways of producing and arranging words, but they are classed as arts of visual shaping because their emphasis is here, rather than on meaning.

Violin-making is an art of visual shape, but is intimately concerned with sound. Music is often verbal, as in song and oratorio; but these are still classed as types of music, in so far as they emphasize the quality of sound.

We can thus divide the arts as to basic process involved, into arts which emphasize *visual shaping*, those which emphasize *sounding*, and those which emphasize *verbalizing*. There are many borderline and variable types, such as religious chants, in which it will be hard to decide where the emphasis falls—for example, on sound or on verbal meaning. At one time the religious meaning of an oratorio may seem more important than the music; at another, the emphasis is shifted.

The category of "combined arts" is not necessary, since there is usually a preponderance of emphasis on one or the other factor, at least at a certain time. Opera is a combined art, but is, for practical purposes, usually grouped under the heading of music because its emphasis is there. The ballet is usually an art with visual emphasis, in spite of its important musical factor. All such classifications must be temporary, and relative to specified periods, styles, and cultural settings.

11. Composing, designing, performing, and manufacturing

To say that music is an art of sounding—that is, of singing or playing—does not accurately describe all the kinds of work done in music. It refers mainly to the final performance. A composer may do little playing or singing, and a great deal of writing notes on paper. To call literature the art of speaking is open to the same criticism: an author usually writes out his products, and may never speak them aloud. If he is a playwright, actors may speak his words. In each art, many different kinds of activity are carried on.

In music, a distinction is made between "composing" and "performing." The artist who writes original music is a "composer." One who sings or plays it is not often called a "performer," for that suggests a circus acrobat; but rather a musician or, more specifically, a singer, pianist, violinist, or the like. In literature, the word "composition" is sometimes used, but the original artist is called an "author" or a "writer," or, more specifically, a poet, novelist, dramatist, playwright, essayist, or the like, according to the type of literary form he produces. The performer of drama is an actor, and other kinds of literary performance are "oratory" and "dramatic reading" (formerly called "elocution"). The word-pronouncing part of an actor's skill is called "diction." In the dance, the performer is a dancer, while choreography is "the art of arranging dances" or of "representing dancing by signs, as music is represented by notes" (Webster). There are few choreographers, and many dancers originate their own dances, often without the aid of choreographic notation. In a broad sense "composition" is used to cover original creation in any of these arts.[18]

Performers as well as composers in all of them are called "artists," in a broadly laudatory way. Arts of performance are sometimes classed as "auxiliary arts" in relation to those of composition. Thus acting and other theater arts are regarded as auxiliary to dramatic literature; piano-playing to musical composition. Of course, one individual may do both, and combine them, as when a composer "improvises" at the piano in a concert. Star performers sometimes regard composition as "auxiliary" to their own talents; a playwright will be asked to write a "vehicle" for a certain actress.

Repeated performance is necessary in all arts involving the presentation of moving, changing forms—the "performing arts." This category includes music, the drama, and some arts of visual shape, such as the dance, pantomime, and marionettes. It is necessary because of the evanescence of the images presented to eyes or ears. These stimuli have to be reactivated in temporal succession, each time the work of art is to be perceived. The performance may be "in person," by living actors or musicians, or through the mechanical operation of a reproductive device such as a motion picture film or a phonograph record.

In static forms such as houses, vases, easel paintings, and statues, repeated performance is not necessary. Such products are built or manufactured once and for all. Under proper conditions of light and position they will automatically issue similar visual stimuli—light waves indicating the details of shape and coloring which make up the form. As long as the object retains its physical structure, it can be perceived at any time without repeated activation. We do not speak, therefore, of "performing" such a work of art, though it may occa-

---

[18] "Compose": "To construct by mental labor; to design and execute, or put together, in a manner involving adaptation of forms of expression to ideas, or to laws of harmony or proportion; as, to compose a sentence, sermon, sonata, picture" (Webster).

sionally be shown under specially favorable conditions, with somewhat theatrical effect. In another sense, however, the final process of manufacturing a vase or a house is a kind of performing. The artist's designs are permanently performed or executed in one process.[19]

There are many intermediate types: for example, the arts of landscape design and gardening. A garden is in some respects a mobile form, even though its basic lay-out is fixed. It may have moving water, its trees sway in the wind, and its colors change with the seasons. A landscape designer may plan it once and for all on paper, leaving to gardeners the task of planting and maintaining healthy vegetation. If it is his own garden, he will be more likely to keep altering the design throughout the years, planting new shrubs here and there, and doing much of the execution himself. However, it is a type of form which requires no special performance each time it is seen. Once the garden is planted, changes thereafter are mostly automatic, produced by the interaction of climate with plant structure. The same can be said of breeding decorative animals, such as goldfish. Their forms are mobile, but the artist's work is mostly done when they are bred and born; after that, their display of moving shapes and colors goes on automatically. An animal trainer, on the other hand, may make his animals go through a sequence of movements which is not automatic, and requires special performance.

In arts producing static visual products, the analogue to musical composition is most often called *designing*.[20] The distinction between

[19] Webster's definition covers both these types of "performance": "1. The act of performing; the carrying out or execution in action, execution in a set or formal manner or with technical or artistic skill; as, the performance of a duty, a play, or a piece of music." To "perform" is "2. To carry on to the finish; to complete or accomplish" and also "3. To go through with or execute; esp. some regular function, prescribed part or obligation, or some action requiring special skill or special capacity; to carry through in due form; as, to perform . . . a musical number." To "execute" is "To follow out or through to the end; to carry out or into complete effect; to complete; finish; effect; perform; as, to execute a purpose, a plan . . . To perform, as a piece of music, either on an instrument or with the voice; as, to execute a part finely."

[20] "Design": "To plan mentally; to conceive of as a whole, completely or in outline; to organize a scheme of; to plot;—disting. from 'execute'; as, A designed this church, but B carried out his plans." A "design" in this sense is "a preliminary sketch; an outline or pattern of the main features of something to be executed, as of a picture, a building, or a decoration; a delineation; a plan" (Webster).

designing and executing in these arts is sometimes obscure and sometimes clear, according to the amount of specialization which has
occurred. The painter conceives, sketches, and executes his own product as a rule; so, in many cases, does the sculptor, etcher, or potter.
He may revise his plan in the process of execution. But this is not
always the case. A painter may sketch a "cartoon" for others to
execute—for example, in tapestry; or leave it to his assistants to be
painted. A sculptor may make a clay model, and have others carve
or cast the statue. An engraver may have others print his pictures. An
architect seldom builds a house himself. His creative task is not
expected to include execution or performance; this is left to builders,
contractors, carpenters, bricklayers, etc., whom he may supervise in
part. His own particular task is to produce a *set of directions* in the
form of drawings, including realistic sketches of the intended building,
mechanical drawings of various elevations in scale and showing inner
construction, explanatory calculations and verbal instructions. To an
increasing extent, a similar trend exists in all the applied arts and
crafts: in textiles, costume, furniture, and the like. Here someone,
usually called a "designer," makes sketches with verbal and other
specifications, to direct others how to execute or manufacture the
product.

In the more highly industrialized arts, designing and executing
are distributed among different, specialized workers and groups of
workers, giving rise to distinct occupations. The case of a solitary
painter who does the whole thing himself represents a comparatively
early, undifferentiated stage in the evolution of the arts. This does not
mean, necessarily, that his method is any better or worse than the
other. It is simply adapted to small-scale production. Whenever a
demand arises for a product too large and difficult for one man to
execute (as in architecture and colossal sculpture), or for many duplicates of the product, the process of production tends to specialize into
separate designing and executing phases. With no volition on the
solitary painter's part, this now happens to him when his works are
in demand. One handmade example of each picture is not enough.
Even a few handmade replicas, as in the middle ages, are not enough.
Large numbers of his admirers want color-print reproductions. Thus
the executive phase is continued elsewhere, and his original painting
is treated as a design or set of directions to the printer.

All arts, then, involve performance or execution as well as designing or composing. In all, the two may become distinct processes. At other times, the two may be merged as phases in an undifferentiated process carried on by some individual or group. All the arts were originally of this type. The primitive bard embodied composer, poet, singer, and harpist. He repeated traditional songs, and altered them a little, consciously or unconsciously. Today, there are frequent throwbacks to the ideal of an old-time artist-craftsman, as in the William Morris movement, urging artists to combine creative imagination with skill in various techniques. But the main trend is the other way, for techniques are becoming too complicated, and designing becomes a specialized, highly paid profession in itself. However, the designer must still have enough "feeling for the medium" and for current manufacturing methods to turn out a workable design.

A distinction can thus be made among arts and artists, as to the degree to which designing and executing are separated at any particular time and place. It can also be made as to the number of performances required: whether one performance is enough, or repeated performances are necessary. This latter point requires more attention, for there are more different kinds of "performance" than we commonly realize.

An architect's drawings, we have seen, are a guide or set of directions to the workers who will "perform" or carry out the building. A composer's musical score is likewise a set of directions to the musical performer, as to how to sing or play. It is an arrangement of visual symbols, used to guide the actual sounding of music. A modern score contains elaborate specifications, not only as to the pitch and instrumentation, but as to the duration, loudness, tone quality, accentuation, rhythm, and phrasing of tones and groups of tones. Even so, it leaves certain nuances of expression unspecified or indeterminate, for the performer to interpret. Early musical scores left much more indeterminate; sometimes even the harmonization of the subordinate voices. In the theater, a dramatic text is a set of directions for the actors to speak, gesture, move here and there. It often leaves a great many details indeterminate: for example, costumes, staging, lighting, exact appearance of actors, tempo, exact tones of voice. Sometimes an author or stage director will mark up a copy of the text which is to be used for acting, with additional directions on such points. A dramatic text or script, then, is an arrangement of visual symbols used to guide speaking and bodily action. An orator's text, in written form, usually guides only the speaking of words, leaving intonation and gesture indeterminate. These are actual, functional relations between the process of authorship or composition and the process of performance, involving the use of symbolic visual forms as instruments of partial control. In so far as an author or composer leaves certain details of the performance unspecified, he leaves the door open to original contributions of others: for example, by the orchestra conductor or stage director.

Persons highly skilled in using musical scores—for example, an experienced orchestra conductor—can read a score silently, and imagine how it would sound. They can, in other words, give it an *imaginary performance*, much more clearly and vividly than an ordinary person could. The score becomes a set of directions for imaginary sounding. All educated people now become skilled in the silent reading of literary texts. One can read silently a play of Shakespeare or an ode of Keats, and imagine to some extent how it would sound. This is an imaginary performance of the literary form. In reading poetry, one tends to imagine the sounds of the words with more care than in reading prose fiction. The conventions of verse form in print give us to understand, in the former case, that this is appropriate. In reading prose, we tend to ignore many of the word-sounds or imagine them very vaguely, paying attention to the other meanings of the printed words as we go along. Here, then, the literary text is a set of directions, not so much for imaginary speaking as for other kinds of verbal thinking—involving many different kinds of sensory image, concept, inference, and other psychic processes. The special characteristic of this kind of thinking is its close connection with printed words as stimuli and guides. It is *verbal thinking,* by contrast with the musical or *sound-image thinking* which occurs when a musical score is silently read. Such silent reading of literature is itself a kind of performance, in a broad sense of that term. It is a carrying out of the author's directions for thought, which is none the less real for being internal and imaginary. Kinds of performance, then, can be distinguished as *overt* or external and *imaginary* or internal. Either kind can be given to literature, and either kind to music.

The peculiar task of the author, then, is to arrange a device which can be used for guiding verbal thought, and perhaps verbal sounding also, either overtly or in silent imagination. The task of the musical composer is to arrange a device which can be used to guide instrumental or vocal sounding in precisely specified ways (pitch, etc.), many of which are left indeterminate by the author of literature. Such sounding, again, may be overt or imaginary, but the latter type is rare at present. The exact nature of the device for guiding such per· formance is optional and variable; it may consist of visible letters or notes, or of something quite different, to be devised in future for a similar purpose.

On the whole, the silent reading of literature is a kind of art appreciation, rather than of performance. It is done by the ultimate consumer himself; not by a special kind of artist who is skilled in presenting visible or auditory forms to the consumer. It is analogous to looking at pictures, or listening to music, rather than to acting or playing a piano. But it is well to recognize that these categories overlap. Appreciation is never a completely passive absorption; it involves active doing of various sorts, often overt as well as sensory and mental. One of the best ways to appreciate a piano sonata is to learn to play it. Quiet appreciation often involves imaginary performance, as in looking at a Chinese brush-drawing and imagining how it must have been painted, with flowing gestures of arm and hand which the visible brush-strokes still record.

The sharp separation between performers and observers, as in the modern theater and concert-hall, is but one example of the general trend toward specializing in modern civilization. In former times, there was more "audience participation"—the roles of performer and observer were more frequently exchanged and combined. On the other hand, an opposite trend has occurred in regard to literature. The power to read printed words has become so common that we no longer need a special kind of performer to read them aloud for us; almost everyone has the technique. We can use it, either to experience a full imaginary performance, including word-sounds when they seem to justify the effort, or in abbreviated form with attention mostly to other kinds of meaning. Even in reading prose, we occasionally imagine word-sounds, as when a character in a story speaks. This is a partial approach to imaginary dramatic performance.

12. Creating and producing; planning and executing

In modern times, as we have seen, the making and performing of many kinds of art has developed into a complex industrial process, involving many kinds of worker. Not all of these are classed as artists, and many of them do little or no designing or composing. The whole process of designing and making works of art, performing them if necessary, or otherwise making them available for ultimate use and enjoyment, is the *production* of art. In economics, to produce means "to make economically valuable; to make, or to create so as to be, available for satisfaction of human wants" (Webster). Its opposite, in economics, is "consumption." [21]

In aesthetics, a similar contrast is often made between the creation and the appreciation or aesthetic experience of art. The general meaning of "creating" and "producing" is about the same.[22] But they are differently used in regard to art. The man who designs and executes an original object of art himself is called a "creative" artist, and his work is called either "creation" or "production." But when the process of making is divided up between a designer and a workman who follows his directions, the term "creative" is usually restricted to the former. The latter is sometimes called a "craftsman" or an "artisan," although these words do not necessarily imply complete lack of creative ability.[23] "Creation" implies originality; production and craftsmanship may be original, or may not.

Production of art, in the sense we are using, includes the work of artists who specialize on composing or designing, and of those who specialize on performing or executing—singers, violinists, artisans, craftsmen. It includes the work of many who are not artists at all, but engineers, technicians, business men, clerks, stage-hands, and the like, in the total process of producing "art goods and services"—a prosaic but factual expression. People who publish and sell fiction, sheet music, phonograph records, and color-prints are all engaged in producing art. In the theater, the word "producer" has taken on a

[21] "Consumption may consist in the active use of goods in such a manner as to accomplish their direct and immediate destruction, as in eating food, wearing clothes, or burning fuel; or it may consist in the mere keeping, and enjoying the presence or prospect of, a thing, which is destroyed only by the gradual processes of natural decay, as in the maintenance of a picture gallery" (Webster).

[22] "create": "To produce as a work of thought or imagination; esp. as a work of art or of dramatic interpretation along new or unconventional lines." "produce": "To give being or form to; to manufacture; make; as, he produces excellent pottery" (Webster).

[23] "craftsman": "One who practices some trade or manual occupation; an artificer or artisan; sometimes, an artist or writer" (Webster).

special meaning: the man who takes financial and administrative responsibility for presenting the performances. We shall not use the word in this restricted sense, but he is certainly one of the many kinds of person engaged in producing art.

Is it correct to infer, then, that the creative phase in art production is that of composing or designing? This is commonly said, to the disparagement of other phases in art production.[24] "Creative" is a eulogistic term; "uncreative" is the opposite. Sometimes whole arts are described as "creative," especially painting, poetry, and musical composition, in contrast with arts of performance such as acting and piano-playing, and with the criticism and teaching of art.

Such use of the term "creative" implies two false assumptions. It implies that composing and designing are always and necessarily original, and that other phases in art production are not. On the first point, it must be remembered that composing and designing have become regular occupations or types of job. In a motion picture company, one man will be employed to write scripts or scenarios, another to compose incidental music, another to design settings, another to design costumes. The furniture, clothing, pottery, and many other industries employ thousands of designers, some of them freshly out of art school. It is flattering to assume that all of them are creative, with the originality which that term implies. Many of them have to take orders from some business or production manager, producing designs of a specified type. They frequently copy or adapt previous products, with very slight change. In advertising and other branches of commercial art, there is often a great difference between the work of the "art director" in a studio, and that of the artists who make the drawings. The former may be strong in original ideas but weak in technique; the latter, just the opposite. Many highly paid commercial artists, though deft with pencil and brush, frankly recognize their lack of creative imagination, and willingly carry out specific instructions from the director.

The actual work of composition and designing is often frank

[24] Colvin credits the designer with the power to make a whole industry a "fine art" rather than merely mechanical "art manufacture." "In the case of the engraver's press, there exists behind the industry of the printer the art of the engraver, which, if the engraver is also the free inventor of the design, is then a fine art, or, if he is but the interpreter of the invention of another, is then in its turn a semi-mechanical skill applied in aid of the fine art of the first inventor" (Article "Fine Art," *loc. cit.*, p. 358).

imitation or adaptation of other products, with slight changes here and there. Much of it is done for financial reasons, to satisfy consumer demand for a certain kind of product. Often the consumer does not demand originality, as in cheap tableware and garments. The so-called designer is needed merely to provide a necessary blue-print for use under present conditions. Even in the less industrialized arts, such as oil painting, it is obvious that a vast majority of the products turned out in any one year has little claim to originality.

On the other hand, we frequently underestimate the amount of original contribution to art made by people who do not call themselves "creative artists," and who do not work as composers or designers. Even the authorship of a play or motion picture is often the work of many persons, in different occupations. Credit for a motion picture is sometimes given in words like these: "scenario by A, from a novel by B, from an idea by C." Not only these three, but scores of nameless persons have had a hand in rewriting the script and contributing suggestions. In other ways, the producer and the film director may exert a creative influence. The film editor has an important role, in final cutting, selecting, and rearranging. Some planning and directing is done by heads of many departments. Suggestions are made regarding various aspects of the film by actors and technicians, cameramen, lighting specialists, and so on. Thus the author of the story or scenario may deserve credit for only a small share of whatever creative originality the film achieves. In fact, the story itself is often extremely banal, while original effects are contributed in photography, montage, and other factors.

We might describe these facts by saying that some "composing and designing" (in a broad sense) is done by people in many different occupations. But composing, designing, and authorship are now regarded as specific occupations in themselves. It is less confusing to say that the creative, originating, planning phase of art production is often the joint product of many different types of worker. It is not always the work of authors, composers, and designers alone; in fact, these are often uncreative by comparison with others in the total productive process. There is room for creativeness in the engineering, administrative, financial, and many other branches of art production, and it occurs in different branches at different times.

This is not a recent state of affairs. Who knows how much credit for the creation of a cathedral or an altar-piece really belongs to the bishop who gave the order for it, or to some obscure master-craftsman who supervised a phase of the building? The condition is not limited to complex industries like the motion picture. The so-called "composer" of a piece of music may be very unoriginal and uninspired; a mere hack worker who had the technique to steal ideas and write them down. A great pianist, taking a dull and hackneyed composition, can sometimes infuse life into it, and make it a vehicle for tonal effects which the "composer" did not anticipate. Many a dull and stereotyped play has been saved by creative acting. Using "creative" in this sense, we must be careful to keep it distinct from any particular occupation or group of occupations, and bestow it wherever it actually belongs. To bestow it or withhold it raises many difficult questions, especially as to the amount of originality which is actually present in a particular case. Complete originality never occurs, and one must always ask how much this individual has contributed over and above that which he took from earlier sources; over and above that which his co-workers contributed. This is a task for art criticism and history, which can also be creative in their own ways.

Aside from questions of originality and value, it is a fact that planning and executing are both distributed widely through the productive process. Writing a story or symphony is one kind of guiding or directing, but not the only kind. It is a very gentle, uncoercive kind, like that of a guide-post or the "directions for using" on some package label; they have power to direct only if one wants to be directed. At most, the work of art can attract or lure one to be guided, unless some outside pressure operates to force compliance. Its directive power is at a minimum, perhaps, in the story printed for individual, silent reading. There the reader, if bored, can at any moment think of something else or lay down the book entirely; his thoughts refuse to be guided as the author indicates. The painter's preliminary sketch for a new picture is a tentative guide to execution, which may be radically changed in the final painting.

As art production becomes industrialized, or placed at the service of some outside power such as church or state, a different type of direction enters it. We have, for example, the stage or motion picture director telling the actors and musicians what to do, while the "producer" or president of the company, speaking with the power of money, or government authority, can tell the "director" what to do. In such a situation, the author, composer, or designer may receive fairly explicit orders as to what to create. We must not assume that he is always in the position of an unmoved mover, originating plans and executing them, or commanding their execution. From a limited, aesthetic point of view, this may seem to be the case, but there are deeper controls in any culture which determine both the designing and the execution of art.

Executing as well as planning is widely distributed throughout the production of art. On the whole, singing and playing are the executive phase of music, while composition is the planning phase. But, just as performance may involve a good deal of planning, so composition may involve some execution of its own. From the standpoint of the composer, the main contrast is between his original plan or vague, germinal conception of the symphony and its final form with all the details of harmony and orchestration. To him, the executive phase consists of writing it out in full, ready for the printer. To the printer, it may present a new task of planning the printed score, perhaps with decorative cover, and the published volume completes the executive phase of his work. Just as physical materials can be raw, semi-processed, or processed, so the total work of producing art is full of ending and recommencing, final executing and further planning, as one man completes his share of the work and another takes it up. The finished fabric is but semi-processed material for the upholsterer; the finished novel for the scenario-writer. In short, planning and executing are relative terms, describing phases in all intelligent activity, and not to be associated exclusively with any particular arts, occupations, or techniques. We shall understand the production of art better if we look for them over a large area and in varied forms, not in a few traditional spots.

At the same time, it is reasonable to assume that both planning and creativeness tend to localize themselves in certain occupations, to some extent. It would be wrong to overstress exceptions to the rule. There is a real distinction in practice between those who are paid mainly for policy-making and original ideas, and those who are paid mainly to carry out the ideas of others. This distinction is expressed not only in differences of pay and authority, but in accepted definitions of various types of job or occupation. Authors, composers, and designers are especially charged with creating original ideas for works of art, and with expressing them in forms suited for use in further manufacture or performance. Sometimes they fail to do so, and are highly paid nevertheless, while someone in another capacity does it for them. But there is a theoretical difference in jobs, which is more or less closely approximated in practice.

13. Six basic types of process in the production of art

Let us now summarize and combine several points made in the foregoing sections.

One type of art is concerned with *visual shaping*. It discloses an executing or performing phase, the actual making or presenting of visual shapes, as in building a house or dancing a tarantella. It discloses also a designing or composing phase, as in sketching plans for a house, or noting the choreography of a dance. This can be summarized as *visual shape guiding*. The specific mode of guiding is optional and variable, but it usually takes the form of sketches, letters, numbers, and other visual symbols. It may be expressed in the spoken words and gestures of a stage-director or ballet-master.

The second type has as its performance phase *sounding,* especially *musical,* through singing or playing.[25] This is usually overt, though it can be imaginary. The composing phase consists in planning and guiding such performance. Musical composition is *sound guiding*. In our culture, it is usually achieved through written, visual notation; but it may be done in other ways—for example, through recording a performance for the phonograph or screen, which can be imitated by others. Much contemporary popular, as well as primitive music, is almost impossible to write down exactly; the rhythmic and tonal qualities considered essential to the piece can only be directed through demonstration.

The third type, comprising the various branches of literature, has been called "the arts of speech." This is hardly adequate, for speaking is only one of the ways in which literature is performed. *Verbalizing* is a broader term, including writing and silent reading. Some branches of literature, such as prose fiction, are seldom read aloud. Drama and poetry, though adapted for audible speech, are often read silently; in that case their performance phase may consist of imaginary speak-

---

[25] Another kind of sounding, which includes non-musical sounds, can be included here. It consists of the realistic "sound effects" which are accessory in radio, theater, motion pictures, etc. It is not yet a distinct art or a recognized, major factor in art.

ing, and perhaps imaginary acting, gesturing, etc. The concept of "verbal thinking" applies to all these modes of performing literature. Accordingly, the universal task of literary composition is *verbal thought guiding*, through organizing groups and sequences of words. Speech directing is now only an occasional function of literary texts; in prose fiction and other branches, even the imaginary sounding of words tends to cease as silent reading accelerates. Action-guiding, as in drama, is another occasional function.[26] The compositional phase, authorship, is now usually carried on through the device of written letters and words, or substitutes such as tactile (Braille) symbols. It may be done through speaking into a recording device, such as dictaphone, phonograph, or sound film. When played, such a device operates to direct verbal thinking in the hearer, but makes it unnecessary for him to imagine or speak aloud the sound of the words.

This classification can be outlined still more briefly:

I. Arts of visual shaping
   A. Designing or composing phase: visual shape guiding
   B. Performing or executing phase: visual shaping

II. Arts of sounding, especially musical
   A. Designing or composing phase: sound guiding
   B. Performing or executing phase: sounding

III. Arts of verbalizing
   A. Designing or composing phase: verbal thought guiding, and sometimes speech and action guiding
   B. Performing or executing phase: verbal thinking, and sometimes speaking and acting, in accordance with verbal guides.

It is hardly necessary to add that these main types overlap, as in opera, which combines all three. We have already seen that designing and performing often merge, in all arts. On the other hand, each main type, and each phase under it, often parts company from the rest, as a specialized occupation.

[26] In regard to all the arts, we are now considering only the processes and functions immediately involved in designing and performance of the work as specified. That is, we are not considering the many kinds of ulterior effect which a work of any art may produce on the observer, or be intended to produce: for example, emotional, moral, patriotic, educative.

14. Overt and psychic phases in art production

There is another way of classifying the processes and abilities involved in all the arts. They can be classified as (a) those emphasizing overt, motor, externally observable behavior; somatic; involving movement of limbs and muscles, and often the use of tools and instruments; (b) those emphasizing inner, psychic, mental activity, conducted largely in the brain and central nervous system.[27]

The first type, of *overt* processes and abilities, includes the use of brushes, chisels, pens, pencils, typewriters, violins, cameras, kilns, and all other tools and instruments. It includes skills of the hands and fingers, of the vocal and sensory organs, and of the limbs and torso. Some are used in the execution and performance of art, and some in its composition. Ability along these lines is always learned; never wholly a matter of inborn reflexes, though inborn aptitude helps determine the ability to learn one or another more successfully. Such skills are consciously taught in all cultures; some of them, such as writing, to almost everyone; others, such as brushwork, only to special groups. They are never purely somatic, manual, or muscular, but always require some mental control. However, some phases of them tend to become automatic, as in typewriting, leaving conscious thought free to deal with other phases. In playing the piano, a virtuoso's fingers move almost automatically through rapid, intricate passages, leaving his attention free to control the subtle shadings of expression and phrasing. Some kinds of artistic performance are carried on in a condition of trance (for example, certain Balinese dances), with conscious control suspended. But even this requires a peculiar kind of psychic control: the ability to enter a trance condition at will, with appropriate aids.

The second type, of *psychic* abilities and processes, is sometimes closely coordinated with overt activity, as in observing outer objects and in directing hand movements. Sometimes it is more detached, so that active mental work goes on while the rest of the body is quiet, or engaged in unrelated routine activities such as eating or walking. Benedetto Croce quotes Michelangelo as saying, "One paints, not with

[27] The terms "mental" and "psychic" are almost synonymous in the sense intended. But "mental" is often restricted to "intellectual," while "psychic" more definitely implies the sensory, emotional, conative, and imaginative activities also. No fundamental dualism, metaphysical or psychological, is implied in this antithesis.

the hands, but with the brain." Leonardo da Vinci, says Croce, would stand for days together, gazing at the Last Supper, and not touching it with the brush. Thereupon, he says, the convent prior remarked, "The minds of men of lofty genius are most active in invention when they are doing the least external work." [28]

This second type of process and ability includes much of what is commonly known as "creative imagination" or "the creative process." But they are not identical. The total process of creating a poem, sonata, or picture includes the overt writing or painting as well as the inner conceiving and imagining. On the other hand, there is more to the psychic phase of art production than conceiving and imagining. It occurs, for example, in the conscious direction and control of a performance, as by an orchestra conductor leading a symphony. This process, with its requisite skills, is not wholly overt, the mere waving of a baton; it involves its own kind of mental activity, to control the movement of arms and hands.

Individual abilities in this realm are determined partly by inborn special aptitude, partly by general environment and personality development, partly by general formal education, and (to a relatively slight degree at present) by special training for artistic pursuits. They are intimately bound up with special skills: for example, when a painter or craftsman thinks out his preliminary conception of a future product. Images derived from his past experience with the medium enter into his thinking, and his thinking later directs the new overt process. Some of these abilities are specially trained, and can be definitely listed as skills or techniques; for example, narrative plot construction; versification; musical counterpoint; perspective drawing. These can be carried on with pen or musical instrument in hand, or in quiet meditation. On the other hand, some of the basic mental or psychic abilities in art production are not special skills, but general character traits, such as an ability to see the humorous side of things, or to persevere under difficulty. But they become linked up with special artistic situations, and focussed on artistic means and ends, thus infusing and directing all the special skills.

The overt and psychic processes in art production are so interwoven as to be indistinguishable in practice. All artistic production involves some of both. But there are differences in emphasis, and it is

[28] *Aesthetic,* p. 10.

often obvious that one phase or the other is dominant for the time being.

The psychic skills are often omitted in accounts of artistic technique. They are commonly regarded as mysterious and indescribable. They are often neglected in the training of artists, on the assumption that they are unteachable, and must be left to inborn talent or genius. This leads to a one-sided, incomplete understanding of artistic ability, and to inadequate methods of art education.

In arts involving highly developed overt technique, such as pottery, such technique looms up so conspicuously that the mental phases in production are often taken for granted. Our whole conception of "technique" or "skill" is then limited to external manipulations. If asked how he makes a vase, the artist will begin by explaining how he prepares the clay, shapes it on the wheel, fires it, glazes it, fires it again, and so on. This seems to him, to the student, and often to the teacher of art, as the whole artistic process: the technique of making pottery. But, in so far as the potter was an intelligent, genuinely creative artist, many steps preceded and accompanied the handling of the clay: in particular, the tentative conception of a design for the vase, and of what detailed characteristics were consistent or inconsistent with it; hence what ones were to be produced or avoided. Sometimes an attempt is made to distinguish between "technique" as overt craftsmanship and "creative imagination" as the psychic phase of art production. The names are of secondary importance if both phases are given due attention. But a very narrow conception of technique results if we regard it as wholly external. There is danger of losing the proper coordination between mental and manual phases of the work; of failing to realize that the psychic phases can be trained as systematically as the manual, and need not be left to spontaneous "talent," "good taste," or "inspiration." In the oriental attitude toward art production, more careful attention was paid to the psychic preliminaries. Instead of rushing into manual execution at once, the artist took time to achieve the right mental and emotional condition, and to visualize the form which was to be produced.[29] An adequate understanding of technique as "expert method in the details of accomplishing something" requires the full recognition that both overt and psychic skills are

[29] *Cf.* A. K. Coomaraswamy, *The Transformation of Nature in Art* (Cambridge, Mass., 1934), p. 5. It is questionable how much of the Indian artist's essentially religious approach can be followed apart from its religious basis.

always involved in art; that both can be trained and developed through experience and scientific knowledge; and that both should be closely coordinated in the productive process.

Knowing as little as we do about the basic factors which make for creative talent or genius in art, we could still do more in training those psychic skills which serve creative talent: for example, skill in sense perception; in sensory discrimination, recognition, and memory; in various kinds of controlled imagining and mental conception of aesthetic forms; in intelligent planning of art projects from a functional standpoint; in the learning of scientific knowledge which may be useful in art production; in the appreciation and criticism of previous works of art, and consideration of how certain elements in them can be adapted to modern needs.[30]

The distinction between mental and physical work in art has been exaggerated in the past, and wrongly applied. It was used to distinguish the "liberal" arts from the "mechanick" arts, the latter being said to "require more the Labour of the Hand and Body than of the Mind; as Carpentry, Carving." [31] No group of arts has a monopoly on mental labor; none is merely physical. Certain phases in the work of every art are largely mental and others more physical; the same can be said of individual workers and specialized occupations in the total process of production.

However, there is a grain of truth in the old attempt to distinguish whole arts on this basis. Everyone knows that writing sonnets takes less manual training, less power to handle tools and physical materials, or even to coordinate one's own bodily movements, than carving, painting, dancing, or piano-playing. Milton, when blind, sat and dictated poetry to an amanuensis. Writing poetry does not necessarily take *more* mental ability than making chairs, but the kind of ability it takes is more exclusively mental; less extended into muscular coordination. Accordingly, our whole approach to the training of an artist is different in literature. Since there are no special overt techniques required, beyond the common ones of reading and writing, it is often assumed that there is no way of training a prospective poet. Even today, in most of our school and college courses in English and other

[30] *Cf.* T. Munro, "Creative Ability in Art and its Educational Fostering," in *Art in American Life and Education* (Bloomington, Ill., National Society for the Study of Education, 1941), p. 289.

[31] Above, Ch. II.

literature, there is no systematic effort to develop creative writers. To a large extent, the educational emphasis is still on studying past products. But there is an increasing number of courses in "composition," and in particular branches of literary craftsmanship such as short story writing, for which there is popular demand.

How can we compare the *composing and performing phases of art* with respect to *types of skill employed?* On the whole, no doubt, performing and executing require more highly developed overt skill than composing does. To write a play is largely a mental process, requiring as overt skills only the ability to handle a pen or typewriter, or to dictate. To present it on the stage requires many overt techniques, including acting, costuming, and scene painting. A man can compose music even though his hands are too badly paralyzed to play, provided he can still write or dictate the notes. The composing or designing phase of many arts is accomplished with little more than a few simple, basic overt skills such as writing words or notes and sketching rough pictures or diagrams. Often some amount of overt skill in execution is necessary to be able to compose well. A musical composer should be able to play some instrument, but not necessarily all for which he writes. An architect does not have to be a carpenter or stone-mason, even though it might help him in some ways. It is impossible for those who design in complex industries to have all the overt skills which they direct. Designing becomes a full-time job in itself, and one has to acquire by observation instead of direct experience the necessary sympathy with most of the tasks to be guided.

There are important exceptions to the general rule that performance takes more overt skill than composition. Some kinds of performance are very simple, or done with only those basic overt skills which all educated people learn to some extent: for example, playing a phonograph, or reading a book. On the other hand, composing and designing are sometimes developed into elaborate processes with overt as well as mental skills of their own, and with their own kind of instruments: architecture, for example, with its rulers, compasses, T-squares, and protractors; its refined technique of drawing plans. This, of course, really amounts to a different kind of execution, preliminary to that of actual building. Certainly, we cannot assume that composition always takes more mental skill than performance does.

In modern industrial production, including that of art, there is a tendency to hand over all planning and directing to certain officials, and to make the rank and file of workers mere automata. This sometimes results in a situation where the composer or designer is treated as an absolute authority, who does all the thinking and basic policy-making; whose directions are obediently carried out by the performing or executing staff. This happens when the composer has great prestige and insists on having his own way: for example, in the presentation of Bernard Shaw's plays. It happens when the composer is also in a position of financial or governmental authority—for example, when he owns the company, or is head of a state-controlled theater. But, more often, counter-trends prevent this extreme specialization. The composer or designer often follows general policies laid down by a publisher, manufacturer, theatrical producer, or by public taste; he has only a limited margin of free initiative. In a democracy, the right to make suggestions is often widely distributed among the rank and file, and good ideas are gladly accepted from workers who are not directly employed for that purpose. Many a play is largely rewritten after a few rehearsals, in response to suggestions from directors, actors, and critics. Many an industrial design is redrawn when the production and sales managers begin to criticize it. Thus mental skill and initiative are encouraged at various points of the productive process, instead of being exclusively allocated to the composing or designing phase. This may seem unfortunate to the modern artist, as he thinks of the freedom which a free-lance enjoys, to produce as he wishes. But that freedom was more often apparent than real, and there are often compensations —to the artist, in greater rewards; to the public, in the collaboration of many minds.

What kinds of performance skill are required in the three main types of art distinguished above? We have noticed how some theorists oversimplify the facts in saying, for example, that the plastic arts use tools; literature and music no tools. Again, there is a grain of truth here: literature and music can do a good deal, if necessary, with nothing but the voice. Visual shapers have almost always used some kind of tool, from paleolithic times. Finger-painting is an attempt to get along without them, and thus to simplify the process of expression for children and nervous patients. Even there, special kinds of paint, paper, and supporting surface are used. In all arts, adequate performance may require manipulation of some physical instrument or accessories, whether it be a brush, a violin, or the scarf a dancer waves. But manual skills are on the whole basic and essential to performance in the arts of visual shaping, whereas they are needed only in instrumental music, and seldom strictly necessary in the performance of literature. For the deaf and dumb, there is a language of symbolic manual gestures; but that is a very exceptional case. Gestures are helpful to the actor, but not indispensable unless his art is pure pantomime. Then it is not a performance of literature, but belongs with the dance as an art of visual shaping.

In the combined arts, such as opera, some versatility is often required of the performer. In opera he is expected to sing and also act—that is, move and gesture expressively, and thus perform visually. The singing skill is so paramount, however, that limitations along other lines are pardoned. A ballet dancer is engaged in a combined, audio-visual art; but he does not have to be as versatile as that suggests. The performance as a whole is presented to eyes and ears both; but different performers carry on the two different phases. The main performance phase of motion pictures takes place while the play is being filmed. Theater performances here are mechanical reproductions. It also is audio-visual, but increasingly specialized except for an occasional star who can sing, dance, and act. The multiplication of performance skills required in a complex art proceeds rather through combining different specialists than through developing versatile individuals.

In the *composing or designing phase of various arts, what skills are involved?* Let us think especially of cases where this phase is relatively distinct from execution. In some highly industrialized arts, such as architecture, we have seen that designing itself comes to develop overt skills, such as mechanical draftsmanship. It develops its own executive phase, distinct from final execution, in that even the plans have to be expressed in a certain elaborate form before they will be effective as guides to building. In others, we have seen that relatively simple, common skills are sufficient, such as the ability to write words or make a rough sketch. In these, there is a minimum of overt skill required of the composer-designer, and his principal tasks are mental: "thinking up" the new idea, and carrying it from a vague germ to a form as clear-cut and complex as the conditions require. In all arts, as designing becomes a specialized task, there is a tendency for it to produce refined forms of its own, even though these forms are merely preliminary guides to final execution. The designer of costumes or furniture has to learn some technique of visual representation, in order to make even his tentative sketches clear and attractive. Theatrical costume sketches by Bakst, Picasso, and others—for example, those of the French Baroque spectacles—have won regard as works of pictorial art in their own right.

To a large extent, composing or designing in any art now requires overt skill in the use of a *visual* medium. This is true, not only in the visual arts, but also in those which are or were primarily auditory, such as literature and music. All composition in these auditory fields used to be unwritten; but today an illiterate author cannot get very far, and neither can a musical composer who has not learned musical notation. Up to the present time, visual symbols have proven to be indispensable as means of preserving compositions, and even in the composing of them. Auditory symbols are too evanescent; the printed word endures. Few artists can think out a story, poem, or sonata completely, away from a piece of paper. They do not create in non-visual terms (spoken words and sound-images) and then merely record the form in visual symbols; they create directly in and with visual symbols. Many musicians compose away from the piano, working directly on the score with visual symbols whose meaning they have learned well enough to imagine vividly the sounds intended. Perhaps other ways of expressing musical and literary form will become adapted for creative work, such as phonographs, films, and dictaphones; but so far they have been little used. Even in making a phonograph record, the orchestra must have the score to look at; and in making the motion picture, the script is almost essential.

This widespread visualization of the process of composing art has important consequences. Not only the composition but the experience of literature is becoming increasingly visualized, through silent reading, with less attention even to the imaginary sounds of words. This militates against the art of poetry as a whole, where word-sounds are essential, and tends to stimulate prose. The whole auditory factor in literature has declined to some extent, although the radio and sound film may revive it. There is no serious threat of this in music; too few people can read music silently. But the need of composing in visual symbols affects the type of music composed. Visual notation is a tremendous help to the composer, in working out exact specifications, revising and preserving them. But it is also a limitation; it prevents him from using effects not easily written down and quickly readable by a performer. This excludes subtle and complex variations of pitch and rhythm, as in oriental and primitive music. Some composers (for example, Reger, and even Bach in "The Art of Fugue") have been charged with writing music "for the eye"—intricate contrapuntal and harmonic patterns that can hardly be followed by the ear, unless one has studied the score and analyzed their convolutions. After the over-refined products of erudite writers and composers, and the colorless voices of educated conversation, the public often feels an exhilarating shock in listening to unwritten folk songs and popular, jazz music. But the major trend is the other way.

Biologists tell us that the trend of human evolution is toward weakening the lower senses. That of civilization has been to put a fatiguing burden on vision, thus impoverishing other forms of art and experience. Learning to compose on paper, in literary language or in the complex vocabulary and syntax of musical notation, is enough to deter many a born story-teller or singer from attempting to create works of art. For the musician, especially, learning a visual language is alien to his main flow of auditory thinking. Having constantly to trans-late sounds into ink-spots and back again is a distracting obstacle to free auditory imagination, unless it can become completely learned and automatic.

The overt skills of a musical composer are usually more diver-sified than that of an author, in that he has to be able to play one or more instruments; not necessarily well, but enough to feel what they can do. His experience is enriched, then, by various types of hand or voice training, derived from his work in performing. The author needs no overt muscular skill, but the common ones of speaking and writing with pencil, pen, or typewriter. His technique in speaking, his penman-ship, and even his spelling may be bad, without affecting his author-ship; others will correct these minor defects in publication.

Our educational methods have wisely recognized the indispen-sability of reading and writing for all occupations, including the arts, and have made the elementary learning of these techniques com-pulsory. Most children now learn to read and sing simple music, but few learn how to write it down, even from dictation and without originality. While it remains the necessary language of musical com-position, an ability to use *notation* more actively could well be made more widespread at an early age, so that it would become automatic.

The same can be said of *drawing,* which has been a basic tech-nique of creative design in all the visual arts for thousands of years.

There is little likelihood of its ceasing to be so, yet few children are taught to draw with facility. Drawing as a basic technique for all kinds of visual art should be distinguished from the kind of drawing which is a special preparation for pictorial art—that is, for becoming a painter. Less detailed study of realistic perspective and anatomy is necessary, and more adaptability to different kinds of visual expression. The student should be able to handle a pencil easily, so as to convey a rough idea of any kind of visible shape he has in mind. This requires some power to represent the third dimension realistically, and the human figure in different attitudes. It also requires some of what is usually classed as "mechanical drawing"—the ability to make diagrams, cross-sections, floor-plans, and the like, with emphasis on expository meaning rather than on visual realism.

15. Theories of creative imagination. Psychic phases in the production of various arts

Much has been written about the "creative process" in art, by critics, philosophers, and psychologists from the time of Plato to the present. Theories on this subject have usually been combined with theories about the nature of the artist as a distinctive type of personality. According to Plato, artistic creation was largely the result of divine madness or inspiration, and the artist was a person unusually capable of receiving such inspiration. This semi-mystical, supernaturalistic conception of artistry was an integral part of the Neo-Platonic strain in Roman and Medieval thought; but it was overshadowed until the Renaissance by the low appraisal placed on most kinds of art as menial. By the Renaissance Platonists, it was revived in a movement to glorify the artist, and this glorification swelled to a chorus of worship (in which artists themselves were not reluctant to join) during the Romantic period. By his superior powers of responding to the Cosmic Mind or Will, his self-forgetfulness and ability to rise above practical, mundane considerations, the artist could assist all humanity to a similar flight. Kant approached the question of the nature of artistic genius with more sober naturalism, showing the roles of reason and imagination therein. The creation of art was for him a natural process, but one in which the cognitive powers of the genius had free play, excited and directed by the imagination.

At the beginning of the twentieth century, Ribot's work on the

Creative Imagination[32] brought many newer psychological conceptions to bear upon the problem of distinguishing between reproductive and creative imagination. He described the latter in terms of sense images, motor needs and desires, association, the intellectual and emotional factors, the unconscious factor, and the development of higher out of lower forms of invention. He attacked the mystical, supernatural view of genius and creativeness, holding imagination to be a function of mind common to all men in some degree. In many ways, he declared, the abilities and mental processes of the artist are like those of the scientist, the practical inventor, and the commercial, social, or religious leader. He also distinguished various types of artistic imagination, but did not correlate them with different arts.

The ancient theory that artistic genius is akin to madness, and that some kinds of psychic disorder may be socially valuable, was revived in 1859 by J. J. Moreau.[33] Lombroso and Kretschmer [34] studied personality types in the field of art, as related to bodily structure. Freud, Jung, and Adler studied them in relation to neurotic types of disposition. Freud's interpretation of dream imagery, as compared with neurotic symptoms and the imagery of religion and folklore, has thrown great light upon the nature of artistic imagination.[35] He also made a start toward the psychoanalysis of artistic personality in his study of Leonardo da Vinci. Recently the psychoanalytic approach has been fruitfully combined with that of anthropology, in the work of Kardiner, Linton, and others, in comparing the psychology of different cultural groups.[36] Again, this throws light on the nature of artistic creation, by showing how each cultural environment predetermines an artist to think, feel, imagine, and produce.

Meanwhile, much empirical data has been collected and sifted by literary biographers and psychologists on the ways in which artists work, as indicated by their letters and other documents, and by per-

[32] T. Ribot, *Essay on the Creative Imagination*. Paris, 1900. English Tr., Chicago, 1906.

[33] *La psychologie morbide dans ses rapports avec la philosophie de l'histoire.* Paris, 1859.

[34] E. Kretschmer, *The Psychology of Men of Genius.* New York, 1931.

[35] S. Freud, *Die Traumdeutung.* Leipzig and Vienna, 1900. *Leonardo da Vinci.* New York, 1916.

[36] A. Kardiner, *The Psychological Frontiers of Society.* New York, 1945. R. Linton, *The Cultural Background of Personality.* New York, 1945.

sonal interviews in the case of living artists. The results are limited by the frequent ignorance of artists about their own mental and emotional processes—a trait not peculiar to them, but often intensified by unusually great unwillingness or inability to analyze themselves objectively. It is limited also by the tendency of human beings to conceal or distort facts which they think would place them in an unfavorable light, and to play as glamorous a role as possible. However, such data can be checked with others, corrected, and fitted into the growing fabric of psychological understanding.

Resultant generalizations about the creative process have distinguished various *personality types,* each with its own way of going to work—for example, some impulsive and some rationally planful; some introverted and some extroverted. They have also distinguished various *stages* in the creative process, believed to be more or less universal among all types of artist. Dessoir described (a) the artist's preliminary mood of vague illumination and emotional, often painful groping; (b) his moment of clear, articulate conception; (c) his objectification of the concept in a sketch; and (d) his difficult, experimental execution of the project. Some of these stages, Dessoir pointed out, may be omitted, telescoped, or changed in order of sequence.[37]

Richard Müller-Freienfels[38] accepts the prevailing view that artistic creativeness is an inborn trait or type of personality rather than an acquired skill. He goes on to characterize it in terms of superior powers of rich, intense, emotionally colored perception and imagination, as well as of expressing inward experience in objective forms, through motor activity which is not practical in purpose. Types of expression are distinguished as free or controlled; direct or ideomotor (as in dancing and acting), indirect (as in vocal or graphic expressions of feeling), or symbolic (as in black to express mourning). He distinguishes three stages in the creative process: preparation, conception, and execution. Inspiration, which may occur at various points, is characterized by suddenness, an unusual mental and emotional condition, and an impersonal, passive condition.

One of the most widely quoted studies of artistic creativeness is

[37] Max Dessoir, *Aesthetik und allgemeine Kunstwissenschaft.* Berlin, 1906; Stuttgart, 1923.

[38] *Psychologie der Kunst.* Berlin, 1923. Vol. II, Book III, is on "The Psychology of Art Creation," with a detailed analysis of its phases and varieties.

The Road to Xanadu, by John Livingston Lowes.[39] It traces in minute detail the steps in Coleridge's creation of "Kubla Khan," "The Ancient Mariner," and other poems, with emphasis on his collection and transformation of source materials from folklore and miscellaneous reading. There are three stages or factors in creative imagination which interplay reciprocally, according to Lowes. They are (a) the long, slow storing of the Well, or stocking of the mind with materials and experiences; (b) the flash of amazing vision through a chance suggestion; and (c) the exacting work of translating this vision into actual, objective form. This hypothesis has been developed by several other aestheticians, notably Max Schoen,[40] who subdivides the artistic process more elaborately. There are two main processes, he says: Adventure and Discovery. Adventure includes Preparation and Elaboration, and the latter of these includes one or more of the following: Reconstruction, Integration, Intuition, Abstraction, Generalization, and Transmutation. All of these Schoen analyzes psychologically. The process of Discovery includes (a) illumination, flash of inspiration or "divine madness"; and (b) laborious execution.

Such accounts of the creative process have been based more on data from the lives of poets than from artists in other fields; largely because more objective, relevant data are available about the preliminary stages. It is not wholly clear to what extent the accounts are applicable to other arts. Paul Plaut,[41] Norman C. Meier, and others have gathered a considerable amount of data on the methods of contemporary painters and craftsmen. Meier remarks that the artists' methods "are as different as are the artists." [42] Some, he says, work directly from nature, while others are inspired by dreams; some make

[39] Boston: Houghton, Mifflin, 1927, 1930.

[40] *Art and Beauty* (New York, 1932), p. 54. Also *Understanding the World,* by M. Schoen, H. G. Schrickel, and Van Meter Ames (New York, 1947), Ch. XXXI, on "Theories about the Artist"; a brief survey of the subject. Another analytical summary is in A. R. Chandler's *Art, Beauty, and Experience* (New York, 1934), Ch. XVI, on "The Artist and his Work." He divides the stages and factors in the creative process as follows: stocking the mind; unconscious reorganization of material; inspiration, the germinal idea; conscious organization of material; elaboration and revision, filling out details.

[41] *Prinzipien und Methoden der Kunstpsychologie.* Berlin, 1935.

[42] *Art in Human Affairs.* New York, 1942. Ch. IV on "Creative Production and Artistic Talent," and Appendix on "Creative Artists at Work."

a few sketches at the scene and reconstruct the picture in the studio, while others plan the composition meticulously before painting, with many detailed, preliminary sketches. Even the same artist may work in different ways at different times.

Nevertheless, it is generally believed by aestheticians that the three main phases, which Lowes picturesquely called "the storing of the Well, the Vision, and the concurrent operation of the Will" occur in all arts.[43] Indeed, Lowes is careful to point out, as Ribot did, that even scientists create in this way. Darwin reports such a flash or leap of the imagination in suddenly grasping the cumulative meaning of his data on the origin of species; and Poincaré reports a similar set of stages in mathematical discovery.[44]

Such accounts of stages in the creative process deal mostly with the few, conspicuous, final steps, just before a particular work of art is formed. They neglect the long, previous conditioning; the building up of a psychophysical organism suited for producing just that kind of art. Lowes hints at this in his phrase, "the storing of the Well," and Chandler in "stocking the mind." But more dynamic concepts are required to describe the complex redirecting of motives, habits, and fantasy life. Long before the artist receives the stimulus which consciously touches off a creative process for him—for example, before he sees the thing about which he is to write a poem or paint a picture —heredity and environment have been shaping him for years to be receptive to such stimuli, and to respond in certain ways. But these preliminary phases in the creative process remain vague, suspended, generalized, until some particular stimulus helps to bring them to a focus, and to precipitate a particular example. It may be any kind of stimulus: in the same medium as that in which he works, or not; it may be something perceived, or an unsought fancy. It may be an order from outside, a utilitarian need; any fact or idea noted. It may be a vague, germ-idea produced in his own medium (for example, on

[43]Julius Portnoy, in *A Psychology of Art Creation* (University of Pennsylvania Ph. D. dissertation, 1942) has assembled some significant material about the methods of artists in music, literature, painting and sculpture. It tends to confirm the belief that the creative process in all these arts is basically similar. It involves, he says, (a) sensory experience; (b) incubation or unconscious elaboration; (c) rise to conscious level, spontaneously or through reflection or introspection (p. 93).

[44] Graham Wallas describes the stages of all creative thought as Preparation, Incubation, Illumination, Verification (*The Art of Thought*. New York, 1926).

the piano) through aimless experimentation. It activates and fuses many relatively inactive, separate trains of thought. For example, long after he has formed the habit of dreaming about dark forests and misty glades, with all they connote emotionally, something suddenly shows him how they can be suggested in piano music, to his satisfaction. But this is only a late step in the whole creative process.

The examples cited by Lowes and others, where a definite "flash" or leap of the imagination has occurred, provide no adequate basis for assuming that it is universal in creative thinking, in art or science. Obviously, there is some kind of reciprocating process in all human experience, of receiving and (at least in part) of reorganizing and giving out or expressing in some way, if only through a change in everyday behavior and conversation. For the inventive artist or scientist, the phase of expressing or producing in an altered form is comparatively definite and conspicuous; it issues in a particular, concrete work of art, or a scientific device or demonstration. The psychic process of selecting and reorganizing material from past experience into the conception of a work of art or science is no doubt partly unconscious and automatic. In some cases, it is shown to be sudden and ecstatic; and this is doubtless characteristic for certain types of personality. On the other hand, it has not been shown that the process of conceiving a new product in art or science is always, or in most cases, sudden and ecstatic enough to be called a "flash" or "leap" of inspiration. Something which can be metaphorically described as "leaping" occurs in all thought, as we quickly shift from data to concepts or from one image or train of inference to another. But something much more than this is meant by the theory of creative "flash."

Max Schoen credits Nietzsche with the most vivid account of the state of flashing inspiration. In this state, says Nietzsche in *Ecce Homo*, one seems to be—

the mere incarnation, or mouthpiece, or medium of some almighty power. The notion of revelation describes the condition quite simply; by which I mean that something profoundly convulsive and disturbing suddenly becomes visible and audible with indescribable definiteness and exactness. One hears—one does not seek; one takes—one does not ask who gives: a thought flashes out like lightning, inevitably without hesitation—I have never had any choice about it. There is an ecstasy whose terrific tension is sometimes released by a flood of tears. . . . There is a feeling that one is utterly out of hand, with the most distinct consciousness of an infinitude of shuddering thrills that pass through one from head to foot. . . . Everything occurs quite without volition, as if in an eruption of freedom, independence, power, and divinity.

Without such inspiration, it has been asserted, great art cannot be produced. "Every product of higher art, every significant *aperçu*, every thought which yields fruit, lies in no man's control, but is raised above all earthly power. The man is controlled by a demon while he believes he is directing his own activities. In such instances a man is a tool of a higher ruling power, a favored receptacle of the divine influences." [45]

Such a statement is hard to prove or disprove. If one points to works of art whose production involved no such ecstatic vision or sense of outside control, they can be set aside as inferior. But the history of the arts is full of steady, quiet workers who made no claims to demonic control, and some of their works are highly rated. It is perhaps significant that most of the artists in modern times who have emphasized the role of flashing inspiration have been Romanticists like Coleridge and Keats; and that some of them, like Nietzsche, have been neurotic to the point of eventual insanity. It is also significant that many neurotic, epileptic, and psychotic cases lay claim to similar divine inspiration, while their products are devoid of merit.

The question calls for more extensive, open-minded investigation into different types and periods of artists, by psychologists who are not prejudiced in favor of sensational results. It is a little misleading to speak of "*the* creative process," "*the* artistic process," or "*the* creative imagination," as if there were only one kind. There is ample evidence to suggest that different kinds of personality, in different cultural environments, create in different ways. No one way is essential to the production of good art, so far as our present knowledge indicates. Many roads to success are open to the aspiring young artist, and he should choose one for which he is suited.

There is some danger in overemphasizing the "flash of inspiration" theory, in that it tends to prolong the old, semi-mystical attitude toward the processes of art. It tends to obscure innumerable cases, in both art and science, where the process of invention is more gradual and undramatic; where the new form emerges step by step through

[45] Quoted from Goethe by Max Schoen, *op. cit.*, p. 67.

patient, intelligent, imaginative effort. If a young, prospective artist believes that no real originality is possible without the mysterious fantasies and sudden illuminations which Coleridge, Nietzsche, and others like them experienced, he is likely to be discouraged at not having them. He may even be turned aside from worth-while conscious labors, in a vain effort to whip up his dreams with opium or some other artificial device, as Coleridge did.

It seems generally agreed that the creative "flash," when it does occur, may occur in any art, and in many kinds of invention outside the arts. Hence it cannot be used as a basis for comparing the arts, or distinguishing between them. Apparently, psychic differences in the creative process occur, not so much between different arts as between different individuals or types of personality. It would appear, for example, that the planful, highly conscious, rational type of artist is to be found in all fields of art; and also the more impulsive, ecstatic, visionary type, which is impelled by some unconscious drive to imagine and express its fantasies, as if by a force from behind.

One distinction among the arts, however, is fairly obvious. The differences in *medium* between the visual arts, music, and literature necessarily entail some difference in the psychic process of creation also. The musical composer must think to a large extent in terms of sound-images; discriminating finely between them as to rhythm, pitch, timbre, and other qualities; devoting his time and energy to combining them this way and that; making, hearing, and dreaming of sound patterns. He tends to translate many of his other types of experience into auditory symbols; to express his attitudes and emotions, desires and aversions, in and through the suggestive power of musical sounds. The writer does the same with words, and the visual artist with visible shapes and colors. There are overlappings, in that the musician thinks partly in terms of words and visual symbols; the poet in terms of auditory rhythm, and so on. But there is a real difference in emphasis. This is further specialized along the lines of particular materials, tools, techniques, and surrounding conditions. A playwright thinks not only in terms of words, but of spoken words, footlights, and action on the stage. A sculptor comes to feel at home with a chisel, a mallet, and a block of stone; a painter with brushes, paint, and canvas. He dreams of them when away, and longs to get back to them. Each plans and imagines in terms of his own medium, and pours into that set of images a large part of his life experience, conscious and unconscious. Few artists are as versatile as Richard Wagner—able to compose in sounds, words, and visual shapes. Even he achieved preeminence only in music.

In short, there is some difference between the arts, as between other occupations, in terms of the psychic process involved. In so far as a man identifies himself with his work, and does not merely perform it in an absent-minded, perfunctory way, he comes to channel a large part of his total psychic activity into the set of images and actions involved in that work. Such channeling, of course, has countless individual and cultural variations; it is not sharply marked off by any abstract distinctions between the arts. But in so far as an art actually develops a distinctive set of materials and overt techniques, the psychic techniques of composing for it tend to be modified accordingly. This includes not only the immediate work of composition itself, but the whole personality structure and life activity which find a partial outlet in that work. Everything connected with it becomes highly symbolic to the artist, and loaded with affective meaning.

This does not mean that all oil painters tend to think alike, and in a way entirely different from wood-carvers. There are many other factors involved in channeling the psychic processes of an artist. Some of them tend to diversify the attitudes of artists dealing with the same medium, and to produce resemblances among those in different arts. Thus we cannot assume a complete correlation between type of medium and type of psychic process.

We are touching here upon the complex and little-understood problem of the growth of personality, and of individual differences in character, within which the artist is only a special case. From this point of view, the choice of a certain art and medium to work upon is itself a result of previous factors determining personality. Why are paint and painting attractive to some students, words and writing to others, music and singing to still others? To what extent are these predispositions inborn and physiological—for example, due to possession of good eyes, good ears, good voice, good muscular coordination, including the related brain and nervous systems? To what extent are they due to early family conditions, disciplines, and conflicts which unconsciously determine his attitudes in art and elsewhere? To what extent are they due to wider social, economic, political, religious, and intellectual influences? To cultural influences in the field of art—for example, to the fact that a certain art commands high or low prestige and financial reward at a certain time? (Remember the low status of the visual artist before the Renaissance.) To what extent are they due to current styles and style trends in the various arts—for example, to a romantic movement in music and literature, which attracts the youth of romantic tendencies, at a time when other arts remain stubbornly classical? What of the influence of great individual artists, who sweep many followers into their train?

No doubt, all these factors and many others combine to produce the artist's personality and consequent ways of thinking, with varying degrees of strength in different instances. Their combined effect is to predispose the artist toward a liking for certain kinds of form or product in art; a dislike for others. They make him want to create certain kinds of art, and to react violently away from others. They make him build up a certain ideal conception of himself as an artist, and of what he intends to do. These preferences may be rationalized by himself and others in terms of conventional standards which do not describe their basic motivation. Certain kinds of art take on strong symbolic, emotional significance for him, as standing for things outside of art which he admires or detests—for example, for obedience to authority or revolt; for rational control or turbulent impulsiveness. The kinds of art which he admires and wants to emulate impel him to go through the appropriate steps to produce them, provided he is strong-willed and intelligent enough to do so. This brings into play certain appropriate types of overt technique and of inward fantasy and reasoning, as means to ends. It operates to channel the artist's mental processes in certain distinctive, complex ways.

The system of channeling or conditioning thus produced may coincide with that impelled by his chosen medium and occupation, or it may not. For example, a certain artist may find that the art of carving statues in marble, with present tools and techniques, provides a completely satisfactory outlet for what he wants to do in art; it is an adequate mode of expression for his personality, and perhaps for that of many others in his cultural setting. If he is fortunate enough to be able to follow that calling, he will have comparatively smooth sailing; and if capable, may produce art which will later be regarded as the typical, outstanding expression of its age. (Shakespeare, Titian, and Bach were such fortunate men.) If not, as often happens, there will be a conflict, more or less conscious, between these various directive influences; consequently, in his creative processes themselves. It may be expressed in a vague, inadequately explained anxiety (as in

Michelangelo); in resentment toward the world, hostility toward rivals, and worry about himself; in a constant struggle with his medium and uncertainty what to do with it; in fitful experimentation along diverse lines. He may try to produce effects which are hard or impossible with that medium, as when Rodin tried to carve marble into vague, melting, dreamlike forms suggesting life and movement. He may try to make painting do things which music has been doing, and music do things hitherto done only in literature. If he is powerful enough, he may be able to alter the medium itself; to devise new tools or materials, new overt techniques; to make the medium say what it has never said before—for example, Walt Disney. He may thus make the name of his art take on a new meaning, rendering obsolete old definitions and old conceptions of its "boundaries."

Differences in the psychic processes of artists, then, correspond only in part with differences in medium and overt technique. They correspond also, in part, with differences in the *type and style of the product*. At the height of the Romantic period, when Coleridge, Keats and Blake lived, dreamlike, ecstatic art was in demand. Accordingly, many artists consciously tried to be ecstatic and visionary. Perhaps Romantic artists did not have any more unconscious fantasies than those of other schools, but they sought after and encouraged them more; they translated them eagerly and directly into works of art. When asked how they worked, they proudly emphasized their flashes of inspiration. At other periods it has been fashionable for the artist to be more calmly practical and rationalistic; hence to restrain his fantasies more, and disguise them in approved forms. Painting and sculpture in the Middle Ages emphasized other-worldly visions; in the late Renaissance, they emphasized faithful observation of nature. Necessarily, the change in aim and style of product entailed some change in the artistic process—for example, to more exact and systematic observation of the visible world, as a subject for artistic representation.

From differences in the form and function of the product, such as we are to consider in the next chapter, it is reasonable to infer some related differences in the artist's mode of thinking. Various literary types, such as the essay, novel, and lyric, tend to call forth somewhat different mental and emotional processes in the artist of any period. The lyric is more likely to emphasize obscure imagery and condensed emotional fantasy. Other types of literature tend to be more discursive and reflective. An essay or semi-scientific detective story, containing a large element of logical reasoning, entails some emphasis on logical reasoning in its author's creative process. A strongly utilitarian, functional object such as a chair, sword, or shoe, entails more practical reasoning in terms of adaptation to intended functions—more, that is, than a poem like the "Ancient Mariner," which has little or no practical utility. On the whole, the more utilitarian, practical arts, such as architecture and furniture, probably tend to involve more practical reasoning, more contriving of effective means to active uses, than the less utilitarian ones such as music and sculpture. But all arts, as we have seen, involve some utilitarian functioning, and some practical thinking by the artist. The facts are much less simple than they seem at first sight. One cannot infer the nature of the process, just by examining the product. The two are not exactly correlated.

Assuming that a work of art is made purely for aesthetic reasons, that it has no aim or function but to serve as an object and stimulus for pleasant contemplation, it still does not follow that the artist's processes were purely aesthetic. There is an essential difference between the *aesthetic* and the *artistic,* as habitual modes of behavior, and as types of personality. Where the former is, on the whole, receptive and compliant toward the outer stimulus, the latter necessarily involves an active effort to control and change something in the outer world; to alter the medium—whether it is paint, words, or tones —so as to give it the desired form. This in turn involves practical reasoning, the adaptation of means to ends. The artist always has to ask himself, in one way or another "how can I use my available resources to produce the desired result?" Whether the result is utilitarian or aesthetic from the consumer's point of view, it still requires practical thinking on the part of the artist. If his aim is merely to amuse or entertain, as in light music and vaudeville, whoever originates the skit must plan and criticize it as means to that end: "Will it make them laugh? Will it offend or bore them at this point? Will it hold their attention? If not, how can I make it do so?"

A product whose aim is purely aesthetic may require even more practical reasoning on the artist's part than one which is highly utilitarian. What we call useful art is not always approached in a genuinely practical spirit. In architecture and furniture, the utilitarian basis often becomes conventional and stereotyped, requiring little study by the artist. He may accept a traditional box-shaped framework for the house, and a traditional method of construction. Bowls of a certain shape and size are made with the same fundamental structure for centuries, and little call for change. In such cases, the artist may lavish nearly all his creative power on a few ornamental details.

Any phase of art-production may become stereotyped, so that the artist no longer thinks creatively about that phase, but executes it in a routine manner, and directs his creative efforts—if any—to other phases. The ideas expressed in sermons, political speeches, and newspaper editorials are often stereotyped clichés or "rubber stamps," devoid of any fresh reasoning on basic arguments and conclusions. Yet such a conventional, intellectual framework can be embroidered with fresh, colorful figures of speech and verbal rhythms, and to that extent creative.

About any work of art we can ask, "How much of it was really originated by the artist who is given credit for it? How much did he take over, ready-made, from earlier works of art? What details or characteristics, if any, did he originate himself?" Those questions cannot be answered by examining his product in isolation; one must compare them with previous ones to which he had access. Accordingly, one cannot infer, by looking at the product, what phases of the artist's process involved fresh, original thinking, planning or dreaming, and which were conventional. To be sure, conventional imitation sometimes gives a lifeless, mechanical quality, and fresh experience a quality of animation, which are evident in the product, at least to a trained observer. But this is not always the case; the best experts can be deceived. In our culture, highly skilful artists usually try to be original, and obviously so. In Egypt, in China, and in the European Middle Ages, they were more content to follow traditional forms. Many of them could copy an older work of art, or execute a conventional design, with the apparent freshness and vitality which we associate with new creations. Even today, there is much more imitation of past art than artists like to admit; but it is usually unacknowledged; concealed by a superficial appearance of novelty. It is not limited to those who, as artisans or craftsmen, frankly execute the designs of others. What passes for creation is often, in large part, an imitation of older forms, with the artist's thought limited to superficial details. If so, a connoisseur observing the work may have a much richer experience, a deeper understanding of the work of art than its maker did. The real artist, in that case, is the ancestral group: the countless forerunners who built up the tradition which this particular artist (or artisan) mechanically follows.

As we learn to understand the nature of art more fully, we see it as an epitome, a symbolic vehicle, of general trends in human nature and in culture. We see in each work of art an expression of recurrent themes and attitudes, whose meanings can be endlessly interpreted. It is not wise or necessary for the artist to dwell upon all the devious forces which have made him what he is, or all the possible implications of what he does. To see his work in such a vast cultural and psychological setting might well diffuse his attention, and weaken his impulse to make a single, simple, definite gesture. His attention is rightly concentrated on his own particular objectives, with some but not too much philosophical consideration of their wider import. It is well, for the sake of his enthusiasm, that the gesture he is making should appear to him as more important, more valuable, more profoundly right and original, than it may seem to historians of the future, in their comfortable perches above the unending battle.

16. Individual and cultural factors in creative activity. Style trends and the individual artist.

The psychology of art, under the influence of romantic individualism, has usually exaggerated the individual, personal aspects of artistic creation as compared with social and cultural aspects. The impression has been given that each individual genius creates his art almost entirely *de novo,* from the ground up, owing little to outside influence, and directly responsive to the inner light of miraculous inspiration. At most, such individualistic theorizing has recognized the artist's use of "source materials," as in the ideas for plots and characters which Shakespeare took from earlier writers; but has regarded the artist's way of organizing those materials as peculiarly his own. Against this extreme individualism, Marxist and other theories arose in the nineteenth century, which stressed various forms of social determinism; but these often went to the opposite extreme of ignoring the artist's personality as a determining factor, and of oversimplifying the nature of social influence—for example, as consisting merely in the struggle for power and wealth between exploiting and exploited classes.

We are trying now to analyze the facts more objectively, and to see in a more balanced way the interaction between heredity and environment. Within the environmental factors themselves, we are trying to distinguish the respective parts played by vast, general movements in culture, and by those more limited forces which play upon the individual artist from before his birth, in his family, neighborhood, schooling, and other personal experience. Recent trends in the psychology of personality development continue to stress the importance of these outside influences, especially in early childhood. But often the psychologist has to rely on the vague conception of inborn difference in disposition, to explain how two children, subject to very similar conditions from birth, respond and develop in very different ways— one into neurotic retreat; the other into passionate expression through art.

The psychoanalytic interpretation of art and artists has already been vividly illuminating, and promises to be more so. But for best results, it should be combined with a study of styles in art and other social trends affecting the artist; not applied as if he were an isolated phenomenon. Historians tend to overemphasize social and stylistic influences. On the other hand, psychologists and biographers with a psychoanalytic approach tend to explain the artist's style, and the symbolism of his work, in terms of some purely individual configuration of personality. Such an explanation may be correct as far as it goes, but it is often too narrowly limited to immediate family influences: for example, to the effects of maternal overprotection and sibling rivalry. It needs to be supplemented by other researches into the artist's wider cultural environment: for example, what moral and ideological attitudes of the time, operating through parents, church, school, and companions, contributed to his conflict and maladjustment on the one hand, while impelling him to a certain kind of artistic compensation on the other? What current trends in art contributed to his style? Granted a particular conflict in the artist, and a particular symbolic expression of it in his art: one must not assume that these are peculiar to him as an individual. Social repressions lead to social fantasies, as in folklore, religion, and taboo. The genesis of any particular symbolic form in art must be attributed, not alone to mechanisms within the individual artist's personality, but also to social trends, institutions and conflicts of his time, toward which he was partly antagonistic, partly compliant. With these he eventually worked out a compromise adjustment, which is partly expressed in his art, if we know how to look for it.

Recent developments in art history [46] have laid great stress on styles and style trends, running all through the arts of a certain period. People at the time are never clearly aware of them; from the perspective of a later date, they stand out as vast movements in which previous styles are partially abandoned, and new ones built instead. Vast as they are, such trends in artistic style are never independent, but parts of still larger cultural trends embracing all forms of thought and behavior: social, political, economic, religious, and scientific.

The role of the individual artist in these impersonal movements must not be too much obscured: he is always the vehicle through which they operate; there is no cultural trend and no abstract *Zeitgeist*, apart from human individuals. The individual still appears to lead and to follow; to give some peculiar twist to the general trend, which it would not have had without him. There is something unique in Keats, in Chopin, in Delacroix, and in each of their works, which is not contained in the Romantic movement as a whole, apart from them. Individual configurations are just as real and unique as they were before, after we have learned to see their place in more inclusive cultural configurations. But they are not quite as unique and distinctive as we used to consider them, when under the spell of the hero-worshipping approach to art history. Their lives and works are less completely inexplicable when we see the social forces which helped to mould them. We cannot explain Chopin completely in terms of them; there still remains the unique combination of genes which produced him as a biological organism; the peculiar set of local and family influences which focussed upon him as an individual. Nothing is ever completely explained. But at least, we are discovering more and more of the factors which operate within and without the individual artist, and which make up his creative, psychic process. We see the artist as never entirely original, never a bolt from the blue, always responsive to the currents about him, and therefore different from what he would have become in another cultural setting.

In general, the individual artist's potentialities are inborn—hereditary and congenital: his brain and nervous system; his muscular

[46] For example, in the works of Fiedler, Riegl, Wölfflin, Cassirer, and Curt Sachs.

coordination or lack of it; his sensitive auditory system, perhaps, along with a weaker visual apparatus, all of which predisposes him toward music. Even temperamental dispositions are inborn to some extent; one child being restless and irritable from birth, another placid; one quickly tiring of any prolonged occupation, ever in search of novelty. No one knows how much to attribute to such factors in the adult artist, whose disposition is markedly rebellious or conservative. But it is equally certain that rebellion and stability move also as great social trends, one or the other dominant for a generation or a century. Each sweeps along personalities of every type, while raising to the crest of the wave those individuals who are, by birth and conditioning, in tune with the age and most fit to express it.

Individual style in art, and individual personality, appear as specific, detailed variants of one or more main cultural trends. There are always many trends and patterns at a given time, especially in our complex modern civilization. Radical and conservative trends eternally conflict and compromise. Yesterday is in conflict with today and tomorrow, and each has its adherents. Conflicting social, religious, and other pressures beat upon the plastic child; they fuse, cancel each other out, and eventually reach some kind of equilibrium in adult personality. No one can be unique. Even the arch-rebel, he who stands out as a lone wolf against society, is borne along by some current of the time which makes lone wolves; the decay and disintegration of some old social pattern; the cry of far-off kindred spirits, which encourage his defiance. The rebellious artist is quick to sense an incipient trend toward some particular kind of revolt, which is congenial to him; the attack on some particular moribund convention. He jumps into the fray, and helps to push the new trend a little further along. One cannot escape social influences by becoming a rebel; one merely chooses a rebellious social trend to swim with, and one's choice is an example of that cultural movement.

A general style-trend—for example, the impressionist movement in painting—never exactly determines the individual styles of its adherents. It moves them toward a general orientation of seeing, thinking, feeling, and imagining. It presents them with a certain range of alternatives, within which there is always room for considerable individual variation. There is room for an infinite number of personal styles within the impressionist movement: for people as different as Monet and Manet, Renoir and Sisley. None of these personal styles is completely covered by the single epithet "impressionist"; they all have some impressionist traits, plus traits of other styles like the Spanish, the Dutch, or the French rococo. Each original personal style is more than a composite of period styles. To show how it is unique, and at the same time how it exemplifies past influence, tradition and trend, is a major problem for the art historian.

In the psychology of art, the time has passed for describing "the creative process" as if it were always the same. It differs profoundly, not only in accord with different types of personality, but with different periods and styles of art. Within the same art and medium, artists at different periods think, feel, and imagine in very different ways, even though they use much the same overt techniques. We must now pay more attention than past biographers did to the cultural influences which play upon the artist: those which shape his mind and character in general, and those within the realm of art, which help to form his personal style, his personal way of working. In describing the mental processes of artists, we must accord a larger place than has been given so far, to the process of assimilating past traditions and current trends in style. We must view the emergence of original ideas as a process of building upon inherited culture-patterns, and adapting them to new conditions, new needs, techniques and goals.

Persons mystified by the bizarre and radically different styles of contemporary artists often jump to the conclusion that each is due to some peculiar aberration of the artist. The paintings of Van Gogh appear to them as crazy distortions, with mad excesses of coloring. Van Gogh died insane, they hear. Obviously, then, his art was a mere expression of his insanity. For the psychologist, the problem is much more complicated. In many respects the style of Van Gogh was not peculiar to him, but an example of certain general, post-impressionist trends in the art of Europe at the end of the nineteenth century: bright, contrasting colors, expressionist distortions, etc. If such traits in Van Gogh occurred to some extent in other artists, and were "in the air" at the time, they cannot be attributed entirely to his own personal make-up, normal or insane. The question remains, why the psychopathic Van Gogh produced notable art, while most psychopathic persons do not; also the question why Van Gogh's style is similar to that of many sane artists. Individual style in art is not exactly correlated with types of personality; it cannot be explained without reference to general trends in art and culture at the time. Trends in art at a certain time—for example, a time of social turmoil and breakdown of tradition—may be such as to attract people of unstable disposition to become artists; to afford an artistic outlet for impulses which have to turn elsewhere in more severe or classical times. On the other hand, there is this to be said for the popular theory that Van Gogh's own personality caused his style of painting. The time in which he lived was one of many diverse trends, and consequently great freedom for individual choice. There were neo-classical trends (as in Puvis de Chavannes) as well as calmly impressionist and wildly expressionist trends. In such times, when many alternatives are clearly open to the artist, his choice is determined more by individual, personal tastes and motives. These in turn must be attributed more to local environmental forces, in the family and immediate milieu, than to broad general trends in the culture as a whole. Our main concern must be to consider all these variable factors in each case, as it arises in art history, biography, or individual psychology; not to be satisfied with any one simple explanation.

The problem, of course, is not limited to insane or neurotic artists. It includes the whole subject of relations between style, personality, and culture. It includes not only causal explanations of style, but the psychology of the creative process: what factors were involved therein, with what relative force, and in what order of development.

To the art historian today, it is a truism that no work of art is completely original; that every artist, even the greatest, stands on the shoulders of the past. There is no artistic creation out of nothing; *ex nihilo nihil fit*. The comparatively original part of an artist's work consists, not in thinking up completely new ideas, but in working out a few variations on one or more of the styles he inherits. By comparison with what he accepts and follows in them, his own contribution is usually smaller than it is supposed to be. Often it consists largely in a combination of selected elements from two rival, contemporary styles. If his contribution, large or small, is accepted and imitated, it becomes part of a tradition. By such gradual increments the traditions of art and of civilization develop. Sudden, large mutations are extremely rare in the history of art. When an artist appears like a bolt from the blue, it is usually because we do not know the sources of his style. Giotto and El Greco still appear as highly original artists, but a little less so as we discover some of the sources of their style. The

"burning of the books" in China destroyed much pre-Confucian literature, and obscured the early development of Chinese civilization.

In every period, certain basic conceptions and techniques, certain
fundamentals of style, are taken for granted by the vast majority of
artists. When the Gothic style dominates, they accept its fundamentals
as a starting-point and produce a few variations within this general
framework. Radical exceptions are few and likely to be ignored or
rejected by contemporary taste, as too much out of step with the times.
The composer in a polyphonic age accepts the general principles of
contrapuntal composition; the painter of the high Renaissance accepts
the general ideal of a good picture as emphasizing noble, statuesque,
solid figures, with realistic lighting and coloring, perspective into deep
space, and subordinate landscape background. As seen by a later age,
most individual artists in a period seem basically similar, much more so
than they seemed to each other. Michelangelo, Leonardo, and Raphael
were acutely conscious of their differences. Today, we see their actual
differences more clearly than they did, but we also see that in many
basic respects they were brothers in the spirit of fifteenth century
Italy, by contrast with contemporary Chinese painters, or with Dutch
painters two centuries later. With more knowledge of art history, we
begin to see the main, distinctive traits, not only of each period, but of
all modern European art; to see how all artists within it were, more or
less unconsciously, expressing various aspects of modern western culture.

Recent advances in cultural psychology show how all members of
a culture express its basic patterns, even in their small revolts from
convention, without knowing it. They cannot imagine, at first, that still
more radically different ways of thinking, feeling, and producing art
are possible. Only the shock of contrast with a radically different
pattern makes them conscious of their own. The artist repeats current
patterns in his art without realizing it, just as he conforms on the
whole to customary standards in other realms. In only a few respects
at any one time is there much individual revolt or variation. These few
seem highly important at the time, and bitter disputes rage over them:
for example, whether the "three unities" must be observed in drama;
whether painters have a right to "distort" natural anatomy and perspective; whether poets have a right to dispense with meter, or
composers to employ a certain dissonance. Later on, such issues often

seem like tempests in a teapot. Aspects of art to which the artists devoted most of their conscious attention often seem in after years to be rather trivial; the real advances were along other lines, hardly noted at the time; perhaps in the work of some obscure popular artist whom the academies despised.

Today, we are in a wave of eclecticism and of straining for novelty, with constant swings of style from one extreme to another. To the layman, much contemporary art seems like a complete, insane break with all tradition. The historian sees, however, that beneath this apparent originality is constant borrowing from older unfamiliar sources; from the orient, and from primitive and exotic styles. The main European traditions in art seem, momentarily, to be thrown aside. But even the break with modern, occidental tradition is more apparent than real; more superficial than profound. Artists keep returning to it, and using it as a main trunk, on which to graft these newly imported, exotic forms.

However far afield the occidental artist goes for inspiration, he still sees other styles of art through occidental eyes. He selects out of them only those aspects which he is prepared to understand and sympathize with; the rest he rejects as merely crude, odd or repulsive. Today, he is ransacking the arts of China, India, Byzantium, the African and Polynesian tribes, for ideas he can use. But he can understand and like them only in certain limited respects: in their visual, decorative aspects, and in their weird or idyllic associations of exotic life as he imagines it to be. The deeper meanings of exotic art as expressing attitudes radically different from our own are still hard for us to grasp. It will be long, if ever, before our culture can accept and fuse them with its main traditions.

In times of great eclecticism and diversified experiment like our own, the artist feels at times an agreeable sense of freedom. No one in authority tells him how to create; almost everyone concedes his right to do whatever he wants to, within legal limits. But at the same time, he is likely to feel a sense of insecurity; of confusion and anxiety as to what he really wants to do. If forced to "prostitute" his skill for a living, he may feel resentful; when free to do what he wants, he is often bewildered and impotent. There is no strong, unified current of tradition behind him, to reassure him that what he is doing is worth while; to solve his basic problems, and steer the main course of his imaginings, while leaving him enough scope for variation to achieve a moderately individual style. Before an equilibrium is again achieved, there must be a long period of cultural assimilation. It is not enough to work out, artificially and superficially, a new synthetic style of art, by selection from all available sources. Our own culture must achieve more fundamental unity in all its phases: political and social, industrial and intellectual, before its artistic expression can again fall into a unified rhythm, and proceed with some assurance of aim.

Broadly speaking, the artist's productive process includes his gradual acquirement of the patterns of his cultural group; the traditions and current fashions of his art; also of those exotic influences which are being accepted by his group, and used by other artists in it. His productive process includes a slow, selective rearrangement of these inherited patterns in his own personality and behavior; partly by conscious thought and partly by unconscious "gestation." In the latter, certain affect-laden images from different sources gradually combine with each other into new complex fantasies, as in a dream; later to be consciously revised and rationalized. The result, if the artist lacks originality, will be to turn out a product which is stereotyped, like the shop-girl's daydream of love, fine clothes, and admiration. The original artist adds some new variations, developments, combinations of hitherto separate elements. In addition, if he is to be recognized as great, creative in the laudatory sense and not a mere freak, his contribution must somehow fill an aesthetic need of the time, and perhaps of later times as well. It must come at the appropriate time in cultural history; not too early or too late. He must be, not only different from his predecessors, but different in a way which is approved and admired by dominant forces in posterity.

The inner sense of such creativeness is, unfortunately, no guarantee of its genuineness. Much the same "creative process" of sudden illumination, detailed elaboration, and so on, is reported by geniuses and mediocrities; by real innovators and by unconscious copyists. To all, what seems to be the "great idea" may appear without conscious volition, through unconscious motivation and fantasy. An ecstatic sense of inspiration is no guarantee that the results will be new or distinctive; mediocrities experience many of the thrills of genius. Often the original artist does not realize where his own originality lies; he is gloomy and dissatisfied when a job is done. He may try hardest for some effect, and feel most proud of its achievement, which posterity throws aside as worthless, while some incidental, minor work that cost him little effort is exalted. It is hard indeed for the artist to realize at the time exactly which moments in his work are creative in the sense of producing something new and important. Alcohol and drugs, it is well known, can give one a sublime awareness of uttering great, profoundly original things. As great artists often go unrecognized in their time, so the most creative, epoch-making moments in the life of an individual, or of a people, often pass unnoticed at the time. Their importance is not seen until later; there was nothing in the activity itself which stamped it, manifestly and intrinsically, as creative.

So, again, it is better not to identify the creative process with any special type of felt experience, such as that of flashing inspiration. The young artist should not strain too anxiously for it, or feel dismayed if it does not come; but do his daily job as well as he can, and steadily cultivate whatever sources of psychic energy may lie within him. Only the future can tell which of his products, and which qualities within them, will turn out to be really creative, as valued additions to civilization. A false conception of the artist's work as purely individual, or purely inspirational, tends to lead both artists and psychologists astray. Both miss the real nature of innovation as building upon the past.

Artists often cherish romantically idealized notions of their own mental processes, especially in the present age, with all its admiration for individual originality. One who regards himself as "creative," and not a mere hack worker, if asked how he works, will usually omit or minimize—even deny indignantly—the extent to which he is following other artists, past and present. However obviously his work may resemble that of some older artist, he is likely to deny that he has been influenced by it, or perhaps that he has ever seen (or heard) it. Unconsciously, he refuses to remember or to recognize the debt. Like all members of a culture, except those who have analyzed it scientifically, he is largely unaware of the ways in which he has accepted its basic attitudes, beliefs and patterns as to life in general; or its aims, techniques, styles, and standards of value in his own occupation. He tends to feel that he is creating or discovering something quite new, and completely his own, when it is basically a restatement of traditions and current trends. Of course, real innovation occurs, but it is usually much less than the artist and his friends believe. It often consists in very slight departures from a traditional form, which they are quite unable to distinguish among the mass of unoriginal characteristics.

They praise him for "creating" what he took from other artists' work, while rejecting or ignoring his real innovations.

It is dangerous to generalize about the psychology of art, on the basis of what artists say about their own methods. Such accounts are highly important for psychology to study, as data; but not to be taken at their face value, as true descriptions of what actually happens. They often contain profound and striking observations on the artist's work in general, and on particular experiences. Indeed, their words often reveal, to the psychologist, far more than they realize. But such illuminating remarks by artists are always combined with obscuring and misleading poses, concealments, rationalizations, and fantasies, of which they are largely unaware. These mechanisms operate even in keen self-analysts, like Goethe and Rousseau. These are usually literary men, and more able than others to explain themselves in words. But, as artists, they produce works of art when they try to lay their souls bare; even when that revelation seems most brutally frank, or coldly objective. Asked how he creates, an artist may reply one day with insults, another with whimsical bantering, a third with romantic self-depreciation, and a fourth with some account highly flattering to himself, with great stress upon his independence and originality.

Artists like to emphasize the mysterious, automatic quality of creative imagination,[47] which indeed they actually feel; but which is due to its largely unconscious nature, and is not necessarily a sign of merit. If asked how they get their ideas, they will seldom acknowledge that another work of art in the same medium has ever suggested one. It is not so humiliating for a painter to admit being inspired by a piece of music, or a composer by a poem. But each is morely likely to insist that his idea came to him quite independently, either by conscious effort or by some mysterious, unsought inspiration. In representational art, such as painting and fiction, he may insist, and honestly believe, that the idea came to him solely through observing nature, the world, human beings—anything but previous works of art in his

---

[47] "Composers are not actually very revealing in their prose writings and can at times say all sorts of nonsense with the greatest seriousness. They seem bent on making the creative process as mysterious as possible." (Review by Charles Jones, himself a composer, of Frederick Dorian's *The Musical Workshop*, New York, 1947. *Journal of Aesthetics,* December, 1948, Vol. VII, No. 2). This is an extreme statement; some writings by composers are highly revealing.

own medium. If this particular face or flower has never been painted before, he assumes that any picture of it must be original and creative, regardless of the fact that his style of painting is largely conventional. If he has painted a human figure, he will make it appear that the whole process was limited to himself and his model; that he created the work of art directly from nature, by his own unaided imagination. If so, he ignores the fact that previous training and looking at pictures have conditioned him to choose, see, and represent this model in certain ways—that is, in terms of a particular style. Without experience of past art, he would have no idea of how to begin. Tradition tells him approximately what to do and how to do it, leaving him only a small range of alternative possibilities to choose from and experiment with. His conscious attention is focused on these possibilities, ignoring the ways in which his work conforms to current style. To posterity, he may appear as a typical example of that style, and even of the influence of some hated rival or predecessor. It is becoming harder and harder for an artist to maintain the delusion that he is completely original. The history and critical analysis of styles in art are becoming better known to the public, and to students of art. Thus they are forced to recognize the existence of styles, and of their own debt to tradition.

The opportunity for conscious choice is comparatively large for most people in our present western culture, in all walks of life. We have great freedom to choose our occupations, our place and manner of living. We can go up or down the social and economic ladder with comparative ease, especially in America. We can use our talents as we please; if not for one employer, then for another, or as free lances. The price of non-conformity is less severe than in most other cultures. We have great mobility as a result of racial and cultural mixture, with diversity and conflict of folkways, including styles of art. This diminishes the area of fixed conformity; it encourages or necessitates individual choice and eclectic combination. Furthermore, we have a special tradition of individual freedom, which approves and rewards some (by no means all) kinds of change and originality.

Education is gradually, in spite of setbacks, increasing powers of rational decision, as opposed to blind conformity. The artist, too, can learn to analyze consciously the various alternatives open to him in producing a work of art. He can consider all the different ways a similar problem has been solved in the past, and the new ones allowed by modern technology. His creative process is becoming more conscious and rational; whether the product will be better is another question. Many artists, teachers and students resent this trend; they resist attempts to make them think rationally about their art, and to read critical discussion. But the trend, for the present, is irresistibly in that direction. Art criticism, history and philosophy are in the air, in popular magazines and over the radio, so that no one can ignore them entirely.

It is a moot question, too large to be considered here, how much artistic creation is dependent on unconscious, fantasy-producing conflicts; how much the well-springs of inspiration are consequently dried up by psychoanalysis or other harmonizing, ego-developing influences. Many artists fear to lose their unconscious tensions. Henry Moore once remarked, "It is a mistake for a sculptor or a painter to speak or write very often about his job; it releases tensions needed for his work." [48] Most people, artists included, have more unconscious conflicts than they need in their work, and they have the wrong kind of tensions. What the right, productive kind are, we may learn as depth psychology progresses; also what to do about them educationally. Some artists depend on automatic fantasy, and try to exploit their own unconscious with the aid of psychoanalysis. Some depend on soberly conscious, daylight methods.

Today, there is much eclectic choice and synthesis between this style and that; much deliberate planning to achieve a certain effect, whether useful or aesthetic, reassuringly familiar or shockingly bizarre. The straining for novelty and the anxiety to be thought original are now familiar parts of our culture-pattern. Thus the artist who exhibits them is not unusual, but following a convention. Not only automobile and clothing designers, but many painters and composers as well, try to startle the jaded public by some radical change of style every year or two. Consequently, it becomes harder and harder to produce the desired shock of surprise.

Eventually, perhaps, there will be less of this straining for novelty. As we develop a more unified, self-conscious culture, one which has assimilated the present stream of exotic influences and become more

[48] *Art in England,* p. 95. Quoted by Richard Seddon, in "Two Modes of Perception and Expression Performed by Artists when Painting," *Journal of Aesthetics,* Vol. VI, No. 1 (Sept., 1947), p. 27.

broadly human in scope, our artists may be more content to express its collective patterns of love and hate, desire and aversion, in forms which are essentially consistent in style, as in the great, homogeneous cultures of the past. Individual variation will not be lacking, but rather released and invigorated. There will be less need to grope for it anxiously. Each artist will see more clearly what things need to be done, the possible ways of doing them, and what his own best contribution can be.

IX

Comparing the Arts as to Nature of Products

1. Importance of this basis of classification

To think of the arts as types of product rather than as types of process is natural to the consumer of art—that is, to its user, enjoyer, and appreciator. It is also natural to those who deal with finished products in a professional way, as in art museum work, literary publication, art criticism and connoisseurship. In an art museum one has to classify and arrange the products of visual art, and may never come in contact with its raw materials or productive processes.

Of course, the artist thinks also of the product. It is his aim and goal; a vague or clear conception of it is more or less constantly in the back of his mind. He regards it, when finished, with pride or dissatisfaction. But it is often obscured from his immediate attention by the present unfinished state of his material, and by problems of technique.

From the standpoint of the consumer, critic, or scholar, the finished work of art is likely to seem more important than either the raw material or task of production. Hence one who takes this point of view tends to define and classify the arts on a basis of their types of product. Sculpture is conceived as the art of making statues; poetry as the art of making poems, and so on. Less concern is felt about differences in medium or method. Whether the sculptor uses stone, wood, or bronze; whether he carves or casts, his art is distinguished primarily on the basis of its end result: the statue.

Such an "end result" is not necessarily a completely finished, static thing. As long as it remains a vital part of the cultural heritage, it functions actively in human experience, as a guide or instrument. The house or city plan goes on affecting and directing behavior, for good or ill. The play or symphony is repeatedly performed. The poem or picture goes on directing thoughts and feelings, conveying beliefs and attitudes. In shifting our attention to the products of art, we find ourselves emphasizing not only their form, but also their functions— how they operate to stimulate various kinds of perceptual and mental experience, and to influence overt action. To describe and classify these products, we have to pay attention to the processes of appreciation and of use, rather than to those of production and performance.

2. Products of the arts, as commonly named and defined

One way to define and classify the arts, then, is in terms of their kinds of product. At first sight, this seems fairly easy. Sculpture is the art of making statues; architecture is the art of making houses, and so on. But we soon encounter difficulties. In some cases, the name of the product is the same as that of the art itself. Music is the art of making music, or musical compositions; painting is the art of producing paintings, or pictures. The word "picture" is derived from the Latin word for painting. Literature is the art of producing literature. Such definitions are tautologous.

If we look up the dictionary definition of a product, we often find that it is defined, at least partly, in terms of the medium and process of production. This again makes for reasoning in a circle. For example, what is a "statue"? According to Webster, a statue is "the likeness of a living being sculptured or modeled in some solid substance, as marble, bronze, or wax." The last part of this definition ("in some solid substance," etc.) refers to material or medium. The central part ("sculptured or modeled") refers to process or technique. As to the product itself, then, we have only this to distinguish it from other uses of these materials and processes: "The likeness of a living being." But is this adequate to describe the products of sculpture? No, for we have many abstract sculptural designs which represent nothing. Also, what about three-dimensional representations of houses (as in the Han Chinese products), of swords, airplanes and cannon, etc.? What are they if not sculpture? Webster leaves the concept of sculpture flexible in this respect; sculpture may produce other things besides a statue. It is the "Act or art of carving, cutting, or hewing wood, stone, metal, etc., into statues, ornaments, etc., or into figures; hence, the act or art of producing figures and groups, whether in plastic or hard materials, but now especially in marble or bronze."

Likewise in the case of architecture and each of the "useful arts," many different kinds of product are turned out. Architecture produces not only "houses," in the strict sense of "human habitations," but other kinds of structure. It is, according to Webster, the "Art or science of building; especially the art of building houses, churches, bridges, and other structures, for the purposes of civil life—often called civil architecture." Broadly defined to cover military building, it would include forts, etc. Shall we say then that architecture is the art of making structures? But this is a very broad, vague word, which can take in many small products. Size is not the only differentia, for a statue can be larger than a house.

In short, it is not easy to pin down the concept of a given art to the making of any one kind of product. Every art produces several different kinds, if the products are described specifically. Literature produces epic poems, lyric poems, novels, short stories, essays, etc. Music produces songs, piano sonatas, symphonies, etc. Weaving produces rugs, tapestries, dress fabrics, and many other things.

A given type of product, on the other hand, is not necessarily restricted to a given "art," in the sense of a given medium or process. Pictures are produced, not only by painting but by photography and etching. Painting can produce, not only pictures but abstract, decorative patterns, or a uniform coat on a house or chair.

Evidently, what we need to do is to clarify certain general concepts of "product-types," each to include many specific varieties. Then we must inquire how these types are correlated with various types of medium and process. To what extent is each main product-type bound up with a certain "art," in the sense of a certain technique and medium? To what extent does it overlap them, in that it can be produced in different ways, out of different materials?

3. Types of form in the arts; the problem of objective description and classification

A somewhat new approach to the classification of art products is provided by the analysis of aesthetic form. A finished work of art is a form, simple or complex; it is analogous in many ways to the plant and animal forms which are described in biological morphology. The attempt to analyze, describe, and classify the forms of art objectively is called "aesthetic morphology," and is a branch of aesthetics.[1]

The chief difficulty in describing works of art is to find ways of doing so without, at the same time, expressing debatable evaluations of

[1] "Morphology" must be understood here as including the dynamic aspects of form; the physiology as well as the anatomy of art. For further details, see T. Munro, "The Morphology of Art as a Branch of Aesthetics," in *Toward Science in Aesthetics*. (New York: Liberal Arts Press; Bobbs-Merrill Co., 1956).

them. It is not objective to "describe" a work of art as beautiful or ugly, pleasant or unpleasant, well or badly drawn. On the other hand, it is not enough to measure and describe works of art in terms of their size and physical structure, for these fail to bring out the differences in appearance, style, and meaning which are important in determining their psychological and social functions. No way of describing art or anything else can be purely objective, for all involve human responses of perception and thinking. But we can try to leave out the more emotional and evaluative terms for the time being, and to emphasize those characteristics which are capable of dispassionate observation by other investigators.

The problem of classifying types of form is not the same as that of classifying whole arts as such. Many types of form cut across the traditional boundaries of the arts, and occur in a wide variety of mediums. Representative form, for instance, occurs in painting, sculpture, drama, motion pictures, and other arts. Within each art, many different types and styles of form occur. Painting and sculpture are not always representative. A classification of abstract types of form is very different from a classification of arts. Its divisions will not correspond with those of the arts, which have been established primarily on a basis of process or medium, rather than of product.

However, all these modes of classification are interrelated. Even though the types of form do not correspond exactly with divisions between the arts, there are important partial correspondences. Certain arts tend on the whole to emphasize and develop certain types of form, and to produce them more often than others do.

In the rest of this section, we shall consider several basic types of aesthetic form, and ways of describing an art or a single work of art as to its formal characteristics. Later on, we shall see how these can be applied in the systematic classification of the arts.

4. Modes of transmission: presented and suggested factors in aesthetic form

What is *form* in art? In Webster's definition, form is "orderly arrangement or method of arrangement; as: order or method of presenting ideas; manner of coordinating the elements of an artistic production or course of reasoning." In brief, the form of a work of art is the way in which its details are organized.[2] Aesthetic form occurs not only in art but in other types of object, natural and artificial. A flower and a machine have aesthetic form; so does a city or a sunset. It is not the same as physical form (molecular and atomic structure). It consists rather in the structure which a scene or other object appears to have, as an object of aesthetic apperception. It is the selection and arrangement of sensory qualities and meanings which the object manifests to the perception and understanding of the observer. The physical form of a painting consists of certain arrangements of atoms and molecules; but this is less important in psychology and aesthetics than the way it functions as a stimulus to perception and understanding.

In terms of the psychology of perception, a work of art consists of certain stimuli to sensory experience, and also to association and interpretation on the basis of memory and past experience. A painting stimulates visual experiences such as those of linear shape, color, lightness and darkness. It *presents* visual images directly to the eyes. In addition, it has the power to *suggest* other images and concepts to a brain which has been conditioned through experience and education. Thus a painting can be analyzed into certain presented factors—the shapes and colors which are directly visible—and certain suggested factors—the other objects and events such as trees, persons, battles, which it tends to call up in imagination; and also, in some cases, more abstract conceptions such as moral ideals and religious doctrines. Presentation and suggestion are the two *modes of transmission* by which a work of art is conveyed to the apperceptive mechanism of the observer or percipient.

No two persons will see exactly the same thing in a picture, for each is led by his nature and habits to select slightly different aspects for special notice. No two will imagine or understand exactly the same things, because of differences in mental constitution, habits and edu-

---

[2] The word "form" is also used in a sense equivalent to "shape" or "solid shape," as in speaking of the elements of visual art as "line, form and color." This is a misleading sense, which makes it hard to compare the arts. The definition adopted here is applicable to all arts, as in speaking of musical or literary form. Another narrow conception of form, not intended here, is the one which makes it exclude "content" or "expression," and comprise only the empty shell or skeleton. The concept of form, as we shall see, also includes adaptation to specific functions.

cation. But presented factors are comparatively easy to verify and agree upon. One can point out that certain lines are straight or curved; certain areas light or dark, blue or yellow; and all persons of normal vision will agree substantially upon their presence. In describing the presented factor in a work of art, one emphasizes the main, determinate sensory characteristics; not accidental variations such as those caused by unusual lighting, acoustics, or deterioration—unless such characteristics are part of the total effect determined by the artist.

As to suggested factors, there is often more disagreement on exactly what is meant or represented. Various modes of suggestion are employed by visual art. One is imitation or *mimesis,* as in a picture of a tree. One is arbitrary *symbolism,* as in the use of a cross to suggest Christianity. In addition, certain visual qualities often derive suggestive power from *common association* in experience. Thus reds and yellows may suggest warmth, blues and greens coolness; horizontal lines rest or stability, and diagonal, wavy or zigzag lines may suggest disbalance, movement, or agitation.

Sometimes the associations suggested in one or more of these ways are so vague, conflicting or fragmentary as to arouse different interpretations. A picture may look somewhat like a tree, but not exactly. A symbol like the swastika may have different meanings. Thus it is often impossible to say objectively just what the suggestive content of a work of art is. However, there is usually a nucleus of comparatively obvious meanings upon which most observers will agree. Within a particular cultural environment, common usage tends to attach fairly definite meanings to particular images and groups of images. Artists come to use certain images with a definite intention, and observers to understand them in the same way, by tradition and convention. Authoritative reference works, such as dictionaries, encyclopedias, and books on the iconography of art, confirm a number of these symbol-meaning relations. On a basis of social custom, then, it becomes possible to say with some objective authority that a certain picture has certain definite meanings, whether uneducated or disputatious persons understand it so or not.

In addition to these established meanings, the same work of art may have others which are less cogent, more subject to personal interpretation. These can hardly be classed among the more objective parts of the form. Likewise, affective responses of liking and disliking, enjoyment and displeasure which are made to a work of art, are not parts of its aesthetic form in a strict sense. They are too individual and variable. But the form of the work of art as a whole, from a standpoint of aesthetic apperception, does include not only the directly presented images but also that portion of its suggestive content which is most definitely demonstrable on a basis of cultural usage. There is no sharp boundary; the established suggestive form shades off into extraneous associations, and it is often doubtful whether a certain alleged meaning should be included as part of the form: of the work of art as an objective entity.

The factors in art which we have been calling "presented" and "suggested" are sometimes called "sensory" and "expressive." To speak of the "sensory" aspects of art is somewhat vague, however. That term can be applied to the sense-images which are suggested by a poem, as well as to the lines and colors which are directly seen in a painting. "Presented," as here defined, refers only to what can be directly seen, heard, or otherwise sensed.

"Expressive" is also an ambiguous term, because of its place in the special theories of Croce and others. It tends to make us think of art from the standpoint of the artist, who is trying to put forth and externalize some of his inner feelings. At the present time, we are not concerned with this mysterious expressive or creative process, but with the more obvious fact that an external object may have the power to suggest associations in the mind of an observer, because of his previous experience. A work of art can be suggestive, as in a portrait or landscape. A natural object, such as a gnarled tree or an insect's markings, can also suggest images and ideas to our minds. Here there is no "expression" by a human artist. The phenomenon of suggestion can be objectively described, as a tendency to arouse associations in the mind of a conditioned observer, apart from any speculations as to what goes on in the artist's mind.

The distinction between presented and suggested becomes clearer if we compare a picture with a literary form, such as a poem. Here the directly presented factors may be auditory images (the sounds of spoken words) or visual images (printed words on a page). Whichever is used, the form of the poem evidently includes something more than these presented images. It includes also an arrangement of meanings; of other images and concepts which the words suggest. Words, written or spoken, are arbitrary symbols endowed with more or less definite suggestive powers through cultural usage. In the case of printing, the visible shape and color of the letters makes little essential difference to the form òf the poem; it can even be conveyed through Braille type for the blind. Of course, the sound of the words is important, as in rhyme and rhythm. But that can be either presented (if spoken aloud) or suggested (if read silently). When read silently, as it now is to a great extent, literary form is largely suggestive. The suggestive factor then includes word-sound patterns as well as arrangements of other images and concepts. Music, on the other hand, is still presented aurally, as a rule, although some experts can understand a printed score without hearing it played. Musical form is thus largely presentative, but it also includes suggested images and emotions, especially in romantic "program" music.

In visual art, the presented factors tend to make up a conspicuous part of the total form, and to be regarded as essential to it. Sometimes, as in abstract decoration, they make up almost the whole form, and there is little definite meaning. (There is always some, for all sense data call up some associations, individual and cultural.) At other times, as in story illustration, the suggestive content may bulk larger in the whole. In the case of useful art, such as a cup or sword, part of the suggestive content consists of associations derived from use. To tell what the object means, one must then tell how it was used, or for what functions it was adapted.

Some types of aesthetic form are addressed principally to one of the lower senses, such as perfume and cookery. The forms which they present are usually simpler, though not necessarily less pleasant or valuable, than those addressed to the so-called higher senses. Lower-sense stimuli may fit into a complex, higher-sense form: for example, incense (olfactory) into a religious ritual (visual and auditory).

5. The components of aesthetic form

We have not described the form of a work of art by merely dividing it into presented and suggested factors. It is necessary to observe what specific *ingredients* are presented, what ones suggested, and how they are organized. Psychology helps us considerably in describing them. Foɩ they are the same as in all conscious experience. The materials of art, from a standpoint of aesthetic apperception, are not chemical pigments, bronze and marble, but visible shapes and colors, joys and sorrows, desires, beliefs, and actions.

To classify the materials of art, we must look to psychology for a classification of the modes of human experience and behavior, and so far there has been no adequate one. The traditional way is under such headings as sensation, emotion, conation (will or volition), reasoning, and so on. This is open to objection as suggesting the old faculty psychology, but has its uses at the present early stage in the psychology of art. However, any approach to general psychology is also, by implication, an approach to describing the materials of art. For art selects and rearranges details from life experience into new concrete form.

Inadequate as they are, the traditional psychological categories are useful in analyzing a work of art. "Sensation" includes vision and other senses. In visual art, by definition, we are concerned only with forms whose main presented ingredients are visual rather than auditory. There are certain concepts by which we compare and describe visual objects: especially shape and color. Under "visual" come linear shape or line, surface shape, and solid shape (sometimes called mass or volume). Under "color" come hue; lightness and darkness (often called "value" in art, and in physics often called "brilliance"); and saturation (often called chroma or intensity). These are the principal visual attributes, but many others can be added. In talking of shape, it is often important to note the shape of voids or empty spaces. In talking of colors, it is often important to notice their luminescence, as in colored electric lights. Effects of texture are produced by many small variations in color, shape, or both. Auditory sense-images are analyzed into pitch, timbre, rhythm, consonance and dissonance, loudness, etc.

These attributes function as *elementary components* in aesthetic form. They are concepts devised by the human mind for describing objects perceptually, and do not refer to independent realities. No such attribute ever occurs alone; line is always the linear shape of some colored area or solid. Under the heading of each attribute or component, common usage recognizes a multitude of names for specific *traits* and *types* of quality. Under hue, for example, come red, green, and violet; under lightness or value, the various shades and tints from very dark to very light. Under linear shape come the various geometric types such as straight line, arc, angle, and the free-flowing or "biomorphic" irregular, wavy line, such as that of a climbing vine or a river. Under solid shape come the geometric types such as cubical, spherical, pyramidal; and others more irregular, such as cloud-shaped or mushroom-shaped. Under timbre (an auditory component) come various specific tone-qualities such as violin-tone, flute-tone, etc. Timbre includes the peculiar tone quality (not the pitch alone) of a man's voice as distinguished from a woman's, a child's, or a bird's; also the sound of the different vowels and consonants spoken by a human voice—for example, the hissing sound of *s;* the humming sound of *m;* the full tone of a long *o.* Non-musical sounds, as of thunder and motor traffic, also have distinctive timbres. These are elementary auditory traits. Countless words are in use to describe the specific sensory qualities of things. They occur in art as *component traits.* Any work of art may be analyzed as to its visual or auditory ingredients in terms of a peculiar set of such component traits.

It is important to realize that the psychological content of a work of visual art is not restricted to visual qualities. "Visual" refers only to its mode of presentation to the observer; to its presented content. A work of visual art may suggest visual images which it does not directly present, as of solid shape and deep space in a painting. In addition, it can suggest a much wider range of sensory images. It can suggest tactile and kinesthetic images, sounds, and even tastes and odors, as in a picture of flowers, food and wine. Its suggestive content can extend beyond the sensory: to emotions, desires, and rational inferences.

In each case, if one asks what sorts of thing are suggested, the answer will be in terms of general *components* of experience such as emotion, and of specific *traits* or *types* under each.[3] Among the specific emotions which art may suggest are joy, grief, and anger. Desire, aversion, indifference, and many more specific types of attitude come under the general heading of conation or volition. Literature can suggest abstract concepts, religious beliefs, logical arguments, overt actions—in short, examples of any mode of experience or behavior. Music, though an auditory art in presentation, can suggest visual images, moods, kinesthetic and volitional attitudes, and other types of

---

[3] Affective responses (emotions, desires, etc.), which are suggested in and by a form are not the same as affective responses to the form by some observer. One may recognize that a pictured face expresses sadness without being moved to sadness by it.

experience. Types of experience derived from one sense come to suggest, through common association, those derived from another. Thus high-pitched sounds come to suggest spatial height, as in bird-songs. They may also suggest children's voices, hence the visual image of children also. Wailing sounds suggest grief. Such bonds in common experience help to provide works of art with their suggestive power, often more poignant because its origins are not realized. Naturally, works of visual and auditory art can have similar associations, since they develop from a common fund of life experience.

Any work of art can be described as to its suggested as well as its presented ingredients, in terms of a peculiar set of specific types of emotion, conation, and so on. Some works of art are more *diversified* than others in terms of the different kinds of experience which they present or suggest. Rembrandt's works are usually restricted in range of presented hues and saturations, but highly varied in light and dark. Dante's Divine Comedy suggests a wide range of human emotions and desires; a Shakespeare sonnet is more limited in range. A Cézanne still life is more *specialized* in suggestive content than Tintoretto's *Paradise* or Michelangelo's *Last Judgment*. A Persian rug is often more diversified in its presented shapes and colors than in its suggestive meanings.

Strictly speaking, the ingredients of a work of art are not really "in" the object (for example, a painting) as a physical thing, but largely in the behavior of humans toward it. People respond to a given type of art in a more or less similar way, because of similarities in their innate equipment and cultural conditioning, and tend to project these responses upon the object which arouses them, as if they were attributes of the object itself. Metaphysically, this raises difficult problems of distinguishing the real from the apparent; but they need not all be raised in aesthetics. To aesthetics, the "real" in a metaphysical or physical sense is less important than the way things appear to human experience. And from a psychological standpoint, "appearing" is a fact in itself—a psychological phenomenon to be explained. To explain it fully, one would have to consider not only the nature of the outside object but that of the individual responding; the mental structure which makes it appear to him in a certain way. Here we are interested in the description of aesthetic forms as they appear to human beings in a cultural environment, including not only the sensory but the meaningful aspects of these forms.

6. Spatial, temporal, and causal organization

One way in which a work of art is organized is in certain dimensions of space and time. Various types of art can be contrasted as to their mode of *spatio-temporal* organization. An oil painting, for example, is presented to the eyes as essentially a flat, two-dimensional area. (The actual thickness of paint and canvas is usually not emphasized.) But as a suggestive form, it can be three-dimensional—that is, represent a scene in deep space. It presents no moving images; its presentation is not developed in time. Its presented factor is static. But it can suggest movement and temporal sequence, as in the early Italian paintings which show successive stages in the ascent to Calvary. A carved relief, a statue or a chair is directly presented to the observer as three-dimensional, even though the third dimension is inferred from images on the retinas of the eyes. It presents a slightly different aspect to each eye; a still more different one as the observer changes position. A relief, as in the Ghiberti doors, can also suggest further three-dimensional development, in deep space. Most rug designs are presented in two dimensions, and have little or no suggestive development in the third, although they occasionally suggest rounded flowers or animals. Raised embroidery or cut velvet involves a slight three-dimensional presentation. Tapestry pictures are often highly developed in the suggestion of deep space. A building, a town, a formal garden, and a flower arrangement on a tray, are all presented in three dimensions of space, but with different degrees of development. The garden is usually less elaborately developed in its vertical than in its other dimensions.

A garden presents movement, when wind and weather move the flowers and trees, but this movement is not definitely determined or regulated by the artist. There is determinate change in the garden when flowers are placed so as to bloom in a definite sequence. An object such as a weathervane or waterwheel, a pair of scissors or a jumping-jack, has mobility of a simple, rudimentary sort. A shadow play or motion picture is presented in two dimensions on a flat screen, but with a determinate sequence of images in time. Its presented factor is fully mobile; that is, it has complex, determinate change or motion. It also suggests three-dimensional space and movement; the motion picture much more definitely than the shadow play of silhouettes. A marionette show, a stage play and a ballet are presented in three dimensions of space and in time, and more or less definitely determined in these four dimensions. In dramatic action, there is usually little development in the vertical dimension, but there may be if action takes place on various levels of the stage, as through ramps, platforms, and balconies. The dancer's movements are developed and presented in all four dimensions.

In music, the presented form is mobile, and developed in definite temporal order; but the spatial arrangement of the sounds (where they are to come from) is indeterminate except in rare examples. Literary form is likewise developed mainly in time, the order of words being essential. When presented visually on a page, the two-dimensional space arrangement of letters is important; but it is not directly essential to literary form, since this can be presented aurally with no definite spatial arrangement. Literature, of course, can develop suggested images of two or three spatial dimensions, as in describing a cathedral interior.

The relative *complexity* of a work of art depends in part on the degree to which it is definitely developed in these various dimensions. It may be highly complex in two-dimensional presentation and very simple or undeveloped in others, as in the case of a Persian rug design. Complexity, in one or in several dimensions, consists of differentiation and integration among parts. It differs from simple unity, as in a stone pyramid; and from disordered multiplicity, as in the wreckage of a bombed house.

Another way of interrelating the images presented and suggested by a work of art is *causal organization*. This occurs in literature, as in the plot of a narrative which shows the effect of one action or character on another. It also occurs in pictures which represent a dramatic situation, as in Leonardo's *Last Supper,* where the effect of Christ's words on the various disciples is shown. It is highly developed in drama and cinema. The observer must interpret and organize the successive details and images, not only in terms of before and after, but in terms of one causing or influencing the other. Here again, the organization can be vague or definite, simple or complex, realistic or fantastic.

7. Developed components

As art forms become more complex, it often becomes necessary to deal with them in terms of components more complex than line, light, and color. For example, motion picture producers and critics discuss a film in terms of continuity, montage, photography, setting, animation, and so on. Dramatists and novelists speak of plot, dialogue, and characterization. These are *developed components* in form. Each is a complex combination of one or more elementary components. In music, the elementary component *pitch* is developed in melody and harmony. Melody involves the organization in close temporal sequence of many detailed variations in pitch and also in rhythm. It thus makes use of two or more elementary components. Instrumental timbre (for example, violin tone) can also contribute to the continuity of a melodic line.

In painting, we speak of drawing, modeling, tonality, color-harmony, perspective, and so on—all involving complex developments of visual shape and color. In poetry, rhythm is developed into meter and rhythmic phrasing. Timbre is developed into organized series and patterns of vowels and consonants, which are described as rhyme, alliteration, assonance, etc. Imagery is a suggested component in literature; it covers a wide range of percepts, derived from all the senses, which can be summoned up in memory and imagination through the power of words.

There is no brief, final list of the developed components in art. New conceptions of them appear in the course of development of a vital art, as means whereby artists plan and organize their works, and critics analyze them.

In a highly diversified art, where much specialization of process has occurred, such developed components often come to be recognized as distinct arts. Their products can be regarded as more or less complete works of art in themselves, capable of being enjoyed independently, in addition to being factors in a still more complex form. This is true of opera, where literature is a *component art,* producing the libretto; and where music, dancing, costuming, lighting, acting, etc., are also component arts. In such cases, one art usually provides the *basic framework,* while the others fit in as *accessories.* In opera, the libretto with its plot and dialogue usually acts as basic framework, even though the singing may be considered most important.

8. Modes of composition

Compositional organization is another way of interrelating the details in a work of art. There are four principal *modes of composi-*

tion: utilitarian, expository, representative (or representational), and thematic. All the modes are used in all the arts, to a different extent at different periods. This is one basis for distinguishing styles. A single work of art may involve all four modes; many are organized in two or more modes at the same time.

(a) Utilitarian composition consists in arranging details in such a way as to be instrumental (or at least apparently or intentionally instrumental) to some active use or end. "Active" refers here to overt bodily action and movement, or direct preparation for it; and in general to all the ordinary business of life as distinguished from aesthetic and intellectual contemplation, dreams and reveries. Utility is fitness for some use over and above being looked at, listened to, understood, or thought about. Utilitarian form is sometimes called "functional." But from a psychological standpoint, art has a function if it serves only as a stimulus to aesthetic perception and enjoyment. Here we are thinking of additional functions in the world of practical behavior.

In so far as a thing is organized in a utilitarian way, its form can be described in terms of fitness for some practical use; of means to an end. We can say this of the blade and handle of a sword; of the legs and seat of a chair; of the walls, roof and openings of a house; and of each moving part in a machine.

Literature can be utilitarian, as in advertising, propaganda, guide-books or exhortations aimed at influencing or directing action; explaining how to do something or why one should do something. Music is also utilitarian at times, as in bugle calls, marches and work songs, adapted for directing or coordinating action.

Even if the form is ineffective for the end sought, it can still be called utilitarian. Sometimes people seek to gain their ends by supernatural means: by magic or by pleasing the gods; at other times by natural means. Each gives rise to its own type of utilitarian forms, such as magic rattles, charms and rituals on the one hand, and on the other tools, garments, houses, weapons, furniture and vehicles. Naturalistic technology is often mixed with supernaturalistic, especially at the prescientific stage.

(b) Representative composition is arrangement of details in such a way as to suggest to the imagination a concrete object, person, scene, or group of them in space. Some representation goes further, and suggests a series of events in time. It tends to arouse a specific, concrete fantasy in the mind of a suitably trained and compliant observer.

There are two main types of representation: mimetic and symbolic. In mimetic or imitative representation, the presented set of images (lines, colors, etc.) resembles to some extent the set of images which it calls up in imagination. It may be comparatively realistic, or much altered, simplified, or stylized, so that its meaning is vague or general. Music can thus represent (usually with very slight resemblance) a brook, a storm, or bird-songs in a forest. In visual art, representation is usually mimetic, as in a painted landscape or a sculptured portrait head.

In the symbolic type, especially literature, the presented images are words or other conventional signs, and usually do not resemble the images which they suggest. Literary representation includes description, narration, and drama. Description suggests the nature and appearance—perhaps the sound and other sensory qualities—of some object, scene, person, or group of these. It may represent the inner thoughts and character of a person. It deals with characteristics or appearances at a certain time, or in general, or at different times; but not as a connected sequence of events. It may include some actions and events. But if a definite, causally connected sequence of events is emphasized, we go over into narration, story-writing, history, or biography. In narration, a story is told by someone, the author or a supposed character, usually as if occurring at another time and place. Drama is written as if to be enacted. Dramatic enactment involves direct mimesis—visual, auditory, or both—of the characters and events represented. A story can be acted or narrated in words, or conveyed through a series of pictures. Dramatic representation is developed visually through gesture, dance, costume, and scenery; verbally through the spoken text. Oriental flower and garden art sometimes involves representation, as of a small tray arrangement to suggest a landscape, or a garden mound to suggest Fujiyama.

The subject and mode of representation provide a basis for distinguishing many types of form in different arts. In painting, we distinguish the landscape, the portrait, the still life, the genre scene, the Holy Family, the Last Supper, and so on, in terms of traditional types of subject and treatment. A portrait is a representation of an individual, with some emphasis on distinctive traits.

(c) Some composition is expository, in that it arranges details so as to set forth general relationships, as of causal or logical connection—abstract meanings, pervasive qualities, common or underlying principles. This mode of composition is more highly developed today in literature than in visual art, but it has visual examples. Much religious art, such as the Dancing Siva in Hindu sculpture, undertakes to convey theological, metaphysical, and moral ideas through visual images. Sometimes their meaning is cryptic and obscure, sometimes explicit. A great deal of medieval and Renaissance painting expresses Christian belief through symbolism. A single symbolic image is not enough to constitute exposition; the latter implies systematic development, involving a number of related meanings. Hieroglyphics and other types of pictography are used, not only to suggest concrete descriptions and narrations, but to express abstract principles and arguments. A coat of arms involves expository composition, in that it undertakes to convey general facts about the owner's rank and privileges in feudal society, and perhaps about his ideals and the accomplishments of his family. The essay and treatise are literary types emphasizing exposition; but many others, such as the novel and meditative lyric, often contain expository passages. Music sometimes tries to set forth abstract ideas (religious, moral, etc.), but does not do so very clearly without the aid of words.

(d) Thematic composition, or "design," is a way of organizing a work of art through the repetition, variation, contrast, and integration of certain traits or characteristics. Such traits may be directly presented to the senses of the observer, or suggested to his imagination, or both. A trait which is repeated with emphasis, or systematically varied or contrasted with others, is a theme. The products of thematic composition, when developed in a fairly complex, unified way, are called "designs." But thematic composition occurs also in more simple, fragmentary, and disorganized ways. It occurs in nature and in all kinds of human products, including those without consciously aesthetic aims. It is deliberately cultivated in art as a source of beauty or enjoyable aesthetic experience in perception, imagination, or both. As such, it is called "decoration" or ornamentation, especially in the visual arts.

Thematic composition differs from utilitarian in that it is not necessarily suited for any use in the world of action, or for any function except to provide an object for aesthetic contemplation. The thematic aspects of an object may or may not have utilitarian functions also. As contrasted with representative form, thematic does not need to resemble anything else, or suggest any other concrete form to the imagination. It may do so, as in a decorative picture, but that is not essential. As contrasted with expository form, thematic does not need to set forth any general concepts, or suggest any abstract relations other than those directly observable in the object itself. A design may also be expository, as in a coat of arms; but that is not essential to its nature.

As a rule, thematic composition occurs in a work of art as one of two or more compositional factors—that is, along with utility, representation, or exposition; with any one of them, or with two or three in the same work of art. It is sometimes called the "decorative element" or "design factor" in such a work. One can then study, for example, the relation between design and representation in a picture. Sometimes design is almost indistinguishable from the other factors, being intimately merged with them. On the other hand, it is often developed along its own distinct lines. When it forms a comparatively distinct and separate part of a work of art, it is sometimes called "surface decoration," "extraneous ornamentation," or the like. In some works of art there is little or no compositional development except thematic; these are called "pure design." However, there are usually traces of some other compositional factor.

The various compositional factors in a work of art overlap and are not mutually exclusive. They are usually different ways of organizing the same parts or ingredients; coexisting systems of relationship between them. They are also different ways in which the observer regards them; he can pay attention to a picture chiefly for its representative meaning, or chiefly for its design or decorative aspects. A particular detail or quality within the form often functions in more than one compositional factor—for example, a spot of red may help represent a rose-garden, and also fit into a design of red and green areas. The utilitarian, representative, or expository factor in a work of art may also function as design, and fit into the thematic arrangement. However, various degrees of cooperation and unity exist between them. The thematic factor often diverges from the others, with an effect of inconsistency, conflict, or mutual frustration.

Design or thematic composition can be described in terms of the following basic thematic relations. (a) *Repetition:* observable resemblances and recurrences within a group or series of parts or units having some continuity in space, time, or both; as in a concrete object, scene, list, process, or connected sequence of events. (b) *Variation:* slight differences among details, parts, qualities, or events of the same general kind. (c) *Contrast:* greater, more obvious and striking differences among them. (d) *Integration:* combination of such details and traits, like or unlike, in such a way as to facilitate unified perception or understanding; especially by juxtaposition in space or time, internal connection, and subordination of parts to some unifying scheme or framework.

To have thematic composition, we must have one or more, but not necessarily all of these relations. We may have repetition with little or no variation or contrast; contrast but no repetition; repetition and contrast but little integration. Highly developed, complex design involves all to some extent, but in varying proportions. It is thus a combination of unity and multiplicity, order and diversity. Some designs are comparatively uniform, some full of contrast; some tightly integrated, some loose and irregular; some have few parts and some have many.

In a painting, thematic relations may appear in the repetition of certain component traits such as blue areas and curving lines; and perhaps their contrast with markedly different traits such as red areas and angular lines. In architecture, designs are built from solid masses and interior spaces, as well as from lines, surfaces, and textures.

Design and thematic relations occur in music and literature (especially poetry) as well as in visual art, but the term "decorative" is not usually applied there. In music, designs are built by repeating, varying, and contrasting themes through the use of melody, harmony, rhythm, instrumental timbre, and other components. Design can be developed to any degree of complexity desired, by differentiating parts and including small pattern-units within larger ones. Ultra-complex designs, as in the façade of a Gothic cathedral, have many levels of inclusion, design within design.

Types of design or thematic composition. In the following outline, these are classified on two bases. First, they are distinguished into main types (with Roman numerals and capital letters) as to *mode of presentative development:* that is, how details are arranged in space or time for perception by the eyes or ears. Second, some of these types are subdivided as to mode of *suggestive development:* especially as to whether the design contains representation of three-dimensional objects.

I. *Visual, static, surface design.* Thematic development presented mostly in two dimensions of space, with little or no determinate movement. Presented on a plane, curving, or polyhedral surface. Components presented: line, color, texture; sometimes, surface shape, masses, voids. There may be some presentative development in the third dimension, as in low relief; but with emphasis on surface arrangement and little extension in the third dimension. "Static" refers to the presented factor only, and has nothing to do with possible suggestions of movement, as in a painting of a battle. Certain types of surface design are distinguished on a basis of which components are emphasized—for example, an "arabesque" is a kind of design involving intricate linear development, with or without representative meaning.

A. *Strip design:* long and narrow, as in ribbons, borders, and architectural mouldings. Extended mostly in one dimension, lengthwise; units of design may be indefinitely repeated or prolonged in either direction. Definitely bounded in the second dimension, and internally adapted to the area between the two boundaries— for example, between the edges of a moulding or border. Conventional types: the fret, guilloche, etc.

Varieties:

1. According to dimensions in which *presentative* development occurs: presentatively *flat* or *three-dimensional.* In the latter, actual differences in surface or solid shape are present, and are systematically arranged, as in mouldings, picture-frames, lace, repoussé, jeweling, embossing.
2. According to dimensions in which *suggestive* development, if any, occurs: suggestively *flat* or *three-dimensional.* In the former, there are no definite suggestions or illusions of solidity or depth. In the latter, there are. Further varieties of the latter can be distinguished as to the realism and precise detail in which such illusions are conveyed.
3. According to degree of *representative* development: whether the design is (a) non-representative, abstract, non-objective, or (b) representative, pictorial, naturalistic. The latter is not necessarily developed in the third dimension, presentatively or suggestively; it may be flat and yet highly realistic through

linear outlines alone. This necessarily involves some three-dimensional suggestion, but it may be slight, without use of shadows, perspective, etc. Strip design is sometimes highly realistic, as in Chinese landscape scrolls, friezes, etc.

4. With pictorial or decorative *framework*. Usually the latter; occasionally pictorial, as in such scrolls, friezes, etc.

B. *Bounded area design*. Definitely limited within a given two-dimensional area, and internally related to the size and shape of the area marked off—for example, to a rectangle or circle. This tends to distinguish it from an arbitrarily severed portion of a strip or allover design; but in practice there is a good deal of overlapping between these types. Varieties are analogous to those of strip design:

1. *Presentatively flat or three-dimensional:* whether the design involves no systematic variation of surface shape, as in an ordinary painting, or does involve it, as in a sculptural relief. Some paintings approximate reliefs through the use of high impasto or raised, gilded areas.

2. *Suggestively flat,* as in most prayer rugs, or *suggestively three-dimensional,* as in most paintings.

3. *Non-representative; representative.*

4. With pictorial or decorative *framework*. When the framework is *pictorial,* as in most paintings, the main area is organized as a representation of a scene in space. Thematic development takes place within it as repetition, variation, and contrast of line, color, etc., among represented objects. When the framework is *decorative* or thematic, as in most rug designs, the units are repeated and arranged arbitrarily to make a pattern, rather than merging into a single scene in the interests of representation. In a decorative framework, the individual units may be representative and realistic, as in a rug with floral and animal motifs.

C. *Allover design.* Unbounded in two dimensions, with a tendency to indefinite repetition or prolongation in two dimensions and in four directions. Termination is usually arbitrary and sudden, as when a piece of cloth is cut from a bolt, or when the edge of a wall or box-top is reached; the internal arrangement is not necessarily adapted to the outside shape thus produced. Units are often arranged on two intersecting systems of lines (horizontal and vertical, or diagonal), and not along a single axis, as usual in strip designs. Conventional types: spot, stripe, scale, imbricated, interlaced, flowered, figured, scenic, etc. Much used in dress fabrics, wall paper, and wherever the design is to be adaptable for further use in products of variable size and shape.

1. Presentatively flat or three-dimensional.
2. Suggestively flat or three-dimensional.
3. Representative or non-representative.
4. With pictorial or decorative framework. Allover design, like strip design, is usually decorative rather than pictorial in its comprehensive framework. Theoretically, a realistic landscape could be indefinitely extended in all directions, as on the inside of a hollow sphere; but this seldom happens. The tendency of allover design is to repeat units. Individually, these are often pictorial and realistically three-dimensional, as in scenic wall paper; but they are usually repeated and contrasted to make a somewhat regular design, instead of being merged into a single scene. In extremely realistic types, the boundary between units is obscured, so that they seem to merge continuously.

II. *Static solid design.* Three-dimensionally presented visual design, considerably extended in thickness or depth as well as in length and breadth. Little or no presented temporal development or determinate mobility. More use of solid masses, voids, and surface shapes than in static surface design; line, color, texture also used.

A. *Exterior* design, as in architecture when viewed from the outside; sculpture, utensils, furniture, etc. The object may present many different designs as seen from different points of view, as solid parts fall into different arrangements. This indicates high three-dimensional development; it is often lacking in solid objects meant to be seen from only one point of view, as in a statue intended for a niche.

B. *Interior* design: surrounding or partly surrounding the observer, as inside a building, room, garden, or city square. Many aspects and vistas as seen from different points of view.

C. Integrated *combinations* of the two, as in a Gothic cathedral.

D. *Non-representative* (as in most architecture) or *representative* (as in most sculpture). As to framework; as to details or individual units.

III. *Mobile surface design.* With visually presented thematic development in time; change and motion in determinate sequence. Mostly in two dimensions of space. In motion pictures, shadow plays, lumia or mobile color, etc., on a flat screen. Varieties: non-representative, representative; with or without three-dimensional suggestions.

IV. *Mobile solid design.* Visually presented thematic development in three dimensions of space and in time; change and motion in determinate sequence. As in ballet, marionettes, acrobatics, theatrical skating, fireworks, and mobile sculpture. Mostly representative; sometimes not, as in most pyrotechnic displays.

V. *Auditory design.* With aurally presented thematic development in time; arranged in temporal sequences. Usually without spatial development, but sometimes with—for example, in music, antiphonal relations between choirs at different positions in a cathedral.

A. *Musical design.* Components presented (elementary): pitch, timbre, consonance and dissonance, etc.; (developed): melody, tempo, dynamics, meter, chord structure and progression, orchestration, etc. Conventional types of framework pattern: theme with variations, rondo, fugue, sonata, symphony, etc.[4]

B. *Word-sound design:* one factor in literary design. Presented aurally when literature is spoken. Highly developed in verse, but more simple and irregular thematic relations occur also in prose; especially rhythmic. Components; timbre developed into rhyme, assonance, alliteration, etc.; rhythm developed into rhythmic phrasing and sometimes into meter. Pitch and tempo usually indeterminate. Conventional framework patterns: for example, the Shakespearean and Petrarchan sonnets.

C. *Verbal-musical design,* as in song, oratorio, opera. Combination of musical and word-sound patterns.

VI. *Audio-visual design.*

A. Mobile surface design combined with auditory, as in motion pictures or shadow plays with music and spoken verses.

[4] Some of these musical form-types are occasionally described as "arts": for example, in Bach's *Die Kunst der Fuge* ("The Art of Fugue").

B. Mobile solid design combined with auditory, as in dance and ballet with music. Including patterned movements executed by groups
of skaters, swimmers, flyers, etc., with musical accompaniment.

VII. *Intermediate types.* There are many combinations of the above
types, and borderline types between them—for example, sculptural
relief varies as to degree of three-dimensional development. When
very low and applied to a flat panel, it is static surface design
within a bounded area; when high and partly detached from the
background, it approximates static solid design. Pictorial scrolls, to
be unrolled and viewed in slow movement, are intermediate between
static and mobile surface design.

This list, as mentioned above, deals mainly with presentative or
directly perceptible differences among the types of design. These are
important and far-reaching, but do not cover the whole subject. Design
is not restricted to the directly visible or audible aspects of form.
Stimuli to the lower senses, and also suggested meanings, can operate
as factors in design, through being arranged thematically. Many additional types of design arise from such development.

Abstract symbolism, for example, often plays a part in design.
A tapestry may contain heraldic figures, to symbolize the union of two
noble families in marriage. Perhaps a lion and a *fleur-de-lis* are repeated alternately in the border, and joined at each corner of the
design. Such repetition, contrast, and integration of themes involve
not only the visual images but their meanings also.

In some arts, especially literature, thematic development is mostly
suggestive. Certain ideas and emotions such as war and peace, love and
hate, and every type of image derived from the senses, can be arranged
to form simple or complex patterns. When poetry is spoken aloud, the
patterns of word-sounds are presented. But when it is read silently to
oneself, all the word-sound patterns become suggestive: rhyme,
rhythm, alliteration, and other auditory components are imagined and
not heard. These word-sound patterns interact with other patterns,
composed of suggested images, concepts, emotions, desires and the like.
The various patterns may or may not coincide; indeed, there is often
a deliberate effort to keep them from coinciding exactly, for fear of
excessive and monotonous regularity.

In analyzing the total design of a work of art, we have to pay attention to all the diverse thematic series and patterns which may be involved in it. Both ingredients and modes of organization vary greatly in different arts, periods, and individual styles.

9. Relations between modes of composition

A given set of component traits can be arranged according to any of these four modes of composition, or according to two or more at once. Some types of art are comparatively *specialized,* from a compositional standpoint, in that they involve development in only one mode. These are sometimes called "pure decoration," "purely utilitarian," and so on. But even if a tool, chair or house is bare and unadorned, and intended only for utilitarian purposes, it is sure to involve some aspects of a thematic nature. In the chair, for example, the four legs will constitute a series of repeated cylindrical masses which fit together as a thematic arrangement. However, the decorative development of the chair may proceed much farther than this, as through the addition of incised grooves and ridges, or the coloring of surfaces. These additions may or may not fit into the utilitarian scheme, that is—be useful in themselves. They may or may not be integrated with the utilitarian scheme from a decorative standpoint, as through making the added lines repeat the contours of the legs, seat, and back. Furthermore, the chair may be developed along representative lines, as in a king's throne ornamented with carved animals in relief. Finally, these details may have expository significance if they fit together into a coat of arms. A Gothic cathedral is highly developed in all four modes of composition, through its utilitarian framework, its decorative treatment of masses and surfaces, its sculptural and stained glass representations, and its theological and moral symbolism. A Dancing Siva contains sculptural representation of a dancing figure, a design of masses, lines and surfaces, and a complex religious and philosophic exposition. It also has utility for purposes of worship. Such works of art are highly *diversified* as to modes of composition.

From the standpoint of form analysis, the modes of composition operate as *factors* in a particular work of art. In other words, a work of art can be described as to the various modes of composition which are involved in it; their relative emphasis and degree of development, and their interrelations in that particular object. For example, we speak of the "design factor" or the "decorative element" in a painting; of the relation between decorative and functional elements in a building. Utilitarian fitness, design, and pictorial representation are often combined in postage stamps and advertising posters.

It becomes important then to notice, not only how each compositional factor is developed in itself, but also how and how thoroughly they are *integrated*. In a painting, we may ask how the design is related to the representative factor or "subject matter." Sometimes the design is conspicuous and clearly organized, while the represented objects are vague and distorted. Then we may say that representation is partly sacrificed to design. Sometimes there is a highly realistic portrait or landscape with little or no definite design. However, there is always some decorative element, if only from the simple lines and colors necessary for representation. Sometimes the design seems clearly integrated with the representation, so that neither can be easily distinguished from the other; the representative form provides a basic structure for the design itself. Sometimes, on the contrary, the decorative factor in a picture or a building is superficial and separate. Such distinctions are used as a basis for standards of value in art criticism; but the descriptive study of form is content to note them as facts.

One way of discovering whether compositional factors are integrated is to look at a number of individual details, and find out whether each is functioning as an element in more than one mode of composition. Does each decorative detail of a building also have a utilitarian function, and does each visible part of the utilitarian scheme contribute to the design? In a picture, does a given spot of red function as part of a represented flower, and also as part of a design of lines and colors?

Whatever compositional factors are present in a work of art, one of them usually acts as a basic *framework* for the whole; the others being *accessories*. For example, in the decorated chair utility is the framework mode of composition, determining the basic structure. But it does not follow that the framework mode is necessarily the most important from a historical or evaluative standpoint. The utilitarian structure of the chair may be quite conventional, like a thousand others. Its decorative factor, though accessory, may be the only one elaborately developed, and the only one which is distinctive and original. The representation of a scene gives a basic framework to most pictures; but accessory effects of decorative color may give to a certain picture its most distinctive characteristic. Decorative composition may provide the general framework for an abstract design, whose representative factor is confined to occasional repetitions of a flower or animal motif. Thus many permutations are possible in the various arts, as to the relative status of compositional factors. Theoretically, any one may provide the framework, and one or more others enter as accessories. But actually, in certain arts, certain factors are most often used as frameworks—for example, representation in sculpture, and design in music.

The relation between modes of composition has important historical aspects, which can be only briefly touched upon here. They concern the *evolution of art forms,* and their relation to science. Important primitive and archaic forms are often undifferentiated as to modes of composition, involving several without clear distinction between them. As historians have pointed out, there is no conception of pure decoration, art for art's sake, or fine as opposed to useful art, in early society. There is little if any in oriental or medieval culture. As we have seen, the tendency to differentiate sharply between beauty and use, the aesthetic and the practical, the decorative and the functional or significant, is comparatively recent. Some extreme dissociation along these lines followed the industrial revolution. It was manifested in many bleak utilitarian products, and on the other hand in an efflorescence of superficial, nonfunctional decoration. Recent years have seen a conscious effort to reintegrate the two, as in artistically designed industrial products. However, there is always a certain pressure toward specialization for the sake of intensive, undistracted progress along one chosen path.

The intensive, specialized development of utilitarian form has led to applied science or technology; that of expository form to pure science and philosophy. The cultural ancestors of modern machines and technical processes, of modern scientific textbooks, are the less differentiated forms of early practical and religious art, including tools, weapons, magic, and ritual. Representation has a scientific development, in exact photographs, maps, models, and diagrams. But other types of representation remain within the accepted province of fine art. Decoration alone has shown no strong tendency to pass from an artistic to a scientific stage. Visual design reached a high intensive development in Islamic textiles (partly because of a taboo against visual representation) and in certain other periods. Auditory design has been intensively developed in modern classical music.

After periods of specialization on one or another mode, there is usually a reaction toward diversity, as in the recent effort to combine design with representation in painting and sculpture; with utility in furniture and architecture. Another example of such reaction is seen in the development of pictorial art for educational purposes, as in illustrations for children's textbooks. Like much ancient art, they include not only representation and decoration, but an expository element: the conveying of information and abstract ideas through concrete illustration. Advertising and propagandist art are similar in this respect.

10. Types and Styles of Art

The description of a particular work of art is best accomplished by classifying it in terms of various *types*. In zoology, a newly found animal or fossil is thus described by classifying it under various types in various respects. It belongs to one type as to its bony structure; another as to its skin covering; another as to its mode of locomotion; another as to its mode of respiration; another as to its mode of reproduction, and so on. Thus the whole is described as a peculiar combination of various characteristics. In art, one may describe the Statue of Liberty in New York as the figure of a goddess from the standpoint of representation, and as a lighthouse from that of utility. One should also indicate how it *differs* from usual cases of each type. For example, its colossal size and interior stairways distinguish it from most statues.

In the paragraphs above, we have noted a number of artistic types. Some works of art are visual and some auditory in respect to principal mode of presentation. Some are diversified and some specialized in range of presented ingredients; some in range of suggested ingredients. Some are specialized on one mode of composition; some on another; some combine several. Some have complex presentative development in three dimensions of space; some in only two. Some are developed in time. Each art contains many recurrent types or genres, such as the epic, lyric, sonata, portrait, landscape, temple, and prayer-rug.

The traditional names for aesthetic types and categories are often confusing because of their evaluative implications. For example, to call an object "beautiful," "ugly," "sublime," or "pretty" not only helps to describe it but in part evaluates it—praises or condemns it. At the same time, there is an objective element in the difference between sublimity and prettiness, which can be expressed in terms of observable characteristics without reference to value. Other aesthetic types such as "romantic" and "tragic" also refer to observable traits, and hence can be used in describing art with less danger of confusion. Some of the so-called "art principles," or alleged rules and standards of good art, also refer to certain objective types of art, and can be so considered apart from questions of value. Whether or not all art should be "balanced" (and many will deny that it should), at least some works of art possess more balance than others.

Sometimes objects can be compared in a way approximating *quantitative* estimate, though rarely with numerical exactness. For example, one can say that a certain Persian rug is more complex in its visual design than a certain Chinese bowl; or that a Rubens battle scene contains more represented movement than a Chardin still-life. These are obvious and will arouse little dispute; but quantitative estimates are often more difficult. At present, measurement can go but a little way in the description of aesthetic form. But much description in other sciences also lacks quantitative exactness.

The description of historic "styles" of art presents an important and difficult task of aesthetics. A style is a distinctive or characteristic mode of presentation, construction, execution or expression in art. Historians attempt to define styles characteristic of certain nations, periods, schools, and persons, as the Greek, medieval, impressionist, or Raphaelesque style. As a rule, the broader the scope thus taken in, the more difficult it is to define the style satisfactorily, for the reason that more varieties of form are encountered. If one defines the style too specifically, one must add that many exceptions to it exist in the historical period included. Even a single artist, such as Raphael, is likely to have painted in several different ways during his life; so distinctions are sometimes made as to the early, middle, and late styles of the artist. It is a perennial problem to define such terms as Gothic, classic, and romantic in brief yet adequate terms.

A historic style is in some ways analogous to a biological species, as a complex type which persists through many successive individuals. (Even a personal style like the Raphaelesque can be followed by many artists.) It is to be described or defined, not in terms of any single type or characteristic, but as a combination of several, such as the usual shape of doors and windows, height of vaults, thickness of walls, type of ornamentation, and so on. However one specifies in these respects, one is likely to find examples which conform in some ways and deviate in others. Artistic styles are much more variable than biological species. They change more rapidly, and merge imperceptibly into other styles. For this reason, it is well to think of styles as dynamic, complex trends, rather than as fixed and definite.

Concepts of historic styles are potentially very useful in describing individual works of art. It saves a great deal of detail if we can classify a building as typically Romanesque, or a piece of music as "Gregorian." However, much depends on the accuracy with which our style-names are defined and applied; often they are vague and inconsistent. Also, one should not overlook the unique characteristics of a work of art, which differentiate it from other examples of its style.

Some of the difficulty arises from confusion in applying the names of styles both to abstract types and to particular historic periods or nations. If one thinks of the Baroque period as equivalent to the seventeenth century in Europe, then the Baroque will include many different types of art. If one thinks of it as an abstract type involving large, sweeping curves, oblique and eccentric patterns, emotional excitement and so on, then examples of the Baroque style will be found in other centuries, and even in other civilizations such as that of India. It is important for the study of cultural history to recognize such resemblances among the arts of remote peoples and places; but to do so we need clearer definitions of various styles as abstract complex types. Many terms used as names of abstract types are also used in the other sense. For example, "classic" refers to the art of Greece and Rome, and also to an abstract type involving comparative regularity, balance, symmetrical proportion, smoothness, gently flowing curves, rationality and cool serenity of expression. "Romantic" refers to European art in the late eighteenth and early nineteenth century, and also to an abstract type involving a tendency to irregularity, rough textures, sentiment, primitive impulse and passion.

Of course, the terms "classic" and "romantic" as so defined do not characterize all the art of any one period or nationality; for every age contains some diversity of styles. If such terms are to be used as names of abstract types, they should be clearly defined as such apart from special historical associations; but it is hard to exclude the latter. Even when abstractly defined, their application to particular cases is troublesome. Cases will appear which embody some but not all characteristics of the type as so defined. Delacroix, Beethoven and Keats, for example, are romantic in some but not all the traits just mentioned; and their individual works vary considerably. However styles are defined, examples will be found which conform to none exactly; which are intermediate or transitional, embodying characteristics of more than one.

Some styles and trends involve several or all the arts of a period, and their analysis provides a useful way of comparing and interrelating different arts. For example, how is the romantic movement of the early nineteenth century manifested in painting, music, and poetry; in the picturesque garden, the novel, and the opera—even in philosophic, political, and economic theory? But we must be careful not to assume that all contemporary works (for example, of the romantic period) share the same style. Works produced at the same time and place are sometimes at opposite poles as to style. Usually a style-trend occurs in certain arts considerably before it does in others.

The causal explanation of the genesis of styles, and of their relation to other cultural factors, is not a problem of form-analysis alone, since it requires much supplementary information. But it can not be effectively pursued without clear description and classification of the forms of art themselves.[5]

11. Varieties of creative process, in relation to varieties of product

Let us return briefly to the psychic phase of art production, which was discussed at the end of Chapter VIII. We can now see more clearly how the artist's mental process is affected by the kind of product he intends to make.

Much depends on the compositional factors which are to appear in the product and on the relative emphasis to be given them. Some works of art, as we have seen, are basically organized along utilitarian or functional lines; the factor of utility is highly developed in them. In others, the form is predominantly representative, expository, or thematic.

[5] For a further discussion of styles, see "Style in the Arts: a Method of Stylistic Analysis," by the author. *Journal of Aesthetics*, Vol. V, No. 2 (Dec., 1946), pp. 128-158. The foregoing account of form analysis is a development of "Form in the Arts: an Outline for Descriptive Analysis," *Ibid.*, Vol. 2, No. 8 (Fall 1943), pp. 5-27. It is more fully set forth in *Evolution in the Arts and Other Theories of Culture History* (Cleveland: Cleveland Museum of Art, 1963).

To develop a certain compositional factor in a work of art, some-one has to think along that line. Each factor entails a certain kind of thinking, imagining, and organizing on the part of its creator. If the work of art is basically representative, but contains some decorative or thematic development within the representative framework, one has a clue to the creative process which preceded it. Someone thought out, before or during execution, the scheme of the whole work, devoting some attention to its representative meaning and some to its design. If a work of art contains expository development, someone must have planned along expository lines; if it contains utility or practical adaptation, someone planned along practical lines. Such development in art does not occur by accident. One may find a weatherbeaten stone or branch which happens to look like something else, or a snow crystal to which nature has given a complex design. Even so, it takes artistic thinking to notice such a form, to photograph it or place it where it can be experienced as an aesthetic object. The existence of any type of complex form in art is *prima facie* evidence that some artist has thought creatively in the way required to produce it.

In all artistic creation, as we have seen, the artist has to think to some extent in a practical way, about the fitness of means to ends. In a broad sense, functional thought and planning are not limited to so-called "functional" art; they may occur as well in designing a play, a poem, or a symphony; wherever the artist asks himself, "How can I produce the effects I want to produce, on the people who will see or hear it?" But, over and above this, the designing of utilitarian forms, if carefully planned, involves a comparatively large amount of practical thinking. Here the artist must devise, not only the means to an aesthetic effect, but the means to some active use as well. Poetry, music, and painting can be produced as direct expressions of free fantasy, as in the case of "Kubla Khan," with a minimum of planning about effects on the reader. But the designer of a bridge or a pleasure-dome can hardly avoid giving some thought to how well it will stand up and serve its purposes.

At the same time, we must recall the fact pointed out in Chapter VIII, that the individual artist whose name is signed to a work has not always created the whole work; indeed, he has never originated the entire conception himself. In many respects, his work necessarily follows tradition and current trends, even if he does not consciously copy any particular examples. Even supplementary documents, such as letters in which the artist describes his methods, or accounts of contemporary observers, are to be taken with a grain of salt; they tend to exaggerate the creative aspects and obscure the imitative.

Utilitarian fitness in a work of art, however complex, does not in itself prove that its designer has done much creative thinking along utilitarian lines. It only shows that *someone* concerned in its making has done so; perhaps a long line of forgotten predecessors, whose work is now merged in the joint product to which he has signed his name. From inspecting the product in isolation, without comparing it with older ones to which he had access, one cannot possibly tell in what way, if any, his product is original. Hence one cannot infer what his mental processes were in making it: where he proceeded by conscious or unconscious imitation, or thought freshly for himself. Architecture and furniture are classed in general as useful or functional arts. But the chief complaint of modern "functionalism" in these fields is that artists have not approached their problems in terms of fitness for use; that they have accepted stereotyped conceptions of basic structure, worked out long ago to meet different needs; that they have treated the house or chair as a mere surface to be decorated. Even in decoration, they have applied conventional motifs mechanically. The resulting form may contain the fruit of creative thinking, but most of it was done long ago, by other artists than the one who claims the credit.

In trying to correlate certain types of process with certain types of product, it is well to speak in general terms, avoiding hasty assumptions about what occurred in any particular artist's mind. If a certain work of art is highly developed along a certain line, much creative thought along that line must have been done somewhere within the cultures which produced it, perhaps during centuries of time. This is the attitude taken in anthropology toward primitive artifacts and orally transmitted folklore. The group as a whole or some subdivision of it (for example, a priestly class) is credited with such achievements. The role of individual geniuses at this level is doubtless underestimated, because it is usually impossible to identify them. In advanced civilization, we tend to overestimate it, and to assume that each famous artist must have thought out for himself whatever we see in his works. In addition, we overestimate the contribution of the few leading artists in each period, forgetting the multitude of lesser ones who were producing along similar lines—not quite as well, but expressing the same cultural trends, and often contributing much to the top-flight geniuses whose names survive.

With these precautions in mind, one is justified in making a few tentative inferences from the type of product as to types of thinking which must have led to it. There is no richer source of data for the psychology of art than the products of art themselves; in no other way does the artist reveal himself and his times more directly and fully. The composer expresses himself in his music, and it is idle to suppose that some casual remark or letter, or some verbal response to questioning, can tell us more about him than his music does. But we have scarcely begun to learn how to interpret works of art psychologically, and there are dangerous pitfalls in the way. Already, we can see that different ways of thinking, different types of personality and psychic process, can lead to similar types of art. The quality of madness or unbridled confusion in a work of art can be the direct expression of such a condition in the artist, or a deliberate, calculated effect arranged by a sane artist for some special reason. On the other hand, apparently similar personalities, with similar methods, may turn out diametrically opposite types of art. Countless variable factors, most of them hidden, determine the total result.

Suppose we are dealing with a work of representational art: a story or play, a picture or statue of something or someone, or a piece of descriptive music. Is it fair to assume that the person or persons who conceived it must have done some observation of similar things in the outside world, so as to give us this fantasy of a concrete scene or story? Yes, in a general way; but there are many possibilities; representative art is not all produced in the same way. Sometimes it is done directly from nature, while observing a model, as a portrait-painter looks back and forth between the real and the painted face. But an equally vivid, realistic face can be painted from imagination, resembling no single face the artist has ever seen; built up from countless memory images of different faces and other objects—perhaps of animals or mountains—each contributing a detail or quality. The same is true of literary representation. Most characters in fiction and drama are composites rather than direct counterparts of any whom the author has encountered in real life. There is wide variation among artists as to the relation between observing and imagining. Some transcribe directly from nature, with little imaginative reconstruction, while in others the original sense data are profoundly modified, perhaps through years of conscious and unconscious memory. This is partly a question of style, for some periods favor visual realism; others conceptual, schematic representation.

From childhood, the artist's observations of nature are mixed with those of art, and his own imaginings are drawn from both sources. From the fact that an artist portrays a certain kind of scene or character vividly, one cannot infer that he has drawn it all from real life. He has been stimulated and guided by previous artistic representations of that kind of scene or character; has been led by them to observe nature in a certain way. Within these inherited frameworks, he has infused a certain amount of fresh, new data from direct experience of nature and life; but how much, it is hard to say from looking at his products, or where one ends and the other begins. A picture or story may seem highly realistic, as if taken directly from life, and yet be like nothing the artist has ever seen in nature. It may be a composite of details from older works of art, or a product of creative fantasy, far removed from any kind of observation. On the other hand, an abstract or schematic representation, which seems like nothing in nature, may be made while directly observing nature. The artist has gone out with a special purpose or attitude; looking for certain abstract qualities, perhaps, as Cézanne looked for geometric shapes in rocks and tree-trunks; or projecting his own kinesthetic and emotional mood, as Van Gogh did, upon the scene that lay before him.

Toward the making of all representative art, there must go some observing of nature and some of art; some selecting and reorganizing into new forms, through conscious and unconscious thought; some translation of previous experience into the terms and technics of a certain art medium. But at present, one can only guess how much of each has occurred in any particular case. The psychologist's task is not only to generalize about the operation of these recurrent, constituent processes, but to infer if possible how they operated in a particular artist's work, in what order and relative proportion. This he must do by putting together shreds of evidence from many different sources; the work of art alone is not sufficient. By doing so, he will learn more about the varieties of creative process in the arts, and avoid the oversimplified accounts in present aesthetic theory.

Since most works of art are developed to some extent in two or more compositional factors, the question arises of how the artist adjusted this double, triple, or quadruple type of development. Again, it must not be assumed that he thought creatively about all of them. In utilitarian art, as we have just seen, it is common for the artist to accept a traditional framework—for example, the basic structure of an armchair—and lavish all his thought upon the surface decoration. In all types of art, this sort of limited creativeness is common; the artist follows convention in one compositional factor, where there is little demand for originality, or where he feels no desire to attempt it. He feels sufficient scope for his creativeness in specializing on a single aspect of the form. When exposition is highly developed, as in medieval visual art, a conventional expository scheme is often followed. Certain iconographic principles are fixed and followed. At certain places in the church and its furnishings, certain symbols are appropriate: for example, the Tree of Jesse in a stained glass window, or in the carved back of a choir-stall. The artist is not encouraged—is rather forbidden —to work out any original system of symbols and meanings; but he is free within limits to embody the traditional system in a new decorative setting. Modes of representation also become conventionalized— for example, the head of Christ; the costume of the Virgin. To a less extent, modern landscape painting has developed conventional framework types, such as the vista down a forest lane. An artist may accept it, claiming no originality on that score, but ingeniously working out new thematic relations of line and color within it.

On the other hand, the thematic factor may be the most conventional. The Petrarchan sonnet, the fugue, sonata-allegro pattern; these are conventional thematic frameworks, which many artists are content to accept. Setting out to write a Petrarchan sonnet, the poet willingly renounces any claim to fundamental originality in word-sound pattern. He finds sufficient scope for his talents in working out a new combination of images and ideas within it; perhaps the representation of a scene or story; perhaps the exposition of his philosophy of life. At the same time, he tries for some novelty of rhyme and rhythm within the sonnet scheme.

To be radically original in several modes of composition at once is a difficult task, which few artists care to attempt. Many of the greatest geniuses have been content to put new wine in old bottles; to accept a traditional framework for at least one compositional factor; to attempt originality through incidental details within this framework, and along other lines.

When we see a work of art which is diversified as to modes of composition, and ask how the artist thought it out, the problem is to discover what elements within it he took over most unthinkingly from other sources, with least alteration. The rest will constitute the area over which his creative efforts played. To find this out, we must compare his work with earlier examples in the same medium. What appear to be the dominant, framework features of the form often turn out to be the least original. For example, Gilbert and Sullivan's operas are works of representative art; stories in dramatic form. Many of their plots and characters are stereotypes; the harmony and orchestration are conventional, and so is the dramatic scheme of dialogues, arias, and choruses. The most original features, and presumably those on which the artists did most creative thinking, are the witty and humorous incidental turns of thought in the verse, and the simple, lively, and appropriate tunes to which the verse is set.

It is not unusual, however, for an artist to attempt some original creation in two or more compositional factors at once: for a painter, let us say, to attempt an original design and also a novel subject, with unusual effects of lighting and perspective. In such cases, the artist's attention tends to *alternate* from one mode of composition to another. At times, he tries to organize his work so as to build up the desired illusion of a scene in space, filled with objects of different texture, and with people in significant postures. He inspects and criticizes his unfinished work from this point of view. At other times, he plans and criticizes from the standpoint of design: changing the outline of an arm or leg to carry out a certain linear theme and link together scattered units; changing the color of an area, not to make it more realistic, but to fill out his color-pattern.

All art contains at least the rudiments of thematic organization, and in most art there is some thematic development in the direction of design, although it may remain comparatively simple and irregular. It is a persistent problem for the artist, then, to carry water on both shoulders, and perhaps on his head as well. He must work out the desired thematic development, simple or complex, along with the other compositional factor or factors. In designing the chair he must think now of utility, now of design. In designing the Tree of Jesse window he must think, now of its expository meaning, now of its design, and now of its durability and function as a window, to withstand the weather and admit light. Throughout preliminary planning and in execution as well, his attention keeps going back and forth between these different ways of organizing the same materials, so as to achieve them all at once; not all to the same extent, but to the extent desired. One painter will be satisfied with the rudiments of design, and think mostly about representation; another will reverse the emphasis.

This again is partly a question of style; in recent years the trend in painting has been toward re-emphasizing design, and it often goes to the extreme of complete abstraction. The extent to which each compositional factor should be developed in each art, the extent to which each may or should be sacrificed for the sake of other factors, is a question which each period decides in a slightly different way. The liking for a certain compromise between them, and for certain ways of adjusting their respective claims, is part of the style and taste of that period. It is rationalized in aesthetic theories about the rules for good art, and in the assurance of critics that the new blend they favor is a great improvement over all old-fashioned ones. In the early Renaissance, conservatives deplored the sacrifice of traditional religious symbolism to the detailed representation of nature. In later generations, a picture was wrong and ugly if it made any noticeable sacrifice of representation to design. Still later, the "right" of the painter to distort anatomy and perspective for the sake of design was maintained and finally taken for granted.

The fact that observers can distinguish two or more compositional factors in a work of art does not imply that the artist clearly distinguished them in his mind. Such distinctions are the result of modern theoretical analysis, which many artists dislike and avoid. They tend to shift from one approach to the other without noticing the change, as if all were parts of the single job of painting a picture. An artist who is sensitive to the requirements of both design and representation—not everyone is—judges each brushstroke by this double standard of rightness, as if it were a single standard. It looks right to him if it takes its place in the imaginary scene and also in the pattern of shapes and colors. When design and representation are smoothly merged in a single pictorial form, the observer himself is not conscious of any difference between them, unless by critical analysis he traces out the double mode of organization. Each detail functions doubly or plurally, as a unit in two or more compositional factors. For example, a red rose-petal is a unit in a representative schema, a garden of flowers in the sunlight; it is also a unit in a thematic schema, a pattern of red, yellow, green, and blue spots. Likewise, the author of a sonnet, in seeking for the words to fill each line, is satisfied when he hits upon a phrase that conveys his meaning and at the same time fits into the pattern of rhyme and meter, satisfying his ear with enough variation to avoid monotony. Each word, each syllable, has a double or *plural functioning:* as a unit in one or more patterns of word-sounds and images; also as a unit in a representative or expository fabric of ideas. Looking over his work with a critical eye, he changes a word here, a punctuation mark there; now because it offends his taste for verbal music; now because it fails to help describe the scene or express the sentiment intended. Whether he will be conscious of these different phases in the composing process, these simultaneous or alternating modes of organization, depends on the extent to which he has studied his art in an abstract, theoretical way.

When two or more compositional factors are developed in the finished work, it is often hard to tell which came first in the artist's mind, or in what order he developed them. Some painters begin with a scene from nature; almost any scene, and not necessarily one which looks "picturesque" to begin with, or presents any readymade design. They sketch its essential features—the representative schema. Some begin with a photographic snapshot or picture postcard. In a portrait, some begin with the characteristic lines and surfaces of the face and head. But soon their design sense comes into play. They seek for potential themes of line, of shape, of light and dark, of hue; some recurrent quality here and there, which suggests the beginning of a design. Then they look elsewhere for details which could be modified a little, so as to carry out one of these themes, to build up the design, and organize the scene from this point of view.

On the other hand, it is possible to begin with a non-representative form, an abstract design or part of one, and then develop it along representative lines. The Gothic manuscript illuminator takes an initial letter, and whimsically turns it into a twisted plant or animal shape; the Greek architect transforms a column into a caryatid. Some modern painters (for example, Thomas Benton) often begin by sketching an abstract pattern of rhythmic lines and masses within the given area; then turn these into human figures and landscape details, so as to build up a scene and tell a story. In writing music, one can begin with representation—for example, a short passage suggesting birdsongs, a waterfall, a clucking hen, a rainstorm or a spinning wheel; then develop the passage thematically, into an ABA pattern, a fugue, or a sonata movement. In the opposite direction, one can begin with a purely thematic, musical pattern in mind, and the germs of several melodies without any representative meaning. In the process of developing a musical design, the composer may find that it is coming to suggest a storm, a battle, a peasant dance, or something else in the outside world. He then decides to develop this resemblance a little more fully, and reinforce it by a descriptive title. Much music, of course, has no representative development at all; it is highly specialized on the single factor of design. Once more, these artistic practices vary greatly from one period to another; the romantic composer is more likely than the classic one, to develop his music along representative, programmatic lines, and to begin with a representative conception.

12. Comparing the arts in regard to modes of transmission; in regard to presented and suggested components

We now return to the problem of comparing and classifying whole arts such as painting and poetry. Several generalizations along this line were made in a previous section; it remains to summarize and develop them a little more systematically. These generalizations are quite tentative, and relative to present knowledge of the history of the arts. They are not intended as boundaries which the arts cannot or should not cross, but merely as rough estimates of common differences among various fields up to date. Original artists may take them as a challenge to attempt quite different emphases in the use of a given medium.

Under the general heading of "modes of transmission," there are several specific bases for comparing the arts. Let us concentrate first on the presented factor, and ask how the arts differ in this regard.

a. *Mode of presentation.* As to the *number of senses* which are directly addressed, the arts can be grouped as unisensory, bisensory, and multisensory. Music is on the whole an art of *unisensory* presentation; it is addressed to the ears alone. This is true of concert or radio music in which the appearance of the performers is not an integral part of the work of art, even though it may contribute to the total aesthetic experience. Music in an operatic performance is in a different category. Drawing, painting, and sculpture are also, on the whole, arts of uni-sensory presentation. They are presentatively specialized. Opera and ballet with music are arts of *bisensory* presentation. Religious rituals with incense, music, visible and sometimes tactile ceremony constitute an art of *multisensory* presentation. They are diversified as to mode of presentation.

b. As to the *particular senses addressed,* the arts have been classified by Külpe and others as visual, auditory, and audio-visual (optic, acoustic, and optic-acoustic). The *visual,* of course, include painting, sculpture, architecture, and the so-called useful or applied arts. Music is wholly or mainly *auditory.* Külpe also lists poetry under this heading, and Piper adds "all Literature, Speech Arts." But this is hardly correct. As we have seen, prose fiction is now almost always an art of visual presentation, and even poetry and drama are frequently so. Literature in all its branches is an art of either visual or auditory presentation. It can be presented to both senses at once, as when one follows the printed text of *Hamlet* while hearing it spoken on the stage or radio.

The *audio-visual* arts are defined by Külpe as those appealing to both the higher senses. They can also be understood as those appealing to *either* of the higher senses interchangeably. In that case, literature is an audio-visual art. The dance is sometimes addressed to both senses, when accompanied by music, and sometimes to vision alone. So are pageants and puppetry, which Piper lists as optic-acoustic. Opera and spoken drama, including their filmed and televised performances, are more consistently audio-visual in the sense of appealing to both sight and hearing at once.

The Külpe-Piper list should be augmented by a class of *lower-sense* arts; Tolstoy's view is to be favored on this point, rather than Kant's. The traditional scorn of occidental philosophers toward the lower senses is based on medieval dualism and asceticism; it is obsolete today. Even the term "lower" should be understood without moral implications, and merely as implying weaker powers of sensory dis-crimination. The arts of lower-sense presentation include the *olfactory* (perfume; incense) and *gustatory* (cuisine). Were it not for Christian asceticism in sexual matters, we should also recognize a *tactile* "art of love" to include the elaborate erotic rituals prescribed by Hindu, Persian, Roman, and Renaissance writers.[6] All lower-sense arts, in isolation, are comparatively lacking in organized, complex form.

To classify certain arts as visual does not imply that their visual aspects are their most important ones, or most characteristic of their nature on the whole. This is certainly true of printed literature. As we noted in a previous chapter, there is some danger of over-simplification in referring to houses, swords, cups, and the like as works of visual art. To do so is to assume a special point of view, that of the art critic or museum worker, whose interest in their visual qualities has become paramount. He thinks of works of art as in a glass case or a book illustration, not as they function in ordinary living. For an account of how these products work in human experience generally, we should have to consider many different functions and effects, including how a cup or sword feels when we lift and use it. A cup or a sword (outside a museum case) is actually presented not only to the eyes but to the tactile and kinesthetic senses also. Many arts are commonly regarded as being addressed primarily to one sense, when as a matter of fact their effect on some other sense is at least as important from certain points of view.

In classification, we can take account of such facts in two ways. We can add a number of headings to indicate appeal to more than one sense—for example, visual-tactile arts—to include many of the useful "minor" arts whose products are commonly handled, worn, or sat upon, as well as looked at. It might also include sculpture, whose products can be perceived through the finger-tips by a blind man. This would considerably complicate our classification of the arts on the presentative basis. The other alternative is to adopt a frankly simplified, special point of view for this particular mode of classification. Biological classifications are always arbitrarily simplified, selecting certain characteristics of a plant or animal which may not seem at all important from the ordinary human standpoint. After all, the way an art affects one or both of the higher senses has come to receive special attention in aesthetics, criticism, and cultural history generally. There is nothing wrong with using this as one among many bases of comparison, if we are aware of its limitations.

[6] Esp. Vatsyayana, *Kama Sutra;* Ovid, *Ars Amatoria,* etc. On cuisine as an art, see J. A. Brillat-Savarin, *The Physiology of Taste.* (English trans., Liveright, New York, 1926.)

c. A closely related basis of comparison is that of *presented components*. By definition, the visual arts all emphasize visual components in presentation. But they differ from each other as to which visual components they emphasize. Some emphasize line, light-and-dark, hue, and texture (drawing, painting, textile design, etc.), and others emphasize solid and surface shape (sculpture, architecture). Architecture often emphasizes interior voids or empty spaces; sculpture usually does not. In architecture, they are large and encompassing, so that the observer can view the form from inside. In music, auditory components dominate in presentation, including pitch, rhythm, and timbre. Literature spoken aloud is an auditory art, but it differs from music in not emphasizing pitch. (Chinese literature is an exception.) Distinctions between the arts along this line are subject to many exceptions, in view of great stylistic variation—for example, painting sometimes emphasizes color, sometimes line.[7]

It must be remembered that we are now considering only "presentative" differences between the arts; their suggestive characteristics have nothing to do with the present case, and will be considered later. It is quite irrelevant here that painting sometimes suggests deep space, sounds, and tactile qualities. It is irrelevant here that music and literature can suggest visual images; that does not make them visual arts in the present sense. It is irrelevant that melodic pattern resembles linear pattern in some respects, and may suggest it. When strictly defined, melody is an auditory component; line, a visual one. Melody is not a presented component in painting; or line, in music. The use of vague metaphors often obscures these facts. The kind of "color" which is presented in music is a different component from visual color; it is an effect of audible timbre and harmony. The kind of "rhythm" which is said to occur in visual art is not the same as musical rhythm, even though they have certain things in common.

d. Another specific basis of comparison, under the general heading of "modes of transmission," is the *degree to which each transmissional*

[7] It is an error to associate a certain art with a single component, as if it were always based on that one. Thus E. Souriau regards painting as the art of color; drawing and arabesque as the arts of line, etc. (*La correspondance des arts*, p. 97). It is not enough to add that other components may cooperate; one must say that other components often predominate in the form as a whole. Painting is, in some styles, primarily an art of line, with color a minor accessory. Drawing is sometimes an art of surface texture, with line a minor accessory. Color and texture sometimes predominate over volume in sculpture.

factor is emphasized and developed. Which arts emphasize the presentative factor, and which the suggestive? Certainly literature today, especially prose literature, usually emphasizes suggestion. The appearance of the letters is of little importance, and even the sound of the words is usually a minor consideration, aside from determining meaning. When literature is read silently to oneself, even the word-sounds, such as rhyme and rhythm in poetry, become parts of the suggestive factor; they are imagined and not directly sensed. At the other extreme is music, where the nature of the sounds directly heard is almost always highly important. Suggested images and emotions may or may not bulk large in the total effect of music. Painting and sculpture are highly variable in this respect, as stylistic trends swing to one extreme or another. In some periods, the subject-matter represented and the moods expressed are emphasized by artist and public alike. In others, "associated values" are denounced as irrelevant, while the directly visible form, the design of lines and colors, is everything. Literature also must be classed as somewhat variable in this respect; for example, radio tends to revive the importance of spoken word-sounds. Contrasts between whole arts must be very cautiously made on this basis, with due attention to the wide range of styles throughout history.

Music and the visual arts, as Volkelt pointed out, exceed literature in bringing us the "sensory abundance of the world" in strength and variety. Their presentative factor is usually greater in vividness and range of effects; in development through variety and complexity. Literature, on the other hand, has a wider range of suggestiveness or expressiveness than any other art. Auguste Comte, for this reason, declared poetry to be the most complex and comprehensive of the arts, with architecture at the other end of the scale.[8] It was, he said, highest in its own special effects and in its power to call up ideally the effects of all the other arts, all phenomena of nature and all experiences of life. It is hard to compare two arts as to their total complexity; but certainly literature is high in power to convey clear, abstract concepts and inferences, as well as a great variety of desires, emotions, and images from all the senses. The minor, applied arts are usually slight in range of suggestions, although they sometimes take on complex symbolic meaning. Music suggests vague emotions and images, but not usually definite concepts or logical arguments.

[8] *Cf.* Colvin, "Fine Arts," *op. cit.*, p. 361.

e. Let us now ask how the arts differ in regard to the particular *mode of suggestion* emphasized. In some, suggestion is mostly *mimetic*. These include painting, sculpture, the mimetic dance and pantomime, and the visual side of acting, including make-up, costume, gesture and tone of voice. Suggestion is achieved through presenting a form which *resembles* the image to be aroused by association.

In literature, on the other hand, it is mostly *symbolic*, depending on the arbitrary suggestive power of written or spoken words. In music, there is some mimesis, through partial resemblance to non-musical sounds; there is also much suggestion by *common association*—for example, a sound like a wail or sob can suggest grief. There are many combined or undifferentiated types of art from this point of view. Spoken and acted drama combines symbolic suggestion, through the meaning of words, with mimetic, through visual appearance.

f. We come now to the *suggested components*. How do the arts resemble each other as to the components which they can suggest? In Chapter VII, we saw how hard it was to identify any art with a particular kind of suggestions, although some theorists have tried to do so. Each art—not only the "major" ones, but handicrafts and other useful arts as well—has an almost limitless range of possible suggestions. This is true even when we consider only those suggestions which are strongly established by physiological or cultural bonds, so that the power of art to call them up is common and predictable, not a matter of occasional, personal coincidence.

Each art seems to have a narrow, peculiar range of suggestions when we are thinking only of (a) some special kind of suggestion, such as mimesis, and ignoring others; (b) some special cultural context, such as western European art, and ignoring others. A statue has the power to suggest, not only what it represents by direct mimesis—for example, a king with a crown—but also the ideas which have been culturally associated with that kind of statue. If it is in the Gothic style, long and slender, it may suggest a Gothic cathedral setting, and hence the whole realm of medieval Christian ideology. Likewise a piece of ordinary craftwork such as a shepherd's crook, a drum, a jar of ointment, a helmet, a mason's square and compass: any of these, in certain contexts, may assume symbolic meaning, and the power to call up far-reaching associations. Such cultural and stylistic connections give each art the power to suggest, under appropriate circumstances, works of other arts which belong to the same historic style or period. Thus a Gregorian chant tends to suggest the medieval cathedral wherein it was sung, and the ceremonies of which it was a part. Of course, one may choose to ignore such associations, as distracting from the essentials of artistic form; but the tendency of art to arouse them is a fact.

In terms of components, it can be said that certain visual images, moods, volitional attitudes, and religious concepts are involved as suggested components in the Gregorian chant. Likewise, a painting such as Giorgione's *Pastoral Concert* contains, as part of the suggestive factor in its form, images of music and pastoral pleasures; the concept of a Renaissance gentleman at ease in a rustic setting; the free, pagan morality of nudes in the open air. In short, a work of visual art may contain, as part of its suggestive factor, not only visual images but all kinds of sensory and other psychological components. So may a work of musical or literary art. The suggestive range of each art is so vast that they overlap and can not be permanently differentiated from each other.

If we observe an art only within a narrow cultural setting, it may exhibit fewer types of suggested component. The art of flower arrangement has had a much narrower range of cultural associations in the occident than in Japan and China. An occidental example of this art is not at present able to convey so many different kinds of meaning. Its suggestive range appears limited to a small group of decorative, domestic, and sentimental associations. No one would think of comparing it with religious painting or architecture as to wealth and variety of serious meanings. But in the orient, the meanings conveyed by these various arts are more similar.

In regard to any one mode of suggestion, the arts differ considerably from each other, and each has a narrower range of meanings. Architecture and the crafts suggest little through mimesis; much through common association based on the utilitarian functioning of their products—for example, a spinning wheel suggests the work of spinning, and the period in which it was used. In painting and sculpture, mimesis is much used, utilitarian association little.

The problem of analogies between the arts is often confused by failure to maintain a clear distinction between "presented" and "suggested" components. If we are talking about the former, line and color are components of painting but not of music; the two arts differ in this respect. But music can suggest linear pattern, and a visual design can suggest melody.

Is visible line, then, part of the aesthetic form of a piece of music? That depends on how definite, cogent, and socially established the suggestion is. Usually, such suggestions are vague and uncertain, so that individuals differ widely in responding to them. The aesthetic form of a work of art does not include all its possible suggestions, but only those which are culturally established, so that the artist can count upon them to some extent in predicting and controlling the responses of observers to them, as the poet can count on the meanings of words. There are many vague and tenuous resemblances between works of different arts, which may cause one to suggest another at times, but which are not sufficiently established in our culture to function as definite meanings. This is true in regard to the power of linear patterns to suggest melodies, and vice versa. We must not include, within the list of suggestive components of a certain art, those types of suggestion which are merely occasional and accidental, but only those which constitute fairly regular means in its equipment for producing desired effects.

Conditions differ as to the nature of such associative bonds, as between one culture and another, or one period or another. One cannot say with finality, then, whether visible line and linear pattern are parts of the suggestive factor in music. They can become so, just as certain meanings become attached to verbal or other symbols, if artists and public come to connect them persistently, and establish bonds between them. In our culture, we commonly associate musical sounds with printed scores; the rises and falls of pitch with the ups and downs of black notes on a white page. These visual associations are so firmly established, for a musically trained person, that the heard melody may be at once translated into visually imagined notes and linear graphs. Even so, it is seldom the composer's intention to arouse visual images of notes on a page. He often wishes to suggest linear patterns of a more abstract sort, and for this purpose the established bonds between heard melodies and printed melodic lines are an aid, even though the latter are not clearly and consciously visualized. If the composer wishes to suggest linear pattern, he must usually seek the additional aid of a descriptive title such as "Arabesque." In that case, if the music also helps to convey the idea, the visual image of an arabesque becomes part of the aesthetic form of the music. In general, our culture is accustomed to quick translations between visual and auditory images, primarily through language; and this tends to make one kind of image constantly suggest the other, even when no definite bond of meaning exists.

Similar questions arise in regard to color and rhythm. As strictly defined, color is presented only to the sense of vision; but it can become a suggested component in music, when the composer consciously tries to convey images of color and light by the means at his command, in addition to verbal titles. (For example, Debussy's *Reflets dans l'eau.*) Some individuals are so constituted as to have strong associations between color and hearing—for example, between certain musical keys and certain colors. But they do not all experience the same associations, and such bonds are not definite enough for the composer to be able to count upon them.

Rhythm is usually regarded as an auditory component; one presented to the sense of hearing. In a broad sense, it occurs also in temporal series of visual and tactile stimuli. We can directly perceive the temporal grouping in a series of electric light flashes. A succession of taps on the skin can be felt as rhythmic. But it is confusing to speak of rhythm as something visible in a motionless painting or statue, as is often done in textbooks on "art principles." A strongly kinesthetic observer may perceive a row of lines, spots, or masses in temporal order, with strong feelings of rhythm, as a succession of thrusts or accented beats. Rhythm occurs here, then, as a *suggested* component in the visual form; as a temporal grouping of imagined visual or auditory events. But such rhythm can never be presented in a static visible object, as line and color are presented. Further confusion arises when the term "rhythm" is applied to all thematic repetition—for example, to the resemblance between a row of curving lines. Such resemblance is not a "component" at all, but a "mode of composition."

In modern western music, melody has characteristically played an influential role, which it has not played in some other styles of music. It has usually exerted a form-giving, architectonic function in the composition as a whole, much like that of line in drawing and painting. It has helped to organize the so-called "color" of timbre and harmony into fairly definite forms, easily grasped by the western listener. Just so, line has helped to organize light, hue, and texture into definite visual shapes. In both arts, a blurred, romantic effect results when the organizing component is softened, as in nineteenth century impressionism. Both line and melody can be developed into thematic designs, in partly analogous ways.

How much of this analogy between visual and auditory components is based on fundamental similarities in the physical stimuli themselves? How much is based on the physiology of the human organism? How much is based on passing cultural and stylistic connections? We know too little, as yet, to say; but these questions deserve research in comparative aesthetics. We shall touch upon them again at the end of this chapter, in relation to the subject of style.

13. Comparing the arts in regard to spatial, temporal, and causal development. Dimensional characteristics

Much has been said, pro and con, about the division of arts into spatial and temporal. These categories are useful as abstract types; the difficulty comes, as we have seen, in trying to force a whole art into one of them. Arts have a way of escaping from such pigeon-holes. As our knowledge of different styles expands, we often see that the art in question has never been really confined there. Is painting really a space art, and nothing more? Then what of Walt Disney's moving picture films from paintings, and what of the Chinese scrolls which were unrolled and looked at in temporal sequence?

A similar difficulty arises in trying to separate the "arts of rest" from the "arts of movement." Volkelt classified sculpture, architecture, and the applied arts as arts of rest. But sculpture becomes a mobile art as soon as we set it in motion, as in marionettes, Calder's "mobiles," and the mechanical figures made by Hero of Alexandria. Even architecture, if we define it broadly, becomes mobile and temporal in ships, automobiles, trains, and airplanes. It is usually restricted to static buildings. But then we need a new category of arts devoted to large mobile structures of the types just listed. They are now grouped as "vehicles of locomotion" under the broad heading of "industrial design," along with a great diversity of other products. Mobile vehicular design is closely related to architecture in that people live and work inside such hollow shells, as they do in static buildings. Living quarters in a motor trailer, a houseboat or a sleeping car are functionally akin to those within a house. One might class this category of arts as "mobile architecture," a division of architecture in general.

It is important to recognize that certain types of art are comparatively static, while others move or change in carefully controlled ways. Sculpture, painting, and architecture, in the narrow traditional senses of these words, are certainly more static than dancing and music. The distinction is not absolute, but the difference in degree is great.

John Dewey objects to the "space and time" classification, mainly on the ground that a work of art—even a stationary one—is perceived in a temporal, cumulative way.[9] This is true, but the fact remains that some arts (for example, ballet) present a moving, physical object to the eye, while in others the work of art remains comparatively fixed while the spectator does most of the moving, as in walking through a cathedral. Even allowing for the shifting play of lights which Dewey mentions, there is an obvious difference in degree of mobility between a statue or cathedral and a dancer.

The worst fallacy in the theory of space and time arts has been the inferring of restrictive rules and value-standards from this distinction. Arts were not only forcibly separated into these two groups, but forbidden to cross the barrier between them, as in Lessing's condemnation of paintings which try to suggest temporal succession. And this referred only to suggestive effects in painting; the possibility of actual, visible movement in the picture was not in question. Said Lessing, "To introduce two necessarily distant points of time into one and the same painting, as . . . Titian has the whole history of the prodigal son . . . is an encroachment by the painter upon the sphere of the poet which good taste could never justify." [10] This is only one example of countless similar rules deduced from the general assumption that the arts have definite boundaries, rightful and permanent, which should not be crossed.[11] Admirers of modern, non-representational art sometimes denounce the story-telling kind of painting as a "confusion of values," in that it invades the "proper field of literature." It is true that art sometimes profits by accepting restrictions, and simplifying its problems; also, it is inevitable that each age should denounce the styles of the previous age, and find arguments for doing so. Lessing spoke as an apologist for what actually was the main Renaissance tendency in painting—to restrict a picture to what could be seen at a single

[9] *Art as Experience*, p. 218.

[10] Laocoön, Ch. XVIII.

[11] *Cf.* I. Babbitt, *The New Laokoön*, p. 233, with ref. to Volkmann, *Grenzen der Künste.*

moment, from a single point in space. But there is no reason whatever why the modern artist or aesthetician should accept such restrictions as binding.

It is worth recalling again, at this point, the importance of the German concept of *bildende Künste*. We have seen that its abstract connotation is broad and vague, coming from a noun *(Bild)* meaning "image" and a verb *(bilden)* meaning "to form." Hence it suggests the forming of visual representations. Its denotation as applied to the arts has varied somewhat. Sulzer, about 1771, applies it especially to the arts of visual representation where the third dimension is actually present: for example, to sculpture, gem-cutting, and stucco-work. Architecture and painting are not included. Kant, however, explicitly includes these two arts in addition to sculpture. The abstract meaning of *bildende Künste* then widens accordingly. Architecture is not a representative art, and painting is not actually three-dimensional. Dancing and mobile color are still left out; so *bildende Künste* comes to mean, in general, "arts of static visual shape."

Urries y Azara, in the twentieth century, defines the *bildende Künste* as arts intended for the eye, affecting it with plane or mass, with or without inner space. He follows Kant in including architecture, painting, sculpture, and minor arts; he makes the *bildende Künste* coincide with "space arts," and does not extend them to cover the space-time arts of dance, drama, and motion pictures. "Arts of static visual shape" seems to be the closest and clearest English equivalent.

In speaking of static and mobile, or spatial and temporal, arts, it is important to recall again the difference between *presented* and *suggested* factors in art. If we call a picture by Rubens "flat" or "motionless," we are thinking only of its presented factor. It suggests depth in space and movement in time. The statue of Laocoön has solidity as a presented component, while a photograph of it merely suggests solidity. For systematic comparison, it is well to confine ourselves for a while to the presented factor alone.

Using as a basis the *spatio-temporal development of the presented factor,* it is possible to distinguish the following groups of arts:

a. *Arts whose main presentative development is spatial; static* arts, lacking complex determinate motion or change. Here belong all the arts which are traditionally listed as *bildende Künste;* most varieties of painting, sculpture, architecture, and minor useful arts—that is, all varieties except those into which complex temporal development has been introduced. The static arts are those whose products, as presented, are comparatively motionless and unchanging. On the borderline of this class are arts involving motion which is simple and repetitious, as in a weathervane, a waterwheel, a jumping-jack, or a pair of scissors; or comparatively uncontrolled, spasmodic, irregular and accidental, as in the blowing of a tree or flag by the wind.

Static arts can be further divided into (a) those of *two*-dimensional presentation and (b) those of *three*-dimensional presentation. The former group includes most paintings and other pictures, and most textiles. The latter includes most sculpture in relief and round, architecture, and most of the minor useful arts. Borderline cases are pictures with areas of high impasto or gilt in relief; also textiles with raised embroidery or appliqué. These become three-dimensional to the extent that the actual raising of parts in relief becomes an important factor in the total visual effect. Arts of three-dimensional presentation can be further subdivided into those with and those without perceptible inner space; the former including most architecture and furniture, and some sculpture; the latter including most sculpture.

b. *Arts whose main presentative development is temporal.* These include music, and literature which is oral and auditory in presentation, such as a recited poem. They are mobile, possessing complex determinate motion or change. Spatial characteristics may enter to a slight extent, as in having sounds or speeches issue from different points; but the basic structure is temporal.

c. *Arts whose main presentative development is spatio-temporal;* in both space and time. These also are mobile arts, with complex determinate motion or change. They include (a) those developed in two dimensions of space and in time, such as filmed motion pictures, shadow plays, etc., and (b) those developed in three dimensions of space and in time, such as ballet, opera, acted drama, marionettes, and most other theater arts. Some types of athletics and acrobatics approach the latter group in so far as they stimulate aesthetic observation. So do certain types of vehicular movement, as in complex aerial evolutions, and complex fireworks with a series of changes.

d. *Arts lacking complex development in either space or time;* arts of rudimentary spatio-temporal development. These include the lower-sense arts mentioned above. For example, the planned succession of courses in a dinner involves a simple organization of taste stimuli in space and time.

Literature is once more hard to classify on this basis. It can jump from one category to another with little ado, and with little effect on the essentials of literary form. In its primitive stages, it is an art of temporal presentation (oral and auditory); it becomes a static art of two-dimensional, visual presentation when written or printed on a page. Determinate motion begins as soon as we have the book, to be unrolled or to have its pages turned in definite order. Such visible motion is highly developed when illuminated words stream along an electric news bulletin. It can become three-dimensional in spatial presentation when presented to the blind through Braille type or cut-out letters. As we saw in the chapter on process, a printed text or musical score is a visible set of directions for performance, audible or imaginary. Aesthetic theory should frankly recognize these variations, and the fact that literature as a whole can not be forced into any one category on the present basis. This extreme variability of the sensory symbols through which literary forms are conveyed is still further augmented by language differences, and provides the art with great flexibility in presentation.

By way of summary, let us see how two bases of classification just examined—mode of presentation and spatio-temporal development—can be combined. Either one may be used first, as the primary basis, with the other determining smaller subdivisions.

Using *mode of presentation* first, we have:

1. Arts of visual presentation

   a. Static visual arts: spatial development only; in 2 or 3 dimensions; without complex determinate change or motion;
   b. Mobile visual arts: spatio-temporal, with complex determinate change or motion; in 2 or 3 dimensions of space.

2. Arts of auditory presentation (mobile).
3. Arts of audio-visual presentation: in 2 or 3 dimensions of space (mobile).
4. Arts of lower-sense presentation: rudimentary spatio-temporal development.

Using first the degree of *mobility* and *temporal development,* we have:

1. Static arts: without complex temporal development; mostly visual.

2. Mobile arts: with complex temporal development
   a. Visual: spatio-temporal;
   b. Auditory: temporal only;
   c. Audio-visual: spatio-temporal.

Lower-sense arts, rudimentary in mobility and spatio-temporal development, can be placed under either heading or in a third, intermediate group.

Now let us turn to the *suggestive* factor in the arts, and how it is developed as to space, time, and other frames of reference. Here the situation is different. All the representative arts can suggest *spatial* relations, in three as well as two dimensions. Depth and solidity are suggested in painting. Sculptural relief presents a slight development of three-dimensional form, and suggests more. That is, a difference in height of half an inch or so between the various planes of a relief may help suggest a deep vista into space, with massive figures here and there. A theater stage, likewise, can suggest more three-dimensional development than it actually presents. Literature can describe all spatial relations of shape and distance with vivid clarity. In music, spatial suggestions are vague, as are most other suggestions. A piece of music may suggest broad expanses of snow or desert, or the shadowy aisles of a forest or cathedral; but never very clearly, unless it is accompanied by literary text or program notes. There is great disagreement on the suggested meanings of music, so they cannot always be classed as determinate parts of the form.

What of *temporal* suggestions? Static painting and sculpture may portray unchanging, immobile subjects, or may show one moment in a sequence of events. They can easily give a slight hint of before and after, as in showing a horse with forelegs raised or the effect of some remark on a group of listeners. This suggests, more or less clearly, what must have immediately preceded or followed the scene portrayed. Before the late Renaissance, a picture often included events which were supposed to have happened at different times; but usually without clear indication of their temporal order. A picture-sequence (a row of pictures in definite order, as from left to right) can tell a long story, suggesting temporal sequence through its spatial arrangement, as in a newspaper "comic strip." Likewise, the spatial arrangement of words on a page and pages in a book can build up an imaginary sequence of events: a story.

Arts in which the presented factor is mobile and developed temporally can easily suggest a temporal sequence of events. In a stage or screen play, great complexity of development is possible along this line. The imaginary sequence does not need to parallel the presented one exactly. A story is often told or enacted in a different order from that in which the events are supposed to have occurred, through "flashbacks" to earlier times. Music can also suggest an ordered sequence of moods and events. By itself, it is never very clear in doing so; but it is a great help to drama, film, and ballet in building up the emotional background of action. It gives a vivid sense of the temporal flow of life in an abstract way.

Architecture and the other useful, visual arts, whose presented aspects are static, do not ordinarily try to suggest a definite temporal sequence of events. They are full of temporal associations: what could suggest time in general, with the passage of hours and days, more strongly than a sundial, a clock, or a calendar? But such suggestions are very abstract and general, unless other factors are present to give them concrete meaning.

Definite classification of the arts on this basis is obviously difficult. One can generalize roughly to the effect that (a) certain arts often lay great emphasis on suggestive temporal development, especially literature (epic poetry and fiction), theater arts, music, and picture sequences; (b) certain arts are intermediate in this respect, especially single still pictures and sculptures; (c) certain arts suggest little or no definite temporal development, especially architecture and the minor useful arts.

One other kind of development must be considered at this point— that of *causal* relations, in which certain events or conditions are shown to be causes or effects of others. Such relations are always suggested by the work of art and inferred by the observer; never directly presented.

In literature, especially epic and fiction, they are elaborately developed into plots and schemes of motivation and mutual influence, while in essays and lyrics causal relations are considered in a more general way. In theater arts, picture sequences, and wherever stories are told, the organization of details is to be described in terms of "because," "therefore," and "in order that," as well as in terms of "before" and "after." In music, suggested causal relations are at a minimum. They are again vague and indefinite, consisting in obscure hints of struggle and overcoming or of inevitability.[12] In architecture and other strongly utilitarian arts, it is often difficult to grasp, through mere observation, the functional relations of parts to the whole and to each other; of all to the intended purpose. But such relations are causal, to be described in terms of means and ends, as in telling why a certain column or buttress is where it is. Static or still pictures sometimes suggest a definite causal scheme, especially when they are of a story-telling kind. They may show, for example, one man lying dead and another bending over him with a dagger, so that the observer infers a murder. But much painting (for example, decorative and semi-abstract) is little concerned with such relations. It is hard to produce elaborate causal development without considerable temporal development, so that the gradual repercussion of factors on each other may be shown.

Thus literature and theater arts lead in emphasis on causal development, especially through story plots and abstract discussion; while the static utilitarian arts often suggest another kind of causal relationship, that of potential or actual cooperation of parts in performing a function. Music is low in this type of organization, while static painting and sculpture are intermediate and variable.

14. Comparing the arts in regard to modes of composition

Volkelt, in comparing the arts on a basis of "psychic content," divides them into "objective" and "non-objective." In the former group he places painting, sculpture, poetry, and drama; they are able to convey precise, individualized, specific representations of things, persons, scenes, actions, and events. On the other hand, music, dance, architecture, and applied art are said to be non-objective in that no specific things, events, or actions are represented; suggested images and emotions are vague, general, and not referred to particular objects. A similar antithesis is used by Urries y Azara, who couples "objective"

[12] It is easy to exaggerate the extent to which music involves causal relations. The suggestion of "inevitability" in a final return to the tonic is largely due to expectancy based on experience of similar patterns; it tends to disappear when styles change, and many compositions avoid such a return. The "inevitable" outcome of a Greek tragedy is based on the working out of accepted causal principles such as Fate, inherited curses, etc. Even there, the "inevitable" is sometimes averted through divine intervention. Causal suggestions are sometimes conveyed in music, but not as definitely as in literature.

with "imitative," and "non-objective" with "free." Adler, instead, contrasts the objective and imitative arts with the "subjective and cosmic." He makes the latter group include architecture, music, and dance; so it coincides with Volkelt's "non-objective."

Several partly valid generalizations are mingled here, in a vague and over-simplified way. It is quite true that some arts tend to emphasize representation, and can easily achieve representation of a fairly definite, concrete type. By either words or pictures, one can suggest a vivid fantasy of a particular person, scene, or event. However, it should not be implied that either painting, sculpture, or literature is always "objective" in this respect. They can all be abstract and indefinite in meaning. Kandinsky's late paintings are now called "non-objective."

It is true on the whole that music, architecture, and the applied arts do not ordinarily stress representation to the extent that painting and sculpture do. Architecture and furniture are full of carved, painted, and woven representations, but these are somewhat secondary interests. Music usually represents natural sounds vaguely if at all; but it can do so vividly if and when the composer wants to do so. If not "bound" by imitative aims, it is bound by whatever aims and customs it does accept, in design or expression.

The term "objective" is full of confusing associations in philosophy and psychology. In some ways, a purely abstract design can be regarded as more objective than a realistic picture: it is there in front of us as an actual, perceptible object. The picture, on the other hand, relies for its effect on stimulating certain fancies within us, which are in some ways "subjective," based on illusion, and devoid of real objective reference. "Representative" or "representational" is a much less confusing term at present. As its opposite, we can say "non-representative" or "non-representational." There are, however, no completely non-representational arts. All arts, including music, architecture, and furniture, sometimes involve representation. Even gardening does so, as in clipping shrubs into bird-shapes and imitating mountain landscapes with rocks and moss.

Within every art, there are different styles and different examples, some of which tend to be more representative and perhaps more realistic than others. Some are very slightly so, and these are often called "abstract," "distorted," "stylized," or "fantastic." Some have no definite representative meaning, whatever vague associations they may arouse. They can be properly called "non-representative" styles or examples. In comparison with the natural forms, from which they may have been derived, they are also called "abstract." This implies that they have left out so many of the details present in these natural forms that they are no longer recognizable as a picture or statue. Non-representative forms are abstract only in this relative sense; a linear pattern or a fugue in music is a concrete work of art in its own right, whether or not it represents anything else.

Strictly speaking, then, the term "non-representative" can be applied only to particular works of art and to certain types and styles of art; not to whole arts. It is incorrect to make a sharp division between representative and non-representative, or objective and non-objective. It is misleading to speak of "the representative arts" with the implication that any arts are wholly non-representative. One can say more correctly that certain arts such as poetry, painting and sculpture, are more strongly or frequently representative; while others, such as architecture, furniture, and music, are less strongly or frequently representative.

It is impossible to divide the arts into sharply contrasting groups on a basis of the modes of composition employed. All arts employ more than one mode of composition. Each of the so-called major arts employs all four of them, to some extent and at certain times. Comparisons can be made only in terms of more and less; as extremely rough generalizations to the effect that a certain art tends to use a certain mode of composition more frequently than another art does, and to develop it with greater emphasis. To demonstrate such generalizations with any approach to conclusiveness would require a vast amount of illustration and evidence, based on greater knowledge than we have at present as to the variety of styles in each art. Even in a single work of art, available for direct observation, it is often hard to say which compositional factor is more emphatic or highly developed. Often two or more seem about equal: for example, in a painting which is detailed and realistic in representation and also complex in design of lines and colors. However, it is usually evident that certain other factors are comparatively neglected. Likewise in regard to whole arts, there is considerable disparity in development of the various factors, especially within the main traditions of European art.

a. Among the arts which have placed comparatively great emphasis on *representation* are literature (especially epic and dramatic poetry and prose fiction), drawing, painting, tapestry, photography, sculpture, dance, and other theater arts. This can be confidently asserted on the whole, in spite of occasional trends toward the "abstract" or non-representative in some of them. This group can be subdivided according to which type of suggestion is used. Literature now ordinarily uses the arbitrary symbolism of words and letters, now that picture-writing is largely obsolete. The rest of the group usually employs mimesis, or suggestion by resemblance.

Comparatively little emphasis on representation has been made in music, when divorced from literary text—that is, when it is purely instrumental concert music. In modern western music, even when there is some representative "program," it is usually subordinated to the musical design. The utilitarian visual arts, such as architecture and furniture, sometimes contain a representative factor in carved, woven, or painted figures. But they rarely stress these as much as they do the functional shape of the object. Recently, the trend has been toward omitting or severely minimizing the representative factor in forms which are mainly utilitarian.

b. The arts which most obviously emphasize *utilitarian* composition are these same visual arts which do not emphasize representation —namely, architecture and the minor useful arts. Most of them are static, but we have just noted the strong development of mobile vehicular design, with dominantly utilitarian frameworks, in automobiles, trains, ships, and aircraft. Music has its utilitarian aspects, as in work songs and bugle calls, but the art as a whole can not be said to emphasize either utility or representation. Certain types of literature are utilitarian (for example, a guidebook), but they are usually not ranked as distinct arts.

c. As to *thematic* composition or *design*, comparison has been hindered by failure to recognize the basic similarity between design in music, in literature, and in the visual arts. Aesthetics has not sufficiently recognized the presence of thematic development in all the arts, through the repetition, variation, contrast, and integration of themes, whether these themes are of lines and colors, melody and harmony, or verbal rhymes and rhythms. Hence comparisons between the arts on this basis are, for most readers, not easy to follow. No single term is in common use to indicate such a thematic or design factor in any art. The term "decorative," for example, is commonly applied only in the visual arts.

By and large, we may hazard the generalization that music, especially since the Renaissance, has most consistently emphasized thematic composition and design. The term "theme" is most commonly used in music, though in a special, restricted sense which we are not at present using. Musical analysis, largely in terms of thematic composition (to include harmony, rhythm, and the larger patterns such as fugue and sonata) has gone farther than thematic analysis in most of the other arts. In post-Renaissance music, the factors of utility, representation, and exposition have been commonly minimized or omitted, but there are important exceptions.

All the other arts have been extremely variable as to the emphasis placed on thematic development, so that comparison of whole arts is very difficult. Within the general field of literature, poetry is recognized as an art distinct from prose. Among its distinguishing factors is emphasis on the organization of word-sounds, which is one kind of thematic development. Images and ideas can also be organized thematically, and contribute to the total design. But even where such thematic development exists in poetry, it is seldom in isolation, for poetry has other important factors. Lyrical poetry often places great stress on exposition (for example, the setting forth of emotional attitudes toward the world), while epic poetry stresses narrative representation. Poetry is thus an art in which there is usually high, but not necessarily highest emphasis on thematic development. In prose, such development is characteristically low.

In the visual arts, there is likewise great variability. Certainly, there is a group called the "decorative arts," in which thematic development of line, color, texture, and pattern is characteristically emphasized. But, again, it is not necessarily the dominant factor in all respects. As we have seen, this group of arts is also characterized, on the whole, by utilitarian emphasis.

The sharp antithesis between decorative arts and representative arts is misleading. Not only are many representative forms—for example, small ivory carvings and painted miniatures—often classed as decorative art; in addition, all great styles of painting and sculpture contain a decorative or design element. This is not restricted to superficial ornamentation, but includes the basic structure of the object or scene itself, as thematic arrangement of the principal lines, colors, masses, light and dark areas. When the two are thoroughly integrated, it is again hard to say whether design or representation is more highly emphasized or developed.

Music, architecture, and textile design stand out as arts with frequent high emphasis on thematic composition. Schelling's dictum that architecture is "frozen music" showed his perception of a genuine analogy betweer these arts, as tending to emphasize non-representative design. He perceived, too, that thematic structure is fundamentally similar whether developed in space or in time, and with visual or auditory ingredients.

Prose literature is characteristically low in presentative thematic development. That is, it lacks emphasis on complex arrangement of word-sounds. Elsewhere in art, thematic development tends to co-exist with one or more of the other compositional factors, in varying degrees of relative emphasis, and in varying degrees of integration with them.

d. Many arts, in earlier times, were often used for *expository* purposes. This was true, as we have seen, of much religious painting and sculpture. Drawing and photography are still used for exposition, especially as diagrams in conjunction with a scientific text. Music can suggest abstract ideas, but is too vague for systematic exposition. In modern times, the task of exposition in art has been taken over more and more by literature; especially in meditative lyric poetry, and in the prose essay and treatise. Literature as a whole can not be classed as typically emphasizing any one mode of composition.

15. Combined arts and component arts; specialized and diversified types of product

Opera is called a combined art, since it combines music and drama. Ballet is similarly classed, as a union of dancing, music, costume, and stage design. Can all the arts be classified on this basis, as to whether they are comparatively simple or compound, homogeneous or heterogeneous?

A mixed or compound product is not necessarily the same as a complex one. A black-and-white sketch in pen and ink can be very complex within its own limits, having a multiplicity of tiny, varying details; but it will still be relatively homogeneous by contrast with an opera, which brings in more radically different factors.

There are many ways in which a work of art can be judged as simple or compound. An art may be diversified in some respects and not in others. One way, considered previously in this chapter, is that of *sensory appeal:* to one, two, or more senses. On this basis, opera and ballet are diversified or heterogeneous, since they appeal to eyes and ears. Religious rituals involving incense as well as music and visible pageantry are still more diversified in this respect.

Another basis of comparison is that of *components,* elementary and developed. How many are involved? A pen-and-ink sketch is limited in this respect by contrast with an oil painting, since it lacks development in hue. A piece for violin alone is specialized by contrast with a symphony, since it lacks timbre-development, or contrast in instrumental coloring. Again, an opera is diversified, since it presents a wide range of visual and auditory components. In addition, it has a large suggestive range, especially through the power of literary text.

Still another basis is that of *modes of composition,* or compositional factors. Some works of art are highly diversified compositionally, in that they involve several such factors; others are much more specialized. The Gothic cathedral was mentioned above as an example of such diversity, since it involves all four compositional factors. Occasional works in various arts are so diversified: for example, the Statue of Liberty, as a utilitarian, representative, and decorative form. But architecture and sculpture are not always so diversified. Opera itself is not highly diversified from this point of view. Most operas have no utilitarian, and little or no expository development. They have a representative, narrative framework, which is enriched thematically by all the resources of music plus visual textures and patterns in motion. Ballet also receives its principal development in two modes of composition: representative and thematic. Most arts likewise specialize on two modes of composition: for example, painting on representation[13] and thematic design; architecture on utility and thematic design. They bring in the others in a more occasional or subordinate way, if at all.

Several modern arts, now distinct, are said to be descended from a *primitive, undifferentiated proto-art:* the dramatic religious dance

---

[13] *Cf.* Herbert Spencer on the differentiation of painting into specialized subject-types such as pure landscape, without figures (*Principles of Sociology,* Vol. II, Pt. VII, p. 313).

with words and music.[14] In Homeric Greece, this was called the *molpê*. Gilbert Murray describes it as a dance-and-song, by a bard and chorus, with choral singing and dancing.[15] Its subjects, he says, were love, strife, death, and that which is beyond death. From this undifferentiated art, some theorists have said, came the separate arts of vocal and instrumental music, epic and lyric poetry, and the dance.

There can be little doubt that, on the whole, the arts have been progressively differentiated; or that the *molpê* contains the germs of several which are now distinct. But we must be careful not to generalize too broadly and simply. It is going too far to say that all the arts came from one germinal art. Comparatively specialized arts, such as the chipping of stone tools, have existed side by side with diversified rituals from paleolithic times. The dramatic religious dance in early Greek culture, which seems primitive by comparison with Greek tragedy at its height, was itself a fairly complex product, with a long previous evolution. Along with such diversified types, and preceding some of them, were more specialized types like simple instrumental music (for example, the shepherd's pipes), singing without dancing, and the recitation of genealogies and legends. All these were practiced in comparative detachment at certain times; in combination at others.

Since diversified types of art have existed from primitive times, it is a little misleading to call their modern descendants (such as opera) "mixed" or "combined." This suggests that they have been artificially assembled out of original, elementary arts. On the contrary, some of them are direct survivals of undifferentiated ancestral arts. In modern times, to be sure, it usually does take artificial assembling or reintegrating, to produce an opera out of several groups of artists whose training has been highly specialized. A more natural, spontaneous kind of diversity persists today in rustic festivals and certain children's games, involving song and rhythmic motion.

[14] Müller-Freienfels calls this the "musal proto-art" *(die musische Urkunst)*. Cf. *Psychologie der Kunst,* Vol. III, Pt. I. Volkelt raises the question "whether the arts developed from a germinal art or arts in the earliest history of man" *(System der Aesthetik,* Vol. III, Ch. XII, p. 380). He attributes to A. Schmarsow the view that "the plastic arts come from mimicry as the original artistic activity" *(Unser Verhältnis zu den bildenden Künsten.* Leipzig, 1903). P. J. Möbius, on the contrary, declares that the chief arts had separate beginnings *(Über Kunst und Künstler.* Leipzig, 1901).

[15] *The Classical Tradition in Poetry* (Cambridge: Harvard U. Press, 1927). Ch. II.

The history of the arts, as far as we can see it now, has always involved some tendencies toward specialization and some toward pro‐ ducing diversified, compound products. Examples of the latter may be found, not only in the dramatic dance, but in the dwelling-house and its furnishings, considered as a functional unit; also in the primitive vil‐ lage and town. Likewise, there have been throughout the known his‐ tory of art many tendencies toward complication—the building up of ultra-complex single forms, such as a medieval cathedral—and many tendencies toward simplification—the abandonment of ultra-complex types in favor of simpler, separate units. An example of the latter is seen in modern women's apparel, as compared with that of the seven‐ teenth and eighteenth centuries.

The precise order of steps by which the modern arts have evolved does not concern us here, and these facts are mentioned merely as a caution against any oversimplified formula. What does concern us is, first of all, the fact that both specialized and diversified types of art product do exist side by side; and, second, that tendencies in both directions are constantly going on. In the rise of modern opera through Wagner's music-dramas, we had a notable example of the tendency to build gigantic, heterogeneous art-forms out of diverse materials. Baroque festivals,[16] spectacles, and pageants were often still more colossal and diversified. At the same time, there has been a great de‐ velopment of music along more specialized lines: those of instru‐ mental, concert-hall music, devoid of words or theatrical accompani‐ ment. Here even Wagner's dramatic music is often detached and enjoyed in isolation. Modern sculpture has been, on the whole, a highly specialized art, avoiding contrasts of color and texture. Small ceramic sculpture has recently pursued an opposite course.

There is no sharp line between the specialized and the diversified type of art or art product. The difference is partly in our point of view; partly a gradual range in degrees of diversification.

The difference in viewpoint operates especially through the spe‐ cialized approaches of modern scholars and critics. In an art museum, for example, we detach one piece of wood carving from a canoe prow, another from a chief's dwelling, another from a group of fetish figures, and regard them all as examples of decorative wood carving. By de‐

[16] The importance of the festival as a cooperation of the arts is stressed by H. Kuhn in "The System of the Arts," *Journal of Aesthetics*, Vol. I, No. 1 (Spring, 1941), p. 66.

taching them, we obscure the fact that each existed as part of a larger, more heterogeneous form. We lose much of its original significance, and even of its visual effect as part of a larger setting. We do the same thing when we publish an anthology of early ballads, regarding them as pure literature, apart from the music and gestures which originally accompanied them. For certain purposes of study and enjoyment, such detached and artificial presentation has its values. It also has its disadvantages, for both enjoying and understanding.

A necessary phase in the study of past art is the reassembling and reintegration of such cultural products into something like the original, diversified complexes in which they flourished. This is easier said than done: for example, a period room, in which all kinds of contemporary objects are grouped together, is often very dead and uninteresting. Its lack of life and movement is even more noticeable, the nearer we approach the original appearance. Once the culture-complex has gone, it can not be actually revived; but we can try to recreate it in imagination. This implies, of course, that the specialized art historian or critic, confined to one art, must be in part replaced by cultural historians and aestheticians with broader scope, more capable of stepping over the artificial boundaries of modern scholarship, and seeing how the different arts are actually interrelated in a living culture. When this is done, many arts and works of art which now seem highly specialized and independent will appear in their true light as integral parts of a larger cultural complex.

In comparing works of art as to their degree of diversity, there is one criterion to be kept especially in mind: *to what extent are radically different parts or components presented together,* used and perceived together, so as to be the object of a single aesthetic experience? To answer this, we must notice (a) how *different* the parts or components are, and (b) to what extent they are *merged* in a single form, capable of unified perception.

We have already noticed several bases for judging the diversity of parts or components: in terms of modes of sensory presentation and suggestion, modes of composition, etc. An opera is highly diversified in presenting both visual and auditory components; also in suggesting through mimesis, verbal symbolism, and common association (in music and gesture). It is, or can be, highly developed along many lines at once: for example, in plot, characterization, stage design, and musical design. These function as developed components in the total form.

Diversity of parts is often felt in terms of *medium or material*. For example, an upholstered armchair appears as a diversified form, in part because it is made of so many different materials: of wood, silk or woolen fabric, paint or varnish, metal tacks, springs, and so on. From the standpoint of form-analysis and the psychology of perception, these differences in material can all be described in terms of presented and suggested components, elementary and developed. The visible difference between a polished wooden area and one of woolen tapestry can be described in terms of texture, hue, light-and-dark, pattern (if any), etc. There is also a difference in suggested tactile qualities and other associations.

The total effect of diversity or mixture is also augmented by the fact that many *different kinds of person,* with different specialized techniques, are contributing to the total effect. Opera is a combined art in that many different kinds of artist have to cooperate in composing, directing, planning, and performing it. When we go to an opera, see one group of people acting and singing, another playing in the orchestra pit; then go back stage and see still others manipulating curtains, lights, costumes, etc., we are impressed by the diversity of the whole undertaking and the difficulty of fusing it all into one perfect unity. This diversity of process exists in the making of a motion picture, but is less apparent in the finished film.

When one versatile craftsman executes or performs the whole work, as in the primitive stages of an art, we are less apt to think of the whole as diversified. Very gradually, individual versatility may give way to division of labor and cooperation: for example, when the drawing, coloring, and gilding of a miniature book illumination are distributed among different craftsmen. Toward the making of a house or an upholstered chair, as we have seen, several different industries in different places cooperate. The knowledge of this is a part of our total appreciation of the house or chair, as a more or less successful unification of radically different elements.

The recognized educational value of theater projects in schools arises partly from the fact that they do require a merging of different arts. Often they require cooperation between classes and teachers of drama, visual arts, and music. Some subordination is made by each to the whole joint effort, and a concrete example is seen of cooperation between the arts.

Some unification is necessary if we are to have a single, diversified art, instead of a loose assemblage of separate arts. The first step toward it is to bring the constituent factors together in space, time, or both, so that they can easily be *coperceived*—that is, perceived together or in close succession. Such rudimentary unity is achieved in an old curiosity shop full of miscellaneous objects; in a scrap-book or shelf of souvenirs; in a miscellaneous vaudeville show or festival comprising different events and performances. Coperception and the effect of unity are increased by similarities among the constituent parts: for example, when all the scraps in a scrap-book are alike in being pieces of paper, cut out of newspapers and magazines.

Unity is further increased by subordination of all details to some comprehensive framework. In any organized work of art, there is usually one basic *framework,* developed in one of the four modes of composition. It determines the main outlines of the whole. Subordinate developments in this and other modes of composition are fitted into it as accessories. By this and other means, which need not be enumerated here, the skillful artist can secure a merging of all diverse elements; an effect of aesthetic unity. Such a work of art, however diverse its elements, is not experienced as "mixed" or heterogeneous. In opera, this complete merging is seldom attained.

In a highly complex and diversified form, several different frameworks may coexist, and it is not always easy to say which is basic, which accessory. In opera and ballet, the basic framework is usually representative, and is provided by the plot or story—the outline of action. In ballet, this is conveyed mainly through visual pantomime, with costume, lighting, and music cooperating. The movements of the dance are also organized thematically, into mobile patterns of line and mass. Some of these contribute to telling the story, while others are more or less independent visual enrichments. While the story gives the unifying framework, it is not necessarily the most important thing aesthetically; people go mainly to see the accessory enrichments—the grace, color, the flowing pattern of movement —which they enjoy intrinsically, and not merely because of the story they tell.

In opera, the plot is again the main framework; it is told by word and gesture, with music and sometimes ballet included and cooperating. Though music is in this sense an accessory art, adapting itself to the action and dialogue, it is usually the factor most highly valued. Indeed, the audience usually pays closest attention to a single component within the musical factor: the tone quality of the voices of the principal singers. Various styles of opera differ as to the extent to which music is subordinated to a plot or dramatic framework. In opera before Wagner, and especially in Italian opera, the musical factor is not consistently adapted to the story framework; it tends to pursue its own independent patterns of thematic development, often irrelevant to the action and suspending it entirely for special arias and choruses. "Subordination" to a framework, in the sense of following a story, does not in the least mean taking a subordinate or inferior place in interest or value. In Wagner, the music is more thoroughly fitted into the plot and characterization of the drama; but this does not prevent its high development as music. Still, it does require some surrender of independence. Many composers and performers prefer to hold the spotlight alone in a separate art, instead of sharing it with others in a cooperative one.

Much of what has just been said about opera and ballet applies also to the modern sound film, with its color-photography, dialogue, pantomime, incidental music and sound effects. It applies also to marionettes and other arts coming under the general heading of *theater arts*. That title refers specifically to the sort of building in which they are performed. It includes a number of important mobile arts. Most of them are diversified, adapting several *component arts* to a single basic framework, usually representative. In Walt Disney's film *Fantasia*, musical compositions were taken as basic frameworks, and color-films fitted into them. Thus either component art can provide the basic framework; but the visual or literary one usually does.

The Japanese *tea ceremony* is another diversified type of art. It is a secular ritual, not primitive but modern and sophisticated in its conscious return to rustic simplicity. It involves a special kind of architectural setting, the tea-house in a garden; special types of costume and utensil, especially the carefully rough-textured tea-bowl. It has a ceremonial of acts and gestures in sequence, with appropriate conversation. The gustatory factor—the actual drinking of the tea— is emphasized, but is not the most important part. Every presented factor is endowed with symbolic meaning of a poetic, moral, or other traditional type.

Architecture as a whole has always been diversified, bringing together many accessory arts. The cathedral included stone sculpture, wood-carving, stained glass, metal-work, mural painting, furniture, and many other arts. In modern times, architecture has become increasingly diversified with the application of scientific technology for use in all kinds of building. The modern *dwelling-house,* located in a garden plot and complete with furniture and accessories for living, is an excellent example of a diversified work of art. The architectural shell itself is diversified, including as it does so many materials, forms and apparatus for heating, plumbing, cooking, lighting, etc. Landscaped and furnished, it is not the product of any one recognized art, unless we can speak of the composite art of home-building or home-designing. There is considerable freedom in selecting and interchanging the furniture, textiles, and minor accessories; but they have to be fitted spatially into the architectural shell, and functionally into the family's plan for living—what it wants to do in and with the various rooms. The basic framework of the dwelling as a whole is utilitarian or functional, and so is that of most of its parts and furnishings individually. Some of them are representative (pictures, statues, etc.) and some are expository (charts, diagrams, texts in the library).

The *book* (including the magazine and related forms) is another composite art product of great importance in modern civilization. It is mainly visual in presentation, with some attention to tactile qualities. It is hardly ever the product of one man, and several radically different arts may enter into it—that of the author, the publisher, the printer, the maker of paper and ink, the binder, and sometimes the illustrator. A modern European book has its own utilitarian framework, different from that of older scrolls and tablets: its scheme of binding together one edge of many rectangular sheets of paper for easy turning, and protecting them between covers. To this framework everything is adapted. The verbal symbols begin on or near the left hand corner of the top page, and proceed in conventional order of lines and numbered pages to the bottom. Within this utilitarian framework, other frameworks are developed: for example, the plot of a novel. Pictorial illustrations and marginal ornaments may be inserted as accessories within this representative framework. Once again, some such accessory may give a particular book its greatest value. In another book, the literary framework will be expository, as in an essay or treatise. This too must be adapted physically and spatially to the structure of the book as a utilitarian framework in itself.

There is no single name for the composite art of *book-making,* a name which will include the author's work of writing, the editor's of arranging, annotating, correcting, etc., the printer's of typography and layout, the pictorial artist's of illustrating, and all the rest. A moment ago, we noticed that there is no adequate name for the composite art of home-making. The products of these arts are, or can be, highly important and highly unified. Their lack of recognized names is a symptom of their failure to receive adequate recognition in aesthetics, in theoretical lists and classifications of the arts.

The same can be said of *city-planning, town-planning,* or *urbanism;* an ancient art of supreme cultural importance, which until recently has received little attention in aesthetics. It exhibits diversification on an extremely large scale. One might go on to speak of the art—as yet unnamed—of combining cities and agricultural communities in larger regional wholes of aesthetic as well as functional, economic and sociological merit. It is community planning, with due attention to social and aesthetic aspects.

Philosophers have spoken of the "art of living" as the ultimate art, embracing all human relations; an aesthetic substitute, perhaps, for the older ethics which sought to regulate life in terms of sin and virtue, right and wrong. There is no limit to the number or scope of composite arts which may in future be evolved and consciously practiced. Certainly the time has long passed when the list of arts, or even of major arts, should be limited to the conventional five or seven. To avoid vagueness, however, it is probably best to reserve the term "work of art" for types of aesthetic product or performance in which there is some definite, distinctive kind of unity; some way of integrating diverse elements under one framework. An art exists where such a mode of organization has been practiced by many successive artists until it has become a social custom or institution.

To *summarize* in terms of classification: examples of high diversification are the theater arts, architecture and home designing, city planning, and book-making (in a broad sense). Examples of specialization or low diversity in the product are monochrome sculpture, pencil drawing, and music for violin alone. Painting ranges from the highly specialized to the moderately diversified, as when it uses gilt or other radically contrasting materials and textures. The smaller useful arts vary greatly in this respect, some of them producing diversified forms such as the upholstered chair.

16. Comparing the arts in regard to stylistic tendencies

Hegel raised an interesting question in cultural history when he asserted that some arts were most suited to express the symbolic spirit, some the classical, and some the romantic. The question can be separated from his transcendentalist theory of the origin and evolution of art styles in the Cosmic Mind and its gradual self-expression. There remains a more naturalistic problem of whether some arts are most suited to embody certain styles, and some to embody others.

Hegel's own answer is largely unacceptable today, not only because of his metaphysical assumptions, but because of his limited understanding of art history. He had a most inadequate appreciation of the ancient and oriental styles which he lumped together as "symbolic." He was on debatable ground in holding that architecture, rather than sculpture or literature, best expressed the spirit of non-Greek antiquity; also in holding that the classical mind of Greece was best expressed in sculpture, rather than in architecture, epic poetry, and drama. He was more plausible in describing music as the art best suited to expressing the romantic spirit. Its restless movement, its vague yet poignant emotional suggestiveness, and other traits are certainly appropriate to certain phases of the romantic spirit. Perhaps the Romantic movement of early nineteenth-century Europe is expressed in music more fully than in any other art. Marble and bronze are so fundamentally static, stiff and heavy as to resist the sculptor's efforts at making them suggest romantic yearnings or the spirit of evanescence. Rodin went, perhaps, as far along this line as anyone could go, and he was not altogether successful.

There are things to be said on the other side, however. Certain phases of European romanticism found characteristic expression in the picturesque garden; in the rustic cottage and artificial ruin; in neo-Gothic architecture and literature; in lyric poetry. And is music not suited to expressing certain phases of classicism—for example, the quality of ordered, regular movement and rational control, which appears in Palestrina, Bach, Handel, and others? Do we know enough yet about ancient and oriental music to say what styles and spiritual attitudes it was or was not fitted to express? In short, Hegel's particular classification of the arts on the basis of their supposed stylistic potentialities must be treated with some reserve. At the same time, it deserves respect as a pioneer step toward a broad, comparative history of the arts and of their cultural settings.

We are now at the stage of discovering the tremendous variety of styles which have flourished in most of the arts, in both eastern and western hemispheres. Through comparative analysis of historic styles in various arts, we may hope to learn a great deal more about the relations between the arts, at different periods and in general. The subject of comparative stylistic analysis is still in its infancy.

To discover empirically whether certain arts are best suited to certain styles, we must observe in which arts each style has manifested itself. Some styles are narrow in distribution, occurring only in a single art and group of artists, for a short time—for example, pointillism in nineteenth-century French painting. Others, such as the baroque and romantic styles, spread through all or nearly all the arts of a period. Their basic, distinctive characteristics appear, along with a host of minor variations, in many different mediums and techniques. Major cultural trends—for example, toward freedom for individual impulse and emotion—are expressed in music, poetry, painting, and many other arts. As a rule, they do not appear everywhere at once; certain arts and certain artists are style leaders, and others join in one by one, as the new spirit gains momentum. Very often contemporary leaders do not know of each others' work, and, if they happen to encounter it, do not grasp its essential kinship with their own. During the early stages of a great historic style, such as baroque, people do not grasp its distinctive nature: the qualities which link together all examples of that style and distinguish it from others. Centuries may elapse before historians can see it clearly in perspective, and define it in general, accurate terms.

Thus we are now coming, with the aid of philosophical historians, to form a conception of baroque style as something characteristic of Rubens in painting, Bernini in sculpture and architecture, Milton in poetry, Monteverdi and Lully in music.[17] Scientific students of cultural

[17] See the *Journal of Aesthetics*, Vol. V, No. 2 (Dec., 1946), for articles on various aspects of baroque style: R. Wellek, "The Concept of Baroque in Literary Scholarship"; W. Stechow, "Definitions of the Baroque in the Visual Arts"; and others. Also E. Roditi, "Torquato Tasso: the Transition from Baroque to Neo-Classicism." *Ibid.*, Vol. VI, No. 3 (March, 1948), p. 235. E. C. Hassold, "The Baroque as a Basic Concept of Art," *College Art Journal*, Vol. VI, No. 1 (Autumn, 1946), p. 3. Some artists formerly classed as baroque are now called "mannerist."

history are not content with vague generalities about the "spirit of the age"; they insist on tracing specific, observable characteristics in works of art. This leads to detailed lists of analogies and common qualities in works of different mediums, nationalities, and subjects. We see how painting changed from sharp, clear outlines to an emphasis on rich colors, lights, and shadows, in which the outlines of individual objects were partly dissolved. We see how, almost at the same time, music tended to blur clear melodic outlines with brilliant polychoral textures and chromatic harmonies which suggest the visual richness of color.[18]

In the past, such stylistic affinities between different arts have been realized only dimly and partially at the time; perhaps in a general sense of fitness for a common purpose, as when the new baroque music, powerful and brilliant, reverberated through a magnificent baroque cathedral, before a pompous audience of richly costumed nobles. These affinities were felt emotionally by artists and the public, long before theorists took the trouble to analyze them intellectually.

In a very abstract way, the idea that all the arts are fundamentally one is at least as old as the Greeks. It is vaguely implicit in their philosophical dictum that the All is One; in the Platonic view that the whole universe is a manifestation of divine mind, and in the Neo-Platonic theory of beauty as an emanation from that mind. Mystics and alchemists, through the middle ages and on into modern times, insisted on the doctrine that earthly man and all his arts are a microcosm, a small, unified summary of the one great cosmos. Hegel and the German romantic idealists only restated this perennial belief in the oneness of all the arts as an expression of the cosmic spirit; and in the merely superficial character of apparent differences between them.

In modern times, specific analogies between the arts are becoming more conscious; more promptly noted and described by critics; more deliberately calculated by the artists themselves. The decline of differences in social status—as formerly existed between the poet and the manual worker—has thrown them more closely into one artistic world.

We have seen how, at the close of the nineteenth century in France, artists in different arts were keenly aware of each other, and fascinated by the relations between their respective mediums. They

[18] See H. Leichtentritt, *Music, History, and Ideas,* Cambridge, Mass., 1938, Ch. 6, "Seventeenth-Century Baroque."

savored with voluptuous refinement the emotional tones of pleasures derived from the different senses. Along with inquiring psychologists, they noted how certain musical keys suggest certain colors, more strongly to some persons than to others. They compared their own technical procedures and problems with those of other arts. They sought to express the same subjects, the same emotional moods, in different mediums, regarding each as a potential "symbol" of the others. Poets, painters, and musicians were especially close together, and often used each others' works explicitly as themes for their own, as in the compositions by Debussy, inspired by poems of Verlaine and Baudelaire. The trend toward melting away the clear outlines of things in a luminous bath of iridescent color, which had begun in the late Renaissance and Baroque, was carried to its final extreme, devoid of baroque power and splendor, in the twilight world of *fin-de-siècle* romanticism.

Elsewhere in nineteenth-century Europe, and outside the Symbolist group, the consciousness of unity or close connection between the arts was also strong. Pater and Whistler in England were stressing the analogy between music and the other arts, or at least the potential analogy, in that other arts might aspire toward the formal beauty of music. Wagner, in his music dramas, had shown how poetry, music, and the visual arts could be reunited through the theater, as they had been in primitive Greece; how they could produce analogous aesthetic effects, and combine to produce a single work of art. Theory and practice reinforced each other in this direction. Being convinced that the arts can and should work for similar effects, artists made them do so to a greater extent than sometimes happens, when leaders in different arts consciously react away from each other. Romantic music, for example, was strongly programmatic on the whole, and thus close to poetry in trying to convey specific moods and ideas.

On the other hand, the influence of Lessing, also potent in modern aesthetics, favored the view that different arts have fundamentally different aims and limitations. Paradoxically, Lessing's influence was not entirely toward divorcing the arts. It tended to free painting from the influence of literature, especially story literature, by insisting that a picture did not need to represent action in time. Apparently, this would divorce painting from music also, since music is a time art and painting (according to Lessing) one of space. But actually, freedom from the need to tell a story opened the way for painting to concentrate on visual form and design—eventually on abstract design. This freedom was not often accepted by the art world for well over a century after Lessing. But it is a central thesis in Whistler's plea that painting should be like music. Painting should be so, not in trying to represent action in time, but in developing its own kind of directly visible beauty—that of colors and shapes. This would be the true "music" and "poetry" of painting. Whistler's art was not one of story-telling, but it was never rigidly static. Like that of impressionism in general, it suggested the evanescent play of lights and shadows.

Much of this long debate about the unity or multiplicity of the arts was based on metaphysical assumptions. Most of it was polemic and evaluative, as to what the arts should do; whether an artist in one medium should try to produce effects considered proper to another. The Lessing tradition goes on today, as we have seen, in the theory that painting should avoid "literary values," and concentrate on the purely visual.

In this book, we have not taken either side of the argument. The trend of the discussion has been to show that both sides express different world-views, different personal tastes, and temporary styles in the arts themselves. Neither is completely wrong. Each side expresses a half-truth. The arts are alike in certain respects and different in others. There are values to be gained from having them cooperate closely at times, and other values to be gained from having each explore its own distinctive potentialities.

Primarily, we have been engaged in a factual inquiry, as to just what these analogies and differences, these potentialities, actually are. We have been trying to bring the discussion down from philosophers' generalities and critics' wrangles to a level of moderately specific analysis. After considering all the chief bases for comparing the arts, we have arrived at the concept of *style,* as one of the most useful. It has been pointed out, from the beginning of this book, that one can not generalize precisely about resemblances or differences between the arts, in an absolute way; one cannot classify them into fixed categories, because of the tremendous variation in styles within each art. Past systems of the arts have been faulty and repressive, largely because they ignored this variation. Their authors assumed that a certain art was always of a certain character, and always should be, because their range of historical knowledge was narrow. They were unaware of, or indifferent to, those styles in which the art took on a different character. We are now discovering this variety, and also the fact that different styles have different values for different cultural groups and periods. There is no theoretical basis for dismissing them as mere aberrations from the correct style.

Granted this extreme variability, where does it leave us in the task of comparing and classifying the arts? In the first chapter of this book, we saw how it led some philosophers to give up the task as impossible. Some were content to reaffirm, vaguely, "all the arts are one." Others declared, "the arts are so variable that no classification of them can be valid." We have taken the intermediate position that such variability is not infinite; that it occurs within certain *ranges of variation*, which can be approximately described. To do so, we must first chart the range of stylistic variations within each art; second, observe the relations between these ranges, as to overlapping, parallelism, and divergence.

Through detailed observation of these changing styles and the roles of different artistic factors in them, we shall develop a better understanding of what each art—each physical medium, technique, and set of components—attempts most frequently, and achieves most easily. Aesthetics will probably not make the mistake again of trying to set down limits in advance for any art; but the experiments of artists in each field, their varying success in trying to achieve desired effects, will indicate what are the lines of most and least resistance.

The problem will be to correlate a given factor in art with a certain range of stylistic variations in which it has been used; some very often, in many cultures, and some infrequently. For what range of aesthetic effects, in what styles and contexts of form and function, is marble used? The same for gold, jade, leather, paper, silk? For what musical effects and in what contexts has the oboe, the English horn, the French horn been employed? More abstractly, in what different ways is color used in painting, in sculpture, architecture, cinema? How in each case, is it related to line, mass, and other visual components? What different uses are made of melodic line, of rhythm, instrumental timbre, tempo, and dynamics? An open-minded, empirical survey of styles will show each art and each factor in art, as doing a much greater variety of things, under different conditions and for different purposes, than we now realize. Greater knowledge of past history and future experiments in art will alike increase our understanding of the potential range of functions, aesthetic and non-aesthetic, for which each can be used.

Incidentally, light will be thrown on perennial questions like that of the degree to which painting and music, or visual color and musical tone-color, can be analogous. The answer will appear in the form of a partial overlapping between two different ranges of variations. Both visual and musical coloring can be used in a representative way, as in building up on the stage an impression of a vast, dim forest with shimmering, rustling leaves and distant bird-calls. Color can be compartmental, contained within sharp outlines; musical harmony and orchestration can be subordinated to clear, sharp melodic lines, with analogous effects. On the other hand, there are things which visual color can do and musical color can not, and vice versa. Musical color can not stand motionless and changeless, like a red-painted wall under uniform lighting.

As to the stylistic tendencies and fitnesses of various arts, again we have much to learn. It is hard to know just how romantic architecture can become, if there is a strong demand for it to be as romantic as possible. In the thatched cottage and the artificial, ivied ruin of the eighteenth century, it went a certain distance, from which it has now receded. But this fact is significant—that architecture does not often try to be very romantic, and that the public does not often want it to be so. Extreme romanticism tends to involve the use of irregular, curving, biomorphic lines and shapes, rough blurred textures, suggestions of evanescence, mystery, sentiment, wildness, the far away and long ago. Ordinarily, people seem to prefer the opposite qualities in their buildings, especially major public buildings. They want a house to look strong, steady, and durable, as they walk through and live in it, or leave their money and important documents in it. For this and many other reasons, architecture has tended toward firm, geometric, regular shapes and textures. Even when exuberant, curvilinear ornament is in favor, as in the late Gothic, Spanish Churrigueresque, and Art Nouveau styles, it usually stays on the surface or near the top, and hence does not seem to weaken the underlying structure. Streets and city plans are also commonly rectilinear, in spite of occasional picturesque winding roads, because (for one reason) a straight line is the shortest route between two points.

In the pictures on our walls, as in the clothes we wear, the music we listen to, and the books we read, we have no such persistent desire for stability. Their forms can go much farther toward the irregular—even to suggestions of violent confusion and disbalance—without upsetting the basic equilibrium we ordinarily demand for daily living. When architecture and large furniture go to extremes of geometric simplicity, their accessory arts often refuse to follow that far. When the house becomes an oblong box, and the rooms inside it are reduced to a few rectangles of various shapes and sizes, the desire remains for something fluid, soft, and biomorphic, like the human body, to contrast with this rigid framework. That desire is answered by picturesque outside planting and small, irregular, curving forms within: by pictures, statuettes, textiles, and garments. The opposite rarely happens.

When there is a marked rapprochement between certain arts, as between French poetry, painting, and music of the late nineteenth century, it does not necessarily follow that all the arts join in with equal ease and thoroughness. It is important to notice which arts stay outside a prevailing style-trend, or join it only slightly and superficially. Some remain stubbornly within a certain limited range of variations, and resist the contagion of opposite styles; others hover about the opposite pole, and still others are volatile, dashing easily from one extreme to the other. Painting in the early twentieth century, for example, has found no difficulty in producing the bare geometry of Léger and Mondrian along with the romanticism and profuse, curvilinear detail of Dali and Berman. Kandinsky has done both.

One must use extreme caution in predicting that any art will continue to show certain stylistic tendencies, just because it has done so in the past. Any apparent "law" of that sort is likely to challenge rebel artists toward attempts at violating it. But eccentric, individual experiments do not take root, and engender lasting, widespread styles, unless they satisfy some deep cultural need and achieve some harmony between form and medium. A *tour de force* in art which runs counter to basic social behavior-patterns is likely to remain an isolated phenomenon.

One must use caution also in explaining any stylistic analogy or divergence between the arts as due to some inherent, inalterable property of the medium itself. Too many factors operate in determining the rise and career of artistic styles: economic, political, religious, technological, the force of great individual artists, and many others. What seems at one time to be a universal law or characteristic of an art—for example, the supposed laws of harmony in eighteenth and early nineteenth century music—often turns out to have been a mere transitory style, when viewed in the perspective of later history. Who, in the time of Lessing, would have predicted that painting would develop forms which not only suggested action, but moved and changed with luminous colors on a screen, before one's very eyes? Great social upheavals, key inventions like the printing press, the combustion engine, the electric light, tend to inaugurate a vast train of innovations in the forms produced by art, as well as in its materials and processes. All that we can do at any one time, in formulating aesthetic theories, is to generalize with careful inductive reasoning on the past and present data within reach, and then project the main apparent tendencies a little way into the future, as tentative predictions.

Part Three

INDIVIDUAL CHARACTERISTICS

OF THE ARTS

X

How Can an Art Be Defined?

1. Medium, process, and product as keys to the nature of an art

Webster defines "sculpture" as "Act or art of carving, cutting, or hewing wood, stone, metal, etc., into statues, ornaments, etc., or into figures; hence, the act or art of producing figures and groups, whether in plastic or hard materials, but now especially in marble or bronze."

Analysis of this definition shows the use of three bases or criteria for distinguishing a particular art from others. These three bases are also employed in classifications of the arts. The types of *process* used in sculpture are specified as "carving, cutting, or hewing." The types of *medium* or material are specified as "wood, stone, metal, etc." The types of *product* are specified as "statues, ornaments, etc., or figures." The second half of the definition, after the semi-colon, is a broader, alternative sense, really a second definition. Here the concept of sculpture is extended to cover other types of process besides carving, cutting, or hewing. In this definition, the only specifications refer to *product* ("figures and groups") and to *medium* ("plastic or hard materials, but now especially in marble or bronze"). By implication, this would include such *processes* as casting, stamping, and pressing, applied to metal, clay, or plastic figures.

Confining ourselves for a moment to the first of these definitions, let us see how these three bases or types of specification fit together. They cooperate in roughly marking off an area of human culture, a field or range of activity, to be called by the name "sculpture." On each basis, a certain area is specified, which we may symbolize in the following way:

PROCESS:	MEDIUM:	PRODUCT:
carving, cutting, hewing	wood, stone, metal, etc.	statues, ornaments, figures, etc.

433

Their combination in one definition may be diagrammed as follows:

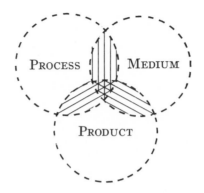

Notice that each circle overlaps each of the others in a certain place, while all three overlap in a smaller area. Some examples of the process-group "carving, cutting, or hewing" are also examples of the medium-group "wood, stone, or metal." Some are also examples of the product-group "statues, ornaments, figures." This is the central area where all three circles overlap; it includes examples and subordinate classes which fulfill all three sets of specifications. It may be called the area of *greatest typicality,* for it includes the examples which are, by this definition, most typical of the art of sculpture; most obviously and unquestionably classed as such. A carved marble statue of Apollo would be, accordingly, a most typical example of sculpture.

Other areas and examples are of *intermediate* typicality; they qualify on only two bases, or at least leave some room for doubt on the question. For example, what about a mathematical model of a cube or sphere, cut out of wood? It is a figure in the mathematical sense, but not used as an ornament. In art, the terms "statue" and "figure" both suggest representation, especially of the human body. Hence we should have to know how these terms are defined, before deciding whether they cover the one in question. A figure of a man, cut and bent out of flat pieces of paper, qualifies as sculpture in regard to product-type and perhaps as to process-type, but not as to medium-type. It is not made from any of the three materials explicitly mentioned, or even from any similar hard material. There is room for **argument, therefore, as to whether such figures should really be called** "sculpture." A figure of a man carved out of soap is perhaps a little closer to the kinds of material specified, being moderately hard, with an appearance not unlike stone. When the definition lists several examples of the type, but indicates by the term "etc." or "such as" that others might also qualify, one has to use one's judgment as to how similar the case in question is to the examples listed as highly typical.

The *least typical* areas and examples fall in the unshaded parts of each circle; they fulfill only one set of specifications, and qualify on one basis only. A rubber doll or balloon in the shape of a man or animal (for example, the inflated figures used at bathing beaches) is a figure and perhaps a statue.[1] So is a Mexican doll, made of tied and twisted bits of straw, or a Japanese kite in the shape of a three-dimensional fish. But it is not "carved, cut, or hewed," and not made of "wood, stone, or metal" or anything like them. Something cut from a block of soft rubber, but not a statue or figure—for example, a cushion —would qualify only as cut and as three-dimensional. It would usually be classed as outside the realm of sculpture.

Some one of the bases is usually given more weight than others when the term is applied, in determining what shall be regarded as an example of the art. In the case of sculpture, the idea that its product must represent some living being is strongly fixed by tradition. A nonrepresentative form, even if carved out of stone—for example, a gravestone or an abstract cubist design—is less likely to be described as sculpture.[2] Thus the degree of typicality is determined, not merely by the number of bases or kinds of specification which the object fulfills, but by the comparative weight which is given to the various specifications.

More and less typical varieties can be distinguished even when only one basis of specification is used. Degree of typicality is not entirely a matter of overlapping between bases. Within each circle of the diagram; within each set of specifications, certain varieties are usually singled out as most typical. There are different ways of doing this. One may first give a broad specification, and then add "especially

---

[1] "Statue": "The likeness of a living being sculptured or modeled in some solid substance, as marble, bronze, or wax; an image" (Webster). Note that a statue is not necessarily made of hard material, although it must be "solid"— that is, three-dimensional.

[2] Witness again the Brancusi case (p. 7).

so-and-so." Or one may begin with a definite list of typical varieties and then add "or others," to indicate that a less typical margin exists. Webster defines "lithography" first in a fairly narrow way, on a basis of medium and process: "The art or process of putting writing or designs on stone with a greasy material, and of producing printed impressions therefrom . . ." That, we are to understand, is the most typical kind of lithography. But a margin of other, partly similar ones is allowed in the rest of the sentence: "also, any process based on the same principle, using zinc, aluminum, or some other substance instead of stone." Nothing is said about the nature of the product: for example, the characteristic appearance or potential values of a lithograph.

Being extremely atypical on one basis only may result in exclusion from the art, even though there is conformity in others. In topiary art, the landscape gardener cuts shrubs and trees into odd forms, often representing animals. This could qualify as sculpture on the basis of product and process, but the medium—living plants, twigs and leaves —is so different from the usual materials of sculpture that, in practice, it would seldom be classed as a branch of that art.

Early aestheticians were fond of talking about the "limits" or "boundaries" of the various arts. "Defining" an art, they assumed, meant primarily the marking off of such limits. From our present standpoint, however, there are no definite limits to an art. In the first place, the extent of territory which the concept of an art shall cover is largely an arbitrary matter, and is changed from time to time. In the second place, the extension of each concept of an art shades off gradually into that of other arts. Their boundaries merge and overlap imperceptibly, so that each has a margin of atypical, borderline cases which can be classed equally well under any of several different arts. How they will be classed in practice depends on the immediate point of view and situation. For example, a small, solid figure of a bird, equipped with a pin and worn on a dress, becomes "jewelry" or "costume accessory," even though it qualifies in several respects as sculpture. A small human head, carved from wood as part of a cabinet, is merged in the art of furniture. The Statue of Liberty, being hollow and equipped as a light-house, is architecture as well as sculpture. In thinking out definitions of the arts, it is not worth while to argue long over just where the lines should be drawn around each one. It is more important to stress the central, most typical areas of each; then to mention how it sometimes combines with others.

Many are the futile, indecisive arguments over whether some kind of product "really deserves the name" of sculpture, or of music, painting, or some other art. The fact usually is that it satisfies some but not all the necessary requirements, as commonly understood. Whether it satisfies the basic or essential requirements, the *sine qua non,* is a question which ought to be easily answered by studying the object in the light of a dictionary definition; but unfortunately even the best definitions are vague in some respects. When the example seems to fall on or near the borderline of the area marked off by the definition, and when there is no clear, accepted usage as to just how the name should be applied, the decision must be largely arbitrary and individual.

Aesthetics is not alone in thus having a debatable margin in most of its concepts. All subjects dealing with complex and variable phenomena, such as those of life and mind, have concepts of this sort. Even mathematics has not entirely eliminated them. Wherever they persist, discussion can never be perfectly clear, or reasoning exact. But each subject can progress scientifically by revising its concepts to make them indicate more definite areas of phenomena and relationship. In law and jurisprudence, it is very important to decide exactly what is and what is not a case of murder, theft, or violation of contract. Brief statutes can never make the meaning fully explicit, and volumes of judicial decisions are often required to indicate how the term is to be applied in practice. Even these always leave a margin of debatable ground, as unforeseen combinations of circumstances arise.

However objective and logical such reasoning appears, there is usually a factor of personal taste involved. People deny that a certain kind of thing is "really sculpture" because they do not like that kind of product—for example, an abstract modern or primitive carving. The name of each particular art, as well as the word "art" in general, can be used in an evaluative sense, as a term of praise. Such usage is not to be recommended in technical discussion, but it is very widespread. By one who follows it, nothing will be classed as sculpture which seems to him ugly or unskillful, no matter how well it satisfies other requirements.

Occupational interests also operate to make one emphasize a certain basis of definition, and a certain way of conceiving an art. As we have seen, the practicing artist or teacher of techniques tends to think in terms of process; he thinks of an art as essentially the exercise of a certain kind of technique in relation to a certain medium. The user, buyer, or student of the finished products tends to think of the art more in those terms; to stress the requirements as to nature of product, in deciding whether or not a certain example is to be included. Dictionaries and other neutral authorities try to combine and condense these various points of view to some extent, although they usually list alternative definitions for use in different realms of discourse.

It is hard for them to ascertain and summarize all the manifold considerations which determine how a concept works when applied. Many such ideas, though basic and influential, may be taken for granted almost unconsciously, and omitted from the formal definition. For example, the definition of sculpture quoted above says nothing about the static or mobile nature of the product. Yet it is taken for granted as a rule that sculptural products are motionless; thus sculpture is, by the German theorists, placed without hesitation among the "arts of rest." It is only when one comes to consider such a special group as marionettes and puppets that the question is likely to arise. They are not usually classed as sculpture, but should they be, as fulfilling its stated requirements on all three bases? Does movement disbar them? Does small size or use by children disqualify marionettes and dolls as sculpture? Does the addition of cloth garments disqualify a shop-window dummy or manikin? In practice, such considerations actually work to restrict the extension of "sculpture" more narrowly than the abstract definition would indicate, if interpreted literally. For the thorough understanding of a concept, as we have often seen, one must study it in action, in concrete application, as well as in formal definition.

An art always involves doing something (a process) to and with something (a medium) in order to make or do something else (a product or performance). By specifying as clearly as we can what all those somethings are, we can best give a clear idea of the nature of the art. In Webster's definition of sculpture, the use of these three bases of specification helps to make the concept a fairly clear and sharp one. It narrows down to a small range the class of things which are most fully and typically sculptural, and leaves an added margin of things which are partly sculptural, or sculptural in certain respects.

Shall we set it up as a rule, then, that an art should be defined in terms of all three bases? Certainly, a concept so defined has the virtues of sharpness and explicitness. If the art is actually distinctive in all three ways, the definition should mention it. If it is not, one may ask whether it really deserves to be called an art. Is "metal-working" an art? It specifies only material, and thus covers so many techniques and products that one might better call it a group of different arts. Is "picture-making" an art? Again, it is rather a name for a group of very different arts, since pictures can be made in so many materials and techniques. The concept of a single, definite art begins to emerge when there is some correlation between certain types of medium and process, on the one hand, and certain types of product on the other.

It is not always possible to specify definitely in terms of all three bases. Even in a well-known, recognized art, many varieties may be included. However, the definition can at least illustrate them and state that other varieties exist. Webster's definition of "architecture" mentions only two bases, and only one specifically. According to this dictionary, architecture is the "Art or science of building; especially the art of building houses, churches, bridges, and other structures, for the purposes of civil life—often called civil architecture." The only specification of process is the vague word "building," which covers a great variety of techniques. Nothing whatever is said about medium or material. Only the product-type is described, as consisting of houses, churches, bridges, and other civil structures. This makes the definition very broad and vague, with only military structures excluded. Should it specify more definitely as to process and material? This would be hard, because so many different ones are used. Presumably, any process or material by which a civil structure can be built would be accepted as "architecture." To require certain ones would make the definition too narrow in the light of the facts concerned. One might, however, illustrate a few common techniques such as carpentry and masonry, and a few common materials such as wood, stone, brick, concrete, and steel.

On the whole, aesthetics has suffered from too narrow conceptions of the particular arts, as well as of art in general, rather than from too broad ones. They have cramped the practice, teaching, and criticism of each art, as well as philosophical theorizing. The tendency has been to conceive of an art on the basis of a few familiar styles and techniques which were known in a small, provincial, European world. The concepts thus produced did not fit the facts of art on a scale of world history; they have constantly to be enlarged as we discover exotic, primitive, and modern styles and techniques which differ from the ones which Aristotle, Kant, and Hegel knew. As we read an old definition of some art, we often find that it is narrowed down to too small a list of approved types as to process, medium, and product. Others are left by implication in the outer limbo of non-recognition. Today, we must include many of these others, and make the list more flexible. Then the specifications as to process, medium, and product are no longer absolute requirements or limits of the art, but examples of common practice within it; characteristic, but not mandatory.

There is no assumption whatever that the most typical examples of an art are necessarily the best or most worth emulating. The path of originality often lies around the margins.

Even in the best dictionaries, survivals persist of old distinctions which are no longer current. These must be preserved for use in understanding old writings; but should not be allowed to limit modern use of the term unduly. Take for instance Webster's limiting of "architecture" to *civil* structures. By implication, this leaves out forts and fortified castles, city walls, etc. In Vitruvius's *De Architectura,* there are chapters on civil buildings such as houses and temples, and also on military engines such as battering rams and catapults. Modern specialization has eliminated weapons and fortifications from the ordinary work and training of an architect, and from that of a "civil engineer." How should this tendency be expressed in the definition of architecture? One way is to distinguish between "civil" and "military" architecture. A second is to restrict "architecture" entirely to the civil type, and call military construction by some other name. The latter is perhaps the usual practice. But it has the disadvantage of obscuring the common elements in civil and military building. These are important when we think of earlier, less specialized periods. No one would think of excluding Carcassonne or the Tower of London from the history of architecture, simply because they involve military construction.

Different viewpoints, different fields of discussion, thus point to different ways of defining a term, and there is no final way of adjusting the matter. One obvious solution, which all dictionaries follow, is to allow alternative meanings of the term, especially in different realms of discourse. Another is to avoid expecting too much from a short, dictionary definition. Even in an unabridged dictionary, it must be extremely terse, for obvious practical reasons. As a result, it must always oversimplify to some extent.

Little help is to be derived, as a rule, from turning back to the original meaning of the name. It will lead through interesting turns and twists of cultural history, as we have seen in tracing the term "fine arts"; but it offers little clue to how the name should be defined today. Many names of arts have wandered far from their original meaning, as in the case of music, from "art of the Muses." There is only confusion in trying to turn the clock backward. "Sculpture" is certainly derived from a Latin word which meant "to carve"; but that is no reason for so restricting it now. It has acquired a broader meaning along certain lines, as more and more different techniques were included under it. Along other lines it has narrowed, as its meaning focussed especially on a certain kind of product—solid representations of living beings. "Music" has certainly narrowed down to one particular section of the Muses' former domain. "Textile," on the other hand, has broadened out to include many processes besides weaving.

There is one thing to be gained from studying the history of the names and definitions of the arts. After doing so, it would be hard for anyone to follow the old mistaken view that an art was a definite, permanent realm of human activity, with quite distinctive aims and boundaries. In that sense, one comes to see that there is no such thing as an art, any more than there is a definite realm of fine art in general. Concepts of particular arts are largely arbitrary ways of dividing up the continuous process of human culture. They are not quite arbitrary, for real distinctions of degree and kind occur. But there is always overlapping around the edges, and ceaseless change in techniques, tools, and styles of product. Every generation divides up the realm in a somewhat different way, for both theoretical and administrative purposes. New arts and new names arise, and old names are assigned to different territories.

2. Requirements of a good definition

There are several points to bear in mind in analyzing a concept, and in seeking to improve its formulation. One, as we have seen in various cases, is to inquire *whether the intension* (connotation or abstract definition) is *consistent with the extension* (the denotation or concrete application). Is the term "sculpture" actually applied in a way that would follow logically from its dictionary definition? Are certain things called sculpture and others not, in accordance with the specifications listed? If not, the concept lacks internal consistency; in theoretical statement it is one thing; in active operation another. The world is full of such dislocation between principles and practice, to the detriment of both.

Two kinds of extension are involved here. One is that which would logically follow from a literal, deductive application of the way the definition is worded. For example, if sculpture is restricted to "carving, cutting, or hewing," with no "etc." added, then casting is not sculpture, and a cast bronze statue is not a piece of sculpture. This is the *implied* extension of the term. In addition, there is the way the term is actually applied in current discussion, whether correct or incorrect, authoritative or not. This is its extension *in usage.* If the term "sculpture" is commonly applied in practice to cast bronze statues, without sanction of the dictionaries, then there is inconsistency between the term's intension and its extension in usage.

The most flagrant sort of inconsistency occurs when examples cited along with the definition itself do not conform with the abstract statement. This is rare in first-class reference works. But a concept, broadly considered, is not limited to the few words a dictionary says about its name. Its dictionary definition can never be more than a verbal skeleton, pieced together from a few approximate synonyms. The concept as a whole, in a functional, dynamic sense, includes all the ways the name and its associated meanings are used in action, in thought, in writing, in conversation; with subtle shades of meaning over and above what the dictionary says, derived from innumerable contrasts and combinations with other ideas. The concept of sculpture in modern western culture, then, is something different from any verbal definition of the term, in dictionaries or elsewhere. It is a complex, changing configuration in social behavior, which various definitions try to outline, and to influence a little in future. A concept in this larger sense is internally inconsistent when its name is used in different senses within the same realm of discourse, in application to the same general subject-matter; when it is theoretically understood in one way, and concretely applied in others. It is a badly working instrument of communication, making for confusion in the mind of an individual, and between individuals.

It would be too much to hope for absolute consistency between dictionary definitions and current usage. A term's abstract definition usually lags behind its active use, as dictionary-writers vainly try to catch up with new trends in usage, and to distinguish authoritative, major trends from ephemeral ones. They cannot possibly give a full and detailed account of a term's extension; it would take up too much space. They can only hint at it with a few brief illustrations; by indicating the field of discourse in which a certain meaning is used, one or two examples of its application, and perhaps a short quotation. Thus, to judge whether intension is consistent with extension, we have to look beyond the dictionary statement itself, and examine actual usage far and wide, deciding as we go which usage is sufficiently reasonable and authoritative to be recognized in a new definition.

Such a change in usage is recognized in the second half of Webster's definition of sculpture, quoted above, where the all-inclusive word "producing" is substituted for "carving, cutting, and hewing." The term's implied extension thus becomes vastly larger in respect to process, taking in every possible kind of technique. With both a narrow and a broad intension, the definition thus fits a narrow and a broad extension in usage, and avoids any definite inconsistency. Likewise in regard to product-type, Webster avoids too precise a limitation of sculpture to the representation of living figures. By saying "into statues, ornaments, etc., or into figures," he makes the term's intension vague and flexible at its margins, thus allowing for different kinds of extension in usage.

Such vagueness in defining the boundaries of a concept would be intolerable in mathematics, and undesirable in any exact science. In aesthetics at present, it is a necessary compromise between the scientific desire for exactness and the shifting ambiguity of current usage. Those who frame definitions in humanistic fields may hope to clarify concepts a little here and there, but not very drastically. Any exact definition of an art will turn out to be unacceptable and unworkable in practice.

We noticed in Chapter I that definition is closely related to *classification,* so that neither can be developed far without some of the other. This is true in regard to any particular art. When we define it, we have to begin by placing it within a genus, which in this case is "art." "Sculpture is the act or art of . . ." Some arts may be classed also as applied sciences: "Architecture is the art or science of . . ." Then follow the differentiae, in terms of one or more bases. Sculpture is said to differ from other arts in that it uses certain kinds of medium and process, and turns out certain kinds of product.

To indicate the extension of the term is to mention some of the smaller groups and perhaps individual examples which fall under it. This involves partial division of the class into sub-classes. Common types of sculptural product, one might say, are low and high reliefs, statues in the round, portrait busts, equestrian statues, etc. Sub-classes divided according to medium are sculptures of marble, bronze, ivory, ceramics, etc. According to process, they include carvings, castings, etc. These can be further subdivided, as in the "lost wax" and other special techniques of casting.

The term "art" is applied, not only to main classes like sculpture and other widespread arts, but to very small subdivisions also. Thus we speak of the arts of dry-point, of color lithography, of lace-making, of bobbin lace-making, etc. To define each of these by placing it directly under "art" as a genus is correct but indefinite, and fails to help us much in locating it with reference to other arts. In biology, we do not define each minor species and variety by calling it merely "an animal which . . ." We place it under its more immediate genus, order or family, as in saying that a porpoise is "any small gregarious cetacean of the genus Phocaena" (Webster). Likewise, *dry point* is defined as "an engraving made with the needle instead of the burin, and differing from an etching in that the plate is engraved without the use of acid" (Webster). That is, dry point is first placed under the nearest genus, "engraving," and then differentiated from other kinds of engraving in terms of medium and process. (It might also be differentiated in terms of product: for example, a fuzzy texture of line, etc.)

Ideally, it would help in defining each of the smaller species of art if we could locate it under some intermediate genus, and this under a slightly broader one, etc. But that would imply a definite hierarchy of types in art, which does not yet exist in any acceptable form. The taxonomy of aesthetics is still in its infancy. However, there are numerous terms for groups of arts or broad types of art, such as visual arts, auditory arts, theater arts, graphic arts, musical arts, pictorial arts, industrial arts, etc. All these terms are still ambiguous, but they are clear enough to help in definition, and should be used more widely in defining minor subdivisions. This is not always done: Webster defines "lithography" as "The art or process of putting writing or designs on stone with a greasy material, and of producing printed impressions therefrom." If it were defined as "a graphic art which . . . ," its close relation to etching, dry point, wood engraving, etc., would be more quickly apparent.

When possible, then, an art of minor scope should be defined by classing it under some broader art or group of arts. Many problems will be met in doing so, however. Almost every term used to designate an art is ambiguous, being used in both broad and narrow senses. Almost every minor species of art can be classed under two or more inclusive headings, on different bases. Scene painting can be put under painting as to its medium; under theater arts as to its locale and function; under pictorial arts or decorative arts as to form of product, and so on. Sometimes only part of an art, or certain phases in it, can be placed under a given heading. Drama is a branch of literature, and also a factor in theater art. Oral diction or public speaking also belongs with literature as a way of performing it, analogous to the playing of music; yet it is likewise classed with theater arts as a factor in acting. Dance is partly a theater art; partly a ballroom art; partly a religious art.

Almost every art can thus be placed under several genera, from different points of view. Such a "genus" is merely a name for a certain type of function which an art carries on, or for other arts with which it sometimes cooperates. When music is played in a theater, as part of a play, it becomes a theater art and a branch of dramatic art. Since every art thus has innumerable connections in the modern world, it would be possible to class it under innumerable genera. However, most of these would seem comparatively adventitious or extraneous in a given case—for example, to class printing as a theater art merely because dramatic scripts and programs are printed. The majority of such uses and connections are best described as such, and not as a genus under which the art is to be classed. The latter mode of description should be reserved for those few functions and connections which seem to be most basic and typical of the art; most directly bound up with its basic activities. "Auditory art" is such a genus for music; "literature" is such a genus for poetry; "graphic art" is such a genus for etching.

At present, there is no clear understanding as to the difference between a *single, particular art* and a *group of arts* or an *abstract type* of art. Painting is usually referred to as a single particular art, with "branches" such as water-color painting, oil painting, etc. Yet each of these branches is itself often called an "art." There are even books on the "art of still-life painting," "the art of the novel," etc., based on special differences in type of product. "Graphic arts" and "theater arts," in the plural, seem to indicate groups of distinct arts, and so they do; but we often hear of "graphic art" or "the art of the theater" as if each were a single art. Still more abstract types are treated as "arts"—for example, "decorative art," "non-objective art," etc. As we have seen from the first, the term "art" is extremely ambiguous as to its extension: it can cover the whole realm of skills, or only that of aesthetic skills, or any large section of that realm, or any small section of it, however minute.

The situation is analogous to that in biology when the word "species" was used very loosely. Now, it refers to a certain kind of class: one of intermediate breadth, between a genus and a subspecies or variety. In that sense, "vertebrates" are not a species. In aesthetics, much of the difficulty in defining particular arts arises from uncertainty as to how large a realm should be included as a single art, or under some particular name like "painting." There are many obvious divisions within the total realm of art, on each of the three bases; but there is a great scarcity of names to designate them. Hence each of the few familiar names of arts is applied to a great variety of divisions, large and small. There is need for some agreement on what relative size of realm shall be called a particular art, and on what shall be called a "branch of art," a "group of arts," a "combined art," or an "abstract type of art." Traditional usage would indicate reserving the term "an art" or "a particular art" for a fairly broad realm; for one of the main divisions of art in general. Hence extremely small divisions should be called by some other name. If distinguished largely on a basis of process, as in the case of lithography, they can be called "techniques" or "processes." If we then wish to distinguish artistic or aesthetic lithography from other kinds, we can call it artistic lithography, or lithography as a branch of art. If distinguished largely on a basis of product, we can say "pictorial form" or "the pictorial type of art" instead of "the art of pictorial representation." Such attempts at clarification may seem hair-splitting now, in casual conversation; but they are a necessary step toward the development of scientific thinking in aesthetics.

The principal aim in definition should be to state as concisely as possible the few facts most necessary to give a person with some general education a rough, preliminary idea of its distinctive nature; of what is covered by the concept of this art, and how it fits into its cultural context. At most, the definition can give a few significant leads, so that anyone can investigate further if he wishes to. It should do this with balance and not one-sided specialization, starting the inquirer on his way to a comprehensive understanding of the whole subject.

What we call the definition of an art is and should be two things: (1) a definition of the *name* of that art; an indication as to how this term is and should be used, as covering certain types of phenomena but not others; (2) a short description of the distinctive *facts* within the field of phenomena covered by that name. The first task is primarily verbal; the second deals more with other facts, to which the words refer; but the two cannot be clearly separated.

The definition of an art should include three principal *steps*. The order in which they are given is not essential, and may be varied to avoid monotony, but the following is most logical:

a. *Classing the art within its genus.* In the case of a major, extensive art, one may need only to class it as an art, in the broad aesthetic sense of that term. Sometimes it is classed as both an art and an applied science. A more restricted, specialized art should be classed, if possible, as a branch of some particular, larger art, rather than simply as an art in general. In some cases, the art to be defined should be classed as belonging to two or more genera: as a branch of one art in certain respects, and of another in other respects. Some such classifications may be thought too obvious for mention, although important in some theoretical connections: for example, that painting is a visual art. Many facts about an art can be assumed as common knowledge, and emphasis placed rather on what the reader of the definition is less likely to know.[3] The genus or genera to which the art is assigned should be indicated in terms of process, medium, product, or a combination of these.

b. *Differentiating the art from others within that genus.* The task here is to indicate briefly the most distinguishing features of the art, again in terms of process, medium, product, or a combination of them;

[3] Torossian repeats his general concept of art in defining each particular art. Each is "the art of expressing a bit of experience in terms of human values through . . ." some particular means (*op. cit.*, pp. 167, 168). This is artificial and cumbersome.

to mark it off from other coordinate species within that genus—that is, from arts of approximately equal scope and importance, not from relatively narrow subdivisions. As a rule, the art can not be precisely marked off from others within that genus, since they all overlap. One should try rather to indicate its central, most typical area, in which it differs most from the central, typical areas of other coordinate arts.

c. *Illustrating the extension of the art* by mentioning some of its most typical subspecies, branches, varieties, and perhaps individual examples (well-known, particular works of art). The branches so listed should fall to a large extent within the art being defined, but not necessarily entirely; they may extend into other fields. They should be indicated in terms of process, medium, product, or a combination of these.

d. *Additional, optional steps.* Dictionaries often give other, useful information about a term, such as its etymological derivation, the historical order in which different meanings have developed, quotations from well-known writers using it, and some approximate synonyms and antonyms, with slight shades of difference among these terms. In defining the name of an art, dictionaries are also careful to list alternative meanings, used in different realms of discussion, or even within the same realm.

It is always unfortunate to have the same name used in different senses within the same realm, and our aim in improving definitions should be to reduce this ambiguity by recommending only one meaning for each realm of discussion. Our realm of discussion is here limited to aesthetics and the fine or aesthetic arts; hence we shall not consider any meanings which the names of arts have elsewhere.

How long should the definition of an art be? We have recognized that no brief definition of a complex idea, or realm of phenomena, can be wholly adequate. Any possible wording will arouse objections, by omitting points which someone considers essential, or by suggesting interpretations which, someone feels, are false or unacceptable. A longer account gives the definer more leeway in which to say exactly what he means, guard against misinterpretation, tone down sweeping generalizations, illustrate with examples. But there are times when extreme brevity is necessary: for example, in a small, abridged dictionary. Even in a long treatise, the author may wish to begin with a short, basic definition of terms, and then go on to amplify them at leisure. Thus several of the *Encyclopaedia Britannica* articles on particular arts are fairly long, but start off with a very brief definition.

Let us distinguish roughly between three ways of explaining the meaning of a term: one short, one medium, and one long. Each has its uses. The first, which we shall call a *basic definition,* is as brief a statement as can be made, to indicate accurately and comprehensibly a certain meaning of the term in a certain context. One sentence, or a part of a sentence, is its limit. (A dictionary will usually list several of these, one for each different meaning.) The second is an *expanded definition,* which often amounts to a paragraph or two. It develops one meaning, or a few closely allied ones, with more informative details. In the case of an art, it will specify some common types of process, medium, and product. It may illustrate some typical and borderline cases. It may even touch on the main styles or stages in the history of the art. It belongs in an unabridged dictionary, a short encyclopedia, or a technical glossary for students. The third is a *detailed account,* which develops one or more of these lines of explanation with some fullness. It may vary in length from a long encyclopedia article to a treatise in several volumes. There is no definite line between these types, and no definite limit to the length of what shall be called a definition. In defining certain particular arts, we shall ordinarily begin with a basic definition, and go on to expand it slightly. The art of literature will receive a more detailed account.

In discussing the definition of each art, we shall begin with current definitions from authoritative reference works. These provide an analytical summary of current usage, with expert recommendations for desirable terminology. To contrast present ideas with those of the nineteenth century, we shall quote several statements from J. A. Symonds's essay on "The Provinces of the Several Arts." [4]

It was mentioned above that the name of every particular art, as well as of art in general, is sometimes used in an evaluative sense. If we do not like a piece of music or literature, and consider it badly done, we say: "that's not really music," or "that doesn't deserve to be called literature." The names of the arts thus become terms of approbation, and products of inferior quality are excluded, however well they may seem to fulfill the definition. We shall not follow this course; on the contrary, every art will be defined in an objective,

[4] *Essays Speculative and Suggestive* (London, 1890), I, 124f.

non-evaluative way, so as to include examples which may be considered good, bad, or indifferent, as long as they conform to the broad aesthetic definition of "art" in general, which we have adopted in Chapter III.

This approach to definition is partly in the spirit of traditional, formal logic; partly in that of modern experimental or pragmatic logic. Some reference to genus and differentiae is almost indispensable to locate a concept within its intellectual context. Modern definitions, especially by individual theorists, are often excessively vague and casual on such points, which makes for hazy thinking.[5] On the other hand, we need not follow the scholastic formula for definition with monotonous uniformity; the order can be varied, and bits of miscellaneous information added which seem to be especially important.

Volumes have been written about the nature and proper definition of each of the principal arts. The following proposals are full of debatable points. They are advanced as illustrating an approach and giving a basis for further discussion.

3. A list of arts for special study

These arts have been selected for individual discussion, as being important or distinctive in modern western culture, though not necessarily the most important from all points of view. Many of them have been important throughout the history of world civilization. A few are only potentially important, being new and in their infancy.

The list is more condensed than the one in Chapter IV. Many of the items listed there are covered here under broader headings. Which ones should be called independent arts, and which mere branches or subdivisions, is a question which can not yet be definitely settled. Current usage bestows the term "art" very loosely, to main divisions and small branches alike. It would be hard and unnecessary to restrict the term's extension exactly at the present time.

It is questionable whether so embryonic an art as mobile color (lumia) has a right to be listed as a main division of art. Certainly, it is not yet extensive or important in actual, cultural influence. Yet it seems unique and potentially important for the future.[6] Hence we

---

[5] For example, in definitions which make "art" synonymous with "expression" or "intuition," as in Croce.

[6] E. Souriau lists *projections lumineuses* as one of his fourteen principal arts (*La correspondance des arts*, p. 97).

may list it, as still undiscovered chemical elements were listed by early chemists, at their proper places in the periodic table.

The order in which the following arts and groups of arts are listed is not necessarily best, and implies no hierarchy of values. Different orders and headings, as we have seen, are best for different purposes. The comparatively static visual arts come first. Some of the forms they produce are mobile, as in transportation design; but on the whole the order of temporal unfoldment is not the main aesthetic consideration, as it is in music. Next come music and literature, which are largely or originally auditory and temporal in presentation. Then come the combined or audio-visual arts, most of which also emphasize mobility and temporal sequence.

1. Sculpture
2. Painting
3. Graphic arts; drawing; typography, commercial arts
4. Architecture
5. Landscape architecture; garden art; horticulture
6. City planning; community planning; regional planning; geo-architecture
7. Industrial design; utilitarian visual design
   a. Transportation design
   b. Furniture design
   c. Utensil design
   d. Weapon design
   e. Book design
   f. Clothing or costume design
   g. Textile design; cloth or fabric design
   h. Ceramics; pottery and porcelain design
   i. Interior design
8. Music
9. Literature: prose, verse, poetry.
10. Dancing and ballet; acting
11. Drama and theater
12. Motion pictures; cinema; film; animated cartoons.
13. Radio and television
14. Mobile color; fireworks; lumia; the clavilux.

XI

Some Arts of Importance Today and Tomorrow

1. Sculpture

We have already considered the Webster definition from various points of view, and found it useful as a summary of the narrow original meaning and the broader modern extension. Even more explicit, instructive, and yet flexible, is that of the *Columbia Encyclopedia:* [1] sculpture is—

the art of representing in solid material, and in three dimensions, forms of nature or objects of the imagination. It includes representation in the round, where the work can be seen from all sides and has true proportions in all three dimensions, and representation in relief, where the figures or designs are not separated from the background and have the true proportions in only length and breadth, with the depth, or thickness, diminished in proportion. The materials commonly used are wood, stone, clay, and metal, although ivory, bone, rock crystal, precious stones, and wax also are used. Clay, wax, and other plastic substances are molded or shaped with the hands, but the block of stone or wood must be carved.[2]

It should be made clear that sculptural forms are directly *presented* to the eye in three dimensions; not merely represented as such through the illusion of shadows as in painting. "Solid material" is correct for most sculpture, especially stone; but metal sculpture is often hollow, and flat or soft materials like paper and straw can be bent and twisted into three-dimensional shapes. In some recent sculpture, such as that of Gargallo and Moore, inner spaces are clearly evident, the shape becoming hollow like a shell or a stringed musical instrument. Unlike architecture, sculpture does not ordinarily produce hollow forms large enough for people to enter, though it may in exceptions like the colossal Statue of Liberty. Sculptural forms are made chiefly to be viewed from the outside, for their representative or

[1] New York: Columbia U. Press, 1935.

[2] The *Encyclopaedia Britannica's* definition is similar: "The art of representing observed or imagined objects in solid materials and in three dimensions" (J. Hudnut, in the 14th ed.). Colvin, in the 11th ed., under "Fine Arts," defined sculpture as "a shaping art, of which the business is to express and arouse emotion by the imitation of natural objects, and principally the human body, in solid form . . ."

decorative interest. But sculptural design has much in common with architectural and other three-dimensional, utilitarian design, and they can not be completely separated.

Practically all definitions of sculpture state that it is an art of representation. The older definitions restricted it to the representation of nature. J. A. Symonds says, for example, that "sculpture and painting distinguish themselves from the other fine arts by the imitation of concrete existences in nature. They copy the bodies of men and animals, the aspects of the world around us, and the handiwork of mankind . . . for the expression of internal, spiritual things." More recent definitions include the representation of imagined objects. This is obviously necessary, to cover religious and fantastic sculptures. The recent trend toward semi-abstract or highly stylized art, as in the works of Brancusi and Lipchitz, and even toward completely non-representative design, make it necessary to expand the concept still further. Most sculpture is representative; but a work may now be classed as sculpture which does not represent anything at all, natural or imaginary, if it presents a three-dimensional design of surfaces. The production of such designs is not new in art; they are as old as obelisks and other monuments, such as gravestones. Architecture brings in many such three-dimensional forms, as ornaments and functional details. Monument-making is sometimes classed as a distinct art, and sometimes as a branch of sculpture. Abstract or highly stylized, unrealistic sculptural designs are now produced by various modernist schools, not as monuments or architectural ornaments, but as statues or decorative forms. There are countless gradations between the highly realistic and the wholly non-representative; but the tendency now is to include them all as sculpture, if so intended and regarded.

Sculpture which is wholly non-representative, or which bears only a slight, vague resemblance to any natural or imaginary object, is usually called "abstract" or "non-objective." [3] Such sculpture is not

[3] A distinction is sometimes made between "abstract" and "non-objective" sculpture or painting, to the effect that abstract art is taken from real objects by leaving out some of their details, while the non-objective "comes from within." This distinction will not hold water. All art is derived from experience of the outer world, as reorganized by inner powers. The difference is in the degree of abstraction: some art stays recognizably close to a particular kind of natural object or phenomenon, and some does not. Art is never purely abstract or nonobjective; it always has the power to suggest outside associations, through slight resemblance or otherwise.

necessarily lacking in suggested meaning, or intended purely as decoration. It is sometimes meant to convey general ideas, feelings, natural forces, or types of experience. For example, a certain arrangement of masses may suggest tension or relaxation, whirling or rising movement, a menacing or cowering attitude.

To allow for all these various styles and trends, the *basic* definition of sculpture should now be extended as follows:

Sculpture is the art of planning and constructing three-dimensional forms, usually to be seen from the outside, having one or all of the following characteristics: (a) representing natural or imagined objects; (b) presenting a design of three-dimensional shapes; (c) suggesting general ideas, feelings, or other types of experience.

This specifies only the general types of product, and the use of a solid medium. No specific material or technique is required. If we now wish to expand this brief, basic definition into one which is more informative, we can add other facts about common types of medium, process, and product, as follows:

The materials commonly used in sculpture are wood, stone, clay, bronze and other metals, ivory, bone, crystal, jade, precious stones, wax, and plastics. Common processes are carving or cutting, molding with the hands, and casting in a mold. The products of sculpture are usually called statues in the round (statuettes or figurines if small) when adapted for perception from all sides. When highly developed in three dimensions, they tend to present different, related designs from different points of view. Reliefs are fully visible only from in front; the represented objects or designs are not completely detached from a background surface. In low relief they project only slightly from the background; in high relief considerably; in hollow relief their highest areas are on the background plane. In the intaglio process, a figure or design is cut below the surrounding surface, so that its usual protuberances become hollows. Masks represent a face or head, usually in a fantastic form that can be worn for disguise. Non-representative solid monuments, architectural ornaments, and other three-dimensional designs are often classed as sculpture. The products of sculpture are usually static, but include some mobile types such as marionettes. They are sometimes polychromed, but are now usually left in the color and texture natural to the material, or in some artificial and comparatively uniform texture (the patina), as in the greenish tinge produced in bronze by age and chemical agents. Ceramic sculpture is often poly-

chromed and glazed. Sculpture is one of the oldest arts, having been produced since paleolithic times for magical, religious, political, ornamental, and other purposes, in a great variety of styles. Common subjects of large statues are figures of supernatural, legendary, noble, or official personages, figures of animals (for example, horses combined with riders as equestrian statues), and individual portraits. Statuettes are often less formal in design and less serious in mood. Especially in relief, sculptural figures may be combined into represented scenes and figures.

2. Painting

Webster's definition 3, for "Fine Arts," is as follows: "The work of the painter; representation or depiction of objects or scenes in color on a surface by means of pigments, generally applied with a brush; also, any work of art so produced." This omits abstract, nonobjective, and decorative painting; it fails to recognize that design of colors, shapes, etc., may be emphasized more than representation. The *Encyclopaedia Britannica* (14th ed.) begins its article on "Painting" with a similarly narrow definition.

The *Columbia Encyclopedia* is again more elastic and informative on this subject:

Painting, in art [is] the process of laying pigments on a surface so as to produce by means of color some decorative arrangement or the representation of objects, presenting a subject or an experience which the painter aims to record. Prehistoric artists painted figures of animals and other natural forms upon their implements and the walls of their caves. Mural painting, through all ages one of the most important forms of art, has come into renewed prominence. The two principal methods are fresco and tempera painting. Decoration seems to have been the chief purpose of painting in the ancient Egyptian, Assyrian, and Babylonian arts, as well as the Persian, Indian, Chinese, and Japanese.

This last sentence is historically incorrect, since religious and moral symbolism and other aims were stressed more than decoration. Oil and water-color painting should be included as typical mediums.

Recommended revision: *Painting is the art of arranging pigments on a surface so as to produce one or more of the following effects: (a) the representation of objects or scenes from nature or imagination;*

(b) a decorative design or texture of lines, shapes, and color areas; (c) a form with symbolic meaning; (d) suggestion of abstract qualities in nature or in human experience. Such a product is called a painting or (especially when representative) a picture; but pictures can be produced in many other ways. Painting as a general process, and as a factor in other arts, is used to spread a film of pigment, oil, etc., over a house, chair, or other object, for protective or decorative purposes, or both. The principal tool of painting is the brush, but others such as airbrush and palette-knife are also used, and paint can be applied directly with the fingers. The principal materials are oil paints, water-colors, and tempera, with pigments derived from mineral and vege-table sources. Human and animal figures, portraits, spirits and super-natural beings, landscapes, and still-life groups have been the chief types of subject. In size, paintings vary from miniatures and easel paintings to large murals, the last of which are often done in fresco, on wet plaster. Since paleolithic times and throughout the world, many different styles in painting have flourished; almost every great epoch in civilized history having produced one or more.

3. Graphic arts; drawing; typography; commercial arts

Webster defines the "graphic arts" as *"a.* Orig., those fine arts, as drawing, painting, engraving, etc., which pertain to representation on a flat surface. *b.* Those arts, including printing, process engraving, etc., which pertain to the expression of ideas by means of lines, marks, or characters impressed on a surface." The word "graphic" is from the Greek and Latin words for "written," and calligraphy or decorative and expressive handwriting is one of the early graphic arts.

Webster includes two concepts: one of a group of fine or aesthetic, mainly hand-executed arts. One might better say here, "which pertain to representation or decoration on a flat surface," for non-representa-tive ornaments were often produced. The second concept includes some modern techniques, largely mechanized, and devoted to reproducing not only pictures and other aesthetic objects, but also scientific or commercial diagrams, charts, printed text, etc. Handwriting also falls in this category.

We can restate the definition as follows:

Graphic arts: the arts of producing pictures or representative, decorative, or symbolic lines, marks, or characters on a surface, by means of drawing, writing, painting, engraving, printing, half-tone, etching, lithography, photography, or other techniques, manual or mechanical. The usual mediums are paper and black or colored ink or paint, in addition to drawing instruments such as pencils, pens, brushes, and sharp-pointed engraving tools; also cameras and printing devices such as wood-blocks, copper plates, silk screens, and presses.

The tendency now is to omit painting, especially oil and fresco painting, from the list of graphic arts, and to restrict the list mainly to work produced on paper; water-colors are often included.

Drawing, says Webster, is "the act or art of representing an object or outlining a figure, plan, or sketch, by means of lines; delineation, as by pen, pencil, or crayon." The *Columbia Encyclopedia* defines it as "the art of portraying form or scene with a hard pointed instrument or with a brush (moistened with liquid color or ink) on any surface, by lines; a delineation itself, as for an illustration, and sometimes in the sense of a study or sketch for work to be executed in painting or sculpture."

The emphasis should certainly be placed on lines; but other components enter in as follows:

Drawing is the art of representing an object or scene, or producing a decorative or symbolic form, especially through lines, shaded areas and textures made with a pencil, crayon, pen, or brush. Drawings are usually made with a pointed instrument on paper, or for reproduction on paper, either in black and white or in colors. Drawing can be (a) an independent art, producing finished forms, or (b) a component in other arts such as painting, where it includes preliminary sketches and shapes directly painted with the brush, or (c) a way of making preliminary sketches to be executed in an entirely different medium, as in architecture and industrial design.

The concept of drawing overlaps that of painting, and several kinds of picture can be placed in either class. A picture made in sharp lines with a pencil is definitely a drawing, not a painting. But a "wash drawing" is defined by Webster as a kind of water-color painting, "done chiefly in washes [that is, thin or watery coats of color], as distinguished from that done in stipple, in body color, etc." If such a picture contains a variety of hues, it is more likely to be called a painting. If done with a brush in black ink or a monochrome wash such as bistre (a dark brown pigment), it may be classed either as a wash drawing or as a monochrome painting. If done with pastel crayons instead of a brush, in one or many colors, it is usually called a pastel drawing. The most typical paintings are done with a brush and pigments of different colors. Paint is sometimes distinguished as opaque, from transparent or translucent washes, varnishes, and stains. But this distinction is not consistently maintained; thin water-colors are also classed as paints.

As we noted in an earlier chapter, the word "design" was formerly used to mean "drawing," and arts which used drawing (painting, sculpture, architecture, etc.) were called "arts of design." But "design" is now used in other senses in aesthetics, and should not be used with this former implication.

Typography, says Webster, is the "art of printing with type; use of type to produce impressions on paper, vellum, etc.; also, the style, arrangement, or appearance of matter printed from type." *Type* is "a rectangular block usually of metal or wood, having its face so shaped as to produce, in printing, a letter, figure, or other character." Broadly, this art would include the printing of pictures as well as linear designs; in practice, it is largely concerned with printing letters and other arbitrary symbols. It is not always classed as a graphic art in itself, but it has many points in common with the others. It produces a visual form in which line, light and dark are the main components. Type faces are drawn with care by their designers, before being made into blocks. Typography may produce pictures and designs, as in colophons and decorative lay-outs. Its basic process of printing from blocks is shared with engraving and other graphic arts. The main difference is in the function, and hence in the forms produced on a surface. Most of the so-called graphic arts, in spite of the original meaning of their name, are concerned with pictorial representation rather than with writing or printing words. Typography, on the other hand, has a strongly utilitarian emphasis; it is a means to the recording and easy reading of words. It is one way of executing literary composition; of giving it a final form of expression. The decorative qualities of type and its arrangement are usually subordinated and restrained, so as not to distract the attention, strain the eyes, or interfere with quick interpretation of the symbol. There have been many cases of decorative emphasis, in typography as in its ancestor, calligraphy; but these are not characteristic of the art as a whole. Enough of the visual and decorative remains, however, to qualify typography as a graphic art. It is usually a factor in the production of books, periodicals, posters, and other combined forms, rather than a complete art in itself.

Let us redefine "typography" as *the art of designing type faces, of printing from type, and of arranging the letters, symbols, words, or other printed figures within a given area, so as to produce a combined form which will have the qualities desired, such as easy legibility, decorative appeal, emphasis, and adaptation to the spirit and purpose of the material printed.*

Commercial art is defined by Webster, only as "art applied to commercial purposes." But it has taken on a more specific meaning, especially in art education and occupational surveys. It refers especially to the designing of advertising pictures, text, and lay-outs, such as are used extensively in periodicals, posters, billboards, and other displays. The aim and resulting type of form are dominantly utilitarian: to persuade or induce the observer to buy or do something, usually by representing it with attractive visual and emotional associations. It is a characteristic expression of modern capitalism, and of the consumer-directed type of economy. It overlaps the general field of propagandist art, including political posters, cartoons, and caricatures. In both, aesthetic appeal is a means to an end. Commercial art is coming to be distinguished, not only by its aim and subject-matter, but by its peculiarly diversified combination of mediums and techniques. Drawing and painting, usually for mechanical reproduction, are still the chief ones. Pictures so produced are often combined, in the same page or lay-out, with photographs and printed text. Various techniques are used to reproduce and distribute them, especially halftone color printing and lithography.

With great freedom and experimental ingenuity, commercial art extends into other mediums. It has no compunctions about stepping over the traditional "limits" of the arts, or about preserving its dignity and fineness. This limits its intellectual and spiritual significance, but encourages innovations in form. Innumerable materials and methods are used in combination, including electric bulbs and neon lighting, mobile sculptural figures, motion pictures, printed or spoken words, etc., with and without auditory accompaniment. Hence commercial art is only in part a graphic art, or a visual art. Pictures still remain its central medium, however.

Let us redefine "commercial art" as *the art of designing pictorial or other displays for advertising and similar purposes, especially to help in selling a commercial product or service by representing it in attractive form and with pleasant associations, or by associating disagreeable images with failure to buy it. Advertising lay-outs are usually designed for mechanical reproduction in periodicals or posters, and often combine literary, typographical, and other elements with drawn, painted, or photographed pictures. Larger displays for use in public places often involve, in addition, luminous and mobile pictorial and sculptural effects.*

4. Architecture

Webster's definition, noted above, is "art or science of building; esp., the art of building houses, churches, bridges, and other structures, for the purposes of civil life;—often called civil architecture." If "civil" means non-military, then the definition is too restrictive, for military and partly military structures such as castles are commonly classed as architecture. If it means "urban, civilized," it is again too restrictive, for primitive and rustic structures are also included in the history of architecture. At most, one should say, "especially for civil life."

An "architect," says the same dictionary, is "a person skilled in the art of building; a professional student of architecture, or one who makes it his occupation to form plans and designs of, and to draw up specifications for, buildings, and to superintend their execution." This has the advantage of pointing out the designing phase (visual shape guiding) in the process of architecture.

What, then, is a "building"? It is, continues Webster, "a fabric or edifice, framed or constructed, designed to stand more or less permanently, and covering a space of land, for use as a dwelling, storehouse, factory, shelter for beasts, or some other useful purpose. Building in this sense does not include a mere wall, fence, monument, hoarding, or similar structure . . . nor a steamboat, ship, or other vessel of navigation."

Vitruvius mentions "convenience, beauty, and strength" as aims in building a temple.[4] These aims find modern expression in H. W.

---

[4] *De Architectura*, Bk. III, ch. III. Under *architectura*, he includes much that we would class under "industrial design," "engineering," or some other heading: for example, the making of clocks, water-screws, and catapults.

Corbett's article on "Architecture" (*Encyclopaedia Britannica,* 14th ed.), where architecture is defined as "the art of building so as to apply both beauty and utility." Its problem, says Corbett, is "how best to enclose space for human occupancy." It should arrange plan, masses, and enrichments so as to give the structure "interest, beauty, grandeur, unity and power without sacrificing convenience." Architecture as an art is thus distinguished from building without an aesthetic aim.

Retaining this aesthetic emphasis, let us restate the definition as follows:

Architecture is the art of designing and guiding the construction of buildings, so as to make them visually satisfying as well as suitable for their intended uses. Buildings are three-dimensional forms, usually enclosing or partly enclosing an interior space large enough for persons or animals to enter and carry on activities within it. They can present a visual design or series of designs on the exterior, interior, or both. Main types of product are distinguished on a basis of function and related form as follows: dwelling-houses (of many varieties from palaces to hotels and apartment houses), temples, churches, monasteries, forts and fortified towns, bridges, dams, theaters, amphitheaters, light-houses, public baths, some kinds of monument, libraries, store and office buildings, factories, warehouses, railroad stations, and airplane hangars. Typical materials are wood, brick, stone, tile, plaster, steel, and concrete; typical structural methods are the post and lintel, the wooden truss, the masonry arch and vault, and the steel skeleton. Architecture often incorporates or provides a setting for products of other arts, such as sculpture, stained glass, furniture, and interior design; hence it can be regarded as a combined art. It often cooperates with landscape design and city planning. Among principal Western styles are the Egyptian, Greek, Roman, Byzantine, Romanesque, Gothic, Renaissance, Baroque, and Rococo; distinctive styles were also produced by the chief oriental civilizations.

5. Landscape architecture; garden art; horticulture

"A landscape architect," says Webster, is "one whose profession is to so arrange and modify the effects of natural scenery over a given tract as to produce the best aesthetic effect considering the use to which the tract is to be put." A "landscape," according to this dictionary, is "a portion of land or territory which the eye can comprehend in a single view, including all the objects so seen, esp. in its pictorial aspect." A "landscape gardener" is "a person who lays out or develops a garden, grounds, etc., by means of decorative planning." A "garden" is "a piece of ground appropriate to the cultivation of herbs, fruits, flowers, or vegetables." "Gardening" is "the laying out or cultivating of gardens." "Horticulture" is "the cultivation of a garden or orchard; the science and art of growing fruits, vegetables, and flowers or ornamental plants. Horticulture is one of the main divisions of agriculture."

Several closely related arts are indicated by these concepts. Let us note their points of distinction. "Horticulture" is both a science and an art. As a science, it is an application of botany and a branch of agriculture. It is devoted to the improvement, not only of flowers and other decorative plants, but also of vegetables and other plants of a more utilitarian sort. It is more concerned with plants as species than with their arrangement in any particular place. *Gardens* and *gardening* may be wholly utilitarian or wholly decorative, or both. *Garden art* implies the laying out or cultivating of gardens with an emphasis on their visual and other aesthetic aspects.

Landscape architecture is not limited to gardens, flowers, or decorative plants, although they constitute an important part of its medium. It also uses lawns and meadows, bodies of water, hills and valleys, rocks and other topographical elements, in addition to man-made structures. Let us define it as *the art of arranging plants and other objects in a particular area of land, and if necessary altering the configurations of ground and water therein, so as to produce a satisfying visual appearance along with other desired qualities and uses. It includes the designing and placing of artificial features such as walls, fountains, statues, terraces, and summer-houses, and the relating of grounds, gardens, approaches, etc., to the main buildings; but not, as a rule, the designing of the main buildings themselves. Among its products are parks, gardens, and the landscape effects of yards, highways, and boulevards. Styles vary from the extremely geometric and formal to the extremely informal, natural, and picturesque. Landscape design is concerned with the designing or planning of such effects, and not with their execution. Garden art is a branch of landscape architecture, especially concerned with flowers and gardens.*

6. City planning; community planning; regional planning; geo-architecture

"City planning," says Webster, is "arranging or laying out by an organized plan (city plan), the streets, parks, recreation centers, business sections, etc., of a city with a view to securing health, convenience, and aesthetic qualities." This art, though ancient, has seldom been recognized in lists of the fine arts. It is being brought to prominence as critics [5] point out the disastrous effects of unplanned urban growth, such as crime-breeding, unhealthy slums and inconvenient traffic facilities. City planning is a combined art which incorporates and transcends architecture, landscape architecture, and many applied sciences. It is now approached primarily from a functional and sociological standpoint, with emphasis on health, convenience, industry, education, culture, recreation, family life, and community life. The community should be planned, it is said, primarily as a means to realizing the highest possible values along all these lines. Visual aspects, such as broad scenic vistas, are now thought to have been overvalued by earlier planners, but are not forgotten in the total aim. In classing the art as visual, in regard to its primary mode of presentation to the observer, one need not imply that its visual or other aesthetic aspects are its most important ones. Even among direct sense-qualities, those of sound and odor also enter the problem.

City planning is also called "town planning" and "urbanism" by various writers. The term "city," as in the Webster definition, has the disadvantage of restricting the concept to large-sized communities. Some of the most successful building of planned communities has been done with small towns and suburbs. On the other hand, the scope of planning may and probably will, in future, extend beyond the limits of the largest cities. It will take in relations between cities, towns, villages, and the intervening countryside, with a view to organizing the whole physical basis of social living as well as possible from the standpoint of utility and beauty.

The term "geo-architecture" has been proposed to cover large regional developments such as the Tennessee Valley Authority, where the architect cooperates with the engineer and landscape architect in

[5] For example, Lewis Mumford, in *The Culture of Cities*. New York, 1938.

planning complex systems of dams, waterways, hydroelectric control, highways and interrelated communities.[6] This can all be broadly classed as community planning, but it deals with large areas of countryside as well as thickly inhabited centers.

Community planning would be a more inclusive name for the art, as applied to social units of any size. Let us define it as *the art of designing and arranging the physical form of a city, town, or other inhabited region, so as to provide the best possible conditions for social and individual living; especially as to physical safety, health, comfort, intellectual and aesthetic experience, education, efficiency of work and transportation, family and neighborhood relations, opportunity for growth, and cooperation with the outside world. As a means to these ends, special attention is paid to the problem of zoning industrial, commercial, and residential sections, providing for all parts of the community safe and adequate traffic and recreational facilities, schools, churches, theaters, libraries, and community centers. The community as a visual form, and its planning as a visual art, cover all possible scenes and vistas observable from points within or near it; including rows and groups of buildings, streets, parks, yards, and waterfronts. Special attention is paid to the larger, more inclusive vistas, and to the interrelation of smaller views in a consistent whole. The products of community planning are (a) the community plan or design, involving maps, pictures, charts, and specifications; (b) the planned community itself, as built wholly or partly in accord with such a design.*

7. Industrial design; utilitarian visual design

In a previous chapter, we examined the terms "industrial arts" and "handicrafts" as names for a large group of skills and occupations, concerned with making products in which decorative form or visual appeal is combined with a relatively strong emphasis on utilitarian functions. The latter determine the basic materials and form of the object to a large extent; the decorative effects being sometimes added in a superficial, extraneous way, and sometimes achieved mainly in and through the utilitarian form itself. (In the latter case, design is called "functional.") Many such objects, we found, are made with little or no decorative intention; in that case they are not industrial

---

[6] *Cf.* C. W. Condit, "Modern Architecture: a New Technical-Aesthetic Synthesis," *Journal of Aesthetics,* Vol. VI, No. 1 (Sept., 1947).

arts, by our definition, but industries, or applied sciences. They are handicrafts when hand methods of manufacture predominate. When on a large scale and mechanized, they can be called "industrial art" in a general way; but the artistic element in them tends to become concentrated in certain specialized phases: in the work of art directors, designers, special types of craftsman, and others to whom the decorative aspect of the product is largely entrusted. A rough distinction can be made along these lines between "industrial arts," on the one hand, which covers execution and manufacture, and "industrial design" on the other, which is especially concerned with designing and composing. "Industrial design" is sometimes made to cover the engineering and utilitarian aspects of planning, as in machine design. But when we class it as an *art* in the aesthetic sense, we restrict it mainly to the planning and designing of the decorative and other aesthetic aspects of the product. Within the field of aesthetics, there is little danger of confusion. When there is, we can specify "artistic industrial design" or "decorative industrial design."

"Design," it will be remembered, has two current meanings in aesthetics, in addition to the obsolete one in which it meant "drawing." These appear in the two parts of Webster's definition:

5. Art. a. A preliminary sketch; an outline or pattern of the main features of something to be executed, as of a picture, a building, or a decoration; a plan. b. The arrangement of elements or details which make up a work of art; esp., a piece of decorative art viewed with reference to the invention and disposition of its forms, colors, etc.; as, the panel is a fine design. Used also of other than plastic or graphic art.

The *Columbia Encyclopedia* gives the second meaning, in defining "design" as "the plan or arrangement of line, form, mass, and space in a pattern to produce an effect pleasing to the eye."

It is sometimes important to distinguish these two meanings, and to call them by other names if necessary: for example, to call the first one a preliminary sketch, plan, scheme, blue-print, or composition, and the second one a decorative or thematic arrangement. In the case of industrial design as an aesthetic art, the two meanings are both implied; both types of designing enter it, in close cooperation.

"Decorative" does not imply being covered with extraneous or superficial ornamentation; it may consist in a severely functional shape which is found to be visually satisfying at the same time. On the other hand, profuse external ornamentation of the Victorian type is not excluded by definition; styles vary, and we are not trying to evaluate them. Aesthetic appeal in a utilitarian product is not always limited to the visual. Tactile and olfactory qualities may be important, as in clothing; auditory qualities, as in a clock. But in industrial design the main emphasis is placed on eye appeal or visually decorative form.

The products of industry differ greatly, as to their decorative and other aspects. They involve different mediums, techniques, and types of form. There is a distinct art of furniture design, and another of clothing design. They are grouped as "industrial arts" because of their similarity in combining aesthetic with utilitarian emphasis. There is also a tendency to speak as if "industrial design" were a single art, in spite of its diversity of products. This appears especially in art education, where courses on "design" are given to prepare a student for designing many different kinds of industrial object. Architectural designing is a world apart; but "industrial design" is made to cover almost all other kinds of visual utilitarian product.

In defining industrial design, how shall we describe its mediums, processes, and products? They may be the same as for the finished product (for example, the chair itself), or they may consist in a special kind of preliminary product (for example, a pictorial sketch for a chair). As we saw in an earlier chapter, the tendency in industry is toward the latter; toward making design a specialized art, distinct from manufacture though cooperating with it. Only the manufacture is called "production" in industry; but in a broader sense the sketch is also a product. Such preliminary products, in which the plan is outlined, do not differ as much from each other as do the finished products. A sketch for a new automobile resembles a sketch for a new electric stove, as to medium, process, and product. This is one reason for considering "industrial design" as a single art, in spite of the diversity of its ultimate products. In so far as it uses drawing and painting, it is a branch of graphic art, and requires similar instruction. But its aims and types of form are different from paintings aimed merely at beautiful representation; it must clearly indicate the structure and operation of the intended product, even at the cost of visual realism. Thus it often uses diagrams, cross-sectional views, imaginary "phantom" views, "exploded" views, etc., which are not used in ordinary representational painting. Also, it uses sculptural models, scientific measurements, and other means entirely outside the realm of ordinary graphic art.

Practically all of the finished products of industrial art are three-dimensional objects, such as dishes and tables. Even a piece of cloth is three-dimensional, although its decorative pattern may be flat and two-dimensional. The preliminary sketches and models in which industrial designs are first embodied can be either flat or solid. Pictorial sketches for industrial design resemble the products of commercial, advertising art in some respects. Both may give, for example, a picture of a new refrigerator with a diagram of its internal structure. But the industrial design or "production illustration" will be intended for the eyes of workmen and production managers, to guide them in making the product. It will try to be clear and explanatory. The advertising picture will be intended for possible buyers, and will try to present the product in a glamorous light which may not be entirely realistic. Sometimes a picture belongs to both categories at once. The prospective buyer of a gown may be shown several preliminary sketches of gowns, all as attractive as possible. The one selected may be used as a plan for the gown itself.

Our definition, being intended like others in this chapter for use in the field of aesthetics, will stress aesthetic aspects rather than technological:

Industrial design is the art of designing or planning the production of objects, mostly three-dimensional, so as to make them suitable for practical, utilitarian ends and also aesthetically satisfying in visual and other ways. Such planning can be done in the process of manufacture, or in advance of it, through pictorial sketches, photographs, diagrams, solid models, verbal and numerical specifications, etc. Industrial design is divided mainly on a basis of the type of finished product: for example, automobile design, furniture design, textile design, clothing design. It can be divided according to the medium and process used in expressing the designs or plans: for example, production illustration, scale models, etc. Architectural design and commercial art are allied to industrial design, but are usually classed separately. Certain styles in art, such as Renaissance and Rococo, have been applied in the designing of many types of industrial product.

Because of the enormous variety of industrial products, it is useful to group them under a few main headings. These also provide names for the principal branches of industrial design.

Architectural design, or the artistic designing of buildings, we have already considered. It overlaps industrial design, but is usually considered as a separate main division of art.

Transportation design is concerned with means of conveying people or property from place to place. It includes *vehicle* design, which covers automobiles, trains, wagons, etc., and sometimes aircraft. Boats are usually classed apart. We thus have automobile design, locomotive design, airplane design, ship design, etc.

Furniture design is concerned with objects of convenience or decoration placed within a house or other building; especially those which are movable but comparatively large and stationary. Those which are permanently built in are part of the architectural interior, or interior construction: for example, a fireplace or doorway. Those attached in a more or less permanent way are *fixtures*, such as electric wall lamps, bathtubs, and kitchen stoves. Those more easily moved but usually solid and left in place, are called *furniture;* they include tables, chairs, bookcases, cabinets, desks, large clocks and radios. *House furnishings*, such as curtains and rugs, are usually less solid and more easily moved. In large stores, many utensils are so classed, such as kitchen hardware. Books and pictures can be regarded as house furnishings, but are so distinct and important in themselves as to be ordinarily excluded.

Utensil design deals with useful objects, most of which are solid, small, and more easily moved than furniture. Most of them are now designed with careful attention to visual appeal. They include *household* utensils such as dishes, table silverware, and coffee-pots; also *personal* utensils such as fountain pens and hairbrushes, which are ordinarily used by one person and often carried around by him. Personal utensils are sometimes treated as costume accessories: for example, purses, eyeglasses, signet rings. Many household and personal utensils are now complex and mechanical, as in vacuum cleaners and electric shavers. They are often called *appliances*. Large radios and electric stoves are usually to be classed as furniture or fixtures. *Tools* are a kind of utensil or instrument, especially one which is used to carry on one's occupation, or to make or repair other objects. Their form is now usually severely functional, and for that very reason admired by critics for its decorative quality, which is often unintended.

Weapons are a special kind of utensil or tool, devoted to hunting and fighting. Modern ones are not usually treated with decorative care, except in the case of expensive shotguns and other luxuries. Most of them have become severely functional, and deliberately inconspicuous. But in earlier times they were often elaborately ornamented, with rich textures and patterns, symbolic figures, and sometimes representative painting or sculpture. Such ornamentation, in addition to the decorative form inherent in their functional structure, admits them to the class of decorative art.

Books are another special type of utensil, not ordinarily so classed. They are a type of three-dimensional form, designed primarily to record and transmit ideas through the printed word, but often embellished with elaborate care. As such, they become a combined art, in which the decorative qualities of typography, paper-making, ink-making, lay-out, binding, embossing, gilding, and decorative hand lettering may all be combined to supplement the literary art of the author and the pictorial art of the illustrator. The modern book is distinguished from scrolls, incised tablets, and other early kinds by being printed on both sides of rectangular, numbered, paper pages, one edge of all the pages being fastened together for easy turning. Tactile and sometimes other sensory qualities are considered in planning the total aesthetic effect.

Clothing or costume design is concerned with wearing apparel of all sorts: garments, hats, shoes, gloves, and accessories. *Jewelry* is usually a costume accessory, aiming less at utility than at ornamentation and prestige value, although sometimes applied to utensils. It may rely mostly on the natural color and texture of precious stones and metals, or combine these into designs. *Armor* is a very special type of clothing, not usually so classed; it is distinguished by its metal material, usually rigid, and by its defensive functional form. It also has been treated with elaborate decoration. The more common types of clothing design are divided on a basis of function and consequent form. In recent times, they have been designed with more attention to the demands of health, comfort, and convenience; but aesthetic and erotic appeal are usually strong additional determinants, often outweighing the utilitarian. There are hat designers, dress designers, shoe designers, sportswear designers, uniform designers (for example, for soldiers, nurses, chauffeurs), and theatrical costume designers.

There is great overlapping between all these classes and concepts. The designing of each type of industrial object, or a small subdivision within it, is often called an art in itself. This is especially true when it presents special technical problems, and when its products are subjected to careful scrutiny and criticism on aesthetic grounds. Clocks and watches, for example, constitute a highly important type of product in the modern world, receiving frequent attention and often placed at conspicuous points. They may be considered as furniture, fixtures, household or personal utensils, jewelry or costume accessory, according to their size and form. Striking and chiming clocks are musical instruments as well as visual forms.

Toys are a heterogeneous class of utensils for children's play. They are not usually given serious attention in aesthetics, but deserve it on several grounds. They are sources of aesthetic and other directly satisfying experience for children. They are important means in the development of personality, especially through the rehearsal of future adult activities, and through giving a vicarious outlet in fantasy for conflicting impulses. They are significant expressions of social culture, through symbolizing characteristic group interests. Toys which are elegantly made for privileged children are often designed and executed with refined craftsmanship and rich ornamentation. Three main types can be distinguished: (a) those which imitate human, animal, and other natural forms, such as dolls, hobby horses, masks; these tend to assume sculptural or pictorial form; (b) small imitations of adult utilitarian forms such as tools, utensils, weapons, vehicles, horse equipment, houses, furniture, balloons; and (c) non-representative utensils for games and play such as marbles, balls, tops, dice, some kites, jumping ropes, tennis rackets. These last may be distinguished from adult games and sporting goods as being smaller and less substantial. All these types, especially *a* and *b,* are used in dramatic mimesis of adult behavior as conceived by children. Some kites are representative, such as those in the shape of fish and other animals, made in China and Japan. The concept of toys overlaps those of other objects made for children, such as clothing, books, pictures, phonograph records, and educational equipment. It includes primarily those intended for amusement rather than instruction and improvement. But, as in the case of art in general, there is a persistent attempt to combine these values.

8. Textile design; cloth or fabric design

The designing of cloth, for its appearance as well as its utilitarian qualities, is a branch of industrial design, distinct enough to receive separate consideration. A piece of cloth is actually three-dimensional, but usually so thin and flat that its decorative development must be largely two-dimensional. In rare cases, it approaches the form of a sculptural relief, as in heavy embroidery and appliqué work. It can be pictorial, as in tapestry; symbolic, as in heraldic and ecclesiastical vestments; or treated with elaborate, two-dimensional design. A piece of cloth may be treated as a finished work of art in itself (for example, a rug), or as a semi-processed material for clothing, upholstery, or other uses. It is usually adapted to specific utilitarian functions, as to keep out cold or moisture. It may be intended purely as decoration, but even then can be utilized in a larger form, as when the interior designer hangs a rich fabric on the wall.

A "textile," according to Webster, is "that which is, or may be, woven; a woven fabric or a material for weaving." Textile art and textile design are thus restricted to the process of weaving. To "weave," according to the same source, is "to form, as a textile, by interlacing yarns or similar strands of material; specif., to make or manufacture (a web, cloth, a certain kind of cloth) on a loom by interlacing warp and filling yarns . . . hence, to interlace into a fabric, esp. on a loom; as, to weave wool; to weave straw braids." No particular material is specified; even metal wire or glass threads can be woven. This is definition in terms of a single basis—that of process or technique.

However, several other kinds of cloth are sometimes classed as textiles. For example, the textile department of an art museum will probably have charge of laces and embroideries, even though they are not woven. "Textile design" thus becomes roughly equivalent to "cloth design." "Cloth" is a much broader term, according to Webster: "A pliable fabric woven, felted, or knitted from any filament; commonly, fabric of woven cotton, woolen, silk, rayon, or linen fibre, used for garments, etc." "Fabric" is also broad, covering "cloth that is woven or knit from fibers, either vegetable or animal, as, silks, or other fabrics. Any similar material."

Either of two courses may be followed in a case like this. (1)

Usage may tend toward the broader interpretation of "textile," so as to cover non-woven kinds of cloth. One would then say "weaving" to indicate a particular technique. (2) The narrow sense of "textile" may be retained, as a synonym for "weaving." In that case, one might say "cloth design" or "fabric art" for the broader field. Either would do, if the meaning were clear. In the past the confusion has not been serious, because woven fabrics (including rugs and tapestries) have been the most important in art. Even when the design itself was not woven, it was ordinarily placed on a woven fabric, as in embroidering or block printing on a woven cloth. Now, the situation is changing a little. New plastic and synthetic materials are coming into use, such as cellophane and artificial rubber, which can be pressed into thin, flexible sheets, with a decorative texture or pattern pressed or printed thereon. It is doubtful whether the term "textile design" will or should be extended so far as to include these; but "cloth design" is already broad enough to do so. Moreover, it will easily cover older varieties of non-woven, decorative cloth, like Polynesian tapa or bark cloth, which is made by steeping, beating, and block printing.

Webster's definition of "cloth" covers knitted and felted, as well as woven, fabrics. Both of these can be made with decorative patterns or textures. Paper is made by the felting process, but is so important in itself that it is rarely classed as felt or cloth.

Without trying for precise distinctions, which are impossible at the present time, let us summarize as follows:

Textile, cloth, or fabric arts: the industrial arts concerned with designing and making thin, pliable sheets of material, especially for use in clothing and house furnishing, with decorative texture, pattern or color, and often with pictorial or symbolic figures; especially, the making of such sheets by weaving animal or vegetable fibers such as wool, cotton, silk, or linen; also, by knitting, felting, embroidering, pressing, block printing, or otherwise treating these or other materials. Important products of decorative weaving are rugs, tapestries, damasks, and brocades; those of other techniques are laces, embroideries, and tapa cloth. Paper may be included as a special kind of felted sheet or fabric, often decoratively treated, as in wall paper. The art of designing patterns or textures suitable for use on cloth or other continuous surfaces is called flat design or flat decorative design.

9. Ceramics; pottery, stoneware, and porcelain

Webster defines "ceramics" as "the art of making articles of baked clay, as pottery, tiles, etc." It is thus defined primarily in terms of the material, clay, and of the general process, baking or the use of fire. Any kind of product is included: not only pottery and tiles, but statues and reliefs, jewelry, dishes, and other utensils. "Pottery" is used in two senses: (a) as equivalent to ceramics, and (b) as restricted to the coarser kinds of earthenware material, especially when made into vessels. In the second sense, it is distinguished from "porcelain" as to material and process; porcelain requiring specially fine clay and special firing methods. The difference in material is apparent in the product, a porcelain dish being fine in texture, and usually translucent, hard, and sonorous. Pottery in the second sense, referring especially to vessels, is also distinguished from brick and tile. This is on a basis of product-type, since both of these are made of coarse earthenware. A vessel is "a hollow or concave utensil for holding anything" (Webster). It may be made of wood, metal, leather, rubber, etc., as well as of clay. Glazes and other materials besides clay are used in all the above types of manufacture. Stoneware is a coarse kind of pottery glazed and fired to density.

On the whole, ceramics is an industrial art or group of arts, producing objects which are strongly utilitarian as well as decorative. In part, it is also a branch of sculpture. It is still practiced as a handicraft, but is becoming increasingly mechanized.

To summarize: *Ceramics or pottery is the art of making articles of baked clay, especially vessels and other utensils, sculpture, bricks, and tiles, usually with the addition of glazes, pigments, and other materials. It includes (a) coarse or ordinary pottery: the making of articles from coarse earthenware; (b) porcelain: the making of articles from certain finer types of clay by special techniques; (c) brick-making and tile-making. Such articles, especially vases, bowls, and statuettes, are often given decorative form through shape, color, texture, and applied pictorial or other patterns, painted or incised.*

10. Interior design

This is *the art of planning and arranging groups of furniture, rugs, curtains, pictures, books, and other furnishings within a room or building, with a view to their visual appearance when combined, as well as to their convenience, healthfulness, comfort, and other desired qualities.* It is sometimes called "interior decoration," but this name is in some disfavor, since it is thought to suggest mere superficial ornamentation, ignoring the functional aspects of the problem.

The interior designer may cooperate with the architect in planning the interior construction itself; more often, he has to accept the construction and fixtures as a basic setting within which to work. He usually advises on the selection or manufacture of some of the interior equipment, as well as on its arrangement. Functional or utilitarian aspects of his problem are closely bound up with the aesthetic. Emotional effects like cheerfulness and restfulness are determined by the visual appearance of the room, and by the ease and efficiency with which one can live and carry on activities there. Each interior, and each family or group of users presents a distinct problem. Large scale, mechanized production enters only into large housing projects, hotel rooms, etc., where many rooms are furnished in almost identical ways.

11. Music

Webster defines music as "the science or art of pleasing, expressive, or intelligible combination of tones; the art of making such combinations, esp. into compositions of definite structure and significance, according to the laws of melody, harmony, and rhythm; the art of inventing or writing, or of rendering, such compositions, whether vocal or instrumental." The *Columbia Encyclopedia* is more brief and indefinite: "any orderly arrangement of tones in patterns and rhythms appealing to the aesthetic sense of human beings. It is an ancient art . . ." and so on, in reference to its history.

The Webster version has the advantage of pointing out various types of process, including composition and performance, vocal and instrumental. To include tone-combinations which are "intelligible" without being pleasing is a little too broad, since it would take in all spoken language, most of which is not considered music. Whether compositions must be built "according to the laws of melody, harmony, and rhythm" is a rather dubious and obsolete way to describe the facts. Many theorists now question whether there are any such laws; also whether "the aesthetic sense" mentioned by the *Columbia* definition exists. To class as music "any orderly arrangement of tones in patterns and rhythms," appealing to anyone's aesthetic taste, is extremely broad. It reflects the fairly recent discovery that many oriental and primitive styles of music exist, which do not conform to our supposed "laws," and yet build up complex forms admired in their own cultural settings. It is perhaps a little too broad. Someone may like the rhythmic pattern made by a saw-mill or by waves on a beach. The problem is to include everything we really wish to include, yet keep the concept from being so broad as to be meaningless. One way to do this, as we have seen, is to leave the concept a little indefinite around the edges, but stress the nature of the central, most typical areas within the art.

Symonds's generalizations on music are almost all exaggerated. "Like architecture," he says, "it imitates nothing." But both architecture and music are occasionally imitative—that is, representative. "It uses pure sound, and sound of the most wholly artificial kind—so artificial that the musical sounds of one race are unmusical, and therefore unintelligible, to another." Vocal sounds are not wholly artificial. Oriental and primitive music is somewhat strange to the occidental, but not wholly unintelligible; it has long influenced ours, and is doing so increasingly. "Like architecture, music relies upon mathematical proportions." Some phases in music are mathematically measured, but not all; and that can be said of any art. "Unlike architecture, music serves no utility." What of martial music and worksongs? "The domain of the spirit over which music reigns, is emotion. . . . The sphere of music is in sensuous perception; the sphere of poetry is in intelligence." These are vague and overdrawn psychological distinctions.

"Program" music often represents the sounds of nature and human life in an abstract, selective way. In a broad sense, this can be called "imitative." But there is a question of degree: whether an exact imitation of non-musical sounds, devoid of all other qualities, can be classed as music. According to present usage, it can not. The question is not one of value or beauty, but of the type of auditory form produced.

It arises today in a new way. In radio and motion pictures, there has been a great development of "sound effects," devoted to the realistic imitation of all sorts of sounds, such as automobiles, machine-guns, foot-steps, creaking doors, breaking glass, and so on. Considerable skill is shown in producing them, and they constitute an important factor in dramatic enactment, providing auditory background. They may, perhaps, be called a distinct type of auditory art, or at least a factor in art. They are not presented as independent works of art, to be enjoyed for their own sake. A distinction is made between these and "incidental music," bits of which are also used in radio drama, as additional background material and to divide the program into parts. To be called music, a series of sounds is expected to have some rudiments of melody and rhythm. Its representation of non-musical sounds is approximate rather than exact, and is usually combined with other kinds of auditory effect.

Both Webster and Columbia define "music" as a combination or arrangement of *tones;* and a tone, according to the former, is "sound quality; a sound considered as of this or that character; as, tone production; variations in tone; a low, high, loud, soft, sweet, or harsh tone." The idea of tone is thus not restricted to sounds having definite pitch, as in our diatonic scale. Primitive drum sounds are tones, even though their pitch and timbre are sometimes extremely mixed and blurred. They are developed, as by some African tribes, into highly complex forms involving counterpoint of several rhythmic themes at once, with little or no melodic development. This would be atypical in western music, but is included in the general concept of music by ethnologists and students of comparative musicology. We cannot make melody or harmony prerequisites of all music, but we can say that melody occurs in most music, and harmony in most modern occidental music.

By classing music as an art, in the aesthetic sense, we imply that it appeals to aesthetic taste or tries to do so. In addition, it may have many other aims and functions. Let us word our definition, then, as follows:

Music is the art of arranging sounds in close temporal succession, and often in simultaneous combinations, in such a way as to present some regularity and continuity of variation in rhythm, and usually in pitch. In most music, repetitions and variations of rhythm and pitch are organized into melody, which may be simple and rudimentary or developed into complex patterns based on definite scales. In occidental music, complex form is also produced through melodic counterpoint, chord-structure, and chord-progression based in part on systematic rules and conventions. Music is produced by voices, instruments, or by both in combination. Varieties of instrumental timbre are organized in the orchestra, different types of which have arisen in different parts of the world. Both simple and complex musical forms have the power to suggest emotions, moods, desires, and other phenomena of human experience and the outside world. They sometimes imitate non-musical sounds, usually in a partial, abstract way, and may represent scenes, activities, and stories. Such representation is usually indefinite unless accompanied by verbal text or dramatic action. The processes of music include the inventing or composing of musical forms, and usually recording them in conventional notation on a written or printed score, suitable for guiding performance. Some of the types of pattern emphasized in modern European music are the fugue, dance suite, sonata, and symphonic poem. Distinctive historic styles have arisen in primitive and oriental cultures, as well as in the western world. Music is often used in combination with other arts: for example, with literature in song and oratorio; with drama in opera and motion pictures; with dance in ballet. New types of timbre are now derived from sources formerly considered as non-musical noises.

12. Literature; prose, verse, poetry

Aesthetics has traditionally listed only poetry among the major arts, and indeed has given scant recognition to prose as an art of any status. This is inconsistent with the high esteem in which many prose writers have been held as artists, from ancient times to the present. In recent years, the trend in literature has been toward even stronger emphasis on prose. Having so much in common, prose and poetry should be defined in close relation to each other. To differentiate literature as an art, including both prose and poetry, from less artistic types of writing as in science and popular journalism, the term *belles-lettres* is occasionally used, but not widely outside France. Current usage favors the term "literature" to cover all developments of verbal form along aesthetic lines. Symonds gives the following definition:

The last of the fine arts is literature; or, in the narrower sphere of which it will be well to speak here only, is poetry. Poetry employs words in fixed rhythms, which we call metres. Only a small portion of its effect is derived from the beauty of its sound. It appeals to the sense of hearing far less immediately than music does. It makes no appeal to the eyesight, and takes no help from the beauty of colour. But language being the storehouse of all human experience . . . it follows that, of all the arts, poetry soars highest, flies widest, and is most at home in the region of the spirit.[7]

[7] *Op. cit.,* p. 143.

This can be criticized, first, for narrowing poetry down too much to metric verse. The recent tendency has been to admit free or non-metric verse as poetry (for example, that of Walt Whitman); and even to speak of "prose poetry." Second, much of Symonds's account is devoted to repeating the traditional eulogy of poetry as superior to the other arts. This appeals to the literary mind, but is more questionable to others; in any case, a definition should be less evaluative.

Webster gives a special definition of poetry for the field of aesthetics. It is quite in the traditional vein, stressing the old antithesis between free and bound: poetry is—

That form of literature which is characteristically free in its imaginative and emotional range but restricted by its acceptance of a form of expression imposing the conditions of musical beauty, and which, though not bound down to the representation and rational interpretation of that which has happened or may happen in real life, must achieve a kind of truth that is appropriate to the poet's conception and results from integrity of treatment affecting both the details and the fundamental principles.

Such a statement is not even an attempt at objective summary of how the word "poetry" is used in aesthetics. It repeats a special philosophical theory about poetry—one which sounds vague, pompous, and dubious to modern ears.

A little simpler is Webster's general definition of poetry as "the embodiment in appropriate language of beautiful or high thought, imagination, or emotion, the language being rhythmical, usually metrical, and characterized by harmonic and emotional qualities which appeal to and arouse the feelings and imagination . . ."[8] It gives room for non-metrical poetry, while correctly calling the metrical more typical. However, it is too full of evaluative terms, which make the concept hard to apply objectively. Who is to say whether the language is appropriate, and whether the thought is beautiful or high? What are harmonic qualities in poetry?

Webster stresses the narrow conception of poetry as metrical in defining *poem:* "A metrical composition; a composition in verse, either blank verse or rhyme, characterized by imagination and poetic dic-

[8] *Cf.* Colvin's definition of poetry, *Encyc. Brit.*, 11th ed., under "Fine Arts": "a speaking or time art, of which the business is to express and arouse emotion by imitating or evoking all or any of the phenomena of life and nature by means of words arranged with musical regularity."

tion; . . . opposed to prose." In the broader, figurative sense, it is any composition or achievement "marked by a quality or qualities ascribed to poetry, such as expressiveness, elevation, beauty, or artistry." This obscures the fact that, even within the art of poetry, it is not strictly necessary for the product to be metrical.

The *Columbia Encyclopedia* relies on the word "elevation" in distinguishing poetry from mere verse; but acknowledges that all such definitions are debatable theses:

> Some measure of predictable regularity of form seems to be the quality which distinguishes poetry from prose. Regularity of form as a whole (as in the case of the sonnet) is not necessary to poetry, but some predictable regularity, be it one of stress, accent, rime, rhythm, pattern, meter, or cadence, is present in every type of literary creation which is dignified by the name of poetry. It is generally acknowledged that poetry is to be distinguished from verse by the presence of those qualities which are able to create, in the consciousness of the reader or listener, imagination, feeling, emotion, or passion, the nature of which is akin to an elevation of the spirit. Discussion of the nature of these creative qualities is the province of poetical criticism. Diction and sound seem to be dominant; meaning, on the other hand, has been held to be nonessential (and in some few cases even detrimental) to true poetry. Since the real nature of poetry is vague and indistinct, definitions of it are and have been mere theses to be defended.

The definition of poetry involves many special difficulties. These arise partly from the omnipresence of its medium—words; and from the fact that words are used in so many different ways. In some arts, the medium itself is distinctive, and so is the process. But here neither one is especially distinctive; so we have to split hairs very carefully to distinguish the poetic from other kinds of product.

Most writers hardly mention the medium in defining poetry or literature, although it would seem to be relevant, especially when we are contrasting the arts. "A word," says Webster, is "an articulate sound or series of sounds which, through conventional association with some fixed meaning, symbolizes and communicates an idea, without being divisible into smaller units capable of independent use. . . . Hence, the written or printed character, or combination of characters, expressing such a unit of discourse." Perhaps we ought to begin the definitions of "literature" and of its main branches, poetry and prose, by saying, "the art of arranging words . . . ."

Nothing whatever is said, in the definitions quoted above, about the process or technique of writing poetry or other literature. As we noted in an earlier chapter, it was long assumed that creative writing could not be taught; that it was the result of inspiration, and not of any special skill which could be learned. One could only learn the fundamentals of vocabulary, grammar, and syntax, read the great authors, and hope for inspiration. Now there are many books and courses on how to write poetry, novels, short stories, etc.; but apparently no particular procedure in stringing words together, or in reading and speaking them, is regarded as essential. The burden of distinguishing poetry and prose from each other and from other verbal skills thus rests largely on the distinction of product-types.

As to product, two specifications are emphasized in most of the recent definitions of poetry: (a) some predictable regularity of form, not necessarily metrical; and (b) an effect of emotional elevation on the spirit of the reader or listener. It is the second of these which raises difficulties, from the standpoint of form-description. If one tries to describe a kind of form in terms of its effects on the percipient, one encounters the objection that people react in different ways. Some people are "elevated" by what others consider bad, and even "great" poetry does not make everyone feel elevated. Shall we consider only people of "good taste," who know real values? But this again is a debatable question of whose tastes and standards are right. Can we interpret "elevation," not in an evaluative sense as a higher, nobler quality of experience, but as emotional excitement in general? In this sense, even alcohol and drugs can make one feel "elevated." But all poetry bores some people. Moreover, these supposed emotional and spiritual effects are not peculiar to poetry, or to literature. The admirers of every art report similar effects, as from a great novel, painting, cathedral, symphony, etc. Thus the effect of elevation can not well distinguish poetry from other arts. To mention it here is merely to repeat the evaluative conception of all "fine art," which restricts it to the superior, the really beautiful examples of work in each medium. We have already rejected this evaluative conception of art, and of each particular art, in favor of a neutral definition which includes good, bad, and indifferent products. Poetry, like every other art, can be defined in this broadly inclusive way, on ᴀ basis of its observable, non-evaluative traits. This does not deny the possibility and the importance of evaluation in literature; but such evaluation can be expressed otherwise than in the definition itself, simply by saying that this poem is good or beautiful, and that one bad.

Observable traits of form are not limited to those which can be directly sensed. In the case of poetry, they are not limited to the sound of words, as in rhyme and rhythm. They can also include culturally established meanings; suggested ideas, images, desires, emotions. We can agree that a certain piece of writing *suggests* emotional intensity, or expresses an agitated mood—not necessarily of the artist; perhaps of an imaginary character—without saying anything about the emotional effect which the piece of writing will have on readers and listeners. We need not evaluate the piece, or make any dubious assumptions about its actual aesthetic effects, in saying that it has certain suggested emotional traits or factors.

We can describe poetry itself in this way: not as producing any special kind of emotional effect, but as tending on the whole to *suggest* emotional intensity more strongly than non-poetic writing does. There is much calm and even prosaic verse, and prose is often excited. But one tends to expect, in a poem, a greater concentration of emotive images, a less inhibited expression of desire and emotion, than modern occidental adults usually permit themselves in ordinary conversation or in prose writing. In the sympathetic reader or listener, these can arouse latent powers of desire and emotion, and produce a heightened sense of psychic vitality. Poets often deal with subjects of great moral, religious, and philosophic import: with love, birth, death, nature, God, freedom, the future life, the universe as a whole. They suggest escape from the limits of everyday, practical life; often with violent protest against things as they are, and visions of things as they ought to be. When such imagining and intensified emotion are directed along lines which the reader consciously approves and welcomes, he tends to feel the result as "elevation of the spirit." But such responses are extremely variable, depending on the personality of the reader. Hence it is safer to describe the work of art in terms of what it definitely presents and suggests, rather than of how people will respond to it.

The kind of affective intensity and release which characterizes poetry is hard to describe psychologically, and impossible to summarize clearly in a short definition. It involves psychological problems too far-reaching to be dealt with here. It is not mere excitement or expression of violent passion, which often occur in prose (for example, in a "blood-curdling" melodrama or adventure story), and which are often absent in poetry. The poet is often concerned with finding adequate expression for milder but more subtle and uncommon feelings. Many types of desire and fantasy can be easily expressed in prose and ordinary conversation: for example, for more money, physical comfort, social and political advancement, and the more obvious types of sexual success. Others are hard to express in ordinary prose, under present occidental customs and conventions, without embarrassment and fear of ridicule. It would tend to violate a strong acquired prejudice against public expression of one's private, personal feelings. The ordinary adult attitude in talking of love and other intimate personal relations is somewhat taciturn, cynical, and rationalistic; partly as a result of scientific psychology. There is also much inhibition in expressing religious feeling, except in church and other special channels. The skilled prose writer can deal effectively with these or any other subjects, but must usually work up to emotive ideas rather gradually, to build up the necessary state of mind in his reader. In verse, and especially in song, intense and subtle personal feeling of an erotic or other sort can be expressed more immediately and with less fear of ridicule, being more expected and socially approved. Of course, all poetry and poets are regarded somewhat askance by the extremely conventional, practical, and matter-of-fact person.

One of the functions of verse form—that is, of separating poetry into linear units, instead of printing them continuously as in prose—is to give the reader visual notice to expect a kind of expression here which is different from that of ordinary prose, and which asks to be appraised by different standards. Otherwise, he might approach it in a prosaic state of mind, and hence regard it merely as affected prose. The verse form warns him to apperceive it with a special kind of anticipatory set; to read or listen in a certain way; to expect certain traits which are commonly approved in verse but regarded as strained or artificial in prose.

These include certain types of diction called "poetic." They consist not only of literary terms like "thou" and "e'er" (now seldom used), but also of departures from ordinary word order and sentence structure for the sake of rhythm, rhyme, emphasis, and other aesthetic effects. The division of verse into lines is often but not always expressed in speech, as on the stage, by slight pauses or inflections of tone.

Verse form, especially with the aid of music, helps to relax the rigid requirements of logic, practical common sense, and everyday modes of thinking and acting, so as to release the flow of fantasy from partly unconscious levels. Such release and relaxation, again, may occur in prose and not in verse; but verse is more conducive to them. Its rhythms tend to exercise a dreamy, hypnotic effect upon conscious reasoning, and a stimulating effect upon semi-conscious impulses.[9] Its slightly artificial speech facilitates the shift from everyday modes of thought and feeling to a different level. This level is not entirely uninhibited or apart from the current conventions of the time and group; it assumes new literary restrictions of its own; but it does help in escaping some of the ordinary ones. Such a straining toward psychic release and liberated fantasy are not universal in works commonly classed as poetry, many of which are quite the opposite. But they are common enough to be listed as specifications for what is most typical of poetry—for poetry in the fullest sense. There is a poetic type of thought and feeling, as well as a poetic type of diction and verbal arrangement; both are closer to myth and folklore than to modern scientific discourse or other extremely rationalistic prose.

Another contribution which verse form makes to poetic effect is to slow down the process of reading. In the visual reading of prose, such as fiction and news reports, the hurried modern learns to speed quickly down a page, taking in a sentence or paragraph at a glance. He learns to pick out a few key words and to skip over many others. At such a pace, he has no time to dwell upon a single word or phrase, allowing it to reverberate in his mind and call up trains of dreamy association. He tends to grasp only the most common, direct, basic, dictionary meanings of each word. By special effort, or in a leisurely mood, he *can* read prose more reflectively, with pauses for meditation and reverie; but the speed of modern living is not conducive to it. Even in reading verse, the habit of fast, superficial skimming often operates, preventing full appreciation of word-sounds and associations. But verse form gives a slight pressure toward slow, freely associative reading or listening. When correctly spoken aloud, verse is not rushed through but pronounced distinctly, with due observation of the emphases and pauses indicated by division into lines, and by punctuation

[9] A musical accompaniment, as in song, greatly increases this effect. John Dewey calls poetry "next to music, the most hypnotic of all the arts"—attributing this to its "self-sufficiency" as self-enclosed and self-limiting (*Art as Experience*, p. 241).

marks. Usually a slight pause is heard or imagined at the end of a line, though sometimes (for variety) the sentence structure makes one run on to the next without pause. By frequent pauses and the consequent detachment of lines and phrases, the reader is invited to dwell upon a single group of words, long enough to allow their evocative power to operate a little within his mind, calling up vague series of emotive images. These may include some purely private associations, based on his own experiences. But they will also be, in part, culturally determined, as by association in the history or literary tradition of his social group, or in commonly shared emotional experiences.

The distinctive nature of poetry is often said to consist in its power of evoking (as if by magic) an aura of dimly felt, emotional meaning in addition to the basic, dictionary meaning of the words. Poetry differs from science, it is shown, in deliberately cultivating ambiguity; not only double but multiple meanings of a word or phrase, whereas science strives to sharpen down the meaning of each word or sign such as "plus" or "triangle" to a single meaning if possible. (It seldom achieves this goal; most nearly, perhaps, in symbolic logic.) Poetry, on the other hand, constantly strives for words and phrases which will set off emotional trains of association if dwelt upon; images which suggest obscure analogies and hidden symbolism, so that their import reaches far beyond the obvious reference or designation of terms, for those who have the power to grasp it. The deliberate emphasis on obscurity and mystification is a trait of romantic style; but to some extent multiple meaning occurs in all periods of literature. Its effectiveness depends partly on the selection of words and images which have become laden with diverse associations and affects in a particular language and culture; laden with the special affects one desires to evoke, for it is easy to call up the wrong ones. Also, they have to be arranged in the proper context, so as to direct association along the desired lines.

No special "poetic" words are needed; those often used, like "June" and "moon," become hackneyed and cheapened by common association. The cultural bonds on which poetic evocation rests are transitory and unpredictable over long periods. Hence all poetry tends to lose part of its magic in a later day, taking on new meanings which may differ widely from the poet's intentions, for better or for worse. Serious, tender sentiments are especially liable to be ruined by parodies and comic associations. It is hard to take seriously today Keats's line, "Emprison her soft hand, and let her rave."

The term "verse" has several meanings. It refers to a single line or rhythmical sequence of words in poetry; also to "metrical writing; that which is composed in measured rhythms; hence, poetry" (Webster). It is sometimes used for evaluative distinctions, as in saying, "this is real poetry; that is mere verse, or versification." We shall not accept this evaluative contrast. But it is well to preserve a distinction between the two terms. *Verse* can be taken to imply a narrower set of specifications, referring only to the arrangement of words and word-sounds which is characteristic of most poetry, in lines and usually in stanzas, with or without meter and rhyme.

"Poetry," then, can imply this and something more: verse form plus a tendency on the whole toward more concentrated, intense emotional suggestion than is usual in prose; more release of thought and fantasy from ordinary, logical, practical, and other conventions, more use of emotive images (often with partly unconscious symbolic meaning), and special types of diction associated therewith. Thus a composition can be "verse" and not "poetry," as in advertising jingles which deal with prosaic subject-matter in a prosaic way.

Can a composition be poetry and not verse? Rarely; this would be an atypical, borderline case. But we must interpret "verse form" broadly, as including the irregular lines of Whitman and modern "free verse." If the composition or passage has concentrated emotional intensity, psychic release, poetic diction, some verbal rhythm, and yet is printed as continuous prose, it may be called "prose poetry" or "poetic prose." In most periods of history, emotional thought and imagination have found easier expression in verse or dithyrambic chanting. One shifted more often and more gradually back and forth between rhythmic and non-rhythmic utterance. Now, both verse form and poetic thought are somewhat out of fashion, for this is a very rational, scientific, and practical age. Many good writers are so exclusively accustomed to prose form that they would never think of shifting over into verse, even if it were in some respects more appropriate to the thoughts being expressed. They continue to write prose since this is an age of prose, and sometimes contrive to make their prose comparatively poetic.

Poetry is not unique among the arts in thus involving emotional concentration, release of fantasy, and the like. These are common attributes of music, painting, and other arts. But it is hardly necessary to mention them in defining other arts, since those arts are more easily differentiated in terms of medium, process, type of subject represented, etc. Here, as mentioned above, we have to analyze product-types more in detail, so as to differentiate the literary arts on this basis, from other ways of using words.

What, then, is *prose?* Again, the term has a variety of accepted meanings from which we may choose. Webster calls it, first, "the ordinary language of men in speaking or writing"; and, in the same definition, "that genus of literature not cast in poetical measure or rhythm; —opposed to verse and to poetry." By extension, it also means "unimpassioned, unimaginative, sometimes, prosy, discourse or expression," and "that which is prosaic in temper; . . . matter-of-factness." Lowell is quoted as saying: "To see things as they are . . . in the frank prose of undissembling noon."

These meanings are very different, but there is an underlying connection between them. Two large areas are marked off: one, that of ordinary speech; another, that of ordinary thought and feeling, matter-of-fact and unemotional. Prose as an art and a branch of literature falls to some extent within both these areas; at least more so than poetry does. But not entirely, for it varies at times in the direction of poetic rhythm and diction, or in that of emotional fantasy, or both.

Prose as an art and a branch of literary art is, by definition, aimed to some extent at an aesthetic effect. When successful, it is not dull, or prosy in the sense of being stodgy and tedious, concerned with uninteresting details. Good prose stories hold the attention, and often involve much excitement; but as a rule, they work up to the latter gradually. They do not involve the immediate break with everyday reality which we encounter when we start to read poetry, or the concentration of emotive images which follows. [10] On the whole, the great mass of prose literature makes less attempt than most poetry does to escape from ordinary rational and practical modes of thought and expression; to indulge in those remoter flights of fancy, inspired by "divine madness," which Pegasus personified.

[10] "The prosaic," says Dewey, "is an affair of description and narration, of details accumulated and relations elaborated. It spreads as it goes. . . . The poetic reverses the process. It condenses and abbreviates, thus giving words an energy of expansion that is almost explosive" (*Art as Experience*, p. 241).

The exceptions in both poetry and prose are numerous and important, so that no sharp line can be drawn. It is a serious mistake to suppose that prose literature is necessarily "prosaic," unimpassioned, and matter-of-fact. It goes to the opposite extreme in countless fairy tales, mystic visions, and tales of violent passion. The beginning "Once upon a time" warns us not to expect sober, credible fact. Prose is sometimes highly condensed and emotive, as in some short stories. In general, prose is more flexible and adaptable, being suited to all types of thought and expression; whereas poetry tends to restrict itself more to the realm of emotive fantasy. When a composition in verse becomes wordy, diffuse, and pedestrian, it is not regarded as poetic in the full sense. Poetry usually makes a strong effort to avoid being dry, cold, and matter-of-fact, even when its subject-matter is intrinsically as commonplace as Burns's field-mouse. Prose is often intentionally so, especially when it verges over toward science. As a medium, prose writing extends far beyond the limits of prose as literary art, and includes much verbal expression which has no claim to aesthetic appeal. As an art, prose is only a division of the art of literature; but as a medium, it is used in many other fields. Literary prose shades imperceptibly over into scientific prose, ordinary journalistic, business, and conversational prose; so that again there is no sharp distinction and many borderline examples exist.

Several writers on literary theory have objected to the antithesis between poetry and prose, and the identification of poetry with verse. "The word 'prose,'" said R. G. Moulton,[11] "has had to do double duty: there is the 'prose' that is antithetic to 'verse,' and there is the 'prose' that is antithetic to 'poetry.' This has had the effect of identifying 'poetry' and 'verse' even in the most cultured minds." He goes on to argue that the distinction between prose and verse is a superficial one, concerned with rhythm, while that between prose and poetry goes down to the essentials of meaning and matter. "The poet is the creator of an imaginary universe, which he fills with imagined personages and incidents. . . . Modern novels, just as much as the *Iliad* and *Odyssey*, are in the fullest sense poetry. In opposition to this, the literature to be called prose shows no such act of creation; prose is limited to the discussion of what already exists. . . . The great bulk of ancient

[11] *The Modern Study of Literature* (Chicago: Univ. of Chicago Press, 1915), p. 13. *Cf.* Edmund Wilson, "Is Verse a Dying Technique?" in *The Triple Thinkers* (New York: Oxford U. Press, 1948), p. 21.

poetry is in verse. The great bulk of modern poetry is in prose."
Moulton thus makes poetry equivalent to all creative literature, which
adds to the sum of existence. Prose, the discussion of existing things
that does not create, includes history, philosophy, oratory, and letters.
Moulton finds a precedent for this conception of poetry in the original
Greek meaning of a poet as a maker or creator.

Once more we are faced with the need to distinguish between
deeper issues of fact and theory and relatively superficial, verbal issues.
It is one step to point out certain basic, perennial types of literature;
it is another to decide what names should be given them. The fact
that "poetry" has been used in an extremely broad sense by the Greeks,
and by modern critics steeped in classical learning, does not imply
that newer uses of the term are wrong. The consensus of modern usage
recognizes a close connection between "poetry" and "verse," while not
identifying the two. It recognizes verse form (metrical or free) as one
of the typical characteristics of poetry, but not the only one. In the
modern sense of the term, to call a piece of literature "poetry" or "a
poem" strongly suggests verse form. One would be surprised and puzzled to find a passage of prose described as a poem. At the same time,
it is recognized that poetry has other requirements, and that verse
form alone does not entitle a verbal composition to be called "poetry."
The modern concept of poetry implies a set of several specifications,
of which verse is only one. The most typical area, the realm of literature which is poetry in the fullest sense, has all these specifications:
verse form plus poetic diction and meaning. By the same token, a
piece of writing can lack verse form—be written in prose—and still
have other poetic characteristics.

It is not necessary to go to Moulton's extreme in nomenclature—
that is, to narrow down the conception of "prose" to "discussion of
what already exists." Here again, modern usage is overwhelmingly
opposed. It includes as prose all sorts of imaginative fiction and drama,
provided they lack verse form. The distinction between "poetry" and
"prose" today is actually made, in nine cases out of ten, on the basis
of whether the piece is in verse or not. This is the simplest, most objective criterion to apply in practical classification. On the other hand,
it is often hard to distinguish between "what actually exists" and
what does not. Much historical, religious, and philosophical writing,
intended as a sober account of reality, is now considered fantasy. Its
attempts to describe and explain reality are "creative" in their own

way. It is often hard to distinguish between writing which has poetic emotional qualities and that which does not.

In short, the contemporary antithesis between prose and verse is still useful, with prose defined primarily in negative terms, as literature not in verse. The extreme of prosiness in prose is reached when not only verse, but poetic diction and meaning as well are lacking. There is at the same time a large and diversified intermediate realm of literature, comprising poetic verse or poetry at its core and center. At one side, it shades off into non-poetic verse, and at the other into poetic prose.

From the historical point of view, it is well to realize that verse was used much more widely in ancient and medieval literature than it is today; that it was used to express very prosy or non-poetic ideas—for example, on science or practical affairs, as in some passages by Lucretius and Hesiod. Prose, as in the modern novel and most modern drama, is now often used for the expression of poetic ideas. Thus prose as an art has been enriched, partly at the expense of verse, which has somewhat declined in recent years. This makes prose writing often verge toward poetry, but does not qualify it as poetry in the full sense. It is quite true, as Edmund Wilson says, that "the most intense, the most profound, the most beautifully composed, and the most comprehensive of the great works of literary art . . . have been written sometimes in verse technique and sometimes in prose technique . . ." [12] But it does not follow that it is "time to discard the word 'poetry' " or define it in some different way, to take account of this fact. Our policy throughout this book, in choosing between rival definitions, has been to choose if possible a fairly conventional, widely used, current meaning. As we have seen, this does not interfere in the least with recognizing all sorts of important facts, or expressing different evaluations, about the phenomena in question.

It is hardly fair to prose to define it merely in negative terms, as non-poetic, non-metric literature, or as that part of literature which is left over when we take away verse. Prose has its own positive characteristics; its own irregular rhythms, cadences, and euphonies, often subtler than those of verse, and effective aesthetically in their own ways. It has its own ways of expressing thought and feeling, which can rise in value as far above the level of ordinary prose con-

[12] *Loc. cit.*

versation as any art can rise above the unskillful use of its medium. Prose literature is not completely bound to "the ordinary language of men" or to their ordinary thoughts. Its forms, which have been less carefully and less respectfully studied by theorists than those of poetry, are no less varied. They are more adaptable than verse to expressing many basic trends in modern thought: especially to the rationalistic, realistic, and practical attitudes. Most moderns prefer it for all long literary works; Pegasus lags too often when forced beyond a brief lyrical flight, and the struggle to keep him flying through a full-sized epic or dramatic poem exceeds the talents of most writers in this or any other day.

Literature is first defined by Webster in its broad linguistic sense, as "the total of preserved writings belonging to a given language or people"; then as an art: "that part of it which is notable for literary form or expression, as distinguished, on the one hand, from journalistic or other ephemeral literary writing; belles-lettres." A quotation from J. Morley illustrates the latter sense in a strongly evaluative way: "Literature consists of all the books . . . where moral truth and human passion are touched with a certain largeness, sanity, and attraction of form."

Broad as they seem, both senses are too narrow for the greatest usefulness in aesthetics and cultural history. In the first place, they are both restricted to *writing*. This seems reasonable from the etymological standpoint, since "literature" is derived from the Latin word for "letter." But modern scholarship recognizes the importance of a vast body of unwritten literature, transmitted orally in prehistoric and primitive cultures, including recent ones like the American Indian. It is not a contradiction in terms to speak of "oral literature," but a useful extension of the concept beyond its original, etymological meaning. The development of literary forms progressed much farther without the aid of written language than early scholars realized. Ancient written works, once regarded as the beginnings of literature, are now seen to be late and sophisticated by comparison with the unwritten sources out of which they grew. Modern works can be recorded on records or films. We must now revise our conception of literature to include all verbal composition, whether written or oral; or else find a new name for this larger art. The former solution is easier, and is gaining ground.

The second sense, as Morley uses it, is evaluative; hence to be avoided in aesthetics for the reasons noted above. To be most useful in scientific investigation of the arts in human culture, our concept of literature should include bad as well as good poems, plays, and novels; also a good deal of journalistic and other writing which is not sure of immortality. In accord with our general definition of art, it should include not only the good and beautiful works, but all other verbal compositions which are intended to have aesthetic value, and all examples of recognized types such as novels, sonnets, and epics, which are commonly produced with an aesthetic aim. There is nothing to prevent our calling a certain novel bad, merely because we have classed it as a novel, and as a literary product.

If we accept the aesthetic definition of "art" to begin with, it is perhaps enough to go on and define literature as "the art of using words"; or, at greater length, as "the art of combining and arranging written or spoken words and their meanings." If that basic conception of "art" needs repetition, one should add "in ways which commonly produce, or are intended to produce, an aesthetic effect." (The word "aesthetic" must of course be separately defined.)

The nature of the medium—written or spoken words and their meanings—is enough in itself to distinguish literature from all other arts, except from those arts such as song and calligraphy which combine words with other ingredients. Among the ways in which this medium differs from that of other arts is its division into radically different languages, associated with racial and national groups. No other artistic medium differs so much from one cultural group to another. In spite of much parallelism in the meaning of different languages, their differences of sound and syntax produce many associated differences in literary form, between various language groups.

No special types of process or technique are recognized as peculiar to literature, except those based on different types of product. We speak of "dramatic technique," of "versification," or of "the craft of short-story writing." But these are merely names for the general occupation of making dramas, verse, or short stories; they indicate no special technique analogous to carving or casting in sculpture.

The principal types of product can, however, be used to help distinguish literature from other arts, and from the non-artistic use of words. They clarify the concept of literature by indicating its extension and main divisions. The two main product-types are poetry and prose. Each of these can be subdivided, but that is better left for the definitions of poetry and prose themselves. Non-poetic verse and poetic prose are borderline, intermediate divisions of literature.

Literature, then, can be defined as *the art of combining and arranging written or spoken words and their meanings in ways which commonly produce, or are intended to produce, an aesthetic effect. As to linguistic medium, it is divided into English literature, Latin literature, etc. As to form of product, it is divided into poetry, verse, and prose, which are overlapping categories. Poetic prose and non-poetic verse are intermediate between them.*

Poetry is a kind of literature, usually composed in lines or verses, with some regularity (metrical or otherwise) in its arrangement of word-sounds, in addition to comparatively concentrated emotional suggestiveness through emotive images, and a tendency to psychic release in expressions of desire, emotion, and fantasy. It is often ambiguous, suggesting analogies through metaphor and symbol, and expressed in distinctive, appropriate types of language and sentence structure called poetic diction. Literature possessing all these traits is poetry in the fullest sense and most typical form; that possessing some but not all of them is less typical, and is on the borderline between poetry and non-poetic verse, or between poetry and prose. A single, complete product or example of the art of poetry is a poem. Poetry may occur as part of a work which is elsewhere non-poetic; for example, as a lyrical passage in a prose play or novel. Parts of a poem may tend toward non-poetic verse or prose. Among the chief traditional types of poetry and poem are the epic, the lyric, and the poetic drama; also types based on verbal pattern such as the sonnet.

Prose is literature composed in a form which resembles that of ordinary discourse in lacking meter, division into lines or verses, or obvious regularity of word-sounds. It is commonly written in continuous paragraphs. Its emotional suggestiveness, if any, tends to be diffuse and gradual rather than concentrated. It is often unimpassioned, matter-of-fact, and in accord with the practical and logical conventions of ordinary thought and speech; but is not necessarily so, and often goes to opposite extremes. It is highly flexible, and adapted to either fantasy or conscious realism and rationalism. Among the principal types of prose literature are the novel, short story, prose drama, essay, and treatise.

Poetic prose or prose poetry is a kind of literature, written in prose form (not in verses) which possesses one or more of the follow-

ing traits to a degree unusually high for prose: (a) rhythms or pat-
terns of word-sounds; (b) poetic diction; (c) poetic feeling and
imagery.

Verse is a kind of literature, written in separate verses or lines,
and with some regularity of word-sounds, as to rhythm, rhyme, allitera-
tion, or other respects. It includes most poetry, which possesses the
additional qualifications mentioned above, and also non-poetic verse,
which does not.

13. Dancing and ballet; acting; pantomime

"Two subordinate arts," says Symonds, "which deserve a place in
any system of aesthetics . . . are dancing and acting. Dancing uses
the living human form, and presents feeling or action, the passions
and the deeds of man, in artificially educated movements of the
body. The element of beauty it possesses, independently of the beauty
of the dancer, is rhythm. Acting or the art of mimicry presents the
same subject-matter, no longer under the conditions of fixed rhythm,
but as an ideal reproduction of reality. The actor is what he represents,
and the element of beauty in his art is perfection or realisation. It is
his duty as an artist to show us Orestes or Othello, not perhaps as
Othello and Orestes were, but as the essence of their tragedies, ideally
incorporate in action, ought to be. He usually interprets a poet's
thought, and attempts to present an artistic conception in a secondary
form of art, which has for its advantage his own personality in play."

We have already rejected the traditional idea that dancing and
dramatic enactment are subordinate or minor arts. Their importance
in cultural history would indicate otherwise, apart from any question
of general aesthetic value. The tendency of theorists to disparage them
is a survival of many obsolete prejudices, based partly on Puritanical
dislike of bodily beauty and gayety; partly on the inferior social
status of actors and dancers. It is also due in part to the fact that no
way has ever been found until modern times to record and preserve
the art of a great dancer or actor. Choreographic notation is quite
inadequate for that purpose. Only the verbal factor in acting, the
dramatic text, has been preserved, aside from minor stage directions.
This has tended to make historians think of acting, and of theatrical
directing, merely as an application or obedient handmaid of dramatic

writing. The art of countless great actors and dancers has vanished, except for glowing and unreliable accounts by their admirers.

The situation now is changing rapidly. Motion picture photography, with sound and color, has not yet succeeded in recording dancing or acting adequately; but it is on its way to doing so. At the same time, it influences these arts along lines appropriate to its own nature as a medium. It can show subtle details which the old-time theater audience missed. The film, for example, can present in rapid succession different aspects of a dancer or actor, from near and far, left and right, above and below. It can record in exact synchronization the musical accompaniment and the overtone of speech, however soft. This new medium not only records, but helps creative composition, planning, and direction, in cooperation with the written word.

Symonds overemphasizes the factor of representation or "mimicry" in dancing. It is important there, but the directly presented factor is often stressed as much or more. The latter includes, not only rhythm, but all other visual components as well—line, color, texture, solid shape, etc.—all set in motion, and perceived as temporal series. With the aid of theatrical costume and lighting, the dance can become a sequence of complex pictorial or sculptural patterns, fused with musical form. With the aid of stage design, it incorporates perspective vistas into deep space.

Webster's definitions of "dance" are clear and specific. To dance is "to perform, either alone or with others, a rhythmic and patterned succession of movements, commonly to music; to trip, glide, or leap rhythmically." Dance, as a noun, according to this dictionary, is—

A series of movements executed by the body or limbs or both, in rhythm; a measured leaping, tripping, or stepping, commonly in unison with music, hand-clapping, or other rhythmic sounds as an expression of group emotion, a religious rite, a theatrical entertainment, a means of physical education, a social amusement, or, esp. in modern times, as a form of art; also, the act or technique of dancing. . . . As applied to European usage, dance commonly denotes a display of skill in rhythmic motion, sometimes with scenic or mimetic elements. . . .

This agrees with the *Encyclopaedia Britannica's* definition [13] of dancing as "the rhythmical movement of any or all parts of the body

[13] "Dance," by Camilla H. Wedgwood (14th ed.).

in accordance with some scheme of individual or concerted action which is expressive of emotions or ideas."

The primary physical medium, then, is the living body with its powers of movement. But the costume and other accessories sometimes used by the dancer should not be overlooked, for they contribute greatly to the total effect. Notable among them are the masks which transform and sometimes dehumanize the dancer's personality, the flowing scarfs whose curving motion carries out the flow of bodily lines, and the tambourines and castanets which accentuate the rhythm.

Dance as a combined art includes among its materials the rhythmic and usually musical sound accompaniment, and the drums or other instruments which make it. Lighting, whether of torches or electric spotlights, is a contributing factor.

Ballet has come to mean "a theatrical dance of an aesthetic character; esp., an ensemble dance. . . . A kind of artistic dancing distinguished from all others by the greater variety, intricacy, and expressiveness of its movements" (Webster). In ballet, as a variety of theater art, the medium takes in all the complex apparatus of the stage, including scenery and ramps or platforms, static or moving. As a combined art, ballet includes three main component arts: dance, music, and décor; the last of which includes several visual arts such as costume, scenery, lighting, and other stage equipment. In addition, a director is required to coordinate them.

The product of dance or dancing as an art is *a* dance or ballet; also the choreographic score or other directions for one of these. As a form, a dance is mobile and temporal; developed in three dimensions of space and in time. To the onlooker, it is usually audio-visual, with the visual factor predominating. The visual rhythms are synchronized with and to some extent aided by the auditory. Sometimes the dancers produce rhythmic sounds, as in tapping the feet or shouting a war-cry, but usually the sounds are made by others. To the dancer himself, his art is strongly kinetic and kinesthetic as well as visual and auditory; he communicates these kinesthetic suggestions as part of the total form. They, in turn, may suggest moods, characters, and stories.

The creation or composition of ballets, especially the dance element in them as distinguished from the music and décor, is called "choregraphy" or "choreography." These names are also applied to the processes and symbols of notation in which dance forms are written down, as directions for performance. The more restricted term "steno-choregraphy" is sometimes used for the notation alone, as distinct from the creative planning. The art of figure skating has also developed a system of notation to direct complex movements on ice by individuals or groups.[14]

Both dancing and ballet are usually performed on a stage or on the ground. But recently, the term "ballet" has been extended to organized group movements with artistic purpose, executed by ice skaters, roller skaters, swimmers on the surface, or swimmers under water in glass tanks.[15] The movements of these last seem to approximate flying. The mass evolutions of aviators also resemble ballets in certain respects, and can be performed as a spectacle. Rhythmic movements of abstract forms, as in the film, have been called "dances." Thus the basic ideas of dance as an art of rhythmic movement, and of ballet as an art of group rhythmic movement, can be extended far beyond their narrow, traditional meanings.

Let us now reword the definitions of "dance" and "ballet" as follows:

Dance is an art of rhythmic bodily movement, presenting to the observer an ordered sequence of moving visual patterns of line, solid shape, and color. The postures and gestures of which these are made suggest kinesthetic experiences of tension, relaxation, etc., and emotional moods and attitudes associated with them. They may also represent imaginary characters, actions, and stories. Dances are performed by one person or by two or more in mutual coordination; some animals and marionettes can be made to dance. The movements are usually synchronized with, and partly aided by, musical or other rhythmic sounds. In theatrical forms, they are often combined with appropriate effects of décor (costume, scenery, lighting, and other stage equipment). They are planned and to some extent recorded through choregraphic notation, sketches, films, and otherwise. Styles of dance include primitive ritual enactments, symbolic gesture, as in India, peasant and rustic folkdance patterns, the light toe-dancing of the classic European ballet, Greek revivals, and modern experiments in decorative and expressive movement. A great variety of interests and motives have influenced the dance at various times, including magic,

[14] See "Skating," *Encyc. Brit.*, 14th ed.
[15] See cover and p. 13 of *Life*, Aug. 27, 1945.

religion, group solidarity, physical education, theatrical entertainment, and recreation.

Ballet is a variety of dance, or of other group movements in rhythm for artistic or entertainment purposes, usually presented in a theater by dancers moving in complex coordination with the aid of music and décor. It usually involves the dramatic enactment of a story through pantomime, as well as the presentation of changing visual designs in ordered sequence.

Social or ballroom dancing is a popular type of group dancing, performed in couples or larger groups, for mass participation rather than for observation, and consisting of simpler forms requiring less technical skill.

Acting, according to Webster, is "the art or practice of performing or impersonating upon the stage." This is at once too broad and too narrow. Acting does not include instrumental musical performance on the stage. On the other hand, acting does not need to be on a stage; it may be in a film, radio or television studio, or in a circus, a living-room, or a public square; in fact, anywhere. It is usually classed as a theater art because the most important acting is thought to be performed or represented there; but, strictly speaking, acting is not restricted to the stage or theater as a physical structure.

Acting overlaps the art of musical performance, as in opera and dramatic concert singing, where impersonation is required. It overlaps the art of dancing; the latter, being frequently dramatic, involves acting ability. It differs from dancing in not developing the decorative sequence of movements as elaborately. Representation is a dominant aim in this art, and grace of movement is often sacrificed to it.

Pantomime, as a distinct art, is a kind of acting or dramatic performance in which characters and stories are represented by "dumb show," or mimetic gesture and facial expression, usually without words. It is now seldom practiced as an independent art,[16] but forms an important factor in most acting and theatrical dancing. In ballet, words are usually dispensed with, and the dance is a combination of pantomime and decorative movement, with varying emphasis on one or the other. Pantomime as mimetic gesture and facial expression occurs along with words and music in the primitive dance and in modern vaudeville. It occurs along with words in most visible acting.

---

[16] E. Souriau classes it as one of the fourteen principal arts, and as the representative correlate of dancing (*La correspondance des arts,* p. 97).

In the silent motion picture, pantomime was supplemented by printed words. Mimetic action in the primitive dance and religious ritual was supposed to have a magical function in causing the sort of action or event portrayed—for example, rainfall or successful hunting.

Speech is usually an important part of acting, and may be all-important, as when the actor is not seen over the radio. Hence acting, to this extent, is bound up with literature, and constitutes its chief mode of overt performance. It is sometimes regarded as a mere speaking aloud of the printed text. But it can become far more than that. The printed text leaves so much unspecified as to manner of utterance, accompanying gesture and facial expression, etc., that the actor is forced to work out these factors in the performance more or less independently. Furthermore, acting varies greatly as to the extent to which it endeavors to follow out the intentions of the writer, or the literal implications of the text. The actor always infuses his own personality to some extent; often a great deal when he is famous and independent; [17] or he may have to follow the director's ideas as to what the public will like.

Acting also resembles the process of ritual or ceremonial observance, as in a church. The Christian clergyman does not usually impersonate anyone, though some of his acts are symbolic. But some rituals are also dramatic enactments, especially in primitive cultures, and some priests therefore have to *act,* in the dramatic sense of the word. The representation may be stylized and mixed with abstract symbolism, as in the sacrificial killing of an animal to symbolize the death of the god.

Let us now redefine "acting" as: *the art of representing an imaginary character, or a real one other than the actor himself, usually in a dramatic performance, through suggestive traits of speech, gesture, carriage, facial expression, or a combination of these, often with the aid of appropriate costume, makeup, accessories, and other theatrical equipment.*

The representation of a real character, such as another well-known actor, is now commonly called "impersonation." This term can also be applied to all dramatic representation.

Acting and dramatic dancing are often called "mimicry" (*Mimik,* in German). But this implies too narrow a conception; they involve

[17] See Marcel Proust's comment on Berma's acting of Racine (*The Guermantes Way,* New York, 1930, p. 57).

not only imitation but creative imagination and the production of new, original forms.

Certain constituent skills in the art of acting are also practiced elsewhere, and can be regarded as independent arts: for example, that of *oral diction, eloquence, or elocution.* This skill is closely related to literature, and may involve the speaking of non-dramatic literature, such as poetic lyrics and prose orations. "Eloquence" is sometimes listed as a fine art in its own right; it once enjoyed high social status, as kings and nobles were not ashamed to be orators.

The definition of acting, just proposed, covers medium, process, and product. It does not imply, of course, that an actor always uses all these means, or that he aims only at representation. He may rely solely on pantomime. His performance as a whole may include, not only acting, but also dancing, flute-playing, juggling, or any other kind of entertainment; he may also be a stage director and a playwright. Many actresses appeal to the public more through their physical beauty than through their acting ability. This does not affect the correctness of defining the art of acting itself in the restricted way proposed.

14. Drama and theater

The term "theater arts" is applied to a group of arts which are usually concerned with performance in a theater, especially of plays or drama. Their interrelations are complex and important, and there is great ambiguity in the terms used to designate them.

The primary meaning of "theater" is "an edifice for dramatic performances or spectacles." By association, it is applied to such dramatic performances themselves, and also to their written texts: "The drama, esp. that of some specified country or period. Dramatic literature or representation; as, the British theater; the modern theater. Dramatic works collectively, as, the theater of Dryden." Also, to "Material or method suitable for a theatrical production; as, a play is not good theater." The word *theatrics* is available, but not in common use, to mean "the art of producing effects suitable to theatrical presentation." (All these definitions are from Webster.) What Webster does not make quite clear is that "theater" is also commonly used as a name for the whole realm of theatrical presentation, with all the various arts involved.

"Drama" is also applied to dramatic literature and to the art of dramatic representation; it is, says Webster—

1. A composition, now usually in prose, arranged for enactment, and intended to portray life or character, or to tell a story by actions and, usually, dialogue tending toward some result based upon them; a play. It is designed, or composed as though designed, to be performed by actors on the stage. 2. Hence, in a generic or collective sense, dramatic art, literature, or affairs; as, a person skilled or versed in drama; a devotee of the drama.

We thus have three basic ideas: (a) the theater building, with its physical equipment; (b) a literary text, or group of them, written for performance in a theater, or as if for such performance; (c) theatrical presentation or dramatic enactment, usually on the stage of a theater.

Each of these ideas indicates a different type of medium, process, and product: a different art or group of arts. Meaning *a* is concerned with architecture; a theater building is a product of architecture and its associated skills, such as electric lighting and acoustic engineering. Its form is largely determined by its function: to provide a setting for theatrical presentation; also, by prevailing styles in architecture and other visual arts. *Theater designing and construction* is thus a branch of architecture and allied arts.

Meaning *b* is concerned largely with a branch of literature: the written drama, in prose or poetry. It is, of course, intimately bound up with dramatic performance; a drama is a set of directions for such details of the acting and staging. However, the drama as literature also has its own separate life apart from the theater. It is read silently and discussed like any other branch of literature. Its medium and skills are different, being mainly concerned with the arrangement of words as written symbols. To avoid confusion, it should be called by a different name. It is more commonly called "drama" than "theater," and the latter name should be avoided in this connection. When there is danger of confusion, one can specify "literary drama," "dramatic literature," "dramatic text," "dramatic script," "dramatic writing," or "playwriting." The definition can be reworded in this sense:

Drama: a verbal composition adapted or arranged as if adapted for theatrical performance; consisting usually of words to be spoken, and usually containing some directions for acting and other details of performance; a play; also, the art of writing such compositions. Main

types of drama are tragedy, comedy, tragicomedy, miracle play, moral-
ity play, opera, farce, melodrama, and film drama or photoplay.

The term "drama" is sometimes restricted to one of these types of play or film, especially that containing tense and serious emotional conflict; but the word in this sense is likely to be misunderstood, and is not recommended. The definition of drama proposed is broad enough to include scripts or written sets of directions for pantomime, containing no words to be spoken, and not intended to appeal as literature. These would, however, not be typical examples of drama.

Meaning *c* refers to presentation or performance. Although usually in a theater building (including amphitheaters, arenas, etc.), it may be given elsewhere. Shakespeare is sometimes presented on a lawn or in a public square, with no stage. Film dramas are presented mechanically in a theater, but not performed there by the actors. In a theater, many things besides dramas can be performed: concerts, lectures, religious services, etc. Nevertheless, the association between drama and theater is so close that each tends to suggest the other.

When this sense is intended, we can avoid confusion by saying "dramatic enactment," "dramatic presentation," or "dramatic perform-ance" instead of the vaguer terms "drama" and "dramatic art." "Theatrical presentation or performance" is equally clear. The term "theatrics" has not found much favor, but "theater arts" is in common use. The plural is favored because of the extreme diversity of skills involved. Our revised definition is as follows:

Theater arts or *theatrics: the arts or combined art of producing*
effects suitable to theatrical presentation or dramatic enactment,
especially of spoken dramas in a theater building. They include as
cooperating skills and as factors in the product, the arts of acting,
directing, scene designing, staging, costuming, make-up, lighting,
music, dancing, and films. Both actual performance of these arts and
writing, planning, directing, preparing, or designing for them are
included. Plays, operas, vaudeville shows, and ballets are common
types of theatrical performance.

15. Motion pictures; cinema; film. Animated cartoons

This is a new art, which is undergoing rapid, fundamental changes, both in technique and in the artistic uses of technique. It has not yet found a single, universally accepted name. It is not, of course, considered in traditional aesthetic classifications of the arts. As we have seen, it upsets many cherished assumptions about the arts—for example that painting is purely a space art and an art of rest, not a time art.

The name "cinema" is now favored in Europe, but little used in the United States, where the art has received much of its early development. It is short for "cinematography," which Webster defines as "the science and art of producing the illusion of motion with the aid of the motion picture," and from "cinematograph," a motion picture camera or projector. "Cinema" itself, says Webster, is "a motion picture; also, with *the,* motion pictures collectively." The name "cinematography" is analogous to "photography," but is too long for popular use. "Motion picture" is defined by the same source as "a series of pictures, usually photographs presented to the eye in very rapid succession, with some or all of the objects in the picture represented in successive positions slightly changed, and producing, because of the persistence of vision, the optical effect of a continuous picture in which the objects move. Specif., a photoplay." "Film" is defined there as "a thin, flexible, transparent sheet of cellulose nitrate or acetate or similar material coated with a light-sensitive emulsion, used for taking photographs. . . . Hence, a motion picture; also, in the plural or attributively, motion pictures collectively." Only one of these definitions refers to an *art,* but current discussion is full of references to "motion picture art," "cinema art," and "the art of the film."

The word "film" refers primarily to one of the materials used in this art: to the strip of film on which the scenes are photographed, and also to the strip which is afterward run through the projector in showing the pictures on a screen. By extension, and because it is a short, easy word, it has come to mean also the whole art of planning, producing, and presenting motion pictures.

History is full of such extensions in meaning, where the concept of a particular material or technique is enlarged to take in a group of associated products, and perhaps a group of other materials and techniques also used to make such products. The result is ambiguous, as to whether the word is meant in its original or extended sense; but experience has shown that the latter may become thoroughly accepted and understood with little confusion. There is little difficulty as long as the original material or technique remains in wide use for making that kind of product. But what if motion pictures come to be made, in future, without the use of films? Then the question would arise whether they ought still to be called "film art." Other things being equal, it is well to start with a name which is likely to survive a long time, so that discussion of the art can be continuous. Moreover, "still" photography is also a film art.

Both "cinema" and "motion pictures" refer primarily to a type of product: to the apparent motion of the pictures presented. Hence they could be applied to the art of making such pictures even though films were no longer used. "Cinema" has been taken over into many languages, sometimes as *Kiné*. "Motion pictures" is more cumbersome, which accounts for its popular shortening into "movies"; also, it is not easily taken over into other languages. "Moving pictures," in a broad sense, would include the ancient shadow-play. "Cinema" is to be preferred on the whole, but all three names will probably be used for some time to come.

The word "photoplay" was once suggested as a name for the art and its products, but is now seldom used.[18] One reason is that so many important films are not "plays" or dramas, but "documentaries," "newsreels," and the like, photographed directly from real life and not "acted out." We still speak of "film plays" and "film dramas" to specify this particular kind of product.

Some films, called "abstract," present non-representative or highly stylized sequences in line, light, and color. Having at present no great popular appeal, they are usually made as amateur experiments, but they have great future possibility from an artistic standpoint. Since the term "picture" usually implies representation, the question arises whether abstract films should be classed as motion pictures.

The definitions quoted do not adequately cover the nature of this art. Because of its rapid change, it will need frequent redefinition. For today, we suggest the following definitions:

Cinema, motion pictures, or film: the art of composing, producing, and presenting on a screen sequences of visual forms, usually pictures, in which scenes and objects apparently move and change, usually with the accompaniment of audible speech and other sound; especially by means of cameras, films, and projectors adapted to this purpose. Presentation, which is mechanical and largely automatic, is accomplished through projecting on the screen, through a long film strip, a series of still pictures, each shown for a fraction of a second, in which

[18] The United States Copyright Office distinguishes between "Motion Picture Photoplays" (Class L) and "Motion Pictures other than Photoplays" (Class M).

some of the objects are shown successively in slightly changed positions, so that the eye interprets them as moving. Synchronized sounds are now produced through a visible track at the side of the film. The art as a whole, which is highly complex and diversified, includes that of composing the story, script, dialogue, music and other sound effects, and color effects if any, directing and acting the performance which is to be recorded, cutting and editing the film to recombine selected sequences in desired ways; also designing and executing sets, costumes, make-up, lighting, and special effects such as montage. The products, most of which are dramatic, differ from ordinary stage dramas in many ways, especially the rapid changing of viewpoint so that successive moments in a story may be seen in the most effective ways; also the freedom and variety of scenic backgrounds. Most films are photographed directly from living actors; some are photographed in whole or part from series of drawn or painted pictures, so that objects in these seem to move; these are now called "animated cartoon films." Abstract or semi-abstract films present non-representational sequences of shapes and colors. Some types of film product aim more at education or information than at entertainment through story-telling. These are called documentary films, newsreels, and educational films; by their use, many subjects are concisely and vividly taught. Films are also used for advertising and propaganda.

A better name is needed for the important type of film just referred to as "animated cartoons." That name suggests the funny, and often crudely childish, pictures of the newspaper "comic strip." It was appropriate for some of the early stages of this type of film, such as those of *Mickey Mouse* by Walt Disney. But his later productions involve complex and subtle pictorial effects, some of which are adapted to a mature artistic taste, as in *Fantasia*. These are apparently moving paintings, rather than moving photographs of real people. "Mobile painting" would be a fairly accurate name for this type of motion picture, or at least for the visual factor in it. Such films are usually synchronized with musical or other sound accompaniment. *Fantasia* was unusual in that well-known musical compositions were taken as basic frameworks, and the visual sequences fitted into these to produce a combined audio-visual form.

16. Radio and television

At the present time, these are not fully developed arts, but new and important means of communication. They are devices whereby a performance can be presented to the ears and eyes of millions of observers, far from where it is given, but at the same time.

The cinema was in a similar condition in its infancy—that of an instrument, a potential new medium of art, which had not yet developed into an art in its own right. At first, it was used to record and reproduce other arts; works composed, not expressly for the motion picture camera, but for the stage and concert hall. Later, its peculiar capacities and limitations led to new types of product; new forms of dramatic and other art, which could not have been made by any other means. The concept of "motion pictures" expanded to imply these new types of product, in addition to a certain medium and process. At the same time, the medium and process themselves developed, to include not only the improved cameras, films, and projectors, the spotlights and sound-devices, but also the actors and other experts whom the film director could manipulate, with all their individual skills.

The radio has already begun to evolve distinctive types of art form, different from those of stage and film. Now, when many radio performers are still invisible, there is great development of auditory effects, both musical and imitative. This is just the opposite of the film's early development, in its silent period, when everything had to be conveyed through the eyes. There is an extreme speeding up and "streamlining" of plays and music, to come within the short timespans allowed. Snatches of music are used to indicate breaks in the action, elapsed time, change of place, etc. Short sentences and words with vivid imagery are used. These are the beginnings of a new type of radio art-form. It is now often joined with television, so that it does not have to rely so much on auditory means. This evolution to an audio-visual stage will stimulate certain lines of growth and discourage others, as in the case of the film. It remains to be seen what new types of form, dramatic and otherwise, will be evolved. Until then, radio-television can not be regarded as an art, but only as a new medium and process, of great artistic potentiality, now in a rudimentary stage.

17. Mobile light and color. Fireworks. Lumia; the clavilux

The display of colored objects in motion is a common factor in the visual arts. Sometimes the visible change and motion are only slightly controlled, as in ordinary clothing, where the movement of the wearer, under different lighting conditions, alters the color-effect of the costume. Definite control of the temporal sequence of color changes is more carefully developed in some types of theater art: in stage scenery, lighting, costume, and gesture; in ballets and other spectacles. In a carefully planned garden, the multicolored flowers blow in the wind, grow and fade, slowly changing their harmonies of hue in a prearranged sequence as the season advances. Motion pictures are using color sequences more and more systematically, through color photographs of "real" objects and of paintings. Artistic film direction makes careful use of contrasts and transitions from one color scheme to the next. Electric advertising signs can change color in simple, prede-termined cycles.

In all these arts, mobile color is combined with other factors, often in a very subordinate way. In costume, it is subordinate to various utilitarian considerations; in most films, to the needs of realistic repre-sentation. But artists and theorists have long wondered whether it could be divorced from such connections and developed in its own right, more or less abstractly, as sounds are developed in music: that is, into temporal sequences of different color designs, to be enjoyed for their own sake rather than for their representative or other meanings. The kaleidoscope can produce a series of color designs in a mechanical, accidental way, but without much contrast or temporal development.

Fireworks or pyrotechnics are an ancient art, highly developed and esteemed in China. They are popular throughout the civilized world, especially to entertain large crowds on the occasion of a holiday or other celebration, such as Bastille Day in Paris. Webster defines them as devices "for producing a striking display, as of light, noise, or smoke, by the combustion of explosive or inflammable compositions, for exhibition, signaling, illumination, or the like." In so far as sound enters, fireworks are audio-visual; but the audible element is so simple and crude, as a rule, that only the visual element now deserves consid-eration as an art.

Sometimes fireworks are representative, and as realistic as the medium permits, as in "set pieces" which imitate the appearance of an animal, flower, or human face. But these are less characteristic than the non-representative displays produced by sky-rockets, pinwheels, and other devices. One quality which distinguishes fireworks from most other kinds of mobile color is their extreme luminescence; these multi-colored flashes, flames, and sparks radiate intense light themselves, out of a black sky. Most paintings and textiles, and even the images on a motion picture screen, merely reflect light rather weakly from another source. (Luminous paint and translucent screens are still exceptional.) Temporal sequences are developed, in the most elaborate rockets, through having different charges burn one after the other, producing a series of patterns and showers of sparks. They are organized in shape as well as in color and texture: for example, as radiating or fringe-like patterns. Their meteoric speed and brevity are at once a limitation and a source of charm; one can never contemplate them at leisure; they soar and burst above us with breathtaking power and immensity, then vanish before we can tire of them. They possess to an unusual degree that evanescence which poets find in all beautiful things. Even the most extended sequences of effects are short, compared to those of music and ballet; seldom more than a few seconds in duration. Hence there is no building up of sustained progressions or really complex temporal forms, capable of acting gradually and profoundly on the spectator's emotions. Perhaps, through the use of neon tube and other kinds of illumination, more easily controlled than burning chemicals, some of the spectacular power of fireworks can be combined with more complex development and subtlety.

The most promising approach to mobile color as an independent art now seems to be that of projecting colored electric lights upon a screen before an audience. By this means, as much intensity can be produced as the human eye can stand. Colors can be made to change fast or slowly, or to stand unchanged. Linear shape is controlled, and illusions of the third dimension are given.

In addition to abstract films, the principal device for this purpose is the Clavilux, invented by Thomas Wilfred.[19] He has composed and

---

[19] See T. Wilfred, "Light and the Artist," *Journal of Aesthetics*, Vol. V (June, 1947), p. 247; "Composing in the Art of Lumia," *Ibid.*, Vol. VII, No. 2 (Dec., 1948), p. 79. See also discussion between Wilfred and E. M. Blake in the same *Journal* for March, 1948 (Vol. VI), p. 265. Blake suggests the name "mobile graphics" instead of lumia.

performed a number of compositions for it, using a notation which he has devised for the purpose, and has written theoretically about the future possibilities of the art. He has suggested that the art be called "lumia," and this name is coming into use. Although technical difficulties and other obstacles have delayed the spread of lumia to a wide group of performers, its potentialities are so unique and obviously great as to justify its inclusion in a list of established arts.[20] It may become a major art in future.

Lumia has been popularly described as "color music." It has many analogies with music: notably its presentation as a time art, and its comparative lack of representation; its emphasis on the direct aesthetic effect of changing sensory stimuli in ordered groups and sequences. It is sometimes presented in combination with music, to produce an audio-visual form; but Wilfred objects to this subordination of lumia to music. He insists on its ability to stand on its own feet as a silent visual art, and on the fallacy of the old belief that an exact correspondence exists between sounds and colors. He usually presents his recitals silently, in an auditorium with a screen shaped much like a motion picture screen, but translucent and placed between the audience and the source of light.

The element of representation is absent or slight in Wilfred's own compositions, but the colors are often presented in definite shapes, geometrical or otherwise. Many of these suggest abstract resemblances to nature and the outside world, such as sunsets, steel girders, and flower forms. Such resemblances are usually subordinate factors in the composition, as they are in music. Another composer might prefer to develop them further, or combine the forms with music; lumia is flexible enough to permit many different lines of progress. But Wilfred has chosen the lines in which his art seems able to proceed most independently and distinctively. Presenting it in combination with music tends to make it a mere accompaniment; increasing realistic representation would tend to compete with motion pictures.

In so far as cinema is used for abstract or non-representational sequences of shape and color, as it is by a few experimental filmmakers, it overlaps the field of lumia and competes with it as a medium. At present, films have an element of flicker from the succession of still

---

[20] This has been recognized by articles in standard reference works: for example, "Clavilux," *Encyc. Brit.*, 14th ed.; "Clavilux" and "Lumia" in *Encyc. of the Arts*, New York, 1946.

images, by contrast with which a clavilux performance is smooth and flowing; but films may overcome this disadvantage. Film-making now lacks spontaneity, the power of direct, immediate expression by a performer on his instrument. Each film must be elaborately and artificially made, long in advance of performance. The clavilux player can sit down and improvise. But this instrument now presents grave difficulties in construction, performance, and repair. It needs simplification.

In a statement written for this book, Wilfred has described "lumia" as "a silent visual art in which the artist's sole medium of expression is light." He defines it as follows: *first, in terms of the artist's object or aesthetic concept, it is the use of light as a medium for artistic expression through the silent visual treatment of form, color, and motion in dark space with the object of conveying an aesthetic experience to a spectator; second, in terms of the physical basis or means employed, it is the composition, recording, and performance of silent visual sequences in form, color, and motion, projected on a white screen by means of a light-generating instrument controlled from a keyboard.*

Wilfred adds—

Lumia is built on a neutral foundation of darkness as music is built on silence. The lumia artist conceives his idea as a three-dimensional evolution of light in dark space. In order to materialize his idea for presentation before the spectator, he must execute it as a two-dimensional sequence of form, color and motion projected on a flat white screen. This he achieves by means of a specially designed light projection instrument, such as the clavilux, in which light from a number of individual sources can be molded into changing form, color and motion and the result projected on the screen so as to create an illusion of volume and depth. The projection instrument is played from a keyboard resembling a pipe-organ console, but equipped with sliding keys. While composing, the artist records the key movements in a special notation from which a skilled player (lumianist) can perform the work with as much latitude for personal interpretations as in music.

Webster defines "clavilux" as "an instrument, invented by Thomas Wilfred, for throwing upon a screen varying patterns of light and color which permit combinations analogous to the successive phrases and themes of music;—called often color organ."

Future technical improvements, perhaps combining some of the advantages of film and clavilux, will doubtless permit developments in mobile light and color which are now unforeseen. For example, the presentation is not necessarily restricted to a rectangular screen. It can cover the walls and ceiling of a room. It can be used outside at night, to play over walls, clouds, smoke, or water. But such dispersions tend to weaken the compactness of the form, and its power of definite, complex organization. Lumia is already used in various accessory functions, as in providing backgrounds for stage drama.

XII

Summary and Recommendations

The foregoing chapters are partly historical, partly theoretical, and partly practical. Beginning with the present situation, with current ideas about the nature and interrelation of the arts, we have looked backward in cultural history, to see how this situation came to exist. We have analyzed the present situation, to reveal the serious ambiguities of terminology and the survival of old, mistaken beliefs, which hamper clear thinking and investigation of the arts. We have observed the practical uses and influence of theories about the arts, and have suggested, at various points, possible improvements in this conceptual apparatus.

1. Historical backgrounds

The historical parts of this book deal with two connected threads in the development of modern thought. One is the history of the concept of fine arts; the other, the history of theories about the classification or systematic interrelation of the arts.

In Chapter II, on "The Concept of Fine Arts," we began with the origin of the English term "fine arts" in the eighteenth century, and traced its meanings—the history of the ideas then attached to it—backward in time through France and Germany, Italy and Greece, to the time of Plato. Out of the original conception of "art" in a broad, technical sense, including all useful skills, we saw the rise of distinctions between different kinds of art, conceived as higher and lower, liberal and servile. This distinction was made largely from an aristocratic point of view, from the Greek period through the eighteenth century, according to which arts were deemed suitable for a freeman or nobleman. But opinions changed considerably as to which particular arts were thus suited. Some of the visual, manual arts rose in social status during and after the Renaissance. The distinction between liberal and servile also implied psychological and moral assumptions about the relative amount of mental or spiritual ability required in various arts, and the effects of different arts in elevating or debasing the spirit. In and after the eighteenth century, the distinction was made more on a hedonistic basis—as to whether the art was aimed mainly at arousing aesthetic pleasure, or at satisfying man's material needs. However, the older associations of high social status, intellectual and moral superiority, still hovered around the group of arts now singled out as "liberal," "polite," "elegant," "beautiful," or "fine." It consisted chiefly of the so-called major arts of poetry, music, painting, sculpture, and architecture. Opinions were divided on whether drama, the dance, and the "minor useful" arts should be included, but there was a gradual tendency to admit them, at least under some conditions.

From the eighteenth century onward, the word "art" and its equivalents in other European languages came to be understood more and more with aesthetic and often hedonistic associations. It became, therefore, less and less necessary to use the prefix "fine" to distinguish the aesthetic arts from other, more utilitarian skills. The latter came to be called, not "arts," but applied sciences, industries, technics, technologies, or branches of engineering. Hence the single word "art" or "arts" gradually replaced, to a large extent, the term "fine arts." The latter term persisted, but with confusingly ambiguous meaning, since it was sometimes understood as covering only certain visual arts (painting, sculpture, architecture, and perhaps the "minor" useful or decorative arts); at other times as including also poetry, music, dancing, and drama.

In Chapter III on "The Meanings of Art," after distinguishing the various current meanings, we traced some further historical trends from the eighteenth century to the present time. Our attention was directed especially to theories about the proper definition of "art," including its relation to "beauty" and "pleasure." At the time of Kant, fine art was conceived as a kind of skill which aimed at beauty, the source of which was pleasure without practical advantage. The problem arose of whether the mere aim or intention of beauty was enough; whether a product must actually *be* beautiful to deserve the name of "art," and if so, how to decide whether it was or was not beautiful. The hedonistic conception of beauty was accepted by some theorists, who defined it as power to convey a pleasurable impression to the spectator or listener, apart from any thought of personal advantage. Art would then be conceived as a kind of skill or product which had this power, although it was not always easy to agree upon in a particular case. Several later theorists objected to the term "pleasure," because of the weaknesses in eighteenth century hedonism. But some of them kept a closely related definition of art, in terms of "power to satisfy aesthetically."

In Chapter III, we considered Tolstoy's attack on the "beauty-pleasure" definition of art, and also his substitute: that art is the "expression and communication of remembered emotion." There were difficulties in this wording also, it appeared. As abstractly stated, it would include a great deal which is not usually classed as "art"; but as Tolstoy himself applied it, the definition would leave out all or most of the works of Wagner, Beethoven, Ibsen, Monet, and others commonly recognized as great artists. There was much to be said for Tolstoy's philosophy of art in general, but his definition of the term "art" seemed inexpedient.

In Chapter IV, on "Different Kinds of Art," we saw how the hedonistic conception of art had been subjected to further attacks up to the present time. It had made, said recent critics, too sharp an antithesis between *fine* and *useful* art; between *beauty* and *utility;* between the *aesthetic* and the *practical.* Such a mistaken separation, it was charged, had been perpetuated in the nineteenth century doctrine of "art for art's sake" and in the "ivory tower" conception of art as something esoteric and aloof from everyday life. The result, it was charged, had been to weaken art by restricting it to a sterile, trivial pursuit of pleasure, and to make practical life more ugly than it need be, through divorcing it from art.

In recent years, the justice of this argument has been generally conceded. Recent definitions of "art" or "fine art" have been careful not to exclude the arts combining utility with beauty, and it is further agreed that all the arts can have valuable social functions. At the same time, in justice to eighteenth century aestheticians, we saw that few if any of them actually made the extreme separation alleged by modern critics. It has never been seriously maintained, by any considerable school of thought, that a thing cannot be useful and at the same time beautiful; or that the fine arts are or should be entirely separate from the useful arts.

In Chapter V, on "Philosophical Classifications of the Arts," we went back again to the eighteenth century as a starting-point; this time to follow another thread in the history of ideas up to the present.

Since there was no clear conception of fine or aesthetic arts before 1700, there would naturally be no attempts to *classify* such arts systematically. But there were partial anticipations of this modern philosophical development, in the writings of Aristotle, Augustine, Francis Bacon, and others.

Since Lessing (1766), the problem has been under almost continuous discussion, especially in Germany, where philosophical systems have often included a division on aesthetics, and in it a section on the *system of the arts*. Lessing's distinction between arts of space and of time has been used ever since, with various interpretations. His service in directing attention to problems of aesthetic form has been somewhat offset by the repressive effect of his theory that each art (especially painting and poetry) has a more or less definite, permanent field of its own, with limits which it should not cross into the domain of another art. Kant's division of the arts, as we saw, covered a longer list of arts, and grouped them much more systematically. His basic division is into (a) arts of speech, (b) plastic or shaping arts, and (c) arts of the beautiful play of sensations. This division, with the subheadings under each class, is somewhat cumbersome today. Nevertheless, it is fairly objective and empirical. It stays close to observable facts as he knew them at the close of the eighteenth century, and is not bound up with any grandiose metaphysical system.

After Kant, a factual approach to the problem was long impeded by the transcendental speculations of Hegel, Schopenhauer, and other metaphysical system-builders. It was impeded also by the persistent tendency of German philosophers to work out a neat, simple, symmetrical formula, and to ignore whatever facts did not fit in with it. Obvious, psychological bases of division, as into "visual arts" and "auditory arts," were dismissed as superficial. Instead, there was a search for more profound, eternal, spiritual distinctions, as into *real* and *ideal, finite* and *infinite, free* and *bound*. Most of these were vague in meaning and controversial in application.

In 1907, Oswald Külpe's division on the basis of sense addressed was a simple, common-sense approach to the problem, though not a complete solution of it. He had three main headings: optic arts, acoustic arts, and optic-acoustic arts. Each of these was redivided on the basis of observable differences in medium and form of product.

Between the two world wars, several more comprehensive systems were published. Max Dessoir arranged his as a table, with the arts in two vertical columns. The space arts, including sculpture, painting, and architecture, are also arts of rest and coexistence; they are plastic arts, whose affective means are visual images. The time arts, including the mimic dance, poetry, and music, are arts of movement and succession; also poetic arts whose means are audible gestures. The two columns are divided horizontally into imitative arts and free arts. Urries y Azara and Leo Adler combined these and a few other bases into complex tables or diagrams, each with several vertical and horizontal divisions. Adler's even brings in a far-fetched theory of the historical sequence in which the arts have developed.

Most of these diagrams and systems give a false account of the nature of the arts, through ignoring differences in style within each art. Their authors tend to oversimplify the nature of a given art, by classing it as a whole under a certain narrow heading such as "imitative" or "non-imitative," and ignoring the fact that many examples do not really conform to it. They are prone to sharp dichotomies, ignoring that many borderline examples occur. Their divisions are based only in part on observation. They insist on bringing in the old metaphysical catchwords, whose vagueness does not seem to bother them, as in Adler's high-sounding declaration that "Architecture and music are abstract, cosmic, subjective art," while "sculpture, mimicry, painting, and poetry are concrete, imitative, objective art."

More *practical* methods of classifying the arts were being worked out during the nineteenth and twentieth centuries, along with these philosophical ones. These were partly inspired by current philosophical theories, and partly worked out afresh, to meet practical problems. We noticed the development of such methods in regard to museum management, encyclopedias, library classifications, and curriculum organization in schools and colleges. They have the virtue of being more or less workable in dealing with concrete objects and activities, such as pictures and textiles, books on various arts, courses, projects, professorships, and departmental organization. But all of them have logical and theoretical flaws, which often impede efficient action more than is realized. All could profit by periodic revision in the light of new knowledge and understanding.

We arrive at the present day with a recognition of two *opposite attitudes* among recent philosophers, toward the problem of defining and classifying the arts. One, as we have just seen, is to persist in building unsound, over-elaborate systems of classification, which fail to take account of the highly variable, changing nature of the arts; which insist on drawing sharp lines of contrast where the facts show only a gradual range of variation; which tend (if taken seriously) to repress the artist's freedom of experiment, by setting up fences which he is forbidden to cross. The other is to denounce all attempts at classifying the arts, or at formally defining individual arts.

At this point we leave the historical approach, by restating the thesis advanced in Chapter I—that *a middle ground exists for flexible, tentative systematization in aesthetics, which will take account of the variable, changing, intangible nature of its phenomena*. In all approaches to scientific method, and in all clear philosophic thinking, an attempt must be made to define and classify concepts, and to arrange phenomena in significant groups. This must be done, not once for all time, but constantly, as a necessary phase in intelligent thinking. It is impossible to make steady progress in aesthetics, or in any other subject, without frequently redefining and reclassifying our principal concepts, to bring them into better conformity with new knowledge and new points of view. As long as we ignore definition and classification in aesthetics, on the ground that it is tedious or impossible, our thinking about art will be archaic and muddled at crucial points, whether we realize it or not. We cannot get along without some kind of definition and classification. As a rule, we remain satisfied with obsolete concepts, because they are sanctified by tradition and because we have never stopped to analyze them critically. The alternative, attempted in this book, is to work out a new, tentative set of definitions and classifications of the arts, admittedly imperfect, but as good as we can fashion in the light of present knowledge.

2. *Recommended definitions of art and the arts*

In Chapter III, on "The Meanings of Art," we distinguished no fewer than eighteen current meanings of that term; current in the sense that leading dictionaries recognize them as correct and not obsolete. These we grouped under five main definitions, each a cluster of closely related concepts: (1) the broad technical sense; (2) the broad intellectual sense; (3) the broad aesthetic senses, eulogistic and non-evaluative; (4) the visual aesthetic senses, eulogistic and non-evaluative; (5) the pictorial aesthetic senses, eulogistic and non-evaluative. All of these are based on the concept of *skill;* art being regarded as a kind of skill, or a process or activity in which that skill is shown, or a product of that skill.

In addition to these dictionary meanings, we noticed a large number of definitions by individual writers. Some of these are slight variations of the dictionary meanings; others are special theories about art, its nature, genesis, values, etc., rather than definitions of the term. The most influential definition, outside the "skill" group, is that of Tolstoy, who defined art as "the expression and communication of remembered emotion." Formally, it is very different from the "skill" group, in using *expression* as the main genus within which art is classed. Tolstoy goes on to differentiate art from other kinds of expression, by restricting it to the skilled expression of the "higher," moral emotions. Véron and others before Tolstoy, and several subsequent writers, have agreed in defining art as a kind of expression. They have not all agreed with his restriction of art to high, moral emotion. We can thus observe a cluster of several connected meanings of art, more or less current though not yet listed in the dictionaries, which can be called the *expression group,* as distinct from the *skill group.* The two groups are not really as different as they appear in formal statement, since "skill" is usually implied at least tacitly, as a differentia of that kind of expression which is art. Those who define art as a kind of skill, on the other hand, often go on to state that it is concerned with the expression and communication of emotion.

Roughly speaking, we can distinguish about twenty different meanings of "art" in current usage, not counting many special, individual definitions. Obviously, such extreme ambiguity is an obstacle to clear discussion, and should be reduced.

We proceeded on the assumption that there is no one correct meaning of "art," and that a choice of meanings should be made on the basis of expediency in discussion. We decided that it would not be expedient or possible to reduce all the current meanings to a single one, or try to formulate a single, short definition of "art" which would be satisfactory as a tool of discussion. It seemed possible to reduce the long list to a few alternative or supplementary meanings, which would be fairly consistent and closely related. The resultant definition would be a little longer and more cumbersome than might be desired, but might be neutral and flexible enough for use by rival schools of opinion. It would help to mark off a field of phenomena, an area of human culture, to be designated by the name "art." The various specifications included in the definition would be various ways of describing this field, and would coincide to a large extent, instead of indicating widely different fields.

The definition recommended in Chapter III is really a group of closely related definitions; a statement of several alternative meanings for the name "art." All are actually in current use, and the context is usually enough to indicate which is intended. It reads as follows:

1. *a. Art is skill in making or doing that which is used or intended as a stimulus to satisfactory aesthetic experience, often along with other ends or functions; especially in such a way that the perceived stimulus, the meanings it suggests, or both, are felt as beautiful, pleasant, interesting, emotionally moving, or otherwise valuable as objects of direct experience, in addition to any instrumental values they may have. b. Art is skill in expressing and communicating past emotional and other experience, individual and social, in a perceptible medium. c. Especially, that phase in such skill or activity which is concerned with designing, composing, or performing with personal interpretation, as distinguished from routine execution or mechanical reproduction.*

2. Also, a product of such skill, or products collectively; works of art. Broadly, this includes every product of the arts commonly recognized as having an aesthetic function, such as architecture and music, whether or not that particular product is considered to be beautiful or otherwise meritorious.

3. Art, as a main division of human culture and a group of social phenomena, includes all skills, activities, and products covered by the above definition. As such, it is comparable in extent to religion and science; but these divisions overlap in part.

4. An art, such as music, is a particular division of the total field of art, comprising certain distinctive kinds of skill, activity, medium, and product. Especially, a division regarded as comparatively large, important, or distinctive; others being often classed as branches or subdivisions of an art.

In Chapter IV, we examined the meaning of several names for kinds or groups of arts. Here the problem of definition merged with that of classification. We agreed that the sharp antithesis between *fine* and *useful* arts is misleading, and should as a rule be avoided.

In the terminology recommended here, the word "art" in itself implies an aesthetic function. Thus any skill or product which is classed as an art is by definition "fine" or aesthetic. Skills and products having little or no direct aesthetic function, such as coal mining, are not to be classed as arts at all, but as utilitarian technics, industries, branches of engineering, etc. All arts have religious, moral, utilitarian, educational, political, and other types of function. Within the field of art, a rough contrast in degree can sometimes be made between "more and less utilitarian arts" or "more and less aesthetic arts," according to which type of function is emphasized. It is hard to generalize about whole arts on this basis, because they vary greatly in different periods. Painting and poetry are sometimes regarded chiefly as handmaids to religion; at other times, chiefly as sources of pleasant entertainment. When certain arts are treated only as sources of aesthetic pleasure, while others are recognized as chiefly utilitarian, it becomes natural to contrast them as "fine" and "useful" or "applied." The antithesis then becomes a true one as applied to those particular types or styles in the arts concerned. But it is usually not so limited, and hence leads to an oversimplified conception of the arts in general.

The arts in which a utilitarian function is usually emphasized, along with the aesthetic, include architecture, furniture, pottery, textiles, metalry, and others. All but architecture are commonly classed as "minor useful arts" or as "decorative arts." These terms are both admissible, since the arts in question have both functions. "Useful" implies "more strongly utilitarian." In so far as pottery, for example, is produced with no directly aesthetic aim or function whatever (as in making drain-pipes which are not to be seen), it falls outside the field of art. A given technique can thus fall partly within the field of art, and partly outside. The term "minor" may imply "smaller" or "inferior," "less valuable." Use in the latter sense should be relative to some particular culture or period. The term "handicrafts" is acceptable as a name for the minor useful arts when made by hand; the term "industrial arts" when made by large-scale, machine processes. The latter term also includes architecture, and certain phases of the other arts, as in the reproduction of prints.

The sense of "art" or "fine art" which excludes music and literature is confusing and undesirable in aesthetics or other technical usage; it should be abandoned. Instead, the term "visual art" or "visual arts" should be used. Its extension should not be limited to the traditional *bildende Künste* or static visual arts of sculpture, painting, architecture, pottery, etc., but should cover the visual phases of such mobile arts as theater, dance, and film.

Types of skill and their products which appeal to the lower senses, such as perfume and cooking, are by implication included in the general field of "art" as defined above. Theoretical objections to recognizing them as arts are insufficient. Their psychological limitations, usual simplicity of form, and other characteristics can be given due recognition in detailed comparisons between the arts. They are sometimes developed into moderately complex groups and sequences, and endowed with special symbolic meanings.

In contrast with the traditional list of five or seven "major arts," plus some half dozen "minor arts," our list of visual, auditory, and audio-visual arts included a hundred names. Some of these concepts overlap, but many more current names of arts could be added. This list of arts, plus whatever lower-sense arts may be added, constitutes an approximate description of the total *field or extension* of the term "art." It is unnecessary and undesirable to mark off the boundaries precisely. Many types of skill and product are on the borderline, since their claims to artistic status are dubious or occasional, as in games, sports, and amusements. The relative emphasis on aesthetic appeal which is given to a particular technic often varies greatly from one culture to another. So does its relative importance in the hierarchy of social status and accepted values, as in the case of tattooing.

Definitions were recommended for about twenty-five *particular* arts, branches of art, or groups of arts, including those which are commonly recognized as most important in our culture, and some which are not. As given in Chapter XI, they vary in length and detail. Those of literature, sculpture, painting, and architecture are comparatively long. They are so stated in order to illustrate how a brief definition can be expanded into a *descriptive account* of the art, suited to an encyclopedia or textbook.

3. Classifications of the arts

There is no such thing as an art, in the traditional sense of a distinct, permanent, integral realm of human activity. What we call an art is a more or less arbitrary way of marking off a particular area within the continuous, shifting fabric of social culture. A particular name such as "poetry" is applied in radically different ways, to different cultural areas. The conception of a particular art stands, to some writers, for a certain kind of technique; to others, for a certain kind of medium; to others, for a certain kind of product; to others, for a vague combination of these.

When we come to study the relations between particular arts, it makes a great deal of difference how they are defined. Whichever basis of definition stands out in our minds, it tends to make us locate each art in a different genus, and divide it into different branches. If we are thinking mainly about the techniques, the arts fall into certain groupings; if about products, into others. These different divisions do not exactly correspond. Many of them overlap and cut across each other. Hence it is impossible to combine them all into a single, clear-cut system of classification. Numerous false "systems" of the arts have resulted from the attempt to make them do so, in order to produce a neat formula.

To avoid such mistakes, it is helpful to divide the problem into three parts. We may then ask, first, "how can the arts be classified according to medium?"—or, still better, "how can the mediums of the arts be classified?" Second, we may ask, "how can the processes of the arts be classified?" and, third, "how can the products of the arts be classified?" Finally, we may ask, "to what extent do these three types of classification coincide?"

4. Kinds of art from the standpoint of medium

We observed that the words "medium" and "material" are both ambiguous; each is understood in several senses. Accordingly, there are several ways to classify the mediums of art, depending on what we are talking about.

If medium is understood to mean "physical materials and instruments," we have the problem of grouping these into main types. The arts can then be classified as to whether they use stone, brick, metal, vegetable fibers, animal bodies, etc. The number and diversity of materials and instruments used by many of the arts prevents any stable correlation between material on the one hand, and type of process or product on the other. Generalizing more broadly, it is possible to distinguish between arts which tend to use (a) simple, raw, crude or unprocessed materials such as a block of stone; (b) semi-processed, complex, but inanimate materials such as upholstery fabrics; or (c) living plants, animals, or human bodies, as in gardening and the dance. Some materials are processed but without complex form, such as oil paints and fine clay.

The distinction is sometimes made between arts using physical bodies (the visual arts), those using tones (music), and those using words (literature). It is dubious, however. Music and literature also use physical bodies (violins and books). If we are thinking about imaginary, suggested bodies, as in representative painting, then we are no longer dealing with actual physical materials. Lessing's concept of painting as an art of bodies in space, and poetry as one of actions in time, dealt with art's imaginary content rather than with its physical medium.

If the concept of medium is expanded to include *suggested* imagery, thoughts, emotions, desires, etc., it becomes too broad and loose for distinguishing the arts. Literature, painting, music, theater, dance, and other arts can all suggest a great variety of psychological experiences. Literature, of course, has the widest range; but this basis of comparison can better be applied to the products or final forms of art than to the medium or unworked material.

A more fruitful way of generalizing about materials is in terms of their *direct, perceptual qualities;* the *types of sense image which they present* to the eye, ear, or other sense organ of the observer. Thus we can speak of arts which use line, arts which use color, arts which use solid shape, etc.; not as suggestions, but as directly observable components in the work of art. Music uses pitch, rhythm, timbre. Poetry, when heard aloud, uses rhythm and certain other auditory traits. There is a great deal of overlapping here. Practically all the visual arts present line, light and dark, texture; many present color.

By generalizing a little more, we come to one of the most serviceable of all bases of comparison: that of *sense primarily addressed.* Some arts use a visual medium, and are called the visual arts. Music uses an auditory medium, and is called an auditory art. Opera uses both types, and is called an audio-visual art. Literature uses either an auditory or a visual medium: spoken or written words. It can fall into any of these three categories, or be given one by itself. Perfume and cooking use lower-sense mediums, and we class them as lower-sense arts.

In the chapter on mediums, we noticed the importance for art and aesthetics of studying their *technological properties*. This does not offer much direct help in classifying the arts, since the properties of mediums are so diverse. But it does point to the desirability of retaining a fairly definite, restricted meaning for "medium," and not expanding it to include all the suggested factors in finished works of art, such as desire and emotion. The subject can well be approached from another direction. Having distinguished a given art in terms of process and product, we can then ask, what materials does it use in these processes, to make the kinds of product aimed at? To what extent are these materials suitable? What are their potentialities, their limitations, advantages and difficulties, when considered as means to ends? To what kinds of technique do they respond most readily, and for what kinds of product, function, and aesthetic effect are they most adaptable?

Investigation along these lines leads to a *functional* basis for classifying the physical and psychological mediums of the arts. It is analogous to "materia medica" in the science of medicine, in which substances are classified according to their uses in treating various diseases; that is, as more or less effective means to various ends, or as things to be avoided under certain conditions. Thus iron is recognized as a material to be avoided on the surface of sculpture, when rust is not desired. More positively, one begins with certain types of form, function, and conditions of use: for example, sculpture in high relief, to be carved by hand as decoration for choir stalls in a church where there will be wide variations in temperature and humidity. Certain types of wood, veneering, joining, etc., will be suitable and others unsuitable. Certain colors—for example, bright red, are usually more suitable for a theater lobby than for a hospital bedroom, because of their psychological effects. One must take due account, however, of the great variability of aesthetic effects according to the context in which a certain material is used, and according to other variables such as the personality of the observer. A beginning has been made along these lines in many technical handbooks on the arts, but there is need (a) for a general synthesis of such knowledge, and (b) for more experiment on the psychological effects of various artistic means: for example, the emotional effects of certain words and images in literature, and of certain instrumental timbres in music.

5. Kinds of art from the standpoint of process

A tremendous number of different skills, processes, and occupations are involved in the arts. Our problem, again, is to group them under a few main headings if possible, so as to bring out their main similarities and differences.

An *occupation,* such as that of an architect, itself involves a number of different activities. In classifying occupations in the realm of art, we are dealing with whole sets of associated processes and skills. One way of grouping them is according to *levels of education and responsibility.* Government occupational surveys usually minimize the idea of higher and lower levels in classification; it might be resented by persons who do not wish to be placed in a lower class.[1] The idea of levels runs counter to our fiction of living in a classless society, in spite of the obvious fact that, like all others, our society falls into different grades according to education, ability, responsibility, social status, and reward. We have, of course, a high degree of individual and family mobility from grade to grade, and the level of one's job is not always correlated with a definite level in social prestige. Nevertheless, there are obvious analogies between the hierarchy of modern occupational levels and the aristocratic hierarchy of liberal and servile arts. Occupations in the arts, like those in all other fields, are graded from the top level of "professional, technical, and managerial work" down to "mechanical work," and at the bottom, "manual work." Such horizontal divisions cut across the particular arts. Workers in visual art, in music, in literature, and in entertainment, are found on all levels. Within a given art such as music, the various occupations are carefully graded on different levels.

Most arts, like music, have become diversified in the modern world; split up into long lists of specialized, interlocking occupations. In the ancient world, a single bard or minstrel could combine all phases of the art, including composition and performance. Today, all the principal arts have become to some extent industrialized, with specialization and diversification of labor. An individual in the field does not always realize it. He may think of himself as a solitary poet in an ivory tower; but if he mails a poem to a magazine and has it printed, he becomes part of the gigantic publishing industry, in which literature is itself but a part.

As to degree of *industrialization, specialization,* and *complexity,* one can grade whole realms of art, and also occupations. We are not concerned here with the historical, evolutionary development by which

---

[1] It is obscured by other coordinate divisions: for example, "agricultural, marine, and forestry." Even there, higher and lower grades of work exist.

primitive, undifferentiated arts and occupations have split up into specialized ones. But in the contemporary world itself, arts exist at various stages of industrialization. Aside from its publishing aspect, the art of poetry is less industrialized than those of architecture and motion pictures. Many individuals—for example, poets and painters— work in comparative solitude, and carry on a variety of tasks.

Two or three different bases of comparison are involved here. As to *nature and conditions of work,* we can distinguish occupations as (a) more solitary, or (b) more cooperative. As to *degree of industrialization,* we can distinguish (a) the comparatively undifferentiated art or branch of art, where one individual tends to do many different kinds of thing, from (b) the comparatively differentiated, industrialized art, where different phases of the work are distributed among different groups of specialized workers. Oil painting is on the whole less differentiated than motion picture making. An occupation or an individual worker within a highly industrialized art tends to be less diversified, more specialized, than in the older type. Along with industrialization goes some tendency to *mechanization;* the use of machines, scientific engineering, and labor-saving devices, especially for mass production. Arts and occupations can be compared as to the *degree to which they are mechanized.* The work of a poet or painter is less mechanized than that of a motion picture photographer. But these tendencies are not exactly correlated. Within the motion picture industry there are many occupations in which machine processes are not directly used.

In comparing artistic occupations, we found it useful to distinguish those concerned mainly with *composing and designing* from those concerned mainly with *performing and manufacturing.* In one way or another, we found that this distinction runs through all the arts. For example, in furniture, there are people who only design furniture, and others who only manufacture it. In music, there are people who only compose songs, and others who only sing them. This is one phase of the general tendency to differentiation which we have been considering, but it is a most important one. Again, there are less differentiated occupations, and again oil painting is one of them, in which the same person tends to do both the designing and the executing. When these phases are differentiated into separate jobs, the designing or composing phase tends to be placed on the high level of "professional, technical, managerial" work. That of executing is done in part by mechanical or manual workers, but (in a large industry) it is supervised by managers or executives who are also on a high level, and often paid more highly than any of the others.

The common distinction between *creative* and *non-creative* arts and activities is mistaken, as usually interpreted. It is a mistake to call certain arts "creative" (for example, painting), with the implication that other arts such as acting and singing are non-creative or merely reproductive. Much work in the so-called "creative arts" is non-creative; while in other arts and occupations connected with the arts, there is room for creation by individuals capable of it. At the same time, responsibility for creating, in the sense of originating ideas, tends to become localized in a specialized type of occupation, such as those of musical composer, author, and designer.

In all artistic work, there is a *psychic, mental, inner phase,* and an *overt, somatic, outer phase.* They are never entirely separate, but one or the other dominates at different times, and in different individuals. Here, too, the differentiating, industrializing tendency has penetrated some of the arts, in setting up one class of people to do most of the planning and thinking; another to do most of the muscular and mechanical work. This is nothing new, of course, but merely a democratic, machine-age version of the ancient cleavage between "planners" and "doers." In the ancient and medieval worlds, the aesthetic arts remained relatively unspecialized. They branched off from each other, but within a given art such as building or acting, there was less division of labor. The old-time artist-craftsman, who used his brains and his hands in close coordination, often appears to us today as a better individual than his modern successors—better balanced, a more complete artist. Attempts are made to revive his type of work; but, aside from leisure hobbies, the trend is mostly the other way.

There is no definite ground for contrasting the arts in regard to *psychic* processes involved. In so far as psychology has described the work of artistic creating, composing, and designing, where the psychic phase is most developed, it seems to be similar in many respects in all arts. Even creative thought in science and practical affairs seems to have much the same general character. Differences in the creative process appear to be correlated rather with differences in personality type and in social culture. The *overt* processes of the arts do differ greatly, in relation to types of medium and product. Composing and designing are not all psychic, any more than performing and executing are all overt. The former have their own overt phases, as in sketching a design or writing down a poem or sonata. Performing and executing have their psychic phases, which may be highly creative, or may consist in faithful obedience to orders.

The psychic phases of artistic work do tend to differ somewhat on the basis of *sense addressed,* inasmuch as the artist tends to organize and channel his thoughts and feelings in terms of either (a) visual shapes and colors, (b) musical tones and rhythms, or (c) written or spoken words. However, many other factors operate to determine the nature of the creative process: among them, the type of product aimed at, and the kind of functions it is intended to carry out; also, as has just been said, the artist's cultural setting and his individual personality configuration. Social trends in artistic style and general cultural attitude are more influential than has been realized, in determining the artist's processes and products.

Building on Kant's triple division of the arts, but changing it considerably, we arrived at the following list of *six basic types of process in the production of art:* [2]

I. *Visual shaping*
    a. Designing or composing phase: visual shape guiding
    b. Performing or executing phase: visual shaping
II. *Sounding*
    a. Designing or composing phase: sound guiding
    b. Performing or executing phase: sounding
III. *Verbalizing*
    a. Designing or composing phase: verbal thought guiding, and sometimes speech and action guiding
    b. Performing or executing phase: verbal thinking, and sometimes speaking and acting, in accordance with verbal guides.

This list of process-types includes all those directly involved in producing the visual, auditory, and audio-visual arts. "Visual shaping" covers a great variety of specific techniques, from carving stone and spreading paint to planting gardens and breeding goldfish. Changing the posture of the limbs in dancing, and the expression of the face in acting, is a kind of visual shaping which occurs in temporal sequence.

[2] This list does not include processes in the lower-sense arts, or in the appreciation and use of the higher-sense arts.

The primary basis of division in this list is that of *sense addressed,* with the usual main categories of visual and auditory, sight and sound. Theoretically, literary verbalizing is covered under these two categories. It is usually conveyed by sight or sound; occasionally by touch. But literary art has become a large and important realm in itself, with its own distinctive techniques in the combining and interpreting of linguistic symbols. Therefore it demands a separate, main category in the description of artistic processes. The phrase "other than verbal" should therefore be understood after "visual shaping" and "sounding." Calligraphy and typography are visual shaping; the writing and speaking of literature are verbalizing.

Any art, and any occupation in the arts, can be analyzed on its productive side into one or more of these basic types, and compared with others on that basis. Some specialize on one type of process, as for example:

I. *Visual shaping.* The designing or composing phase, visual shape *guiding,* is emphasized in architecture, industrial design, and choreography. They emphasize making preliminary sketches, notations, and specifications for others to execute in final form. The performing or executing phase, *visual shaping* or the actual giving of visual form, is emphasized in building, carpentry, furniture-making, dress-making, bronze-casting, and actual dancing as distinct from choreography. Painting commonly includes *both* phases, practiced by one man. Many arts and occupations are variable in this respect. The art of sculpture in general includes both designing and executing statues; but an individual sculptor may design a statue in clay, and turn over to a bronze-caster its final execution. A dancer may originate some dances, and also perform dances composed by others.

II. *Sounding.* Sound *guiding* is the work of the musical composer, or of the director of sound effects in radio and motion pictures. Actual *sounding* is the performance of musical or other sound effects, as in singing and playing. A musician who is both composer and instrumentalist combines both phases.

III. *Verbalizing.* Verbal thought *guiding* is the work of the author; of the poet, novelist, short story writer, and dramatist. In theater art, *speech and action guiding* is done by the playwright whose plays are acted; also by the stage or motion picture director.

Verbal *thinking* is a type of imaginary performance, done by all literate persons in reading literature silently. Verbal *speaking and acting* is the overt performance of literature, as in the work of the actor or the orator.

IV. *Visual shaping and sounding.* The combined art of dance or pantomime with music involves both these types. An artist may devote himself to composing and designing for the combined art, or to performing it, or both.

V. *Sounding and verbalizing.* The art of song, combining words and music, involves both of these types. The composer of songs guides the combined process; the singer performs it.

VI. *Visual shaping, sounding, and verbalizing.* The art of opera includes all six processes. *Visual shape guiding* occurs in designing and planning the scenery, staging, lighting, costuming, gesturing, dancing, and other visible aspects. *Visual shaping* occurs in executing these stage effects, and performing the visible movements. *Sound guiding* occurs in composing the music, writing it down as a set of directions, and instructing the performers how to sing and play it. *Sounding* occurs in the actual singing and playing. The work of an orchestra conductor is a highly specialized, modern development, intermediate between guiding and actual sounding. He usually does not play himself, as early orchestra leaders did. He is expected to do some creative interpreting and directing, and not to follow the notes mechanically; he may even alter the score in minor details. Yet his work is directly bound up with the performance phase of music, rather than with the preliminary composing. *Verbal thought, speech, and action guiding* occurs in writing the text or libretto, and instructing actors and singers how to utter the words, with appropriate movements. *Verbal thinking* occurs in reading the text; *verbal speaking and acting* occur in the performance by actors and singers.

6. Kinds of art from the standpoint of product

We first noticed the multiplicity of specific types of product in the arts, such as picture, statue, house, poem, novel, sonnet, sonata, symphony, etc., and the need of classifying them under a few main headings. This line of inquiry led to the subject of form analysis or aesthetic morphology. A brief survey was given of the principal factors in aesthetic form, and of the way in which they combine into different types of form. The principal factors and modes of organization are as follows:

I. *Modes of transmission:* presented and suggested factors in aesthetic form. The modes of suggestion (which may operate as factors in a single work of art) are (a) mimesis; (b) symbolism; (c) common association.

II. Psychological *ingredients* in aesthetic form are classified (a) according to their mode of transmission in a particular work of art, as presented or suggested; (b) under various *components,* based on psychological conceptions of the principal types of experience, psychic functions, etc. *Elementary* components include sensation, conation, emotion, reasoning, etc. Sensation includes visual, auditory, and other sensory types of component. Visual components include hue, linear shape, solid shape, etc. Auditory components include pitch, timbre, etc. Under each elementary component is a multitude of elementary *traits:* for example, under "hue," traits are red, blue, yellow, etc. The ingredients in a work of art include the suggested ones, such as emotional traits of joy, sorrow, etc., suggested in a picture or poem.

III. The ingredients or component traits in a work of art are always *organized* in certain general ways: especially in space, time, and causality. One has to distinguish the ways in which presented factors are organized from those in which suggested factors are organized. A picture, for instance, is presentatively organized in two dimensions of space; it may suggest deep space with actions going on in time. Causal organization is in terms of suggested cause-and-effect relations among the things and events portrayed, as in the plot of a story.

IV. *Developed components* are factors in form, each of which involves one or more elementary components, developed in space, time, or causality. For example, melody is a developed component in music, involving the organization in close temporal sequence of many detailed variations in pitch and rhythm.

V. *Modes of composition* are another way of interrelating the details in a work of art. The four principal modes of composition are utilitarian, representative, expository, and thematic. Each of the major arts employs them all. A single work of art may involve one, two, three, or four modes of composition at once. They are then regarded as compositional factors in the work of art: for example, a picture may have a representative factor (the scene portrayed) and also a thematic or design factor (the patterns of line, color, etc., which are presented to the eye).

VI. *Particular works of art,* types, and styles of art can be analyzed and compared in terms of these various factors. One must consider (a) how each factor is developed; what component traits are used and how they are organized within this factor; (b) how much diversity exists; (c) how the various main factors are interrelated; for example, how utility, representation and thematic design are related in a chair carved with animal figures; (d) how and to what extent all details are integrated through subordination to a comprehensive framework.

Using these principles of aesthetic morphology as bases, we then compared the various arts with respect to each. The aim was to find out *whether different arts tended to produce different kinds of form.* Generalization was found to be difficult here because of the great variety of types and styles of product which have been produced by each art. In many cases, a certain type of product can be turned out by several different arts, mediums, and processes. Representative forms (works of art involving representation of concrete objects, scenes, situations, or events) are produced in the visual arts, music, and literature. Nevertheless, a few rough generalizations can be made to the effect that certain arts have usually—especially in the modern, western world—emphasized certain types of form. It is not implied that they ought to continue doing so, or to restrict themselves to the types which are usually considered most suitable for them. The arts mentioned below are examples only, and not a complete list of those which belong under each heading.

I. *Comparing the arts as to modes of presentation*

    A. As to *number* of senses addressed; extent of presentational *diversity:*

        1. Arts of unisensory presentation: for example, music (auditory); painting (visual).

2. Arts of bisensory presentation: for example, opera, ballet with music (visual and auditory).

3. Arts of multisensory presentation: for example, religious rituals with incense plus visual and auditory forms.

B. As to the *particular senses* addressed:

1. Visual arts: for example, painting, sculpture.
2. Auditory art: music.
3. Audio-visual arts: opera, ballet (to sight and hearing); literature (to sight or hearing or both).
4. Lower-sense arts: subdivided as olfactory (perfume); gustatory (foods, beverages), etc.

C. As to *components* emphasized in presentation:

1. Among the visual arts: (a) those often emphasizing color (painting, textile design, costume, ceramics, interior design, horticulture, ballet, cinema, and others); (b) those emphasizing solid shape (sculpture, architecture, industrial design); (c) those often emphasizing line (drawing, calligraphy, typography and some other graphic arts); (d) those emphasizing interior space (architecture, some furniture and utensils); (e) light and dark (some painting, photography, and graphic arts).

2. Among the auditory and audio-visual arts: (a) emphasizing rhythm and pitch (music); (b) emphasizing rhythm but not pitch (poetry).

II. *Comparing the arts as to modes of transmission*

A. As to comparative emphasis on *presented or suggested* factors:

1. Emphasis usually on suggestion: literature.
2. On presentation: music.
3. Variable: painting. (Some styles stress the represented subject or the symbolic meaning; some the visible design).

B. As to which *modes of suggestion* are usually emphasized:

1. Mimesis and common association: painting, sculpture, dance, pantomime, visible acting, music.
2. Symbolism (verbal) and common association: literature.
3. Mimesis, symbolism, and common association; dramatic enactment; sound film.

III. *Comparing the arts as to spatial, temporal, and causal development*

A. As to development of the *presented* factor:

1. Mainly spatial: (a) two-dimensional: most pictures and textiles; (b) three-dimensional: sculpture, architecture, furniture, utensils.
2. Mainly temporal: music; spoken literature.
3. Spatio-temporal; presented in both space and time: (a) in two dimensions of space and in time: cinema, shadow plays; (b) in three dimensions of space and in time: ballet, opera, acted drama, marionettes.
4. Arts usually lacking complex development in either space or time: lower-sense arts.

B. As to development of the *suggested* factor:

1. Arts suggesting three-dimensional spatial development: all representative arts (painting, sculpture, textiles, literature, theater, etc.). Minor useful arts, less so.
2. Arts suggesting temporal development; that is, suggesting sequence in time: (a) to a large extent: theater arts, literature, music; (b) to a less extent: painting, sculpture, architecture.

C. As to *causal* development:

1. Usually high: literature, theater.
2. Medium or variable: painting, sculpture.
3. Usually low: music; textile, ceramic, and other abstract visual design.

IV. *Comparing the arts as to modes of composition*

A. As to degree of emphasis on *representation:*

1. Usually high: literature, especially epic and dramatic poetry and prose fiction, drawing, painting, tapestry, photography, sculpture, dance, and other theater arts.
2. Usually low: music, architecture, furniture, utensils, horticulture.

B. As to degree of emphasis on *utility:*

1. Now usually high: architecture, furniture, utensils and other industrial arts.
2. Now usually low: music, poetry.

    C. As to degree of emphasis on *thematic design:*

       1. Usually high: music, poetry, textile design, architecture.
       2. Usually low: prose fiction and essays.
       3. Variable: painting, sculpture.

    D. As to degree of emphasis on *exposition:*

       1. Usually high: today, only in certain branches of literature, especially the prose essay and lyric poetry; formerly high in oriental and medieval painting, sculpture, literature, architecture.
       2. Usually low: music; modern painting and sculpture.

V. *Comparing the arts as to degree of differentiation within a single work of art; diversity of details combined in a single product*

    A. Relatively undifferentiated arts: the primitive religious dance with words and music; modern survivals in religious rituals, children's games, etc.
    B. Highly specialized arts: for example, modern instrumental concert music.
    C. Complex, diversified arts, involving combination of many diverse factors in a single product, with distinct development of each: opera, ballet, cinema, books, architecture, interior design, industrial design (for example, of ships), community planning; homemaking.

VI. *Comparing the arts as to stylistic tendencies*

    A. Persistently geometric and often rectilinear in basic structure: architecture, large furniture, city planning.
    B. More susceptible to fundamentally irregular, biomorphic, curvilinear, and romantic styles: painting, textiles, costume, music, literature, garden arts.

    The above outline is not a mere topical classification. It suggests approaches to many persistent problems of comparative aesthetics. Among these is the question, to what extent are the arts analogous, similar? To what extent are they different? To what extent is it possible to "translate" or take over into one art effects produced in another?

In particular, what correspondences can exist between such apparently diverse arts as music and visual design?

The outline just given, on different ways of comparing the arts, seems to emphasize division and contrast. On each basis of comparison, it separates the arts into two or more groups which differ in this respect. It thus suggests many detailed answers to the question, how do the arts differ? But at the same time, it suggests analogies and similarities by grouping certain arts together, as alike in a certain respect.

For example, the following arts are grouped as often emphasizing *color:* painting, textile design, costume, ceramics, interior design, horticulture, ballet, cinema, and others. In the outline, such listings are only illustrative, not complete. They do, however, take the question "How analogous are the arts?" down from a level of vague generality, to a level on which it can be dealt with point by point. In respect to frequent emphasis on color, certain arts resemble each other, while others stand out in contrast. In respect to frequent emphasis on *representation,* the arts fall into a different grouping: painting now stands side by side with literature, leaving music outside. As to frequent emphasis on design, music is grouped with architecture, poetry, and textile design.

When we have thus grouped certain arts together, as roughly similar in a certain respect, the task of comparative aesthetics has just begun. Any such vague affirmation, to the effect that arts A and B are more alike than A and C, is sure to be debatable. Our outline is intended more as a set of challenging hypotheses than as a final statement of the facts. Even if one grants, for the sake of argument, that music, architecture, and textiles are alike in often emphasizing design, the important problem still remains of exactly how design occurs in each of these arts, and to what extent it is emphasized in each. What is design in music? What is design in architecture, in painting, in a Persian rug? What have they all in common, and how do they differ? What varieties of design occur within each art? What analogous roles are played by certain components, such as melody and line? With these further problems we have hardly begun to deal in the present book. Our aim has been, primarily, to break down a few of such extremely general problems into many more specific ones, which can be investigated one at a time.

7. Combined classifications; a functional approach to systems of the arts

There are many correct ways of classifying and dividing the arts, and no one of them is always the right or best way. Different ones are preferable for different purposes. In working out a classification, one should first decide what uses are to be made of it, in theory or practice.

There is no one right way of dividing up a territory such as North America. Sometimes we are interested in political units and their relationships; sometimes in types of physical terrain such as mountains and plains; sometimes in climatic zones; sometimes in economic zones such as wheat, corn, and manufacturing regions. We can put several different kinds of division into one large map; but if too many are combined the map becomes confusing and unwieldy, a maze of overlapping boundaries. It is often preferable to use a series of different maps. In the same way, it is usually preferable to make several different divisions of the arts for different purposes, rather than to try to combine them all in a single table or outline. The boundaries would soon become hopelessly confused. It is usually impossible to divide the arts into sharply distinct regions, whatever basis of division we employ. There is always a gradual shading off from one to another, with many variable, borderline cases.

It is well to ask at the start whether one is most interested in mediums, processes, or products. This will determine the choice of appropriate bases. Let us suppose that one's problem is to make an inventory of the equipment available for work in the arts, in a university or in a state educational system, so as to order whatever is needed. One will need to classify different kinds of raw *material* such as paint, clay, paper, ink; different kinds of *instrument* and apparatus such as brushes, kilns, violins, typewriters. Under each main art or group of arts will be listed the things used in it. Suppose, on the other hand, that one's problem is to organize educational activities, such as courses in a university. Then one may wish to classify according to the types of *product* aimed at: for example, courses in how to produce short stories, plays, paintings, statues, musical compositions, photographs, color films, and so on. Also, one may wish to classify according to *process* or technique: for example, courses in glazing and firing porcelain; in stage direction; in orchestration.

In working out a classification for some practical purpose, it is not always necessary to be logically consistent, or scientifically up to date. Sometimes the main requirement is that the headings be easily understood by those who will use them. Then it may be better to break down the field in some conventional way, such as Art, English, French, Music, Shopwork, just because it is familiar, even though it is theoretically faulty. Concepts devised by theorists, such as "audio-visual," often take a long time working down into popular usage. Illogical classifications persist for decades or centuries, as in library systems, because it would be too much trouble to change them. Nevertheless, it is well for administrative leaders in any field to be aware of improvements, so as to introduce them when it seems expedient.

In aesthetics itself, we are less concerned with practical uses than with understanding; with intellectual organization for the sake of greatest clarity and enlightenment. Even here there is a practical, functional aspect: we seek for conceptual systems that will be useful as tools for further investigation; that will serve us well in assembling and interpreting new data.

It is not always satisfactory to have a number of different, specialized classifications, each for a different purpose. Sometimes we desire an *all-purpose classification*. This is true of library systems, because books are written on every aspect of the arts, and readers choose them from every conceivable point of view. However, there is no such thing as an all-purpose classification. The moment we choose our *primary basis* of division,[3] we irrevocably shape the whole system into one which will suit some people and some uses better than others. Some people are interested in the arts mainly from a standpoint of cultural history; they wish to think in terms of chronological and geographical divisions. They would like to divide the field at once into "The Arts of Ancient Greece," "The Arts of Medieval Europe," "The Arts of Asia," etc., so as to pick out one such block of history and ignore all the rest. It is inconvenient for them to think first in terms of different arts, such as architecture and sculpture, even if architecture is later divided into Architecture, Greek; Architecture, Medieval, etc.

In philosophy and aesthetics we are not indifferent to history, but are usually more concerned with recurrent, general types: for example,

[3] In the tables by Dessoir and Urries y Azara, two or more primary bases are used, or at least two of equal rank: one for vertical and one for horizontal divisions.

with painting, poetry, and music as perennial avenues of expression for the human mind.[4] Education on the higher levels also tends to follow this subject division on the whole. Hence there is a demand for some way of breaking down the total field of art on an abstract, non-historical basis, into subdivisions suited to different specialized studies.

For this purpose it is important to choose a *primary basis* of division which will not be superficial or highly specialized, but which will indicate some deep, far-reaching cleavage among types of art. It may not be the best for all uses, but should be the most adaptable to a variety of uses. It should imply distinctions which are fairly obvious and universally recognized; not based on some debatable theory of metaphysics or value.

These considerations lead us to the choice of *sense primarily addressed* as usually best for an all-round, multi-purpose classification of the arts. It is suitable for use as the primary basis of division, to be supplemented by others later on.

The distinction between the senses, and the types of perceptual experience associated with each, is a fundamental one psychologically. It seems to run through human experience from its primitive, infantile beginnings through the most sophisticated forms of art. Opposing tendencies are at work from the start, to bridge over the gulfs between the senses; to enable us to translate back and forth between them, with alternative sets of symbols as in written and spoken words. We learn to make our senses cooperate in building up conceptions of the external world. We produce forms addressed to the eyes which resemble and supplement those addressed to the ears, so that both convey analogous experiences of design, fantasy, and the like. Thus the boundary between the arts addressed to different senses is frequently bridged. It is far from adequate in itself for bringing out the most important types of artistic phenomena. Mystics and transcendentalists have minimized it as superficial; they oppose any way of thinking which attributes much importance to sensory data. But their own attempts at a spiritual basis for comparing the arts have not produced anything definite. The conception of "sense addressed" does not take us very far into the deeper intellectual and emotional aspects of art, but it is useful as a first step in dividing up the field for deeper examination. It is so obvious and natural a way of distinguishing the arts that even a mystic like St. Augustine uses it.

[4] There are exceptions; Hegel's aesthetics was strongly historical in approach.

One advantage of this basis of division is that it applies to the mediums, processes, and products of art. As to medium, light and the physical substances which reflect it are visual; so are color, line, and texture as psychological materials of art, while sound is an auditory medium. As to the productive processes of art, we have seen how they can be grouped as visual shaping or shape guiding; sounding or sound guiding. As to products or finished forms, they too can be grouped as visual forms, auditory forms, and so on. Thus the concept of sense addressed allows us to analyze and classify the arts from the triple standpoint of medium, process, and product.

Just how shall the division be made on this basis? There are various possibilities, equally correct.

I. The simplest division is into two parts: *visual* and *auditory* arts; visual and auditory mediums, processes, and products. Theoretically, almost all the traditional realm of art can be placed under one or the other. Some arts can be placed under both: opera is a visual art, and also an auditory art.

II. But it is often useful to make a third main division of *audiovisual* (or audivisual or optic-acoustic) arts. This takes account of the difference between arts of unisensory presentation and those addressed to two senses at once. The latter are also called "combined arts."

III. Proceeding on a purely sensory basis, it is easy to divide the field more specifically, (a) into *four* types: visual, auditory, audiovisual, and lower-sense; or even (b) into *seven*: visual, auditory, audiovisual, gustatory, olfactory, tactile (cutaneous), and kinesthetic. But this is abstract psychologizing, and it is hard to find definite arts to fill all these categories.

IV. Paying more attention to the concrete facts of art, we can set up a separate class of *literature* or *verbal art*. This is a little inconsistent, since it abandons the strictly sensory basis. But it recognizes that the construction of verbal forms has tended to become a major realm of culture in itself. This realm has affiliations with both the visual and the auditory arts, but its divergences from both almost outweigh them. We do not behave toward literature, most of the time, as if it were either a visual or an auditory art; as if either its appearance or its sound were important. In comparing the arts, it is often convenient to use only three main categories: *visual art, music* (as the only great auditory art), and *literature*.

V. More specifically, again, we can enlarge this to five: *visual art, auditory art, audio-visual art, literature,* and *lower-sense art.* This is a very workable list of main categories. Opera can be classed as "audio-visual," as "audio-visual-verbal," or (for brevity) as "combined."

VI. If necessary, this list can be further enlarged as before by splitting up the class of lower-sense arts.

When we erect literature into a main class by itself, on the ground that it uses a distinctive kind of form and method based on linguistic symbolism, we are really introducing another basis of division. We are referring to the principal *modes of transmission* used in the arts. This, rather than sense addressed, becomes our principal criterion. We are implying that the arts called "visual" operate mainly through direct visual presentation (along with various kinds of suggestion); that "auditory" art operates mainly through auditory presentation (along with suggestion); while "literary" art operates mainly through linguistic suggestion, in which the presentative aspect is less essential.

Which of these six modes of division is the best? Again, the answer must depend entirely on the end in view, and the circumstances. If one is classifying courses in a university, and there is no course on lower-sense art or demand for one, it would be absurd to mention it just because it is theoretically possible. If one is organizing a public school agency for circulating educational equipment, and there is great demand for sound films and film projectors, then it may be necessary to talk about "audio-visual" materials. It may be worth while to class them apart from purely visual pictures and purely auditory phonograph records. A minute psychological analysis into gustatory, olfactory, and other lower-sense objects may be irrelevant as a rule, but important in a thorough survey of aesthetic psychology.

Let us suppose that we wish to survey and reorganize instruction in a university where all the arts are taught. We group them under four main headings: *visual, auditory, literary,* and *combined* (audio-visual or audio-visual-verbal).

A second step might be to subdivide each of these classes according to types of *product.* We undertake to teach the production and appreciation of the following kinds of art-work:

I. *Visual arts:* paintings, statues, houses and public buildings, parks and gardens, vases, rugs, chairs and tables, etc.
II. *Auditory (musical) art:* sonatas, fugues, symphonies, etc.

III. *Literature:* dramas, novels, short stories, essays, poems, etc.

IV. *Combined arts:* operas, ballets, stage productions, sound films, etc.

Working backward from the ends to the means, we then ask what techniques or *processes of production* are to be taught in connection with each of these product-types. Which of them can we undertake to teach? How can we organize and divide their instruction, by departments and courses? This leads to a third step in division, on the basis of process-types; for example,

IV. *Combined arts*

    A. Operas

        1. Operatic *writing;* the composition of operas.

        2. Operatic *performance:* singing, acting, playing, directing, costuming, make-up, lighting, etc.

This, of course, can be further subdivided on the same basis, as we specify the particular techniques involved in acting; those involved in directing, etc. Any number of steps can use the same basis of division. On the other hand, we may now wish to plan about the *materials* and *instruments* used in each technique.

    2. *Operatic performance*

        f. *Make-up:* cosmetics used, such as grease paints, charcoal, mascara, putty, etc. Their technological properties; which to use for various effects.

This in turn can be subdivided as minutely as desired. Small subdivisions would probably be omitted from a general prospectus or catalogue of the institution. But the teacher of a class on make-up could be expected to prepare his own syllabus, in which that item would be broken down in detail.

The total outline, produced by all these successive steps, would be a system or systematic classification of the arts, devised for practical purposes. True, we have not used the word "arts" at each step, because it is vague and redundant. Each of these items is commonly called an "art"—the art of make-up, for example—and we have been arranging them in various orders. It is more specific to refer to them as process-types, product-types, etc.

If this is a "practical" system, what is a theoretical one? What sort of classification of the arts is suitable for a textbook on aesthetic theory? There is no great difference, except that the end in view is more general and intellectual. Sometimes it is not clearly thought out. The function of a theoretical classification, as we have seen, is to aid the reader in understanding the nature and varieties of the material classified; and perhaps to aid him also in further investigation of it. There is no one perfect classification for theoretical purposes, any more than for practical. The question is, what particular phases of the subject-matter does one wish to explain and organize? If one is writing a book on "Creative Processes in the Arts," one will divide the field in a certain way for detailed treatment, chapter by chapter. If one is writing on "Types of Form in the Arts," one will divide it differently. A general text on aesthetics may try to work out an all-purpose theoretical system, to explain everything about the arts at once. The result will probably be fallacious; deceptively simple. It will stress some few relationships which the author considers essential, and ignore or minimize countless others.

"Sense addressed" is not always the best primary basis of division. In some connections it may be irrelevant or of minor importance, and used far down in the series of subdivisions. A study of artistic products might be divided first into main types of form, such as the utilitarian, the representative, the decorative, etc. Later on, one might ask how each type is produced in the visual arts, in music, and in literature. A study of artistic processes might be divided first on a basis of personality types or of cultural settings.

Several bases of division can be combined, in ways which *coincide* with each other; the overlapping is not universal. For example, the arts have been divided into "time" and "space" arts, and arts of rest and motion.. More accurately, there are arts which emphasize mobility and temporal development in the presented factor, and there are arts which emphasize static spatial development in the presented factor. Music, acting, and ballet belong in the first group; sculpture, architecture and painting belong largely in the second, aside from a few exceptional varieties.[5]

Now let us turn to *processes of execution and performance* as a

---

[5] Some writers distinguish ballet and theater as "spatio-temporal" from music as purely temporal. We have covered these distinctions in discussing modes of presentative development.

basis of division. There is one group of arts which requires repeated performance, each time the product is to be perceived. They are necessarily "time" arts. Techniques of repeated performance are important in such arts. On the other hand, the static space arts require no such performance. Their products are performed or executed once for all when first made, and have only to be maintained and exhibited under specified conditions.

In addition, it can be said that all auditory arts are arts of temporal succession; of change and motion rather than of rest and coexistence. This includes music and spoken literature. It follows from the evanescence of any particular sound-form. Also, the auditory arts do comparatively little mimetic representation. There is some of this in music and less in poetry (through onomatopoeia); but most literary representation is by verbal symbols, and musical mimesis is usually vague and subordinate. Most of the arts emphasizing imitative or mimetic representation are visual or audio-visual, as in painting and theater. Most of those emphasizing utility are also visual, as in architecture and the minor useful arts.

Such occasional correspondences are significant, but should not be exaggerated. One must resist the temptation to bring still other bases into line; to identify static arts or "arts of rest" with "visual arts," and "arts of motion" with music and literature. These categories simply part company, and there is no forcing them all into line. Let us not deplore the fact, as a stubborn rebellion of nature against our neat formulas. On the contrary, it is stimulating to see how infinitely rich and variable are the manifestations of art; how they fall into new arrangements each time that we look at them from a different point of view.

There is need for much study and experiment on different ways of classifying the arts and phenomena within the arts; not as a mere intellectual pastime, but for definite values. It can lead to more intelligent, efficient ways of organizing and conducting all kinds of practical activity in the arts. Through showing what kinds of art have been produced, and what others are possible but still undeveloped, it can point the way to new creative experiments.

In aesthetics, it can lead to new and fruitful ways of dividing and interrelating the phenomena of art for investigation. Every scholar in the realm of art faces the problem of how to divide and interrelate his own field of study. In publishing his findings, he must decide how to divide his book into chapters and sections. These are but special aspects of the larger problem, which we have been considering throughout this book, of division and classification in art. Progress in this larger problem can give far-reaching help to scholars and teachers working on innumerable special topics within it, by showing them new ways to organize their materials.

Too much study, writing, and teaching in the arts is organized on a simple *historical* basis of geography, chronology, or individual biography. For example, one studies "the art of eighteenth-century England," or "the life and times of Shelley." This is an easy, obvious way of marking off a field of study, and many students and teachers follow it because no other way occurs to them. It is one very good way, but not the only one. It has its limitations, and should not be overdone to the exclusion of others. For progress in the scientific understanding of the arts, we need more *comparative* studies, which will reach back and forth between different periods and nationalities, in search of significant recurrences, major tendencies, and determining factors. These will eventually help us to a better understanding of art history itself, and of individual artists. They will help us to see an artist or period in relation to broader cultural contexts; not as a string of detached, inexplicable happenings. Such studies will help us to understand and control the arts of our own time, by showing how they fit into major types and tendencies; where they came from and where they are going; where, to some extent, they can be made to go.

Through dividing the field of art in various ways, and studying the relationship of parts thus revealed, we become aware of new problems and promising clues to further knowledge. As long as we stay inside the old compartments of thought, we tend to retravel the same old paths within them. It is time for new surveys of the territory of the arts, and for new explorations within it.

XIII

Four Hundred Arts and Types of Art: A Systematic Classification*

The previous chapter explained several possible ways of constructing a many-purpose classification of the arts, but did not actually construct one. In an earlier section one hundred visual and auditory arts were listed alphabetically, without theoretical classification, so as to show that many more arts exist than is commonly realized. The present list is still longer, including over four hundred arts and types of art, some of which are addressed to the lower senses. It could be still further enlarged.

To include so many kinds of activity and product as "arts" is at variance with the traditional belief that there are only seven arts, or some other very small number. Since the conception of "art" employed here is a broad one, many arts are listed which do not ordinarily find a place in conventional treatises on aesthetics and art history. Traditional aesthetics held to a narrow, exclusive conception of art, ignoring or disparaging a great variety of skills and products with aesthetic functions, many of which were and are highly respected by art critics and historians, as well as by the general public. Reasons are given in the foregoing chapters for recognizing in aesthetics the existence of these other skills, and their claim to be classed as arts. This does not imply, however, that they are all of equal or nearly equal importance and value. On the contrary, some have played major roles in cultural history and still do so, while others are relatively trivial. Some are old, some new; some have grown in importance while others have declined. Some are potentially great in cultural value, others more limited. New ones are constantly arising, whose potential value is yet unknown. Such questions of relative value are not raised in the present outline, and nothing is said or implied about which arts are major and which are minor, at present or in general.

The present list is classified according to some of the categories or

* Reprinted with revisions from the *Journal of Aesthetics and Art Criticism*, Vol. XVI, No. 1, September, 1957.

"bases of classification" which seem to be most true to fact, most useful in practice, and most significant in bringing out major distinctions and analogies among the arts. These are: (a) sense primarily addressed; (b) medium, materials, instruments; (c) processes, techniques; (d) nature of products, as to form or mode of organization in space and time, and as to uses, functions, and modes of operation. Since all these bases are employed, the resulting groups and divisions overlap some-what; a certain art or type of art may fall under more than one heading in the list, in regard to different traits and relations. Art A may be classed with Art B in respect to material and process; with Art C in respect to the social use or function of its products.

The arts are constantly changing as well as overlapping, merging, and redividing, so that sharp and permanent divisions are impossible. Whatever concept one employs as the main, primary basis of division, one renders the system less advantageous for persons whose main interest lies along other lines. For example, to divide the arts at once into "visual," "auditory," etc., tends to unfit the list for those whose main present interest is in chronological, geographical, or sociological distinctions such as that between medieval and renaissance, European and Asiatic, tribal and urban, or handmade and mechanized. Different interests and problems lead to different ways of naming and grouping the arts, with emphasis on different characteristics. Nevertheless, the following list is adaptable to a considerable variety of purposes, both theoretical and practical.

No sharp distinction is currently made between "arts" and "types" or "branches" of art, and they are not sharply distinguished in the following outline. Thus reference is sometimes made to the "art of still-life painting," the "art of dramatic writing," and the "art of the fugue" as if these were separate, independent arts. At other times, they are regarded as mere types or branches of painting, literature, and music. A minor skill or specialized type of art may at first be regarded merely as a branch of a larger one, then gradually develop into a recognized, independent art in its own right.

In listing a certain art as a main heading or as a branch or sub-division, nothing is implied as to its relative importance, its aesthetic, moral, spiritual, or cultural value. Section I, on the visual arts, must be divided into many subdivisions within subdivisions, because these arts are in fact highly specialized and differentiated. Sections V and VI, on the other hand, require fewer subdivisions.

I. VISUAL ARTS

A. INTRODUCTION: This group of arts is addressed primarily to the sense of sight. Some of their products appeal to other senses also, as in the sound of a clock or the feeling of clothes and furniture; but their visual qualities are ordinarily considered more important from the aesthetic point of view. They are presented mostly as static forms in two dimensions, on flat surfaces, but they often suggest the third dimension. Some involve movement, as in vehicles of transportation, but they do not usually present to the eyes a complex sequence of movements or changes in definite, temporal order. Details must usually be grasped in some sort of temporal succession (not all at once), but the exact order in which they are seen is usually not essential; hence these are not called "time arts." Some other visual or partly visual arts, in which temporal order is emphasized, are listed under §IV, ARTS OF PUBLIC PERFORMANCE.

B. PICTORIAL ARTS AND TYPES OF ART:

1. INTRODUCTION: The word "picture" comes from the Latin word for "painting." But, in its present sense, a picture is not necessarily painted; it can be made in many other ways, such as engraving and photography. Most pictures are representations of objects, persons, scenes, etc., but sometimes the term is applied to a non-representative painting or design, especially when framed and used as a picture. In pictures classed as artistic, an aesthetic effect is emphasized, but much pictorial art has other functions also, such as the religious and moral. Some pictures are symbolic, and stand for certain things or ideas without looking like them. Some try to express an emotion, mood, or abstract idea. Some pictorial arts are also called "graphic arts," especially drawing. This word comes from the Greek for "writing" (see §C on the non-pictorial graphic arts of writing and printing). The following subheadings are somewhat interchangeable in that those listed under each main heading can be regarded as subdivisions of the others: e.g., under "Painting," Mural, Religious, Figure, etc. (For definitions, see pages 455ff., 457ff.)

2. TYPES OF PICTORIAL ART AS TO MEDIUM AND PROCESS: MATERIALS, INSTRUMENTS, TECHNIQUES.

    a. *Painting*.

        I'. Oil painting.

II'. Tempera painting.

III'. Watercolor and gouache.

IV'. Fresco.

V'. Encaustic.

VI'. Sand painting.

  b. *Drawing.*

I'. Pencil drawing.

II'. Pen and ink drawing.

III'. Brush drawing; wash drawing.

IV'. Crayon and pastel drawing.

  c. *Print-making.*

I'. Engraving, hand; on wood, metal, etc.

II'. Etching, drypoint, aquatint.

III'. Mezzotint.

IV'. Lithography.

V'. Photo-engraving; half-tone.

VI'. Collotype; gelatine processes.

VII'. Silkscreen; serigraphy.

  d. *Photography (still).* In black and white; in color. Microphotography; telephotography; X-ray photography.

  e. *Mosaic, pictorial.*

  f. *Wood inlay; intarsia, pictorial.*

  g. *Tapestry; pictorial weaving.*

  h. *Embroidery* and other needlework, lace, etc., pictorial.

  i. *Collage and montage,* pictorial; cut paper pictures; silhouettes.

  j. *Colored lights,* static and pictorial.

3. TYPES OF PICTORIAL ART AS TO NATURE OF PRODUCT.

  a. *As to form, size, location:*

I'. Mural pictures; on walls and ceilings.

II'. Floor pictures, esp. in tiles and mosaics.

III'. Easel pictures.

IV'. Scroll pictures.

V'. Miniature pictures; separately or as manuscript and book illumination.

VI'. Vase painting.

VII'. Screen painting.

VIII'. Various shapes in the above: rectangular, round, triangular, pendentive, irregular.

b. *As to subject, function, and mode of treatment.*

    I′. *Figure* pictures: of humans or supernatural and imaginary beings in human or partly human form. Religious, secular, aristocratic, mythological, fantastic, "genre" or everyday subjects. Single figures and groups with or without landscape or architectural backgrounds. Portraits (head, bust, full-length); more or less realistic, individualized. Equestrian and other combinations of humans and animals.

    II′. *Animal* pictures.

    III′. *Landscapes* and seascapes.

    IV′. *Still-life* pictures.

    V′. *Decorative, semi-abstract, abstract,* and non-objective pictures; non-representative designs.

    VI′. *Symbolic* pictures; emblems, insignia. These may be abstract designs or representative pictures with an additional, symbolic meaning; allegories. Types of symbolic picture.

        A′. Religious symbols, such as the Cross, Crescent, and Star of David; symbols of particular gods and saints such as the owl for Minerva, the wheel for St. Catherine.

        B′. Political symbols: national, city, etc. Flags, seals, coats of arms.

        C′. Heraldic symbols, of a family or hereditary rank or title. Coats of arms, crests.

        D′. Commercial symbols; trade marks.

        E′. Club and association symbols.

    VII′. *Illustration* (for books, magazines, posters, etc.).

    VIII′. *Fashion-illustration.*

    IX′. *Cartooning;* caricaturing.

C. WRITING AND PRINTING; NON-PICTORIAL GRAPHIC ARTS.

  1. INTRODUCTION: These arts are now mainly used as means for the visual presentation of verbal compositions, including literature. Thus literature can become an art of visual presentation. Writing and printing can also be presented tactually, as in Braille type for the blind. Letters and words can also be communicated aurally. Writing and printing can be combined with pictures.

They are visual *arts,* rather than mere utilitarian devices for ordinary communication, only when they involve some aesthetic refinement and development, as in calligraphy and artistic typography. This is not necessarily conspicuous or ornamental, however; it can be subordinated to clear communication and easy readability. (For definitions, see pp. 456f.).

2. *Calligraphy and hand lettering;* in cursive or detached characters; manuscript writing.
3. *Typography.*
   a. Type designing.
   b. Printing.
   c. Layout (non-pictorial); page-arrangement.
4. Other kinds of lettering and visual wording, as by carving in stone, by electric lights, etc.

D. COMBINED PICTORIAL-VERBAL ARTS AND TYPES OF ART.
1. Picture-writing, primitive and modern; pictographs; hieroglyphics, pictorial symbols. (In primitive culture, preceded the separation of writing from pictures; but still used, as for educational and advertising purposes.)
2. Manuscript and page illumination and illustration; hand painting combined with calligraphy.
3. Printed layouts, pictorial-verbal; page, poster, and cover design, book and magazine illustrations with text. Advertising and other commercial devices.
4. Packaging, as involving printed pictorial-verbal arrangements.
5. Postage stamps, banknotes, and other common types of form, combining pictorial and decorative elements with words, numbers, etc.
6. Maps, charts, pictorial diagrams and displays for explanatory and utilitarian purposes; often combining realistic details with arbitrary symbols.
7. Luminous displays combining pictorial and graphic elements.

E. SCULPTURAL ARTS AND TYPES OF ART.
1. INTRODUCTION: Sculpture is the art of making three-dimensional forms, usually to be seen from the outside, which represent human or animal figures or other natural objects, compose a design of solid shapes and surfaces, and/or suggest feelings or abstract ideas. Some sculpture is representational and realistic; some highly stylized or abstract. (See pp. 452f.)

2. TYPES OF SCULPTURE AS TO MEDIUM AND PROCESS.
   a. Stone sculpture.
   b. Ceramic sculpture; clay, earthenware, porcelain, terra cotta, plaster, etc.
   c. Metal sculpture, in bronze, iron, copper, gold, silver, lead, etc.; casting and other processes.
   d. Glass sculpture.
   e. Ivory and bone sculpture.
   f. Wood sculpture (including totem poles, fetish figures, etc.).
   g. Wax sculpture; soap sculpture.
   h. Gem carving, cameo and intaglio, with effect of sculptural relief.
   i. Paper and papier-maché sculpture.
   j. Sculpture in plastic and synthetic materials, string, cloth, etc.
   k. Taxidermy; habitat groups; animal figures reconstructed and arranged.
   l. Embalming and mummifying (of human and animal bodies; esp. in ancient Egypt). Use of skulls and dried heads as statues.

3. TYPES OF SCULPTURE AS TO FORM OF PRODUCT.
   a. *As to form, size, and function:*
       I'. In the round.
       II'. In relief; low, high; steles, tablets, on walls and monuments.
       III'. Free-standing.
       IV'. Engaged, attached to a building (e.g., as caryatid) or to a piece of furniture or utensil. As architectural ornaments.
       V'. For magical use, as in amulets, fetishes.
       VI'. Mobiles, stables; combined types. Wind-moved; hand-moved; mechanical. String figures.
       VII'. For religious use, as in idols and ikons.
       VIII'. For commemorative monuments, often with architectural bases.
       IX'. As interior ornaments; esp. small reliefs and statuettes.
       X'. For wear, esp. ceremonial and theatrical, such as masks.
       XI'. For theatrical use, as in marionettes and puppets.

XII'. As emblems, insignia, for identification, as in carving heraldic crests.

XIII'. As advertising devices, displays (three-dimensional).

XIV'. Dolls and similar toys involving three-dimensional representation.

XV'. As to size: colossal, heroic; lifesize; small (statuettes, figurines, bibelots, netsukes, toys, etc.). Small reliefs, as in coins, medals, amulets, cameos, sculptural jewelry.

b. *As to subjects represented:*

I'. Figures: human, animal, supernatural, diabolical, fantastic. Equestrian groups; totem poles.

II'. Portraits; busts; full-length portrait statues. Masks, realistic and fantastic.

III'. Sculptured plants, flowers, fruit, and other natural objects.

IV'. Reliefs with scenic, quasi-pictorial backgrounds.

V'. Semi-abstract and non-representative sculpture; constructivist designs.

F. USEFUL AND DECORATIVE ARTS AND TYPES OF ART; UTILITARIAN DESIGN; INDUSTRIAL DESIGN. (For definitions, see pp. 467ff.)

1. INTRODUCTION: These arts fulfill a great variety of functions which can be broadly classed as useful or practical. They serve as means in many overt activities such as work, war, education, worship, and everyday living. Their products, mostly three-dimensional, are correspondingly varied in form, size, and mode of operation. Those classed as useful *art,* rather than as purely utilitarian devices, pay some attention also to aesthetic qualities: to visual appearance or "eye appeal." Other sense-qualities may also be emphasized, as in the tone of a violin or piano. Most of their products are non-representational, especially in contemporary styles, but some involve carved, painted, or other representational features for ornament. The "functional" or utilitarian aspects are sometimes considered more important; at other times, the aesthetic and decorative.

2. TYPES OF USEFUL AND DECORATIVE ART AS TO MEDIUM OR MATERIAL: those using

a. *Hard, inanimate materials, and soft materials which harden. To be carved, molded, hammered, etc.*

I'. Masonry; stonework (decorative).

II'. Ceramics (non-sculptural); earthenware, pottery, porcelain.

III'. Tilework and brickwork, decorative.

IV'. Plasterwork, stucco, cementwork.

V'. Glassware.

VI'. Enameling.

VII'. Lacquerwork.

VIII'. Ivory and bone-carving (non-sculptural).

IX'. Gem-cutting; lapidary art (non-sculptural).

X'. Goldsmithing and silversmithing.

XI'. Jewelry, as including gems and metal settings, costume jewelry of non-precious materials, etc.

XII'. Ironwork and steelwork, decorative.

XIII'. Coppersmithing.

XIV'. Bronze casting, non-sculptural.

XV'. Plastics.

XVI'. Woodcarving (non-sculptural).

XVII'. Cabinet-making; fine and decorative carpentry.

b. *Those using soft and pliable, inanimate materials. To be twisted, woven, tied, knitted, felted, sewed, pasted, etc.*

I'. Basketry.

II'. Cordwork and stringwork, decorative.

III'. Weaving; textiles; rug and tapestry weaving.

IV'. Lace-making.

V'. Knitting and crocheting.

VI'. Needlework, embroidery, appliqué, etc. (esp. non-pictorial).

VII'. Feltwork.

VIII'. Tapa or barkcloth-making.

IX'. Paper-making, decorative.

X'. Paperwork, decorative; products of cut, folded, pasted papers, plain and colored.

XI'. Plastic cloth-making, decorative.

XII'. Leatherwork.

XIII'. Featherwork.

XIV'. Beadwork and quillwork.

XV'. Fur-making; designing and executing garments, rugs, etc., of fur along with other materials.

    c. Those using *plants,* and related natural objects (earth, water, stones, etc.). To be cultivated, trained, and arranged into groups and sequences for aesthetic as well as utilitarian purposes.

    d. Those using *animals;* animal breeding and husbandry, for aesthetic as well as other qualities; e.g., for shape, coloring, graceful motion, etc., as in horses, deer, cattle, dogs, cats, goldfish, birds. (Song is also cultivated in some kinds of birds.) Also, in some cases, as pets for friendly disposition, intelligence, watchfulness; for racing, working, etc.; but not classed as "art" if for utilitarian purposes only.

3. TYPES OF USEFUL ART AS TO PROCESS OR TECHNIQUE.

    a. Handcrafts.

    b. Machine crafts; mechanized industries.

    c. Partly mechanized; combinations of hand and machine technique.

    d. Large-scale, mass production methods (e.g., specialized work and assembly line, whether by hand or machinery).

4. AS TO NATURE OF PRODUCT; FORM AND FUNCTION.

    a. *Clothing arts;* design and manufacture of garments and accessories for personal wear; also for dolls, marionettes, etc. For ordinary use or for theater, dance, ritual, ceremonial, or other special occasions.

        I'. Tailoring and dressmaking.

        II'. Hat-making; millinery; head-dresses.

        III'. Shoemaking, bootmaking.

        IV'. Glove-making.

        V'. Lingerie, underwear, corsetry, etc.

        VI'. Costume accessories.

        VII'. Masks, adapted for wear.

    b. *Products for war and hunting.*

        I'. Weapons.

        II'. Armor, helmets, etc., for man and horse.

    c. *Tools, utensils, furniture; equipment for home, work, school, church, recreation.*

        I'. Tools and machines for occupational use.

        II'. Utensils, instruments, smaller home and personal accessories such as dishes, cutlery, tableware, desk equipment, watches, writing materials, games, and sports equipment.

III'. Furniture and fixtures; larger appliances, movable and immovable.

IV'. Rugs, carpets, linoleum, and other floor coverings.

V'. Draperies, upholsteries, and other decorative fabrics adapted for use in rooms, trains, vehicles, etc.

VI'. Wallpapers and other wall-coverings.

VII'. Book-manufacture, including folding and sewing pages, binding, etc.

VIII'. Toymaking, including dolls and children's games, utensils for play, small copies of products used by adults, etc.

IX'. Food-preparation, visual aspects of; shape, color, texture of foods, esp. ornamental cakes, candies, desserts.

X'. Consumable and disposable products, made with attention to visual and other aesthetic qualities: soaps, paper handkerchiefs and napkins, etc.

d. *Interior design and decoration.* Room composition. The art of planning and arranging furniture and other objects within a room or group of rooms, so as to achieve a satisfactory appearance as well as convenience, health and comfort, efficiency, or other desired qualities.

I'. *Selection and arrangement* of furniture, fixtures, appliances, wall-coverings, floor-coverings, lamps, pictures, utensils, house-plants, etc., in relation to the architectural setting and to particular needs and ways of living.

II'. *Table setting and decoration;* selection and arrangement of tableware, cloths, flowers, etc., especially for the service of meals.

e. *Displays* (of solid objects in three-dimensional space). *Decorative and educational displays:* in museums, schools, libraries, etc. *Commercial* displays: for merchandising, advertising, etc. Arrangements of objects (esp. for sale) in or out of doors; in shops, store windows, exhibit areas; with appropriate backgrounds, lighting; sometimes sound effects.

f. *Stage and scene design;* large representations of rooms, outdoor scenes, etc.; built, painted, lighted, and equipped for dramatic presentation.

g. *Dioramas, peep-shows, small-scale model rooms and house interiors,* built in three dimensions. Solid objects and figures arranged in deep space, often so as to be seen from a certain point of view.

h. *Building arts; architecture, civil engineering.* (For definitions, see pp. 460f.)

    I′. *Civil and military architecture* (the latter including castles, forts, and fortifications).

    II′. *Religious architecture:* designing and building temples, churches, baptistries, pagodas, stupas, mosques, shrines, monasteries, etc. Altars, pulpits, fonts, sarcophagi, and other interior fixtures are on the borderline between architecture and furniture.

    III′. *Secular architecture:* designing and building dwelling-houses, palaces, arches and complex monuments, hotels, apartments, theaters, office buildings, schools, railway stations, libraries, laboratories, hospitals, factories, warehouses, stores, shopping centers, etc.

    IV′. *Other types of building,* often involving architecture and engineering: bridges, dams, highways, piers, harbors, aqueducts, viaducts, lighthouses, airplane fields and hangars, amusement parks and expositions.

i. *Landscape and garden arts.* Arts involving the cultivation and arrangement of plants and other natural objects such as rocks, water, etc., and of planted areas out of doors, with or without accessory products such as small buildings, statuary, garden furniture, lighting, etc.

    I′. *Landscape architecture:* the art of arranging plants and other objects and cultivated areas in a certain region, perhaps with alterations in ground-level, bodies of water, etc., so as to produce a satisfactory visual effect from various points of view and also to serve other uses.

    II′. *Water-designing:* fountains, cascades, pools; usually in relation to architecture and gardens.

    III′. *Gardening:* as an art, the arrangement, planting, and care of flowering and other plants for their appearance, scent, or other aesthetic qualities as well as for their useful functions.

IV'. *Horticulture:* the science and art of growing plants, including flowers, trees, fruit, and other ornamental plants; including applied genetics, breeding and cultivating plants for better appearance, hardiness, and other desired qualities.

V'. *Topiary art;* ornamental clipping and training of plants.

VI'. *Flower arrangements;* set pieces, bouquets, wreaths, garlands.

VII'. *Arrangements* of driftwood, shells, and other natural objects.

VIII'. *Tray landscapes* (esp. Japanese).

j. *Community designing; town, city, and regional planning.* The art of planning and arranging the form of an inhabited area so as to provide the best possible means to social and industrial living; especially as to health, safety, comfort, education and cultural advantages, efficient work and transportation, recreation and travel, family and neighborhood relations. Special care is taken with zoning industrial, commercial, and residential centers, safe and speedy traffic, public buildings and utilities. Relation of buildings, roads, and parks to natural topography, climate and resources is considered. Visual appearance can be planned with respect to all scenes and vistas within or near it, especially the main or central, inclusive ones. Community designing involves architecture, civil engineering, landscape architecture, and many other arts and applied sciences. (For further details see pp. 463f.)

I'. *Civil and town planning; urbanism.* Community planning and designing in the case of large or small cities, towns and villages.

II'. *Regional planning and designing; geo-architecture.* Community and environmental planning in the case of large areas, which may include many towns and villages with intervening farms or vacant land, parks, highways, bridges, waterways and waterfronts, dams, irrigation, etc.

k. *Transportation; vehicle design,* for appearance, outside and inside, as well as for comfort, safety, speed, quiet operation, etc. Large, complex vehicles can be regarded as mobile architecture.

I'. *Land transportation:*
  A'. *Saddles, harness,* etc., for riding on animals.
  B'. *Litters; sedan chairs, human power.*
  C'. *Sleds and sledges; without wheels; human or animal power.*
  D'. *Chariots; animal power.*
  E'. *Carriages, carts, wagons; human and animal power.*
  F'. *Bicycles, tricycles, motorcycles.*
  G'. *Railroad trains; steam, petroleum, electricity;* cars for sleeping, dining, etc., comparable to hotel rooms.
  H'. *Automobiles:* steam, petroleum, electricity.
  I'. *Trailers,* built and equipped as dwellings, offices, etc.

II'. *Water transportation; surface and submarine:*
  A'. *Canoes, rowboats, gondolas, galleys* (human power).
  B'. *Sailboats and sailships* (windpower).
  C'. *Automotive ships, boats, and submarines.* (Steam, petroleum, electricity, atomic energy.) Passenger ships as complex, floating hotels.
  D'. *Combined types.*

III'. *Air and space transportation:*
  A'. *Balloons;* lighter than air; some automotive, dirigible.
  B'. *Airplanes; heavier than air.* Gliders. Automotive planes; propeller type; jet and rocket types.

II. MUSIC; AUDITORY ARTS

A. INTRODUCTION. Music is the art or group of arts concerned with arranging sounds simultaneously and in close succession, with some regularity and continuity of rhythm, and usually of changes in pitch and timbre. (For fuller definition, see pp. 474f.)

B. MUSICAL ARTS AND TYPES OF ART, AS TO MEDIUM AND PROCESS OR TECHNIQUE.

1. *Composition and performance.*
   a. Musical composition, transcription and adaptation.
   b. Musical performance, including playing instruments, singing, and conducting.
2. *Kinds of music as to medium or instrument used.* (Each kind includes both composing and performing.)
   a. *Vocal music;* singing, with or without instrumental accompaniment. (N.B.: Humming, whistling, and other types of vocal sound are sometimes developed musically. Some are intermediate between singing and speaking.)
      I'. *Solo; soprano, alto, tenor, bass.* (Usually with instrumental accompaniment.)
      II'. *Choral: men's, women's, mixed; vocal group.* (Often without instrumental accompaniment.)
   b. *Instrumental music.*
      I'. *Solo:* alone or with subordinate accompaniment; piano, violin, pipe organ, clarinet, drum, etc.
      II'. *Small and medium-sized groups; ensemble; chamber music, dance orchestras; bands.*
      III'. *Orchestra; large groups of different sizes.*
   c. *Combined vocal and instrumental music, as in chorus or solo singer with orchestra;* anthems, oratorios, operas, cantatas.
   d. *Concrete, electronic,* and other music from sources formerly regarded as non-musical. Recordings adapted from natural sounds, traffic, industry, and machinery. Artificial combinations of sounds with different timbres and wave-lengths.
3. *Techniques and processes in musical composition; often regarded as distinct arts.*
   a. *Melody-writing.*
   b. *Counterpoint; polyphony.*
   c. *Harmony-writing.*
   d. *Orchestration.*
   e. *Atonal, twelve-tone, or serial music.*
4. *Skills and activities related to music and sometimes classed within it.*
   a. Sound effects in drama, film, radio, television.
   b. Breeding and training birds for song and speech.

C. MUSICAL ARTS AND TYPES OF ART AS TO NATURE OF PRODUCT; FORMS
AND FUNCTIONS.
1. *Music for active use.* (The same piece of music may be put to
different uses.)
   a. For worship and ritual; religious music.
   b. For work, war, marching, etc.
   c. For dancing, games, festivals, etc.
   d. For psychotherapy.
2. *Concert music: mostly for quiet listening; for aesthetic perception.*
   a. *With words: songs, chants, hymns, oratorios, cantatas.* (Non-
theatrical; without acting.)
   b. *Instrumental music with little or no use of words.* (Voices can
be used as instruments, without words.)
        I′. *Fugues, toccatas, madrigals, and other polyphonic
        pieces.*
       II′. *Suites, sonatas,* and other types of music for one or
        more instruments.
      III′. *Symphonies; symphonic poems* and other forms for
        full orchestra.
       IV′. *Quartets, quintets, sextets, etc. for chamber group.*
        (Often in sonata form.)
        V′. *Concerti for orchestra and solo instrument or instru-
        ments.*
3. *Music as a component in a combined, diversified art.* (Such music
can often be performed separately, for concert use.)
   a. *Operatic, ballet, film, and ceremonial music.* Where music is
   an important part of a more complex work of art, including
   acting, costume, scenery, etc.
   b. *Incidental music;* music as a subordinate accompaniment to
   dance and theatrical programs, radio, TV, films, etc.

III. LITERATURE; ARTS OF VERBAL COMPOSITION

A. INTRODUCTION: Literature is an art or group of arts devoted to combining words and their meanings into forms which give or are intended to give a satisfactory aesthetic effect. It can be heard when
spoken aloud or silently read through visual or other symbols, thus
becoming either auditory or visual in presentation. It can be read
by touch as in Braille type for the blind. Literature is a time art in

that the order of presented details is important. Unwritten, orally transmitted literature existed before writing was invented. Literature was originally an auditory art, but is now usually communicated visually. Much verbal composition is not ordinarily classed as literature because it serves purely practical, scientific, or other non-aesthetic ends; but such writing can sometimes achieve literary quality also. (See pp. 477, 492.)

B. TYPES OF LITERATURE, AS TO LINGUISTIC MEDIUM.
1. Ancient languages: Greek, Latin, etc.
2. Modern languages: English, French, etc.

C. LITERARY ARTS AND TYPES OF ART AS TO FORM AND FUNCTION OF PRODUCTS.
1. *As to development of word-sounds* (with related characteristics of emotional intensity, diction, etc.).
   a. *Prose literature.* Prose is composed in a form like ordinary conversation in that it lacks rhyme, regular meter, division into verses of even length, or other definite regularity of sound. It is usually divided into paragraphs, and is usually (but not necessarily) less intense emotionally than poetry.
   b. *Poetry writing; verse and versification; prosody.* "Verse" is literature composed in lines or verses with some regularity in the sounds of words. Prosody or versification is the science and art of writing verse. "Poetry" usually implies not only verse form but concentrated emotional and imaginative expression, especially through metaphors or other figures.
      I'. *Metrical verse.*
      II'. *Free or non-metrical verse.*
      III'. *Rhymed verse.*
      IV'. *Unrhymed verse; blank verse.*
      V'. *Alliterative verse.*
   c. *Prose poetry; poetic or lyrical prose.* Intermediate between prose and poetry; not in verse form but with considerable regularity of word-sounds, concentrated imagery and emotion, etc.
2. *Literary arts and types of art as to development of ideas: as to function and general mode of composition.* (All the following types overlap. Many combined and intermediate examples exist.)
   a. *Narrative literature; narration.* Tells a story or connected sequence of actions and events from the standpoint of the

author or of some imaginary character or characters represented by him. May involve plot construction, dialogue, characterization, imagery, local coloring, verbal style, and other components. May be in prose or verse; may be communicated orally or visually. As pure literature, does not include the arts of speech.

    I'. *Epic and verse romance: long verse narratives.*

    II'. *Ballads and other short or medium-length tales in verse.*

    III'. *Novels and prose romances; long fictional narratives; sagas.*

    IV'. *Short story, novelette, prose tale, fable, anecdote; short or medium-length fiction in prose.*

    V'. *Journalism; short factual narrative; news reporting, in newspaper, magazine, or book form.*

    VI'. *Symbolic stories and moral tales; allegories, parables, fables.*

b. *Dramatic literature; play writing; composition of verbal texts, scripts, or scenarios in a form suited for enactment.* May be in prose, verse, or a combination of both, as in many of Shakespeare's plays. The text is organized as a guide to dramatic speaking and acting. It is intended to be spoken aloud with appropriate movements and gestures, or is written as if it were so intended. Sometimes the dramatic form is used even when it would be impossible to present the action on a stage, and when the text is really intended for reading only. As a branch of literature, drama does not include the arts of public speaking and acting, but they are often grouped together. (See also §IV, ARTS OF PUBLIC PERFORMANCE.)

    I'. *Tragedy, high and low; dramas of pathos, failure, and suffering.*

    II'. *Comedy; high and low; comedy of manners; farce, burlesque, satire. Dramas of success, happiness, and amusement.*

    III'. *Tragi-comedy; mixed and intermediate types of play, esp. serious plays with happy or partly happy endings.*

    IV'. *Morality, miracle, mystery, and passion plays.*

    V'. *Masques.*

c. *Lyric writing.* Lyrics are written to be read independently, and also to be set to music as songs. A lyric may include some narration, drama, or exposition. A lyric is usually in verse, with a fairly regular design of word-sounds and ideas, and is fairly short. Emotional expression is emphasized.

I'. *Songs; lyrics suited for singing.*

II'. *Sonnets.*

III'. *Odes.*

IV'. *Pastoral poetry; idyls, bucolics, eclogues.*

V'. *Poems for special occasions:* elegies, epithalamia, etc.

VI'. *Dramatic poems; dramatic lyrics and monologues; lyrical dramas.* Intermediate between dramas and pure lyrics. Written in dramatic or partly dramatic form, but intended for reading rather than for stage performance. Short, single speeches of imaginary characters revealing character and events. Longer poems, written mostly in dialogue form, but not suited for acting; often including shorter lyrics.

d. *Expository and hortatory literature; explanation and rhetoric.* Writing to explain, instruct, discuss, or persuade. Exposition deals especially with general topics such as virtue or democracy. Rhetoric is the use of language to persuade. These types are classed as literary art only when possessing some claim to aesthetic value, as through sound of words, imagery, poetic diction and fantasy, emotional ardor, incidental narratives, etc. In prose or verse; when in verse, usually classed as "didactic" poetry.

I'. *Essays (short).*

II'. *Treatises (long).*

III'. *Speeches, orations, sermons, hortatory letters, etc.* (Considered here as literature only.)

e. *Mixed and variable types of literature:*

I'. *History;* supposedly factual narration and explanation of events, in the description of characters and conditions. Often there is some departure from fact, especially in early histories, where the imaginative element is strong.

II'. *Biography and autobiography;* also supposedly factual, but often with much imagination or bias.

III'. *Conversations,* as reported in writing, more or less

factually; not as dialogue in stories or plays. Often more literary when somewhat formalized and planned in advance, as in aristocratic salons of Renaissance Italy.

IV'. *Philosophic dialogues;* mostly expository but in dramatic form; expressing different opinions on controversial subjects; often with persuasion of some speakers.

V'. *Prayers and rituals;* of various religions. As literature, the verbal text rather than speech or action. Often lyrical and hortatory. Hymns and songs are often in prayer form. Rituals may enact sacred stories in somewhat dramatic form.

VI'. *Letters (factual or fictional).*

VII'. *Diaries; journals; meditations.* Daily or occasional notes, usually unsystematic. Events, thoughts, comments.

VIII'. *Epigrams; proverbs.* Very short poems or prose sentences with concentrated, often wise or witty, meaning; terse generalizations about life and people.

IX'. *Epitaphs.* For tomb inscriptions, or as if so intended.

IV. ARTS OF PUBLIC PERFORMANCE; THEATER ARTS; CEREMONIES AND ENTERTAINMENTS (OTHER THAN MUSIC ALONE)

A. INTRODUCTION: These arts are mostly audio-visual, in that they present to the observer's eyes, ears, or both, an organized sequence of images or stimuli. These usually come from the appearance, actions, spoken words, or musical performance of living actors, seen in deep space. Sometimes they come from representations of these or from changing designs on a screen with accompanying sound, as in marionettes, motion pictures, and television. The temporal order in which they are presented is important for the desired effect. Spatial organization is also important. Hence these arts can be called "space-time" arts. (See definitions on pages 493f. and 499f.)

B. DANCE; BALLET; BALLROOM DANCING: "Dance" is rhythmic bodily movement, usually seen as an orderly sequence of moving patterns of line, shape, and color. Such postures and gestures suggest feelings of tension and relaxation, and related moods and ideas. Sometimes they act out a story. Dancing is usually done to music or rhythmic sounds. "Ballet" is a kind of dancing, usually by several dancers in a theater, with music and lighting. They move in complex visual designs and often act out a story. "Ballroom" dancing is performed by couples or small groups, with simpler movements, more for amateur participation—dance for the dancers—than for observation by others. But all art can be enjoyed by artists and performers as well as by observers; the difference is one of degree. In ballroom dancing, the dancers observe each other in addition to participating. *Ballet includes as component arts:* (1) Dancing and sometimes pantomime; solo and group dances; (2) Choreography; composing dances and recording them in written notation; (3) Costuming; (4) Stage and scene design, lighting, etc.; (5) Music; (6) Direction; coordination.

C. PANTOMIME; EXPRESSIVE GESTURE AND POSTURE, INCLUDING FACIAL EXPRESSION: Especially as used for dramatic representation of characters and stories, often with music. In India, this is done with conventionalized symbolic gestures and postures called "mudras."

D. SPEECH ARTS: Speaking or chanting words, other than as musical singing. Recitation of a prepared text or composed as one goes along. Attention to tones of voice, expressiveness, diction and pronunciation, etc.

1. *Oratory; eloquence; speech-making; lecturing.* The art of delivering speeches with suitable tones of voice, gestures, facial expression, and manner. Oratory as an art is usually defined as including also the writing of speeches; the latter is classed in this outline as a branch of literature.

2. *Dramatic speaking; dramatic diction as a part of stage, film, or television performance by two or more actors.* The vocal element in acting and theater, especially where each actor takes a single part in a group performance, and where theatrical costumes, make-up, settings, and lights help in representing the imaginary characters.

3. *Spoken literature; recitation; elocution; dramatic reading.* Oral presentation of any kind of literature—poetry, prose, drama, fiction, etc.—as an independent art, usually without theatrical costumes or settings to help represent the characters. The art of the bard, minstrel, or modern diseuse or monologist, but usually without musical accompaniment. Oral literature preceded the

written word, and has always existed as a distinct art, in addition to theater. The spread of silent reading of literature in modern times has made it less necessary, but it is frequently revived now, especially on radio and television.

  a. *Monologue,* where one speaker presents the whole composition, including all parts if it is a dramatic work.

  b. *Story-telling* as a special type of oral, literary presentation. Usually prose narration by a single speaker, with freedom to vary the wording of the story.

  c. *Choral and other group speaking.* Several speakers deliver different parts of the piece and perhaps combine in choruses. Not limited to dramatic compositions. Story-telling in which several speakers take part.

4. *Acting (dramatic)* as a combined art of speech, gesture, and other components. Singing and dancing are sometimes included.

5. *Conversation (as an art of speech).* Two or more persons, real or imaginary, speaking to each other and exchanging ideas without explicit, prepared text. To be classed as art, it requires some approach to literary form and style in wording, sequence and importance of ideas, etc. As dialogue, it is incorporated in plays and stories. A conversational style in speaking is more informal and unsystematic than an oratorical or ceremonial one. Conversations, partly spontaneous and partly planned in advance, are often presented on radio and television.

E. DRAMATIC REPRESENTATION; STAGE PERFORMANCE (AUDIO-VISUAL): A complex, diversified art or group of cooperating arts. A single dramatic presentation may involve many component arts: (1) Dramatic writing; playwriting; script or scenario writing; (2) Play direction and production; (3) Stage construction; (4) Stage setting; scene designing; (5) Stage lighting; (6) Costuming; (7) Make-up; theatrical cosmetics, coiffure, etc.; (8) Acting; dramatic speech, movement, gesture, facial expression; stage business; (9) Dance, ballet; (10) Tableaux vivants; set group poses; (11) Singing and other music (as a minor, incidental feature); (12) Sound effects, non-musical (as of storms, gunfire, etc.).

F. OPERA; MUSIC DRAMA: This is a special type of theater art involving music (vocal and orchestral) as one of its main features throughout. It may involve all the theater arts just listed, plus a musical score. All or most of the text or libretto is sung rather than spoken. The music is often considered more important than the plot or dialogue. "Lyric drama" is often in verse, with occasional music and dancing.

1. *Grand opera; serious opera.*
2. *Light opera; comic opera, operettas, revues, musical shows, musical comedies.*

G. VAUDEVILLE: Light entertainment in mixed sequences of diverse acts and performances; usually on a stage. May include small plays and skits, music, acrobatics, sleight of hand, trained animals, etc.

H. PUPPETRY, MARIONETTES, SHADOW PLAYS: Performance only; for manufacture, see SCULPTURAL ARTS. Usually includes speaking a dramatic text as well as manipulating figures, lights, etc. Shown widely on television.

I. MOTION PICTURES; FILM ARTS; CINEMA: The art of preparing and presenting on a screen, by means of film, camera, and projector, sequences of visual images, usually pictures, in which objects and scenes move. Pictures are in black and white or color. Most films are now used for dramatic enactment of plays, with audible speech, music, and sound effects. (See pp. 501f.)

1. *Types of film art:*
   a. *Film dramas or photoplays,* including comedies, tragedies, crime and detective plays, farces, etc., photographed from life.
   b. *Documentaries, newsreels, educational films.* Informative as well as entertaining; usually without definite plot, though a story element is often introduced.
   c. *Animated cartoons; mobile drawings and paintings.* Usually acting out a story or drama.
   d. *Mixed cartoon and "real life" films.*
   e. *Abstract and semi-abstract films;* sequences of non-representational or slightly representational images and designs.

2. *Some component arts and processes in film-making:* (a) Production; (b) Direction; (c) Scenario and script writing; (d) Costuming and make-up; (e) Scene designing; (f) Lighting; (g) Acting; (h) Motion-picture photography; cinematography; (i) Editing and continuity; (j) Montage and special effects; (k) Animation; drawing and painting for films; (l) Three-dimensional effects.

J. RADIO AND TELEVISION: Not yet independent arts, but means of communicating other auditory and audio-visual forms. Now developing original forms and changes in the older arts with which they deal.

K. FIREWORKS; PYROTECHNICS: Rockets, set pieces, etc. Usually for spectacular visual effect; sometimes to represent objects, characters, scenes, events.

L. LUMIA; THE CLAVILUX; MOBILE COLOR: Directly projected on screen or walls, without films. Usually non-representational "color music" with sequences of changing forms; with or without sound music accompaniment.

M. CIRCUSES, PAGEANTS, AND OTHER SPECTACLES: Entertainments and celebrations on a large and sometimes lavish scale, with many participants. Held in the open air, a stadium, tent, or large hall. Such a show often includes many component arts: (1) *Acrobatics; tumbling;* (2) *Clowning;* (3) *Animal training and performance;* (4) *Parades, processions, triumphs, regattas,* often with special costumes, boats, floats or ornamented vehicles, bands, actors portraying characters and situations, animals, fireworks, etc.; (5) *Theatrical and exhibition swimming, diving, figure skating, stunt and formation flying; water and ice ballets and spectacles;* (6) *Bullfighting;* formalized combats against animals. (Considered in Spain as an art with stylized techniques and aesthetic qualities.)

N. RELIGIOUS RITUALS, CEREMONIES, FESTIVALS: Considered as works of art, these are often spectacular, with costumes, parades, and music, in addition to verbal text, prescribed acts and gestures; sometimes also pantomime, dancing, incense, lights, ritual food and drink. Aesthetic aspects are usually considered secondary but often highly developed. Religious and secular rituals were less separate from each other and from art in early cultures. Each religion has distinctive rituals and ceremonies. Certain types of ceremony are common to many religions.

O. FEASTS AND FESTIVALS; SECULAR RITUALS AND FORMALIZED AMUSEMENTS: Some were formerly religious but are now more or less secular. They are considered as arts only when involving fairly definite skills and contrived forms of action or product, with attention to sensory and emotional effects.

  1. *Seasonal festivals;* traditional holiday observances: Christmas trees, Hallowe'en, New Year's Day, and other regular celebrations.
  2. *Ceremonies and festivities for special occasions:* wedding parties, inaugurations, etc. The Japanese tea ceremony.
  3. *Children's games of a ritual type* (often descending from

primitive adult rituals): London Bridge, Farmer in the Dell, etc.

4. *Feasts, entertainments, formalized parties,* with more or less planned participation by those attending; esp. when elaborately organized as in Renaissance and Baroque periods.

V. LOWER-SENSE ARTS AND FACTORS IN ART

A. INTRODUCTION: Regarded as arts insofar as (a) producing or intending to produce controlled aesthetic enjoyment through sensory stimulation; (b) somewhat refined, complex, skillful, meaningful, and formalized, rather than crudely instinctive satisfactions. The "lower senses" in man are incapable of perceiving as subtle or complex forms as are the "higher" senses of sight and hearing. Hence artistic forms addressed to the lower senses are comparatively simple, although often emotionally powerful. They differ greatly in different cultures as to social prestige and technical development. All kinds of lower-sense imagery are suggested in literature and other representational arts.

B. COOKING; CUISINE AND BEVERAGE-MAKING; ARTS OF TASTE OR GUSTATORY ARTS.

1. *Cooking* as the manufacture and preparation of foods, with respect especially to their taste, odor, and tactile qualities, as well as to their nutritiousness. Visual qualities also considered. The aesthetic aspect of the sciences of dietetics, nutrition, etc.; gastronomy.

2. *Beverage-making;* production of wine, beer, liquors, tea, coffee, and other drinks, with special attention to their qualities of taste, odor or "bouquet," alcoholic content, etc.

3. *Meal-planning; organizing repasts.* Included in the "art of cuisine" as broadly defined. Combinations and sequences of foods, drinks, etc., with regard to their combined effects and interrelations, especially as to taste and appetite. May be accompanied by attention to visual arts of table-decoration, to incidental "table-music," etc.

C. PERFUME AND INCENSE; OLFACTORY ARTS OF ODOR, SCENT, SMELL.

1. *Incense;* fragrant smoke and gases from combustion. Esp. from burning woods, herbs, and dried sap of trees. Used in religious rituals and to make rooms fragrant.

2. *Tobacco-making; other plant preparations for smoking.*

3. *Perfume:* fragrant odors from volatile liquids, esp. floral essences. Esp. for wearing on clothes and body. Includes *sachet,* a mixture of ground roots, blossoms, and herbs.

D. TACTILE QUALITIES IN ART.

1. As presented factors in the total aesthetic effect of clothing, furniture, food, etc.

2. Tactile presentation of sculpture, literature, and other arts, esp. for the blind.

3. *Ars amatoria,* erotic arts of ancient Rome, Orient, and Renaissance, as complex, transmitted skills. (Cf. Ovid, Aretino, and the Indian *Kama-Sutra.*)

VI. ARTS OF PERSONAL APPEARANCE AND ATTRACTIVENESS

A. INTRODUCTION: Combined arts addressed to various senses. Personal appearance, voice, posture and carriage, as well as lower-sense qualities are involved. The informal adaptation to ordinary life and social relations of many skills and devices which are developed elsewhere into separate arts.

B. BODILY APPEARANCE AND FRAGRANCE; PERSONAL BEAUTIFICATION.

1. *Cosmetics;* as artificial embellishment of skin, features, hands. Attention to desired visual, tactile, and olfactory qualities. Includes use of soaps, powders, perfumes, creams, dentifrices, coloring for hair, eyes, and lips, etc.

2. *Hairdressing, coiffure;* with or without combs, pins, ribbons, etc.

3. *Medical aids to beautification;* plastic surgery, orthodontia, etc. Artistic phases of medicine, surgery, and dentistry.

4. *Tattooing,* a major art in some tribal cultures; degenerate and disparaged in our culture.

C. DRESS; COSTUME: The art of choosing and combining various garments and accessories for aesthetic effect in relation to requirements of use, function, durability, etc., and to one's personal appearance, the occasion and conditions, as well as current taste and fashion. Combining such items as hats, shoes, dresses, suits, shirts, coats, furs, underwear, stockings, jewelry, handbags, floral corsages and boutonnieres.

D. VOICE AND SPEECH: The development of pleasing or otherwise effective tones and expressions of voice, as suited to one's personality, social customs, and special occasions.

E. POSTURE AND CARRIAGE.

F. SOCIAL BEHAVIOR: As an art, involves etiquette, or conformity to accepted group conventions of appearance, speech, and action. More broadly, involves also tact, grace, refinement of manner, consideration for the enjoyment of others, insofar as these are expressed in perceptible forms. The art of social living, especially in direct, personal relations. Involves ethical and practical as well as aesthetic aims and standards. Involves more than mere conformity to custom, since original innovations occur. These are often influenced by new patterns of behavior suggested in other arts, especially painting, the novel, and theater arts.

INDEX *